Lecture Notes in Computer Science 3114

Commenced Publication in 1973
Founding and Former Series Editors:
Gerhard Goos, Juris Hartmanis, and Jan van Leeuwen

Springer
Berlin
Heidelberg
New York
Barcelona
Hong Kong
London
Milan
Paris
Tokyo

Rajeev Alur   Doron A. Peled (Eds.)

Computer Aided Verification

16th International Conference, CAV 2004
Boston, MA, USA, July 13-17, 2004
Proceedings

 Springer

Volume Editors

Rajeev Alur
University of Pensylvania, Department of Computer und Information Science
3330 Walnut Street, Philadelphia, PA 19104, USA
E-mail: alur@cis.upenn.edu

Doron A. Peled
University of Warwick, Department of Computer Science
Coventry, CV4 7AL, UK
E-mail: pdoron@dcs.warwick.ac.uk

Library of Congress Control Number: 2004108215

CR Subject Classification (1998): F.3, D.2.4, D.2.2, F.4.1, I.2.3, B.7.2, C.3

ISSN 0302-9743
ISBN 3-540-22342-8 Springer-Verlag Berlin Heidelberg New York

Springer-Verlag is a part of Springer Science+Business Media

springeronline.com

© Springer-Verlag Berlin Heidelberg 2004
Printed in Germany

Typesetting: Camera-ready by author, data conversion by Olgun Computergrafik
Printed on acid-free paper   SPIN: 11015802   06/3142   5 4 3 2 1 0

Preface

This volume contains the proceedings of the conference on *Computer Aided Verification*, CAV 2004, held in Boston, Massachusetts, USA, July 13–17, 2004. CAV 2004 was the 16th in a series of conferences dedicated to the advancement of the theory and practice of computer-assisted formal analysis methods for software and hardware systems. The conference covers the spectrum from theoretical results to concrete applications, with an emphasis on practical verification tools and the algorithms and techniques that are needed for their implementation. The conference has traditionally drawn participation from researchers as well as practitioners in both academia and industry.

CAV 2004 was colocated with the ACM International Symposium on Software Testing and Analysis (ISSTA 2004), and was partially sponsored by the ACM SIGSOFT. The colocation reflects the increasing synergy between research on verification and testing, and emerging applications of formal verification to software analysis. Joint CAV-ISSTA events included a distinguished plenary lecture by David Harel and a special session exploring various approaches to the specification and verification of concurrent software organized by Shaz Qadeer. The program of the conference consisted of 32 regular papers and 16 tool papers, selected from a total of 144 submissions. The conference was preceded by a tutorial on processor verification, on July 12, 2004, with three invited lectures by Randal E. Bryant, David L. Dill and Warren A. Hunt, Jr. The conference also included invited talks by Mary Jean Harrold and Thomas W. Reps. Two workshops were associated with CAV 2004:

- BMC 2004: Second International Workshop on Bounded Model Checking
- GDV 2004: Games in Design and Verification

We would like to thank all the program committee members and the subreferees for their excellent work in evaluating the submissions and the selection of the program. Our thanks also go to the steering committee members and the organizers of CAV 2003 for their helpful advice. Special thanks go to George Avrunin, the ISSTA General Chair, and Erin Dolan of ACM, for their help with the local organization. We would like to acknowledge the generous sponsorship of Cadence Design Systems, IBM Research, Intel Research, Microsoft Research and the John Von Neumann Minerva Center for Verification of Reactive Systems. Their support helped us reduce the registration fee for the graduate students.

The CAV community is deeply saddened by the sudden demise of Dr. Rob T. Gerth. Rob was a highly regarded researcher with many notable contributions to the theory and practice of formal verification. For CAV 2004, we had invited Rob to join the program committee as well as to give a tutorial on processor verification. This LNCS volume containing the CAV 2004 proceedings is dedicated to Rob, and includes a special presentation, commemorating his scientific accomplishments and collaborations.

May 2004   Rajeev Alur and Doron A. Peled

Jason Baumgartner
Bernd Becker
Michael Benedikt
Saddek Bensalem
Sergey Berezin
Mikhail Bernadsky
Jesse Bingham
Roderick Bloem
Johan Blom
Bernard Boigelot
Dragan Bosnacki
Ahmed Bouajjani
Marius Bozga
Tevfik Bultan
Donald Chai
Jacob Chang
Marsha Chechik
Ling Cheung
Alessandro Cimatti
Scott Cotton
Thao Dang
Conrado Daws
Johann Deneux
Jyotirmoy Deshmukh
Peter Dillinger
Xiaoqun Du
Elena Dubrova
Avijit Dutta
Marco Faella
Manuel Fahndrich
Ansgar Fehnker
Xiushan Feng
David Fink
Bernd Finkbeiner
Carsten Fritz
Marc Geilen
Blaise Genest
Philippe Gerner
Alain Girault
Amit Goel
Gregor Goessler
Peter Habermehl
Malek Haroud
John Hatcliff

Marc Herbstritt
Gerard Holzmann
Jozef Hooman
Michael Huth
Franjo Ivancic
Paul Jackson
Sadegh Jahanpour
Petr Jancar
Geert Janssen
Bertrand Jeannet
Sven Johr
Rajeev Joshi
Vineet Kahlon
Huthasana Kalyanam
Joost-Pieter Katoen
Nathan Kitchen
Felix Klaedtke
Nils Klarlund
Christos Kloukinas
Matthias Kuntz
Orna Kupferman
Shuvendu Lahiri
Yassine Lakhnech
Frederic Lang
Ruggiero Lanotte
Joyce Lauer
Ranko Lazic
Axel Legay
Martin Leucker
Bing Li
Scott Little
Rupak Majumdar
Shawn Manley
Heiko Mantel
Marco Maratea
Eric Mercer
Markus Mueller-Olm
Aniello Murano
Madan Musuvathi
David N. Jansen
Kedar Namjoshi
Margherita Napoli
Kelvin Ng
Dejan Nickovic

Marcus Nilsson
Iulian Ober
Alfredo Olivero
Joel Ouaknine
Domenico Parente
Gennaro Parlato
Viresh Paruthi
Corina Pasareanu
Mark Pichora
Nir Piterman
Andreas Podelski
Ramanujam
Kavita Ravi
Theo Ruys
Gerardo Schneider
Viktor Schuppan
Sanjit Seshia
Ilya Shlyakhter
Eric Smith
Oleg Sokolsky
Sudarshan Srinivasan
Ian Stark
Martin Steffen
Colin Stirling
Marielle Stoelinga
Val Tannen
P.S. Thiagarajan
Tayssir Touili
Richard Trefler
Stavros Tripakis
Yaroslav Usenko
Antti Valmari
Helmut Veith
Miroslav Velev
Willem Visser
Daron Vroon
Thomas Wahl
David Walter
Thomas Wilke
Aleksander Zaks
Yunshan Zhu
Lenore Zuck
Rob van Glabbeek

Table of Contents

Kijereshi, Tanzania, 1994

HET KOMT WEL VOOR

"Gedaan in het gesloten
seizoen der dromen"
Lucebert

het komt wel voor
dat de deur in het slot valt
de stilte plotseling intreedt
de angst toeslaat
men in een leegte staart –

het komt wel voor
dat een man van in de veertig
met ontstelde ogen toeziet
hoe de vingers zich in elkaar
wringen, voelen moet hoe de
adem stokt in de keel –

het komt wel voor
dat men dan de dood ontmoet

Wim Gerth
28 November 2003

Rob Tristan Gerth: 1956–2003

On Friday November 28, 2003, computer scientist and logician Rob Gerth died from sudden cardiac arrest. It is impossible to say all that the loss of Rob means to Intel, to the verification community, and to each of us personally.

As a corporation, Intel has lost a world-renowned authority on formal modeling and verification. Rob brought an independence of thought and agility of mind that are the hallmarks of a rare intellect. He was one of the few people with the knowledge and experience to meet the challenges we face in verifying micro-architectural protocols; we hope we can find a way to carry on his legacy.

As a community, we have lost not just a key technical contributor but part of our scientific conscience. It was in Rob's nature to ask "Why?", even when the answer seemed obvious. He brought a commitment to truth and high standards that was alternately challenging, frustrating, and inspiring; we will sorely miss it.

As family, friends and colleagues, we will remember and cherish Rob's warmth and love, his knowledge and openness in sharing it, his dry sense of humor, the way only he could read Toon Tellegen stories, and – perhaps most of all – his contagious laughter.

Rob's passion for knowledge reached far beyond computer science and logic: it embraced science, history, literature, art and music. The 2004 Proceedings of the 16th International Conference on Computer Aided Verification are dedicated to him. This article in the Proceedings surveys highlights of Rob's scientific career, followed by excerpts taken from some of the many tributes sent for Rob's funeral by friends and colleagues from around the world. The list of contributors, though too long to be printed here, is itself a tribute to Rob's impact on us all.

May 2004

John O'Leary & Marly Roncken
Intel

R. Alur and D.A. Peled (Eds.): CAV 2004, LNCS 3114, pp. 1–14, 2004.
© Springer-Verlag Berlin Heidelberg 2004

Rob Gerth, Program Verifier par Excellence: His Research

Going through Rob Gerth's contributions to program semantics and verification, and tools for the latter, one is struck by his almost incredible versatility, total commitment, and scientific depth.

Starting in 1981 with a proof system for Brinch Hansen's monitor-based language Distributed Processes [1], he followed with an important paper on "Transition Logic: How to Reason about Temporal Properties in a Compositional Way" [2], coauthored papers on "Compositional Semantics for Real-Time Distributed Computing" for the predecessor of LICS [3], with its Full-Abstraction proof [4], a (sound and relatively complete) "Proof System for Concurrent Ada Programs" in *Science of Computer Programming* [5], and a far reaching paper in 1986 "Monitors Revisited: A First Step towards Verifying Object-Oriented Systems" [6], far before the general research public in computer science realized the importance of concepts like compositionality, formalized real-time semantics, or relatively complete proof systems for monitor-based and object-oriented languages.

This list continues to be extended in the same break-through baffling fashion: Coauthor of full-abstract semantics for Statecharts and concurrent Prolog [7, 8], "Rooting UNITY" [9], his Program Refinement and Self-Modifying Code [10, 11], coauthored papers for CONCUR [12, 13] or Reliable Distributed Systems [14]. Who else in those years cared for investigating fully abstract program semantics, verifying fault-tolerant distributed programs, self-modifying programs, interface refinement, and the now crucial concept of compositional refinement?

Having reached the limits of what can reasonably be verified *in principle* by hand, Rob saw that the time of automated verification had arrived and devoted himself with the same ruthless interest and intrepidity to developing foundations of abstract interpretation, model checking and automated refinement tools – to allow applications at industrial scale. The focus in his work now shifts to handling state explosion in (real-time) model checking.

To this end, he developed partial-order techniques [15, 16] and other advanced techniques like on-the-fly model checking [17] and abstraction [18] – the latter with his "very own" Ph.D. student Dennis Dams and with Orna Grumberg. The foundational aspects of abstract interpretation in model checking were first presented at a memorable PROCOMET workshop in San Miniato [19], and culminated in 1997 in a TOPLAS seminal paper [20] and application paper [21].

At the end of this period, Rob organised the ESPRIT project VIRES (Verifying Industrial Reactive Systems) where the developed theory and tools were applied to the verification of an industrial bus protocol. This project was his legacy to Europe, and the beginning of a new era in the verification of large systems. When Rob left the Technical University Eindhoven for Intel at the end of 1997, VIRES found a suitable new project lead in his former Ph.D student Dennis Dams.

Rob's "warming up" exercise at Intel was the ambitious exploratory project of formally verifying arithmetic hardware units to their IEEE specifications [22]. The technology and methodology developed in that project are used routinely today to verify floating-point functionality in Intel's Microprocessor design projects.

He subsequently went back to a more familiar domain, developing a linear-time temporal logic – dubbed ForSpec [23]. The uniqueness of Forspec lies in its many special features for hardware specification, motivated by many Intel engineering years of both edge-cutting and practical design and validation. Rob's unique blend of theoretical knowledge and practical experience in formal semantics and model checking invariably prevented inconsistencies and efficiency hazards, and helped solve the most difficult roadblocks. ForSpec is widely used in Intel, and has been incorporated in OpenVera^{TM}, a language for hardware testbenches and assertions that is supported by a broad network of CAD companies.

Just weeks before his death, Rob presented the first results of what he called his "bit-vector compiler" – software he had been developing to relate protocol models over abstract data types to ditto models over "hardware" datatypes, i.e. bits and bit-vectors. Following up on [24], the compiler is part of Rob's protocol verification programme and perhaps the most cherished and ambitious project of his life. A life which he did not anticipate would end any time soon.

If Edsger Wiebe Dijkstra, another Dutchman, opened the eyes of computer scientists for the value of proving programs correct, then in Rob Tristan Gerth a worthy modern-day successor and polymath was incarnated, whose own unique vision furthered the feasibility of Dijkstra's programme. We shall all miss Rob's enthusiasm, ruthless intellectual curiosity, and relentless energy.

Selected List of Publications

1. M. Roncken, R. Gerth, and W. P. de Roever. A proof system for Brinch Hansen's distributed processes. In *Proceedings of the GI Jahrestagung*, pages 88–95, 1981.
2. R. Gerth. Transition logic: How to reason about temporal properties in a compositional way. In *16th ACM Symp. on Theory of Computing*, pages 39–50. ACM Press, 1984.
3. R. Koymans, R. K. Shyamasundar, W. P. de Roever, R. Gerth, and S. Arun-Kumar. Compositional semantics for real-time distributed computing. In R. Parikh, editor, *Logic of Programs*, volume 193 of *LNCS*, pages 167–189. Springer, 1985.
4. C. Huizing, R. Gerth, and W. P. deRoever. Full abstraction of a real-time denotational semantics for an OCCAM-like language. In *14th ACM Symp. on Principles of Programming Languages*, pages 223–236. ACM Press, 1987.
5. R. Gerth and W. P. de Roever. A proof system for concurrent Ada programs. *Science of Computer Programming*, 4(2):159–204, 1984.
6. R. Gerth and W. P. de Roever. Proving monitors revisited: a first step towards verifying object oriented systems. *Fundamenta Informatica*, 9(4):371–399, 1986.
7. C. Huizing, R. Gerth, and W. P. de Roever. Modeling statecharts behaviour in a fully abstract way. In M. Dauchet and M. Nivat, editors, *13th Colloq. on Trees in Algebra and Programming*, volume 299 of *LNCS*, pages 271–294. Springer, 1988.
8. R. Gerth, M. Codish, Y. Lichtenstein, and E. Y. Shapiro. Fully abstract denotational semantics for flat concurrent Prolog. In *3rd Symp. on Logic in Computer Science*, pages 320–335. IEEE Computer Society, 1988.

9. R. Gerth and A. Pnueli. Rooting UNITY. *ACM SIGSOFT Software Engineering Notes*, 14(3):11–19, 1989.

10. R. Gerth. Foundations of compositional program refinement - safety properties. In J. W. de Bakker, W. P. de Roever, and G. Rozenberg, editors, *Stepwise Refinement of Distributed Systems: Models, Formalisms, Correctness*, volume 430 of *LNCS*, pages 777–807. Springer, 1989.

11. R. Gerth. Formal verification of self modifying code. In *Int. Conf. for Young Computer Scientists*, pages 305–313. International Acad. Publishers, China, 1991.

12. R. Gerth, R. Kuiper, and J. Segers. Interface refinement in reactive systems. In R. Cleaveland, editor, *3rd Int. Conf. on Concurrency Theory*, volume 630 of *LNCS*, pages 77–93. Springer, 1992.

13. S. Zhou, R. Gerth, and R. Kuiper. Transformations preserving properties and properties preserved by transformations in fair transition systems. In E. Best, editor, *4th Int. Conf. on Concurrency Theory*, volume 715 of *LNCS*, pages 353–367. Springer, 1993.

14. H. Schepers and R. Gerth. A compositional proof theory for fault tolerant real-time distributed systems. In *12th Symp. on Reliable Distributed Systems*, pages 34–43. IEEE Computer Society, 1993.

15. D. Dams, R. Gerth, B. Knaack, and R. Kuiper. Partial-order reduction techniques for real-time model checking. *Formal Aspects of Computing*, 10(5-6):132–152, 1998.

16. R. Gerth, R. Kuiper, D. Peled, and W. Penczek. A partial order approach to branching time logic model checking. *Inf. and Comp.*, 150(2):132–152, 1999.

17. R. Gerth, D. Peled, M. Y. Vardi, and P. Wolper. Simple on-the-fly automatic verification of linear temporal logic. In *15th IFIP WG6.1 Int. Symp. on Protocol Specification, Testing and Verification*, volume 38 of *IFIP Conference Proceedings*, pages 3–18. Chapman & Hall, 1995.

18. D. Dams, O. Grumberg, and R. Gerth. Generation of reduced models for checking fragments of CTL. In *CAV*, LNCS, pages 479–490. Springer, 1993.

19. D. Dams, O. Grumberg, and R. Gerth. Abstract interpretation of reactive systems: Abstractions preserving ∀CTL*, ∃CTL* and CTL*. In E.-R. Olderog, editor, *IFIP WG2.1/WG2.2/WG2.3 Working Conf. on Programming Concepts, Methods and Calculi*, IFIP Transactions. North-Holland/Elsevier, June 1994.

20. D. Dams, R. Gerth, and O. Grumberg. Abstract interpretation of reactive systems. *ACM Trans. on Programming Languages and Systems*, 19(2):253–291, 1997.

21. D. Dams and R. Gerth. The bounded retransmission protocol revisited. In F. Moller, editor, *2nd Int. Workshop on Verification of Infinite State Systems*, volume 9 of *Electronic Notes in Theoretical Computer Science*. Elsevier, 1997.

22. J. O'Leary, X. Zhao, C.-J. H. Seger, and R. Gerth. Formally verifying IEEE compliance of floating-point hardware. *Intel Technical Journal*, First Quarter 1999.

23. R. Armoni, L. Fix, A. Flaisher, R. Gerth, B. Ginsburg, T. Kanza, A. Landver, S. Mador-Haim, E. Singerman, A. Tiemeyer, M. Y. Vardi, and Y. Zbar. A new temporal property-specification language. In J.-P. Katoen and P. Stevens, editors, *Tools and Algorithms for the Construction and Analysis of Systems*, volume 2280 of *LNCS*, pages 296–311. Springer, 2002.

24. R. Gerth. Sequential consistency and the lazy caching algorithm. *Distributed Computing*, 12(2-3):57–59, 1999.

Rob and Masja, Eindhoven, 1993

Rob Gerth: Personal Recollections

I had the pleasure of knowing Rob for over 10 years. He first appeared in the department of Computer Science at the Technion when I was doing a Phd, for a visit in Israel, while he collaborated with Liuba Shrira.

When I finished the Phd, during my work at Bell Labs, Rob invited me several times to Eindhoven. We worked on several topics, and published together two papers. We worked with Ruurd Kuiper, Wojciech Penczek, Moshe Vardi and Pierre Wolper. It was always a lot of fun and great inspiration.

We all know these people that we try to communicate with about our research, and they are busy and postpone their reply indefinitely, so after some time we give up and never hear from them again. Rob was the striking exception to that: it took me some time to understand that I can always and fully trust that even if we did not achieve a fully published results on a visit, there will be one day, where Rob is going to send some really interesting new and original thread of ideas. I learned that I do not need to remind him. He is just thinking of it, and when he realizes he has something substantial to say, he will. Rob was a perfectionist. We worked on a third subject, and decided the results are not so great. Rob would never send a paper unless he thinks it's an important result and the writing is clear.

I was looking forward to meet Rob again soon. We talked about me visiting Intel in December. I also waited for him to clear his invited talk about the verification of the new Intel processor in the CAV 2004 conference in Boston with his management. I would have reminded anyone else, but with Rob I knew he is taking care of things. Rob has influenced the CAV community with his important contributions. We will remember him.

Doron Peled
University of Warwick

It is with great pain that I struggle with the unacceptably tragic news of Rob's death. For me, Rob always signified the spirit of youth and intellectual rebellion – uncompromising insistence on finding out things for himself and establishing his own truth in the way that would satisfy him personally. This independence of thought and idealistically high standards often led him in paths infrequently traveled achieving many original, ingenious, and fresh insights that were Rob's unique trade mark in science.

It is extremely difficult to reconcile oneself with the thought that this youthful and energetically fresh creative person has been cut in mid stream. The loss to science, industry, and each of us personally, is too great to encompass in few words.

Amir Pnueli
New York University & Weizmann Institute

I have known and shared many happy times with Rob. He and I shared a grant from the EU for many years, which let us eat, drink, and (sometimes) work around Europe. Most of all I remember fierce arguments, highlighted by the intensity of Rob's in-your-face burning eyes. These were all totally enjoyable, and happily resolved over a more-than-few drinks.

Mike Reed
Oxford University

Fig. 1. Rob, Amir Pnueli and Mike Reed in Loutro, Crete, 1995.

Remembering Rob Gerth, I am deeply saddened by the loss of a real friend. He was my first Ph.D. student. The difference between him as supervisee and me, his supervisor, quickly evaporated because of his rare, incisive intellect, his passionate devotion to our field – program verification – his integrity, his admirable courage, and his honesty. He was a man to steal horses with.

He surpassed me scientifically shortly after finishing his thesis. Both of us knew that, and for me this was a reason for pride and enjoyment – The Torch of Scientific Research had been passed on to a Worthy Successor.

Rob, Marly Roncken, Niek van Diepen, and I met in the beginning of the 1980's as part of an informal research group in program verification at the University of Utrecht. We had a proof theory for Brinch Hansen's monitor-based language Distributed Processes as goal in mind. Marly contributed our first representative example, her Monkey-Bananas puzzle, and Rob observed that its correctness proof involved Owicki's interference-freedom test. These efforts led eventually to our first joint publication in 1982.

This goal of a proof theory for monitors subsequently evolved into the subject of Rob's thesis, finished after my group had already moved to Eindhoven. But Rob wanted to obtain his Ph.D. degree at "his own" University, that of Utrecht. Jan van Leeuwen made this possible. I still remember sitting along one of Utrecht's beautiful medieval canals after the ceremony, with my wife Corinne and our daughter Jojanneke, trying to convince Rob that a meal for his doctoral committee and his guests would be the appropriate end to a wonderful day. Marly convinced him in the end, and I finally noticed they had become a real couple.

Fig. 2. Jan van Leeuwen handing over Rob's Ph.D. certificate, 8 May 1989 (left). After the ceremony (right), Rob exchanged his tails for a T-shirt version – a present from WP in response to Rob's (reluctant) yielding to the University's ceremonial dress code.

In the meantime we had started participating in the ESPRIT research programme of the European Commission. This was made possible by an eminent team of research students, consisting of Rob, Ruurd Kuiper, Kees Huizing, Ron Koymans, and Jozef Hooman at Eindhoven, and Frank Stomp and Job Zwiers at Nijmegen University. Amir Pnueli commented later that they constituted the most gifted single group of Ph.D. students he had ever collaborated with.

In my second EU research project Rob became Eindhoven's team leader. Those projects led, among others, to the birth of the now dominant CAV series of conferences on Computer-Aided Verification. Frequent guests of the chair were Allen Emerson, Amir Pnueli, Joseph Sifakis, and many others who were to lift program verification later to its current level. Within a couple of years Rob Gerth had evolved from a proud citizen of Utrecht to a researcher having a world-wide view of program verification with an established scientific reputation, and had changed his main line of research to computer-aided verification.

His parting gift to Eindhoven University was the ESPRIT project VIRES, the proposal of which he wrote single-handedly, on the verification of a mobile phone protocol. That project was subsequently led at Eindhoven University by his first Ph.D. student, Dennis Dams. It constitutes still a topic for invited lectures!

I had moved in the meantime to the University of Kiel, Germany, Rob moved later to Intel, and Dennis Dams to Bell-Labs. An era of scientific excellence and vision in program verification in the Netherlands had come to an end.

Willem-Paul de Roever
University of Kiel

Fig. 3. Two Ph.D. generations: Dennis Dams with Rob at the PROCOMET workshop in Italy, 1994 (left), and Rob with Willem-Paul, Corinne and Sanne de Roever and the Shyamasundar family in Utrecht, 1983 (right).

I had not seen Rob for two years, but when I got the message of his death he was suddenly there again, in a long sequence of memories. The many years in Eindhoven, first as M.Sc. advisor, then co-promotor of my PhD thesis. In that sense he was my "scientific father", a role that he fulfilled with dedication.

Thinking back, what I found most characteristic about Rob was his calmness. Always was he willing, and took ample time, to listen patiently to what I had to tell him. We discussed long, and often late hours about work and many other things. He could continue working on a joint paper, unstirred, until just before, or after the submission deadline. And I remember how relieved I was when he finally showed up on the platform escalator of Eindhoven station, half a minute before the departure of our international train. His face showing only a slight surprise about my state of panic.

With that self-evident calmness he allowed me to continue working on my PhD thesis, even well beyond the regulatory four years. I do not actually remember whether I ever told him how grateful I am for that.

Between 1989 and 1997 we have done many things together: working, eating, running, traveling. Memories that we talked about together, not so long ago. Memories that now suddenly take a different role. The PROCOMET workshop in San Miniato. That restaurant in Haifa where we had dinner each night during our working visit to the Technion. Those memories now turn into memories of Rob himself.

Dennis Dams
Bell Labs

I am deeply grateful for having had the privilege to work with Rob for the past five years. Rob was always one of the first people I consulted whenever I had questions on a scientific topic. He was one of the very first people who recognized the importance and significance of the GSTE work, and even encouraged me on many occasions to write a book on the subject. I remember that he carefully read the first draft of the theory paper, and walked into my cubicle one day with the copy full of his valuable comments ... and a coffee stain. He apologized for the mess, but I thanked him and told him jokingly that I would like to keep it as it would become a great souvenir when he'd be a very famous computer scientist some day. I have kept the copy and I will keep it forever as a memory of Rob.

Recently, Rob and I worked closely on mentoring the protocol verification project by Professor Lin in China. He was very enthusiastic and upbeat about it. I still remember the words he said when we discussed how to steer this project. With his unforgettable smile and an emphatic "No", he said "Jin, we should define the problem very clearly, but we cannot constrain how he is going to solve it". How could one argue with that?

Jin Yang
Intel

Rob, and Marly almost equally long, I have known since their post-university days at the University of Utrecht. We were coached, quite independently and at different places, by Willem-Paul de Roever. Initially with him, Rob and I at a later stage spent a period of about 10 years at Eindhoven Technical University, Rob as leader and later initiator of projects with European Community funding.

Workwise, that meant interaction on a day-to-day basis, where Rob's scientific perceptiveness, and his perseverance and integrity were a constant pleasure and inspiration. Spotting a new idea like a vague shadow of a fish, but then also catching it - making it precise and finding the appropriate formalism to describe it; accomplished artist and craftsman both. To honour Rob's love for books: Il Miglior Fabbro - certainly. Socially it meant isolated, few, pinpointed, but intense and happy interactions. Like triggered when our children were born (there still lives a toy-frog in our bathtub donated by Rob and Marly, though politely named after Rob), or when the mood was right, tired-out after work on a project assignment at the Weizmann Institute of Science in Israel.

This mix felt absolutely right. To me Rob was, apart from the driven, talented scientist, an unusually complete human being, in his tastes as well as in his priorities. Leaving a cinema late at night I once saw Rob and Marly cycling around rather hollow-eyed: having worked together on some paper, they had forgotten about time and food. But at that moment work was far away; their being together radiated happiness and was a joy to look at.

A furtive try to phrase what Rob means to me:

A good thing about a friend is that you understand and value him; the better thing is that he understands and values you - Rob did. The book "Pallieter" of which he once gave me a fine old copy (hunting down one, after noticing that I admired his) will always be on my shelf, as Rob will remain in my life.

Ruurd Kuiper
Technical University Eindhoven

Rob and Marly, Eindhoven, 1990

Fig. 4. Jozef Hooman, Rob, Ruurd Kuiper, Kees Huizing, and Ron Koymans, Israel.

Rob was my co-promotor and we worked together at the Eindhoven University. He was also my daily supervisor during my Ph.D. work and I learned so many things from him. About English writing, for instance. Maybe also a few bad habits, but what I remember most is his attitude to science. He combined strong opinions with a very open mind, which is exceptional, I think. Sometimes, when I had made a nice exposition of some point of view, he could ask with his eyes wide open in what seemed true surprise: "Why?". This single word made me rethink my whole position and suddenly every assumption I made seemed questionable. Although he had a very broad knowledge of computer science, he managed to approach the research field every time in a fresh and original way.

His original and sharp thinking also lightened up our coffee break discussions and now that he died I realise that I still miss him, even after these years. And not only for his conversation, but also for his independent mind, whether it be science, politics, or conventions and manners.

Kees Huizing
Technical University Eindhoven

I have written two papers with Rob. He was a challenging collaborator. He took nothing for granted and challenged everything. Working with him was like a furious tennis match. At times, you could not tell whether it was collaborative or competitive, it was so intense. When the end result finally emerged, it was always of superb quality, having been polished by clashing intellects. Rob's uncompromising quest for scientific truth forced his collaborators to bring forth their best ideas. His untimely departure leaves us with a gaping hole.

Moshe Vardi
Rice University

When I first met Rob in 1987 he was a student at TU-Eindhoven. All of Willem-Paul's group were impressive, but Rob stood out somehow. His brilliance and intensity were so plainly visible. He wasn't like a student. Instead, he already had the maturity and judgement of an excellent junior faculty member.

I followed Rob's career with interest. He brought much needed clarity and illumination to everything he worked on. I myself was doubly impressed with Intel's seriousness regarding formal verification when I learned they had hired Rob.

Rob was both a gentlemen and a scientist. I myself, his friends and colleagues, and the community will miss him enormously.

Allen Emerson
University of Texas

I was shocked to hear the sad news about Rob. Rob was a well respected member of our community – an international community of researchers working on specification and verification. I met him frequently at workshops and conferences.

Rob's intelligence was obvious, and he contributed a great deal to the progress of our field. But what impressed me most was his good sense and openness to new ideas. He was free of preconceived notions of how things should be done, and he was always willing to listen to what others had to say.

Leslie Lamport
Microsoft

Rob was very kind and welcoming to me whenever I visited Intel. Although we never worked on a project together, I had a tremendous respect for his scientific knowledge and often popped by his desk to consult him on tricky technical points. Rob was a generous man and always willing to share his time.

Rob also had a wonderful sense of humor and was a simulating and enjoyable lunch-time companion. I remember well how his face would light up with a smile, as he would agree with a gently ironical "of course" to some absurdity or other we were discussing.

In his work, I think what characterised Rob was his tremendous dedication to really getting to the bottom of difficult scientific questions. He wasn't content just to have an approximate understanding of a problem and its solution. He wanted to really *know* – and as a first-class computer scientist he had the ability to get there too.

Tom Melham
University of Oxford

Rob, Utrecht, 17 October, 2002

Rob had a remarkable mind. He had a deep understanding of computer science theory, particularly automata theory. He explained many concepts to me and to others on my team. Yet, he was never condescending. He enjoyed sharing his knowledge, and he didn't give up on an explanation until it was clear.

I knew that Rob had many interests outside of work, but sadly I didn't learn the full scope of those interests until after his death. I have come to understand that Rob was a true "Renaissance Man". He had a library with thousands of books and CDs, and the home he shared with Marly is filled with art and sculpture from around the world. I'm amazed at the breadth and depth of his interests and knowledge.

Rob had a subtle, wry sense of humor. He was often amused by my (usually futile) attempts to effect change despite the bureaucracy inherent in a large company like Intel. After one of my skirmishes with the powers-that-be, Rob presented me with a special award–something that he had invented just for the occasion. It was the inaugural Strategic CAD Labs "Don Quixote" award: a small porcelain Dutch windmill. He told me that tilting at that windmill would often be more productive than "tilting" at bureaucracy.

Robert Jones
Intel

Long before I met him, I actually tried to ignore Rob. Everywhere I went, people were raving about how smart he was, what a great guy he was, etc. At some level, I guess I was jealous, and I arrogantly said to myself, "If this Rob Gerth guy is such a hot shot in verification, why haven't I met him yet?" I should have heeded my own advice: you can't tell the difference between someone who is two steps ahead of you and someone who is two steps behind you. When someone is a bit ahead of you, you can understand what they're doing and why, and you acknowledge that they're ahead; similarly, when someone is a bit behind you, you understand exactly what they're missing and how they are behind you. But when someone is too far ahead, what they say and do is incomprehensible, and thereby becomes indistinguishable from gibberish. For me and Rob, it took me a lot of hard work and tough thinking before I reached the point that I could start to appreciate his comments and insights, and work he had done long before. Let me give a few concrete examples:

- I've long considered the verification of multiprocessor memory systems to be one of my specialties. This was how I got started in verification, and I've done quite a bit of work in this area. Only in the past few years, though, have I started looking at verifying the conformance of the system to a formal memory model, rather than verifying simple ad hoc assertions. As I moved into this "next step" in verification, I found that Rob had been there already. In fact, he had already edited an entire journal special issue on this topic!

- I have always ignored work on strange automata variations as interesting, but irrelevant theory. When I visited Intel SCL to work on the eminently practical GSTE, Rob remarked, "Oh, it's basically forall-automata. I'm more interested in alternating automata." After weeks of concentrating on GSTE, I eventually came to realize, "Oh yeah, I guess it *is* a forall-automaton." And I've started seeing alternating automata (the generalization of forall) popping up everywhere in my own research and that of others.

- The other comment Rob made to me about GSTE was that it was "using a graph to structure fixed-point computations". At the time, I understood his comment at a syntactic level: GSTE does indeed use a graph, and various fixed-point computations are done in accordance to the graph. Only after a year and a half am I starting to see that there was more to his comment, that there is a general principle, that there might be promising ways to generalize and exploit that general principle. I still don't think I can see what he saw, but I'm starting to catch a glimpse of his ideas.

Given how far ahead Rob's thinking and research has been, I take solace in knowing that he will continue to teach me things for years, perhaps decades, to come. I expect that, with enough hard work and hard thinking, I'll yet again rediscover something of Rob's, and I'll be able to see him, with that it's-really-very-obvious-if-you-think-about-it look on his face, showing me the way forward when I'm finally ready to follow him.

Alan Hu
University of British Columbia

Static Program Analysis via 3-Valued Logic*

Thomas W. Reps[1], Mooly Sagiv[2], and Reinhard Wilhelm[3]

[1] Comp. Sci. Dept., University of Wisconsin
reps@cs.wisc.edu
[2] School of Comp. Sci., Tel Aviv University
msagiv@post.tau.ac.il
[3] Informatik, Univ. des Saarlandes
wilhelm@cs.uni-sb.de

Abstract. This paper reviews the principles behind the paradigm of "abstract interpretation via 3-valued logic," discusses recent work to extend the approach, and summarizes on-going research aimed at overcoming remaining limitations on the ability to create program-analysis algorithms fully automatically.

1 Introduction

Static analysis concerns techniques for obtaining information about the possible states that a program passes through during execution, without actually running the program on specific inputs. Instead, static-analysis techniques explore a program's behavior for *all* possible inputs and *all* possible states that the program can reach. To make this feasible, the program is "run in the aggregate" – i.e., on abstract descriptors that represent collections of many states. In the last few years, researchers have made important advances in applying static analysis in new kinds of program-analysis tools for identifying bugs and security vulnerabilities [1–7]. In these tools, static analysis provides a way in which properties of a program's behavior can be verified (or, alternatively, ways in which bugs and security vulnerabilities can be detected). Static analysis is used to provide a safe answer to the question "Can the program reach a bad state?"

Despite these successes, substantial challenges still remain. In particular, pointers and dynamically-allocated storage are features of all modern imperative programming languages, but their use is error-prone:

- Dereferencing NULL-valued pointers and accessing previously deallocated storage are two common programming mistakes.

- Pointers and dynamically-allocated storage allow a program to build up complex graph data structures. Even when some simple data structure is intended, one or more incorrect assignments to pointers, or indirect assignments through pointers, can cause bugs whose symptoms are hard to diagnose.

Because tools for finding bugs and detecting security vulnerabilities need answers to questions about pointer variables, their contents, and the structure of the heap[1], the

---

* Supported by ONR contract N00014-01-1-0796, the Israel Science Foundation, and the A. von Humboldt Foundation.

[1] The term "heap" refers to the collection of nodes in, and allocated from, the free-storage pool.

R. Alur and D.A. Peled (Eds.): CAV 2004, LNCS 3114, pp. 15–30, 2004.
© Springer-Verlag Berlin Heidelberg 2004

usage of pointers in programs is a major obstacle to the goal of addressing software reliability by means of static analysis. In particular, the effects of assignments through pointer variables and pointer-valued fields make it hard to determine the aliasing relationships among different pointer expressions in a program. When less precise pointer information is available, the effectiveness of static techniques decreases.

Although much work has been done on algorithms for flow-insensitive points-to analysis [8–10] (including algorithms that exhibit varying degrees of context-sensitivity [11–15]), all of this work uses a very simple abstraction of heap-allocated storage: *All nodes allocated at site s are folded together into a single summary node n_s.* Such an approach has rather severe consequences for precision. If allocation site s is in a loop, or in a function that is called more than once, then s can allocate multiple nodes with different addresses. A points-to fact "p points to n_s" means that program variable p may point to *one* of the nodes that n_s represents. For an assignment of the form p->selector1 = q, points-to-analysis algorithms are ordinarily forced to perform a "weak update": that is, selector edges emanating from the nodes that p points to are *accumulated*; the abstract execution of an assignment to a field of a summary node cannot "kill" the effects of a previous assignment because, in general, only *one* of the nodes that n_s represents is updated on each concrete execution of the assignment statement.

Such imprecisions snowball as additional weak updates are performed (e.g., for assignment statements of the form r->selector2 = p->selector1), and the use of a flow-insensitive algorithm exacerbates the problem. Consequently, most of the literature on points-to analysis leads to almost no useful information about the structure of the heap. One study [16] of the characteristics of the results obtained using one of the flow-insensitive points-to-analysis algorithms reports that

> Our experiments show that in every points-to graph, there is a single node (the "blob") that has a large number of outgoing flow edges. In every graph, the blob has an order of magnitude more outgoing edges than any other node.

Such imprecision, in turn, leads to overly pessimistic assessments of the program's behavior. Moreover, most of the representations of pointer relationships that have been proposed in the literature on points-to analysis cannot express even as simple a fact as "x points to an acyclic list". Such representations are unable to confirm behavioral properties, such as (i) when the input to a list-insert program is an acyclic list, the output is an acyclic list, and (ii) when the input to a list-reversal program that uses destructive-update operations is an acyclic list, the output is an acyclic list. Instead, most points-to-analysis algorithms will report that a possibly cyclic structure can arise. For programs that use two lists, most points-to-analysis algorithms will report that at the end of the program the two lists might share list elements (even when, in fact, the two lists must always remain disjoint).

The failings of conventional pointer-analysis algorithms discussed above are just symptomatic of a more general problem: in general, tools for finding bugs and detecting security vulnerabilities need answers to questions about a wide variety of behavioral properties; these questions can only be answered by tracking relationships among a program's runtime entities, and in general the number of such entities has no fixed upper bound. Moreover, the nature of the relationships that need to be tracked depends on both the program being analyzed and the queries to be answered.

The aim of our work [17] has been to create a *parametric framework for program analysis* that addresses these issues. A parametric framework is one that can be instantiated in different ways to create different program-analysis algorithms that provide answers to different questions, with varying degrees of efficiency and precision. The key aspect of our approach is the way in which it makes use of 2-valued and 3-valued logic: 2-valued and 3-valued *logical structures* – i.e., collections of predicates – are used to represent concrete and abstract stores, respectively; individuals represent entities such as memory cells, threads, locks, etc.; unary and binary predicates encode the contents of variables, pointer-valued structure fields, and other aspects of memory states; and first-order formulas with transitive closure are used to specify properties such as sharing, cyclicity, reachability, etc. Formulas are also used to specify how the store is affected by the execution of the different kinds of statements in the programming language.

The analysis framework can be instantiated in different ways by varying the predicate symbols of the logic, and, in particular, by varying which of the unary predicates control how nodes are folded together (this is explained in more detail in Sect. 2). The specified set of predicates determines the set of properties that will be tracked, and consequently what properties of stores can be discovered to hold at different points in the program by the corresponding instance of the analysis.

As a methodology for verifying properties of programs, the advantages of the 3-valued-logic approach are:

1. No loop invariants are required.

2. No theorem provers are involved, and thus every abstract execution step must terminate.

3. The method is based on abstract interpretation [18], and satisfies conditions that guarantee that the entire process always terminates.

4. The method applies to programs that manipulate pointers and heap-allocated data structures. Moreover, analyses are capable of performing *strong updates* during the abstract execution of an assignment to a pointer-valued field.

5. The method eliminates the need for the user to write the usual proofs required with abstract interpretation – i.e., to demonstrate that the abstract descriptors that the analyzer manipulates correctly model the actual heap-allocated data structures that the program manipulates.

A prototype implementation that implements this approach has been created, called TVLA (Three-Valued-Logic Analyzer) [19, 20].

Points (1) and (2) may seem counterintuitive, given that we work with an undecidable logic (first-order logic plus transitive closure – see footnote 4), but they are really properties shared by any verification method that is based on abstract interpretation, and hence are consequences of point (3). Points (4) and (5) may be equally surprising – even to many experts in the field of static analysis – but are key aspects of this approach:

- Point (4) has a *fundamental effect on precision*. In particular, our approach is capable of confirming the behavioral properties mentioned earlier, i.e., (i) when the input to a list-insert program is an acyclic list, the output is an acyclic list, and (ii) when the input to a list-reversal program that uses destructive-update operations is an acyclic list, the output is an acyclic list. In addition, when a program uses multiple lists that always remain disjoint, our approach can often confirm that fact.

Table 1. (a) Declaration of a linked-list datatype in C. (b) Core predicates used for representing the stores manipulated by programs that use type List. (We write predicate names in *italics* and code in typewriter font.)

```
typedef struct node {
    int data;
    struct node *n;
} *List;
```

(a)

Predicate	Intended Meaning
$eq(v_1, v_2)$	Do v_1 and v_2 denote the same memory cell?
$q(v)$	Does pointer variable q point to memory cell v?
$n(v_1, v_2)$	Does the n-field of v_1 point to v_2?
$dle(v_1, v_2)$	Is the data-field of v_1 less than or equal to that of v_2?

(b)

- Point (5) is one of the keys for *making the approach accessible for users*. With the methodology of abstract interpretation, it is often a difficult task to obtain an appropriate abstract semantics; abstract-interpretation papers often contain complicated proofs to show that a given abstract semantics is sound with respect to a given concrete semantics. With our approach, this is not the case: the abstract semantics falls out automatically from a specification of the concrete semantics (which has to be provided in any case whenever abstract interpretation is employed); the soundness of *all* instantiations of the framework follows from a single meta-theorem ([17, Theorem 4.9]).

The remainder of the paper is organized as follows: Sect. 2 summarizes the framework for static analysis from [17]. Sect. 3 describes several applications and extensions. Sect. 4 discusses related work.

2   The Use of Logic for Program Analysis

Modeling and Abstracting the Heap with Logical Structures. In the static-analysis framework defined in [17], concrete memory configurations – or *stores* – are modeled by logical structures. A logical structure is associated with a vocabulary of predicate symbols (with given arities): $\mathcal{P} = \{eq, p_1, \ldots, p_n\}$ is a finite set of predicate symbols, where $\mathcal{P}_k$ denotes

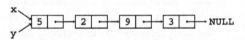

Fig. 1. A possible store, consisting of a four-node linked list pointed to by x and y.

the set of predicate symbols of arity k (and $eq \in \mathcal{P}_2$). A logical structure supplies a predicate for each of the vocabulary's predicate symbols. A concrete store is modeled by a 2-valued logical structure for a fixed vocabulary $\mathcal{C}$ of *core predicates*. Core predicates are part of the underlying semantics of the language to be analyzed; they record atomic properties of stores. Tab. 1 gives the definition of a C linked-list datatype, and lists the predicates that would be used to represent the stores manipulated by programs that use type List, such as the store shown in Fig. 1. 2-valued logical structures then represent memory configurations: the individuals are the set of memory cells; a nullary predicate represents a Boolean variable of the program; a unary predicate represents either a pointer variable or a Boolean-valued field of a record; and a binary predicate represents a pointer field of a record[2].

The 2-valued structure S, shown in the upper-left-hand corner of Fig. 2, encodes the store of Fig. 1. S's four individuals, u_1, u_2, u_3, and u_4, represent the four list cells.

The following graphical notation is used for depicting 2-valued logical structures:

- An individual is represented by a circle with its name inside.

- A unary predicate p is represented by having a solid arrow from p to each individual u for which $p(u) = 1$, and by the absence of a p-arrow to each individual u' for which $p(u') = 0$. (If predicate p is 0 for all individuals, p is not shown.)

- A binary predicate q is represented by a solid arrow labeled q between each pair of individuals u_i and u_j for which $q(u_i, u_j) = 1$, and by the absence of a q-arrow between pairs u'_i and u'_j for which $q(u'_i, u'_j) = 0$.

Thus, in structure S, pointer variables x and y point to individual u_1, whose n-field points to individual u_2; pointer variables t and e do not point to any individual.

Often we only want to use a restricted class of logical structures to encode stores. To exclude structures that do not represent admissible stores, integrity constraints can be imposed. For instance, the predicate $x(v)$ of Fig. 2 captures whether pointer variable x points to memory cell v; x would be given the attribute "unique", which imposes the integrity constraint that $x(v)$ can hold for at most one individual in any structure.

The concrete operational semantics of a programming language is defined by specifying a structure transformer for each kind of edge that can appear in a control-flow graph. Formally, the structure transformer τ_e for edge e is defined using a collection of *predicate-update formulas*, $c(v_1, \ldots, v_k) = \tau_{c,e}(v_1, \ldots, v_k)$, one for each core predicate $c \in \mathcal{P}_k$ (e.g., see [17]). These define how the core predicates of a logical structure S that arises at the source of e are transformed to create structure S' at the target of e; they define the value of predicate c in S' – denoted by c' in the update formulas of Fig. 2 – as a function of predicates in S. Edge e may optionally have a *precondition formula*, which filters out structures that should not follow the transition along e.

Canonical Abstraction. To create abstractions of 2-valued logical structures (and hence of the stores that they encode), we use the related class of 3-valued logical structures over the same vocabulary. In 3-valued logical structures, a third truth value, denoted by $1/2$, is introduced to denote uncertainty: in a 3-valued logical structure, the value $p(\vec{u})$ of predicate p on a tuple of individuals $\vec{u}$ is allowed to be $1/2$.

Definition 1. The truth values 0 and 1 are *definite values*; $1/2$ is an *indefinite value*. For $l_1, l_2 \in \{0, 1/2, 1\}$, the *information order* is defined as follows: $l_1 \sqsubseteq l_2$ iff $l_1 = l_2$ or $l_2 = 1/2$. The symbol $\sqcup$ denotes the least-upper-bound operation with respect to $\sqsubseteq$.

---

[2] To simplify matters, our examples do not involve modeling numeric-valued variables and numeric-valued fields (such as data). It is possible to do this by introducing other predicates, such as the binary predicate *dle* (which stands for "data less-than-or-equal-to") listed in Tab. 1; *dle* captures the relative order of two nodes' data values. Alternatively, numeric-valued entities can be handled by combining abstractions of logical structures with previously known techniques for creating numeric abstractions [21].

Structure Before — S

unary preds.

indiv.	x	y	t	e
u_1	1	1	0	0
u_2	0	0	0	0
u_3	0	0	0	0
u_4	0	0	0	0

binary preds.

n	u_1	u_2	u_3	u_4
u_1	0	1	0	0
u_2	0	0	1	0
u_3	0	0	0	1
u_4	0	0	0	0

eq	u_1	u_2	u_3	u_4
u_1	1	0	0	0
u_2	0	1	0	0
u_3	0	0	1	0
u_4	0	0	0	1

Structure Before — T

unary preds.

indiv.	x	y	t	e
u	1	1	0	0
u'	0	0	0	0

binary preds.

n	u	u'
u	0	1/2
u'	0	1/2

eq	u	u'
u	1	0
u'	0	1/2

Statement

$$y = y\text{-}{>}n$$

Predicate Update Formulas

$$x'(v) = x(v)$$
$$y'(v) = \exists v_1 : y(v_1) \wedge n(v_1, v)$$
$$t'(v) = t(v)$$
$$e'(v) = e(v)$$
$$n'(v_1, v_2) = n(v_1, v_2)$$

Structure After — S'

unary preds.

indiv.	x	y	t	e
u_1	1	0	0	0
u_2	0	1	0	0
u_3	0	0	0	0
u_4	0	0	0	0

binary preds.

n	u_1	u_2	u_3	u_4
u_1	0	1	0	0
u_2	0	0	1	0
u_3	0	0	0	1
u_4	0	0	0	0

eq	u_1	u_2	u_3	u_4
u_1	1	0	0	0
u_2	0	1	0	0
u_3	0	0	1	0
u_4	0	0	0	1

Structure After — T''

unary preds.

indiv.	x	y	t	e
u_1	1	0	0	0
u_2	0	1	0	0
u''	0	0	0	0

binary preds.

n	u_1	u_2	u'
u_1	0	1	0
u_2	0	0	1/2
u'	0	0	1/2

eq	u_1	u_2	u'
u_1	1	0	0
u_2	0	1	0
u''	0	0	1/2

Structure After — T'

unary preds.

indiv.	x	y	t	e
u	1	0	0	0
u'	0	1/2	0	0

binary preds.

n	u	u'
u	0	0
u'	0	1/2

eq	u	u'
u	1	0
u'	0	1/2

abstracts to

embeds into

$$\begin{aligned}
x'(v) &= x(v)\\
y'(v) &= \exists v_1 : y(v_1) \wedge n(v_1, v)\\
t'(v) &= t(v)\\
e'(v) &= e(v)\\
n'(v_1, v_2) &= n(v_1, v_2)
\end{aligned}$$

$$y = y\text{-}{>}n$$

Fig. 2. The top row illustrates the abstraction of 2-valued structure S to 3-valued structure T with $\{x, y, t, e\}$-abstraction. The boxes in the tables of unary predicates indicate how individuals are grouped into equivalence classes; the boxes in the tables for n and eq indicate how the "truth-blurring quotients" are performed. The commutative diagram illustrates the relationship between (i) the transformation on 2-valued structures (defined by predicate-update formulas) for the concrete semantics of $y = y\text{-}{>}n$, (ii) abstraction, and (iii) a sound abstract semantics for $y = y\text{-}{>}n$ that is obtained by using the same predicate-update formulas to transform 3-valued structures.

The abstract stores used for program analysis are 3-valued logical structures that, by the construction discussed below, are *a priori* of bounded size. In general, each 3-valued logical structure corresponds to a (possibly infinite) set of 2-valued logical structures. Members of these two families of structures are related by *canonical abstraction*.

The principle behind canonical abstraction is illustrated in the top and bottom rows of Fig. 2, which show how 2-valued structures S and S' are abstracted to 3-valued structures T and T'', respectively. The abstraction function is determined by a subset $\mathcal{A}$ of the unary predicates. The predicates in $\mathcal{A}$ are called the *abstraction predicates*. Given $\mathcal{A}$, the act of applying the corresponding abstraction function is called $\mathcal{A}$-*abstraction*. The canonical abstraction illustrated in Fig. 2 is $\{x, y, t, e\}$-abstraction.

Abstraction is driven by the values of the "vector" of abstraction predicates for each individual w – i.e., for S, by the values $x(w)$, $y(w)$, $t(w)$ and $e(w)$, for $w \in \{u_1, u_2, u_3, u_4\}$ – and, in particular, by the equivalence classes formed from the individuals that have the same vector of values for their abstraction predicates. In S, there are two such equivalence classes: (i) $\{u_1\}$, for which x, y, t, and e are 1, 1, 0, and 0, respectively, and (ii) $\{u_2, u_3, u_4\}$, for which x, y, t, and e are all 0. (The boxes in the table of unary predicates for S show how individuals of S are grouped into two equivalence classes.) All of the members of each equivalence class are mapped to the same individual of the 3-valued structure. Thus, all members of $\{u_2, u_3, u_4\}$ from S are mapped to the same individual in T, called u' [3]; similarly, all members of $\{u_1\}$ from S are mapped to the same individual in T, called u.

For each non-abstraction predicate p^S of 2-valued structure S, the corresponding predicate p^T in 3-valued structure T is formed by a "truth-blurring quotient". The value for a tuple $\vec{u}_0$ in p^T is the join ($\sqcup$) of all p^S tuples that the equivalence relation on individuals maps to $\vec{u}_0$. For instance,

- In S, $n^S(u_1, u_1)$ equals 0; therefore, the value of $n^T(u, u)$ is 0.
- In S, $n^S(u_2, u_1)$, $n^S(u_3, u_1)$, and $n^S(u_4, u_1)$ all equal 0; therefore, the value of $n^T(u', u)$ is 0.
- In S, $n^S(u_1, u_3)$ and $n^S(u_1, u_4)$ both equal 0, whereas $n^S(u_1, u_2)$ equals 1; therefore, the value of $n^T(u, u')$ is $1/2 (= 0 \sqcup 1)$.
- In S, $n^S(u_2, u_3)$ and $n^S(u_3, u_4)$ both equal 1, whereas $n^S(u_2, u_2)$, $n^S(u_2, u_4)$, $n^S(u_3, u_2)$, $n^S(u_3, u_3)$, $n^S(u_4, u_2)$, $n^S(u_4, u_3)$, and $n^S(u_4, u_4)$ all equal 0; therefore, the value of $n^T(u', u')$ is $1/2 (= 0 \sqcup 1)$.

In the upper-left-hand corner of Fig. 2, the boxes in the tables for predicates n and eq indicate these four groupings of values.

In a 2-valued structure, the eq predicate represents the equality relation on individuals. In general, under canonical abstraction some individuals "lose their identity" because of uncertainty that arises in the eq predicate. For instance, $eq^T(u, u) = 1$ because u in T represents a single individual of S. On the other hand, u' represents three individuals of S and the quotient operation causes $eq^T(u', u')$ to have the value $1/2$. An individual like u' is called a *summary individual*.

---

[3] The names of individuals are completely arbitrary: what distinguishes u' is the value of its vector of abstraction predicates.

A 3-valued logical structure T is used as an abstract descriptor of a set of 2-valued logical structures. In general, a summary individual models a *set* of individuals in each of the 2-valued logical structures that T represents. The graphical notation for 3-valued logical structures (cf. structure T of Fig. 2) is derived from the one for 2-valued structures, with the following additions:

- Individuals are represented by circles containing their names. (In Figs. 3 and 4, we also place unary predicates that do not correspond to pointer-valued program variables inside the circles.)
- A summary individual is represented by a double circle.
- Unary and binary predicates with value $1/2$ are represented by dotted arrows.

Thus, in every concrete structure $\tilde{S}$ that is represented by abstract structure T of Fig. 2, pointer variables x and y definitely point to the concrete node of $\tilde{S}$ that u represents. The n-field of that node may point to one of the concrete nodes that u' represents; u' is a summary individual, i.e., it may represent more than one concrete node in $\tilde{S}$. Possibly there is an n-field in one or more of these concrete nodes that points to another of the concrete nodes that u' represents, but there cannot be an n-field in any of these concrete nodes that points to the concrete node that u represents.

Note that 3-valued structure T also represents

- the acyclic lists of length 3 or more that are pointed to by x and y.
- the cyclic lists of length 3 or more that are pointed to by x and y, such that the back-pointer is not to the head of the list, but to the second, third, or later element.
- some additional memory configurations with a cyclic or acyclic list pointed to by x and y that also contain some garbage cells that are not reachable from x and y.

That is, T is a finite representation of an infinite set of (possibly cyclic) concrete lists, each of which may also be accompanied by some unreachable cells. Later in this section, we discuss options for fine-tuning an abstraction. In particular, we will use canonical abstraction to define an abstraction in which the acyclic lists and the cyclic lists are mapped to different 3-valued structures (and in which the presence or absence of unreachable cells is readily apparent).

Canonical abstraction ensures that each 3-valued structure has an *a priori* bounded size, which guarantees that a fixed-point will always be reached by an iterative static-analysis algorithm. Another advantage of using 2- and 3-valued logic as the basis for static analysis is that the language used for extracting information from the concrete world and the abstract world is identical: *every* syntactic expression – i.e., every logical formula – can be interpreted either in the 2-valued world or the 3-valued world[4].

The consistency of the 2-valued and 3-valued viewpoints is ensured by a basic theorem that relates the two logics. This explains Point (5) mentioned in Sect. 1: the method eliminates the need for the user to write the usual proofs required with abstract interpretation. Thanks to a single meta-theorem (the Embedding Theorem [17, Theorem 4.9]),

---

[4] Formulas are first-order formulas with transitive closure: a *formula* over the vocabulary $\mathcal{P} = \{eq, p_1, \ldots, p_n\}$ is defined as follows (where $p^*(v_1, v_2)$ stands for the reflexive transitive closure of $p(v_1, v_2)$):

$$p \in \mathcal{P}, \varphi \in \textit{Formulas}, \quad \varphi ::= \mathbf{0} \mid \mathbf{1} \mid p(v_1, \ldots, v_k) \mid (\neg\varphi_1) \mid (\varphi_1 \wedge \varphi_2) \mid (\varphi_1 \vee \varphi_2)$$
$$v \in \textit{Variables} \qquad\qquad \mid (\exists v: \varphi_1) \mid (\forall v: \varphi_1) \mid p^*(v_1, v_2)$$

which shows that information extracted from a 3-valued structure T by evaluating a formula φ is sound with respect to the value of φ in each of the 2-valued structures that T represents, an abstract semantics falls out automatically from the specification of the concrete semantics. In particular, the formulas that define the concrete semantics when interpreted in 2-valued logic define a sound abstract semantics when interpreted in 3-valued logic (see Fig. 2). Soundness of *all* instantiations of the analysis framework is ensured by the Embedding Theorem.

Program Analysis via 3-Valued Logic. A run of the analyzer carries out an abstract interpretation to collect a set of 3-valued structures at each program point. This involves finding the least fixed-point of a certain set of equations. Because canonical abstraction ensures that each 3-valued structure has an *a priori* bounded size, there are only a finite number of sets of 3-valued structures. This guarantees that a fixed-point is always reached. The structures collected at program point P describe a superset of all the execution states that can occur at P. To determine whether a property always holds at P, one checks whether it holds in all of the structures that were collected there.

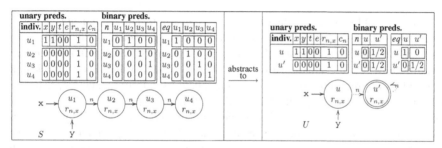

Fig. 3. The abstraction of 2-valued structure S to 3-valued structure U when we use $\{x, y, t, e, r_{n,x}, c_n\}$-abstraction. In contrast with T, T', and T'' from Fig. 2, U represents only acyclic lists of length 3 or more (with no garbage cells).

Instrumentation Predicates. Unfortunately, unless some care is taken in the design of an analysis, there is a danger that as abstract interpretation proceeds, the indefinite value $1/2$ will become pervasive. This can destroy the ability to recover interesting information from the 3-valued structures collected (although soundness is maintained). A key role in combating indefiniteness is played by *instrumentation predicates*, which record auxiliary information in a logical structure. They provide a mechanism for the user to fine-tune an abstraction: an instrumentation predicate p of arity k, which is defined by a logical formula $\psi_p(v_1, \ldots, v_k)$ over the core predicate symbols, captures a property that each k-tuple of nodes may or may not possess. In general, adding additional instrumentation predicates refines the abstraction, defining a more precise analysis that is prepared to track finer distinctions among nodes. This allows more properties of the program's stores to be identified during analysis.

The introduction of unary instrumentation predicates that are then used as abstraction predicates provides a way to control which concrete individuals are merged together into summary nodes, and thereby to control the amount of information lost by abstraction. Instrumentation predicates that involve reachability properties, which can be defined using transitive closure, often play a crucial role in the definitions of abstractions (cf. Fig. 3). For instance, in program-analysis applications, reachability properties from specific pointer variables have the effect of keeping disjoint sublists or subtrees summarized separately. This is particularly important when analyzing a program in which two pointers are advanced along disjoint sublists. Tab. 2 lists some instrumentation predicates that are important for the analysis of programs that use type List.

Table 2. Defining formulas of some commonly used instrumentation predicates. Typically, there is a separate predicate symbol $r_{n,x}$ for every pointer-valued variable x.

p	IntendedMeaning	ψ_p
$t_n(v_1, v_2)$	Is v_2 reachable from v_1 along n-fields?	$n^*(v_1, v_2)$
$r_{n,x}(v)$	Is v reachable from pointer variable x along n-fields?	$\exists v_1 : x(v_1) \wedge t_n(v_1, v)$
$c_n(v)$	Is v on a directed cycle of n-fields?	$\exists v_1 : n(v, v_1) \wedge t_n(v_1, v)$

From the standpoint of the concrete semantics, instrumentation predicates represent cached information that could always be recomputed by reevaluating the instrumentation predicate's defining formula in the current store. From the standpoint of the abstract semantics, however, reevaluating a formula in the current (3-valued) store can lead to a drastic loss of precision. To gain maximum benefit from instrumentation predicates, an abstract-interpretation algorithm must obtain their values in some other way. This problem, the *instrumentation-predicate-maintenance problem*, is solved by incremental computation; the new value that instrumentation predicate p should have after a transition via abstract state transformer τ from state σ to σ' is computed incrementally from the known value of p in σ. An algorithm that uses τ and p's defining formula $\psi_p(v_1, \ldots, v_k)$ to generate an appropriate incremental predicate-maintenance formula for p is presented in [22].

The problem of automatically identifying appropriate instrumentation predicates, using a process of abstraction refinement, is addressed in [23]. In that paper, the input required to specify a program analysis consists of (i) a program, (ii) a characterization of the inputs, and (iii) a query (i.e., a formula that characterizes the intended output). This work, along with [22], provides a framework for eliminating previously required user inputs for which TVLA has been criticized in the past.

Other Operations on Logical Structures. Thanks to the fact that the Embedding Theorem applies to any pair of structures for which one can be embedded into the other, most operations on 3-valued structures need not be constrained to manipulate 3-valued structures that are images of canonical abstraction. Thus, it is not necessary to perform canonical abstraction after the application of each abstract structure transformer. To ensure that abstract interpretation terminates, it is only necessary that canonical abstraction be applied as a widening operator somewhere in each loop, e.g., at the target of each back-edge in the control-flow graph.

Unfortunately, the simple abstract semantics obtained by applying predicate-update formulas to 3-valued structures can be very imprecise. For instance, in Fig. 2, y = y->n sets y to point to the next element in the list. In the abstract semantics, the evaluation in structure T of predicate-update formula $y'(v) = \exists v_1 : y(v_1) \wedge n(v_1, v)$ causes $y^{T'}(u')$ to be set to 1/2. Consequently, all we can surmise in T' is that y may point to one of the cells that summary node u' represents. In contrast, the canonical abstraction of S' is T'', which demonstrates that the abstract domain is capable of representing a more precise abstract semantics than the T-to-T' transformation illustrated in Fig. 2.

In [24], it is shown that for a Galois connection defined by abstraction function α and concretization function γ, the best abstract transformer for a concrete transformer τ, denoted by $\tau^{\sharp}$, can be expressed as: $\tau^{\sharp} = \alpha \circ \tau \circ \gamma$. This defines the limit of precision obtainable using a given abstract domain; however, it is a non-constructive definition: it does not provide an *algorithm* for finding or applying $\tau^{\sharp}$.

To help prevent an analysis from losing precision, several other operations on logical structures are used to implement a better approximation to the best transformer [17]:

- *Focus* is an operation that can be invoked to elaborate a 3-valued structure – allowing it to be replaced by a set of more precise structures (not necessarily images of canonical abstraction) that represent the same set of concrete stores.

- *Coerce* is a clean-up operation that may "sharpen" a 3-valued structure by setting an indefinite value (1/2) to a definite value (0 or 1), or discard a structure entirely if the structure exhibits some fundamental inconsistency (e.g., it cannot represent any possible concrete store).

The transformers used in TVLA make use of *Focus*, *Coerce*, and incremental predicate-maintenance formulas to implement a better approximation to the best transformer than the T-to-T' transformation of Fig. 2. In particular, TVLA is capable of "materializing" non-summary nodes from summary nodes. For instance, given T, TVLA's transformer for y = y->n would create structure T'' (among others) – in essence, materializing u_2 out of u'. Materialization permits the abstract execution of an assignment to a pointer-valued field of a newly created non-summary node to perform a *strong update*.

Dynamically Allocated Storage. One way to model the semantics of x = malloc() is to model the free-storage list explicitly [22], so as to exploit materialization:

A malloc is modeled by advancing the pointer freelist into the list, and returning the memory cell that it formerly pointed to. A free is modeled by inserting, at the head of freelist's list, the cell being deallocated.

3   Applications and Extensions

Interprocedural Analysis. The application of canonical abstraction to interprocedural analysis of programs with recursion has been studied in both [25] and [26]. In [25], the main idea is to expose the runtime stack as an explicit "data structure" of the concrete semantics; that is, activation records are individuals, and suitable core predicates are introduced to capture how activation records are linked together to form a stack. Instrumentation predicates are used to record information about the calling context and the "invisible" copies of variables in pending activation records on the stack.

The analysis in [26] is based on logical structures over a doubled vocabulary $\mathcal{P} \uplus \mathcal{P}'$, where $\mathcal{P}' = \{p' \mid p \in \mathcal{P}\}$ and $\uplus$ denotes disjoint union. This approach creates a finite abstraction that relates the predicate values for an individual at the beginning of a transition to the predicate values for the individual at the end of the transition. Such two-vocabulary 3-valued structures are used to create a *summary transformer* for each procedure P, and the summary transformer is used at each call site at which P is called.

Checking Multithreaded Systems. In [27], it is shown how to apply 3-valued logic to the problem of checking properties of multithreaded systems. In particular, [27] addresses the problem of state-space exploration for languages, such as Java, that allow dynamic creation and destruction of an unbounded number of threads (as well as dynamic storage allocation and destructive updating of structure fields). Threads are modeled by individuals, which are abstracted using canonical abstraction – in this case, the collection of unary thread properties that hold for a given thread. The use of this naming scheme automatically discovers commonalities in the state space, but without relying on explicitly supplied symmetry properties, as in, for example, [28]. The analysis algorithm given in [27] builds and explores a 3-valued transition system on-the-fly. Unary core predicates are used to represent the program counter of each thread object; *Focus* is used to implement nondeterministic selection of a runable thread.

Numeric Abstractions. The abstractions described in Sect. 2 are capable of representing pointer variables, their contents, and the structure of the heap, but have no direct way of representing the actual data items that are stored in the nodes of data structures. Recent work [21] has coupled canonical abstraction with a variety of previously known numeric abstractions: intervals, congruences, polyhedra [29], and various restrictions on polyhedral domains (such as difference constraints [30, 31] and 2-variable constraints [32]). These overapproximate the states that can arise in a program using sets of points in a k-dimensional space. However, when canonical abstraction is used to create bounded-size representations of memory configurations, the number of nodes in an abstract descriptor is different at different points in the program; for numeric abstractions, this means that the number of *axes* changes from program point to program point – i.e., there is not a fixed value of k. To capture numeric properties in such a *summarizing* framework, an analysis needs to be able to capture the relationships among values of *groups* of numeric objects, rather than relationships among values of *individual* numeric objects [21].

Best Abstract Transformers. As mentioned in Sect. 2, for a Galois connection (α, γ), a non-constructive definition of the best abstract transformer $\tau^\sharp$ for concrete transformer τ can be expressed as $\tau^\sharp = \alpha \circ \tau \circ \gamma$. This defines the limit of precision obtainable using a given abstract domain, but does not provide an *algorithm* for finding or applying $\tau^\sharp$. Graf and Saïdi [33] showed that decision procedures can be used to generate best abstract transformers for abstract domains that are finite Cartesian products of Boolean values. (The use of such domains is known as *predicate abstraction*.)

The ability to perform abstract interpretation using best abstract transformers could play a key role in combating indefiniteness in 3-valued structures. It would ensure that an abstract interpretation computes answers that are *precise up to the inherent limitations of the abstraction in use*. In recent work, we have made a start towards this goal. In particular, we have defined two approaches to computing best transformers for applications that use canonical abstraction [34, 35].

Applications. Some of the problems to which the 3-valued-logic approach has been applied include the following: In [36], TVLA was used to establish the partial correctness of bubble-sort and insert-sort routines for sorting linked lists. The abstraction-refinement method of [23] was used to extend this work to address stability and anti-stability properties of sorting routines. TVLA has also been used to demonstrate the total correctness of a mark-and-sweep garbage collector operating on an arbitrary heap. In Java, once an iterator object o_i is created for a collection o_c, o_i may be used only as long as o_c remains unmodified, not counting modifications made via o_i; otherwise a "concurrent modification exception" is thrown. In [37], TVLA was used to create a verification tool for establishing the absence of concurrent modification exceptions.

In the area of multithreaded systems, the 3-valued-logic approach has been used to establish the absence of deadlock for a dining-philosophers program that permits there to be an unbounded number of philosophers [27], as well as to establish the partial correctness of two concurrent queue algorithms; these results were obtained without imposing any *a priori* bound on the number of allocated objects and threads [38].

4 Related Work

Predicate Abstraction. Canonical abstraction is sometimes confused with predicate abstraction, which has been used in a variety of systems [33, 39, 6, 40]. At one level, predicate abstraction and canonical abstraction use essentially the same mechanism:

- Predicate abstraction can be used to abstract a possibly-infinite transition system to a finite one: concrete states of the transition system are grouped into abstract states according to the values of a vector of properties. The transition relation is quotiented by the equivalence relation induced on concrete states.
- Canonical abstraction is used to abstract a possibly-infinite logical structure to a finite 3-valued one: concrete individuals are mapped to abstract individuals according to the values of a vector of unary abstraction predicates; all other predicates are quotiented by the equivalence relation induced on concrete individuals.

However, as used in [17], canonical abstraction is applied to encodings of stores as logical structures, and machinery is developed to use 3-valued structures to define a parametric abstract domain for abstract interpretation. Predicate abstraction has also been used to define a parametric abstract domain [41]. Thus, an alternative comparison criterion is to consider the relationship between the two parametric abstract domains:

- Predicate abstraction yields a parametric abstract domain based on finite Cartesian products of Booleans (i.e., nullary predicates). An abstract value consists of a finite set of finite-sized vectors of nullary predicates [41].
- Canonical abstraction yields a parametric abstract domain based on 3-valued logical structures. An abstract value consists of a finite set of finite-sized 3-valued structures [17].

A special case of canonical abstraction occurs when *no* abstraction predicates are used at all, in which case all individuals are collapsed to a single individual. When this is done, in almost all structures the only useful information remaining resides in the *nullary* core and instrumentation predicates. Predicate abstraction can be seen as going one step further, and retaining *only* the nullary predicates. From this point of view, canonical abstraction is *strictly more general* than predicate abstraction.

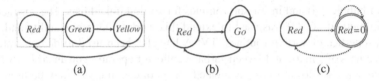

(a)   (b)   (c)

Fig. 4. (a) Transition diagram for a stoplight; (b) transition diagram abstracted via the method of [42] when *green* and *yellow* are mapped to *go*; (c) transition diagram abstracted via canonical abstraction, using $red(v)$ as the only abstraction predicate.

Existential Abstraction. Canonical abstraction is also related to the notion of *existential abstraction* used in [43, 42]. However, canonical abstraction yields 3-valued predicates and distinguishes summary nodes from non-summary nodes, whereas existential abstraction yields 2-valued predicates and does not distinguish summary nodes from non-summary nodes. Fig. 4 shows the transition diagram for a stoplight – an example used in [42] – abstracted via the method of [42] (Fig. 4(b)) and via canonical abstraction, using $red(v)$ as the only abstraction predicate (Fig. 4(c)). With existential abstraction, soundness is preserved by restricting attention to universal formulas (formulas in ACTL*). With canonical abstraction, soundness is also preserved by switching logics, although in this case there is no syntactic restriction; we switch from 2-valued first-order logic to 3-valued first-order logic. An advantage of this approach is that if φ is any formula for a query about a concrete state, the same syntactic formula φ can be used to pose the same query about an abstract state.

One-Sided versus Two-Sided Answers. Most static-analysis algorithms provide 2-valued answers, but are *one-sided*: an answer is *definite* on one value and *conservative* on the other. That is, either 0 means 0, and 1 means "maybe"; or 1 means 1, and 0 means "maybe". In contrast, by basing the abstract semantics on 3-valued logic, definite truth and definite falseness can both be tracked, with $1/2$ capturing indefiniteness. (To determine whether a formula φ holds at P, it is evaluated in each of the structures that are collected at P. The answer is the *join* of these values.) This provides insight into the true nature of the one-sided approach. For instance, an analysis that is definite with respect to 1 is really a 3-valued analysis that conflates 0 and $1/2$ (and uses 0 in place of $1/2$). (It should be noted that with a two-sided analysis, the answers 0 and 1 are definite with respect to the concrete semantics *as specified*, which may itself overapproximate the behavior of the actual system being modeled.)

Acknowledgments

We thank our many students and collaborators.

References

1. Havelund, K., Pressburger, T.: Model checking Java programs using Java PathFinder. Softw. Tools for Tech. Transfer **2** (2000)
2. Wagner, D., Foster, J., Brewer, E., Aiken, A.: A first step towards automated detection of buffer overrun vulnerabilities. In: Network and Dist. Syst. Security. (2000)
3. Engler, D., Chelf, B., Chou, A., Hallem, S.: Checking system rules using system-specific, programmer-written compiler extensions. In: Op. Syst. Design and Impl. (2000) 1–16
4. Corbett, J., Dwyer, M., Hatcliff, J., Laubach, S., Pasareanu, C., Robby, Zheng, H.: Bandera: Extracting finite-state models from Java source code. In: Int. Conf. on Softw. Eng. (2000) 439–448
5. Bush, W., Pincus, J., Sielaff, D.: A static analyzer for finding dynamic programming errors. Software–Practice&Experience **30** (2000) 775–802
6. Ball, T., Rajamani, S.: The SLAM toolkit. In: Int. Conf. on Computer Aided Verif. Volume 2102 of Lec. Notes in Comp. Sci. (2001) 260–264
7. Chen, H., Wagner, D.: MOPS: An infrastructure for examining security properties of software. In: Conf. on Comp. and Commun. Sec. (2002) 235–244
8. Andersen, L.O.: Binding-time analysis and the taming of C pointers. In: Part. Eval. and Semantics-Based Prog. Manip. (1993) 47–58
9. Steensgaard, B.: Points-to analysis in almost-linear time. In: Princ. of Prog. Lang. (1996) 32–41
10. Das, M.: Unification-based pointer analysis with directional assignments. In: Prog. Lang. Design and Impl. (2000) 35–46
11. Fähndrich, M., Rehof, J., Das, M.: Scalable context-sensitive flow analysis using instantiation constraints. In: Prog. Lang. Design and Impl. (2000) 253–263
12. Cheng, B.C., Hwu, W.: Modular interprocedural pointer analysis using access paths: Design, implementation, and evaluation. In: Prog. Lang. Design and Impl. (2000) 57–69
13. Foster, J., Fähndrich, M., Aiken, A.: Polymorphic versus monomorphic flow-insensitive points-to analysis for C. In: Static Analysis Symp. (2000) 175–198
14. Whaley, J., Lam, M.: Cloning-based context-sensitive pointer alias analyses using binary decision diagrams. In: Prog. Lang. Design and Impl. (2004) To appear.
15. Zhu, J., Calman, S.: Symbolic pointer analysis revisited. In: Prog. Lang. Design and Impl. (2004) To appear.
16. M.Das, Liblit, B., Fähndrich, M., Rehof, J.: Estimating the impact of scalable pointer analysis on optimization. In: Static Analysis Symp. (2001) 260–278
17. Sagiv, M., Reps, T., Wilhelm, R.: Parametric shape analysis via 3-valued logic. Trans. on Prog. Lang. and Syst. **24** (2002) 217–298
18. Cousot, P., Cousot, R.: Abstract interpretation: A unified lattice model for static analysis of programs by construction of approximation of fixed points. In: Princ. of Prog. Lang. (1977) 238–252

19. Lev-Ami, T., Sagiv, M.: TVLA: A system for implementing static analyses. In: Static Analysis Symp. (2000) 280–301
20. (TVLA system) "http://www.math.tau.ac.il/~rumster/TVLA/".
21. Gopan, D., DiMaio, F., N.Dor, Reps, T., Sagiv, M.: Numeric domains with summarized dimensions. In: Tools and Algs. for the Construct. and Anal. of Syst. (2004) 512–529
22. Reps, T., Sagiv, M., Loginov, A.: Finite differencing of logical formulas for static analysis. In: European Symp. On Programming. (2003) 380–398
23. Loginov, A., Reps, T., Sagiv, M.: Abstraction refinement for 3-valued-logic analysis. Tech. Rep. 1504, Comp. Sci. Dept., Univ. of Wisconsin (2004)
24. Cousot, P., Cousot, R.: Systematic design of program analysis frameworks. In: Princ. of Prog. Lang. (1979) 269–282
25. Rinetzky, N., Sagiv, M.: Interprocedural shape analysis for recursive programs. In: Comp. Construct. Volume 2027 of Lec. Notes in Comp. Sci. (2001) 133–149
26. Jeannet, B., Loginov, A., Reps, T., Sagiv, M.: A relational approach to interprocedural shape analysis. Tech. Rep. 1505, Comp. Sci. Dept., Univ. of Wisconsin (2004)
27. Yahav, E.: Verifying safety properties of concurrent Java programs using 3-valued logic. In: Princ. of Prog. Lang. (2001) 27–40
28. Emerson, E., Sistla, A.: Symmetry and model checking. In Courcoubetis, C., ed.: Int. Conf. on Computer Aided Verif. (1993) 463–478
29. Cousot, P., Halbwachs, N.: Automatic discovery of linear constraints among variables of a program. In: Princ. of Prog. Lang. (1978)
30. Dill, D.: Timing assumptions and verification of finite-state concurrent systems. In: Automatic Verification Methods for Finite State Systems. (1989) 197–212
31. Miné, A.: A few graph-based relational numerical abstract domains. In: Static Analysis Symp. (2002) 117–132
32. Simon, A., King, A., Howe, J.: Two variables per linear inequality as an abstract domain. In: Int. Workshop on Logic Based Prog. Dev. and Transformation. (2002) 71–89
33. Graf, S., Saïdi, H.: Construction of abstract state graphs with PVS. In: Int. Conf. on Computer Aided Verif. Volume 1254 of Lec. Notes in Comp. Sci. (1997) 72–83
34. Reps, T., Sagiv, M., Yorsh, G.: Symbolic implementation of the best transformer. In: Verif., Model Checking, and Abs. Interp. (2004) 252–266
35. Yorsh, G., Reps, T., Sagiv, M.: Symbolically computing most-precise abstract operations for shape analysis. In: Tools and Algs. for the Construct. and Anal. of Syst. (2004) 530–545
36. Lev-Ami, T., Reps, T., Sagiv, M., Wilhelm, R.: Putting static analysis to work for verification: A case study. In: Int. Symp. on Softw. Testing and Analysis. (2000) 26–38
37. Ramalingam, G., Warshavsky, A., Field, J., Goyal, D., Sagiv, M.: Deriving specialized program analyses for certifying component-client conformance. In: Prog. Lang. Design and Impl. (2002) 83–94
38. Yahav, E., Sagiv, M.: Automatically verifying concurrent queue algorithms. In: Workshop on Software Model Checking. (2003)
39. Das, S., Dill, D., Park, S.: Experience with predicate abstraction. In: Int. Conf. on Computer Aided Verif., Springer-Verlag (1999) 160–171
40. Henzinger, T., Jhala, R., Majumdar, R., Sutre, G.: Lazy abstraction. In: Princ. of Prog. Lang. (2002) 58–70
41. Ball, T., Podelski, A., Rajamani, S.: Boolean and Cartesian abstraction for model checking C programs. In: Tools and Algs. for the Construct. and Anal. of Syst. (2001) 268–283
42. Clarke, E., Grumberg, O., Jha, S., Lu, Y., Veith, H.: Counterexample-guided abstraction refinement. In: Int. Conf. on Computer Aided Verif. (2000) 154–169
43. Clarke, E., Grumberg, O., Long, D.: Model checking and abstraction. Trans. on Prog. Lang. and Syst. 16 (1994) 1512–1542

Deductive Verification of Pipelined Machines Using First-Order Quantification[*]

Sandip Ray and Warren A. Hunt, Jr.

Department of Computer Sciences, University of Texas at Austin
{sandip,hunt}@cs.utexas.edu
http://www.cs.utexas.edu/users/{sandip,hunt}

Abstract. We outline a theorem-proving approach to verify pipelined machines. Pipelined machines are complicated to reason about since they involve simultaneous overlapped execution of different instructions. Nevertheless, we show that if the logic used is sufficiently expressive, then it is possible to relate the executions of the pipelined machine with the corresponding Instruction Set Architecture using (stuttering) simulation. Our methodology uses first-order quantification to define a predicate that relates pipeline states with ISA states and uses its *Skolem witness* for correspondence proofs. Our methodology can be used to reason about *generic* pipelines with interrupts, stalls, and exceptions, and we demonstrate its use in verifying pipelines mechanically in the ACL2 theorem prover.

1 Introduction

This paper is concerned with formal verification of pipelined machines. Pipelining is a key feature in the design of today's microprocessors. It improves performance by temporally overlapping execution of different instructions; that is, by initiating execution of a subsequent instruction before a preceding instruction has been completed. To formally verify modern microprocessors, it is imperative to be able to effectively reason about modern pipelines.

Formal verification of microprocessors normally involves showing some correspondence between a microarchitectural implementation (MA) and its corresponding Instruction Set Architecture (ISA). The ISA is typically a non-pipelined machine which executes each instruction atomically. For non-pipelined microprocessors, one typically shows *simulation correspondence* (Fig. 1): If an implementation state is externally equal to a specification state, then executing one instruction in both the microarchitecture and the ISA results in states that are externally equal [1,2]. This implies that for every (infinite) execution of MA, there is a *corresponding* (infinite) execution of the ISA with the same visible behavior. However, for pipelined machines, such correlations are difficult to establish because of *latency* in the pipelines. As a result, a large number of correspondence notions have been used to reason about pipelined machines.

---

[*] Support for this work was provided in part by the SRC under contract 02-TJ-1032.

R. Alur and D.A. Peled (Eds.): CAV 2004, LNCS 3114, pp. 31–43, 2004.

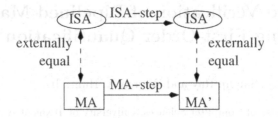

Fig. 1. Commutative Diagram for Simulation Correspondence

As features like interrupts, and out-of-order instruction execution have been modeled and reasoned about, notions of correctness have had to be modified and extended to account for these features. Consequently, the correspondence theorems have become complicated, difficult to understand, and even controversial [3]. Further, the lack of uniformity has made composition of proofs of different components of a modern processor cumbersome and difficult.

In this paper, we argue that in a logic that allows arbitrary first-order quantification and Skolemization, simulation-based correspondence is still effective and sufficient for reasoning about modern pipelines. Our notion of correctness is *stuttering simulations* [2], and preserves both *safety* and *liveness* properties. The chief contribution of this work is to show how to effectively use quantification to define a correspondence relating the states of a pipelined machine with those of its ISA. Our work makes use of the Burch and Dill *pipeline flushing diagram* [4] (Fig. 2), to derive the correspondence without complicated invariant definitions or characterization of the precise timing between the execution of different instructions in the pipeline. Indeed, our techniques are generic and we are able to apply the *same* notion of correspondence to pipelines with stalls, interrupts, exceptions, and out-of-order execution, and verify such machines mechanically with reasonable automation.

In this section, we first survey related approaches and notions of correctness used in verification of pipelined machines. We then describe our approach and proof methodology in greater detail.

1.1   Related Work

Reasoning about pipelines has been an active area of research. Aagaard *et al.* [3] provides an excellent survey and comparison of the different techniques. Some of the early studies have used *skewed abstraction functions* [5,6] to map the states of the pipeline at different moments to a single ISA state. The skewed abstraction functions need to precisely characterize all timing delays and hence their definitions are both complex and vulnerable to design modifications. By far the most popular notion of correctness used has been the Burch and Dill *pipeline flushing diagram* [4] (Fig. 2). The approach is to use the implementation itself to flush the pipeline by not permitting new instructions to be fetched, and projecting the programmer-visible components of the flushed state to de-

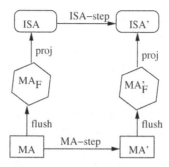

Fig. 2. Burch and Dill Pipeline Flushing Diagram

fine the corresponding ISA state. Sawada and Hunt [7, 8] use a variant called
flush point alignment to verify a complicated pipelined microprocessor with exceptions, stalls, and interrupts using the ACL2 theorem prover. They use an
intermediate data structure called MAETT to keep track of the history of execution of the different instructions through the pipeline. Hosabettu *et al.* [9]
use another variant, *flush point refinement*, and they verify a deterministic out-
of-order machine using *completion functions*. Both of these approaches require
construction of complicated invariants to demonstrate correlation between the
pipelined machine and the ISA. In addition, there have also been compositional
model checking approaches to reason about pipelines. For example, Jhala and
McMillan [10] use symmetry, temporal case-splitting, and data-type reduction
to verify out-of-order pipelines. While more automatic than theorem proving,
applicability of the method in practice requires the user to explicitly decompose
the proof into manageable pieces to alleviate *state explosion*. Further, it relies
on symmetry assumptions which are often violated by the heterogeneity of modern pipelines. Finally, there has been work on using a combination of decision
procedures and theorem proving to verify modern pipelines [11, 12], whereby decision procedures have been used to assist the theorem prover in verifying state
invariants.

Manolios [13] shows logical problems with the Burch and Dill notion and provides a general notion of correctness using *well-founded equivalence bisimulation*
(WEB) [14]. He uses it to reason about several variants of Sawada's pipelines [7].
This, to our knowledge, is the first attempt in reasoning about pipelines using
a general-purpose correctness notion expressing both safety and liveness properties. Our notion of correctness and proof rules are a direct consequence of the
work with WEBs. The basic difference between our approach and that of Manolios is in the methodology used for relating pipeline states with ISA states. Since
this methodology is a key contribution of this paper, we compare our approach
with his in greater detail after outlining our techniques in Section 3.

1.2   Overview of Our Approach

We now describe how it is possible to relate pipeline states with the corresponding ISA using simulation-based correspondence in spite of overlapped execution

of different instructions. Note that our quest here is for a *generic* approach rather than the verification of one specific design. To convey the basic idea we present a simplified view of pipelined machines, namely in-order execution and completion of at most one instruction in a clock cycle. A precise mathematical description is presented later in Section 3, and features like interrupts, out-of-order execution etc., are dealt with in Section 4.

Consider the pipelined machine in some state MA, where a specific instruction i_1 is poised to complete. Presumably, then, before reaching MA, the machine must have encountered some state MA_1 in which i_1 was poised to enter the pipeline. Call MA_1 the *witnessing state* of MA. Assuming that instructions are completed in order, all and only the incomplete instructions at state MA_1 (meaning, all instructions before i_1) must complete before the pipeline can reach state MA starting from MA_1. Now consider the state MA_{1F} obtained by flushing MA_1. The flushing operation also completes all incomplete instructions without fetching any new instructions; that is, MA_{1F} has all instructions before i_1 completed, and is poised to fetch i_1. If only completed instructions affect the visible behavior of the machine, then this suggests that MA_{1F} and MA must be externally equal[1].

Based on the above intuition, we define a relation *sim* to correlate pipeline states with ISA states: MA is related to ISA if and only if there exists a witnessing state MA_1 such that ISA is the projection of the visible components of MA_{1F}. Recall that projection preserves the visible components of a state. From the arguments above, whenever states MA and ISA are related by *sim* they are externally equal. Thus to establish simulation correspondence (Fig. 1), we need to show that if MA is related to ISA, and MA' and ISA' are states obtained by 1-step execution from MA and ISA respectively, then MA' and ISA' are related by *sim*. Our approach is shown in Fig. 3. Roughly, we show that if MA and ISA

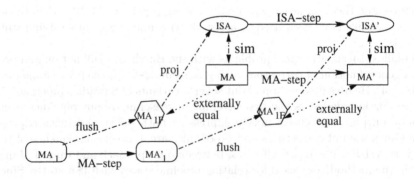

Fig. 3. Use of Burch and Dill and Symbolic Execution to obtain Simulation-based refinement proofs

---

[1] Notice that MA and MA_{1F} would possibly have different values of the program counter. This is normally addressed [13] by excluding the program counter from the observations (or *labels*) of a state.

are related, and MA_1 is the corresponding witnessing state for MA, then one can construct a corresponding witnessing state for MA' by running the pipeline for a sufficient number of steps from MA_1. In particular, ignoring the possibility of stalls (or bubbles) in the pipeline, the state following MA_1, which is MA'_1, is a witnessing state of MA', by the following argument. Execution of the pipeline for one cycle from MA completes i_1 and the next instruction, i_2, *after* i_1 in program order is poised to complete in state MA'. The witnessing state for MA' thus should be poised to initiate i_2 in the pipeline. And indeed, execution for one cycle from MA_1 leaves the machine in a state in which i_2 is poised to enter the pipeline. (We make this argument more precise in the context of an example pipeline using Lemma 2 in Section 3.) Finally, the correspondence between MA'_1 and ISA' follows by noting that the MA states MA_1, MA'_1, and ISA states ISA and ISA' satisfy the Burch and Dill *pipeline flushing diagram*.

The reader should note that the above proof approach depends on our determining the witnessing state MA_1 given MA. However, since MA_1 is a state that occurs in the "past" of MA, MA might not retain sufficient information for *computing* MA_1. In general, to compute witnessing states, one needs to define an intermediate machine to keep track of the history of execution of the different instructions in the pipeline. However, an observation of this paper is that given a sufficiently expressive logic, the witnessing state need not be constructively computed. Rather, we can simply define a predicate specifying "some witnessing state exists". Skolemization of the predicate then produces a witnessing state.

In the presence of stalls, a state MA might not have *any* instruction poised to complete. Even for pipelines without stalls, no instruction completes for several cycles after the initiation of the machine. Correspondence in the presence of such bubbles is achieved by allowing finite stutter in our verification framework. In other words, if MA is related to ISA, and MA has no instruction to complete, then MA' is related to ISA instead of ISA'. Our proof rules guarantee such stuttering is finite, allowing us to preserve both safety and liveness properties. Note that correspondence frameworks allowing a finite stutter are known to be effective in relating two system models at different levels of abstraction using simulation and bisimulation. In ACL2, stuttering has been used with simulation and bisimulation to verify concurrent protocols [15, 14], and indeed, pipelined machines [13].

The remainder of the paper is organized as follows. We discuss our notion of correspondence and the associated proof rules in Section 2. In Section 3, we discuss the correspondence proof for an example pipelined machine. In Section 4, we show how our method can be used to reason about pipelines with interrupts, out-of-order execution etc. Finally, we conclude in Section 5. All the theorems described here have been proven with the ACL2 theorem prover [16, 17]. ACL2 is an essentially first-order logic of total recursive functions, with induction up to ϵ_0 and support for first-order quantification via Skolemization. However, this paper does not assume any prior exposure to ACL2; we use traditional mathematical notations for our presentation.

2   Refinements

Our proof rules relate infinite executions of two computing systems using single-step theorems. The rules are adapted from the proof rules for *stuttering simulation* [2], and a direct consequence of work with WEBs [14].

Computing systems are typically modeled in ACL2 as state machines by three functions namely *init*, *step*, and *label*, with the following semantics:

- The constant function *init*() returns the initial state of the system.
- Given a state s and an external input i, the function $step(s, i)$ returns the state of the system after one clock cycle.
- For a state s, the function $label(s)$ returns valuations of the observable components of s [2].

Such models are common in ACL2 and have been found useful in verification of several hardware and software systems [18, 1]. Also, since ACL2 is a logic of total functions, the functions *step* and *label* above are total.

We now describe the proof rules. Given models $impl = \langle init_I, step_I, label_I \rangle$, and $spec = \langle init_S, step_S, label_S \rangle$, the idea is to define binary predicates *sim* and *commit* with the following properties:

1. $sim(init_I(), init_S())$,
2. $\forall p_I, p_S : sim(p_I, p_S) \Rightarrow label_I(p_I) = label_S(p_s)$,
3. $\forall p_I, p_S, i, \exists j : sim(p_I, p_S) \land commit(p_I, i) \Rightarrow sim(step_I(p_I, i), step_S(p_S, j))$,
4. $\forall p_I, p_S, i : sim(p_I, p_S) \land \neg commit(p_I, i) \Rightarrow sim(step_I(p_I, i), p_S)$.

Informally, *sim* relates the states of *impl* with the states of *spec*, and *commit* determines whether the "current step" is a stuttering step for *spec*. The above four conditions guarantee that for every (infinite) execution of *impl*, there exists a corresponding (infinite) execution of *spec* that has the same observations up to stuttering. To guarantee that stuttering is finite, we define a unary function *rank* with the following properties:

5. $\forall p : rank(p) \in W$, where W is a set known to be well-founded according some ordering relation $\prec$.
6. $\forall p_I, p_S, i : sim(p_S, p_I) \land \neg commit(p_I, i) \Rightarrow rank(step_I(p_I, i)) \prec rank(p_I)$.

We say that *impl* is a (stuttering) *refinement* of *spec*, denoted ($impl \gg spec$), if there exist functions *sim*, *commit*, and *rank* that satisfy the six conditions above. The proof rules essentially guarantee that *impl* is a simulation of *spec* up to finite stuttering. The rules are analogous to proof rules for *stuttering simulation* [2] with the difference that our rules allow only one-sided stutter. We have not yet found a problem in which two-sided stutter has been necessary. Notice also that the notion of refinements is transitive, and this allows us to hierarchically compose proofs of different components of large practical systems.

Our description above shows how to relate two non-deterministic system models. A computing system $M = \langle init, step, label \rangle$ is *deterministic* if *step* is a

---

[2] The *label* is analogous to the valuation of atomic propositions in a Kripke Structure.

function of only the first argument, namely the current state. If *impl* is deterministic, then *commit* is a function of the current state alone. In addition, if *spec* is deterministic, then the condition 3 is modified to eliminate the choice of input for the next step of *spec*:

3. $\forall p_I, p_s, : sim(p_I, p_S) \land commit(p_I) \Rightarrow sim(step_I(p_I), step_S(p_S))$.

3   Pipeline Verification

We now show how to reason about pipelines using the correctness notion described in Section 2. For clarity of presentation, we consider a deterministic 5-stage example pipeline with in-order execution. Features like arbitrary stalls, interrupts, and out-of-order execution are dealt with in Section 4.

Our pipeline (Fig. 4) has *fetch*, *decode*, *operand-fetch*, *execute*, and *write-back* stages. The machine has a decoder, an ALU, a register file, and 4 latches

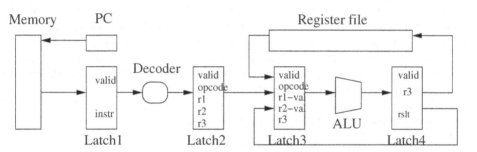

Fig. 4. A simple 5-stage pipeline

to store intermediate computations. Instructions are fetched from the memory location pointed to by the program counter (PC) and loaded into the first latch. The instructions then proceed in sequence through the different pipe stages in program order until they retire. Every latch has a *valid* bit to indicate if the latch is non-empty. We use a 3-address instruction format consisting of an opcode, two source registers, and a target register. While the machine allows only in-order execution, data forwarding is implemented from latch 4 to latch 3. Nevertheless, the pipeline can still have 1-cycle stall: If the instruction i_2 at latch 2 has as one of its source registers the target of the instruction i_3 at latch 3, then i_2 cannot proceed to latch 3 in the next state when i_3 completes its ALU operation.

The executions of the pipeline above can be defined as a *deterministic* model $MA = \langle init_I, step_I, label_I \rangle$. We assume that $init_I$ has *some* program loaded in the memory, and *some* initial configuration of the register file, but an empty pipeline. Since we are interested in the updates of the register file, we let $label_I$ preserve the register file of a state. Finally, the ISA machine $ISA = \langle init_S, step_S, label_S \rangle$ is merely one that executes the instruction pointed to by PC atomically; that is, it fetches the correct operands, applies the corresponding ALU operation, updates the register file, and increments PC in one atomic step.

Notice that we have left the actual instructions unspecified. Our proof approach does not require complete specification of the instructions but merely the constraint that the ISA performs analogous atomic update for each instruction. In ACL2, we use constrained functions for specifying the updates applied to instructions at every stage of the pipeline.

Our goal now is to show that (MA >> ISA). We define *commit* so that *commit*(*MA*) is true if and only if latch 4 is *valid* in *MA*. Notice that whenever an MA state *MA* satisfies *commit*, some instruction is completed at the *next step*. It will be convenient to define functions characterizing partial updates of an instruction in the pipeline. Consequently, we define four functions run_1, run_2, run_3, and run_4, where $run_i(MA, inst)$ "runs" instruction *inst* for the first i stages of the pipe and updates the i-th latch. For example, $run_2(MA, inst)$ updates latch 2 with the decoded value of the instruction. In addition, we define two functions, *flush* and *stalled*. Given a pipeline state *MA*, *flush*(*MA*) returns the flushed pipeline state MA_F, by executing the machine for sufficient number of cycles without fetching any new instruction. The predicate *stalled* is true of a state *MA* if and only if both latches 2 and 3 are *valid* in *MA*, and the destination for the instruction at latch 3 is one of the sources of the instruction at latch 2. Notice that executing a pipeline from a *stalled* state does not allow a new instruction to enter the pipeline. Finally the function *proj*(*MA*) projects the PC, memory, and register file of *MA* to the ISA.

Lemma 1 is the Burch and Dill correctness for pipelines with stalls and was proved automatically by ACL2 using symbolic simulation.

Lemma 1. *For each pipeline state MA,*

$$proj(flush(step_I(MA))) = \begin{cases} step_S(proj(flush(MA))) & if \ \neg stalled(MA) \\ proj(flush(MA)) & otherwise \end{cases}$$

We now define *witnessing states*. Given states MA_1 and *MA*, MA_1 is a *witnessing state* of *MA*, recognized by the predicate *witnessing*(MA_1, *MA*), if (1) MA_1 is not stalled, and (2) *MA* can be derived from MA_1 by the following procedure:

1. *Flush* MA_1 *to get the state* MA_{1F}.
2. *Apply the following update to* MA_{1F} *for* $i = 4, 3, 2, 1$:
   - *If latch* i *of MA is valid then apply* run_i *with the instruction pointed to by PC in* MA_{1F}, *correspondingly update latch* i *of* MA_{1F}, *and advance PC; otherwise do nothing.*

We now define predicate *sim* as follows:

- $sim(MA, ISA) \doteq (\exists MA_1 : (witnessing(MA_1, MA))$
  $\wedge (ISA = proj(flush(MA_1))))$

Now we show how the predicate *sim* can be used to show the conditions 1-6 in Section 2. First, the function *rank* satisfying conditions 5 and 6 can be defined by simply noticing that for any state MA, *some* instruction always advances. Hence if i is the maximum number in MA such that latch i is *valid*, then the quantity $(5 - i)$ always returns a natural number (and hence a member of a well-founded set) that decreases at every step. (We take i to be 0 if MA has no *valid* latch.) Also, $witnessing(init_I(), init_I())$ holds, implying condition 1. Further, condition 2 is trivial from definition of *witnessing*. We therefore focus here on only conditions 3 and 4. We first consider the following lemma:

Lemma 2. *For all MA, MA_1 such that $witnessing(MA_1, MA)$:*

1. $witnessing(MA_1, step_I(MA))$ if $\neg commit(MA)$
2. $witnessing(step_I(step_I(MA_1)), step_I(MA))$ if $commit(MA)$
   $\wedge stalled(step_I(MA_1))$
3. $witnessing(step_I(MA_1), step_I(MA))$ if $commit(MA) \wedge \neg stalled(step_I(MA_1))$

The lemma merely states that if MA is not a *commit* state, then stepping from MA preserves the witnessing state, and otherwise the witnessing state for $step_I(MA)$ is given by the "next non-stalled state" after MA_1. The lemma can be proved by symbolic execution of the pipelined machine. We can now prove the main technical lemma that guarantees conditions 3 and 4 of Section 2.

Lemma 3. *For all MA and ISA, such that $sim(MA, ISA)$:*

1. $sim(step_I(MA), ISA)$ *if* $\neg commit(MA)$.
2. $sim(step_I(MA), step_S(ISA))$ *if* $commit(MA)$.

Proof. Let MA_1 be the Skolem witness of $sim(MA, ISA)$. Case 1 follows from Lemma 2, since $witnessing(MA_1, step_I(MA))$ holds. For case 2, we consider only the situation $\neg stalled(step_I(MA_1))$ since the other situation is analogous. But by Lemma 1 and definition of *witnessing*, $proj(flush(step_I(MA_1))) = step_S(ISA)$. The result now follows from Lemma 2.   □

We end this section with a brief comparison between our approach and that of Manolios [13]. We focus on a comparison with this work since unlike other related work, this approach uses a uniform notion of correctness that is applicable to both pipelined and non-pipelined microarchitectures. Indeed our use of stuttering simulation is a direct consequence of this work. The basic difference is in the techniques used to define the correspondence relation to relate MA states with ISA states. While we define a quantified predicate to posit the existence of a witnessing state, Manolios defines a refinement map from the states of MA to states of ISA as follows: Point the PC to the next instruction to complete and invalidate all the instructions in the pipe[3]. Notice immediately that the method requires that we have to keep track of the PC of each intermediate instruction. Also, as the different pipeline stages update the instruction, one needs

---

[3] Manolios also describes a "flushing proof" and shows that flushing can relate inconsistent MA states to ISA states. But our application of flush is different from his in that we flush MA_1 rather than the current state MA. Our approach has no such problems.

some invariant specifying the transformations on each instruction at each stage. Short of computing such invariants based on the structure of the pipeline and the functionality of the different instructions, we believe that any generic approach to determine invariants will reduce his approach to ours, namely defining a quantified predicate to posit the existence of a witnessing state.

4 Generalization

Stuttering simulation can be used to verify pipelines with advanced features. In this section, we consider arbitrary but finite stalls, interrupts, and out-of-order instruction execution. Stuttering simulation cannot be used directly for machines with out-of-order completion and multiple instruction completion. In Section 4.4 we discuss an approach to circumvent such limitations.

4.1 Stalls

The pipeline in Fig. 4 allowed single-cycle stalls. Pipelines in practice can have stalls ranging over multiple cycles. If the stall is finite, it is easy to use stuttering simulation to reason about such pipelines. Stalls affect Lemma 2 since given a witnessing state MA_1 of MA, the witnessing state for $step_I(MA)$ is given by the "next non-stalled state" after MA_1. But such a state is given by $clock(step_I(MA_1))$, where the function $clock$ (defined below) merely counts the number of steps to reach the first non-stalled state. Finiteness of stalls guarantees that the recursion terminates.

$$clock(s) \doteq \begin{cases} 0 & \text{if } \neg stalled(s) \\ 1 + clock(step_I(s)) & \text{otherwise} \end{cases}$$

4.2 Interrupts

Modern pipelines allow interrupts and exceptions. To effectively reason about interrupts, we model both MA and ISA as non-deterministic machines, where the "input parameter" is used to decide whether the machine is to be interrupted at the current step or proceeds with normal execution. Recall that our notion of correspondence can relate non-deterministic machines. Servicing the interrupt might involve an update of the visible components of the state. In the ISA, we assume that the interrupt is serviced in one atomic step, while it might take several cycles in MA.

We specify the witnessing states for an interruptible MA state as follows: MA_1 is a witnessing state of MA if either (i) MA is not within any interrupt and MA_1 initiates the instruction next to be completed in MA, or (ii) MA is within some interrupt and MA_1 initates the corresponding interrupt. Then *commit* is true if either the current step returns from some interrupt service or completes an instruction. Assuming that pipeline executions are not interleaved with the interrupt processing, we can then show (MA >> ISA) for such non-deterministic machines. We should note here that we have not analyzed machines with nested interrupts yet. But we believe that the methodology can be extended for nested interrupts by the witnessing state specifying the initiation of the most recent interrupt in the nest.

4.3   Out-of-Order Execution

Our methodology can handle pipelines with out-of-order instruction execution as long as the instructions are initiated to the pipeline and completed in program order. For a pipeline state MA, we determine the instruction i_1 that is next to be completed, by merely simulating the machine forward from MA. We then specify MA_1 to be a witnessing state of MA if i_1 is initiated into the pipeline at MA_1. Notice that since instructions are initiated and completed in-order, any instruction before i_1 in program order must have been already initiated in the pipeline in state MA_1. Since flushing merely involves executing the pipeline without initiating any instruction, flushing from state MA_1 will therefore produce the state MA_{1F} with the same visible behavior as state MA.

4.4   Out-of-Order and Multiple Instruction Completion

Modern pipelines allow completion of multiple instructions at the same clock cycle, and out-of-order completion of instructions. Such features cannot be directly handled by our approach. In this section, we outline the problem and discuss a possble approach. We admit, however, that we have not attempted to verify pipelines with these features and our comments are merely speculative.

Consider a pipeline state MA poised to complete two instructions i_1 and i_2 at the same cycle. Assume that i_1 updates register r_1 and i_2 updates register r_2. Thus the visible behavior of the pipeline will show simultaneous updates of the two registers. The ISA, however, can only update one register at any clock cycle. Thus, there can be *no* ISA state ISA with the properties that (i) MA and ISA are externally equal, and (ii) executing both machines from MA and ISA results in states that are externally equal, even with possible stutter. In other words, there can be no simulation relation relating MA and ISA. The arguments are applicable to out-of-order completion as well, where the updates corresponding to the two instructions are "swapped" in the pipelined machine.

Since multiple and out-of-order completion affect the visible behavior of the pipelined machine, we need to modify the execution of the ISA to show correspondence. We propose the following approach: The ISA, instead of executing single instructions atomically, non-deterministically selects a *burst* of instructions. Each *burst* consists of a set of instruction sequences with instructions in *different* sequences not having any data dependency. The ISA then executes each sequence in a burst atomically, choosing the order of the sequences non-deterministically, and then selects the next burst after completing all sequences. Notice that our "original" ISA can be derived from such an ISA by letting the bursts be singleton sets of one instruction.

We are pursuing the "modified ISA" approach to verify practical pipelines. However, we have not verified any complicated machine using this approach, and investigation of the technique is a future area of research.

5   Summary and Conclusions

We have shown how to apply a uniform and well-studied notion of correspondence, namely stuttering simulation, to verify pipelined machines. Since the notion is compositional, proofs of pipelines can be directly composed with proofs of other components of a microprocessor. Further, the use of *witnessing states* enables us to merely "flush" the pipelined machine to define the simulation relation without constructing complicated structural invariants.

Our work demonstrates the importance of first-order quantification in verification of practical computing systems. We have seen how quantification enables us to specify the witnessing state non-constructively by using the Skolem witness of a quantified predicate. Since the witnessing state is a state that has been encountered in the "past", constructing the state would require keeping track of the history of execution via an intermediate machine, and definition of a complicated invariant on that machine. The importance of first-order quantification is often overlooked in the use of a general-purpose theorem prover, especially by the ACL2 community. While ACL2 allows arbitrary first-order quantification, ACL2 proofs typically use constructive recursive functions. In this context, it should be noted that a key advantage of the use of theorem-proving over algorithmic decision procedures like model-checking is the expressivity of the logic. Beyond this, theorem-proving normally involves more manual effort. Thus to successfully use theorem-proving with reasonable automation, it is important to make effective use of expressivity. We have found quantification to be particularly useful in many circumstances for "backward simulation", when the property preserved in a state is guaranteed by a state encountered by the machine in the past. Aside from defining witnessing states for pipelined machines, backward simulation is useful, for example, in specifying weakest preconditions for operationally modeled sequential programs. We are working on identifying other situations in which quantification can significantly reduce manual effort in deductive verification of modern computer systems.

We have demonstrated the application of our approach to verify pipelines with stalls, interrupts, and out-of-order execution using stuttering simulation. As mentioned in Section 4.4, we cannot yet handle out-of-order completion and multiple instruction completion. We plan to analyze the extention outlined in Section 4.4 to reason about more complicated, practical pipelines.

Acknowledgments

Rob Sumners was involved with the initial discussions about the use of quantification for reasoning about pipelines. Anna Slobodová read a draft of this paper and made several useful suggestions.

References

1. W. A. Hunt, Jr.: FM8501: A Verified Microprocessor. Springer-Verlag LNAI 795, Heidelberg (1994)
2. Manolios, P.: Mechanical Verification of Reactive Systems. PhD thesis, Department of Computer Sciences, The University of Texas at Austin (2001)
3. Aagaard, M.D., Cook, B., Day, N., Jones, R.B.: A Framework for Microprocessor Correctness Statements. In: Correct Hardware Design and Verification Methods (CHARME). Volume 2144 of LNCS., Springer-Verlag (2001) 443–448
4. Burch, J.R., Dill, D.L.: Automatic Verification of Pipelined Microprocessor Control. In Dill, D., ed.: Computer-Aided Verification (CAV). Volume 818 of LNCS., Springer-Verlag (1994) 68–80
5. Srivas, M., Bickford, M.: Formal Verification of a Pipelined Microprocessor. IEEE Software (1990) 52–64
6. Bronstein, A., Talcott, T.L.: Formal Verification of Pipelines based on String-functional Semantics. In Claesen, L.J.M., ed.: Formal VLSI Correctness Verification, VLSI Design Methods II. (1990) 349–366
7. Sawada, J., W. A. Hunt, Jr: Trace Table Based Approach for Pipelined Microprocessor Verification. In: Computer-Aided Verification (CAV). Volume 1254 of LNCS., Springer-Verlag (1997) 364–375
8. Sawada, J., W. A. Hunt, Jr: Processor Verification with Precise Exceptions and Speculative Execution. In Hu, A.J., Vardi, M.Y., eds.: Computer-Aided Verification (CAV). Volume 1427 of LNCS., Springer-Verlag (1998) 135–146
9. Hosabettu, R., Gopalakrishnan, G., Srivas, M.: Verifying Advanced Microarchitectures that Support Speculation and Exceptions. In: Computer-Aided Verification (CAV). Volume 1855 of LNCS., Springer-Verlag (2000)
10. Jhala, R., McMillan, K.: Microarchitecture Verification by Compositional Model Checking. In: Proceedings of Twelveth International Conference on Computer-aided Verification (CAV). Volume 2102 of LNCS., Springer-Verlag (2001)
11. Bryant, R.E., German, S., Velev, M.N.: Exploiting Positive Equality in a Logic of Equality with Uninterpreted Functions. In N. Halbwachs and D. Peled, ed.: Computer-Aided Verification (CAV). Volume 1633 of LNCS., Springer-Verlag (1999) 470–482
12. Lahiri, S.K., Bryant, R.E.: Deductive Verification of Advanced Out-of-Order Microprocessors. In W. A. Hunt, Jr, Somenzi, F., eds.: Computer-Aided Verification (CAV). Volume 2275 of LNCS., Springer-Verlag (2003) 341–354
13. Manolios, P.: Correctness of pipelined machines. In W. A. Hunt, Jr, Johnson, S.D., eds.: Third International Conference on Formal Methods in Computer-Aided Design (FMCAD). Volume 1954 of LNCS., Springer-Verlag (2000) 161–178
14. Manolios, P., Namjoshi, K., Sumners, R.: Linking Model-checking and Theorem-proving with Well-founded Bisimulations. In Halbwacha, N., Peled, D., eds.: Computer-Aided Verification (CAV). Volume 1633 of LNCS. (1999) 369–379
15. Sumners, R.: An Incremental Stuttering Refinement Proof of a Concurrent Program in ACL2. In Kaufmann, M., Moore, J.S., eds.: Second International Workshop on ACL2 Theorem Prover and Its Applications, Austin, TX (2000)
16. Kaufmann, M., Manolios, P., Moore, J.S.: Computer-Aided Reasoning: An Approach. Kluwer Academic Publishers (2000)
17. Kaufmann, M., Manolios, P., Moore, J.S., eds.: Computer-Aided Reasoning: ACL2 Case Studies. Kluwer Academic Publishers (2000)
18. Moore, J.S.: Proving Theorems about Java and the JVM with ACL2. Models, Algebras, and Logic of Engineering Software (2003) 227–290

A Formal Reduction
for Lock-Free Parallel Algorithms

Hui Gao and Wim H. Hesselink

Department of Mathematics and Computing Science, University of Groningen
P.O. Box 800, 9700 AV Groningen, The Netherlands
{hui,wim}@cs.rug.nl

Abstract. On shared memory multiprocessors, synchronization often turns out to be a performance bottleneck and the source of poor fault-tolerance. Lock-free algorithms can do without locking mechanisms, and are therefore desirable. Lock-free algorithms are hard to design correctly, however, even when apparently straightforward. We formalize Herlihy's methodology [13] for transferring a sequential implementation of any data structure into a lock-free synchronization by means of synchronization primitives *Load-linked* (*LL*)/*store-conditional* (*SC*). This is done by means of a reduction theorem that enables us to reason about the general lock-free algorithm to be designed on a higher level than the synchronization primitives. The reduction theorem is based on refinement mapping as described by Lamport [10] and has been verified with the higher-order interactive theorem prover PVS. Using the reduction theorem, fewer invariants are required and some invariants are easier to discover and easier to formulate.

The lock-free implementation works quite well for small objects. However, for large objects, the approach is not very attractive as the burden of copying the data can be very heavy. We propose two enhanced lock-free algorithms for large objects in which slower processes don't need to copy the entire object again if their attempts fail. This results in lower copying overhead than in Herlihy's proposal.

Keywords & Phrases: Distributed algorithms, Lock-free, Simulation, Refinement mapping

1   Introduction

On shared-memory multiprocessors, processes coordinate with each other via shared data structures. To ensure the consistency of these concurrent objects, processes need a mechanism for synchronizing their access. In such a system the programmer typically has to explicitly synchronize access to shared data by different processes to ensure correct behaviors of the overall system, using synchronization primitives such as semaphores, monitors, guarded statements, mutex locks, etc. Consequently the operations of different processes on a shared data structure should appear to be serialized: if two operations execute simultaneously, the system guarantees the same result as if one of them is arbitrarily executed before the other.

R. Alur and D.A. Peled (Eds.): CAV 2004, LNCS 3114, pp. 44–56, 2004.

Due to blocking, the classical synchronization paradigms using locks can incur many problems such as convoying, priority inversion and deadlock. A *lock-free* (also called non-blocking) implementation of a shared object guarantees that within a finite number of steps always some process trying to perform an operation on the object will complete its task, independently of the activity and speed of other processes [13]. As lock-free synchronizations are built without locks, they are immune from the aforementioned problems. In addition, lock-free synchronizations can offer progress guarantees. A number of researchers [1, 4, 5, 13–15] have proposed techniques for designing lock-free implementations. The basis of these techniques is using some synchronization primitives such as *compare-and-swap* (*CAS*), or *Load-linked* (*LL*)/*store-conditional* (*SC*).

Typically, the implementation of the synchronization operations is left to the designer, who has to decide how much of the functionality to implement in software using system libraries. The high-level specification gives lots of freedom about how a result is obtained. It is constructed in some mechanical way that guarantees its correctness and then the required conditions are automatically satisfied [3]. We reason about a high-level specification of a system, with a large grain of atomicity, and hope to deduce an implementation, a low-level specification, which must be fine grained enough to be translated into a computer program that has all important properties of the high-level specification.

However, the correctness properties of an implementation are seldom easy to verify. Our previous work [6] shows that a proof may require unreasonable amounts of effort, time, or skill. We therefore develop a reduction theorem that enables us to reason about a lock-free program to be designed on a higher level than the synchronization primitives. The reduction theorem is based on refinement mappings as described by Lamport [10], which are used to prove that a lower-level specification correctly implements a higher-level one. Using the reduction theorem, fewer invariants are required and some invariants are easier to discover and easier to formulate, without considering the internal structure of the final implementation. In particular, nested loops in the algorithm may be treated as one loop at a time.

2   Lock-Free Transformation

The machine architecture that we have in mind is based on modern shared-memory multiprocessors that can access a common shared address space. There can be several processes running on a single processor. Let us assume there are P (≥ 1) concurrently executing sequential processes.

Synchronization primitives LL and SC, proposed by Jensen et al. [2], have found widespread acceptance in modern processor architectures (e.g. MIPS II, PowerPC and Alpha architectures). They are a pair of instructions, closely related to the CAS, and together implement an atomic Read/Write cycle. Instruction LL first reads a memory location, say X, and marks it as "reserved" (not "locked"). If no other processor changes the contents of X in between, the subsequent SC operation of the same processor succeeds and modifies the value stored;

otherwise it fails. There is also a validate instruction VL, used to check whether X was not modified since the corresponding LL instruction was executed. Implementing VL should be straightforward in an architecture that already supports SC. Note that the implementation does not access or manipulate X other than by means of $LL/SC/VL$. Moir [12] showed that $LL/SC/VL$ can be constructed on any system that supports either LL/SC or CAS. A shared variable X only accessed by $LL/SC/VL$ operations can be regarded as a variable that has an associated shared set of process identifiers $V.X$, which is initially empty. The semantics of LL, VL and SC are given by equivalent atomic statements below.

proc $LL(\textbf{ref } X : \textbf{val}) : \textbf{val} =$
$\quad \langle \quad V.X := V.X \cup \{self\}; \textbf{ return } X; \rangle$

proc $VL(\textbf{ref } X : \textbf{val}) : \textbf{boolean} =$
$\quad \langle \quad \textbf{return } (self \in V.X) \rangle$

proc $SC(\textbf{ref } X : \textbf{val}; \textbf{in } Y : \textbf{val}) : \textbf{boolean} =$
$\quad \langle \quad \textbf{if } self \in V.X \textbf{ then } V.X := \emptyset; \ X := Y; \textbf{ return } true$
$\quad \textbf{else return } false; \textbf{ fi } \rangle$

where *self* is the process identifier of the acting process.

At the cost of copying an object's data before an operation, Herlihy [13] introduced a general methodology to transfer a sequential implementation of any data structure into a lock-free synchronization by means of synchronization primitives LL and SC. A process that needs access to a shared object pointed by X performs a loop of the following steps:(1) read X using an LL operation to gain access to the object's data area; (2) make a private copy of the indicated version of the object (this action need not be atomic); (3) perform the desired operation on the private copy to make a new version; (4) finally, call a SC operation on X to attempt to swing the pointer from the old version to the new version. The SC operation will fail when some other process has modified X since the LL operation, in which case the process has to repeat these steps until consistency is satisfied. The algorithm is non-blocking because at least one out of every P attempts must succeed within finite time. Of course, a process might always lose to some faster process, but this is often unlikely in practice.

3   Reduction

We assume a universal set $\mathcal{V}$ of typed variables, which is called the *vocabulary*. A state s is a type-consistent interpretation of $\mathcal{V}$, mapping variables $v \in \mathcal{V}$ to values $s[\![v]\!]$. We denote by Σ the set of all states. If $\mathcal{C}$ is a command, we denote by $\mathcal{C}_p$ the transition $\mathcal{C}$ executed by process p, and $s[\![\mathcal{C}_p]\!]t$ indicates that in state s process p can do a step $\mathcal{C}$ that establishes state t. When discussing the effect of a transition $\mathcal{C}_p$ from state s to state t on a variable v, we abbreviate $s[\![v]\!]$ to v and $t[\![v]\!]$ to v'. We use the abbreviation $Pres(V)$ for $\bigwedge_{v \in V}(v' = v)$ to denote that all variables in the set V are preserved by the transition. Every private variable name can be extended with the suffix "." + "*process identifier*". We sometimes use indentation to eliminate parentheses.

3.1 Observed Specification

In practice, the specification of systems is concerned rather with externally visible behavior than computational feasibility. We assume that all levels of specifications under consideration have the same observable state space Σ_0, and are interpreted by their observation functions $\Pi : \Sigma \to \Sigma_0$. Every specification can be modeled as a five-tuple $(\Sigma, \Pi, \Theta, \mathcal{N}, \mathcal{L})$ where $(\Sigma, \Theta, \mathcal{N})$ is the *transition system* [16] and $\mathcal{L}$ is the supplementary property of the system (i.e., a predicate on Σ^ω).

The supplementary constraint $\mathcal{L}$ is imposed since the transition system only specifies safety requirements and has no kind of fairness conditions or liveness assumptions built into it. Since, in reality, a stuttering step might actually perform modifications to some internal variables in internal states, we do allow stuttering transitions (where the state does not change) and the next-state relation is therefore reflexive. A finite or infinite sequence of states is defined to be an *execution* of system $(\Sigma, \Pi, \Theta, \mathcal{N}, \mathcal{L})$ if it satisfies initial predicate Θ and the next-state relation $\mathcal{N}$ but not necessarily the requirements of the supplementary property $\mathcal{L}$. We define a *behavior* to be an infinite execution that satisfies the supplementary property $\mathcal{L}$. A (concrete) specification $\mathcal{S}_c$ *implements* a (abstract) specification S_a iff every externally visible behavior allowed by $\mathcal{S}_c$ is also allowed by S_a. We write $Beh(\mathcal{S})$ to denote the set of behaviors of system $\mathcal{S}$.

3.2 Refinement Mappings

A *refinement mapping* from a lower-level specification $\mathcal{S}_c = (\Sigma_c, \Pi_c, \Theta_c, \mathcal{N}_c, \mathcal{L}_c)$ to a higher-level specification $\mathcal{S}_a = (\Sigma_a, \Pi_a, \Theta_a, \mathcal{N}_a, \mathcal{L}_a)$, written $\phi : \mathcal{S}_c \sqsubseteq \mathcal{S}_a$, is a mapping $\phi : \Sigma_c \to \Sigma_a$ that satisfies:

1. ϕ preserves the externally visible state component: $\Pi_a \circ \phi = \Pi_c$.
2. ϕ is a *simulation*, denoted $\phi : \mathcal{S}_c \preccurlyeq \mathcal{S}_a$:
    ① ϕ takes initial states into initial states: $\Theta_c \Rightarrow \Theta_a \circ \phi$.
    ② $\mathcal{N}_c$ is mapped by ϕ into a transition (possibly stuttering) allowed by $\mathcal{N}_a$:
    $\mathcal{Q} \wedge \mathcal{N}_c \Rightarrow \mathcal{N}_a \circ \phi$, where $\mathcal{Q}$ is an invariant of $\mathcal{S}_c$.
3. ϕ maps behaviors allowed by $\mathcal{S}_c$ into behaviors that satisfy $\mathcal{S}_a$'s supplementary property: $\forall\, \sigma \in Beh(\mathcal{S}_c) : \mathcal{L}_a(\phi(\sigma))$.

Below we need to exploit the fact that the simulation only quantifies over all reachable states of the lower-level system, not all states. We therefore explicitly allow an invariant $\mathcal{Q}$ in condition 2 ②. The following theorem is stated in [11].

Theorem 1. *If there exists a refinement mapping from $\mathcal{S}_c$ to $\mathcal{S}_a$, then $\mathcal{S}_c$ implements $\mathcal{S}_a$.*

Refinement mappings give us the ability to reduce an implementation by reducing its components in relative isolation, and then gluing the *reductions* together with the same structure as the implementation. Atomicity guarantees that a parallel execution of a program gives the same results as a sequential and non-deterministic execution. This allows us to use the refinement calculus for stepwise refinement of transition systems [8]. Essentially, the reduction theorem allows us to design and verify the program on a higher level of abstraction. The big advantage is that substantial pieces of the concrete program can be dealt with as atomic statements on the higher level.

The refinement relation is transitive, which means that we don't have to reduce the implementation in one step, but can proceed from the implementation to the specification through a series of smaller steps.

3.3   Correctness

The safety properties satisfied by the program are completely determined by the initial predicate and the next-state relation. This is described by Theorem 2, which can be easily verified.

Theorem 2. *Let $\mathcal{P}_c$ and $\mathcal{P}_a$ be safety properties for $\mathcal{S}_c$ and $\mathcal{S}_a$ respectively. The verification of a concrete judgment $(\Sigma_c, \Theta_c, \mathcal{N}_c) \models \mathcal{P}_c$ can be reduced to the verification of an abstract judgment $(\Sigma_a, \Theta_a, \mathcal{N}_a) \models \mathcal{P}_a$, if we can exhibit a simulation ϕ mapping from Σ_c to Σ_a that satisfies $\mathcal{P}_a \circ \phi \Rightarrow \mathcal{P}_c$.*

We make a distinction between safety and liveness properties (See [10] for the proof schemes). The proof of liveness relies on the fairness conditions associated with a specification. The purpose for fairness conditions is to rule out executions where the system idles indefinitely with control at some internal point of a procedure and with some transition of that procedure enabled. Fairness arguments usually depend on safety properties of the system.

4   A Lock-Free Pattern

We propose a pattern that can be universally employed for a lock-free construction in order to synchronize access to a shared node of *nodeType*. The interface $\mathcal{S}_a$ is shown in Fig. 1, where the following statements are taken as a schematic representation of segments of code:

1. *noncrit*(**ref** *pub* : *aType*, *priv* : *bType*; **in** *tm* : *cType*; **out** *x* : 1..*N*) : representing an atomic non-critical activity on variables *pub* and *priv* according to the value of *tm*, and choosing an index *x* of a shared node to be accessed.
2. *guard*(**in** *X* : *nodeType*, *priv* : *bType*) a non-atomic boolean test on the variable *X* of *nodeType*. It may depend on private variable *priv*.
3. *com*(**ref** *X* : *nodeType*; **in** *priv* : *bType*; **out** *tm* : *cType*) : a non-atomic action on the variable *X* of *nodeType* and private variable *tm*. It is allowed to inspect private variable *priv*.

```
CONSTANT
  P = number of processes; N = number of nodes
Shared Variables:
  pub: aType; Node: array [1..N] of nodeType;
Private Variables:
  priv: bType; pc: {a1, a2}; x: 1..N; tm: cType;
Program:
      loop
  a1:    noncrit(pub, priv, tm, x);
  a2:    ⟨ if guard(Node[x], priv) then com(Node[x], priv, tm); fi ⟩
      end
Initial conditions Θₐ : ∀ p:1..P: pc = a1
Liveness   Lₐ : □ ( pc = a2  ⟶  ◇ pc = a1 )
```

Fig. 1. Interface S_a

```
CONSTANT
  P = number of processes; N = number of nodes
Shared Variables:
  pub: aType; node: array [1..N+P] of nodeType;
  indir: array [1..N] of 1..N+P;
Private Variables:
  priv: bType; pc: [c1.. c7];
  x: 1..N; mp, m: 1..N+P; tm, tm1: cType;
Program:
      loop
  c1:    noncrit(pub, priv, tm, x);
         loop
  c2:       m := LL(indir[x]);
  c3:       read(node[mp], node[m]);
  c4:       if guard(node[mp], priv) then
  c5:          com(node[mp], priv, tm1);
  c6:          if SC(indir[x], mp) then
                  mp := m; tm := tm1; break;
               fi
  c7:       else
               if VL(indir[x]) then break; fi
           fi
         end
      end
Initial conditions Θ_c :
  (∀ p:1..P: pc = c1 ∧ mp=N+p) ∧ (∀ i:1..N: indir[i]=i)
Liveness   L_c : □ ( pc = c2  ⟶  ◇ pc = c1 )
```

Fig. 2. Lock-free implementation S_c of S_a

The action enclosed by angular brackets $\langle \ldots \rangle$ is defined as atomic. The private
variable x is intended only to determine the node under consideration, the private

variable tm is intended to hold the result of the critical computation com, if executed. By means of Herlihy's methodology, we give a lock-free implementation S_c of interface S_a in Fig. 2. In the implementation, we use some other schematic representations of segments of code, which are described as follows:

4. $read(\mathbf{ref}\ X : nodeType,\ \mathbf{in}\ Y : nodeType)$: a non-atomic read operation that reads the value from the variable Y of $nodeType$ to the variable X of $nodeType$, and does nothing else. If Y is modified during $read$, the resulting value of X is unspecified but type correct, and no error occurs.
5. LL, SC and VL : atomic actions as we defined before.

Typically, we are not interested in the internal details of these schematic commands but in their behavior with respect to lock-freedom. In S_c, we declare P extra shared nodes for private use (one for each process). Array $indir$ acts as pointers to shared nodes. $node[mp.p]$ can always be taken as a "private" node (other processes can read but not modify the content of the node) of process p though it is declared publicly. If some other process successfully updates a shared node while an active process p is copying the shared node to its "private" node, process p will restart the inner loop, since its private view of the node is not consistent anymore. After the assignment $mp := m$ at line $c6$, the "private" node becomes shared and the node shared previously (which contains the old version) becomes "private".

Formally, we introduce N_c as the relation corresponding to command $noncrit$ on $(aType \times bType \times cType,\ aType \times bType \times 1..N)$, P_g as the predicate computed by $guard$ on $nodeType \times bType$, R_c as the relation corresponding to com on $(nodeType \times bType, nodeType \times cType)$, and define

$$\Sigma_a \triangleq (Node[1..N],\ pub) \times (pc,\ x,\ priv,\ tm)^P,$$
$$\Sigma_c \triangleq (node[1..N+P],\ indir[1..N],\ pub) \times (pc,\ x,\ mp,\ m,\ priv,\ tm,\ tm1)^P,$$
$$\Pi_a(\Sigma_a) \triangleq (Node[1..N],\ pub),\quad \Pi_c(\Sigma_c) \triangleq (node[indir[1..N]],\ pub),$$
$$\mathcal{N}_a \triangleq \bigvee_{0 \leq i \leq 2} \mathcal{N}_{ai},\quad \mathcal{N}_c \triangleq \bigvee_{1 \leq i \leq 7} \mathcal{N}_{ci},$$

The transitions of the abstract system can be described: $\forall s, t : \Sigma_a,\ p : 1..P$:

$$s[\![(\mathcal{N}_{a0})_p]\!]t \triangleq s = t \quad \text{(to allow stuttering)}$$
$$s[\![(\mathcal{N}_{a1})_p]\!]t \triangleq pc.p = a1 \ \wedge\ pc'.p = a2 \ \wedge\ Pres(\mathcal{V} - \{pub,\ priv.p,\ pc.p,\ x.p\})$$
$$\wedge\ ((pub,\ priv.p,\ tm.p),(pub,\ priv.p,\ x.p)') \in N_c$$
$$s[\![(\mathcal{N}_{a2})_p]\!]t \triangleq pc.p = a2 \ \wedge\ pc'.p = a1 \ \wedge\ (P_g(Node[x],\ priv.p)$$
$$\wedge\ ((Node[x],\ priv.p),(Node[x],\ tm.p)') \in R_c$$
$$\wedge\ Pres(\mathcal{V} - \{pc.p,\ Node[x],\ tm.p\})$$
$$\vee\ \neg P_g(Node[x],\ priv.p) \ \wedge\ Pres(\mathcal{V} - \{pc.p\})).$$

The transitions of the concrete system can be described in the same way. Here we only provide the description of the step that starts in $c6$: $\forall s, t : \Sigma_c,\ p : 1..P$:

$$s[\![(\mathcal{N}_{c6})_p]\!]t \triangleq pc.p = c6 \ \wedge\ (p \in V.indir[x.p]$$
$$\wedge\ pc'.p = c1 \ \wedge\ (indir[x.p])' = mp.p \ \wedge\ mp'.p = m.p$$
$$\wedge\ tm'.p = tm1.p \ \wedge\ (V.indir[x.p])' = \emptyset$$
$$\wedge\ Pres(\mathcal{V} - \{pc.p,\ indir[x.p],\ mp.p,\ tm.p,\ V.indir[x.p]\})$$
$$\vee\ p \notin V.indir[x.p] \ \wedge\ pc'.p = c2 \ \wedge\ Pres(\mathcal{V} - \{pc.p\}))$$

4.1 Simulation

According to Theorem 2, the verification of a safety property of concrete system $\mathcal{S}_c$ can be reduced to the verification of the corresponding safety property of abstract system $\mathcal{S}_a$ if we can exhibit the existence of a simulation between them.

Theorem 3. *The concrete system $\mathcal{S}_c$ defined in Fig. 2 is simulated by the abstract system $\mathcal{S}_a$ defined in Fig. 1, that is, $\exists \phi : \mathcal{S}_c \preccurlyeq \mathcal{S}_a$.*

Proof: We prove Theorem 3 by providing a simulation. The simulation function ϕ is defined by showing how each component of the abstract state (i.e. state of Σ_a) is generated from components in the concrete state (i.e. state of Σ_c). We define ϕ : the concrete location $c1$ is mapped to the abstract location $a1$, while all other concrete locations are mapped to $a2$; the concrete shared variable $node[indir[x]]$ is mapped to the abstract shared variable $Node[x]$, and the remaining variables are all mapped to the identity of the variables occurring in the abstract system.

The assertion that the initial condition Θ_c of the concrete system implies the initial condition Θ_a of the abstract system follows easily from the definitions of Θ_c, Θ_a and ϕ.

The central step in the proof of simulation is to prove that every atomic step of the concrete system simulates an atomic step of the abstract system. We therefore need to associate each transition in the concrete system with the transition in the abstract system.

It is easy to see that the concrete transition $\mathcal{N}_{c1}$ simulates $\mathcal{N}_{a1}$ and that $\mathcal{N}_{c2}$, $\mathcal{N}_{c3}$, $\mathcal{N}_{c4}$, $\mathcal{N}_{c5}$, $\mathcal{N}_{c6}$ with precondition "$self \notin V.indir[x.self]$", and $\mathcal{N}_{c7}$ with precondition "$self \notin V.indir[x.self]$" simulate a stuttering step $\mathcal{N}_{a0}$ in the abstract system. E.g., we prove that $\mathcal{N}_{c6}$ executed by any process p with precondition "$p \notin V.indir[x.p]$" simulates a stuttering step in the abstract system. By the mechanism of SC, an active process p will only modify its program counter $pc.p$ from $c6$ to $c2$ when executing $\mathcal{N}_{c6}$ with precondition "$p \notin V.indir[x.p]$". According to the mapping of ϕ, both concrete locations $c6$ and $c2$ are mapped to abstract location $a2$. Since the mappings of the pre-state and the post-state to the abstract system are identical, $\mathcal{N}_{c6}$ executed by process p with precondition "$p \notin V.indir[x.p]$" simulates the stuttering step $\mathcal{N}_{a0}$ in the abstract system.

The proof for the simulations of the remaining concrete transitions is less obvious. Since simulation applies only to transitions taken from a reachable state, we postulate the following invariants in the concrete system $\mathcal{S}_c$:

$Q1$: $(p \neq q \Rightarrow mp.p \neq mp.q) \wedge (indir[y] \neq mp.p)$
$\qquad \wedge (y \neq z \Rightarrow indir[y] \neq indir[z])$

$Q2$: $pc.p = c6 \wedge p \in V.indir[x.p]$
$\qquad \Rightarrow ((node[m.p], priv.p), (node[mp.p], tm1.p)) \in R_c$

$Q3$: $pc.p = c7 \wedge p \in V.indir[x.p] \Rightarrow \neg P_g(node[m.p], priv.p)$

$Q4$: $pc.p \in [c3..c7] \wedge p \in V.indir[x.p] \Rightarrow m.p = indir[x.p]$

$Q5$: $pc.p \in \{c4, c5\} \wedge p \in V.indir[x.p] \Rightarrow node[m.p] = node[mp.p]$

$Q6$: $pc.p = \{c5, c6\} \Rightarrow P_g(node[mp.p], priv.p)$

In the invariants, the free variables p and q range over $1..P$, and the free variables y and z range over $1..N$. Invariant $Q1$ implies that, for any process q, $node[mp.q]$ can be indeed treated as a "private" node of process q since only process q can modify that. Invariant $Q4$ reflect the mechanism of the synchronization primitives LL and SC.

With the help of those invariants above, we have proved that $\mathcal{N}_{c6}$ and $\mathcal{N}_{c7}$ executed by process p with precondition "$p \in V.indir[x.p]$" simulate the abstract step $\mathcal{N}_{a2}$ in the abstract system. For reasons of space we refer the interested reader to [7] for the complete mechanical proof.   □

4.2 Refinement

Recall that not all simulation relations are refinement mappings. According to the formalism of the reduction, it is easy to verify that ϕ preserves the externally visible state component. For the refinement relation we also need to prove that the simulation ϕ maps behaviors allowed by S_c into behaviors that satisfy S_a's liveness property, that is, $\forall \sigma \in Beh(S_c) : \mathcal{L}_a(\phi(\sigma))$. Since ϕ is a simulation, we deduce

$$
\begin{aligned}
\sigma \models \mathcal{L}_c &\equiv \sigma \models \Box(pc = c2 \longrightarrow \Diamond pc = c1) \\
&\Rightarrow \sigma \models \Box(pc \in [c2..c7] \longrightarrow \Diamond pc = c1) \\
&\Rightarrow \phi(\sigma) \models \Box(pc = a2 \longrightarrow \Diamond pc = a1) \\
&\equiv \mathcal{L}_a(\phi(\sigma))
\end{aligned}
$$

Consequently, we have our main reduction theorem:

Theorem 4. *The abstract system S_a defined in Fig. 1 is refined by the concrete system S_c defined in Fig. 2, that is, $\exists \phi : S_c \sqsubseteq S_a$.*

The liveness property $\mathcal{L}_c$ of concrete system S_c can also be proved under the assumption of the strong fairness conditions and the following assumption:

$$
\begin{aligned}
\Box \, (\Box pc.p &\in [c2..c7] \wedge \Box \Diamond p \in V.indir[x.p] \\
&\longrightarrow \Diamond(pc.p = c6 \vee pc.p = c7) \wedge p \in V.indir[x.p]).
\end{aligned}
$$

The additional assumption indicates that for every process p, when process p remains in the loop from $c2$ to $c7$ and executes $c2$ infinitely often, it will eventually succeed in reaching $c6$ or $c7$ with precondition "$p \in V.indir[x.p]$".

5 Large Object

To reduce the overhead of failing non-blocking operations, Herlihy [13] proposes an exponential back-off policy to reduce useless parallelism, which is caused by failing attempts. A fundamental problem with Herlihy's methodology is the overhead that results from making complete copies of the entire object ($c3$ in Fig. 2) even if only a small part of an object has been changed. For a large object this may be excessive.

We therefore propose two alternatives given in Fig. 3. For both algorithms the fields of the object are divided into W disjoint logical groups such that if one field is modified then other fields in the same group may be modified simultaneously. We introduce an additional field *ver* in *nodeType* to attach version numbers to each group to avoid unnecessary copying. We assume all version numbers attached to groups are positive. As usual with version numbers, we assume that they can be sufficiently large. We increment the version number of a group each time we modify at least one member in the group.

All schematic representations of segments of code that appear in Fig. 3 are the same as before, except

3. *com*(**ref** X : *nodeType*; **in** g : 1..W, *priv* : *bType*; **out** *tm* : *cType*) : performs an action on group g of the variable X of *nodeType* instead of on the whole object X.
4. *read*(**ref** X : *nodeType*; **in** Y : *nodeType*, g : 1..W) : only reads the value from group g of node Y to the same group of node X.

The relations corresponding to these schematic commands are adapted accordingly.

In the first implementation, *mp* becomes an array used to record pointers to private copies of shared nodes. In total we declare $N * P$ extra shared nodes for private use (one for each process and each node). Note that $node[mp[x].p]$ can be taken as a "private" node of process p though it is declared publicly. Array *indir* continues to act as pointers to shared nodes.

At the moment that process p reads group $i.p$ of $node[m.p]$ (line $l5$), process p may observe the object in an inconsistent state (i.e. the read value is not the current or historical view of the shared object) since pointer $m.p$ may have been redirected to some private copy of the node by some faster process q, which has increased the modified group's version number(in lines $l9$ and $l10$). When process p restarts the loop, it will get higher version numbers at the array *new*, and only needs to reread the modified groups, whose *new* version numbers differ from their *old* version numbers. Excessive copying can be therefore prevented. Line $l6$ is used to check if the read value of a group is consistent with the version number.

The first implementation is fast for an application that often changes only a small part of the object. However, the space complexity is substantial because $P+1$ copies of each node are maintained and copied back and forth. Sometimes, a trade-off is chosen between space and time complexity. We therefore adapt it to our second lock-free algorithm for large objects (shown in Fig. 3 also) by substituting all statements enclosed by $(* \ldots *)$ for the corresponding statements in the first version. As we did for small objects, we use only one extra copy of a node for each process in the second implementation.

In the second implementation, since the private copy of a node may belong to some other node, a process first initializes all elements of *old* to be zero (line $l1$) before accessing an object, to force the process to make a complete copy of the entire object for the first attempt. The process then only needs to copy part of the object from the second attempt on. The space complexity for our second

```
CONSTANT
   P = number of processes; N = number of nodes;
   W = number of groups;
   K = N + N * P;                           (*  II : K = N + P;  *)
Type nodeType = record
      val: array [1..W] of valType;
      ver: array [1..W] of posnat;
   end
Shared Variables:
   pub: aType; node: array [1..K] of nodeType;
   indir: array [1..N] of 1..K;
Private Variables:
   priv: bType; pc: [l1..l11];
   x: 1..N; m: 1..K;
   mp: array [1..N] of 1..K;               (*  II : mp: 1..K;  *)
   new: array [1..W] of posnat; old: array [1..W] of nat;
   g: 1..W; tm, tm1: cType; i: nat;
Program:
      loop
   l1:    noncrit(pub, priv, tm, x);
          choose group g to be modified;
          old := node[mp[x]].ver;          (*  II : old := λ (i:1..W): 0;  *)
          (*  II : replace all ''mp[x]'' below by ''mp''  *)
          loop
   l2:       m := LL(indir[x]);
   l3:       i := 1
   l4:       while i ≤ W do
                new[i] := node[m].ver[i];
                if new[i] ≠ old[i] then
   l5:             read(node[mp[x]], node[m], i); old[i] := 0;
   l6:             if not VL(indir[x]) then goto l2; fi;
   l7:             node[mp[x]].ver[i] := new[i]; old[i] := new[i];
                fi;
                i++;
              end;
   l8:       if guard(node[mp[x]], priv) then
   l9:          com(node[mp[x]], g, priv, tm1); old[g] := 0;
                node[mp[x]].ver[g] := new[g]+1;
   l10:         if SC(indir[x], mp[x]) then
                   mp[x] := m; tm := tm1; break;
                fi
   l11:      elseif VL(indir[x]) then break;
             fi
          end
      end
```

Fig. 3. Lock-free implementation I (* implementation II *) for large objects

version saves $(N - 1) \times P$ times of size of a node, while the time complexity is more due to making one extra copy of the entire object for the first attempt. To see why these two algorithms are correct, we refer the interested reader to [7] for the complete mechanical proof.

6   Conclusions

This paper shows an approach to verification of simulation and refinement between a lower-level specification and a higher-level specification. It is motivated by our present project on lock-free garbage collection. Using the reduction theorem, the verification effort for a lock-free algorithm becomes simpler since fewer invariants are required and some invariants are easier to discover and easier to formulate without considering the internal structure of the final implementation. Apart from safety properties, we have also considered the important problem of proving liveness properties using the strong fairness assumption.

A more fundamental problem with Herlihy's methodology is the overhead that results from having multiple processes that simultaneously attempt to update a shared object. Since copying the entire object can be time-consuming, we present two enhanced algorithms that avoid unnecessary copying for large objects in cases where only small part of the objects are modified. It is often better to distribute the contents of a large object over several small objects to allow parallel execution of operations on a large object. However, this requires that the contents of those small objects must be independent of each other.

Formal verification is desirable because there could be subtle bugs as the complexity of algorithms increases. To ensure our hand-written proof presented in the paper is not flawed, we use the higher-order interactive theorem prover PVS for mechanical support. PVS has a convenient specification language and contains a proof checker which allows users to construct proofs interactively, to automatically execute trivial proofs, and to check these proofs mechanically. For the complete mechanical proof, we refer the reader to [7].

References

1. B. Bershad: Practical Considerations for Non-Blocking Concurrent Objects. In Proceedings of the 13th International Conference on Distributed Computing Systems, May 1993.
2. E.H. Jensen, G.W. Hagensen, and J.M. Broughton: A new approach to exclusive data access in shared memory multiprocessors. Technical Report UCRL-97663, Lawrence Livemore National Laboratory, November 1987.
3. E. Clarke, O. Grumberg, and D. Long: Model checking and abstraction ACM Transactions on Programming Languages and Systems 16(5), January 1994.
4. G. Barnes: A method for implementing lock-free data structures. In Proceedings of the 5th ACM symposium on Parallel Algorithms & Architecture, June 1993.
5. Henry Massalin, Calton Pu: A Lock-free Multiprocessor OS Kernel. Technical Report CUCS-005-91, Columbia University, 1991

6. H. Gao, J.F. Groote and W.H. Hesselink.: Efficient almost wait-free parallel accessible dynamic hashtables. Technical Report CS-Report 03-03, Eindhoven University of Technology, The Netherlands, 2003. To appear in the proceedings of IPDPS 2004.
7. http://www.cs.rug.nl/~wim/mechver/LLSCreduction
8. J.W. de Bakker, W.-P. de Roever, and G. Rozenberg, editors: Stepwise Refinement of Distributed Systems: Models, Formalism, Correctness. Lecture Notes in Computer Science 430. Spinger-Verlag, 1990.
9. Anthony LaMarca: A Performance Evaluation of Lock-free Synchronization Protocols. In proceedings of the thirteenth symposium on priniciples of distributed computing, 1994.
10. L. Lamport: The Temporal Logic of Actions. ACM Transactions on Programming Languages and Systems 16(3), 1994, pp. 872–923.
11. M. Abadi and L. Lamport: The existence of refinement mappings. Theoretical Computer Science, 2(82), 1991, pp. 253–284.
12. Mark Moir: Practical Implementations of Non-Blocking Synchronization primitives. In Proceedings of the sixteenth symposium on principles of Distributed computing, 1997. Santa Barbara, CA.
13. M. P. Herlihy: A methodology for implementing highly concurrent objects. ACM Transactions on Programming Languages and Systems 15, 1993, pp. 745–770.
14. Maurice Herlihy, Victor Luchangco and Mark Moir: The Repeat Offender Problem: A Mechanism for Supporting Dynamic-Sized, Lock-Free Data Structures. In Proceedings of the 16th International Symposium on DIStributed Computing, 2002.
15. Victor Luchangco, Mark Moir, Nir Shavit: Nonblocking k-compare-single-swap. In Proceedings of the Fifteenth Annual ACM Symposium on Parallel Algorithms, 2003, pp. 314-323.
16. Manna, Z., Pnueli, A.: The Temporal Logic of Reactive and Concurrent Systems: Specification. Springer-Verlag, 1992.

An Efficiently Checkable, Proof-Based Formulation of Vacuity in Model Checking

Kedar S. Namjoshi

Bell Labs, Lucent Technologies
kedar@research.bell-labs.com

Abstract. Model checking algorithms can report a property as being true for reasons that may be considered vacuous. Current algorithms for detecting vacuity require either checking a quadratic size witness formula, or multiple model checking runs; either alternative may be quite expensive in practice. Vacuity is, in its essence, a problem with the justification used by the model checker for deeming the property to be true. We argue that current definitions of vacuity are too broad from this perspective and give a new, narrower, formulation. The new formulation leads to a simple detection method that examines only the justification extracted from the model checker in the form of an automatically generated proof. This check requires a small amount of computation after a *single* verification run on the property, so it is significantly more efficient than the earlier methods. While the new formulation is stronger, and so reports vacuity less often, we show that it agrees with the current formulations for linear temporal properties expressed as automata. Differences arise with inherently branching properties but in instances where the vacuity reported with current formulations is debatable.

1 Introduction

The problem of detecting a vacuous model check of a property has received much attention in the literature [2, 3, 17, 24, 6, 1]. A vacuous model check often indicates a problem, either with the precise formulation of an informal correctness property, or with the program itself. A classic example is that of the property: "Every request is eventually granted", which is true vacuously of a program in which no request is ever made! Most model checkers produce independently checkable evidence for a negative answer in the form of a counterexample trace, but typically are not designed to produce any such evidence of their reasoning for success. Without further checking, therefore, one may end up trusting in vacuously justified properties.

Several algorithms for vacuity detection have been proposed in the papers above. Essentially, these algorithms look for a sub-formula of the correctness property whose truth value does not matter for property verification (a precondition is that the property has been verified). In [3], vacuity is defined as follows: a program M satisfies a formula ϕ vacuously iff M satisfies ϕ, and there is some subformula ψ of ϕ such that ψ does not affect the satisfaction of ϕ – this

R. Alur and D.A. Peled (Eds.): CAV 2004, LNCS 3114, pp. 57–69, 2004.
© Springer-Verlag Berlin Heidelberg 2004

last condition holds if the formula obtained by replacing ψ with any formula ξ (this is written as $\phi[\psi := \xi]$) is true of M. The detection method is to check an automatically generated witness formula for each subformula ψ, one that demonstrates redundancy of ψ if it is true – the witness formula for the property above is "No request is ever made". In [17], this test is simplified and generalized to all of CTL* from the fragment of ACTL considered in [3]. It is shown that to determine whether ψ affects ϕ, it suffices to check whether $\phi[\psi := false]$ ($\phi[\psi := true]$) holds of M if ψ occurs with positive (negative) polarity in ϕ (i.e., under an even (odd) number of negations). These methods treat multiple occurrences of the same subformula independently. A recent paper [1] extends the method above to take into account such dependencies. We adopt their term, *formula vacuity*, to refer to the definition that treats subformulas independently.

A major drawback of these algorithms is that they either require multiple model checking runs to test each subformula, or a single run checking a quadratically long witness formula. (The witnesses are of linear length for the w-ACTL fragment of [3].) Although the cost of model checking increases only linearly in the length of the formula, even a linear blowup can be quite significant in terms of the resources used (time, space, processors), since it is common for large verification runs to take hours to run on a single formula. Remedies have been proposed: in [1], formula structure is used to reduce the number of witness checks, and [24, 6] show how to share intermediate results while checking a single witness formula.

A vacuous verification is, in its essence, a problem with the justification used by the model checking algorithm for deeming the property to be true. Recent work has shown how to extract and present such this justification in the form of a deductive proof (see [21, 22] and the references therein). The central question this paper discusses is whether one can analyze *this justification alone* in order to detect a vacuous verification? The premise seems reasonable, but there are subtleties involved in making it work, and in determining the precise relationship to formula vacuity.

To make this relationship clearer, we examine formula vacuity from the viewpoint of justifications. We show that a mu-calculus formula ϕ is formula-vacuous if, and only if, there exists a valid correctness proof showing that ϕ is true of M in which the invariant for some subformula contains only unreachable states or is empty. Call such a proof *vacuous*. Formula vacuity, then, is equivalent to asking the question: "Does there exist a vacuous correctness proof?". Viewed from this angle, the criterion appears rather odd: why should one discard a valid, non-vacuous correctness proof, just because there is an alternative proof that is vacuous? Examples given later in the paper support this conclusion, by showing that formula vacuity can sometimes produce debatable reports of vacuity.

We propose a new, stronger, formulation of vacuity, which we call *proof vacuity*. This consists of checking whether the correctness proof produced by the model checker as justification is vacuous. Since our vacuity criterion is stronger than formula vacuity, one may expect the new check to report vacuity less often.

However, we show that this may happen only for properties that are inherently branching in nature.

Besides correcting some anomalies in the formula vacuity criterion, the new formulation is, moreover, significantly more efficient to check in practice. All that is required is to examine for emptiness the invariants produced during a model checking run. As these invariants are readily available, this process is even simpler and requires less resources than the generation of a full proof of correctness. As the two formulations coincide for linear time automaton properties, this also gives a significantly more efficient way of checking formula vacuity for such properties.

The next section introduces the concept of proof used in new formulation. In Section 3, we characterize formula vacuity in terms of proofs, motivate and present proof vacuity, and show their equivalence for automaton representations of linear time properties. Section 4 discusses related work, and some future research directions, including "partial vacuity" detection.

2   Preliminaries

We assume that properties are specified as alternating tree automata. In this section, we define the automaton syntax and semantics, and also give the proof system used to represent the justification of model checking results.

Transition Systems. We represent a program by the *transition system* (TS, for short) that it generates – this is also called a *Kripke Structure*. A TS is a tuple $(S, \hat{S}, R, L)$, where S is a non-empty set of *states*, $\hat{S} \subseteq S$ is the set of *initial states*, $R \subseteq S \times S$ is a *transition relation*, and $L : S \to 2^{AP}$ (AP is a set of *atomic propositions*) is a *labeling function* that maps each state to the the propositions true at that state. We assume that R is *total*: i.e., for every s, there exists t such that $(s, t) \in R$.

Temporal Logics. While our results are based on alternating tree automata, we also consider properties defined in one of several well-known temporal logics. The syntax of these logics is defined below; please see [8] for the precise semantics.

LTL [23], linear temporal logic, is a logic that defines infinite sequences over subsets of AP. In positive normal form, formulas of LTL are given by the grammar: $\Phi ::= P(P \in AP) \mid \neg P(P \in AP) \mid \Phi \wedge \Phi \mid \Phi \vee \Phi \mid X(\Phi) \mid (\Phi U \Phi) \mid (\Phi W \Phi)$. The temporal operators are X (next-time), U (until), and W (weak-until or unless). Other operators are defined through abbreviation: $F(\Phi)$ (eventually Φ) is $(true U \Phi)$, and $G(\Phi)$ (always Φ) is $(\Phi W false)$.

CTL* [7], a branching time logic, is given by adding path quantifiers A (over all paths) and E (over some path) to LTL; the set of state formulas are defined inductively as: $\Phi ::= P(P \in AP) \mid \neg P(P \in AP) \mid \Phi \wedge \Phi \mid \Phi \vee \Phi \mid A(\psi) \mid E(\psi)$. Here, ψ is the set of path formulas, which are LTL formulas where atomic propositions come from Φ. CTL [5] is obtained from CTL* by restricting the set of path formulas so that they contain a single, top-level, temporal operator. Its sub-logic ACTL (ECTL) is obtained by allowing only the A (E) path quantifier; ACTL* (ECTL*) is the analogous restriction of CTL*.

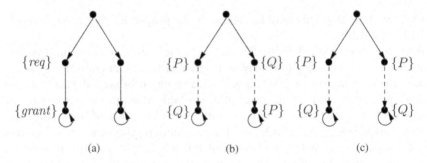

Fig. 3. Transition Systems

there exists an alternate, vacuous justification for the property. To illustrate this point further, we consider some examples.

Existential Properties. The existential analogue of the example defined in the introduction is "There exists a computation where every request is eventually granted". This may be formulated in ECTL as EG($req \Rightarrow$ EF($grant$)). For the TS shown in Figure 3(a), the property is true, as on the left-hand path, a request is sent and subsequently granted. This witness does make use of every subformula, so is non-vacuous. However, replacing the subformula EF($grant$) with *false*, we obtain the property EG($\neg req$), which is true of the right-hand branch; thus, the verification is considered vacuous by the formula-vacuity criterion. This is clearly odd: a perfectly reasonable, non-vacuous proof is disregarded because of the existence of an alternative, vacuous proof.

Universal, Non-linear Properties. Consider another property, in this case a universal one, but one that is not expressible in linear-time logics: "At every successor state, either inevitably P holds, or inevitably Q holds", where P and Q are atomic propositions. The property can be written in ACTL as AX(AF(P) $\vee$ AF(Q)). Consider the TS shown in Figure 3(b), with the dashed arrow representing a long path to a state satisfying the target proposition. The property is clearly true of the TS. The shortest proof will favor satisfying AF(P) for the left successor of the initial state, since it can be done in fewer steps than satisfying AF(Q), and it will favor satisfying AF(Q) for the other successor, for the same reason. This is a non-vacuous proof, since all subformulas are used. However, replacing the subformula AF(Q) by *false* results in the property AX(AF(P)), which is also true of the TS; hence, the verification is vacuous by formula vacuity. This conclusion is debatable: again, a perfectly reasonable proof (in fact, the shortest one) is disregarded because of a vacuous proof that is non-optimal.

3.1   Proof Vacuity

Given these anomalies resulting from the formula-vacuity criterion, we seek to define a stronger criterion based on the justification actually given by the model checker. One possible approach is to examine only the justification provided

The mu-calculus [16] is a branching time temporal logic which subsumes the logics defined above [10]. Formulas in positive form are defined using the following grammar, where V is a set of symbols denoting fixpoint variables, and μ (ν) is the least (greatest) fixpoint operator: $\Phi ::= P(P \in AP) \mid Z(Z \in V) \mid \Phi \wedge \Phi \mid \Phi \vee \Phi \mid EX(\Phi) \mid AX(\Phi) \mid (\mu Z : \Phi) \mid (\nu Z : \Phi)$. A formula must have each variable under the scope of an even number of negation symbols; it is *closed* iff every variable in it is under the scope of a fixpoint operator. The evaluation of a formula f with free variables is a subset of S, defined inductively relative to a context that maps free variables to subsets of S. A state s in M *satisfies* a closed mu-calculus formula f iff s is in the evaluation of f relative to the context that maps every variable to the empty set; M satisfies f (written as $M \models f$) iff all of its initial states satisfy f.

Alternating Tree Automata. An alternating automaton over AP is specified by a tuple $(Q, \hat{q}, \delta, F)$, where Q is a non-empty set of states, $\hat{q} \in Q$ is the initial state, δ is a transition function, and F is a parity acceptance condition. F is given by a partition $(F_0, F_1, \ldots, F_{2N})$ of Q. An infinite sequence over Q satisfies F iff the smallest index i for which a state in F_i occurs infinitely often on the sequence is even. We use a simple normal form for the transition relation: it maps an automaton state and an input from 2^{AP} to one of $(\wedge R), (\vee R), EXr, AXr, true, false$, where r is a state, and R a non-empty subset of states.

Given a mu-calculus formula, one can obtain an equivalent automaton whose transition relation is just the parse graph of the formula (so that each subformula is represented by an automaton state), and the parity condition is determined by an analysis of the alternation between least and greatest fixpoints in the formula [9].

These automata accept computation trees of programs, where tree nodes are labeled with subsets of atomic propositions. For a labeled tree t, let λ_t be the labeling function that maps tree nodes to their labels. The acceptance of a labeled tree t by the automaton is defined in terms of a two-player infinite game. A *configuration* of the game is a pair (x, q), where x is a tree node and q is an automaton state. The moves of the game are as shown in Figure 1.

A *play* of the game is a maximal sequence of configurations generated in this manner. A play is a win for player I iff either it is finite and ends in a configuration that is a win for I, or it is infinite and satisfies the automaton

---

At configuration (x, q), based on the form of $\delta(q, \lambda_t(x))$,

- *true*: Player I wins, and the play is halted
- *false*: Player II wins, and the play is halted
- $(\vee R)$: Player I picks $r \in R$; the next configuration is (x, r)
- $(\wedge R)$: Player II picks $r \in R$; the next configuration is (x, r)
- EXr: Player I picks a child y of x; the next configuration is (y, r)
- AXr: Player II picks a child y of x; the next configuration is (y, r)

Fig. 1. Model Checking Game Moves

acceptance condition. The play is winning for player II otherwise. A *strategy* for player I (II) is a partial function that maps every finite sequence of configurations to a choice at each player I (II) position. A strategy is a *win* for player I if every play following that strategy is a win for I, regardless of the strategy for II. The automaton *accepts* the tree t iff player I has a winning strategy for the game starting at $(\epsilon, \hat{q})$, where ϵ is the root node of the tree t. M *satisfies* A (written as $M \models A$) iff the automaton accepts the computation trees obtained from each initial state by "unwinding" the transition relation of M.

The Proof System. The proof system presented in [21] is as follows. For a TS $M = (S, \hat{S}, R, L)$ and automaton $A = (Q, \hat{q}, \delta, F)$, a proof (ϕ, ρ, W) of A over M is given by specifying (i) [Invariants] for each automaton state q, an invariant predicate ϕ_q (i.e., a subset of S), and (ii) [Rank Functions] for each automaton state q, a partial rank function, ρ_q, from S to a well-founded set $(W, \preceq)$, with induced rank relation $\lhd_q$ over $W \times W$. For vacuity checking, the precise nature of the rank functions and relations is not important[1]. The invariants and rank function must satisfy the three local conditions given in Figure 2 for the proof to be valid. In these conditions, the variable w ranges over elements of W, the notation $[f]$ means that f is valid, and a term of the form $\rho_r \lhd_q w$ ($\rho_r = w$) represents the predicate $(\lambda s : \rho_r(s) \lhd_q w)$ $((\lambda s : \rho_r(s) = w))$.

- ***Consistency:*** (ρ_q is defined for every state in ϕ_q) For each $q \in Q$, $[\phi_q \Rightarrow (\exists w : (\rho_q = w))]$
- ***Initiality:*** (the initial states satisfy the initial invariant) $[\hat{S} \Rightarrow \phi_{\hat{q}}]$
- ***Invariance and Progress:*** For each $q \in Q$, depending on the form of $\delta(q, l)$, where l is a propositional formula over AP, check the following.
  - *true*: nothing to check.
  - *false*: $[\phi_q \Rightarrow \neg l]$
  - ($\lor R$): $[\phi_q \land l \land (\rho_q = w) \Rightarrow (\lor r : r \in R : \phi_r \land (\rho_r \lhd_q w))]$
  - ($\land R$): $[\phi_q \land l \land (\rho_q = w) \Rightarrow (\land r : r \in R : \phi_r \land (\rho_r \lhd_q w))]$
  - EXr: $[\phi_q \land l \land (\rho_q = w) \Rightarrow \mathsf{EX}(\phi_r \land (\rho_r \lhd_q w))]$
  - AXr: $[\phi_q \land l \land (\rho_q = w) \Rightarrow \mathsf{AX}(\phi_r \land (\rho_r \lhd_q w))]$

Fig. 2. The Proof System Rules

Theorem 0 *([21])* **(Soundness)** *If there is a valid proof of A over M, then $M \models A$. **(Completeness)** If $M \models A$, there is a valid proof for A over M.*

The proof of the completeness theorem is important to vacuity detection, so we sketch it here. This proof considers the "run tree" formed by a winning strategy in the game, where the tree contains a single player I move at a node

---

[1] For F of size $2N + 1$, W is the product of N well-founded sets $(W_i, \preceq_i)$, and $\preceq$ is the lexicographic order induced by $\prec_0 \ldots \prec_N$. For $a, b \in W$, $a \lhd_q b$ holds if, and only if, for the unique k such that q is in F_k, either $k = 2i$, for some i, and $(a_1, \ldots, a_i) \preceq (b_1, \ldots, b_i)$, or $k = 2i - 1$, for some i, and $(a_1, \ldots, a_i) \prec (b_1, \ldots, b_i)$.

labeled by a configuration for player I, and all player II moves at a node labeled for player II. The choices of a move for player I are resolved uniquely by the winning strategy. One can extract a proof from this run tree. In particular, the invariant ϕ_q for q is the set of program states s for which there is a configuration of the form (x, q) in the run tree where x contains s.

3   Defining and Detecting Vacuity

We assume that all formulas are in positive normal form. Let Φ be a closed mu-calculus formula. For a subformula ψ of Φ, we define the strict positive subformulas of ψ to be those subformulas of ψ that are not fixpoint variables from a scope outside that of ψ. For instance, in the fairness property $(\nu Z : (\mu Y : \mathsf{EX}(P \wedge Z) \vee \mathsf{EX}(Y)))$ ("There exists a path where P holds infinitely often"), Z is not a strict subformula of $\mathsf{EX}(P \wedge Z)$, although $(P \wedge Z)$ is one.

Theorem 1 *Let Φ be a closed mu-calculus formula, and ψ be a strict positive subformula. Let $\mathcal{A}_\Phi$ be the automaton formed from the parse graph of Φ, with state q corresponding to ψ. Then, $\Phi[\psi := false]$ holds of M iff there is a proof that M satisfies $\mathcal{A}_\Phi$ in which the invariant for q is the empty set.*

Proof. (left-to-right) Let $\Phi' = \Phi[\psi := false]$. The parse graph for Φ' can be obtained from that of Φ by deleting nodes that correspond to strict subformulas of ψ, and replacing ψ with $false$. Thus, an automaton for Φ', $\mathcal{A}_{\Phi'}$, can be obtained from $\mathcal{A}_\Phi$ by deleting states that correspond to strict sub-formulas of ψ, and by setting $\delta'(q, l) = false$ for all l. As Φ' holds for M, by the completeness theorem, there is a valid deductive proof (ϕ', ρ', W') which, of course, is based only on the states in $\mathcal{A}_{\Phi'}$. As this proof is valid, the assertion $[\phi'_q \Rightarrow \neg l]$ must be valid for all l; thus, $\phi'_q = \emptyset$. Now we form a proof (ϕ, ρ, W) as follows: let $W = W'$, and for r in $\mathcal{A}_{\Phi'}$, let $\phi_r = \phi'_r$ and $\rho_r = \rho'_r$. For any other state p, let $\phi_p = \emptyset$, and let ρ_p be some fixed element of W (the choice is arbitrary).

We claim that this is a valid proof for $\mathcal{A}_\Phi$ over M. Since each state p missing from $\mathcal{A}_{\Phi'}$ represents a strict subformula of ψ, it is reachable only from q; hence, setting its invariant to the empty set does not affect the validity of the checks for states of $\mathcal{A}_{\Phi'}$. Furthermore, since the invariants are set to empty, the own checks for these states, which have the form $[(\phi_p \wedge \alpha) \Rightarrow \beta]$, are trivially valid. Hence, the new proof is valid, and it has an empty invariance set for q.

(right-to-left) Suppose that there is a proof (ϕ, ρ, W), where $\phi_q = \emptyset$. Then, the rule for q holds trivially. Consider a state p that corresponds to a strict subformula of ψ. As p is reachable only from q, its invariant does not affect the validity of the check for any state r that does not correspond to a strict subformula of ψ. Hence, dropping states that correspond to strict subformulas of ψ, and replacing $\delta(q, l)$ with $false$ for all l, yields a valid proof of $\mathcal{A}_{\Phi'}$ over M. By the soundness theorem, this implies that M satisfies Φ'. $\square$

Given this theorem, the existing methods for vacuity detection can be viewed as searching for a vacuous proof. This seems to be too broad a formulation: it disregards a non-vacuous proof produced by a model checker simply because

by a given model checker for vacuity. This is simple, but has the disadvantage of being sensitive to the choice of the model checker. This sensitivity may not be a problem if a particular model checker is standardized for use within an organization.

We explore, however, the consequences of a definition that is insensitive to the model checking strategy. As a preliminary, given M and $\mathcal{A}_\Phi$, for a mu-calculus formula Φ, call a state of M *game-reachable* iff it occurs in some configuration of the game for $M \models \mathcal{A}_\Phi$. Note that all unreachable states of M are also game-unreachable, but that some reachable states of M may also be game-unreachable. For instance, the game for the formula $\Phi = P$ examines only the initial states of M; thus, all other states are game-unreachable. The proof of the soundness theorem in [21] shows that each valid proof defines a history-free winning strategy for the model checking game. Thus, removing game-unreachable states from each invariant set does not change the validity of a proof. We can now define a proof to be vacuous for some subformula as follows.

Definition 0 *(Vacuous Proof)* *A proof for an automaton property is vacuous for automaton state q iff the invariant for q is empty or contains only game-unreachable states. A proof is vacuous iff it is vacuous for some automaton state.*

Theorem 1 can then be amended so that it is also possible for the invariant for q to contain game-unreachable states. We rely on this amended form in the subsequent discussion. We can now define proof vacuity as follows. Notice that the crucial difference with formula vacuity is that a verification is considered to be vacuous only if all *all* model checking strategies give rise to vacuous proofs.

Definition 1 *(Proof Vacuity)* *For an automaton property $\mathcal{A}$ and a TS M, the verification of $\mathcal{A}$ on M is proof-vacuous iff for some automaton state q, every proof that M satisfies $\mathcal{A}$ is vacuous for q.*

The rationale for excluding game-unreachable, rather than just unreachable states is as follows. Consider the property $AX(P \Rightarrow AX(Q))$. This is true vacuously of a TS M for which all successors of the initial state satisfy $\neg P$. However, there may be a proof where the invariant for the state corresponding to $AX(Q)$ includes reachable states of M that satisfy $AX(Q)$; thus, the weaker criterion would not properly detect the vacuous verification. Game-reachability is not that stringent a criterion; for instance, COSPAN [12], a symbolic model checker for linear-time automaton properties, restricts the model checking to the reachable states of the product of the TS and a negated property automaton. This product defines the game configurations: thus, all invariants include only game-reachable states.

Although proof-vacuity has a universal quantification over all proofs, we can show that it suffices to consider a maximally inclusive proof, produced by including every game reachable state that satisfies an automaton state q in ϕ_q – this is just the proof provided by the completeness theorem.

Theorem 2 *For an automaton property $\mathcal{A}$ and TS M, the property is true proof-vacuously for M iff the maximally inclusive proof is vacuous.*

Proof. It is slightly easier to show the contrapositive. Suppose that the property is true non-proof-vacuously. Then there is a non-vacuous proof, one in which the invariant for every automaton state contains some game-reachable state. This state must be present, by inclusiveness, in the invariant for that automaton state in the maximally inclusive proof. Hence, the maximally inclusive proof is non-vacuous. In the other direction, if the maximally inclusive proof is non-vacuous, the verification is non-proof-vacuous by definition. □

Vacuity Checking. Suppose that the states of M are represented symbolically by a vector of Boolean variables $\vec{b}$, and that the states of $\mathcal{A}_\Phi$ are represented by a vector of Boolean variables $\vec{c}$. Let $Win(\vec{b}, \vec{c})$ be the set of reachable, winning game configurations that is generated by the model checker, as indicated above for COSPAN. The vacuity check then amounts to detecting whether the encoding of some valid automaton state q is not associated with any state in Win – this means that the invariant for q is empty. Such a check can be performed through symbolic (BDD) calculations. One such method is to calculate the set of automaton states with non-empty invariants, $nonempty(\vec{c})$, as $(\exists \vec{b} : Win(\vec{b}, \vec{c}))$, and check whether $valid \Rightarrow nonempty$, where $valid(\vec{c})$ defines valid automaton states.

An interesting point is that proof-vacuity, as defined, does not take into account the distinction between optimal and non-optimal proofs. For instance, consider the ACTL formula $\mathsf{AX}(\mathsf{AF}(P) \lor \mathsf{AF}(Q))$ and the TS in Figure 3(c). An optimal proof, in which player I makes choices that satisfy eventualities as early as possible, has an empty invariant for $\mathsf{AF}(Q)$; a less-than-optimal proof would include the third-level states (which are game-reachable) in the invariant for $\mathsf{AF}(Q)$. Thus, the verification is non-proof-vacuous due to the existence of the less-than-optimal, non-vacuous proof. However, it might be of interest to know that the shortest proof of correctness does not use a certain subformula. The construction for the completeness theorem can be adjusted to create a proof that is optimal (vs. maximally inclusive) as follows. The construction already results in ranks that define the shortest path to satisfying eventualites. All that remains is to prune the maximally inclusive invariants so that states that do not contribute to the shortest path to fulfilling any eventuality (e.g., the third-level states in this example) are eliminated from the invariants. It is not clear, though, whether an analogue of Theorem 2 can be obtained. Note that a discussion of optimality differences is based on quantifying progress through rank functions; progress concerns have so far not played a role in the identification of vacuous justifications. As shown below, differences in optimality are of concern only for certain branching-time properties.

Theorem 3 *For a mu-calculus property ϕ and TS M, if there is a unique run tree for the model checking game on M and $\mathcal{A}_\phi$, then formula-vacuity for ϕ coincides with proof-vacuity (optimal-proof-vacuity) for $\mathcal{A}_\phi$.*

Proof. Each run tree corresponds to a winning strategy for player I, which is history-free (due to the parity winning condition) and so corresponds to a proof (cf. [21]). As there is a unique run tree, there is only a single valid proof. If ϕ is true formula-vacuously, this proof is vacuous, and hence the verification is also proof-vacuous, since there are no other valid proofs to consider. The other direction follows as proof-vacuity is stronger than formula-vacuity. □

This theorem has some interesting consequences for linear and branching time properties. Consider the case where a linear-time property is specified by expressing its negation as a a Büchi word automaton – this is the usual approach to model checking a linear-time property. From such an automaton B, one may construct a *universal* dual automaton $\tilde{B}$ with the same transition relation and a complemented Büchi acceptance condition [20]. Universality means that $\tilde{B}$ accepts a computation if *all* runs on it are accepting. This dual automaton can also be viewed as a universal tree automaton for the branching time property "All computations of M are accepted by $\tilde{B}$". As $\tilde{B}$ is universal, there is a single run tree of $\tilde{B}$ on M. Applying Theorem 3, one obtains the consequence given below. For pure branching time properties, proof-vacuity is strictly stronger, as shown by the examples discussed previously.

Theorem 4 *Let $\tilde{B}$ be a universal co-Büchi tree automaton that expresses that a linear-time correctness property holds for all computations of M. If $M \models \tilde{B}$, the verification is formula vacuous iff it is proof (optimal-proof) vacuous.*

Linear Properties as LTL Formulas. Theorem 4 showed that, for linear-time properties expressed as (negated) automata, proof vacuity coincides with formula vacuity. The situation is different if formula vacuity is applied to LTL formulas. Intuitively, this is because model checking is carried out with an automaton derived from an LTL formula (cf. [11]), where each automaton state represents a *set* of subformulas. Thus, vacuity at the level of the automaton states makes possible finer distinctions than vacuity at the level of formulas.

This difference can be seen with an LTL formula that is similar – though not equivalent – to the ACTL formula defined previously: $\mathsf{X}(\mathsf{F}(P) \vee \mathsf{F}(Q))$. This holds for the TS in Figure 3(b); however, so does $\mathsf{X}(\mathsf{F}(P))$, which is obtained by setting the $\mathsf{F}(Q)$ subformula to *false*. A universal co-Büchi automaton for this formula is defined by the state set $\{0, 1, 2\}$ with initial state 0, and transitions $0 \xrightarrow{true} 1, 1 \xrightarrow{(\neg P \wedge \neg Q)} 1, 1 \xrightarrow{(P \vee Q)} 2$, and $2 \xrightarrow{true} 2$, and the co-Büchi acceptance condition $\mathsf{FG}(2)$. This automaton is verified without vacuity (either by the old or, from Theorem 4, by the new formulation).

We can show equivalence of the formula and automaton vacuity definitions, however, for a subclass of LTL formulas. This class, LTL^{det}, is defined in [19], where it is shown that it represents exactly those LTL properties that are definable in ACTL. In fact, the ACTL property equivalent to checking that ϕ holds on all computations can be obtained simply by attaching the A path operator to each temporal operator in ϕ; we refer to this ACTL formula as ϕ^+. Any ACTL property has a direct translation to an equivalent mu-calculus property, so we may consider ϕ^+ also as a mu-calculus property. The precise syntax is given below. In this syntax, p is a propositional state predicate, so that every $\vee$-choice can be resolved deterministically at a state.

$\Phi ::= p \mid \Phi \wedge \Phi \mid (p \wedge \Phi) \vee (\neg p \wedge \Phi) \mid \mathsf{X}(\Phi) \mid ((p \wedge \Phi)\mathsf{U}(\neg p \wedge \Phi)) \mid ((p \wedge \Phi)\mathsf{W}(\neg p \wedge \Phi))$.

Theorem 5 *For an LTL^{det} formula ϕ and TS M, the verification of ϕ on M is formula-vacuous iff the verification of $\phi+$ on M is proof-vacuous.*

Proof. Consider any positive sub-formula ψ of ϕ. Then, $\mathsf{A}(\phi[\psi := false])$ is equivalent to $(\phi[\psi := false])^+$, which is identical to $\phi^+[\psi^+ := false]$ by the nature of the transformation. Thus, ϕ is true formula-vacuously for M with ψ as the witness subformula iff ϕ^+ is true formula-vacuously for M, with ψ^+ as the witness subformula. From the determinism inherent in the syntax, there is a unique run tree for the verification of ϕ^+. By Theorem 3, formula-vacuity for ϕ^+ coincides with proof-vacuity. $\square$

4   Conclusions and Related Work

This paper argues that the current formulation of vacuity is too broad. This conclusion is supported both by examples, and by a theorem showing that formula-vacuity is equivalent to the existence of a vacuous proof. We propose a new, narrower formulation, which needs to inspect only the invariants of a single, maximally inclusive proof. Besides resolving anomalies with the earlier formulation, the new one can be checked more efficiently, by using information that is easily gathered during model checking. This should translate to a significant advantage in practice. In fact, checking proof vacuity with COSPAN is trivial, since the model checker produces a list of game-unreachable automaton states; the verification is vacuous iff this list contains a valid automaton state.

The most closely related work in vacuity detection has been discussed throughout the paper. As pointed out in [18], vacuity is but one of several approaches to further inspecting a valid answer from a model checker. One may also examine the state "coverage" (cf. [14, 13, 4]). Vacuity may be viewed, dually, as a form of specification coverage, since it checks whether certain sub-formulas are redundant for the verification. More generally, producing justifications in the form of deductive proofs (cf. [21, 22]) or as interactive games or tableaux [15, 26, 25] can offer deeper insight into why a property holds (or fails) of the program, since these take ranking functions also into account (cf. the discussion on optimality).

An interesting research topic is to recognize "partial" vacuity in a way that produces useful results. For instance, consider a tree-structured transition system where the left subtree of the root satisfies the request-grant property vacuously (by never sending requests), while the right subtree satisfies it non-vacuously (there is at least one request). Neither the earlier formulation nor the one proposed here would consider this to be a vacuous verification, yet there is clearly something odd in this proof. It seems likely that a more detailed analysis of correctness proofs will enable the detection of such instances.

Acknowledgements

This work was supported in part by grant CCR-0341658 from the National Science Foundation.

References

1. R. Armoni, L. Fix, A. Flaisher, O. Grumberg, N. Piterman, A. Tiemeyer, and M.Y. Vardi. Efficient vacuity detection in linear temporal logic. In *CAV*, volume 2725 of *LNCS*. Springer-Verlag, 2003.
2. D. Beatty and R. Bryant. Formally verifying a microprocessor using a simulation methodology. In *31st DAC*. IEEE Computer Society, 1994.
3. I. Beer, S. Ben-David, C. Eisner, and Y. Rodeh. Efficient detection of vacuity in ACTL formulas. In *CAV*, volume 1254 of *LNCS*, 1997. (full version in FMSD, 18(2), 2001).
4. H. Chockler, O. Kupferman, R.P. Kurshan, and M.Y. Vardi. A practical approach to coverage in model checking. In *CAV*, volume 2102 of *LNCS*. Springer-Verlag, 2001.
5. E.M. Clarke and E. A. Emerson. Design and synthesis of synchronization skeletons using branching time temporal logic. In *Workshop on Logics of Programs*, volume 131 of *LNCS*. Springer-Verlag, 1981.
6. Y. Dong, B. Sarna-Starosta, C.R. Ramakrishnan, and S.A. Smolka. Vacuity checking in the modal mu-calculus. In *AMAST*, volume 2422 of *LNCS*. Springer-Verlag, 2002.
7. E. A. Emerson and J. Y. Halpern. "Sometimes" and "Not Never" revisited: on Branching versus Linear Time Temporal Logic. *J.ACM*, 33(1):151–178, January 1986.
8. E.A. Emerson. Temporal and modal logic. In Jan van Leeuwen, editor, *Handbook of Theoretical Computer Science, Vol. B: Formal Methods and Semantics*. Elsevier and MIT Press, 1990.
9. E.A. Emerson and C.S. Jutla. Tree automata, mu-calculus and determinacy (extended abstract). In *FOCS*, 1991.
10. E.A. Emerson and C-L. Lei. Efficient model checking in fragments of the propositional mu-calculus (extended abstract). In *LICS*, 1986.
11. R. Gerth, D. Peled, M.Y. Vardi, and P. Wolper. Simple on-the-fly automatic verification of linear temporal logic. In *PSTV*. Chapman & Hall, 1995.
12. R.H. Hardin, Z. Har'el, and R.P. Kurshan. COSPAN. In *CAV*, volume 1102 of *LNCS*, 1996.
13. Y. Hoskote, T. Kam, P-H. Ho, and X. Zhao. Coverage estimation for symbolic model checking. In *37th DAC*. ACM Press, 1999.
14. S. Katz, D. Geist, and O. Grumberg. "Have I written enough properties?" A method for comparison between specification and implementation. In *CHARME*, volume 1703 of *LNCS*. Springer-Verlag, 1999.
15. A. Kick. Generation of witnesses for global mu-calculus model checking. available at http://citeseer.ist.psu.edu/kick95generation.html, 1995.
16. D. Kozen. Results on the propositional mu-calculus. In *ICALP*, volume 140 of *LNCS*. Springer-Verlag, 1982.
17. O. Kupferman and M.Y. Vardi. Vacuity detection in temporal model checking. In *CHARME*, number 1703 in LNCS. Springer-Verlag, 1999. (full version in STTT 4(2), 2003).

18. O. Kupferman and M.Y. Vardi. Vacuity detection in temporal model checking. *STTT*, 4(2), 2003.
19. M. Maidl. The common fragment of CTL and LTL. In *FOCS*, 2000.
20. Z. Manna and A. Pnueli. Specification and verification of concurrent programs by ∀-automata. In *POPL*, 1987.
21. K. S. Namjoshi. Certifying model checkers. In *CAV*, volume 2102 of *LNCS*, 2001.
22. D. Peled, A. Pnueli, and L. D. Zuck. From falsification to verification. In *FSTTCS*, volume 2245 of *LNCS*, 2001.
23. A. Pnueli. The temporal logic of programs. In *FOCS*, 1977.
24. M. Purandare and F. Somenzi. Vacuum cleaning CTL formulae. In *CAV*, volume 2404 of *LNCS*. Springer-Verlag, 2002.
25. P. Stevens and C. Stirling. Practical model-checking using games. In *TACAS*, volume 1384 of *LNCS*. Springer-Verlag, 1998.
26. S. Yu and Z. Luo. Implementing a model checker for LEGO. In *FME*, volume 1313 of *LNCS*, 1997.

Termination of Linear Programs

Ashish Tiwari*

SRI International
333 Ravenswood Ave, Menlo Park, CA, USA
tiwari@csl.sri.com

Abstract. We show that termination of a class of linear loop programs is decidable. Linear loop programs are discrete-time linear systems with a loop condition governing termination, that is, a while loop with linear assignments. We relate the termination of such a simple loop, on all initial values, to the eigenvectors corresponding to only the positive real eigenvalues of the matrix defining the loop assignments. This characterization of termination is reminiscent of the famous stability theorems in control theory that characterize stability in terms of eigenvalues.

1   Introduction

Dynamical systems have been studied by both computer scientists and control theorists, but both the models and the properties studied have been different. However there is one class of models, called "discrete-time linear systems" in the control world, where there is a considerable overlap. In computer science, these are unconditional while loops with linear assignments to a set of integer or rational variables; for example,

while (*true*) { $x := x - y; y := y$ }.

The two communities are interested in different questions: stability and controllability issues in control theory against reachability, invariants, and termination issues in computer science. In recent years, computer scientists have begun to apply the rich mathematical knowledge that has been developed in systems theory for analyzing such systems for safety properties, see for instance [17, 12, 11].

One of the most basic results in the theory of linear systems, both discrete-time and continuous-time, is the characterization of the stability of linear systems in terms of the eigenvalues of the corresponding matrix. In this paper, we are interested in termination of simple while loop programs, such as the one described above, but with nontrivial loop guards. We present results that relate the termination of such linear programs to eigenvalues of the corresponding matrix, analogous to the stability characterization in control theory. Our characterization also yields decidability of the termination problem for such programs. Although linear programs are similar to discrete-time linear systems, the termination characterization of linear programs is more complex than, though reminiscent of, the stability characterization for both continuous- and discrete-time linear systems.

---

* Research supported in part by the National Science Foundation under grant CCR-0311348 and CCR-0326540.

R. Alur and D.A. Peled (Eds.): CAV 2004, LNCS 3114, pp. 70–82, 2004.
© Springer-Verlag Berlin Heidelberg 2004

Linear loop programs, as studied in this paper, are specialized piecewise affine systems, which themselves are special kinds of nonlinear systems. While several properties, such as reachability, stability, and controllability, are decidable for linear systems [10, 16], they soon become undecidable even when a "little" non-linearity is introduced [16]. In particular, this is also true for piecewise affine systems [3, 4], see also Section 6. In this context, it is interesting to note that termination is decidable for linear loop programs.

Techniques to prove termination of programs have attracted renewed attention lately [7, 5, 6, 13]. The popular approach to prove termination is through the synthesis of a ranking function, a mapping from the state space to a well-founded domain, whose value monotonically decreases as the system moves forward. This line of research has focused mostly on generating *linear* ranking functions – some effective heuristics have been proposed [5, 6] and recently a complete method was presented in [13] for a model motivated by [14]. This paper investigates termination at a more basic theoretical level. The main result establishes the decidability of the termination problem for programs of the form (in matrix notation)

  while $(Bx > b)$ { $x := Ax + c$ }

where $Bx > b$ represents a conjunction of linear inequalities over the state variables x and $x := Ax+c$ represents the linear assignments to each of the variables. The variables are interpreted over the reals $\Re$ and hence the state space is $\Re^n$. This class of programs is simpler than the ones considered in [5, 6, 13]. Although a program may not be presented in this form, termination questions can often be reduced to this basic form after suitable simplifications and transformations.

We approach the termination issue of the above program as follows. We first consider the homogeneous version,

  while $(Bx > 0)$ { $x := Ax$ },

and note that the condition $Bx > 0$ defines a region smaller than a half space of $\Re^n$. Now if a state $x = c$ is mapped by A (in one or more iterations) to something on the other side of the half space, then the program will terminate on this state (since the loop condition will become false). In particular, this means that the program always terminates on states specified by eigenvectors c corresponding to negative real eigenvalue and complex eigenvalues. The former ones are mapped by A to their negative image, while the latter ones are rotated gradually until they reach the other half space (where $Bx > 0$ is false). Thus, our first result is that, for purposes of termination, the eigenspace corresponding to only the *positive real* eigenvalues of A is relevant (Section 2 and Section 3).

In the case when all eigenvalues are positive, the eigenvectors corresponding to larger eigenvalues dominate the behavior of the program, that is, after sufficiently many iterations, the values of the state variables will be governed almost solely by the influence of the largest eigenvalue. Based on this, we can guess a witness to nontermination and test if the guess is correct by checking satisfiability of a set of constraints (Section 4). Finally, we show that the nonhomogeneous case can be reduced to the homogeneous case (Section 5).

1.1   Notation

We use standard mathematical notation for representing vectors and matrices. We follow the convention that upper case letters $I, J, \ldots$, denote integer constants and lower case letters $i, j, \ldots$ denote indices ranging over integers. In particular, a $(N \times 1)$ column matrix is called a vector, and it is denoted by c, d whenever the components of the vector are known constants; and by x, y whenever the components of the vector are all variables. A $(N \times N)$-matrix with constant entries a_{ij} at the (i, j)-position is denoted by $A = (a_{ij})$. A diagonal matrix $A = (a_{ij}) = diag(\lambda_1, \ldots, \lambda_N)$ has $a_{ii} = \lambda_i$ and $a_{ij} = 0$ otherwise. The transpose of a matrix $A = (a_{ij})$ is a matrix $B = (b_{ij})$ such that $b_{ij} = a_{ji}$, and it is denoted by A^T. Note that the transpose of a column vector c is a row vector c^T. Using juxtaposition for matrix multiplication, we note that $c^T d$ denotes the inner product, $\sum_i c_i d_i$, of the vectors c and d.

We will also denote matrices by specifying the submatrices inside it. So, for instance, $diag(J_1, \ldots, J_K)$ would denote a matrix which has matrices $J_1, \ldots, J_K$ on its "diagonal" and 0 elsewhere. If A is a $(N \times N)$-matrix and c is a vector such that $Ac = \lambda c$, then c is called an *eigenvector* of A corresponding to the *eigenvalue* λ. The effect of repeated linear assignments ($x := Ax$) becomes much more explicit when we do a change of variables and let the new variables y be the eigenvectors of A. In particular, we get transformed assignments of the form $y := \lambda y$. If there are N linearly independent eigenvectors, then A is said to be *diagonalizable* and the assignments on the new variables will be of the form $y := diag(\lambda_1, \ldots, \lambda_N)y$. But this is not possible always. However, instead of a diagonal matrix, we can always get an almost diagonal, the so-called *Jordan form*, matrix [9].

2   The Homogeneous Case

The presentation in this paper is incremental – going from syntactically simple to more complex programs. In this section, we consider linear programs of the following form:

    P1: while ($c^T x > 0$) { $x := Ax$ }.

The variables in x are interpreted over the set $\Re$ of reals. The assignment $x := Ax$ is interpreted as being done simultaneously and not in any sequential order. A list of sequential assignments can be modified and presented in the form $x := Ax$, see Example 1. We say that the Program P1 *terminates* if it terminates on *all* initial values in $\Re$ for the variables in x.

Theorem 1. *If the linear loop program P1, defined by an $(N \times N)$-matrix A and a nonzero $N \times 1$-vector c, is nonterminating then there exists a real eigenvector v of A, corresponding to positive eigenvalue, such that $c^T v \geq 0$.*

Proof. (Sketch) Suppose the linear loop program is nonterminating. Define the set NT of all points on which the program does not terminate.

$$NT = \{x \in \Re^N : c^T x > 0, c^T Ax > 0, c^T A^2 x > 0, \ldots, c^T A^i x > 0, \ldots\}.$$

By assumption, $NT \neq \emptyset$. The set NT is also A-invariant, that is, if $v \in NT$, then $Av \in NT$. Note that NT is an affine subspace of $\Re^N$, that is, it is closed under addition and scalar multiplication by positive reals. Hence, it is convex[1]. Define $T = \Re^N - NT$ to be the set of all points where the program terminates. Define the boundary, ∂NT, of NT and T as the set of all v such that (for all ϵ) there exists a point in the ϵ-neighborhood of v that belongs to T and another that belongs to NT.

Let NT' be the completion of NT, that is, $NT' = NT \cup \partial NT$. Since NT is A-invariant, it means that A maps NT into NT. By continuity we have that A also maps NT' into NT'. Now, NT' is convex, and if we identify points x and y, written as $x \sim y$, that are nonzero scalar multiples of each other ($x = \lambda y$), then the resulting set $(NT'/\sim)$ is closed and bounded (as a subset of $\Re^{n-1}$). By Brouwer's fixed point theorem [15], it follows that there is an eigenvector v (with positive eigenvalue) of A in NT'. For all points $u \in NT$, we know $c^T u > 0$. By continuity, for all points $u \in NT'$, we have $c^T u \geq 0$.   ∎

If, in fact, it is the case that $c^T v > 0$, then v is a witness to nontermination of the loop. Thus, Theorem 1 can be used to get the following conditional characterization of nontermination.

Corollary 1. *If there is no real eigenvector v of A such that $c^T v = 0$, then the linear loop program defined by A and c is nonterminating iff there exists an eigenvector v on which the loop is nonterminating.*

Example 1. The effect of two *sequential* assignments $x := x - y; y := x + 2y$ is captured by the *simultaneous* assignment

$$\begin{pmatrix} x \\ y \end{pmatrix} = \begin{pmatrix} 1 & -1 \\ 1 & 1 \end{pmatrix} \begin{pmatrix} x \\ y \end{pmatrix}$$

The matrix A has no real eigenvalues. Let $c \neq 0$ be any (nonzero) vector. The condition of Corollary 1 is trivially satisfied. And since there is no real eigenvalue, we immediately conclude that the linear loop program specified by A and (any nonzero vector) c is terminating.

Example 2. Let θ be a fixed number. Consider the following program: `while` $(z - y > 0)$ { $x := Ax$ }, where $A = [\cos\theta, -\sin\theta, 0; \sin\theta, \cos\theta, 0; 0, 0, 1]$. Thus, A simply rotates the 3-D space by an angle θ about the z-axis. The set of points where this program is nonterminating is $NT = \{(x, y, z) : z > x\sin\phi + y\cos\phi :$ $\phi = n\theta, n = 0, 1, 2, \ldots\}$. For θ that is not a factor of π, $\partial NT = \{(x, y, z) : z^2 = x^2 + y^2\}$ (eliminate ϕ from above). Note that there is the eigenvector $(0, 0, 1)$ in NT corresponding to positive eigenvalue 1. As another example of the boundary, note that if $\theta = \pi/4$, then ∂NT contains 8 hyperplanes, each one is mapped by A to the next adjacent one.

2.1   Generalizing the Loop Condition

The loop condition can be generalized to allow for a conjunction of multiple linear inequalities. We continue to assume that all linear inequalities and linear

---

[1] A set NT is convex if $\alpha u + (1 - \alpha)v \in NT$ whenever $u, v \in NT$ and $0 \leq \alpha \leq 1$.

assignments consist only of homogeneous expressions. Let B be a $(M \times N)$-matrix (with rational entries) and A be a $(N \times N)$-matrix. We consider programs of the following form:

P2: while $(Bx > 0)$ { $x := Ax$ } .

Theorem 1 and Corollary 1 immediately generalize to programs of the form P2.

Theorem 2. *If Program P2, specified by matrices A and B, is nonterminating, then there is a real eigenvector v of A, corresponding to a positive real eigenvalue, such that $Bv \geq 0$.*

Corollary 2. *Assume that for every real eigenvector v of A, corresponding to a positive eigenvalue, whenever $Bv \geq 0$, then it is actually the case that $Bv > 0$. Then, the Program P2, defined by A and B, is nonterminating iff there exists an eigenvector v on which the loop is nonterminating.*

Example 3. Consider the program:

while $(x - y > 0)$ { $x := -x + y; \; y := y$ } .

The matrix $A = [-1, 1; 0, 1]$ has two eigenvalues, 1 and -1. The eigenvector corresponding to the eigenvalue 1 is $[1; 2]$ and we note that $1 - 2 \not> 0$. Hence, it follows from Corollary 2 that the above loop is terminating.

2.2   Two Variable Case

Theorem 1 and Theorem 2 show that nonterminating linear loops almost always have a witness that is an eigenvector of the matrix A. The only problematic case is when the eigenvector is on the boundary, ∂NT, so that it is not clear if indeed there are points where the program is nonterminating. However, in the 2-dimensional case, that is, when there are only two variables, the region NT will be a sector and it can be specified by its two boundary rays. Thus, if $NT \neq \emptyset$, then there exists an A-invariant sector, given by $a^T x \triangleright 0 \; \wedge \; b^T x \triangleright 0 \; \wedge \; x \neq 0$ where $\triangleright \in \{>, \geq\}$, on which the loop condition always evaluates to true. This can be expressed as a quantified formula over the theory of (linear) arithmetic interpreted over the reals, which is a decidable theory.

Theorem 3. *A two variable linear loop program,*

while $(Bx > 0)$ { $x := Ax$ },

is non-terminating iff the following sentence in true in the theory of reals

$$\exists a, b. [\exists x. \phi(a, b, x) \; \wedge \; \forall x. (\phi(a, b, x) \; \Rightarrow \; (Bx > 0 \; \wedge \; \phi(a, b, Ax)))]$$

where $\phi(a, b, x)$ denotes $a^T x \triangleright 0 \; \wedge \; b^T x \triangleright 0 \; \wedge \; x \neq 0$ and $\triangleright \in \{>, \geq\}$.

This theorem gives a decision procedure for termination of two variable loops since the formula in Theorem 3 can be tested for satisfiability. Theorem 3 cannot be generalized to higher dimensions since there may not be finitely many hyperplane boundaries, as Example 2 illustrates.

3   Reducing the Homogeneous Case

Corollary 2 falls short of yielding decidability of termination of homogeneous linear programs. But it hints that the real eigenvalues and the corresponding eigenvectors are relevant for termination characteristics of such programs. In this section, we will formally show that the nonpositive eigenvalues (and the corresponding eigenspace) can be ignored and the termination problem can be reduced to only the eigenspace corresponding to positive real eigenvalues of the matrix A.

We first note that the Program P2 from Section 2.1 can be transformed by an invertible (bijective) transformation, preserving its termination properties.

Proposition 1. *Let P be an invertible linear transformation. The program*
    P2: while $(Bx > 0)$ { $x := Ax$ }
is terminating iff the program
    P3: while $(BPy > 0)$ { $y := P^{-1}APy$ }
is terminating.

Proof. If Program P2 does not terminate on input $x := c$, then Program P3 will not terminate on input $y := P^{-1}c$. Conversely, if Program P3 does not terminate on input $y := d$, then Program P2 will not terminate on input $x := Pd$.   ∎

Thus, Proposition 1 is just about doing a "change of variables". It is a well known result in linear algebra [9, 1] that using a suitable change of variables, a real matrix A can be transformed into the form, $diag(J_1, J_2, \ldots, J_K)$, called the *real Jordan form*, where each J_i is either of the two forms:

$$\begin{pmatrix} \lambda_i & 1 & 0 & \ldots & 0 \\ 0 & \lambda_i & 1 & \ldots & 0 \\ & & & \ddots & \\ 0 & 0 & & \ddots & 1 \\ 0 & 0 & 0 & \ldots & \lambda_i \end{pmatrix} \qquad \begin{pmatrix} D_i & I & 0 & \ldots & 0 \\ 0 & D_i & I & \ldots & 0 \\ & & & \ddots & \\ 0 & 0 & & \ddots & I \\ 0 & 0 & 0 & \ldots & D_i \end{pmatrix}$$

where $\lambda_i \in \Re$ is a real whereas D_i is a (2×2)-matrix of the form $\begin{pmatrix} \alpha_i & -\beta_i \\ \beta_i & \alpha_i \end{pmatrix}$. For uniformity, the second Jordan block will denote both the forms. When it denotes the first form, then D_i and I are both (1×1)-matrices and we will say $D_i \in \Re$ and treat it as a real. We define $|D_i| = |\lambda_i|$ in the first case and $|D_i| = \sqrt{\alpha_i^2 + \beta_i^2}$ in the second case.

Let P be the real $(N \times N)$-matrix such that $P^{-1}AP = diag(J_1, \ldots, J_K)$. Thus, Program P2, specified by matrices A and B,
    P2: while $(Bx > 0)$ { $x := Ax$ },
can be transformed into the new Program P3,
    P3: while $(BPy > 0)$ { $y := diag(J_1, \ldots, J_K)y$ }.
Proposition 1 means that we can focus on termination of Program P3. Partition the variables in y into $y_1, y_2, \ldots, y_K$ and rewrite the Program P3 as
    P3: while $(B_1y_1 + \cdots + B_Ky_K > 0)$ { $y_1 := J_1y_1; \ldots; y_K := J_Ky_K$ },
where B_i's are obtained by partitioning the matrix BP. Let $S = \{1, 2, \ldots, K\}$ be the set of indices. Define the set $S_+ = \{i \in S : D_i \in \Re, D_i > 0\}$. The following

technical lemma shows that we can ignore the state space corresponding to negative and complex eigenvalues, while still preserving the termination behavior of the Program P3.

Lemma 1. *The Program P3, as defined above, is terminating iff the program*
  P4: while $(\sum_{j \in S_+} B_j y_j > 0)$ { $y_j := J_j y_j$; for $j \in S_+$ }
is terminating.

Proof. (Sketch) If the Program P4 does not terminate on input $y_j := c_j$, where $j \in S_+$, then the Program P3 does not terminate on input $y_j := c_j$ for $j \in S_+$ and $y_j := 0$ for $j \notin S_+$.

For the converse, assume that Program P3 does not terminate on input $y_j := c_j$, $j \in S$. Consider the m-th loop condition, $\sum_{j \in S} B_{jm} y_j > 0$, where B_{jm} denotes the m-th row of B_j. Assume that y_j has N_j components, $y_{j0}, y_{j1}, \cdots, y_{j\,N_j-1}$, where each y_{j_k} is either a 2×1 or a 1×1 matrix (depending on whether D_j is 2×2 or 1×1.) The value of y_j, at the i-th iteration, is given by

$$
y_j(i) =
\begin{pmatrix}
D_j^i & i D_j^{i-1} & \binom{i}{2} D_j^{i-2} & \cdots & \binom{i}{N_j-1} D_j^{i-(N_j-1)} \\
0 & D_j^i & i D_j^{i-1} & \cdots & \binom{i}{N_j-2} D_j^{i-(N_j-2)} \\
\vdots & \vdots & \ddots & \vdots & \vdots \\
0 & 0 & \cdots & D_j^i & i D_j^{i-1} \\
0 & 0 & \cdots & 0 & D_j^i
\end{pmatrix}
c_j
\tag{1}
$$

Define $f_m(i)$ to be the value of the expression of the m-th condition at i-th iteration, that is, $f_m(i) = \sum_{j \in S} B_{jm} y_j(i)$. Let J be an index such that $N_J = max\{N_j : |D_j| = max\{|D_i| : i \in S\}\}$. We claim, without further proof, that for large i, the term $\binom{i}{N_J-1} D_J^{i-N_{J'}+1} y_{J'\,N_{J'}-1}(0)$ will dominate the value of $f_m(i)$. If $J \notin S_+$, then the sign of this dominating term, and consequently the sign of $f_m(i)$, will fluctuate (between positive and negative) as i increases. By assumption, this does not happen. Hence, $J \in S_+$ and hence, for a large enough i, say $i \geq I_m$, we have $\sum_{j \in S_+} B_{jm} y_j(i) > 0$. For each condition m, we get an index I_m. Set I to be the maximum of all I_m's. For $i \geq I$, it is the case that $\sum_{j \in S_+} B_{jm} y_j(i) > 0$ for all m.

Define new initial conditions for Program P3 and Program P4 as follows: $y_i(0) := y_i(I)$ for all $i \in S_+$ and $y_i(0) := 0$ for all $i \notin S_+$. Program P3 does not terminate on this new initial conditions. Hence, Program P4 also does not terminate on it. This completes the proof. ∎

Example 4. We borrow the following example from [13],
  Q1: while $(x > 0 \wedge y > 0)$ { $x := -2x + 10y$; $y := y$ }.
The matrix A has two eigenvalues -2 and 1, and it is clearly diagonalizable. In fact, consider the transformation matrix P,

$$
A = \begin{pmatrix} -2 & 10 \\ 0 & 1 \end{pmatrix} \quad P = \begin{pmatrix} 1 & 10 \\ 0 & 3 \end{pmatrix} \quad P^{-1}AP = \begin{pmatrix} -2 & 0 \\ 0 & 1 \end{pmatrix} \quad BP = P
$$

Transforming Program Q1 by P, we get

    Q2: while $(x_1 + 10x_2 > 0 \ \wedge \ 3x_2 > 0)$ $\{$ $x_1 := -2x_1;\ x_2 := x_2$ $\}$.

Lemma 1 says that the termination of Program Q1 and Program Q2 can be decided by just considering the termination characteristics of:

    Q3: while $(10x_2 > 0 \ \wedge \ 3x_2 > 0)$ $\{$ $x_2 := x_2$ $\}$.

In fact, the point $x_1 = 0, x_2 = 1$ makes Program Q3 nonterminating, and correspondingly, the point $x = 10, y = 3$ makes Program Q1 nonterminating.

4   All Positive Eigenvalues

Lemma 1 reduces the termination of Program P2 of Section 2.1 to testing termination of Program P4, which is given as:

    P4: while $(B_1 y_1 + \cdots + B_r y_r > 0)$ $\{$ $y_1 := J_1 y_1; \ldots; y_r := J_r y_r$ $\}$

where each of the Jordan blocks J_i corresponds to a *positive real* eigenvalue λ_i.

The value of variables in y_j, after the i-th iteration, are given by Equation 1, where $D_j = \lambda_j$ is a positive real now. As before, assume that the k-th loop condition is written as $B_{1k} y_1 + B_{2k} y_2 + \cdots + B_{rk} y_r > 0$. We can express the requirement that the k-th loop condition be true after the i-th iteration as

$$B_{1k} y_1(i) + B_{2k} y_2(i) + \cdots + B_{rk} y_r(i) > 0.$$

Expand this using Equation 1 and let C_{klj} denote the result of collecting all coefficients of the term $\binom{i}{j-1}\lambda_l^{i-(j-1)}$. Now, the k-th loop condition after i-th iteration can be written as

$$\lambda_1^i C_{k11} y(0) + i\lambda_1^{i-1} C_{k12} y(0) + \cdots + \binom{i}{n_1 - 1} \lambda_1^{i-(n_1-1)} C_{k1n_1} y(0) +$$

$$\cdots +$$

$$\lambda_r^i C_{kr1} y(0) + i\lambda_r^{i-1} C_{kr2} y(0) + \cdots + \binom{i}{n_r - 1} \lambda_r^{i-(n_r-1)} C_{krn_r} y(0) > 0,$$

which we will denote by $Cond_k(y(i))$. If two eigenvalues λ_l and λ_m are the same, then we assume that the corresponding coefficients (of $\binom{i}{j}\lambda_l^{i-j}$ and $\binom{i}{j}\lambda_m^{i-j}$) have been merged in the above expression, so that without loss of generality, we can assume that each λ_l is distinct and such that $0 < \lambda_1 < \lambda_2 < \cdots < \lambda_r$.

Define the set $Ind = \{11, 12, \ldots, 1n_1, 21, 22, \ldots, 2n_2, \ldots, r1, r2, \ldots, rn_r\}$ and an ordering $\succ$ on this set so that elements on the right are greater-than elements on the left in the above set. The idea here is that nonzero terms in $Cond_k$ that have larger indices grow faster asymptotically (as i increases).

We decide the termination of Program P4 using the following three step nondeterministic algorithm:

(1) For each of the m loop conditions, we guess an element from the set Ind. Formally, we guess a mapping $index : \{1, 2, \ldots, m\} \mapsto Ind$. Intuitively if $y(0)$ is a witness to nontermination, then $index(k)$ is chosen so that $C_{k,index(k)} y(0) > 0$ (and this is the dominant summand) and $C_{k,ind} y(0) = 0$ for all $ind \succ index(k)$.

(2) Build a set of linear equality and inequality constraints as follows: from the k-th loop condition, generate the following constraints,

$$C_{k,ind}z = 0, \qquad \text{if } ind \succ index(k)$$
$$C_{k,ind}z > 0, \qquad \text{if } ind = index(k)$$
$$Cond_k(z(i)) > 0, \qquad \text{if } 0 \leq i \leq \Pi_2(index(k))$$

where Π_1 and Π_2 denote the projection onto the first and second components respectively. Note that the unknowns are just z (the initial values for y).

(3) Return "nonterminating" if the new set of linear inequalities and linear equations is satisfiable (in $\Re^n$), return "terminating" otherwise.

We state the correctness of the algorithm, without proof, in Lemma 2 and follow it up by a summary of the complete decision procedure in the proof of Theorem 4.

Lemma 2. *The nondeterministic procedure returns "nonterminating" iff the Program P4*

    P4: while $(B_1 y_1 + \cdots + B_r y_r > 0)$ $\{$ $y_1 := J_1 y_1; \ldots; y_r := J_r y_r$ $\}$

is nonterminating.

Theorem 4. *The termination of a homogeneous linear program of the form*

    P2: while $(Bx > 0)$ $\{$ $x := Ax$ $\}$

is decidable.

Proof. We decide termination of the Program P2 as follows: If A has no positive real eigenvalues, then return "terminating" (Corollary 2). If every real eigenvector v corresponding to a positive real eigenvalue of A satisfies $Bv < 0$, then return "terminating" (Theorem 2). If there is a real eigenvector v corresponding to a positive real eigenvalue of A such that $Bv > 0$, then return "nonterminating" (Corollary 2). If none of the above cases is true, then clearly A has positive real eigenvalues. Compute the Jordan blocks and the generalized eigenvectors *only corresponding to the positive real eigenvalues* of A. Generate a transformation P by extending the computed set of generalized eigenvectors with *any* set of vectors in space orthogonal to that of the generated eigenvectors. Transform Program P2 by P as in Proposition 1. It is an easy exercise[2] to note that we can apply Lemma 1 and reduce the termination problem to that for Program P4 of Lemma 1. Finally, we decide termination of Program P4 using the nondeterministic procedure of Section 4 (Lemma 2). ∎

Example 5. Consider the program

    Q4: while $(x > 0 \wedge y > 0)$ $\{$ x := x - y; y := y $\}$

This contains only two variables, and hence we can use Theorem 3, but for purposes of illustration, we apply Theorem 4 here. The matrix $A = [1, -1; 0, 1]$ has a positive real eigenvalue 1. The vector given by $x = 1, y = 0$ is an eigenvector corresponding to this eigenvalue. Hence, we cannot apply Theorem 2 or

---

[2] We cannot apply Lemma 1 directly since we did not compute the real Jordan form of the "full" matrix A, but only of a part of it. But we do not need to compute the full real Jordan form to get Program P4.

Corollary 2. The real Jordan form of A is $A' = [1, 1; 0, 1]$ and the corresponding transformation matrix is $P = [-1, 0; 0, 1]$. The new program is:

    Q5: while $(-x > 0 \land y > 0)$ { x := x + y; y := y }

The general solutions are given by

$$x(i) = 1^i x(0) + iy(0) = x(0) + iy(0)$$
$$y(i) = \qquad 1^i y(0) = y(0)$$

The condition $Cond_1$ corresponding to the loop condition $-x > 0$ is $-x(0) - iy(0) > 0$ and similarly $Cond_2$ is $y(0) > 0$. There is no choice for $index(2)$, but there is a choice for $index(1)$: it can be either 11 or 12.

In the first case, we generate the following constraints from the first loop condition: $\{-y = 0, -x > 0, -x - 0y > 0\}$. From the second loop condition, we only generate the constraint $y > 0$. Together, we detect an inconsistency.

In the second case, we generate the following constraints from the first loop condition: $\{-y > 0, -x - 0y > 0, -x - 1y > 0\}$. Again, from the second loop condition, we generate the constraint $y > 0$, which is inconsistent with the above constraints. Hence, we conclude that the Program Q4 is terminating.

5   Nonhomogeneous Programs

Now we consider linear programs of the following form:

    P5: while $(Bx > b)$ { $x := Ax + c$ }

We can homogenize this program and add an additional constraint on the homogenizing variable to get the following

    P6: while $(Bx - bz > 0 \land z > 0)$ { $x := Ax + cz; z := z$ }

where z is a new variable. The homogeneous program reduces to the original program if we substitute 1 for z.

Proposition 2. *The nonhomogeneous Program P5 does not terminate iff the homogeneous Program P6 does not terminate.*

Proof. If Program P5 does not terminate, say on input $x_i = d_i, i = 1, 2, \ldots, n$, then Program P6 does not terminate on input $z = 1, x_i = d_i, i = 1, 2, \ldots, n$.

For the converse, assume that Program P6 does not terminate on input $x_0 = d_0, x_i = d_i, i = 1, 2, \ldots, n$. If $d_0 > 0$, then we can scale this input to get a new state $x_0 = 1, x_i = d_i/d_0, i = 1, 2, \ldots, n$. The behavior of Program P6 will be the same on the scaled input, and hence Program P5 would not terminate on this input either. ∎

Thus we can reduce the decidability of termination of nonhomogeneous programs to that of homogeneous programs. Together with Theorem 4, we get the following result.

Theorem 5. *The termination of a nonhomogeneous linear program of the form*

    P5: while $(Bx > b)$ { $x := Ax + c$ }

is decidable.

Remarks on Computability and Complexity. The three step nondeterministic algorithm described in Section 4 is clearly in class NP. However, the nondeterminism can be eliminated by a careful enumeration of choices. The idea is that we always start with the guess $index(k) = rn_r$ for each loop condition k and if the resulting formula is unsatisfiable, then we readjust the guess and gradually set $index(k)$ to smaller elements in the set Ind. We do not formalize this detail in this paper because it is not central to the decidability result.

The reduction described in Section 3 requires computation of a real eigenvector. Computing with real numbers is not easy, but if the input matrices are over the rationals, then all the real numbers that arise in the computation are *algebraic*. Computing with algebraic numbers is theoretically possible, but it can be expensive (since the theory of real-closed fields has a double exponential lower bound). But this should not be a serious problem for two reasons. First, for most problems arising in practice, we expect the eigenvalues to be rational, and computation with rationals can be done very efficiently. Second, even if the eigenvalues are irrational, the dimension of the problem is unlikely to be so high that computing with algebraic numbers will become a bottleneck. However, these issues have to be experimented with and that is left as future work.

We believe that the Jordan form computation step in the decision procedure outlined in this paper can be eliminated in most cases in practice. This can be achieved by perturbing the system by a little (for example, replacing conditions $c > 0$ by $c > \epsilon$ for some small constant ϵ) and studying the termination property of the perturned system. We conjecture that Corollary 2 can be strengthened for the case when the homogenization variable violates the condition. This would allow us to avoid the Jordan decomposition step in many cases.

The decision procedure for termination of linear loop programs can be adapted to the case when the variables are interpreted over the integers and rationals. If there are "a lot" of witnesses to nontermination, then there will be a rational witness too, since the rationals are dense in reals. If not, then we can detect this case using a specialized wrapper. This leads us to conjecture the following.

Conjecture 1. The termination of Program P5, as defined in Theorem 5, when all variables are interpreted over the set of integers, is decidable.

6   The General Case

We consider the termination of a *set* of nondeterministic linear conditional assignments, written in a guarded command language [8] as,

$$P7: \quad \begin{array}{ll} [& B_1 x > b_1 \quad \longrightarrow \quad x := A_1 x + c_1 \\ [] & B_2 x > b_2 \quad \longrightarrow \quad x := A_2 x + c_2 \\ & \cdots \\ [] & B_k x > b_k \quad \longrightarrow \quad x := A_k x + c_k \,] \end{array}$$

which we will write in shorthand as

P7: $[]_{i=1}^{k}(B_i x > b_i \quad \longrightarrow \quad x := A_i x + c_i)$

Counter machines can be naturally encoded as Program P7. We introduce one variable x_i for each counter and one variable x for the finite control (program counter). Encodings of conditional branches, counter increments, and counter decrements are straightforward. The problem of deciding if a counter machine halts on all inputs is undecidable, see [3], where this problem is called the mortality problem. Therefore, the problem of deciding if a program of the above form halts on all *integer* inputs is also undecidable. Note however that for the restricted forms of assignments ($x := x \pm 1$) generated by the translation, termination over reals is equivalent to termination over integers. Thus, we conclude that the *termination problem for Program P7 is undecidable*.

Theorem 5 can be used to get an incomplete test for nontermination for Program P7 – If Program P7 is terminating, then for each i, the program `while` ($B_i x > b_i$) { $x := A_i x + c_i$ } is terminating. The converse is also true under additional *commutation* properties [2] amongst the k binary relations, say $R_1, \ldots, R_k$, induced by the k guarded commands. In particular, one immediate consequence of a result in [2] is the following.

Proposition 3. *Let Program P7 and relations $R_1, \ldots, R_k$ be as defined above. Let $R = R_1 \cup \cdots \cup R_k$. Assume that whenever $i < j$, it is the case that $R_j \circ R_i \subseteq R_i \circ R^*$. Then, the Program P7 terminates if and only if each R_i do.*

Note that the condition above is dependent on the order $R_1, \ldots, R_k$, which we are free to choose. Testing for the quasi-commutation property [2] $R_j \circ R_i \subseteq R_i \circ R^*$ is possible if we restrict the search to $R_j \circ R_i \subseteq R_i \circ R^l$, for some finite l. In the special case when the i-th guarded command cannot be enabled after execution of the j-th guarded command (that is, $R_j \circ R_i = \emptyset$), then the above inclusion is trivially true.

In the case when the quasi-commutation property cannot be established, the test for nontermination can be made "more complete" by including new guarded transitions obtained by composing two or more of the original guarded commands. It is easy to see that the composition results in a *linear* guarded command. These new guarded commands can be tested for nontermination using Theorem 5 again.

7   Future Work and Conclusion

We have presented decidability results for termination of simple loop programs. The loops are considered terminating if they terminate on all initial real values of the variables. The decision procedure is based on the observation that only the eigenvectors (and the generalized eigenspace) corresponding to positive real eigenvalues of the assignment matrix are relevant for termination. The generalization to multiple linear nondeterministic guarded commands makes the problem undecidable. Under certain restrictive commutation conditions, termination of multiple linear guarded commands can be reduced to termination of each individual simple linear loops.

We believe that results and tools from systems theory, such as Lyapunov functions and control Lyapunov functions, can yield powerful tools for analyzing software, especially for termination analysis and invariant generation. This avenue should be explored further in the future.

Acknowledgments

We wish to thank Andreas Podelski, Andrey Rybalchenko, and their colleagues at MPI for motivation and initial discussions and the reviewers for insightful comments and references.

References

1. D. K. Arrowsmith and C. M. Place. *An introduction to dynamical systems.* Cambridge, 1990.
2. L. Bachmair and N. Dershowitz. Commutation, transformation, and termination. In J. H. Siekmann, editor, *Proc. 8th Int. Conf. on Automated Deduction*, volume 230 of *LNCS*, pages 5–20, Berlin, 1986. Springer-Verlag.
3. V. D. Blondel, O. Bournez, P. Koiran, C. H. Papadimitriou, and J. N. Tsitsiklis. Deciding stability and mortality of piecewise affine dynamical system. *Theoretical Computer Science*, 255(1–2):687–696, 2001.
4. V. D. Blondel and J. N. Tsitsiklis. A survey of computational complexity results in systems and control. *Automatica*, 36:1249–1274, 2000.
5. M. Colon and H. Sipma. Synthesis of linear ranking functions. In T. Margaria and W. Yi, editors, *Tools and Algorithms for the Construction and Analysis of Systems, 7th Intl. Conf. TACAS 2001*, volume 2031 of *LNCS*, pages 67–81. Springer, 2001.
6. M. Colon and H. Sipma. Practical methods for proving program termination. In E. Brinksma and K. G. Larsen, editors, *Computer Aided Verification, 14th Intl. Conf. CAV 2002*, volume 2034 of *LNCS*, pages 442–454. Springer, 2002.
7. D. Dams, R. Gerth, and O. Grumberg. A heuristic for the automatic generation of ranking function. In *Workshop on Advances in Verification WAVe 2000*, pages 1–8, 2000.
8. E. W. Dijkstra. *A Discipline of Programming.* Prentice Hall PTR, 1997.
9. K. Hoffman and R. Kunze. *Linear Algebra.* Prentice-Hall, second edition, 1971.
10. R. Kannan and R. J. Lipton. Polynomial-time algorithm for the orbit problem. *J. of the ACM*, 33(4):808–821, 1986.
11. G. Lafferriere, G. J. Pappas, and S. Yovine. Symbolic reachability computations for families of linear vector fields. *J. Symbolic Computation*, 32(3):231–253, 2001.
12. J. Musset and M. Rusinowitch. Computing metatransitions for linear transition systems. In *12th Intl. FME symposium*, 2003.
13. A. Podelski and A. Rybalchenko. A complete method for synthesis of linear ranking functions. In *VMCAI 2004: Verification, Model Checking, and Abstract Interpretation*, LNCS. Springer-Verlag, 2004.
14. A. Podelski and A. Rybalchenko. Transition invariants. In *Logic in Computer Science, LICS*. IEEE Computer Society, 2004.
15. D. R. Smart. *Fixed Point Theorems.* Cambridge University Press, 1980.
16. E. Sontag. From linear to nonlinear: Some complexity comparisons. In *34th IEEE Conf. on Decision and Control, CDC*, 1995.
17. A. Tiwari. Approximate reachability for linear systems. In O. Maler and A. Pnueli, editors, *Hybrid Systems: Computation and Control HSCC*, volume 2623 of *LNCS*, pages 514–525. Springer, April 2003.

Symbolic Model Checking of Non-regular Properties

Martin Lange

Institut für Informatik
Ludwig-Maximilians-Universität
Munich, Germany

Abstract. This paper presents a symbolic model checking algorithm for Fixpoint Logic with Chop, an extension of the modal μ-calculus capable of defining non-regular properties. Some empirical data about running times of a naive implementation of this algorithm are given as well.

1 Introduction

Automatic hardware verification has proved to be one of the most fruitful areas in computer science of the last two decades. Since the introduction of Linear Time Temporal Logic, LTL, to computer science [Pnu77], it is known that the problem of automatically verifying correctness of a program can be reduced to the logical problem called model checking: given a structure $\mathfrak{A}$ and a formula φ, does $\mathfrak{A}$ have the property described by φ.

Since the structures that computer scientists are interested in are often sets of states with transitions between them that describe a program's behaviour in time, the logics used for verification are mostly modal and temporal ones. A lot has been argued about which is *the* right logic to use; whether it should be a linear or a branching time logic [Sti89, Var98]; whether it should rather be expressive or admit efficient model checking, etc.

Regardless of which of these logics one favours, in almost all cases it will turn out to be a fragment of or embeddable into the modal μ-calculus $\mathcal{L}_\mu$, [Koz83], which extends basic multi-modal logic with extremal greatest and least fixpoints. In fact, $\mathcal{L}_\mu$ incorporates the well-known temporal logics LTL, CTL [EH85], CTL* [EH86], as well as other logics which have gained more attention outside of computer science: PDL [FL79], Description Logics [WS92], etc.

$\mathcal{L}_\mu$ has a commonly accepted weakness: its formulas cannot in general be called readable. Even though $\mathcal{L}_\mu$ might therefore not be of great use to someone who wants to do program verification but is unfamiliar with modal logics, it is nevertheless important to have efficient decision procedures for such a logic. They can automatically yield efficient decision procedures for more readable logics as well. Model checking algorithms for (fragments of) the μ-calculus have been presented in [Cle90, SW91, BC96, SS98] for example. Even though most of these algorithms are local – they do not necessarily need to exploit the entire underlying structure – they are all based around explicit representations of its state space.

R. Alur and D.A. Peled (Eds.): CAV 2004, LNCS 3114, pp. 83–95, 2004.
© Springer-Verlag Berlin Heidelberg 2004

The state-of-the-art in automatic verification however is symbolic model checking [BCM$^+$92] which avoids explicit representations of states. The structures to be checked for correctness are encoded as boolean functions which can space-efficiently be represented using Reduced Ordered Binary Decision Diagrams [Bry86], or BDDs for short. What makes them so suitable and popular for program verification is the fact that all the operations needed to do model checking for the modal μ-calculus – hence all the operations needed to do model checking for a lot of other logics – can easily be carried out on BDDs.

Many people would argue that full $\mathcal{L}_\mu$ is more than anyone would ever want because of two reasons: most people's favourite temporal logic is embeddable into a rather small fragment of $\mathcal{L}_\mu$, and anything in $\mathcal{L}_\mu$ with an alternation depth greater than 2 is incomprehensible anyway. However, it is not only alternation depth that can limit expressive power.

Formulas of $\mathcal{L}_\mu$ can be translated into finite automata over infinite trees [SE84]. This shows that properties definable in the modal μ-calculus cannot be everything anyone would ever want. Every formula of $\mathcal{L}_\mu$ expresses a "regular" property. However, lots of properties of programs one might want to check are inherently non-regular: something behaves like a stack, action sequences get repeated, something happens at the same time in all execution paths, etc.

In [MO99], Müller-Olm has introduced Fixpoint Logic with Chop, FLC for short, which extends $\mathcal{L}_\mu$ with a sequential composition operator. This extension yields a far greater expressive power. FLC can define certain properties which are not even context-free. [Lan02a] gives an idea of what properties actually are definable in FLC.

Of course, there are two sides to a coin: extending $\mathcal{L}_\mu$ to FLC does not retain the finite model property nor decidability of its satisfiability problem. However, it maintains attractiveness for automatic verification purposes since its model checking problem on finite models is decidable, yet PSPACE-hard. Model Checking algorithms for FLC based on explicit state space representations were given in [LS02, Lan02b].

Here we show that despite the PSPACE-hardness, model checking for FLC is feasible – even on rather large transition systems – when symbolic representations are used. Section 2 defines syntax and semantics of FLC, and recalls the definition of BDDs and how to symbolically encode labelled transition systems. Section 3 presents a symbolic model checking algorithm for FLC and proves its correctness. The algorithm is based on the insight that not only all the operations needed for $\mathcal{L}_\mu$ model checking can easily be carried out on BDDs but even those needed for FLC model checking. Finally, Section 4 supports the claim that FLC model checking is feasible. It describes a quick and naive symbolic implementation of a family of transition systems and the model checking algorithm. Furthermore, it contains some empirical data about running times of the algorithm on some FLC formulas. One of those is not equivalent to any $\mathcal{L}_\mu$-formula.

We omit a complexity analysis of the algorithm mainly because it is known that BDD-based model checking can defeat intractability results. Moreover, it is the experimental results which yield a better answer to the questions of feasibility.

2 Preliminaries

2.1 Fixpoint Logic with Chop

Let $\mathcal{P} = \{\mathtt{tt}, \mathtt{ff}, q, \bar{q}, \ldots\}$ be a set of propositional constants that is closed under complementation, $\mathcal{V} = \{Z, Y, \ldots\}$ a set of propositional variables, and $\mathcal{A} = \{a, b, \ldots\}$ a set of action names. A *labelled transition system* is a graph $\mathcal{T} = (\mathcal{S}, \{\xrightarrow{a} \mid a \in \mathcal{A}\}, L)$ where $\mathcal{S}$ is a set of states, $\xrightarrow{a}$ for each $a \in \mathcal{A}$ is a binary relation on states and $L : \mathcal{S} \to 2^{\mathcal{P}}$ labels the states such that, for all $s \in \mathcal{S} : q \in L(s)$ iff $\bar{q} \notin L(s)$, $\mathtt{tt} \in L(s)$, and $\mathtt{ff} \notin L(s)$. We will use infix notation $s \xrightarrow{a} t$ for transition relations.

Formulas of FLC are given by the following grammar.

$$\varphi \quad ::= \quad q \mid Z \mid \tau \mid \langle a \rangle \mid [a] \mid \varphi \vee \varphi \mid \varphi \wedge \varphi \mid \mu Z.\varphi \mid \nu Z.\varphi \mid \varphi; \varphi$$

where $q \in \mathcal{P}$, $Z \in \mathcal{V}$, and $a \in \mathcal{A}$ [1]. We will write σ for μ or ν. To save brackets we introduce the convention that ; binds stronger than $\wedge$ which binds stronger than $\vee$. To keep a strong resemblance to the syntax of the modal μ-calculus we will sometimes write $\langle a \rangle \varphi$ or $[a]\varphi$ instead of $\langle a \rangle; \varphi$, resp. $[a]; \varphi$.

Formulas are assumed to be well-named in the sense that each binder variable is distinct. Our main interest is with formulas that do not have free variables, in which case there is a function $fp : \mathcal{V} \to \text{FLC}$ that maps each variable to its defining fixpoint formula (that may contain free variables).

The set $Sub(\varphi)$ of subformulas of φ is defined as usual, with $Sub(\sigma Z.\psi) = \{\sigma Z.\psi\} \cup Sub(\psi)$.

An *environment* $\rho : \mathcal{V} \to (2^{\mathcal{S}} \to 2^{\mathcal{S}})$ maps variables to monotone functions of sets to sets. $\rho[Z \mapsto f]$ is the function that maps Z to f and agrees with ρ on all other arguments. The semantics $[\![\cdot]\!]^{\mathcal{T}} : 2^{\mathcal{S}} \to 2^{\mathcal{S}}$ of an FLC formula, relative to $\mathcal{T}$ and ρ, is a monotone function on subsets of states with respect to the inclusion ordering on $2^{\mathcal{S}}$. These functions together with the partial order given by

$$f \sqsubseteq g \text{ iff } \forall X \subseteq \mathcal{S} : f(X) \subseteq g(X)$$

form a complete lattice with joins $\sqcup$ and meets $\sqcap$. By the Tarski-Knaster Theorem [Tar55] the least and greatest fixpoints of functionals $F : (2^{\mathcal{S}} \to 2^{\mathcal{S}}) \to (2^{\mathcal{S}} \to 2^{\mathcal{S}})$ exist. They are used to interpret fixpoint formulas of FLC.

To simplify the notation we assume a transition system $\mathcal{T}$ to be fixed, and write $[\![\cdot]\!]_\rho$ instead of $[\![\cdot]\!]_\rho^{\mathcal{T}}$ for the semantics given in Figure 1.

A state s satisfies a formula φ under ρ, written $s \models_\rho \varphi$, iff $s \in [\![\varphi]\!](\mathcal{S})$. If φ is a closed formula then ρ can be omitted and we write $[\![\varphi]\!](\mathcal{S})$ as well as $s \models \varphi$.

Two formulas φ and ψ are *equivalent*, written $\varphi \equiv \psi$, iff their semantics are the same, i.e. for every $\mathcal{T}$ and every ρ: $[\![\varphi]\!]_\rho^{\mathcal{T}} = [\![\psi]\!]_\rho^{\mathcal{T}}$.

We introduce *approximants* of fixpoint formulas. Let $fp(Z) = \mu Z.\varphi$ for some φ and let $\alpha, \lambda \in \mathbb{O}\text{rd}$, the ordinals, where λ is a limit ordinal. Then

$$Z^0 := \mathtt{ff} \ , \quad Z^{\alpha+1} = \varphi[Z^\alpha/Z] \ , \quad Z^\lambda = \bigvee_{\alpha < \lambda} Z^\alpha$$

---

[1] In [MO99], τ is called $\mathtt{term}$.

$$\begin{aligned}
[\![q]\!]_\rho &:= \lambda X.\{s \in \mathcal{S} \mid q \in L(s)\} \\
[\![Z]\!]_\rho &:= \rho(Z) \\
[\![\tau]\!]_\rho &:= \lambda X.X \\
[\![\varphi \vee \psi]\!]_\rho &:= [\![\varphi]\!]_\rho \sqcup [\![\psi]\!]_\rho \\
[\![\varphi \wedge \psi]\!]_\rho &:= [\![\varphi]\!]_\rho \sqcap [\![\psi]\!]_\rho \\
[\![\langle a \rangle]\!]_\rho &:= \lambda X.\{s \in \mathcal{S} \mid \exists t \in X, \text{ s.t. } s \xrightarrow{a} t\} \\
[\![[a]]\!]_\rho &:= \lambda X.\{s \in \mathcal{S} \mid \forall t \in \mathcal{S}, s \xrightarrow{a} t \Rightarrow t \in X\} \\
[\![\mu Z.\varphi]\!]_\rho &:= \bigsqcap\{f : 2^{\mathcal{S}} \to 2^{\mathcal{S}} \mid f \text{ monotone}, [\![\varphi]\!]_{\rho[Z \mapsto f]} \sqsubseteq f\} \\
[\![\nu Z.\varphi]\!]_\rho &:= \bigsqcup\{f : 2^{\mathcal{S}} \to 2^{\mathcal{S}} \mid f \text{ monotone}, f \sqsubseteq [\![\varphi]\!]_{\rho[Z \mapsto f]}\} \\
[\![\varphi; \psi]\!]_\rho &:= [\![\varphi]\!]_\rho \circ [\![\psi]\!]_\rho
\end{aligned}$$

Fig. 1. The semantics of FLC formulas.

If $fp(Z) = \nu Z.\varphi$ then

$$Z^0 := \mathbf{tt} \ , \quad Z^{\alpha+1} = \varphi[Z^\alpha/Z] \ , \quad Z^\lambda = \bigwedge_{\alpha < \lambda} Z^\alpha$$

Note that $\mu Z.\varphi \equiv \bigvee_{\alpha \in \mathbb{O}rd} Z^\alpha$ and $\nu Z.\varphi \equiv \bigwedge_{\alpha \in \mathbb{O}rd} Z^\alpha$. If only finite transition systems are considered $\mathbb{O}rd$ can be replaced by $\mathbb{N}$.

We will give a few examples of FLC formulas to make the reader familiar with the logic and to show how one can express certain non-regular properties in it. Remember that FLC is an extension of the modal μ-calculus whose formulas are commonly perceived as not being the most understandable already. For a better understanding of what property actually is expressed by a given FLC formula consider [Lan02b], which defines model checking games for FLC, or [Lan02a], which maps FLC on linear models into the Chomsky-hierarchy.

Example 1. The standard example of a non-regular and even non-context-free property is the following, taken from [MO99]. It describes the language $\{a^n b^n c^n \mid n \in \mathbb{N}\}$ on finite, linear models.

$$\begin{aligned}
\varphi &:= \psi(a, b); \chi(c) \wedge \chi(a); \psi(b, c) \\
\psi(x, y) &:= \mu X.\tau \vee \langle x \rangle; X; \langle y \rangle \\
\chi(x) &:= \mu X.\tau \vee \langle x \rangle; X
\end{aligned}$$

Note how the modal constructs $\langle \cdot \rangle$ and $[\cdot]$ can be used *behind* variables to produce genuine context-free effects.

The best way to understand FLC formulas is to think of them as alternating, context-free grammars [IJW92]. Variables are non-terminals, formulas of the form $\langle a \rangle$ or $[a]$ are terminals, the boolean operators translate into non-deterministic, resp. universal choices in these grammars, and τ plays the role of the empty word. Finally, least fixpoint variables can only be replaced finitely often (recursion) while greatest fixpoint variables can be replaced infinitely often (co-recursion).

Then formula $\psi(x, y)$ for example generates words of the form $\langle x \rangle^n; \langle y \rangle^n$ for any $n \in \mathbb{N}$.

Example 2. [LS02] Let $\mathcal{A} = \{a, b\}$ and

$$\varphi := \nu Y.[b]\text{ff} \wedge [a](\nu Z.[b] \wedge [a](Z; Z)); (([a]\text{ff} \wedge [b]\text{ff}) \vee Y)$$

Formula φ expresses "the number of bs never exceeds the number of as" which is non-regular and, therefore, is not expressible in $\mathcal{L}_\mu$. This is an interesting property of protocols when a and b are the actions *send* and *receive*.

The subformula $\psi = \nu Z.[b] \wedge [a](Z; Z)$ expresses "there can be at most one b more than there are as". This can be understood best by unfolding the fixpoint formula and thus obtaining sequences of modalities and variables. It is easy to see that replacing a Z with a $[b]$ reduces the number of Zs whereas replacing it with the other conjunct adds a new Z to the sequence.

Then, $[b]\text{ff} \wedge [a]\psi$ postulates that at the beginning no b is possible and for every sequence of n actions a there can be at most n actions b. Finally, the Y in φ allows such sequences to be composed or finished in a deadlock state.

2.2   Binary Decision Diagrams

When we speak about *Binary Decision Diagrams* or BDDs we mean in fact *Reduced Ordered Binary Decision Diagrams*. These are compact representations of boolean functions. For a proper introduction to BDDs see for example [Bry86] or [And97]. In [BCM+92] it is shown how to use BDDs for verification purposes in general and for a variant of the modal μ-calculus due to Park and the temporal logic CTL in particular. Here we will briefly define BDDs and mention some of the standard algorithms for manipulating them.

Definition 1. Let $\mathbb{B} = \{\text{tt}, \text{ff}\}$ be the well-known boolean algebra of boolean values.

A BDD over a totally ordered set $\{x_1, \ldots, x_n\}$ of boolean variables is a directed acyclic graph (DAG) t with the following properties.

- There are two distinguished nodes called tt and ff which are not labelled and have out-degree zero.
- Every other node is labelled with a variable x_i and has out-degree two. The successors are ordered as well, i.e. for a node u they are called $low(u)$ and $high(u)$.
- The DAG has a root and on every path from the root to one of the nodes tt or ff the node labels respect the given variable ordering.
- No two nodes have the same label and the same *high* and *low* successors.
- For no node *high* and *low* successor are identical.

Let BDD_n denote the set of all BDDs over n variables, presumably called $x_1, \ldots, x_n$.

Every BDD t over n variables represents a boolean function $f_t : \mathbb{B}^n \to \mathbb{B}$. The value b of f_t under an assignment of the variables $x_1, \ldots, x_n$ is given by the path in t

- that starts at its root, and
- at every node labelled with x_i branches to the *high*-successor if the variable is assigned the value tt and to the *low*-successor otherwise, and
- ends in the node b.

We will also write $t(b_1, \ldots, b_n)$ for this value if b_i is the value assigned to x_i for $i = 1, \ldots, n$. Note that $t(b_1, \ldots, b_n) = f_t(b_1, \ldots, b_n)$ in this case.

The algorithm of the next section will make use of variable substitutions in a BDD. With $t[y_1/x_1, \ldots, y_n/x_n]$ we denote the BDD that arises from t by simultaneously replacing all node labels x_i with y_i for $i = 1, \ldots, n$.

The converse of the previously sketched result is also true. Every boolean function can be represented by a BDD. In fact, the following stronger result holds.

Theorem 1. [Bry86] *For every function $f : \mathbb{B}^n \to \mathbb{B}$ and a given variable ordering there is a unique BDD t_f representing f.*

[Bry86] also shows how to manipulate BDDs. For example, there are (efficiently) computable functions

- **makeBDD**: $(\mathbb{B}^* \to \mathbb{B}) \to BDD_n$. It takes as an argument a boolean function f and returns the BDD representing it. We will only use it for $f = $ tt or $f = $ ff. In these cases the roots of the returned BDDs are the respective distinguished nodes tt or ff.
- **applyBDD**: $(\mathbb{B} \to \mathbb{B} \to \mathbb{B}) \to BDD_n \to BDD_n \to BDD_n$. It takes as arguments a binary boolean operator $\oplus$ and two BDDs over n variables and returns another BDD over these n variables. Assuming the two input arguments represent the boolean functions f and g, **applyBDD** yields the unique BDD representing the boolean function $f \oplus g$.
- **existsBDD**: $\mathcal{V}^* \to BDD_n \to BDD_n$. It takes as arguments a list of variables $\{x_{i_1}, \ldots, x_{i_m}\} \subseteq \{x_1, \ldots, x_n\}$, and a BDD t representing a function f_t. It returns the BDD representing the function $f' = \exists x_{i_1} \ldots \exists x_{i_m}.f_t$, which has as free variables at most those not in $\{x_{i_1}, \ldots, x_{i_m}\}$. Note that $\exists x.f \equiv f[0/x] \lor f[1/x]$.
- **forallBDD**: $\mathcal{V}^* \to BDD_n \to BDD_n$. Similar to the previous one. However, this one returns a BDD representing the function $f' = \forall x_{i_1} \ldots \forall x_{i_m}.f_t$ where $\forall x.f \equiv f[0/x] \land f[1/x]$.

2.3 Encoding a Labelled Transition System

For the remainder of the paper we assume a $\mathcal{T} = (\mathcal{S}, \{\xrightarrow{a} \mid a \in \mathcal{A}\}, L)$ to be fixed. This is not a restriction but simplifies notation since the number of variables used in the algorithm presented in the next section depends on the size of the transition system at hand.

Also, w.l.o.g. we assume that $|\mathcal{S}| = 2^n$ for some $n \in \mathbb{N}$ [2]. Then every state has a unique number between 0 and $2^n - 1$ and one can identify a state s with its binary representation $s_1 \ldots s_n$, $s_i \in \mathbb{B}$.

---

[2] Note that it is always possible to add further states to an LTS that are not reachable from any state in it already.

```
procedure MC(φ : FLC,  t : BDD)

   case φ of
      q           →   return t_q
      τ           →   return t
      X           →   error "found free variable"
      ⟨a⟩         →   t' = applyBDD(and, t_a, t[y₁/x₁, ..., y_n/x_n])
                       return existsBDD(y₁ ... y_n, t')
      [a]         →   t' = applyBDD(implies, t_a, t[y₁/x₁, ..., y_n/x_n])
                       return forallBDD(y₁ ... y_n, t')
      ψ₀ ∨ ψ₁    →   return applyBDD(or, MC(ψ₀, t), MC(ψ₁, t))
      ψ₀ ∧ ψ₁    →   return applyBDD(and, MC(ψ₀, t), MC(ψ₁, t))
      ψ₀; ψ₁     →   return MC(ψ₀, MC(ψ₁, t))
      σX.ψ        →   if σ = μ then X⁰ = ff else X⁰ = tt
                       t' = makeBDD(X⁰)
                       X¹ = ψ[X⁰/X]
                       t'' = MC(X¹, t)
                       i = 1
                       while t' ≠ t''
                          t' = t''
                          i = i + 1
                          Xⁱ = ψ[X^{i-1}/X]
                          t'' = MC(Xⁱ, t)
                       return t'
```

Fig. 2. A BDD-based model checking algorithm for FLC.

$\mathcal{T}$ can be represented by $|\mathcal{A}| + |\mathcal{P}|$ many BDDs from BDD_{2n}. We fix the variable names and the ordering as $x_1 < y_1 < \ldots < x_n < y_n$.

- For every proposition $q \in \mathcal{P}$ we have a BDD t_q over the variables $x_1, \ldots, x_n$ s.t. $t_q(x_1, \ldots, x_n) = \text{tt}$ iff $q \in L(x_1 \ldots x_n)$.
- For every action $a \in \mathcal{A}$ we have a BDD t_a over the variables $x_1, \ldots, x_n$, $y_1, \ldots, y_n$ s.t. $t_a(x_1, y_1, \ldots, x_n, y_n) = \text{tt}$ iff $x_1 \ldots x_n \xrightarrow{a} y_1 \ldots y_n$.

3   The Model Checking Algorithm

Figure 2 contains the pseudocode of the symbolic model checking algorithm for FLC. The procedure $\mathbf{MC}(\varphi, t)$ takes as arguments an FLC formula φ and a BDD t and returns a BDD t' representing all the states that satisfy φ relative to the states represented by t.

Theorem 2. *The algorithm* $\mathbf{MC}(\varphi, t)$ *terminates for all* $\varphi \in FLC$ *and all* $t \in BDD_n$.

Proof. By induction on the structure of φ. The claim is easily seen to be correct for $\varphi = q$, $\varphi = \tau$, $\varphi = X$ for some $X \in \mathcal{V}$, $\varphi = \langle a \rangle$ or $\varphi = [a]$ for some $a \in \mathcal{A}$. Using the induction hypothesis on ψ_0 and ψ_1 it is also not hard to see that the claim holds for $\varphi = \psi_0 \vee \psi_1$, $\varphi = \psi_0 \wedge \psi_1$ and $\varphi = \psi_0; \psi_1$ – always assuming that the involved function calls terminate.

Suppose now that $\varphi = \sigma X.\psi$. By assumption, any call of $\mathbf{MC}(\psi, t)$ for any t terminates. Thus, it suffices to show that that while–loops terminate. Note that its i-th iteration computes the i-th approximant X^i to $\sigma X.\psi$. Thus, the function that maps t' to t'' in each iteration is monotone. According to [Tar55] it possesses a fixpoint. This fixpoint is eventually found by the while–loop and causes it to terminate. Note that the underlying domain is finite.   □

For a $t \in BDD_n$ let $[\![t]\!] := \{b_1 \ldots b_n \mid t(b_1, \ldots, b_n) = \mathtt{tt}\}$ be the set of all variable assignments that evaluate to $\mathtt{tt}$ in t. Thus, if t encodes a set of states of a transition system then $[\![t]\!]$ is exactly this set.

Theorem 3. *For all closed $\varphi \in FLC$ and all $t \in BDD_n$ we have:* $[\![\mathbf{MC}(\varphi, t)]\!] = [\![\varphi]\!]([\![t]\!])$.

Proof. By induction on the structure of φ. Note that $\varphi \in \mathcal{V}$ is impossible.

Case $\varphi = q$: $[\![\mathbf{MC}(q, t)]\!] = [\![t_q]\!] = \{s \in \mathcal{S} \mid q \in Ls\} = [\![q]\!](T)$ for any $T \subseteq \mathcal{S}$, in particular $T = [\![t]\!]$.

Case $\varphi = \tau$: $[\![\mathbf{MC}(\tau, t)]\!] = [\![t]\!] = [\![\tau]\!]([\![t]\!])$.

Case $\varphi = \langle a \rangle$: Let t be given and $t' = \mathrm{applyBDD}(and, t_a, t[y_1/x_1, \ldots, y_n/x_n])$. Then $[\![t']\!] = \{(s, u) \in \mathcal{S} \mid s \xrightarrow{a} u$ and $u \in [\![t]\!]\}$. Therefore $[\![\mathbf{MC}(\langle a \rangle, t)]\!] = [\![\mathrm{existsBDD}(y_1, \ldots, y_n, t')]\!] = \{s \in \mathcal{S} \mid \exists u \in \mathcal{S}$ s.t. $(s, u) \in [\![t']\!]\} = \{s \in \mathcal{S} \mid \exists u \in \mathcal{S}$ s.t. $s \xrightarrow{a} u$ and $u \in [\![t]\!]\} = [\![\langle a \rangle]\!]([\![t]\!])$.

Case $\varphi = [a]$: Similar to the previous case with $\forall$ instead of $\exists$ and *implies* instead of *and*.

Case $\varphi = \psi_0 \vee \psi_1$: Let $t' = \mathbf{MC}(\psi_0, t)$ and $t'' = \mathbf{MC}(\psi_1, t)$. By assumption we have $[\![t']\!] = [\![\psi_0]\!]([\![t]\!])$ and $[\![t']\!] = [\![\psi_1]\!]([\![t]\!])$. Now, $[\![\mathbf{MC}(\psi_0 \vee \psi_1, t)]\!] = [\![\mathrm{applyBDD}(or, t', t'')]\!] = \{s \in \mathcal{S} \mid s \in [\![t']\!]$ or $s \in [\![t'']\!]\} = [\![t']\!] \cup [\![t'']\!] = [\![\psi_0]\!]([\![t]\!]) \cup [\![\psi_1]\!]([\![t]\!]) = [\![\varphi]\!]([\![t]\!])$.

Case $\varphi = \psi_0 \wedge \psi_1$: Similar to the previous case with $\cap$ instead of $\cup$.

Case $\varphi = \psi_0; \psi_1$: Let $t' = \mathbf{MC}(\psi_1, t)$. By assumption we have $[\![t']\!] = [\![\psi_1]\!]([\![t]\!])$. Furthermore, let $t'' = \mathbf{MC}(\psi_0, t')$. Using the hypothesis again we have $[\![t'']\!] = [\![\psi_0]\!]([\![t']\!]) = [\![\psi_0]\!]([\![\psi_1]\!]([\![t]\!])) = [\![\psi_0; \psi_1]\!]([\![t]\!])$.

Case $\varphi = \mu X.\psi$: Note that by assumption the call of $\mathbf{MC}(\varphi, t)$ computes a sequence of approximants X^i to φ. According to Theorem 2, only finitely many approximants are evaluated. For each i we have $[\![\mathbf{MC}(X^i, t)]\!] = [\![X^i]\!]([\![t]\!])$. According to [Tar55], the sequence of the latter converges to $[\![\mu X.\psi]\!]([\![t]\!])$ which is returned by the algorithm.

Case $\varphi = \nu X.\psi$: The same as the previous case.   □

The last two cases of this proof show why model checking for FLC still is feasible despite being PSPACE-hard. In order to computer the states in $[\![\mu X.\varphi]\!](T)$ it is not necessary to compute the least fixpoint of the functional $F(f) = [\![\varphi]\!]_{[X\mapsto f]}$ where $f : 2^S \to 2^S$. Using fixpoint approximation this could take a number of steps double exponential in $|S|$.

In fact, it suffices to compute the value of the least fixpoint of F on the argument T. If $T = \emptyset$ or $T = S$ then the number of steps needed in the worst case is bounded by $|S|$. In all other cases the number is bounded by the width of the subset-lattice of S which is exponential in $|S|$. However, in order to fully exploit an exponential number of approximations, φ has to describe an exponentially long "walk" through this subset-lattice. This is not easily achieved since it necessarily means that $[\![\varphi]\!]$ maps exponentially many sets of states to something which is neither a subset nor a superset of it.

An example of such a formula is given in [Lan02b]. One can argue that the transition system used there is rather unnatural and constructed since the described phenomenon only occurs because it is build of components whose sizes are prime numbers.

4   A Simple Case Study

In this section we describe a small case study which supports the claim that BDD-based FLC model checking is feasible. The implementation was carried out using Java™ and the JavaBDD package [Wha03] which is a front-end to the BDD library BuDDy [LN03] written in C. All the tests were run on a machine with 3 GB of main memory and two Intel® Xeon™ processors running at 2.40 GHz[3]. The results presented in this section do not have a broad meaning. They simply show that non-regular properties can in principle be verified on finite models up to a decent size.

Definition 2. *Let* $\mathcal{P} = \{\mathtt{tt}, \mathtt{ff}\}$ *and* $\mathcal{A} = \{push, pop, reset, idle\}$. *An N-bounded stack is a* $T = (S, \{\xrightarrow{a} \mid a \in \mathcal{A}\}, L)$ *with* $S = \{0, \ldots, 2^N - 1\}$ *and for all* $s, t \in S$:

$$s \xrightarrow{push} t \quad \textit{iff} \quad t = s + 1$$
$$s \xrightarrow{pop} t \quad \textit{iff} \quad t = s - 1$$
$$s \xrightarrow{reset} t \quad \textit{iff} \quad t = 0$$
$$s \xrightarrow{idle} t \quad \textit{iff} \quad s = t$$

In other words, an N-bounded stack models a counter that can be increased and decreased between the values 0 and $2^N - 1$, reset to 0 and do nothing. According

---

[3] To the best of our knowledge, the fact that the computer has two processors instead is neither a prerequisite nor does it have any effect on the data presented here.

to the previous sections, an N-bounded stack can be represented using 4 BDDs over $2 \cdot N$ variables. We use the variable ordering suggested in Section 2.3.

Figure 3 depicts the BDDs' sizes as a function of N. Note that in explicit state representation, the size of a bounded stack is exponential in N.

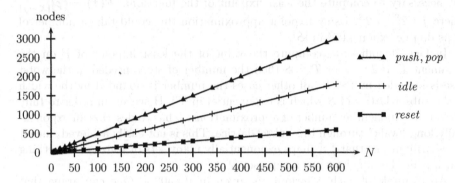

Fig. 3. The BDDs' sizes.

Example 3. Let

$$\psi := \nu X.[pop]; \mathrm{ff} \ \wedge \ [reset]; X \ \wedge \ [idle]; X \ \wedge$$
$$[push]; (\nu Z.[pop] \ \wedge \ [reset]; Z \ \wedge \ [idle]; Z \ \wedge \ [push]; Z; Z); X$$

This is essentially the same formula as the one of Example 2 – tailored to N-bounded stacks. Thus, ψ says that on every path consisting of any of the actions *push, pop, reset* and *idle*, the number of *pop*'s so far is always bounded by the number of *push*'s so far. Note that this formula is not equivalent to any μ-calculus formula.

It is only state 0 of any N-bounded stack which has this property. The times needed to verify this can be found in Figure 4.

5 Discussion

We have shown that – using an appropriate extension of the modal μ-calculus – BDDs can be used to verify properties which are not definable in the modal μ-calculus. It is known that the model checking problem for FLC is PSPACE-hard, even for fixed formulas. But when using symbolic representations and calculations on those, it is not foreseeable whether a problem that is intractable from a complexity-theoretic point of view does not have instances which can be solved in reasonable time. Our case study shows that this is indeed true for FLC's model checking problem – even for instances (see formula ψ of Example 3) that describe interesting properties.

Note that the aim of this case study was just to show that in principle BDD's can be used to do model checking for FLC. The implementation consists of approximately 230 lines of normal Java code. Another 870 lines are used to make

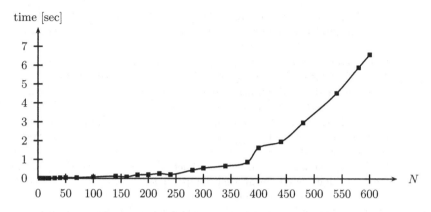

Fig. 4. The model checking running times.

the program understand full FLC which would not have been necessary to acquire the data of the previous section. No optimisation whatsoever has been carried out apart from trying two different variable orderings. The implementation relies on a generic BDD library and uses the naive model checking algorithm of Figure 2. Nevertheless, it was possible to model check a universal formula in less than 7 seconds on a transition system which in explicit representation would require to visit far more states than there are atoms in the universe – keeping PSPACE-hardness in mind.

Note that the algorithm we used is based on the principle of *fixpoint elimination*: formulas are unfolded whenever necessary. In order to keep notation as simple as possible we have not used environments, i.e. an algorithm based on *fixpoint calculation* which can easily be implemented in a functional language. Maybe such an algorithm would constitute an improvisation over the one used here since fixpoint calculations would not require quadratic time anymore.

Acknowledgments

We would like to thank the anonymous referee who suggested the variable ordering used in this version. It hugely improved the performance compared to the previous version.

References

[And97]   H. R. Andersen. An introduction to binary decision diagrams, 1997. URL: http://www.itu.dk/people/hra/bdd97-abstract.html.

[BC96]   G. Bhat and R. Cleaveland. Efficient local model-checking for fragments of the modal μ-calculus. In T. Margaria and B. Steffen, editors, *Proc. 2nd Int. Workshop on Tools and Algorithms for Construction and Analysis of Systems, TACAS'96*, volume 1055 of *LNCS*, pages 107–126. Springer, March 1996.

[BCM+92]   J. R. Burch, E. M. Clarke, K. L. McMillan, D. L. Dill, and L. J. Hwang. Symbolic model checking: 10^{20} states and beyond. *Information and Computation*, 98(2):142–170, June 1992.

[Bry86]   R. E. Bryant. Graph-based algorithms for boolean function manipulation. *IEEE Transactions on Computers*, 35(8):677–691, August 1986.

[Cle90]   R. Cleaveland. Tableau-based model checking in the propositional μ-calculus. *Acta Informatica*, 27(8):725–748, 1990.

[EH85]   E. A. Emerson and J. Y. Halpern. Decision procedures and expressiveness in the temporal logic of branching time. *Journal of Computer and System Sciences*, 30:1–24, 1985.

[EH86]   E. A. Emerson and J. Y. Halpern. "Sometimes" and "not never" revisited: On branching versus linear time temporal logic. *Journal of the ACM*, 33(1):151–178, January 1986.

[FL79]   M. J. Fischer and R. E. Ladner. Propositional dynamic logic of regular programs. *Journal of Computer and System Sciences*, 18(2):194–211, April 1979.

[IJW92]   O. H. Ibarra, T. Jiang, and H. Wang. A characterization of exponential-time languages by alternating context-free grammars. *TCS*, 99(2):301–315, June 1992.

[Koz83]   D. Kozen. Results on the propositional μ-calculus. *TCS*, 27:333–354, December 1983.

[Lan02a]   M. Lange. Alternating context-free languages and linear time μ-calculus with sequential composition. In P. Panangaden and U. Nestmann, editors, *Proc. 9th Workshop on Expressiveness in Concurrency, EXPRESS'02*, volume 68.2 of *ENTCS*, pages 71–87, Brno, Czech Republic, August 2002. Elsevier.

[Lan02b]   M. Lange. Local model checking games for fixed point logic with chop. In L. Brim, P. Jančar, M. Křetínský, and A. Kučera, editors, *Proc. 13th Conf. on Concurrency Theory, CONCUR'02*, volume 2421 of *LNCS*, pages 240–254, Brno, Czech Republic, August 2002. Springer.

[LN03]   J. Lind-Nielsen. BuDDy - Binary Decision Diagrams Library Package v2.2, 2003. http://www.itu.dk/research/buddy/.

[LS02]   M. Lange and C. Stirling. Model checking fixed point logic with chop. In M. Nielsen and U. H. Engberg, editors, *Proc. 5th Conf. on Foundations of Software Science and Computation Structures, FOSSACS'02*, volume 2303 of *LNCS*, pages 250–263, Grenoble, France, April 2002. Springer.

[MO99]   M. Müller-Olm. A modal fixpoint logic with chop. In C. Meinel and S. Tison, editors, *Proc. 16th Symp. on Theoretical Aspects of Computer Science, STACS'99*, volume 1563 of *LNCS*, pages 510–520, Trier, Germany, 1999. Springer.

[Pnu77]   A. Pnueli. The temporal logic of programs. In *Proc. 18th Symp. on Foundations of Computer Science, FOCS'77*, pages 46–57, Providence, RI, USA, October 1977. IEEE.

[SE84]   R. S. Streett and E. A. Emerson. The propositional μ-calculus is elementary. In J. Paredaens, editor, *Proc. 11th Coll. on Automata, Languages, and Programming, ICALP'84*, volume 172 of *LNCS*, pages 465–472. Springer, Berlin, 1984.

[SS98]   P. Stevens and C. Stirling. Practical model checking using games. *LNCS*, 1384:85–101, 1998.

[Sti89]   C. Stirling. Comparing linear and branching time temporal logics. In
            B. Banieqbal, H. Barringer, and A. Pnueli, editors, *Proc. Conf. on Temporal Logic in Specification*, volume 398 of *LNCS*, pages 1–20, Berlin, April
            1989. Springer.

[SW91]   C. Stirling and D. Walker. Local model checking in the modal μ–calculus.
            TCS, 89(1):161–177, 1991.

[Tar55]   A. Tarski. A lattice-theoretical fixpoint theorem and its application. *Pacific J.Math.*, 5:285–309, 1955.

[Var98]   Vardi. Linear vs. branching time: A complexity-theoretic perspective. In
            LICS: IEEE Symposium on Logic in Computer Science, 1998.

[Wha03]   J. Whaley. JavaBDD - Java Binary Decision Diagram library, 2003.
            http://javabdd.sourceforge.net/.

[WS92]   W. A. Woods and J. G. Schmolze. The KL-ONE family. In Fritz Lehmann,
            editor, *Semantic Networks in Artificial Intelligence*, pages 133–177. Pergamon Press, Oxford, 1992.

Proving More Properties
with Bounded Model Checking*

Mohammad Awedh and Fabio Somenzi

University of Colorado at Boulder
{Awedh,Fabio}@colorado.edu

Abstract. Bounded Model Checking, although complete in theory, has been thus far limited in practice to falsification of properties that were not invariants. In this paper we propose a termination criterion for all of LTL, and we show its effectiveness through experiments. Our approach is based on converting the LTL formula to a Büchi automaton so as to reduce model checking to the verification of a fairness constraint. This reduction leads to one termination criterion that applies to all formulae. We also discuss cases for which a dedicated termination test improves bounded model checking efficiency.

1   Introduction

The standard approach to model checking an LTL property [17, 9] consists of checking language emptiness for the composition of the model at hand and a Büchi automaton that accepts all the counterexamples to the LTL property. A competing approach consists of encoding the problem as propositional satisfiability (SAT) [2]. In this approach, known as Bounded Model Checking (BMC), a propositional formula is constructed such that a counterexample of bounded length for the LTL formula exists if and only if the propositional formula is satisfiable.

The basic BMC just described is not complete in practice: It often finds a counterexample if it exists, but it cannot prove that a property passes unless a tight bound on the *completeness threshold* [6] of the state graph is known. Such a bound is difficult to obtain. The issue of completeness is addressed by recourse to an induction proof in [14] and [7], or by the use of interpolants in [10] so that BMC can be used for both verification and falsification of invariants.

The approach of [14] is based on the observation that if a counterexample to an invariant exists, then there is a simple path from an initial state to a failure state that goes through no other initial or failure state. Every infinite path that extends this simple path violates the invariant. Therefore, an invariant holds if all states of all paths of length k starting from the initial states satisfy the invariant, and moreover, there is no simple path of length $k + 1$ starting at an initial state or leading to a failure state, and not going through any other initial or failure states.

This method can be easily extended to prove LTL safety properties. For full LTL, one can convert the check for a liveness property into the check of a safety property

---

* This work was supported in part by SRC contract 2003-TJ-920.

R. Alur and D.A. Peled (Eds.): CAV 2004, LNCS 3114, pp. 96–108, 2004.

following [13]. However, the conversion doubles the number of state variables. An approach that does not incur this penalty is the subject of this paper. We translate the given LTL formula into a Büchi automaton and compose the latter with the model as in [17, 6]. This step reduces the checking of any LTL property to the one of F G ¬p for a propositional formula p, on the composed model.

A counterexample to F G ¬p exists if there is a simple path from an initial state of the composed model followed by a transition to some state on the path[1]. If there is no simple path from an initial state of length k, then there cannot be a counterexample of length $k + 1$. This condition is the counterpart of the one for invariants that checks for simple paths from initial states. However, there is no strict analog of the states failing an invariant in the general case. Hence, the check for no simple paths of length k into failure states must be replaced by a criterion that guarantees that no loops satisfying certain acceptance conditions may be closed by extending paths of length k.

In this paper, we present such a criterion to prove LTL properties in general. We also discuss a more efficient criterion for a common special case. The translation of the LTL formula can be accomplished in several ways. In Sect. 4 we discuss the impact of various choices on the efficiency of the model checker.

As in the case of invariants, the effectiveness of our termination criteria depends on the lengths of the simple paths in a state graph. However, our experiments, presented in Sect. 5, show that many properties that defy verification attempts by either standard BMC or BDD-based model checking can be proved by our approach.

2 Preliminaries

The goal of LTL model checking is to determine whether an LTL property is satisfied in a finite model of a sequential system. The behavior of this sequential system is described by a *Kripke structure*. A Kripke structure $\mathcal{K} = \langle S, \delta, I, L \rangle$ consists of a finite set of states S whose connections are described by the transition relation $\delta \subseteq S \times S$. If $(s, t) \in \delta$, then there is a transition form state s to state t in $\mathcal{K}$. The transition relation δ is total: For every state $s \in S$ there is a state $t \in S$ such that $(s, t) \in \delta$. $I \subseteq S$ is the set of initial states of the system. The labeling function $L : S \rightarrow 2^{AP}$ indicates what atomic propositions hold at each state. We write $\delta(s, t)$ for $(s, t) \in \delta$; that is, we regard δ as a predicate. Likewise, we write $I(s)$ to indicate that s is an initial state, and, for $p \in AP$, $p(s)$ to indicate that $p \in L(s)$.

Definition 1. *A sequence of states* $(s_0, \ldots, s_k)$ *forms a* path *of length k of Kripke structure* $\mathcal{K}$ *if it satisfies*

$$path_k = \bigwedge_{0 \leq i < k} \delta(s_i, s_{i+1}) \ .$$

The path is initialized *if* $I(s_0)$ *holds. A* simple path *of length k satisfies:*

$$simplePath_k = path_k \wedge \bigwedge_{0 \leq i < j \leq k} (s_i \neq s_j) \ .$$

---

[1] Precisely, this is the case when BMC starts from paths of length 0, and increases the length by 1 every time.

The simple path condition can be easily expressed with a number of CNF clauses that is quadratic in the length k of the path. Recent work [8] reduces the number of required clauses to $O(k \log^2 k)$.

Definition 2. *A loop condition L_k is true of a path of length k if and only if there is a transition from state s_k to some state of the path.*

$$L_k = \bigvee_{0 \leq l \leq k} \delta(s_k, s_l) .$$

Definition 3. *The* LTL *formulae over atomic propositions AP are defined as follows*

- *Atomic propositions,* true, *and* false *are LTL formulae.*
- *if f and g are LTL formulae, then so are $\neg f$, $f \wedge g$, $f \vee g$, $\mathsf{X} f$, and $f \mathsf{U} g$.*

An LTL formula that does not contain the temporal operators (X and U) is propositional. We write $f \mathsf{R} g$ for $\neg(\neg f \mathsf{U} \neg g)$, $\mathsf{F} f$ for true $\mathsf{U} f$*, and $\mathsf{G} f$ for* false $\mathsf{R} g$*.*

LTL formulae are interpreted over infinite paths. An atomic proposition p holds along a path $\pi = (s_0, s_1, \ldots)$ if $p(s_0)$ holds. Satisfaction for true, false, and the Boolean connectives is defined in the obvious way; $\pi \models \mathsf{X} f$ iff $\pi^1 \models f$, where $\pi^i = (s_i, s_{i+1}, \ldots)$; and $\pi \models f \mathsf{U} g$ iff there exists $i \geq 0$ such that $\pi^i \models g$, and for $j < i, \pi^j \models f$.

A *safety* linear-time property is such that every counterexample to it has a finite prefix that, however extended to an infinite path, yields a counterexample. A *liveness* property, on the other hand, is such that every finite path can be extended to a model of the property. Every linear time property can be expressed as the intersection of a safety and a liveness property [1].

Though in principle a counterexample to a linear-time property is always an infinite sequence of states, for safety properties it is sufficient and customary to present an initialized simple path that leads to a *bad state*—one from which all extensions to infinite paths result in counterexamples. For liveness properties, on the other hand, counterexamples produced by model checkers are ultimately periodic sequences of states. Such sequences can be presented in the form of an initialized path followed by a transition to one of its states. As an example, in a counterexample to the liveness property $\mathsf{F} p$ all states of the path satisfy $\neg p$. In a counterexample to $\mathsf{F} \mathsf{G} \neg p$, the transition from the last state of the path reaches back far enough that a state satisfying p is included in the loop.

Definition 4. *A Büchi automaton over alphabet Σ is a quadruple*

$$\mathcal{A} = \langle Q, \Delta, q_0, F \rangle ,$$

where Q is the finite set of states, $\Delta \subseteq Q \times \Sigma \times Q$ is the transition relation, $q_0 \in Q$ is the initial state, and $F \subseteq Q$ is a set of accepting states (or fair set).

A run *of $\mathcal{A}$ over an infinite sequence $w = (w_0, w_1, \ldots) \in \Sigma^\omega$ is an infinite sequence $\rho = (\rho_0, \rho_1, \ldots)$ over Q, such that $\rho_0 = q_0$, and for all $i \geq 0$, $(\rho_i, w_i, \rho_{i+1}) \in \Delta$. A run ρ is accepting if there exists $q_j \in F$ that appears infinitely often in ρ.*

Boolean satisfiability (SAT) is a well-known NP-complete problem. It consists of computing a satisfying variable assignment for a propositional formula or determining that no such assignment exists.

3   Proving Properties with Bounded Model Checking

Bounded Model Checking (BMC) [2] reduces the search for a counterexample to an LTL property to propositional satisfiability. Given a Kripke structure $\mathcal{K}$, an LTL formula f, and a bound k, BMC tries to refute $\mathcal{K} \models f$ by proving the existence of a witness of length k to the negation of the LTL formula.

BMC generates a propositional formula $[\![\mathcal{K}, \neg f]\!]_k$ that is satisfiable if and only if a counterexample to f of length k exists; $[\![\mathcal{K}, \neg f]\!]_k$ is defined as follows:

$$[\![\mathcal{K}, \neg f]\!]_k = I(s_0) \wedge path_k \wedge [\![\neg f]\!]_k , \tag{1}$$

where $[\![\neg f]\!]_k$ expresses the satisfaction of $\neg f$ along that path. Of particular interest to us are three cases:

$$[\![\neg \mathsf{G}\, p]\!] = \bigvee_{0 \le i \le k} \neg p(s_i) \tag{2a}$$

$$[\![\neg \mathsf{F}\, \mathsf{G}\, \neg p]\!] = \bigvee_{0 \le l \le k} (\delta(s_k, s_l) \wedge \bigvee_{l \le i \le k} p(s_i)) \tag{2b}$$

$$[\![\neg \mathsf{F}\, p]\!] = L_k \wedge \bigwedge_{0 \le i \le k} \neg p(s_i) , \tag{2c}$$

where p is a propositional formula. The first of the three cases is encountered when checking invariants. The second occurs when checking fairness constraint [4]. It is important because model checking any LTL formula f can be reduced to checking for the satisfaction of a fairness constraint by translating the LTL formula to a Büchi automaton. This translation allows us to deal in a uniform manner with all of LTL. However, common cases may benefit from special treatment. We illustrate these benefits for formulae of the form $\mathsf{F}\, p$, which is our third interesting case.

For an invariant $\mathsf{G}\, p$, no counterexample of length greater than or equal to k exists if $[\![\mathcal{K}, \neg \mathsf{G}\, p]\!]_k$ is unsatisfiable, and either of the following predicates is unsatisfiable [14]:

$$\chi(k) = I(s_0) \wedge simplePath_k \wedge \bigwedge_{0 < i \le k} \neg I(s_i) \tag{3a}$$

$$\zeta(k) = simplePath_k \wedge \neg p(s_k) \wedge \bigwedge_{0 \le i < k} p(s_i) . \tag{3b}$$

For checking fairness constraints, an unsatisfiable $\chi(k)$ does not guarantee termination because all counterexamples may have to go through more than one initial state. Therefore, a weakened form must be used:

$$\chi'(k) = I(s_0) \wedge simplePath_k . \tag{3a'}$$

If $\chi'(k)$ is unsatisfiable, then there can be no simple path of length k that can be extended to a counterexample by a transition back to a state along the path. For (3b), dropping the requirement that all states except the last one satisfy p is not sufficient. In the next two sub-sections we develop termination criteria that replace (3b) when $f = \mathsf{F}\, \mathsf{G}\, \neg p$, and when $f = \mathsf{F}\, p$.

3.1   Proving F G ¬p

Theorem 1. *Let* $\mathcal{K} = \langle S, \delta, I, L \rangle$ *be a Kripke structure, let* $p \in AP$ *be an atomic proposition, and let the following predicates denote sets of paths in* $\mathcal{K}$:

$$\alpha(k) = I(s_0) \wedge simplePath_k \wedge p(s_k) \tag{4a}$$

$$\beta(k) = simplePath_{k+1} \wedge \neg p(s_k) \wedge p(s_{k+1}) \tag{4b}$$

$$\beta'(k) = simplePath_{k+1} \wedge \bigwedge_{0 \leq i \leq k} \neg p(s_i) \wedge p(s_{k+1}) \tag{4b'}$$

$$[\![\mathcal{K}, \neg\, \mathsf{F\,G}\, \neg p]\!]_k = I(s_0) \wedge path_k \wedge \bigvee_{0 \leq l \leq k} [\delta(s_k, s_l) \wedge \bigvee_{1 \leq i \leq k} p(s_i)]\ . \tag{4c}$$

Let m *be the least value of* k *for which* $\beta'(k)$ *is unsatisfiable, and* n *the least value of* k *for which* $(\alpha \vee \beta)(k)$ *is unsatisfiable. Then,* $[\![\mathcal{K}, \neg\, \mathsf{F\,G}\, \neg p]\!]_k$ *is unsatisfiable unless it is satisfiable for* $k \leq n + m - 1$.

Proof. Since $\beta'(k+1)$ is satisfiable only if $\beta'(k)$ is, and $\beta'(|S| + 1)$ is unsatisfiable, there is a minimum $m \geq 0$ such that $\beta'(m)$ is unsatisfiable, and for $k > m$, $\beta'(k)$ remains unsatisfiable. A similar argument applies to $\beta(k)$.

If $\alpha(k)$ is unsatisfiable, every initialized simple path of length k in $\mathcal{K}$ ends with a state s_k such that $\neg p(s_k)$. In addition, if $\beta(k)$ is unsatisfiable, no simple path of length k that ends in a state s_k such that $\neg p(s_k)$ can be extended to a simple path of length $k + 1$ such that $p(s_{k+1})$. Hence, every initialized simple path of length $k + 1$ ends in a state s_{k+1} such that $\neg p(s_{k+1})$. Therefore, $(\alpha \vee \beta)(k+1)$ is satisfiable only if $(\alpha \vee \beta)(k)$ is. Since $\alpha(|S| + 1)$ is unsatisfiable, there is a minimum $n \geq m$ for which $(\alpha \vee \beta)(n)$ is unsatisfiable. In addition, for $k > n$ $(\alpha \vee \beta)(k)$ remains unsatisfiable.

If $[\![\mathcal{K}, \neg\, \mathsf{F\,G}\, \neg p]\!]_k$ is satisfiable for $k = n' \leq n$, then the theorem holds for $\mathcal{K}$. Suppose it is satisfiable for $k = n' > n$, but not for any value of k less than or equal to n. Then

$$\gamma(k) = I(s_0) \wedge simplePath_k \wedge \bigvee_{0 \leq l \leq k} [\delta(s_k, s_l) \wedge \bigvee_{1 \leq i \leq k} p(s_i)] \tag{4c'}$$

is also satisfiable for some $k = n''$, $n < n'' \leq n'$. Since every initialized simple path of length $n'' \geq n$ satisfies $\neg(p(s_n) \vee \cdots \vee p(s_{n''}))$, if there is a path of length $k > n$ satisfying $\gamma(k)$, no state s_i in (4c') such that $p(s_i)$ holds can have $i \geq n$. Hence, the maximum length of such a path is $m + n - 1$; otherwise, there would be a simple path of length $m' > m$ satisfying (4b') from s_n to a state that satisfies p. Therefore, if there is no path of length at most $m + n - 1$ that satisfies $\gamma(k)$, then $[\![\mathcal{K}, \neg\, \mathsf{F\,G}\, \neg p]\!]_k$ is unsatisfiable for any $k \geq 0$. □

Theorem 2. *There exists a family of structures* $\{\mathcal{K}_i\}$, $i \geq 0$, *such that the minimum value of* k *for which* $\gamma(k)$ *is satisfiable is* $m + n - 1 = 2n - 1$.

Proof. Structure $\mathcal{K}_i$ is defined as follows:

$$S_i = \{s_0, \ldots, s_{2i+1}\} \qquad\qquad I_i = \{s_0\}$$

$$\delta_i = \{(s_j, s_{j+1}) \mid 0 \le j \le 2i\} \qquad L(s_j) = \begin{cases} \{p\} & \text{if } j = i \\ \emptyset & \text{otherwise} \end{cases}.$$
$$\cup \{(s_{2i+1}, s_i)\}$$

For this structure, $m = n = i + 1$; $\gamma(k)$ is satisfiable for $k = 2i + 1$ and for no other value of k. (Regarding criterion (3a′), $\chi'(k)$ is unsatisfiable for $k > 2i + 1$.) $\qquad\square$

As shown in Sect. 5, for many models and properties, the termination criterion based on Theorem 1 is more effective than the one based on (3a′).

The conditions of Theorem 1 can be checked efficiently by observing that (4b) is unsatisfiable only if (4b′) is, and that the satisfiability of (4a) is immaterial until (4b) becomes unsatisfiable. Initially, it is therefore sufficient to check (4b′); when this becomes unsatisfiable, one records the value of m and switches to checking (4b). When the latter also becomes unsatisfiable, then one starts monitoring (4a) until the value of n is found. Naturally, if (4c) becomes satisfiable, the process terminates. It is not required to check one of (4a)–(4b′) for all values of k, though, obviously, skipping some checks may lead to trying larger values of k than strictly necessary.

3.2 Trap States

Suppose that a predicate τ is given such that from a state s that satisfies $\tau(s)$, no state s' satisfying $p(s') \vee \neg\tau(s')$ can be reached. Then, when checking $\mathsf{F\,G}\,\neg p$, (3a′) can be strengthened as follows:

$$\chi''(k) = I(s_0) \wedge simplePath_k \wedge \neg\tau(s_k) . \tag{3a″}$$

The model on which $\mathsf{F\,G}\,\neg p$ is checked is normally obtained by composition of the given Kripke structure with a Büchi automaton for the negation of an LTL property. The automaton may contain a *trap state*, that is, a non-accepting state with a self-loop as only outgoing transition. Such a state is often introduced when making the transition relation Δ of the automaton complete. In such cases, one can take τ as the predicate that is true of all states of the composition that project on the trap state of the automaton.

3.3 Proving $\mathsf{F}\,p$

Theorem 3. *Let $\mathcal{K} = \langle S, \delta, I, L\rangle$ be a Kripke structure, let $p \in AP$ be an atomic proposition, and let the following predicates denote sets of paths in $\mathcal{K}$:*

$$\theta(k) = I(s_0) \wedge simplePath_k \wedge \bigwedge_{0 \le i \le k} \neg p(s_i) \tag{5a}$$

$$[\![\mathcal{K}, \neg\,\mathsf{F}\,p]\!]_k = I(s_0) \wedge path_k \wedge L_k \wedge \bigwedge_{0 \le i \le k} \neg p(s_i) . \tag{5b}$$

Let n be the least value of k such that $\theta(k)$ is unsatisfiable. Then $[\![\mathcal{K}, \neg\,\mathsf{F}\,p]\!]_k$ is unsatisfiable unless it is satisfiable for $k \le n$.

Proof. Since $\theta(|S|+1)$ is unsatisfiable, there exists a minimum k such that $\theta(k)$ is unsatisfiable. Let this minimum be n. Since $\theta(k+1)$ implies $\theta(k)$, if $\theta(n)$ is unsatisfiable, for $k > n$, $\theta(k)$ remains unsatisfiable.

If $[\mathcal{K}, \neg \mathsf{F}\, p]_k$ is satisfiable for $k = n' \leq n$, then the theorem holds for $\mathcal{K}$. Suppose it is satisfiable for $k = n' > n$, but not for any value of k less than or equal to n. Then

$$\sigma(k) = I(s_0) \wedge simplePath_k \wedge L_k \wedge \bigwedge_{0 \leq i \leq k} \neg p(s_i) \tag{5b'}$$

is also satisfiable for some $k = n''$, $n < n'' \leq n'$. Since $\sigma(k)$ implies $\theta(k)$, assuming that $\sigma(k)$ is satisfiable for $k = n'' > n$ leads to a contradiction.   □

Note that the value of n in Theorem 3 corresponds to the (predicated) recurrence $\neg p$-radius of [13].

4   Minimum-Length Counterexamples

One virtue of the standard BMC algorithm is that it can produce counterexamples of minimum length for all LTL properties if the lengths of the paths whose existence is checked by SAT starts at 0 and is increased by 1 every time. With BDD-based LTL model checking this is not the case for two reasons. The first is that the shortest fair cycle problem is solved only heuristically [5, 12]. The second reason is that in BDD-based LTL model checking, a counterexample is a path in the composition of Kripke structure and property automaton. Such a counterexample may be longer than the shortest counterexamples found in the Kripke structure.

Example 1. Figure 1 shows a Kripke structure $\mathcal{K}$ with $S = \{a, b\}$, $\delta = \{(a, b), (b, a)\}$, $I = \{a\}$, $L(a) = \{r\}$, and $L(b) = \emptyset$. This structure is composed with a Büchi automaton $\mathcal{A}$ for the negation of $\varphi = \mathsf{G}(r \rightarrow \mathsf{F}\, q)$. The alphabet Σ of $\mathcal{A}$ is 2^{AP}. In the figure, an arc of the automaton is annotated with the characteristic function of all the labels for which there is a transition between the two states connected by the arc. Hence, $\mathcal{A}$ can follow an arc into a state if it reads a letter of the input word that satisfies the arc's formula. The doubly-circled states are accepting. The shortest counterexample to $\mathcal{K} \models \varphi$ found in $\mathcal{K} \parallel \mathcal{A}$ includes three states, $a0$, $b1$, and $a1$, even though there is a counterexample consisting of two states, a and b, in $\mathcal{K}$.

Even when it is possible to retrieve a shortest path in the Kripke structure from the shortest path in the composition—as in the case of Example 1—the computation on $\mathcal{K} \parallel \mathcal{A}$ is likely to be more expensive than the one on $\mathcal{K}$ alone because the transition relation is unrolled more times.

An LTL formula may be translated into many distinct Büchi automata. Though they all accept the same language, they may differ in "style" (labels on the states vs. labels on the transitions; one acceptance condition vs. several), or simply in the numbers of states and transitions.

Automata with labels on the transitions react to the evolution of the Kripke structure with which they are composed with a delay of one step. This is an obstacle in producing shortest counterexamples. Automata with labels on the states do not have this disadvantage, but do not guarantee shortest counterexamples either.

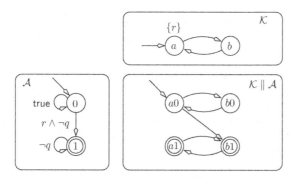

Fig. 1. The composition with the Büchi automaton affects the length of the counterexample

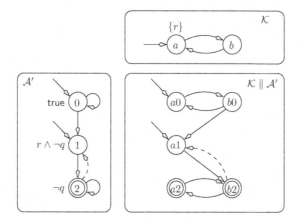

Fig. 2. The position of the labels in the Büchi automaton and its transition relation affect the length of the counterexample

Example 2. Figure 2 shows the Kripke structure of Example 1 composed with a Büchi automaton $\mathcal{A}'$ for the negation of $\varphi = G(r \rightarrow F q)$ with labels on the states. The transition drawn with a dashed line from State 2 to State 1 can be added or removed without changing the language accepted by $\mathcal{A}'$ [16]. However, whether it is present or not affects the counterexample found to $\mathcal{K} \models \varphi$. With the optional transition, the language emptiness check applied to $\mathcal{K} \parallel \mathcal{A}'$ returns the cycle $(a1, b2)$, which is of minimal length. By contrast, when the transition is omitted, the shortest counterexample to $\mathcal{K} \models \varphi$ has three states: $a1$, $b2$, and $a2$.

Example 2 shows that adding transitions to an automaton may lead to shorter counterexamples. On the other hand, more transitions may result in longer simple paths which may delay the triggering of the termination conditions. To avoid these problems, the check for existence of counterexamples of length k is performed according to the original algorithm of [2], while the termination criteria are applied to the composition of Kripke structure and Büchi automaton. The overhead of building two distinct models for each value of k is more than compensated by the ability to terminate sooner for failing properties.

5   Experimental Results

We have implemented the termination criteria of Theorems 1 and 3, (3a′), and (3a″) in VIS [3, 18]. VIS includes an implementation of the BMC algorithm of [2] that uses zChaff [11] to check for the satisfiability of propositional formulae. VIS detects LTL formulae of special types and treats them accordingly.

- For invariants and formulae that are syntactically safe according to the definition of [15], VIS returns a simple path to a bad state in case of failure. The termination criteria (3a) and (3b) of [14] are applied.
- LTL formulae that contain no temporal operators except X are called *bounded*. The *depth* of a bounded formula is the maximum nesting level of X operators in it. VIS concludes that a bounded formula holds unless it finds a counterexample whose length does not exceed the formula's depth. Propositional formulae are bounded formulae of depth 0.

For formulae that fall into one of the above categories, we use the termination checks already implemented. For the others, we have implemented two approaches.

- The first approach applies the standard BMC algorithm augmented with the termination check of (3a″) to the composition of the original model and a Büchi automaton for the negation of the formula.
- The second approach checks if the given formula is of the form F p, in which case, the standard BMC algorithm augmented with the termination check of Theorem 3 is applied. Otherwise, the termination checks of (3a″) and Theorem 1 are applied to the composition of the original model and a Büchi automaton for the negation of the formula, while standard BMC is applied to the original model to check for violations of the property as discussed in Sect. 4.

The results presented in the following tables are for models that are either from industry or from the VIS Verification Benchmark set [18]. For each model, we count each LTL property as a separate experiment. We exclude experiments such that all the methods we compare finish in less than 1 s. Experiments that take more than 1800 s are considered timed out. For all experiments, we set the maximum value of k to 30 and we check for termination at each step. The experiments were run on an IBM IntelliStation with a 1.7 GHz Pentium IV CPU and 2 GB of RAM running Linux. The datasize limit was set to 1.5 GB.

Table 1 shows the results of applying four algorithms to LTL properties for which VIS did not already implement termination criteria. We compare the performance of our method based on Theorems 1 and 3, and the termination criterion (3a″) (*aut_sat*) to the standard BMC algorithm (*bmc*), to the use of the termination criterion (3a″) (*bmc_et*) only, and to the BDD-based LTL model checking algorithm in VIS (*ltl*).

The first column in Table 1 is the name of the model, the second is the number of state variables, and the third is the property number. The remaining columns are divided into four groups, one for each algorithm. The first column in each group indicates

Table 1. Comparison of aut_sat, bmc, bmc_et, and ltl

Model	state vars	#	aut_sat ⊨	k	Time(s)	bmc ⊨	k	Time(s)	bmc_et ⊨	k	Time(s)	ltl ⊨	Time(s)
Am2910	99	1	yes	3	**3.03**	?	30	112.58	?	30	557.48	?	Timeout
Bakery	16	1	no	13	96.86	no	13	78.05	no	13	91.3	no	**0.35**
Blackjack	102	1	yes	1	**1.01**	?	30	148.76	yes	1	1.49	yes	282.6
Chameleon	7	1	yes	3	0.92	?	30	68.81	?	30	639.57	yes	**0.1**
Coherence	1	1	yes	3	2.32	?	30	40.31	?	30	178.46	yes	**0.7**
		2	no	5	4.32	no	5	0.99	no	5	2.19	no	**0.9**
		3	?	21	Timeout	?	30	1231.59	?	19	Timeout	yes	**1.0**
D18	506	1	no	23	1378.21	no	23	**82.68**	no	23	342.52	?	Timeout
		2	yes	0	**0.4**	?	30	123.45	yes	1	13.92	?	Timeout
D24	238	1	no	9	34.53	no	9	**15.12**	no	9	29.35	?	Timeout
Dcnew	10	1	no	6	3.03	no	6	0.88	no	6	1.94	no	**0.26**
		2	no	5	1.62	no	5	0.38	no	5	1.31	no	**0.3**
Dekker	6	1	no	5	2.61	no	5	0.86	no	5	1.31	no	**0.09**
Fabric	85	1	yes	17	**11.21**	?	30	21.57	?	30	116.95	yes	20.9
Feistel	293	1	yes	19	44.43	?	30	39.35	yes	19	35.54	yes	**0.6**
Lock	9	1	yes	7	1.16	?	30	24.4	?	30	359.63	yes	**0.13**
Microwave	4	1	no	2	0.21	no	2	0.05	no	2	0.11	no	**0.01**
		2	yes	3	0.34	?	30	5.87	yes	3	0.29	yes	**0.02**
		3	yes	7	0.95	?	30	16.72	yes	8	1.3	yes	**0.1**
MinMax	27	1	yes	5	13.16	?	30	183.28	?	24	Timeout	yes	**0.41**
Nim	33	1	no	6	19.54	no	6	**4.67**	no	6	11.76	no	464.1
Palu	37	1	no	0	0.1	no	0	**0.05**	no	0	**0.05**	?	Timeout
		2	no	1	0.41	no	1	**0.14**	no	1	**0.14**	?	Timeout
PL_BUS	307	1	yes	5	5.53	?	30	155.11	yes	6	15.68	yes	**1.76**
RetherRTF	43	1	no	2	1.31	no	2	**0.56**	no	2	0.79	no	1.03
		2	?	20	Timeout	?	30	1242.82	?	25	Timeout	no	**1.84**
		3	no	2	1.0	no	2	**0.54**	no	2	0.94	no	0.91
		4	?	25	Timeout	?	30	1014.33	?	28	Timeout	yes	**0.99**
		5	?	30	823.12	?	30	182.49	?	30	332.99	yes	**1.43**
s1269	37	1	yes	9	0.95	?	30	21.37	yes	9	**0.78**	?	Timeout
s1423	74	1	no	9	6.61	no	9	**2.55**	no	9	3.38	?	Timeout
		2	yes	3	0.57	?	30	12.21	yes	3	**0.49**	?	Timeout
Silvermau	17	1	yes	1	**0.14**	?	30	13.72	yes	1	0.16	yes	0.12
Smult	95	1	no	1	0.0.27	no	1	**0.07**	no	1	0.09	no	37.45
		2	?	30	446.67	?	30	7.52	?	30	382.23	yes	**35.47**
three_processor	48	1	yes	3	**2.5**	?	30	56.44	?	30	934.23	yes	184.6
Timeout	31	1	no	0	**0.06**	no	0	**0.06**	no	0	**0.06**	no	1.13
		2	no	2	0.76	no	2	**0.35**	no	2	0.42	no	1.64
UniDec	18	1	yes	3	2.76	?	30	143.84	yes	10	28.81	yes	**0.16**
		2	yes	8	12.6	?	30	112.87	yes	9	18.42	yes	**0.18**
		3	no	6	5.32	no	6	1.58	no	6	2.33	no	**0.36**
		4	no	6	6.93	no	6	3.47	no	6	3.7	no	**0.15**
UsbPhy	87	1	?	30	380.54	?	30	34.59	?	30	130.72	yes	**192.1**

Table 2. Comparison for special cases

Model	state vars	#	Theorem 1 and (3a″) $\models$	k	Time(s)	Special cases $\models$	k	Time(s)	Property type
Arbiter	16	1	?	30	432.6	?	30	**391.95**	Invariant
Blackjack	102	1	yes	1	2.4	yes	1	**1.01**	F p
Bpb	36	1	yes	3	4.72	yes	0	**0.35**	Safety
D4	230	1	?	30	356.7	yes	9	**6.87**	F p
D18	506	2	yes	1	14.66	yes	0	**0.4**	F p
D21	92	1	?	24	Timeout	?	24	Timeout	Invariant
D24	238	2	yes	21	532.24	yes	9	**45.25**	Invariant
Dekker	6	2	?	27	Timeout	yes	18	**266.96**	Invariant
Fabric	85	2	yes	19	15.32	yes	8	**3.76**	Invariant
FPMult	43	1	yes	7	4.36	yes	2	**0.35**	Safety
PLBUS	307	1	yes	6	18.89	yes	5	**5.53**	F p
Rrobin	5	1	yes	3	0.2	yes	0	**0.02**	Safety
s1269	37	2	yes	5	2.26	yes	1	**0.22**	Invariant
Timeout	31	3	?	30	1023.22	yes	0	**0.07**	Invariant
		4	?	30	923.45	yes	16	**24.91**	Invariant
UniDec	18	2	yes	9	22.09	yes	8	**12.6**	F p
		5	yes	8	17.87	yes	8	**1.62**	Bounded LTL

whether each property passes (*yes*), fails (*no*), or remains undecided (*?*); the column labeled k, when present, reports the length of the longest counterexamples that were considered. The columns labeled *Time* give the times in second for each run. Boldface is used to highlight best run times.

As usual, SAT-based model checking does much better than BDD-based model checking on some examples, and much worse on others. Within the SAT-based approaches, *aut_sat* is the only one to prove (as opposed to falsify) a significant number of properties. In fact, all passing properties in Table 1 are proved by either *aut_sat* or *ltl*.

The termination criterion (3a″) is not very effective by itself. It only proves 11 of the 23 passing properties; 5 of them are proved by Theorems 1 and 3 for smaller values of k. By contrast, Theorems 1 and 3 prove 18 of the 23 passing properties.

Augmenting the standard BMC with the termination criteria of Theorems 1 and 3, and (3a″) helps to prove properties that are hard for the BDD-based method. In Table 1, *ltl* times out before deciding 9 properties, whereas *aut_sat* times out before deciding 3 properties. In addition, *aut_sat* proves some properties faster than *ltl*. For example, for model *Am2910*, *aut_sat* proves the property true in 3.03 s, while *ltl* does not reach a decision in 1800 s. As another example, for model *three_processor*, *aut_sat* proves the property true in 2.5 s, while *ltl* takes 184.6 s to prove it.

Table 2 illustrates the importance of checking for special cases. These include invariants, syntactically safe properties, bounded LTL properties, and liveness properties of the form F p, where p is a propositional formula. All properties in this table are passing properties. The column labeled k has the same meaning as in Table 1. If the value of k is 0, the corresponding property is an *inductive* invariant.

In Table 2, the general method is slower. There are two reasons for that: The first is that using the termination criteria of Theorem 1 and (3a″) generate more clauses for a given value of k. The second reason is that longer counterexamples are examined. For instance, for *Fabric*, the general method needs 19 steps to prove the property, while the special case takes only 8 steps. As another example, *s1269* has a bounded depth of 1; however, the method based on Theorem 1 and (3a″) needs 5 steps to prove the property. The termination check of Theorem 3 is better than the termination check of Theorem 1 when checking properties of the form F p. For example, for model *D4*, Theorem 1 fails to prove the property for k up to 30, while Theorem 3 proves it for k equal to 9 in only 6.87 s.

6   Conclusions and Future Work

We have presented an approach to proving general LTL properties with Bounded Model Checking even without prior knowledge of a tight bound on the completeness threshold of the graph [6]. The approach translates the LTL property to a Büchi automaton—as is customary in BDD-based LTL model checking—so as to apply a uniform termination criterion. Experiments indicate that this criterion is significantly more effective than the straightforward generalization of the termination criteria for invariants of [14]. Compared to the completeness threshold of [6], our bound takes into account the position of the fair states in the graph; hence, it may lead to much earlier termination. The experiments also underline the importance of detecting those cases for which special termination criteria are known. Comparison with BDD-based model checking shows a good degree of complementarity. Neither method proved uniformly better than the other, and together, the two could prove all passing properties in our set of experiments.

Our current implementation uses Büchi automata with labels on the transitions. As discussed in Sect. 4, we need to explore the alternative provided by automata with labels on the states as a way to cause earlier termination. Another aspect needing further attention is that our approach only considers Büchi automata with one fair set. Generalized Büchi automata can be converted to non-generalized, but it is not clear that this would be preferable to an extension of Theorem 1 to handle multiple fair sets.

Acknowledgment

The authors thank the referees for their suggestions, including an improved Theorem 3.

References

1. B. Alpern and F. B. Schneider. Defining liveness. *Information Processing Letters*, 21:181–185, Oct. 1985.
2. A. Biere, A. Cimatti, E. Clarke, and Y. Zhu. Symbolic model checking without BDDs. In *Fifth International Conference on Tools and Algorithms for Construction and Analysis of Systems (TACAS'99)*, pages 193–207, Amsterdam, The Netherlands, Mar. 1999. LNCS 1579.
3. R. K. Brayton et al. VIS: A system for verification and synthesis. In T. Henzinger and R. Alur, editors, *Eighth Conference on Computer Aided Verification (CAV'96)*, pages 428–432. Springer-Verlag, Rutgers University, 1996. LNCS 1102.

4. A. Cimatti, M. Pistore, M. Roveri, and R. Sebastiani. Improving the encoding of LTL model checking into SAT. In *Proceedings of the Workshop on Verification, Model Checking, and Abstract Interpretation*, pages 196–207, Venice, Italy, Jan. 2002. LNCS 2294.

5. E. Clarke, O. Grumberg, K. McMillan, and X. Zhao. Efficient generation of counterexamples and witnesses in symbolic model checking. In *Proceedings of the Design Automation Conference*, pages 427–432, San Francisco, CA, June 1995.

6. E. Clarke, D. Kroening, J. Ouaknine, and O. Strichman. Completeness and complexity of bounded model checking. In *Verification, Model Checking, and Abstract Interpretation*, pages 85–96, Venice, Italy, Jan. 2004. Springer. LNCS 2937.

7. L. de Moura, H. Rueß, and M. Sorea. Bounded model checking and induction: From refutation to verification. In W. A. Hunt, Jr. and F. Somenzi, editors, *Fifteenth Conference on Computer Aided Verification (CAV'03)*, pages 1–13. Springer-Verlag, Boulder, CO, July 2003. LNCS 2725.

8. D. Kröning and O. Strichman. Efficient computation of recurrence diameters. In *Verification, Model Checking, and Abstract Interpretation*, pages 298–309, New York, NY, Jan. 2003. Springer. LNCS 2575.

9. O. Lichtenstein and A. Pnueli. Checking that finite state concurrent programs satisfy their linear specification. In *Proceedings of the Twelfth Annual ACM Symposium on Principles of Programming Languages*, pages 97–107, New Orleans, Jan. 1985.

10. K. L. McMillan. Interpolation and SAT-based model checking. In W. A. Hunt, Jr. and F. Somenzi, editors, *Fifteenth Conference on Computer Aided Verification (CAV'03)*, pages 1–13. Springer-Verlag, Berlin, July 2003. LNCS 2725.

11. M. Moskewicz, C. F. Madigan, Y. Zhao, L. Zhang, and S. Malik. Chaff: Engineering an efficient SAT solver. In *Proceedings of the Design Automation Conference*, pages 530–535, Las Vegas, NV, June 2001.

12. K. Ravi, R. Bloem, and F. Somenzi. A comparative study of symbolic algorithms for the computation of fair cycles. In W. A. Hunt, Jr. and S. D. Johnson, editors, *Formal Methods in Computer Aided Design*, pages 143–160. Springer-Verlag, Nov. 2000. LNCS 1954.

13. V. Schuppan and A. Biere. Efficient reduction of finite state model checking to reachability analysis. *Software Tools for Technology Transfer*, 5(2–3):185–204, Mar. 2004.

14. M. Sheeran, S. Singh, and G. Stålmarck. Checking safety properties using induction and a SAT-solver. In W. A. Hunt, Jr. and S. D. Johnson, editors, *Formal Methods in Computer Aided Design*, pages 108–125. Springer-Verlag, Nov. 2000. LNCS 1954.

15. A. P. Sistla. Safety, liveness and fairness in temporal logic. *Formal Aspects in Computing*, 6:495–511, 1994.

16. F. Somenzi and R. Bloem. Efficient Büchi automata from LTL formulae. In E. A. Emerson and A. P. Sistla, editors, *Twelfth Conference on Computer Aided Verification (CAV'00)*, pages 248–263. Springer-Verlag, Berlin, July 2000. LNCS 1855.

17. M. Y. Vardi and P. Wolper. An automata-theoretic approach to automatic program verification. In *Proceedings of the First Symposium on Logic in Computer Science*, pages 322–331, Cambridge, UK, June 1986.

18. URL: http://vlsi.colorado.edu/~vis.

Parallel LTL-X Model Checking
of High-Level Petri Nets Based on Unfoldings

Claus Schröter[1] and Victor Khomenko[2]

[1] Institut für Formale Methoden der Informatik
Universität Stuttgart, Germany
schroeter@fmi.uni-stuttgart.de
[2] School of Computing Science
University of Newcastle upon Tyne, UK
Victor.Khomenko@ncl.ac.uk

Abstract. We present an unfolding-based approach to LTL-X model-checking of high-level Petri nets. It is based on the method proposed by Esparza and Heljanko for low-level nets [4, 5] and a state of the art parallel high-level net unfolder described in [15, 13]. We present experimental results comparing our approach to the one of [4, 5] and the model-checker SPIN [12].

1 Introduction

The main drawback of model-checking (see, e.g., [2]) is that it suffers from the *state space explosion* problem. That is, even a relatively small system specification can (and often does) yield a very large state space. To alleviate this problem, a number of techniques have been proposed. They can roughly be classified as aiming at an implicit compact representation of the full state space of a reactive concurrent system, or at an explicit generation of a reduced (though sufficient for a given verification task) representation (e.g., *abstraction* and *partial order reduction* techniques [2]). Among them, a prominent technique is McMillan's (finite prefixes of) Petri net unfoldings (see, e.g., [6, 16, 13, 17]). It relies on the partial order view of concurrent computation, and represents system states implicitly, using an acyclic net. More precisely, given a Petri net Σ, the unfolding technique aims at building a labelled acyclic net Unf_Σ (a *prefix*) satisfying two key properties [6, 16, 13]:

– *Completeness.* Each reachable marking of Σ is represented by at least one 'witness', i.e., a marking of Unf_Σ reachable from its initial marking. Similarly, for each possible firing of a transition at any reachable state of Σ there is a suitable 'witness' event in Unf_Σ.
– *Finiteness.* The prefix is finite and thus can be used as an input to model-checking algorithms, e.g., those searching for deadlocks.

A finite complete prefix satisfying these two properties can be used for model-checking as a condensed (symbolic) representation of the state space of a system.

R. Alur and D.A. Peled (Eds.): CAV 2004, LNCS 3114, pp. 109–121, 2004.

Indeed, it turns out that often such prefixes are exponentially smaller than the corresponding reachability graphs, especially if the system at hand exhibits a lot of concurrency. At least, they are never larger than the reachability graphs [6, 16, 13].

The unfolding techniques and algorithms described in [6–8, 10, 13, 14, 16–18, 20] help to alleviate the state space explosion problem when model-checking low-level Petri nets. Moreover, the construction of the prefix can be efficiently parallelised [11, 13]. However, the applicability of these techniques is restricted by the fact that low-level Petri nets are a very low-level formalism, and thus inconvenient for practical modelling. Therefore, it is highly desirable to generalise this technique to more expressive formalisms, such as high-level (or 'coloured') Petri nets. This formalism allows one to model in quite a natural way many constructs of high-level specification languages used to describe concurrent systems (see, e.g., [1]). Though it is possible to translate a high-level net into a low-level one and then unfold the latter, it is often the case that the intermediate low-level net is exponentially larger than the resulting prefix. Moreover, such a translation often completely destroys the structure present in the original model. In [15, 13], an approach allowing one to build a prefix directly from a high-level net, thus avoiding a potentially expensive translation into a low-level net, was described. Experiments demonstrated that this method is often superior to the traditional one, involving the explicit construction of an intermediate low-level net.

Petri net unfolding prefixes have been used for verification of simple safety properties, such as deadlock freeness, mutual exclusion and various kinds of reachability analysis [10, 13, 17, 18]. (The LTL model checking algorithm proposed in [22] is quite complicated and a corrected version of the approach requires memory exponential in the size of the prefix in the worst case [4, 5].) Recent work [4, 5, 8] suggested a method for checking LTL-X properties of low-level Petri nets. It uses a particular non-standard way of synchronising a Petri net with a Büchi automaton, which preserves as much concurrency as possible, in order to avoid a blow up in the size of the resulting prefix.

In this paper, we build on the ideas of [4, 5, 11, 13, 15] and propose a parallel algorithm for verification of LTL-X properties based on high-level Petri net unfoldings. To our knowledge, no such an algorithm existed before.

2   Basic Notions

We use *M-nets* [1] as the main high-level Petri net model, as we believe that it is general enough to cover many other existing relevant formalisms. The full description of M-nets can be found in [1]; here we give only an informal introduction, omitting those details which are not directly needed for the purposes of this paper. In particular, [1] devotes a lot of attention to the composition rules for M-nets, which are relevant only at the construction stage of an M-net, but not for model-checking an already constructed one. We assume the reader is familiar with the standard notions of the Petri nets theory, such as *places*, *transitions*, *arcs*, *presets* and *postsets* of places and transitions, *marking* of a Petri net, the *enabledness* and *firing* of a transition and marking *reachability* (see, e.g., [6]).

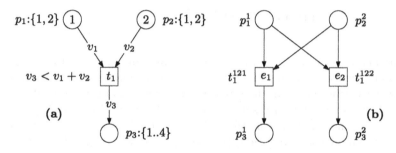

Fig. 1. An M-net system (a) and its unfolding (b).

2.1 High-Level Petri Nets

Let *Tok* be a (finite or infinite) set of elements (or 'colours') and *VAR* be a set
of variable names, such that $Tok \cap VAR = \emptyset$. An *M-net* is a Petri net such that:

- Each of its places has a *type*, which is a subset of *Tok* and indicates the
  colours this place can contain. We assume that the types of all places are
  finite[1]. Valid markings of an M-net can be obtained by placing in each of its
  places a (possibly empty) multiset of tokens consistent with the type of the
  place.
- Each transition is labelled by a *guard*, which is a well-formed Boolean expression over $Tok \cup VAR$.
- Each arc is labelled with a multiset of variables from *VAR*.

For a transition t, we will denote by $VAR(t)$ the set of variables which appear
in its guard and its incident arcs[2].

The enabling and firing rules of M-nets are as follows: when tokens flow along
the incoming arcs of a transition t, they become bound to variables labelling
those arcs, forming a (partial) mapping $\sigma : VAR(t) \to Tok$. If this mapping can
be extended to a total mapping σ' (such an extension can be non-unique) in such
a way that the guard of t evaluates to **true** and the values of the variables on
the outgoing arcs are consistent with the types of the places these arcs point to,
then t is called *enabled* and σ' is called a *firing mode* of t. An enabled transition
can *fire*, consuming the tokens from its preset and producing tokens in places
in its postset, in accordance with the values of the variables on the appropriate
arcs given by σ'.

As an example, consider the M-net system shown in Figure 1(a). At the
initial marking, t_1 can fire with the firing modes $\sigma' \stackrel{\text{df}}{=} \{v_1 \mapsto 1, v_2 \mapsto 2, v_3 \mapsto 1\}$
or $\sigma'' \stackrel{\text{df}}{=} \{v_1 \mapsto 1, v_2 \mapsto 2, v_3 \mapsto 2\}$, consuming the tokens from p_1 and p_2 and
producing respectively the token 1 or 2 in p_3.

---

[1] In general, allowing infinite types yields a Turing-powerful model. Nevertheless, this
   restriction can be omitted in certain important cases [13, 15].
[2] If some variable appears in the guard of t but not on its incident arcs, it must be
   explicitly given a finite type.

2.2   Translation into Low-Level Nets

For each M-net system it is possible to build an 'equivalent' low-level one (the construction is given in [1, 15, 13]). Such a transformation is called 'unfolding' in [1], but since we use this term in a different meaning, we adopt the term 'expansion' instead. One can show that the reachability graphs generated by an M-net and its expansion are isomorphic, i.e., the expansion faithfully models the original M-net. This means that LTL properties of high-level nets can be verified by building its expansion. However, the disadvantage of this transformation is that it typically yields a very large net. Moreover, the resulting Petri net is often *unnecessarily* large, in the sense that it contains many unreachable places and many dead transitions. This is so because the place types are usually overapproximations, and the transitions of the original M-net system may have many firing modes, only few of which are realised when executing the M-net from its initial marking. Therefore, though the M-net expansion is a neat theoretical construction, it is often impractical.

2.3   Petri Net Unfoldings

The *finite complete prefix* of a low-level Petri net Σ is a finite acyclic net which implicitly represents all the reachable states of Σ together with transitions enabled at those states. Intuitively, it can be obtained through *unfolding* Σ, by successive firings of transition, under the following assumptions: (a) for each new firing a fresh transition (called an *event*) is generated; (b) for each newly produced token a fresh place (called a *condition*) is generated. The unfolding is infinite whenever Σ has at least one infinite run; however, if Σ has finitely many reachable states then the unfolding eventually starts to repeat itself and can be truncated without loss of information, yielding a finite and complete prefix.

One can show that the number of events in the complete prefix can never exceed the number of reachable states of Σ, for a precise statement see [6, 13, 16]. However, complete prefixes are often exponentially smaller than the corresponding reachability graphs, especially for highly concurrent Petri nets, because they represent concurrency directly rather than by multidimensional 'diamonds' as it is done in reachability graphs. For example, if the original Petri net consists of 100 transitions which can fire once in parallel, the reachability graph will be a 100-dimensional hypercube with 2^{100} nodes, whereas the complete prefix will coincide with the net itself.

In [13, 15] unfoldings of high-level Petri nets were defined, and the parallel unfolding algorithm proposed in [11, 13] was generalised to high-level nets. It turns out that the unfolding of a high-level net is isomorphic to the unfolding of its low-level expansion. (However, it can be constructed directly from the high-level net, without building this expansion.) Thus this approach is conservative in the sense that all the verification tools using traditional unfoldings as input can be reused with high-level ones. Figure 1(b) shows a finite and complete prefix of the M-net in Figure 1(a), coinciding with the finite and complete prefix of the expansion.

3   An Unfolding Approach to LTL-X Model-Checking

In [4, 5], an approach for unfolding based LTL-X model-checking of safe low-level Petri nets was proposed. It makes use of the automata-theoretic approach to model-checking [21]. A synchronised net system is constructed as the product of the original net system and a Büchi automaton accepting the negation of the property to be checked. Then the model-checking problem is reduced to the problem of detecting illegal ω-traces and illegal livelocks in the synchronised net system. Both problems are solved by exploiting finite complete prefixes of the unfolded synchronised net system. The main advantage of this approach over Wallner's [22] is its efficiency. Wallner first calculates a complete finite prefix and then constructs a graph, but the definition of the graph is non-trivial, and the graph grows exponentially in the size of the prefix [4, 5]. The approach of Esparza and Heljanko [4, 5] avoids the construction of the graph, but builds a larger prefix.

In this paper we follow the approach of [4, 5], but we are using *strictly safe* M-nets (i.e., ones which cannot put more than one token in a place) instead of safe low-level Petri nets. We will explain our approach by means of the example shown in Figure 2(a) (and in the following denoted by $\varUpsilon$). It is an M-net model of a buffer which can store at most 2 items (in places p_2 and p_4). To distinguish these two items they are represented by coloured tokens 0 and 1. The M-net contains 4 places and 3 transitions whereas its expanded low-level net contains 8 places and 8 transitions. One can see that if this example is scaled then its expansion grows exponentially in the size of the buffer and the cardinalities of place types, e.g., if the places have types $\{0..150\}$ then the expansion contains 604 places and 23103 transitions, whereas the prefix of such an M-net has just 10 conditions and 7 events (in this particular example place types do not influence the size of the prefix). Thus the prefix is often much smaller than the low-level expansion because the latter can contain many dead transitions and unreachable places which disappear in the prefix. Furthermore, for larger systems the expansion cannot be constructed within a reasonable time. The main advantage of our approach over the one of [4, 5] is that we unfold the M-net directly and do not have to build its expansion.

Let us assume that we want to check the property $\varphi \overset{\mathrm{df}}{=} \Diamond\Box(p_2 \neq 0)$, i.e., "eventually the item 0 is never stored in the buffer cell p_2 again." First of all, we have to construct a Büchi automaton accepting $\neg\varphi$. This means that the property φ is violated by a system run in which $\neg(p_2 \neq 0)$ is **true** over and over again. The corresponding Büchi automaton $A_{\neg\varphi}$ is shown in Figure 2(b). We identify it with an M-net system (also denoted by $A_{\neg\varphi}$) which has a place for each state q of the automaton, with only the initial state q_0 having a token. (The type of all its places is $\{\bullet\}$.) For each transition (q, x, q') of $A_{\neg\varphi}$ the M-net has a transition (q, x, q'), where q and q' are the input and output places of the transition, and x is its guard. This M-net is shown in Figure 2(c), and in the following its places and transitions are called *Büchi places* and *Büchi transitions*, respectively.

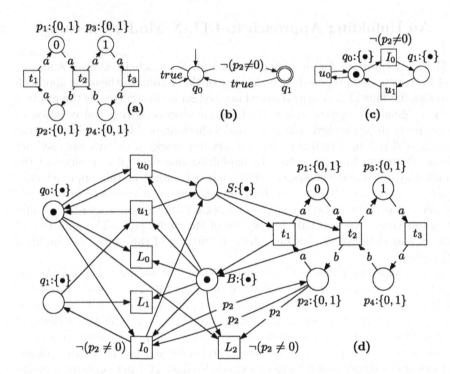

Fig. 2. M-net Υ: buffer of capacity 2 (a), Büchi automaton $A_{\neg\varphi}$ constructed for the property $\varphi \stackrel{\mathrm{df}}{=} \Diamond\Box(p_2 \neq 0)$ (b), the M-net corresponding to $A_{\neg\varphi}$ (c), and the product net $\Upsilon_{\neg\varphi}$ (d).

In the next step a *synchronised M-net system* $\Upsilon_{\neg\varphi}$ is constructed as the product of Υ and $A_{\neg\varphi}$. A standard approach would synchronise the system and the Büchi automaton on all transitions. A drawback of such a synchronisation is that it completely sequentialises the system. Since a strength of the unfolding technique is to exploit concurrency, such a product net would not be very suitable for unfolding based verification techniques. Therefore, we use the synchronisation construction of [4, 5] generalised to high-level nets. In order to exploit concurrency, Υ and $A_{\neg\varphi}$ are only synchronised on those transitions of Υ which 'touch' the places that appear in the atomic propositions of φ. In the following such transitions are called *visible*. For our example this means that Υ and $A_{\neg\varphi}$ only synchronise on the visible transitions t_1 and t_2, because they touch the place p_2 which is the only place referred to in φ.

The resulting product net $\Upsilon_{\neg\varphi}$ is shown in Figure 2(d). Unlabelled arcs denote that only $\bullet$ can flow along them.

Construction of $\Upsilon_{\neg\varphi}$:

1. Put Υ and $A_{\neg\varphi}$ side by side.
2. Connect each Büchi transition with Υ in such a way that it 'observes' the places whose names appear in the guard of the transition. Let (q, x, q') be

a Büchi transition. For each place p which appears in the guard x add arcs from p to (q, x, q') and back; both arcs are labelled with "p". In our example this rule only applies to I_0 because it is the only Büchi transition whose guard refers to p_2. Therefore I_0 and p_2 are connected by arcs which are labelled with p_2.

3. Add *scheduler places* B and S (forming a flip-flop) in such a way that:
   - initially $A_{\neg \varphi}$ can make a step, and all the *visible* transitions of Υ are disabled.
   - after a step of $A_{\neg \varphi}$ only Υ can make a step.
   - after Υ has made a *visible* step, $A_{\neg \varphi}$ can make a step, and until that all the visible transitions of Υ are disabled.

   The intuition behind B and S is that $A_{\neg \varphi}$ (respectively, Υ) can make a step if there is a token on B (respectively, S). The types of these places are $\{\bullet\}$. B is connected by arcs going from B to every Büchi transition (u_0, u_1 and I_0), and going from every visible transition (t_1 and t_2) to B. S is connected by arcs going from S to every visible transition (t_1 and t_2), and going from every Büchi transition (u_0, u_1 and I_0) to S. Only $\bullet$ can flow along the new arcs. Initially, B contains $\bullet$ and S is empty, which allows $A_{\neg \varphi}$ to observe the initial marking of Υ.

Taking a look at the construction of $\Upsilon_{\neg \varphi}$ so far (see Figure 2(d) without transitions L_0, L_1, and L_2) it is clear that an infinite transition sequence that touches the accepting Büchi place q_1 infinitely often violates the property φ because in this case p_2 stores 0 over and over again. To detect such system runs we introduce the set $I \stackrel{\text{df}}{=} \{t \mid t^{\bullet} \text{ contains an accepting place of } A_{\neg \varphi}\}$ of all the transitions putting a token into an accepting Büchi place.

Now we claim that an infinite transition sequence of $\Upsilon_{\neg \varphi}$ which is fireable from the initial marking and contains infinitely many occurrences of I-transitions violates φ. In the following such sequences are called *illegal ω-traces*.

Unfortunately, not every sequence that violates the property φ is detected by illegal ω-traces because we synchronise just on the *visible* transitions. Consider a system that contains amongst others a "loop" of *invisible* transitions. Since we just synchronise on the visible transitions this "loop" would not take part in the synchronisation at all. Suppose the system reaches a marking M from which it is possible to fire a loop of invisible transitions. That is, the system would fire an infinite sequence of transitions without $A_{\neg \varphi}$ being able to observe it. Thus one can imagine a scenario where φ is violated but $A_{\neg \varphi}$ cannot detect this. Therefore, such a situation must be dealt with separately.

Since the firing of invisible transitions cannot change the marking of the *visible* places (i.e., those appearing in the atomic propositions of φ), as well as the places of the scheduler and $A_{\neg \varphi}$, we simply have to check for each marking enabling an infinite sequence of invisible transitions the existence of an accepting run of $A_{\neg \varphi}$ restricted only to those Büchi transitions which are enabled by this marking. (In such a case φ is violated.)

Formally, we augment the product net $\Upsilon_{\neg \varphi}$ with a set L of *livelock monitors* in such way that a new transition $t \in L$ iff there exists a place q in $A_{\neg \varphi}$ such that

$q \in t^{\bullet}$ and, starting from q, the $A_{\neg\varphi}$ accepts an infinite sequence of transitions. Then the situation described above can be formalised by an *illegal livelock*, which is an infinite firing sequence of the form $\tau t^{\sigma} \tau'$ such that $M_0 \xrightarrow{\tau t^{\sigma}} M \xrightarrow{\tau'}$, $t \in L$ and τ' contains only invisible transitions. A formal description for adding L-transitions to $\Upsilon_{\neg\varphi}$ is given in [5].

Theorem 1 (LTL-X Model-Checking of M-Nets). *Let Υ be a strictly safe M-net system whose reachable markings are pairwise incomparable with respect to set inclusion[3], and φ be an LTL-X formula. It is possible to construct a product net system $\Upsilon_{\neg\varphi}$ satisfying the following properties:*

- *Υ satisfies φ iff $\Upsilon_{\neg\varphi}$ has neither illegal ω-traces nor illegal livelocks.*
- *The input and output places of the invisible transitions are the same in Υ and $\Upsilon_{\neg\varphi}$ [4].*

From [4,5] we know that the number of L-transitions can grow exponentially in the size of the M-net system Υ, and so inserting them explicitly into the product net $\Upsilon_{\neg\varphi}$ would seriously hamper this approach. Therefore we follow the trick of [4,5] and generate such transitions on-the-fly during the unfolding procedure. In order to do so we extend the construction of the product net $\Upsilon_{\neg\varphi}$ by the following step:

4. For each Büchi transition, add a copy of it with exactly the same guard and preset, but empty postset. (In our example, these new copies of u_0, u_1 and I_0 are L_0, L_1 and L_2, respectively.) All these new copies form a subset of transitions which are *candidates* to become livelock monitors (L-*transitions*) during the unfolding procedure.

The unfolding procedure makes use of these candidates in such a way that every time when an L-labelled event e could be inserted into the prefix it is checked whether starting from the marking M which is reached by firing e $A_{\neg\varphi}$ accepts an infinite run. If this is the case then the L-event is inserted into the prefix (otherwise it is not), and its preset is expanded to the whole marking M, and its postset is a copy of the preset with instances of the visible, scheduler and Büchi places removed. This guarantees that from this marking only invisible transitions can be fired in the future.

The check whether $A_{\neg\varphi}$ can start an accepting run from M restricted to the Büchi places can be done as follows. Let q be the Büchi place marked under M. We remove from $A_{\neg\varphi}$ all the transitions whose guards are evaluated to **false** under M (and thus cannot fire). Now, in order to check whether there exists an accepting run of $A_{\neg\varphi}$ it is enough to search for a strongly connected component in the obtained graph which is reachable from q and contains at least one I-transition.

---

[3] The latter condition is technical and can be removed [5].

[4] And thus much concurrency is preserved.

4 Tableaux System

We showed in Section 3 that the model-checking problem for LTL-X can be reduced to the problem of finding illegal ω-traces and illegal livelocks. In [4, 5] these problems are solved by considering the prefix as a "distributed" tableaux, in which the conditions are "facts" and the events represent "inferences", with the cut-off events being the *terminals* of the tableaux. We follow this approach, and informally describe how illegal ω-traces and illegal livelocks are detected.

The tableaux $\mathcal{T}$ for $\Upsilon_{\neg\varphi}$ is shown in Figure 3. It contains three terminals, e_{15}, e_{16}, and e_{17}, but for the moment let us concentrate on e_{17}. Since it is a cut-off event of the prefix, there exists a partially ordered execution (po-execution) C ($C = \{e_2\}$ in our example) with the same marking $\{q_0, S, p_1^0, p_3^1\}$ of $\Upsilon_{\neg\varphi}$ as the po-execution $[e_{17}] = \{e_1, \ldots, e_8, e_{12}, e_{14}, e_{17}\}$, where $[e]$ is defined as the minimal (w.r.t. $\subset$) causally closed set of events containing e. Since $C \subset [e_{17}]$, the execution $[e_{17}] \setminus C = \{e_1, e_3, \ldots, e_8, e_{12}, e_{14}, e_{17}\}$ starts and ends at the same marking $\{q_0, S, p_1^0, p_3^1\}$ of $\Upsilon_{\neg\varphi}$, i.e., it can be repeated arbitrarily many times. Moreover, it contains an I-event e_{12}, and thus an illegal ω-trace $\tau\tau'^{\omega}$ is detected, where $\tau \stackrel{\text{df}}{=} u_0$ corresponds to C and $\tau' \stackrel{\text{df}}{=} t_3t_2t_3u_0t_1u_0t_2I_0t_1u_1$ corresponds to $[e_{17}] \setminus C$.

The way of detecting illegal livelocks is quite similar, but in this case a terminal e occurring after an L-event e_L is considered. This means that there exists a po-execution $C \subset [e]$ (which also contains e_L) such that the execution $[e] \setminus C$ starts and ends at the same marking. Now we can use the same argument as above to find an infinite trace $\tau\tau'^{\omega}$, but τ' will contain only transitions of $\Upsilon_{\neg\varphi}$ corresponding to the events occurring after e_L. Since an L-transition empties the scheduler places of tokens, and they are never put back, no visible or Büchi transition of $\Upsilon_{\neg\varphi}$ can be enabled after firing an L-transition. Thus τ' consists only of invisible transitions, i.e., an illegal livelock is detected. (See [4, 5, 10] for more details.)

5 Experimental Results

In this section we present experimental results for the verification of LTL-X properties. We compare our implementation (in the following denoted by PUNF) with the unfolding based LTL-X model-checker for low-level nets UNFSMODELS [5], and with the model-checker SPIN [12]. All experiments are performed on a Linux PC with a 2.4 GHz Intel(R) Xeon(TM) processor and 4 GB of RAM. All times are measured in seconds.

We used UNFSMODELS version 0.9 of 22nd of October 2003, and invoked it with the option -*l* (for LTL-X model-checking).

We used SPIN version 4.0.7 of 1st of August 2003, and invoked it with the options -*DMEMCNT=32* (to allow the use of all 4 GB of memory) and -*DNOFAIR* (as no fairness assumptions were needed). SPIN's partial order reductions were used in all cases (they are enabled by default).

We used PUNF version 7.03 (parallel). In order to have a fair competition against the other tools we invoked PUNF in all examples with the option -*N=1*

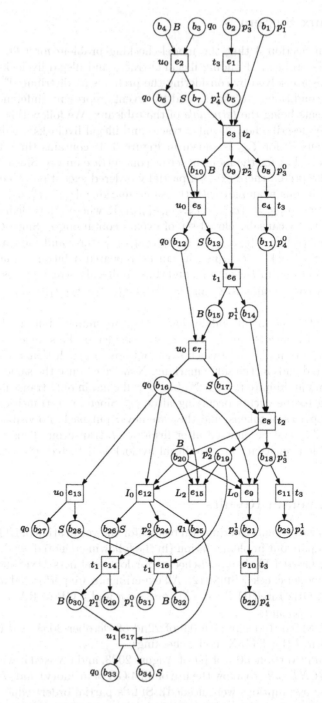

Fig. 3. The tableaux $\mathcal{T}$ for the product net $\Upsilon_{\neg\varphi}$. The colours of conditions are not shown when they are •. The firing modes of events are not shown as they can be derived from their pre- and postsets.

Table 1. Experimental results for LTL-X model-checking.

(a)

Net	Formula	Result	UNFSMDLS	SPIN	PUNF
ABP	$\Box(p \to \Diamond q)$	True	0.19	0.01	0.08
BDS	$\Box(p \to \Diamond q)$	True	199	0.71	8.47
DPD(7)	$\Diamond\Box\neg(p \wedge q \wedge r)$	True	507	2.14	7.25
FURNACE(3)	$\Diamond\Box p$	True	1057	1.00	26.90
GASNQ(4)	$\Diamond\Box p$	True	240	0.14	8.46
RW(12)	$\Box(p \to \Diamond q)$	True	2770	0.44	47.67
FTP	$\Diamond\Box p$	True	>12000	3.99	836
OVER(5)	$\Diamond\Box p$	True	66.01	0.44	0.12
CYCLIC(12)	$\Box(p \to \Diamond q)$	True	0.38	11.25	0.08
RING(9)	$\Diamond\Box p$	True	2.13	1.64	0.13
DP(12)	$\Diamond\Box\neg(p \wedge q \wedge r)$	True	13.05	117	0.36
PH(12)	$\Diamond\Box\neg(p \wedge q \wedge r)$	True	0.04	0.61	0.02
COM(15,0)	$\Box(p \to \neg\Diamond q)$	True	—	3.11	0.02
PAR(5,10)	$\Box(p \to \neg\Diamond q)$	True	—	3.60	0.02

(b)

Net	SPIN	PUNF
CYCLIC(15)	168	0.08
CYCLIC(16)	478	0.07
CYCLIC(17)	1601	0.10
RING(12)	75.38	0.30
RING(13)	274	0.50
RING(14)	1267	0.85
DP(13)	559	0.53
DP(14)	2123	0.75
PH(15)	16.69	0.01
PH(18)	1570	0.01
COM(20,0)	232	0.02
COM(21,0)	686	0.03
COM(22,0)	2279	0.02
PAR(6,10)	161	0.02
PAR(7,10)	mem	0.04

Table 2. Experimental results for the parallel mode.

Net	SPIN	PUNF(1)	PUNF(2)
COM(20,3)	mem	8.58	6.01
COM(22,3)	mem	11.51	8.51
COM(25,3)	mem	17.29	12.84
PAR(20,100)	mem	8.60	4.84
PAR(20,150)	mem	31.98	18.28
BUF(20)	—	22.70	16.95
BUF(25)	—	142.72	89.40

which means that the unfolding procedure is not parallelised, and PUNF uses only one CPU.

The benchmarks (except PH(n), COM(n, m) and PAR(n, m)) are taken from J.C. Corbett [3]. We used only *deadlock-free* examples because our semantics for LTL-X for deadlocking systems is different from SPIN's semantics and thus the results would not be comparable. These benchmarks together with the corresponding result files are available at

http://www.fmi.uni-stuttgart.de/szs/people/schroeter/CAV/cav.tgz.

In order to have a fair contest against SPIN all systems were modelled in *Promela*, all of them (except PH(n), COM(n, m) and PAR(n, m)) by J.C. Corbett [3], but we scaled up some of the benchmarks. The M-nets used as the input for PUNF were automatically derived (using a routine implemented by one of the authors) from SPIN's automata representations of the *Promela* models. The low-level nets used as the input for UNFSMODELS were obtained from the M-nets with the help of the HL2LL utility of the PEP tool [9].

Table 1(a) confirms that our approach outperforms UNFSMODELS on all examples, with an increase of speed up to 550 times (OVER(5) example). But we should mention that as noted in [5] UNFSMODELS is more or less an academic prototype, whereas PUNF is a high-performance unfolding engine. COM(15,0) and PAR(5,10) could not been verified with UNFSMODELS because either the Büchi automaton corresponding to the LTL-X formula for the low-level net (in the former case) or the low level net itself (in the latter case) could not be generated within reasonable time. Comparing PUNF and SPIN one can see that SPIN performs better on the examples over the line. In contrast, PUNF outperforms SPIN on the examples under the line. We wanted to investigate this further and therefore we scaled up these systems and checked them again.

The results are shown in Table 1(b). They seem to confirm that SPIN's verification time grows exponentially with the size of the benchmark, whereas the verification time of PUNF remains less than a second in all cases. All these systems have a high degree of concurrency, and the results show that our partial order technique handles these systems quite well. In contrast, SPIN's partial order reductions are not very efficient on these examples. In our current theory this seems to be related to a reduction condition for LTL-X model-checking which is known as the *reduction proviso* (see, e.g., [2, 19] for further details).

As it was already mentioned, our unfolding routine supports multiple threads running in parallel. To demonstrate this we performed some experiments on a two processor machine.

The results are shown in Table 2. PUNF(n) means that PUNF makes use of n processors. The results confirm that the process of LTL-X model checking can be parallelised quite efficiently. This speeds up the verification, in the best case up to n times. Also the results show that these examples are not verifiable with SPIN because it runs out of memory. (We did not verify the BUF(n) system with SPIN because it was modelled directly as an M-net).

6   Conclusions

We have presented an efficient algorithm for verification of LTL-X properties of high-level Petri nets. We followed an approach proposed by Esparza and Heljanko in [4, 5] for low-level nets, generalised it to M-nets, and implemented it using a state of the art parallel unfolding engine for high-level nets described in [15, 13]. Finally, we presented results showing that our implementation outperforms UNFSMODELS on all examples, and beats SPIN on some examples, mainly those having a high degree of concurrency. To the best of our knowledge, this is the first parallel algorithm for verification of LTL-X properties of high-level Petri nets based on unfoldings.

Acknowledgements

We would like to thank Javier Esparza and Keijo Heljanko for valuable discussions and comments on this topic. This research was supported by EPSRC grants GR/R64322 (AUTOMATIC SYNTHESIS OF DISTRIBUTED SYSTEMS) and GR/R16754 (BESST), and EC IST grant 511599 (RODIN).

References

1. E. Best, H. Fleischhack, W. Fraczak, R. Hopkins, H. Klaudel and E. Pelz: An M-net Semantics of $B(PN)^2$. Proc. of *STRICT'1995*, Berlin (1995) 85–100.
2. E. M. Clarke, O. Grumberg and D. Peled: *Model Checking*. MIT Press (1999).

3. J. C. Corbett: Evaluating Deadlock Detection Methods for Concurrent Software. *IEEE Transactions on Software Engineering* 22(3) (1996) 161–180.
4. J. Esparza and K. Heljanko: A New Unfolding Approach to LTL Model Checking. Proc. of *ICALP'2000*, LNCS 1853 (2000) 475–486.
5. J. Esparza and K. Heljanko: Implementing LTL Model Checking with Net Unfoldings. Proc. of *SPIN'2001*, LNCS 2057 (2001) 37–56.
6. J. Esparza, S. Römer and W. Vogler: An Improvement of McMillan's Unfolding Algorithm. Proc. of *TACAS'1996*, LNCS 1055 (1996) 87–106. Full version: FMSD 20(3) (2002) 285–310.
7. J. Esparza and C. Schröter: Net Reductions for LTL Model-Checking. Proc. of *Correct Hardware Design and Verification Methods*, LNCS 2144 (2001) 310–324.
8. J. Esparza and C. Schröter: Unfolding Based Algorithms for the Reachability Problem. *Fundamenta Informaticae* 47:(3,4) (2001) 231–245.
9. B. Grahlmann, S. Römer, T. Thielke, B. Graves, M. Damm, R. Riemann, L. Jenner, S. Melzer and A. Gronewold: PEP: Programming Environment Based on Petri Nets. Technical Report 14, Universität Hildesheim (1995).
10. K. Heljanko: *Combining Symbolic and Partial Order Methods for Model Checking 1-Safe Petri Nets*. PhD thesis, Helsinki University of Technology (2002).
11. K. Heljanko, V. Khomenko and M. Koutny: Parallelization of the Petri Net Unfolding Algorithm. Proc. of *TACAS'2002*, LNCS 2280 (2002) 371–385.
12. G. J. Holzmann: *The SPIN Model Checker*. Addison-Wesley (2003).
13. V. Khomenko: *Model Checking Based on Prefixes of Petri Net Unfoldings*. PhD Thesis, School of Computing Science, University of Newcastle upon Tyne (2003).
14. V. Khomenko and M. Koutny: Towards An Efficient Algorithm for Unfolding Petri Nets. Proc. of *CONCUR'2001*, LNCS 2154 (2001) 366–380.
15. V. Khomenko and M. Koutny: Branching Processes of High-Level Petri Nets. Proc. of *TACAS'2003*, LNCS 2619 (2003) 458-472.
16. V. Khomenko, M. Koutny and V. Vogler: Canonical Prefixes of Petri Net Unfoldings. Proc. of *CAV'2002*, LNCS 2404 (2002) 582–595. Full version: Acta Informatica 40(2) (2003) 95–118.
17. K. L. McMillan: Using Unfoldings to Avoid State Explosion Problem in the Verification of Asynchronous Circuits. Proc. of *CAV'1992*, LNCS 663 (1992) 164–174.
18. S. Melzer and S. Römer: Deadlock Checking Using Net Unfoldings. Proc. of *CAV'1997*, LNCS 1254 (1997) 352–363.
19. D. Peled: All from One, One for All — on Model Checking Using Representatives. Proc. of *CAV'1993*, LNCS 697 (1993) 409–423.
20. S. Römer: *Entwicklung und Implementierung von Verifikationstechniken auf der Basis von Netzentfaltungen*. PhD thesis, Technische Universität München (2000).
21. M. Y. Vardi and P. Wolper: An Automata Theoretic Approach to Automatic Program Verification. Proc. of *LICS'1986*, Cambridge (1986) 322–331.
22. F. Wallner: Model Checking LTL Using Net Unfoldings. Proc. of *CAV'1998*, LNCS 1427 (1998) 207–218.

Using Interface Refinement to Integrate Formal Verification into the Design Cycle*

Jacob Chang, Sergey Berezin, and David L. Dill

Stanford University
{Jacob.Chang,berezin,dill}@stanford.edu

Abstract. We present a practical compositional interface refinement methodology which helps to integrate formal verification with the design process. One of the main verification challenges is to keep up with the changes to the specifications as the design evolves, and in particular, the transformations to the interfaces between the components. Interface changes are usually incremental, and therefore, the verification efforts after each change should also be incremental in order to be scalable. This paper presents a compositional interface refinement methodology which addresses all of these issues.

We have applied this methodology in the design process of a network controller that will be used in the Smart Memory project at Stanford. The design is split into modules which are modeled as transition systems, and the properties of their interfaces are described in the First-Order LTL. We perform interface refinement by compositional reasoning with the help of an additional interface converter module. Unlike in previous approaches, the inverse converter does not need to be constructed, thus, making the verification of the refinement step simpler.

1 Introduction

The advantage of formal verification over simulation is that one can verify all possible behaviors of a design. This is especially important if the design is complex and has many corner cases that might not be covered by simulation. However, automated methods of formal verification have been limited to relatively small designs [15,5,8,1]. In order to verify a large design formally, one can apply compositional reasoning and refinement techniques [6,9] to split the verification of the low-level implementation into manageable parts. Compositional refinement techniques guarantee that such decomposition preserves the correctness of the entire design.

In this paper, we describe a new compositional interface refinement technique, which is similar to the traditional compositional refinement techniques, except that when an abstract component is refined to its concrete version, its interface is also allowed to change.

---

* This research was supported in part by DARPA contract F29601-032-0117 and NSF grant CCR 0121403.

R. Alur and D.A. Peled (Eds.): CAV 2004, LNCS 3114, pp. 122–134, 2004.

1.1   Interface Refinement

It is a long held belief that if one could integrate formal verification into the design process, then it would make formal verification easier to perform, and improve the design process. Such tight integration was the key to successful microprocessor verification by Kroening in [11].

Integration of formal verification into a top-down design methodology means that a design starts at an abstract level for which exhaustive verification is done. Then, as the design evolves to a more detailed implementation, compositional techniques can be used in order to verify the more detailed design.

However, most of the existing compositional refinement approaches require that the interfaces among the components do not change in the refinement process. This is not an easy requirement to meet, because engineering specifications become more detailed as the design evolves, and this necessitates the refinement of the interfaces. In order to integrate formal verification into the design process, the verification methodology must allow for interface changes that will occur during the course of the design. The problem of verifying that the changes to the interfaces preserve the correctness of the design is called the *interface refinement problem*.

In this paper, we present a methodology that addresses the interface refinement problem in the context of compositional verification. This allows the verification effort to follow the interface changes during the design and avoids the unnecessary restriction on the interfaces imposed by the traditional refinement techniques.

1.2   Our Approach

The problem of interface refinement has been recognized in the past, and a few approaches provide formalization of this problem [3,18,4,7,12]. These results have built several theoretical foundations for interface refinement, but their practical application in real engineering projects so far have been limited.

The most practical approach to interface refinement, to the best of our knowledge, is the method presented by Brinksma et al [3]. Their approach is based on a process algebra framework, and the interfaces are refined through the use of a converter module that converts between the abstract and the concrete interfaces. One of the requirements of this methodology is that the converter must have an inverse.

From our experience with the verification of the Smart Memory network controller, we found that the specifications are more naturally expressed in LTL rather than in process algebra. It is also natural to define the converter as a circuit which translates from the abstract interface to the concrete interface. Furthermore, the inverse of the converter may not exist.

In section 2 we present a generic interface refinement methodology. In particular, it works with the LTL specifications and does not require the existence of the inverse converter. We illustrate our interface refinement methodology by a simple example, then discuss its practical application to the Smart Memory network controller in section 3, and section 4 concludes the paper.

2   Compositional Interface Refinement

Compositional refinement has been extensively studied in the past [6,14], and is now a standard approach to verification of complex systems. We briefly remind the basics of this approach and introduce the formal notation.

For simplicity, let us consider a design consisting of just two modules, X and Y, connected together in parallel by the *parallel composition operator*: $X \| Y$, which we deliberately leave undefined. This operator is assumed to be associative: $(X \| Y) \| Z = X \| (Y \| Z)$, so a composition of more than two modules can be written simply as $X \| Y \| Z$.

Provided that our design $X \| Y$ satisfies the property ϕ (denoted $X \| Y \models \phi$), our goal is to replace each component with a more detailed (or *refined*) implementations X' and Y', respectively, and show that the resulting system $X' \| Y'$ also satisfies ϕ.

More formally, we introduce a *refinement relation* $\preceq$ over modules which preserves the correctness properties from a certain class (e.g. properties expressible in LTL). That is, if $X \models \psi$ and $X' \preceq X$, then $X' \models \psi$ for any property ψ from the chosen class. The refinement relation must be transitive: $X'' \preceq X'$ and $X' \preceq X$ imply $X'' \preceq X$. In addition, we require that the parallel composition operator is associative and monotonic w.r.t. $\preceq$ for both arguments. That is, if $X' \preceq X$, then $X' \| Y \preceq X \| Y$ and $Y \| X' \preceq Y \| X$.

For this section, we leave the operators $\|$ and $\preceq$ undefined, and only assume the following algebraic properties: associativity of $\|$, transitivity of $\preceq$, and monotonicity of $\|$ w.r.t. $\preceq$. This allows the results to be used in various contexts. In particular, we define these operators in a somewhat unusual fashion, over LTL formulas, in section 2.2.

Since the refined components X' and Y' may be rather complex, in order to simplify the verification problem, we would like to reason about each component individually, and avoid verifying $X' \| Y'$ directly. A well-known approach to this problem is know as *compositional refinement* [9], which essentially boils down to showing that

$$X' \preceq X \quad \text{and} \quad Y' \preceq Y. \tag{1}$$

By the monotonicity of $\|$ and transitivity of $\preceq$ the properties (1) imply $X' \| Y' \preceq X \| Y$, and hence, $X' \| Y' \models \phi$, provided that $X \| Y \models \phi$.

Notice that we can show (1) only if modules X' and Y' have the same interfaces as X and Y, respectively. However, in real designs, the interfaces often change as the specifications get refined, as described in section 1, and it is often desirable to refine the interfaces together with the modules.

The problem of *interface refinement* consists in verifying the refinement of a composite module $X \| Y \preceq X' \| Y'$ when the communication interface between the two components changes. For example, we have module X and Y communicating through an abstract interface c as shown in the top portion of figure 1. We want to refine X and Y to X' and Y' such that they communicate over a different protocol d, but their composition $X' \| Y'$ should still have a combined property ϕ, given that the abstract system $X \| Y$ satisfies the same property ϕ.

Notice that if we do indeed change the protocol, the direct compositional refinement does not go through, since the refinement of the individual modules (1) fails.

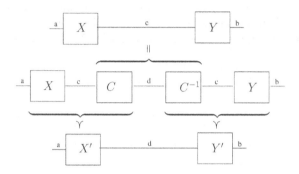

Fig. 1. Interface refinement by Brinksma et al

The interface refinement technique suggested by Brinksma et al [3] (translated to our notation) is to show the following refinements:

$$X' \preceq X \| C \quad \text{and} \quad Y' \preceq C^{-1} \| Y, \tag{2}$$

where C and C^{-1} are *protocol converters* (figure 1). From the monotonicity of $\|$, it immediately follows that $X' \| Y' \preceq X \| C \| C^{-1} \| Y$. Since C^{-1} is the inverse of C, the composition of the two converters $C^{-1} \| C$ is exactly equivalent to the identity function (that is, any input to C appears as the output of C^{-1}). This implies that $X \| C \| C^{-1} \| Y = X \| Y$, and hence, $X' \| Y' \preceq X \| Y$, which is the desired result of the refinement verification.

The problem with this approach is that it is often difficult to find the inverse C^{-1} of the converter C. For instance, if the interface changes from a wide parallel bus (abstract interface) that sends data in a single clock cycle to a serial bus (concrete interface) sending the same data over several clock cycles, the serial-to-parallel converter C would have to "predict the future" in order to output the data the moment it enters the inverse converter C^{-1}. One way to get around this problem is to use the concept of stuttering equivalence [13]. However, we have found that showing that the composition of the converters is the identity model is also difficult under this model.

2.1 Compositional Interface Refinement: Our Approach

Since the abstract interface and the converters will not appear in the concrete implementation, we would like to take advantage of this flexibility in our refinement proof. Thus, we propose the following method for interface refinement.

First, we only perform the refinement on one of the modules, say module Y, by showing that $C\|Y' \preceq Y$, where C is a converter module translating the abstract protocol c to the concrete protocol d. By compositional reasoning, $X\|C\|Y' \preceq X\|Y$ (figure 2), and thus, $X\|C\|Y'$ also satisfies property φ. Next, instead of performing the same refinement step on module X, we show that the concrete module X' is a refinement of the composition $X\|C$. Putting the two refinements together completes the refinement chain: $X'\|Y' \preceq X\|C\|Y' \preceq X\|Y$.

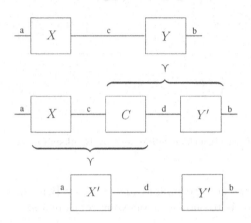

Fig. 2. Interface refinement: our method

Note, that our approach requires only one interface converter, in the direction of our choice; the inverse converter is not needed. This method is also quite general, since it relies on the same algebraic properties of the composition $\|$ and refinement $\preceq$ as the traditional compositional reasoning, and therefore, can be applied in any framework where such properties are satisfied. In particular, the method is applicable even when the composition and refinement operators are defined in non-standard ways (one of which is described in the next section), as long as the required algebraic properties are satisfied.

2.2 First-Order LTL

In the practical application of our compositional interface refinement method, we use a version of First-Order Linear-time Temporal Logic (LTL) similar to the one used in the STeP tool [2] at Stanford. LTL properties are preserved by *trace inclusion*, the type of refinement relation where the refined component has fewer *behaviors*, or *traces* than the abstract component. This logic is expressive enough to permit compositional reasoning with interface refinement directly in the logic. Additionally, LTL is the specification language of Cadence SMV[16], the primary tool we have used to perform the actual verification.

Syntax. We assume two disjoint sets of logical and state variables, V_L and V_S. The syntax of an LTL formula ϕ is given by the following BNF form:

$$\phi ::= \quad p \mid \phi_1 \wedge \phi_2 \mid \neg\phi_1 \mid \mathbf{G}\,\phi_1 \mid \mathbf{F}\,\phi_1 \mid \mathbf{X}\,\phi_2 \mid \phi_1\,\mathbf{U}\,\phi_2 \mid \exists^s u.\,\phi_1 \mid \forall^s u.\,\phi_1$$

where p is an atomic formula, ϕ_1 and ϕ_2 are formulas and $u \in V_S$ is a state variable. Atomic formulas are predicates over state variables.

Semantics. The semantics of an LTL formula ϕ is defined over all paths in a model (Kripke structure) $M = (S, S_0, \rightarrow, D)$, where S is the set of states, $S_0 \subseteq S$ is the set of *initial* states, $\rightarrow \subseteq S \times S$ is the transition relation, and D is the domain of state and logical variables. A state $s \in S$ is an assignment of values from D to state variables; that is $s : V_S \rightarrow D$. We also introduce a logical variable assignment $e : V_L \rightarrow D$.

The semantics of a LTL formula ϕ is defined over a sequences of states called *paths* π that represent execution traces of the model. A state is an assignment to variables that occur in ϕ and, possibly, to other variables. The temporal operators are the same as in propositional LTL. For example, $\pi \models \mathbf{G}\,\phi$ means that ϕ is true everywhere along the path. A quantified formula $\pi \models \forall^s u.\,\phi$ holds if ϕ holds for all paths π' such that π' is the same as π except for assignment to the state variable u. An existential formula $\pi \models \exists^s u.\,\phi$ is defined similarly except that we only need to find one such π' which satisfies ϕ.

An LTL formula ϕ holds in a model M (denoted $M \models \phi$) whenever it holds on any path starting from an initial state of M. We say that a formula ϕ is *valid* ($\models \phi$) whenever it holds in any model.

Compositional Refinement in LTL. The refinement property in this framework is defined as *trace inclusion*, where trace is an execution path π of a particular module A starting from some initial state of A. Recall that in the previous section, we left $\|$ and $\preceq$ undefined and only require that they satisfy certain algebraic properties. In this section, we define these operator in a non-standard way: over LTL formulas. If two modules A and A' satisfy LTL properties ϕ_A and $\phi_{A'}$ respectively, then $A' \preceq A$ is defined by the following formula:

$$\phi_{A'} \rightarrow \exists^s \boldsymbol{u}.\,\phi_A,$$

where $\boldsymbol{u}$ is the vector of all the state variables of ϕ_A which do not occur in $\phi_{A'}$.

Parallel composition of two modules $A\|B$ is simply a conjunction of their respective properties: $\phi_A \wedge \phi_B$. The fact that a composition of modules satisfies some property ϕ can now be derived by

$$\phi_A \wedge \phi_B \rightarrow \phi. \tag{3}$$

These definitions of $\|$ and $\preceq$ clearly satisfy the required algebraic properties stated in section 2.1. Effectively, the actual modules are replaced by their LTL formulas, and all the compositional reasoning is now done completely in LTL.

Interface Refinement in LTL. Our approach to compositional interface refinement translates to the LTL framework as follows. Suppose that the properties $X \models \phi_X$ and $Y \models \phi_Y$ have already been verified, and the desired property of their composition $X\|Y \models \phi$ follows from the fact that

$$\models \phi_X \wedge \phi_Y \to \phi. \tag{4}$$

Additionally, we assume that the concrete modules satisfy their respective properties:

$$X' \models \phi_{X'}, \ Y' \models \phi_{Y'}. \tag{5}$$

Recall in section 2.1, in order to show that the concrete design also satisfies ϕ, that is, $X'\|Y' \models \phi$, it is sufficient to show that $C\|Y' \preceq Y$ and $X' \preceq X\|C$, which translates to LTL as follows:

$$\phi_C \wedge \phi_{Y'} \to \phi_Y \tag{6}$$
$$\phi_{X'} \to \exists^s c. \, \phi_X \wedge \phi_C \tag{7}$$

where ϕ_C is some formula representing the converter module C. Equation (6) does not have the existential quantifier because all the free variables in ϕ_Y appear on the left hand side of the implication. Note, that there are no restrictions on the formula ϕ_C. In particular, the actual converter C does not have to be built (and may, in fact, be unimplementable), and $C \models \phi_C$ does not need to be checked.

3 Examples and Applications

In this section, we first demonstrate the practical application of our method on a very simple example: composition of two modules passing an L-bit value from input to output over an L-bit wide bus, and its refinement to the two modules which communicate through a serial bus (1-bit wide). Then we describe a more realistic example of an actual design in the context of the Smart Memory Project.

3.1 A Simple Example for Illustration

Suppose that we have two modules X and Y that pass the input from a to c and from c to b as shown in figure (3a), modifying the data with functions f_X and f_Y; that is, given the input D, the corresponding output will be $f_Y(f_X(D))$. Signal c is a parallel interface that is L bits wide, and is represented as a record

$$c : \{\text{valid} : \textbf{bool}, \text{ data} : \textbf{bool}[L]\} \,.$$

The transmission of data occurs when the valid bit is set to 1, and the data field is supposed to contain the valid data in the same cycle. The property that the

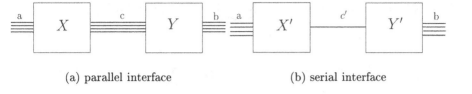

(a) parallel interface   (b) serial interface

Fig. 3. Systems with parallel and serial interfaces

data D : **bool**$[L]$ is sent over the channel c at the current cycle is expressed in LTL as follows:

$$c \rightrightarrows D \triangleq [c.\text{valid} = 1 \wedge c.\text{data} = D].$$

The property of the composed system is then written as follows:

$$\phi \triangleq \forall(D : \textbf{bool}[L]). \, \textbf{G} \, (a \rightrightarrows D \rightarrow \textbf{F} \, [b \rightrightarrows f_Y(f_X(D))]).$$

Suppose that the abstract components X and Y satisfy the properties ϕ_X and ϕ_Y, respectively, where

$$\phi_X \triangleq \forall D. \, \textbf{G} \, (a \rightrightarrows D \rightarrow \textbf{F} \, [c \rightrightarrows f_X(D)])$$
$$\phi_Y \triangleq \forall D. \, \textbf{G} \, (c \rightrightarrows D \rightarrow \textbf{F} \, [b \rightrightarrows f_Y(D)]),$$

and we have already established that

$$\phi_X \wedge \phi_Y \rightarrow \phi. \tag{8}$$

The concrete implementation of the system consists of two components X' and Y' which communicate over a serial bus c' as shown in figure (3b).

A serial interface c' is a record, similar to the concrete interface, only the data field is one bit wide:

$$c' : \{\text{first\_bit} : \textbf{bool}, \text{bit} : \textbf{bool}\}.$$

A valid transmission of an L-bit data D over the serial bus c' starts when the first_bit field becomes 1; at this point, the bit field contain the first bit of the data, $D[0]$, and in the subsequent $L-1$ cycles first_bit remains 0 while the bit field takes the values of the remaining bits $D[1]$ through $D[L-1]$. Such a transmission is expressed in LTL as the following formula:

$$c' \rightsquigarrow D \triangleq \quad c'.\text{first\_bit} = 1 \wedge \text{bit} = D[0]$$
$$\wedge \bigwedge_{i=1}^{L-1} \textbf{X}^i(c'.\text{first\_bit} = 0 \wedge c'.\text{bit} = D[i]),$$

where $\mathbf{X}^i\phi$ is an abbreviation for $\underbrace{\mathbf{X}\ldots\mathbf{X}}_{i}\phi$. The properties of the concrete modules can now be written as follows:

$$\phi_{X'} \triangleq \forall D.\, \mathbf{G}\,(a \rightrightarrows D \to \mathbf{F}\,[c' \rightsquigarrow f_X(D) \wedge \bigwedge_{i=0}^{L-1} \mathbf{X}^i X'.d = f_X(D)])$$

$$\phi_{Y'} \triangleq \forall D.\, \mathbf{G}\,(c' \rightsquigarrow D \to \mathbf{F}\,[b \rightrightarrows f_Y(D)]).$$

Here $X'.d$ is the internal buffer of X' holding the data currently being transmitted on its output bus c'. The formula $\phi_{X'}$ states that X' will eventually start sending the data it receives on the input a, and while the transmission is active, the buffer $X'.d$ will hold the entire data being transmitted. In this case, we would like to establish that

$$\phi_{X'} \wedge \phi_{Y'} \to \phi. \tag{9}$$

However, we do not want to prove this formula directly, and instead, use the already proved property (8). As the first step, we come up with the following property:

$$\phi_C \triangleq \forall D.\, \mathbf{G}\,(c \rightrightarrows D \to c' \rightsquigarrow D)$$

which a protocol converter C would satisfy if we were to build it. Note, that the converter has no delay between receiving the parallel data and starting to send the same data over the serial output. As such, this module is unimplementable, since the parallel input may exceed the data rate of the serial output. However, this property is sufficient to prove the correctness of the refinement.

According to our methodology, in order to establish (9), it is sufficient to show that the following two formulas hold:

$$\phi_C \wedge \phi_{Y'} \to \phi_Y \tag{10}$$

$$\phi_{X'} \to \exists c.\, \phi_X \wedge \phi_C. \tag{11}$$

These two refinements are illustrated in figures 4(a) and 4(b). In (11), the parallel composition $X\|C$ has a nondeterministic state variable c, which is the state of the internal wire between X and C. In order to show that X' is a refinement of $X\|C$, we need to show that for any trace of X' there exists an equivalent trace of $X\|C$. A particular trace of $X\|C$ can be chosen by a particular sequence of values for the variable c. This fact is denoted by the existential quantifier over c. When we provide an instantiation for c as

$$c \triangleq \{\mathsf{valid} = c'.\mathsf{first\_bit},\ \mathsf{data} = X'.d\}\,,$$

then it will yield the equivalent trace of $X\|C$ for any trace of X'. Note, that this instantiation also prevent overflowing the converter C with excessive data on the input, since it can only receive the data as fast as X' can send it, which is exactly the rate of the serial bus. From this point, proving (10) and (11) is a relatively simple exercise.

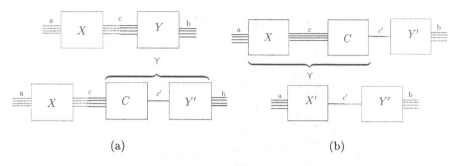

(a)   (b)

Fig. 4. Refinement of X and Y.

3.2   Application to Smart Memory Network Controller

The Smart Memory project aims at developing a single chip multi processor system with reconfiguration capabilities to support various computing models. An on-chip network is required in this project to allow different sets of processors on the chip to communicate with each other.

When the design of the Smart Memory network controller was started, it was clear that getting it right would be a quite difficult task due to the complex interactions among multiple nodes in the network. Therefore, we decided to use formal verification in the design process to guarantee the correctness from the early stages, and preserve it as the design evolves. The practical demands of this engineering effort required the use of effective compositional reasoning together with interface refinement techniques, which eventually led to the results presented in this paper.

Smart Memory Network description. The Smart Memory chip is divided up into 16 nodes. The Smart Memory network passes short control messages as well as large chunks of data between these nodes. The topology of the network is such that each node connects to its four neighbors as well as the nodes that are two spaces away. Thus each quad has six input and output ports as shown in figure 5. Since the messages are of different sizes, we split the messages into smaller fixed length data unit called *flits* which are then transmitted over the network. To meet the latency constraints, all the routing information is placed in the header flit, and the data flits follow the same route. The route is determined dynamically by allocating physical connections, which constitute a limited shared resource. Since messages are sent in parallel, it is possible for the system to deadlock when two streams of flits are waiting for each other's resources.

Problem Statement. To formally verify the correctness of the network, we need to prove the guaranteed delivery of messages to the correct destination

Network Topology

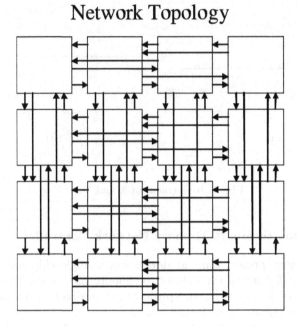

Fig. 5.

without duplication or loss. Proving that the routing algorithm correctly routes messages is already an interesting verification problem. The fact that messages are not atomic but consist of individual flits makes the verification problem even more difficult.

High level description of the interface refinement process. To simplify the verification process, we generalize the network to have arbitrary number of nodes and a parameterized connection scheme with certain restrictions on the topology (e.g. each input port is connected an output port, there is a route between every two nodes, etc.). At the abstract level, we describe the messages delivered by the network in terms of packets. The specification of each node acting on packets are specified by their properties in the assume-guarantee style. These restriction and specifications are easily encoded in LTL. We prove the correctness of packet routing given the node specifications without having to worry about the complexity of breaking up the packet into flits.

Then we refine the interface such that the communication between nodes are flits instead of packets. The correctness of the refined interface are checked by using our tool to process the LTL specifications and converted into verification conditions (7) and (10) which are then proved by Cadence SMV. The problem of refining the message interface to the flit interface is similar in spirit as the example illustrated in section 3.1. However, the fact that each node is connected to many other nodes, the message length can be of different size, and the presence of a flow control mechanism make the problem much more complex.

We then perform another refinement of the interface by adding the flow control to the flit interface using the same methodology.

We estimate that the the first refinement step took us about 10 hours, and about 10 hours were spent on expanding the existing toolset, although this does not include the time spent in our preliminary work with a similar simpler example to develop this methodology. The verification run performed by SMV for each verification condition our tool generate all finish within a minute.

4 Conclusion

We have demonstrated that interface refinement allows us to reuse the correctness proof of a design as the designer makes changes to the interface or makes the interface more concrete during the design cycle. Interface refinement also allows us to apply the divide-and-conquer technique to a large design by incrementally making the protocol more complex.

By applying our technique to the Smart Memory network controller during the design process, we have demonstrated that our interface refinement methodology can be used to allow formal verification to be done in parallel with design. Currently, the Smart Memory Network controller is still in the design stage and no concrete design have been written, therefore we have not made the link between the Hardware Description Language (HDL) description of the design with the LTL specification we have used for the modules. However, SMV is known for proving the LTL specification of the HDL description [10,17], and we foresee that it is possible to verify the HDL description of the network controller.

In addition to the method presented in this paper, we developed additional techniques specific to our toolset to perform the interface refinement of the network controller presented in this paper. These techniques allow us to describe the specifications in a more intuitive manner and deal with the more complex configuration such as a circular configuration.

The interface refinement methodology is being developed as a part of the larger project to formally verify the Smart Memory network controller, showing that formal verification can be applied to a large engineering design. In the future, we hope to demonstrate the feasibility of formally verifying a large design project by integrating verification into the design process. We believe that developing a methodology with the feedback and the pressure of the design team will allow us to address the important issues that are hindering formal verification from being commonly used.

Acknowledgements. The authors would like to thank Mark Horowitz and the Smart Memory design team for guiding the direction of this research. We would also like to thank the anonymous reviewers for helpful comments on the paper.

References

1. C. Barrett, D. L. Dill, and J. Levitt. Validity checking for combinations of theories with equality. In Mandayam Srivas and Albert Camilleri, editors, *Formal Methods In Computer-Aided Design*, volume 1166 of *Lecture Notes in Computer Science*, pages 187–201. Springer-Verlag, November 1996.
2. N. Bjørner, A. Browne, M. Colon, B. Finkbeiner, Z. Manna, H. Sipma, and T. Uribe. Verifying temporal properties of reactive systems: A STeP tutorial. *Formal Methods in System Design*, 1999.
3. E. Brinksma, B. Jonsson, and F. Orava. Refining interfaces of communicating systems. In S. Abramsky and T. S. E. Maibaum, editors, *TAPSOFT '91, Volume 2*, volume 494 of *LNCS*, pages 297–312. SV, 1991.
4. M. Broy. Interaction refinement—the easy way. In *Program Design Calculi: Proceedings of the 1992 Marktoberdorf International Summer School*. Springer-Verlag, 1993.
5. J. R. Burch and D. L. Dill. Automatic verification of pipelined microprocessor control. In D. L. Dill, editor, *Computer Aided Verification (CAV'94)*, volume 818 of *LNCS*. Springer-Verlag, 1994.
6. E. M. Clarke, D. E. Long, and K. L. McMillan. Compositional model checking. In *Fourth Annual Symposium on Logic in Computer Science*, pages 353–62. Washington, DC, USA : IEEE Comput. Soc. Press, 1989, June 1989.
7. R. Gerth, R. Kupiter, and J. Segers. Interface refinement in reactive systems. In *CONCUR '92 Third International Conference on Concurrency Theory*, pages 77–93. Springer-Verlag, Aug 1992.
8. D. Greve. Symbolic simulation of the JEM1 microprocessor. In *Formal Methods in Computer-Aided Design (FMCAD '98)*, volume 1522 of *Lecture Notes in Computer Science*, pages 321–333, 1998.
9. O. Grumberg and D. E. Long. Model checking and modular verification. *ACM Transactions on Programming Languages and Systems*, 16(3):843–871, May 1994.
10. R. Jhala and K. L. McMillan. Microarchitecture verification by compositional model checking. In A. Finkel G. Berry, H. Comon, editor, *Computer Aided Verification: 13th International Conference*, volume 2102 of *Lecture Notes in Computer Science*, pages 396–410. Springer-Verlag, 2001.
11. D. Kroning. *Formal Verification of Pipelined Microprocessors*. PhD thesis, Saarland University, 2001.
12. R. Kurki-Suonio. Component and interface refinement in closed-system specifications. In *World Congress on Formal Methods (1)*, pages 134–154, 1999.
13. L. Lamport. What good is temporal logic? In R.E.A. Mason, editor, *Information Processing*, pages 657–668. Elsevier, 1983.
14. D. E. Long. *Model Checking, Abstraction, and Compositional Verification*. PhD thesis, Carnegie Mellon University, 1993.
15. K. L. McMillan. Verification of an implementation of Tomasulo's algorithm by compositional model checking. In A. J. Hu and M. Y. Vardi, editors, *Computer Aided Verification (CAV'98)*, volume 1427 of *LNCS*. Springer-Verlag, June 1998.
16. K. L. McMillan. *Getting started with SMV*, March 1999.
17. K. L. McMillan. Parameterized verification of the flash cache coherence protocol by compositional model checking. In *Correct Hardware Design and Verification Methods: 11th IFIP WG10.5 Advanced Research Working Conference*, volume 2144 of *Lecture Notes in Computer Science*, pages 179–195. Springer-Verlag, 2001.
18. A. Rensink and R. Gorrieri. Vertical implementation. *Information and Computation*, 170:95–133, 2001.

Indexed Predicate Discovery
for Unbounded System Verification[*]

Shuvendu K. Lahiri and Randal E. Bryant

Carnegie Mellon University, Pittsburgh, PA
shuvendu@ece.cmu.edu, Randy.Bryant@cs.cmu.edu

Abstract. Predicate abstraction has been proved effective for verifying several infinite-state systems. In predicate abstraction, an abstract system is automatically constructed given a set of predicates. Predicate abstraction coupled with automatic predicate discovery provides for a completely automatic verification scheme. For systems with unbounded integer state variables (e.g. software), counterexample guided predicate discovery has been successful in identifying the necessary predicates.

For verifying systems with function state variables, which include systems with unbounded memories (microprocessors), arrays in programs, and parameterized systems, an extension to predicate abstraction has been suggested which uses predicates with *free* (index) variables. Unfortunately, counterexample guided predicate discovery is not applicable to this method. In this paper, we propose a simple heuristic for discovering indexed predicates. We illustrate the effectiveness of the approach for verifying safety properties of two systems: (i) a version of the Bakery mutual exclusion protocol, and (ii) a directory-based cache coherence protocol with unbounded FIFO channels per client.

1 Introduction

Predicate abstraction [15] has emerged as a successful technique for analyzing infinite-state systems. The infinite-state systems consist of both hardware and software systems, where the state variables can assume arbitrarily large sets of values. Predicate abstraction, which is a special instance of the more general theory of *abstract interpretation* [9], automatically constructs a finite-state abstract system from a potentially infinite state concrete system, given a set of *predicates* (where a predicate describes some property of the concrete system). The abstract system can be used to synthesize inductive invariants or perform model checking to verify properties of the concrete system.

For synthesizing inductive invariants, predicate abstraction can be viewed as a systematic way to compose a set of predicates $\mathcal{P}$ using the Boolean connectives ($\land$, $\lor$, $\neg$) to construct the strongest inductive invariant that can be expressed with these predicates. This process can be made efficient by using symbolic and Boolean techniques based on incremental SAT and BDD-based algorithms [21, 7]. Thus, predicate abstraction can construct complex invariants given a set of predicates.

---

[*] This research was supported in part by the Semiconductor Research Corporation, Contract RID 1029.001.

For systems which do not require quantified invariants, it suffices to use simple atomic predicates (predicates do not contain $\vee$, $\wedge$ or $\neg$). The simplicity of the predicates make them amenable to automatic predicate discovery schemes [2, 6, 17]. All these methods use the framework of counterexample-guided abstraction refinement [19, 8] to add new predicates which eliminate spurious counterexample traces over the abstract system. Automatic predicate discovery coupled with the automatic abstraction provided by predicate abstraction makes the verification process fully automatic. This has been the cornerstone of many successful verification systems based on predicate abstraction [2, 6, 17].

To verify systems containing unbounded resources, such as buffers and memories of arbitrary size and systems with arbitrary number of identical, concurrent processes, the system model must support state variables that are mutable functions or predicates [25, 10, 5]. For example, a memory can be represented as a function mapping an address to the data stored at an address, while a buffer can be represented as a function mapping an integer index to the value stored at the specified buffer position. The state elements of a set of identical processes can be modeled as functions mapping an integer process identifier to the state element for the specified process.

To verify systems with function state variables, we require quantified predicates to describe global properties of state variables, such as "At most one process is in its critical section," as expressed by the formula $\forall i, j : \mathtt{crit}(i) \wedge \mathtt{crit}(j) \Rightarrow i = j$. Conventional predicate abstraction restricts the scope of a quantifier to within an individual predicate. System invariants often involve complex formulas with widely scoped quantifiers. The scoping restriction (the fact that quantifiers do not distribute over Boolean connectives) implies that these invariants cannot be divided into small, simple predicates. This puts a heavy burden on the user to supply predicates that encode intricate sets of properties about the system. Recent work attempts to discover quantified predicates automatically [10], but it has not been successful for many of the systems that we consider.

Our earlier work [21, 20] and the work by Flanagan and Qadeer (in the context of unbounded arrays in software) [13] overcome this problem by allowing the predicates to include free variables from a set of *index* variables $\mathcal{X}$. We call these predicates as *indexed* predicates. The predicate abstraction engine constructs a formula ψ^* consisting of a Boolean combination of these predicates, such that the formula $\forall \mathcal{X} \psi^*(s)$ holds for every reachable system state s. With this method, the predicates can be very simple, with the predicate abstraction tool constructing complex, quantified invariant formulas. For example, the property that at most one process can be in its critical section could be derived by supplying predicates $\mathtt{crit(i)}$, $\mathtt{crit(j)}$, and $\mathtt{i} = \mathtt{j}$, where $\mathtt{i}$ and $\mathtt{j}$ are the index variables.

One of the consequences of adding indexed predicates is that the state space defined over the predicates does not have a transition relation [20]. This is a consequence of the fact that the abstraction function α maps each concrete state to a *set* of abstract states, instead of a single abstract state as happens in predicate abstraction [15]. The lack of an abstract transition relation prevents us from generating an abstract trace and thus rules out the counterexample-guided refinement framework.

In this work, we look at a technique to generate the set of predicates iteratively. Our idea is based on generating predicates by computing the *weakest liberal precondition* [11], similar to Namjoshi and Kurshan [27] and Lakhnech et al. [23]. Our method differs from [27] in that we simply use the technique as a heuristic for discovering useful indexed predicates. We rely on predicate abstraction to construct invariants using these predicates. The method in [27] proposed computing the abstract transition relation on-the-fly using the weakest precondition. The methods in [23, 6] can be seen as generating new (quantifier-free) predicates using the counterexample-guided refinement framework with some acceleration techniques in [23].

The techniques have been integrated in UCLID [5] verifier, which supports a variety of different modeling and verification techniques for infinite-state systems. We describe the use of the predicate inference scheme for verifying the safety properties of two protocols: (i) A version of the N-process Bakery algorithm by Lamport [24], where the reads and writes are atomic and (ii) A extension of the cache-coherence protocol devised by Steven German of IBM [14], where each client communicates to the central process using unbounded channels. The protocols were previously verified by manually constructing predicates in [20]. In contrast, in this work the protocols are verified almost automatically with minimal intervention from the user.

Related Work. The method of invisible invariants [28, 1] uses heuristics for constructing universally quantified invariants for parameterized systems automatically. The method computes the set of reachable states for finite (and small) instances of the parameters and then generalizes them to parameterized systems to construct the inductive invariant. The method has been successfully used to verify German's protocol with single entry channels and a version of the Bakery algorithm, where all the tickets have an upper bound and a loop is abstracted with an atomic test. However, the class of system handled by the method is restricted; it can't be applied to the extension of the cache-coherence protocol we consider in this paper or an out-of-order processor that is considered in our method [22].

McMillan uses compositional model checking [25] with various built in abstractions and symmetry reduction to reduce an infinite-state system to a finite state version, which can be model checked using Boolean methods. Since the abstraction mechanisms are built into the system, they can often be very coarse and may not suffice for proving a system. Besides, the user is often required to provide auxiliary lemmas or to decompose the proof to be discharged by symbolic model checkers. The proof of safety of the Bakery protocol required non-trivial lemmas in the compositional model checking framework [26].

Regular model checking [18, 4] uses regular languages to represent parameterized systems and computes the closure for the regular relations to construct the reachable state space. In general, the method is not guaranteed to be complete and requires various *acceleration* techniques (sometimes guided by the user) to ensure termination. Moreover, several examples can't be modeled in this framework; the out-of-order processor or the Peterson's mutual exclusion (which can be modeled in our framework) are few such examples. Even though the Bakery algorithm can be verified in this framework, it requires user ingenuity to encode the protocol in a regular language.

Emerson and Kahlon [12] have verified the version of German's cache coherence protocol with single entry channels by reducing it to a snoopy protocol, which can in turn be verified automatically by considering finite instances of the parameterized problem. However, the reduction is manually performed and exploits details of operation of the protocol, and thus requires user ingenuity. It can't be easily extended to verify other unbounded systems including the Bakery algorithm or the out-of-order processors.

Predicate abstraction with locally quantified predicates [10,3] require complex quantified predicates to construct the inductive assertions, as mentioned in the introduction. These predicates are often as complex as invariants themselves. The method in [3] verified (both safety and liveness) a version of the cache coherence protocol with single entry channels, with complex manually provided predicates. In comparison, our method constructs an inductive invariant automatically to prove cache coherence. Till date, automatic predicate discovery methods for quantified predicates [10] have not been demonstrated on the examples we consider in this paper.

2 Preliminaries

The concrete system is defined in terms of a decidable subset of first-order logic. Our implementation is based on the CLU logic [5], supporting expressions containing uninterpreted functions and predicates, equality and ordering tests, and addition by integer constants. The logic supports Booleans, integers, functions mapping integers to integers, and predicates mapping integers to Booleans.

2.1 Notation

Rather than using the common *indexed vector* notation to represent collections of values (e.g., $v \doteq \langle v_1, v_2, \ldots, v_n \rangle$), we use a *named set* notation. That is, for a set of symbols $\mathcal{A}$, we let $\mathbf{v}$ indicate a set consisting of a value v_x for each $x \in \mathcal{A}$.

For a set of symbols $\mathcal{A}$, let $\sigma_{\mathcal{A}}$ denote an *interpretation* of these symbols, assigning to each symbol $x \in \mathcal{A}$ a value $\sigma_{\mathcal{A}}(x)$ of the appropriate type (Boolean, integer, function, or predicate). Let $\Sigma_{\mathcal{A}}$ denote the set of all interpretations $\sigma_{\mathcal{A}}$ over the symbol set $\mathcal{A}$. Let $\sigma_{\mathcal{A}} \cdot \sigma_{\mathcal{B}}$ be the result of combining interpretations $\sigma_{\mathcal{A}}$ and $\sigma_{\mathcal{B}}$ over disjoint set of symbols $\mathcal{A}$ and $\mathcal{B}$.

For symbol set $\mathcal{A}$, let $E(\mathcal{A})$ denote the set of all expressions in the logic over $\mathcal{A}$. For any expression $e \in E(\mathcal{A})$ and interpretation $\sigma_{\mathcal{A}} \in \Sigma_{\mathcal{A}}$, let $\langle e \rangle_{\sigma_{\mathcal{A}}}$ be the value obtained by evaluating e when each symbol $x \in \mathcal{A}$ is replaced by its interpretation $\sigma_{\mathcal{A}}(x)$. For a set of expressions $\mathbf{v}$, such that $v_x \in E(\mathcal{B})$, we extend $\langle \mathbf{v} \rangle_{\sigma_{\mathcal{B}}}$ to denote the (named) set of values obtained by applying $\sigma_{\mathcal{B}}$ to each element v_x of the set.

A *substitution* π for a set of symbols $\mathcal{A}$ is a named set of expressions, such that for each $x \in \mathcal{A}$, there is an expression π_x in π. For an expression e we let $e\,[\pi/\mathcal{A}]$ denote the expression resulting when we (simultaneously) replace each occurrence of every symbol $x \in \mathcal{A}$ with the expression π_x.

2.2 System Description and Concrete System

We model the system as having a number of *state elements*, where each state element may be a Boolean or integer value, or a function or predicate. We use symbolic names to represent the different state elements giving the set of *state symbols* $\mathcal{V}$. We introduce a set of *initial state* symbols $\mathcal{J}$ and a set of *input* symbols $\mathcal{I}$ representing, respectively, initial values and inputs that can be set to arbitrary values on each step of operation. Among the state variables, there can be *immutable* values expressing the behavior of functional units, such as ALUs, and system parameters such as the total number of processes or the maximum size of a buffer.

The overall system operation is described by an *initial-state* expression set $\mathbf{q}^0$ and a *next-state* expression set $\boldsymbol{\delta}$. That is, for each state element $\mathbf{x} \in \mathcal{V}$, the expressions $q_{\mathbf{x}}^0 \in E(\mathcal{J})$ and $\delta_{\mathbf{x}} \in E(\mathcal{V} \cup \mathcal{I})$ denote the initial state expression and the next state expression for $\mathbf{x}$.

A concrete system state assigns an interpretation to every state symbol. The set of states of the concrete system is given by $\Sigma_{\mathcal{V}}$, the set of interpretations of the state element symbols. For convenience, we denote concrete states using letters s and t rather than the more formal $\sigma_{\mathcal{V}}$.

From our system model, we can characterize the behavior of the concrete system in terms of an initial state set $Q_C^0 \subseteq \Sigma_{\mathcal{V}}$ and a next-state function operating on sets $N_C \colon \mathscr{P}(\Sigma_{\mathcal{V}}) \rightarrow \mathscr{P}(\Sigma_{\mathcal{V}})$. The initial state set is defined as $Q_C^0 \doteq \{\langle \mathbf{q}^0 \rangle_{\sigma_{\mathcal{J}}} | \sigma_{\mathcal{J}} \in \Sigma_{\mathcal{J}}\}$, i.e., the set of all possible valuations of the initial state expressions. The next-state function N_C is defined for a single state s as $N_C(s) \doteq \{\langle \boldsymbol{\delta} \rangle_{s \cdot \sigma_{\mathcal{I}}} | \sigma_{\mathcal{I}} \in \Sigma_{\mathcal{I}}\}$, i.e., the set of all valuations of the next-state expressions for concrete state s and arbitrary input. The function is then extended to sets of states by defining $N_C(S_C) = \bigcup_{s \in S_C} N_C(s)$. We define the set of reachable states R_C as containing those states s such that there is some state sequence $s_0, s_1, \ldots, s_n$ with $s_0 \in Q_C^0$, $s_n = s$, and $s_{i+1} \in N_C(s_i)$ for all values of i such that $0 \leq i < n$.

3   Predicate Abstraction with Indexed Predicates

We use indexed predicates to express constraints on the system state. To define the abstract state space, we introduce a set of *predicate* symbols $\mathcal{P}$ and a set of *index* symbols $\mathcal{X}$. The predicates consist of a named set ϕ, where for each $\mathbf{p} \in \mathcal{P}$, predicate $\phi_{\mathbf{p}}$ is a Boolean formula over the symbols in $\mathcal{V} \cup \mathcal{X}$.

Our predicates define an abstract state space $\Sigma_{\mathcal{P}}$, consisting of all interpretations $\sigma_{\mathcal{P}}$ of the predicate symbols. For $k \doteq |\mathcal{P}|$, the state space contains 2^k elements. We can denote a set of abstract states by a Boolean formula $\psi \in E(\mathcal{P})$. This expression defines a set of states $\langle \psi \rangle \doteq \{\sigma_{\mathcal{P}} | \langle \psi \rangle_{\sigma_{\mathcal{P}}} = \mathbf{true}\}$.

We define the *abstraction function* α to map each concrete state to the set of abstract states given by the valuations of the predicates for all possible values of the index variables: $\alpha(s) \doteq \{\langle \phi \rangle_{s \cdot \sigma_{\mathcal{X}}} | \sigma_{\mathcal{X}} \in \Sigma_{\mathcal{X}}\}$. We then extend the abstraction function to apply to sets of concrete states in the usual way: $\alpha(S_C) \doteq \bigcup_{s \in S_C} \alpha(s)$.

We define the concretization function γ for a set of abstract states $S_A \subseteq \Sigma_{\mathcal{P}}$: $\gamma(S_A) \doteq \{s | \forall \sigma_{\mathcal{X}} \in \Sigma_{\mathcal{X}} : \langle \phi \rangle_{s \cdot \sigma_{\mathcal{X}}} \in S_A\}$, to require universal quantification over the index symbols.

The universal quantifier in this definition has the consequence that the concretization function does not distribute over set union. In particular, we cannot view the concretization function as operating on individual abstract states, but rather as generating each concrete state from multiple abstract states.

Predicate abstraction involves performing a reachability analysis over the abstract state space, where on each step we concretize the abstract state set via γ, apply the concrete next-state function, and then abstract the results via α. We can view this process as performing reachability analysis on an abstract system having initial state set $Q_A^0 \doteq \alpha(Q_C^0)$ and a next-state function operating on sets: $N_A(S_A) \doteq \alpha(N_C(\gamma(S_A)))$.

It is important to note that there is no transition relation associated with this next-state function, since γ cannot be viewed as operating on individual abstract states. In previous work [20], we provide examples where a pair of abstract states s_a and s_a' each has an empty set of abstract successors, but the set of successors of $\{s_a, s_a'\}$ is non-empty.

We perform reachability analysis on the abstract system using N_A as the next-state function: $R_A^0 = Q_A^0$ and $R_A^{i+1} = R_A^i \cup N_A(R_A^i)$. Since the abstract system is finite, there must be some n such that $R_A^n = R_A^{n+1}$. The set of all reachable abstract states R_A is then R_A^n. Let $\rho_A \in E(\mathcal{P})$ be the expression representing R_A. The corresponding set of concrete states is given by $\gamma(R_A)$, and can be represented by the expression $\forall \mathcal{X} : \rho_A [\phi/\mathcal{P}]$. In previous work [20], we showed that the concretization of R_A (or equivalently $\forall \mathcal{X} : \rho_A [\phi/\mathcal{P}]$) is the strongest universally quantified inductive invariant that can be constructed from the set of predicates.

Since there is no complete way for handling quantifiers in first order logic with equality and uninterpreted functions [16], we resort to sound quantifier instantiation techniques to compute an overapproximation of the abstract state space. The quantifier instantiation method uses heuristics to choose a finite set of terms from the possible infinite range of values and replaces the universal quantifier by a finite conjunction over the terms. More details of the technique can be found in [20] and details of the quantifier instantiation heuristic can be found in [22]. The method has sufficed for all the examples we have seen so far. The predicate abstraction is carried out efficiently by using Boolean techniques [21].

The inductive invariant is then used to prove the property of interest by the decision procedure inside UCLID. If the assertion holds, then the property is proved. We have used this method to verify safety properties of cache-coherence protocols, mutual exclusion algorithms, out-of-order microprocessors and sequential software programs with unbounded arrays [20]. However, most predicates were derived manually by looking at failures or adding predicates that appear in the transition function.

4 Indexed Predicate Discovery

This section presents a syntactic method for generating indexed predicates, based on *weakest liberal precondition* [11] transformer. A similar idea has been used in [23], but they do not consider indexed predicates. As a result, they can use methods based on analyzing abstract counterexample traces to refine the set of predicates. In our case, we only use it as a syntactic heuristic for generating new predicates. An inexpensive syntactic heuristic is also more suited to our approach since computing the inductive invariant is an expensive process [20] for large number of predicates (> 30), even with the recent advances in symbolic methods for predicate abstraction [21]. More importantly, the simple heuristic has sufficed for automating the verification of non-trivial problems.

The *weakest precondition* of a set of states S_C is the largest set of states T_C, such that for any state $t_c \in T_C$, the successor states lie in S_C. If Ψ_C is an expression representing the set of states S_C, then the expression which represents the WP(Ψ_C) is $\forall \mathcal{I} : \Psi_C [\delta/\mathcal{V}]$. To obtain this expression in terms of the state variables, one would have to perform quantifier elimination to eliminate the input symbols $\mathcal{I}$. In general, eliminating quantifiers over integer symbols in the presence of uninterpreted functions in $\Psi_C [\delta/\mathcal{V}]$ is undecidable [16].

Let us see the intuition (without any rigorous formal basis, since its only a heuristic) for using WP for predicate discovery. Consider a predicate ϕ without any index variables. A predicate represents a property of the concrete system, since it is a Boolean formula over the state variables. Thus, if WP(ϕ) (WP($\neg\phi$)) is true at a state, then ϕ (respectively $\neg\phi$) will be true in the next state. Therefore the predicates which appear in WP(ϕ) are important when tracking the truth of the predicate ϕ accurately. Since computing WP(ϕ) as a predicate over $\mathcal{V}$ is undecidable in general, we choose predicates from $\Psi_C [\delta/\mathcal{V}]$ without explicitly eliminating the quantifiers over $\mathcal{I}$. We later provide a strategy to deal with predicates which involve input symbols. This intuition can be naturally extended to indexed predicates. In this case, our aim is to generate predicates which involve the index symbols. For a predicate ϕ over $\mathcal{V} \cup \mathcal{X}$, the predicates in $\phi [\delta/\mathcal{V}]$ involve $\mathcal{X}$ and is a good source for mining additional indexed predicates.

We start with the set of predicates in the property to be proved. If the final property to be proved is $\forall \mathcal{X} : \Psi(\mathcal{V}, \mathcal{X})$, we extract the indexed predicates that appear in $\Psi(\mathcal{V}, \mathcal{X})$. At each predicate discovery step, we generate new predicates from the weakest precondition of the existing predicates. An inductive invariant over the combined set of predicates is constructed by predicate abstraction. If the invariant implies the property, we are done. Otherwise, we iterate the process. This process can be repeated until no more predicates are discovered or we exhaust resources.

There are several enhancements over the simple idea that were required to generate meaningful predicates. The problems encountered and our solutions are as follows:

If-then-Else Constructs. To generate atomic predicates, the *if-then-else* (*ITE*) constructs are eliminated from the WP expression by two rewrite rules. First, we distribute a function application over an *ITE* term to both the branches i.e. $f(ITE(G, T_1, E_1)) \longrightarrow ITE(G, f(T_1), f(E_1))$. Second, we distribute the comparisons over *ITE* to both the branches, i.e. $ITE(G_1, T_1, E_1) \bowtie T_2 \longrightarrow (G_1 \wedge T_1 \bowtie T_2) \vee (\neg G_1 \wedge E_1 \bowtie T_2)$, where $\bowtie \in \{<, =\}$. Since the only arithmetic supported in our modeling formalism is addition by constants [5], the final predicates (after all the rewrites are applied) are of the form $T_1 \bowtie T_2 + c$, where T_i is an integer symbol or a function application.

Input Symbols. Since predicates relate state variables, input symbols in $\mathcal{I}$ should not be considered as part of predicates (the input symbols are universally quantified out while computing the WP). Boolean valued input variables can be safely ignored. However, integer input variables are different.

The principal source of integer inputs is the arbitrary index that is generated for choosing a process or an instruction to execute non-deterministically. Ignoring predicates containing inputs can often result in loosing useful predicates. Consider a fragment of a code for modeling a simple protocol in UCLID, where pc is a function state variable, representing the state of each process and cid is an arbitrary process identifier (input) generated to at each step.

```
next[pc]  :=                    (* next state of 'pc' state variable *)
Lambda (i).  case               (* next state for the ith index       *)
   i != cid       : pc(i) ;     (* if i != cid, remain unchanged      *)
   pc(cid) = A    : B ;         (* else if pc(i) = A, update to B     *)
   pc(cid) = B    : C ;         (* else if pc(i) = B, update to C     *)
   default        : pc(i);      (* else remain unchanged              *)
esac;
```

Let us assume that we are generating the set of predicates for $pc(x) = C$, where $x \in \mathcal{X}$. The set of predicates generated from this code fragment is $\{x = cid, pc(cid) = A, \ldots, \}$. Ignoring predicates containing cid returns an empty set of new predicates.

To circumvent this problem, we check if an input variable inp appears in any predicate $inp = x$, where $x \in \mathcal{X}$. In such a case, we say x is a *match* for inp. We repeat this for each input symbol in $\mathcal{I}$. We can have multiple input variables to index into a multidimensional array. Let $\mathcal{X}^\mathcal{I}$ be the named set of index variables, such that $\mathcal{X}_a^\mathcal{I}$ represents the match for input a.

We first ignore predicates that contain input variables without any matches. For any other predicate ϕ, we generate the predicate $\phi\left[\mathcal{X}^\mathcal{I}/\mathcal{I}\right]$. For the above example, the predicates generated are: $\{x = x, pc(x) = A, \ldots, \}$, which generates important predicates. Trivial predicates such as $x = x$ are ignored.

Arithmetic Predicates. In the presence of even simple arithmetic in the model, e.g. $\delta(v_1) \doteq v_1 + 1$, predicate abstraction generates too many predicates, often generating towers such as $v \bowtie v_2 + 1, \ldots, v \bowtie v_2 + k$. Most often these predicates are not essential for the property to be proved.

To prevent such predicates, we only generate predicates of the form $T_1 = T_2$ or $T_1 < T_2$, where T_i is a integer state variable or a function application. The first time we see a predicate $T_1 \bowtie T_2 + c$ (where $c \neq 0$), we generate the predicates $T_1 = T_2$ and $T_1 < T_2$. We ignore the predicate $T_1 \bowtie T_2 + c$ for the next step of predicate generation. This step is automatically performed. If predicates involving $+c$ are required, the user is expected to provide them. This step can be seen as a lightweight acceleration approach.

Nested Function Applications. While generating predicates for a given index variable, say i, we add new index variables to be placeholders for nested function applications. For instance, if the predicate discovered is $F(G(i)) = T_1$, where F and G are state variables, we introduce a new index variable j, add the predicate $j = G(i)$ and replace the predicate (with the nested function application) with a new predicate $F(j) = T_1$. All nested occurrences of $G(i)$ are replaced with j for subsequent predicates. At present, the user determines if new index variables have to be added, as the addition of too many index variables often overwhelm the predicate abstraction engine. We are currently automating this step.

Generalizing from a Fixed Index. Suppose we have a state variable v and we have a predicate that involves $P(v)$, (where P is a function or predicate state variable). If at some point in the future, we see the predicate $x = v$, where $x \in \mathcal{X}$, then we rewrite all the predicates which contains v as an argument to a function or predicate state variable by substituting x for v. For example, the predicate $P(v) = 5$ is rewritten as $P(x) = 5$. This rule has the effect of generalizing a predicate. It also removes the predicate $P(v) = 5$, since it can be constructed as a combination of $x = v$ and $P(x) = 5$. We have found this rule crucial for generating important predicates and also keep the size of the predicate set small.

5   Case Studies

5.1   Bakery Protocol

In this section, we describe the verification of mutual exclusion property for a version of N-process Bakery algorithm proposed by Lamport [24]. For this verification, we only model atomic reads and writes. A version with non-atomic reads and writes has been verified with manually supplied predicates [20].

Each process has a Boolean variable choosing, a ticket number and a loop index j. Each process can be in one of 6 program locations $\{L_0, \ldots, L_5\}$. A program counter variable pc holds the current program location a process is in. All the statements for a particular program location are executed atomically. The test $(a_1, a_2) \le (b_1, b_2)$ stands for $a_1 < b_1 \lor a_1 = b_1 \land a_2 \le b_2$.

The variables are initialized as:

```
choosing := Lambda i. false ;  j := Lambda i. 0 ;
number := Lambda i. 0 ; pc := Lambda i. L0 ;
```

and the overall protocol for the process at index i is described in the following pseudo code:

```
L0 : choosing[i] := true; goto L1 ;
L1 : number[i] := max(number[0],..,number[N-1]) + 1;
     choosing[i] := false; j[i] := 0; goto L2 ;
L2 : if (!choosing(j[i])) then  {goto L3;}
     else {goto L2;}
L3 : if (number(j[i]) = 0 ||
         (number[i],i) <= (number[j[i]],j)) then {goto L4;}
     else {goto L3;}
L4 : if (j[i] < N) then {j[i] := j[i]+1; goto L2;}
     else {goto L5;}
L5 : Critical-Section; number[i] := 0 ; goto L0;
```

We model the computation of the maximum value of $number(0), \ldots, number(N-1)$, in program location L_1 as an atomic operation. This is modeled by introducing a state variable max which takes on arbitrary values at each step, and an axiom that says: $\forall i : \text{max} \ge number(i)$. At each step, at most one process (at index cid) is scheduled to execute.

Proving Mutual Exclusion. The property we want to prove is that of mutual exclusion, namely $\forall i, j : pc(i) = L_5 \land pc(j) = L_5 \Rightarrow (i = j)$. We start out with a single index variable i. We start with the predicates in the property, namely $\{pc(i) = L_5\}$.

The predicates discovered after the first round are: $P^1 \doteq \{$ $\mathtt{j}(i) = \mathtt{N}$, $\mathtt{N} < \mathtt{j}(i)$, $\mathtt{pc}(i) = L_4$, $i = \mathtt{j}(i)$, $i < \mathtt{j}(i)$, $l = \mathtt{j}(i)$, $\mathtt{number}(i) = \mathtt{number}(l)$, $\mathtt{number}(i) < \mathtt{number}(l)$, $\mathtt{number}(l) = 0$, $\mathtt{pc}(i) = L_3$, $\mathtt{choosing}(l)$, $\mathtt{pc}(i) = L_2$, $\mathtt{pc}(i) = L_1$, $\mathtt{pc}(i) = L_0$, $i = \mathtt{N}$, $\mathtt{N} < i$, $i < 0$ $\}$. We introduced a second index symbol l when the predicate $\mathtt{number}(i) = \mathtt{number}(\mathtt{j}(i))$ with nested function application was encountered. We replaced this predicate with $\{l = \mathtt{j}(i), \mathtt{number}(i) = \mathtt{number}(l)\}$. Similarly the predicates $\mathtt{number}(i) = \mathtt{number}(\mathtt{j}(i))$ and $\mathtt{choosing}(\mathtt{j}(i))$ were replaced with $\mathtt{number}(i) = \mathtt{number}(l)$ and $\mathtt{choosing}(l)$ respectively. We ignored one redundant predicate $\mathtt{j}(i) > \mathtt{N}$, since both $\mathtt{j}(i) = \mathtt{N}$ and $\mathtt{j}(i) < \mathtt{N}$ are present. We also encountered the predicate $i = \mathtt{cid}$, and thus we will replace all future occurrences of $\mathtt{cid}$ with i in subsequent predicates. It took 0.81 seconds to discover that the initial set of predicates was not sufficient and to discover these predicates.

It took 55.8 seconds to find a counterexample with this set of predicates. The next set of predicates generated are: $P^2 \doteq \{$ $i = 0$, $l = 0$, $l < \mathtt{j}(i)$, $\mathtt{number}(i) = 0$, $\mathtt{pc}(l) = L_5$, $\mathtt{pc}(l) = L_1$, $l = i$, $l = \mathtt{N}$, $\mathtt{N} < l$, $l < 0$, $\mathtt{number}(i) < 0$, $0 < \mathtt{number}(l)$, $\mathtt{pc}(l) = L_0$, $0 < N$, $N < 0$ $\}$. We filtered out quite a number of predicates using our rules. First the predicate $\mathtt{j}(i) + 1 = \mathtt{N}$ gave rise to $\{\mathtt{j}(i) = \mathtt{N}, \mathtt{j}(i) < \mathtt{N}\}$, both of which are already present. Similarly $\mathtt{j}(i) + 1 < \mathtt{N}$ did not give rise to any new predicates. Likewise, the predicates generated from $i = \mathtt{j}(i) + 1$ are also present in P^1. We ignored predicates which involve $\mathtt{max}$ since it is merely a input. The predicate $l < \mathtt{j}(i)$ was generated from $l = \mathtt{j}(i) + 1$ ($l = \mathtt{j}(i)$ is already present). Finally $l = i$ was generated from $l = \mathtt{cid}$ by substituting i for $\mathtt{cid}$ in the predicate. All the filtering happened automatically inside the tool, we describe them to point out the effectiveness of the various rules.

With this set of 33 predicates, we were able to derive an inductive invariant in 471 seconds and 18 iterations of the abstract reachability. The inductive invariant implies the mutual exclusion property.

5.2   Directory-Based Cache Coherence Protocol

For the directory-based German's cache-coherence protocol, an unbounded number of clients (cache), communicate with a central *home* process to gain *exclusive* or *shared* access to a memory line. The state of each cache can be {*invalid, shared, exclusive*}. The home maintains explicit representations of two lists of clients: those sharing the cache line (sharer_list) and those for which the home has sent an invalidation request but has not received an acknowledgment (invalidate_list).

The client places requests {*req_shared, req_exclusive*} on a channel ch_1 and the home grants {*grant_shared, grant_exclusive*} on channel ch_2. The home also sends invalidation messages *invalidate* along ch_2. The home grants exclusive access to a client only when there are no clients sharing a line, i.e. $\forall i : \mathtt{sharer\_list}(i) = \mathbf{false}$. The home maintains variables for the current client (current_client) and the current request (current_command). It also maintains a bit exclusive_granted to indicate that some client has exclusive access. The cache lines acknowledge invalidation requests with a *invalidate_ack* along another channel ch_3. At each step an input cid is generated to denote the process that is chosen at that step. Details of the protocol operation with single-entry channels can be found in many previous works including [28]. We will refer to this version as *german-cache*.

Since the modeling language of UCLID does not permit explicit quantifiers in the system, we model the check for the absence of any sharers $\forall i :$ sharer_list$(i) =$ false alternately. We maintain a Boolean state variable empty_hsl, which assumes an arbitrary value at each step of operation. We then add an axiom to the system: empty_hsl $\Leftrightarrow \forall i :$ sharer_list$(i) =$ false [1].

In our version of the protocol, each cache communicates to the home process through three directed unbounded FIFO channels, namely the channels ch_1, ch_2, ch_3. Thus, there are an unbounded number of unbounded channels, three for each client[2]. It can be shown that a client can generate an unbounded number of requests before getting a response from the home. We refer to this version of the protocol as *german-cache-fifo*.

Proving Cache Coherence. We first consider the version *german-cache* which has been widely used in many previous works [28, 12, 3] among others and then consider the extended system *german-cache-fifo*. In both cases, the cache coherence property to prove is $\forall i, j :$ cache$(i) = exclusive \land i \neq j \Rightarrow$ cache$(j) = invalid$. Details of the verification of both *german-cache* and *german-cache-fifo* can be found at the authors homepage[3]. Here, we briefly sketch the highlights of the experiments. All the experiments are run on an 2.1GHz Pentium machine running Linux with 1GB of RAM. Let P^k denote the predicates discovered after k iterations of WP computation.

Invariant Generation for *German-Cache*. For this version, we derived two inductive invariants, one which involves a single process index i and other which involves two process indices i and j. For brevity, we will only describe the dual indexed invariant.

For the dual indexed invariant, we start off with the predicates in the property, namely $P^0 \doteq \{$ pc$(i) = exclusive$, pc$(j) = invalid$, $i = j \}$. The predicates discovered in subsequent iterations are listed below:

$P^1 \doteq \{$ ch2$(i) = grant\_exclusive$, ch2$(i) = grant\_shared$, ch3$(i) = empty$, ch2$(i) = invalidate$, ch2$(j) = grant\_exclusive$, ch2$(j) = grant\_shared$, ch3$(j) = empty$, ch2$(j) = invalidate \}$.

$P^2 \doteq \{$ ch2$(i) = empty$, current_command $= req\_exclusive$, $i =$ current_client, invalidate_list(i), $j =$ current_client, current_command $= req\_shared$, exclusive_granted, ch3$(i) = invalidate\_ack$, current_command $= empty$, ch2$(j) = empty$, invalidate_list(j), ch3$(j) = invalidate\_ack \}$.

$P^3 \doteq \{$ sharer_list(i), ch1$(i) = empty$, ch1$(i) = req\_exclusive$, ch1$(i) = req\_shared$, sharer_list$(j) \}$.

The inductive invariant which implies the cache-coherency was constructed using these 28 predicates in 1266 seconds using 15 steps of abstract reachability. The entire process took less than 2000 seconds of CPU time.

Invariant Generation for *German-Cache-Fifo*. The addition of an unbounded number of FIFOs increases the complexity of the model. We constructed an inductive invariant (which implies cache coherence) with a process index i and an index j for the channels.

---

[1] Our current implementation only handles one direction of the axiom, $\forall i :$ empty_hsl $\Rightarrow$ sharer_list$(i) =$ false, which is sufficient to ensure the safety property.

[2] The extension was suggested by Steven German himself.

[3] http://www.ece.cmu.edu/~shuvendu/papers/cav04a-submit.ps

We needed to add two predicates for the FIFOs manually, which contain constant offsets (e.g. $x < y - 1$). The time taken to construct the inductive invariant with 29 predicates was 3 hours.

6 Conclusions

In this work, we have demonstrated that predicate abstraction with indexed predicates coupled with simple heuristics for indexed predicate discovery can be very effective for automated or systematic verification of unbounded systems. The verification is carried out without knowledge about the operation of any of the protocols. The technique has also been applied for the systematic generation of invariants for an out-of-order microprocessor engine and a network protocol.

There is a lot of scope for improving the performance of invariant generation procedure by finding a minimal set of predicates. For instance, the inductive invariant for *german-cache-fifo* could be computed using 26 manually specified predicates in 581 seconds. Hence, there is a scope of almost 20X improvement that can be possibly obtained by a suitable selection of predicates. We are also experimenting with proof-based predicate discovery, where the proof that no concrete counterexample exists within a finite number of steps is used to discover new predicates.

References

1. T. Arons, A. Pnueli, S. Ruah, Y. Zhu, and L. Zuck. Parameterized verification with automatically computed inductive assertions. In G. Berry, H. Comon, and A. Finkel, editors, *Computer-Aided Verification (CAV '01)*, LNCS 2102, pages 221–234, 2001.
2. T. Ball, R. Majumdar, T. Millstein, and S. K. Rajamani. Automatic predicate abstraction of C programs. In *Programming Language Design and Implementation (PLDI '01)*, Snowbird, Utah, June, 2001. *SIGPLAN Notices, 36*(5), May 2001.
3. K. Baukus, Y. Lakhnech, and K. Stahl. Parameterized Verification of a Cache Coherence Protocol: Safety and Liveness. In A. Cortesi, editor, *Verification, Model Checking, and Abstract Interpretation, VMCAI 2002*, LNCS 2294, pages 317–330, January 2002.
4. A. Bouajjani, B. Jonsson, M. Nilsson, and T. Touili. Regular model checking. In A. Emerson and P. Sistla, editors, *Computer-Aided Verification (CAV 2000)*, LNCS 1855, pages 403–418, July 2000.
5. R. E. Bryant, S. K. Lahiri, and S. A. Seshia. Modeling and Verifying Systems using a Logic of Counter Arithmetic with Lambda Expressions and Uninterpreted Functions. In E. Brinksma and K. G. Larsen, editors, *Computer-Aided Verification (CAV'02)*, LNCS 2404, pages 78–92, July 2002.
6. S. Chaki, E. M. Clarke, A. Groce, S. Jha, and H. Veith. Modular Verification of Software Components in C. In *International Conference on Software Engineering (ICSE)*, pages 385–395, May 2003.
7. E. Clarke, D. Kroening, N. Sharygina, and K. Yorav. Predicate Abstraction of ANSI-C Programs using SAT. Technical Report CMU-CS-03-186, Carnegie Mellon University, 2003.
8. E. M. Clarke, O. Grumberg, S. Jha, Y. Lu, and H. Veith. Counterexample-guided abstraction refinement. In E. A. Emerson and A. P. Sistla, editors, *Computer Aided Verification (CAV '00)*, LNCS 1855, pages 154–169, 2000.
9. P. Cousot and R. Cousot. Abstract interpretation : A Unified Lattice Model for the Static Analysis of Programs by Construction or Approximation of Fixpoints. In *Symposium on Principles of Programming Languages (POPL '77)*, 1977.

10. S. Das and D. L. Dill. Counter-example based predicate discovery in predicate abstraction. In M. D. Aagaard and J. W. O'Leary, editors, *Formal Methods in Computer-Aided Design (FMCAD '02)*, LNCS 2517, pages 19–32, 2002.

11. E. W. Dijkstra. Guarded commands, nondeterminacy and formal derivation of programs. *Communications of the ACM*, 18:453–457, 1975.

12. E. A. Emerson and V. Kahlon. Exact and efficient verification of parameterized cache coherence protocols. In D. Geist and E. Tronci, editors, *Correct Hardware Design and Verification Methods (CHARME '03)*, LNCS 2860, pages 247–262, 2003.

13. C. Flanagan and S. Qadeer. Predicate abstraction for software verification. In J. Launchbury and J. C. Mitchell, editors, *Symposium on Principles of programming languages (POPL '02)*, pages 191–202, 2002.

14. Steven German. Personal communication.

15. S. Graf and H. Saidi. Construction of abstract state graphs with PVS. In O. Grumberg, editor, *Computer-Aided Verification (CAV '97)*, LNCS 1254, June 1997.

16. Y. Gurevich. The decision problem for standard classes. *The Journal of Symbolic Logic*, 41(2):460–464, June 1976.

17. T. A. Henzinger, R. Jhala, R. Majumdar, and G. Sutre. Lazy Abstraction. In J. Launchbury and J. C. Mitchell, editors, *Symposium on Principles of programming languages (POPL '02)*, pages 58–70, 2002.

18. Y. Kesten, O. Maler, M. Marcus, A. Pnueli, and E. Shahar. Symbolic model checking with rich assertional languages. In O. Grumberg, editor, *Computer-Aided Verification (CAV '97)*, LNCS 1254, pages 424–435, June 1997.

19. R. P. Kurshan. *Computer-Aided Verification of Coordinating Processes: The Automata-Theoretic Approach*. Princeton University Press, 1995.

20. S. K. Lahiri and R. E. Bryant. Constructing Quantified Invariants via Predicate Abstraction. In G. Levi and B. Steffen, editors, *Conference on Verification, Model Checking and Abstract Interpretation (VMCAI '04)*, LNCS 2937, pages 267–281, 2004.

21. S. K. Lahiri, R. E. Bryant, and B. Cook. A symbolic approach to predicate abstraction. In W. A. Hunt, Jr. and F. Somenzi, editors, *Computer-Aided Verification (CAV 2003)*, LNCS 2725, pages 141–153, 2003.

22. S. K. Lahiri, S. A. Seshia, and R. E. Bryant. Modeling and verification of out-of-order microprocessors in UCLID. In J. W. O'Leary M. Aagaard, editor, *Formal Methods in Computer-Aided Design (FMCAD '02)*, LNCS 2517, pages 142–159, Nov 2002.

23. Y. Lakhnech, S. Bensalem, S. Berezin, and S. Owre. Incremental verification by abstraction. In T. Margaria and W. Yi, editors, *Tools and Algorithms for the Construction and Analysis of Systems (TACAS'01)*, volume LNCS 2031, pages 98–112, April 2001.

24. L. Lamport. A new solution of Dijkstra's concurrent programming problem. *Communications of the ACM*, 17:453–455, August 1974.

25. K. McMillan. Verification of an implementation of Tomasulo's algorithm by compositional model checking. In A. J. Hu and M. Y. Vardi, editors, *Computer-Aided Verification (CAV 1998)*, LNCS 1427, pages 110–121, June 1998.

26. K. McMillan, S. Qadeer, and J. Saxe. Induction in compositional model checking. In A. Emerson and P. Sistla, editors, *Computer-Aided Verification (CAV 2000)*, LNCS 1855, July 2000.

27. K. S. Namjoshi and R. P. Kurshan. Syntactic program transformations for automatic abstraction. In A. Emerson and P. Sistla, editors, *Computer Aided Verification*, LNCS 1855, pages 435–449, 2000.

28. A. Pnueli, S. Ruah, and L. Zuck. Automatic deductive verification with invisible invariants. In T. Margaria and W. Yi, editors, *Tools and Algorithms for the Construction and Analysis of Systems(TACAS'01)*, volume LNCS 2031, pages 82–97, 2001.

Range Allocation for Separation Logic

Muralidhar Talupur[1], Nishant Sinha[1], Ofer Strichman[2], and Amir Pnueli[3]

[1] Carnegie Mellon University, Pittsburgh, PA, USA
[2] Technion - Israel Institute of Technology, Haifa, Israel
[3] The Weizmann Institute of Science, Rehovot, Israel

Abstract. *Separation Logic* consists of a Boolean combination of predicates of the form $v_i \geq v_j + c$ where c is a constant and v_i, v_j are variables of some ordered infinite type like `real` or `integer`. Any equality or inequality can be expressed in this logic. We propose a decision procedure for Separation Logic based on allocating small domains (ranges) to the formula's variables that are sufficient for preserving satisfiability. Given a Separation Logic formula φ, our procedure constructs the *inequalities graph* of φ, based on φ's predicates. This graph represents an abstraction of the formula, as there are many formulas with the same set of predicates. Our procedure then analyzes this graph and allocates a range to each variable that is adequate for all of these formulas. This approach of finding small finite ranges and enumerating them symbolically is both theoretically and empirically more efficient than methods based on case-splitting or reduction to Propositional Logic. Experimental results show that the state-space (that is, the number of assignments that need to be enumerated) allocated by our procedure is frequently exponentially smaller than previous methods.

1 Introduction

Separation Logic, also known as Difference Logic, consists of a Boolean combination of predicates of the form $v_i \rhd v_j + c$ where $\rhd \in \{>, \geq\}$, c is a constant, and v_i, v_j are variables of some ordered infinite type like `real` or `integer`. All the other equality and inequality relations can be expressed in this logic. Uninterpreted functions can be handled as well since they can be reduced to Boolean combinations of equalities [2]. In this paper, we consider Separation Logic with `integer` variables and constants only, assuming that only minor adaptations are needed for other cases. Further we consider only predicates with $\geq$ relations as it does not reduce expressivity in any way.

Separation predicates are used in verification of timed systems, scheduling problems, and more. Hardware models with ordered data structures have inequalities as well. For example, if the model contains a queue of unbounded length, the test for *head $\leq$ tail* introduces inequalities. In fact, as observed by Pratt [7], most inequalities in verification conditions are of this form. Furthermore, since theorem provers can decide mixed theories (by invoking an appropriate decision procedure for each logic fragment [8]), an efficient decision procedure

R. Alur and D.A. Peled (Eds.): CAV 2004, LNCS 3114, pp. 148–161, 2004.
© Springer-Verlag Berlin Heidelberg 2004

for Separation Logic will be helpful in verification of any formula that contains a significant number of these predicates.

There are various known methods for solving Separation Logic (see tools such as CVC [11] and MATHSAT [3] that solves this logic), which we survey in detail in the full version of this article [12]. Let us just mention here the most recent one, which is based on a reduction to Propositional Logic. In [10, 9] such a reduction is proposed, based on an analysis of a graph derived from the formula, called the *inequalities graph*. The inequalities graph is based on the formula's predicates, regardless of the Boolean connectives between them. It encodes each predicate of the form $x \geq y + c$ with a new Boolean variable e_{xy}^c, and then gradually removes nodes from the graph while adding transitivity constraints (similar to the Fourier-Motzkin technique). The following example illustrates this method. Consider the formula $\varphi : x \geq y + 1 \wedge (y \geq z + 2 \vee z \geq x + 1)$. As a first step, abstract this formula with Boolean constraints, i.e. $\varphi' : e_{xy}^1 \wedge (e_{yz}^2 \vee e_{zx}^1)$.

Next, nodes (variables) are eliminated one at a time while adding proper constraints to the formula. Given the order x, y, z it first eliminates x, deriving from the first and third predicates the new constraint $z - 1 \geq y + 1$. It consequently adds the constraint $e_{xy}^1 \wedge e_{zx}^1 \rightarrow e_{zy}^2$. Eliminating y it derives from the second and fourth constraint the new unsatisfiable constraint $z - 2 \geq z + 2$ and adds, accordingly, the constraint $e_{yz}^2 \wedge e_{zy}^2 \rightarrow$ FALSE . This procedure may result in an exponential number of constraints and a quadratic number of variables. In contrast, the Range-Allocation approach which we present now, requires in the worst case $n \cdot \log n$ variables and no additional constraints.

Our Approach. Our approach is based on the small model property of Separation Logic. That is, if a formula in this theory is satisfiable, then there is a finite model that satisfies it. Furthermore, in the case of Separation Logic there exists an efficiently computable bound on the size of the smallest satisfying model. This implies that the given formula can be decided by checking all possible valuations up to that bound.

In the case of predicates of the form $x > y$ (since we treat integers and weak inequalities this is the same as $x \geq y + 1$) the range $[1 \ldots n]$ is sufficient, where n is the number of variables. In other words, it is possible to check for the satisfiability of such formulas by enumerating all n^n possible valuations within this range. Informally, the reason that this range is sufficient is that every satisfying assignment imposes a partial order on the variables, and every assignment that preserves this order satisfies the formula as well. Since all orderings are possible in the range $[1 \ldots n]$, this range is sufficient, or, as we later call it, it is *adequate*. In the case of full Separation Logic (when there are arbitrary constants), it was shown [4] that in the worst case a range $[1 \ldots n + maxC]$ is required for each variable, where $maxC$ can be as high as the sum of all constants in the formula. This result leads to a state-space of $(n + maxC)^n$. These results refer to a *uniform* range allocation to all variables, regardless of the formula structure. In this article we investigate methods for reducing this number, based on an analysis of the formula's structure, which typically results in *non-uniform* range allocation.

A similar approach was taken in the past by Pnueli et al. [6] in the context of Equality Logic (Boolean combinations of equalities). This article can be seen as a natural continuation of that work.

As an example of the reduction in state-space that our method can achieve consider the 'diamond' graph shown below. For such a graph with n nodes and all edge weights equal to 1, the uniform range allocation results in a state-space of size $O(n^n)$. In contrast, our approach allocates a single constant to one node, and 2 values to all the rest, which results in a state-space of size $O(2^n)$. If the graph has arbitrary edge weights, the state-space resulting from a uniform range allocation can grow up to $O((n+maxC)^n)$, while in our approach it would remain $O(2^n)$ (it will, however, increase the values themselves, which has a relatively minor effect on performance).

2 Problem Formulation

Let $Vars(\varphi)$ denote the set of variables used in a Separation formula φ over the set of integers $\mathbb{Z}$. A domain (or range) $R(\varphi)$ of a formula φ is a function from $Vars(\varphi)$ to $2^{\mathbb{Z}}$. Let $Vars(\varphi) = \{v_1, \dots v_n\}$ and $|R(v_i)|$ be equal to the number of elements in the set $R(v_i)$. The size of domain $R(\varphi)$, denoted by $|R(\varphi)|$ is given by $|R(\varphi)| = |R(v_1)| \cdot |R(v_2)| \cdot \dots \cdot |R(v_n)|$. Now, let $SAT_R(\varphi)$ denote that φ is *satisfiable* in a domain R. Our goal is the following:

Find a small domain R such that

$$SAT_R(\varphi) \quad \Longleftrightarrow \quad SAT_{\mathbb{Z}}(\varphi) \tag{1}$$

We say that a domain R is *adequate* for φ if it satisfies formula (1). It is straightforward to see that if $SAT_{\mathbb{Z}}(\varphi)$ holds then the minimal adequate domain has size 1: simply assign the variables in $Vars(\varphi)$ a constant value according to one of the satisfying assignment. Thus, finding the smallest domain for a given formula is at least as hard as checking the satisfiability of φ. So, rather than examining φ we investigate the set of all Separation formulas with the *same set of predicates* as φ, denoted by $\Phi(\varphi)$. Thus, our new, less ambitious goal is the following:

Given a Separation formula φ, find the smallest domain R which is adequate for $\Phi(\varphi)$.

The problem of finding the smallest adequate domain for $\Phi(\varphi)$ is still too computationally expensive (it is still exponential, although we will not prove it here). We will therefore concentrate on finding over-approximations which are easier to compute. As was previously indicated, our solution is based on a graph-based analysis of the formula's structure.

Input Formula. We define a normal form for Separation logic as follows: 1) 'greater-equal than' ($\geq$) is the only allowed predicate, and 2) there are no negations in the formula. Every Separation logic formula can be transformed to this form by first translating it to NNF, reversing negated inequalities, reversing 'less than' ($<, \leq$) predicates and finally, replacing strong inequalities of the form $x > y + c$ with weak inequalities of the form $x \geq y + c + 1$.

A Graph Representation. Given a Separation Logic formula φ, we construct the *inequalities graph* $G_\varphi(V, E)$ as follows (we will write G_φ from now on).

Definition 1 (Inequalities graph). *The* inequalities graph $G_\varphi(V, E)$ *is constructed as follows: Add a node to V for each $v \in Vars(\varphi)$. For each predicate of the form $x \geq y + c$ in φ, add an edge to E from the node representing x to the node representing y, with a weight c.*

We will say that a domain is *adequate for a graph* G_φ if it is adequate for $\Phi(\varphi)$.

Definition 2 (Consistent subgraphs). *A subgraph of an inequalities graph G_φ is* consistent *if it does not include a cycle with positive accumulated weight (positive cycle for short).*

Intuitively, a consistent subgraph represents a set of edges (predicates) that can be satisfied simultaneously. Restating in graph-theoretic terms, our goal is:

Given G_φ, find a domain R for each node in V such that every consistent subgraph of G_φ can be satisfied from values in R.

Example 1. The set of constants associated with each vertex in the following graph constitute an adequate domain. Each edge is assumed to have weight 1. There exists a solution from these sets to every consistent subset of edges in the graph.

For example, the set of edges $\{(x_1, x_2), (x_2, x_3), (x_3, x_4)\}$ can be satisfied by the assignment $x_1 = 10, x_2 = 9, x_3 = 8, x_4 = 7$. Note that there is no need to satisfy the subset containing all the edges because it is inconsistent.

It can be shown that for every simple cycle there exists an adequate domain with size $2^{|V|-1}$. In our example the size of the domain is 8. If we try to reduce this size, for example by setting $R(x_1) = \{6\}$, the domain becomes inadequate, because the subset $(x_1, x_2), (x_2, x_3), (x_3, x_4)$ is unsatisfiable under R.   □

It is obvious that we should find small ranges with an overhead smaller than what is saved compared to the other methods mentioned earlier. In this respect we were not entirely successful, as in the worst case our algorithm is exponential (it requires at some point to look for all negative cycles in the graph). In practice, however, we did not encounter an example that takes a long time to allocate ranges for. It is left for future research to find polynomial approximations to our algorithm.

3   The Range Allocation Algorithm

As mentioned in the introduction, it is known that for every inequalities graph (with all edge weights equal to 1), the range $1\ldots|V|$ is adequate, resulting in a state-space of size $|V|^{|V|}$. However Example 1 shows that analysis of the graph structure may yield smaller state-spaces. For example, if a graph has two unconnected subgraphs then they can be allocated values separately, hence reducing the overall state-space. In fact, it is possible to analyze every Strongly Connected Component (SCC) separately. The edges between the SCCs can then be satisfied by appropriately shifting the allocated domains of each SCC. Thus, a solution to this problem for SCCs implies directly a solution for the general problem.

The pseudo-code in Figure 1 shows the overall structure of our algorithm. The main procedure, *Allocate-Graph* receives a graph as input and returns a graph where all its nodes are annotated with adequate ranges. For each node x we denote the corresponding range by $R(x)$. It allocates values for SCCs with the procedure *Allocate-SCC* and then shifts them so that these ranges are valid in relation to the other SCCs present in the graph. Given an SCC S, *Allocate-SCC* calls itself recursively on a smaller SCC derived from S (the recursion stops when S is the trivial SCC comprised of a single node). When returning from the recursive call, the values assigned to the smaller SCC are used to allocate values for all the nodes in SCC S. The description of *Allocate-SCC*, which requires several definitions, appears in the next subsection.

3.1   Range Allocation for SCCs

The goal of *Allocate-SCC* is to annotate each node x of a given SCC S with a finite and adequate range $R(x)$ (not necessarily continuous). The primary source of difficulty in assigning adequate values to SCCs is the presence of cycles. We introduce the notion of *cutpoints* to deal with cycles in the SCC.

Definition 3 (Cutpoint-set). *Given a directed graph $G(V, E)$, a set of nodes $v \subseteq V$ is a* Cutpoint-set *if removing them and their adjacent nodes makes the graph cycle free.*

The notion of cutpoints is also known in the literature as *Feedback Vertex Sets* [5]. Finding a minimal set of cutpoints is an NP-$Hard$ problem, so our implementation uses a polynomial approximation (several such approximations are

Annotated-Graph *Allocate-Graph*(directed graph G)

1. For each non-trivial SCC $S \in G$, $S = $ *Allocate-SCC* (S)
2. Following the *partial-order forest*, allocate values to non-SCC
   nodes and shift the allocated values of the SCCs so they satisfy
   all predicates. // If every SCC is contracted to a single node, the
                       // resulting graph is a forest
3. Return the Annotated graph G.

Annotated-Graph *Allocate-SCC*(SCC S)

1. If S has a single node x assign $R(x) = \{0\}$ and return S.
2. Find the set of cutpoints C of S // See Definition 3
3. Construct the *Cutpoint-graph* S_C // See Definition 4
4. *Allocate-SCC* (S_C).
5. For each regular node x: // See description of the four phases in Sec. 3.2
   (a) (Phase 1) Find the *cycle-values* of x
   (b) (Phase 2) Find the *dfs-values* of x
   (c) (Phase 3) Let $\{C_{1x}, C_{2x}, \ldots, C_{nx}\}$ be the set of cutpoints that can
       reach x. Then assign

   $$R(x) = \bigcup_{C_{ix}} (\{u+v | u \in R(C_{ix}) \wedge (v \in (cycle\text{-}values^0_{C_{ix}}(x) \cup dfs\text{-}values^0_{C_{ix}}(x)))\})$$

   (d) (Phase 4) Add a *dfs-value* corresponding to the virtual level
6. Return the annotated SCC S.

Fig. 1. Procedures *Allocate-Graph* calls *Allocate-SCC* for each SCC. Both procedures
receive a directed graph as input, and annotates each node x in this graph with a set
of adequate values $R(x)$.

described in the above reference). We will refer to non-cutpoint nodes simply as
regular nodes. This distinction refers to the current recursion level only. As we
will soon see, all graphs at recursion levels other than the highest one comprise
only of the cutpoints of the original SCC S.

Next, we define a *collapsing* of an SCC S on to its Cutpoint-set, which we
call the *Cutpoint-graph* of S:

Definition 4 (Cutpoint-graph). *Given an SCC S and a Cutpoint-set C of
S, a cutpoint graph of S with respect to C is a directed graph $S_C(C, E)$ such
that for $u, v \in C$, $u \neq v$, edge $(u, v) \in E$ with weight w if and only if there is
a path in S from u to v not passing through any other vertex in C and with an
accumulated weight w*

Note that according to this definition there are no self loops in Cutpoint-graphs.
As an example, consider the graph shown in the left of Figure 2. One possible
Cutpoint-set for this graph is the set $\{A, C\}$. The Cutpoint-graph over these
nodes is shown on the right hand side of the figure. We will use this graph as a
running example to illustrate our algorithm.

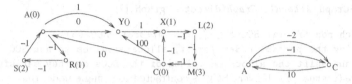

Fig. 2. An SCC S (left) and its Cutpoint-graph with respect to the Cutpoint-set $\{A,C\}$.

Allocate-SCC (Figure 1) progresses by calling itself recursively on the graph S_C. It is easy to see that S_C is also an SCC, but smaller. This ensures that *Allocate-SCC* terminates. This observation is proven in Lemma 1 below.

Lemma 1. *A Cutpoint-graph S_C of an SCC S is an SCC and has less vertices than S.*

(All proofs appear in the full version of this article [12]).

In case S is a single node *Allocate-SCC* assigns it the range $\{0\}$ and returns. The set of values returned from the recursive call are then used to assign values to the rest of the graph (the regular nodes at this level). The process of assigning these values is involved, and is done in four phases as described in the next subsection.

3.2   The Four Phases of Allocating Ranges to Regular Nodes

Ranges are assigned to regular nodes in four phases. In the first two phases the assigned ranges, called *cycle-values* and *dfs-values* respectively, should be thought of as *representative* values: they do not necessarily belong to the final ranges assigned by the algorithm. In Phase 3, these values will be combined with the ranges assigned to the cutpoints to compute the final ranges for all the regular nodes. In the description of these phases we will use the notion of *tight assignments*, defined as follows:

Definition 5 (Tight assignments). *Given a directed weighted path from node x to node y with an assignment of a single value to each node, this assignment is called* tight *with respect to the value assigned to x, if and only if all the inequalities represented by the path are satisfied and the value at each node other than x is the largest possible. In that case, the path is said to be* tight *with respect to the value at x.*

Phase 1. *The role of Phase 1 is to find values that satisfy all non-positive cycles in the graph, assuming that the cutpoints in the cycles are assigned the value 0 (this assumption will be removed in Phase 3).*

We find all the non-positive cycles, each of which, by definition, has one or more cutpoints. For every path p on that cycle from cutpoint C_i to cutpoint C_j, we then assign 0 to C_i and *tight* values with respect to C_i's assignment, to the other nodes in p except C_j. Typically there is only one cutpoint in the cycle, which can be thought of as a particular case of the above one where $C_2 = C_1$. If in this step a node x on p is assigned a value v, we say that this value is *obtained from* C_i.

At the end of this phase regular nodes have one value for each non-positive cycle that goes through them, while cutpoints have the single value 0. In Figure 2 these values are shown in parenthesis. Note that Y has an empty set of values as there are no non-positive cycles going through it.

The set of values associated with each node x is called the *cycle-values* corresponding to *level* 0 and is denoted by $cycle\text{-}values^0(x)$ (0 being the value assumed at cutpoints). Further, the subset of *cycle-values* at x obtained from C_i is denoted by $cycle\text{-}values^0_{C_i}(x)$.

Phase 2. *The role of Phase 2 is to assign values that satisfy all acyclic paths in the SCC starting from a cutpoint, assuming that the cutpoint has a value 0 (this assumption will be removed in Phase 3).* In the second phase, we begin by creating a new set of values at each node called *dfs-values*. Regular nodes have one *dfs-value* corresponding to each cutpoint that can reach it *directly* (that is, without going through any other cutpoint). For a node x and a cutpoint C_i that can reach it directly (i.e. not through other cutpoints), denote the *dfs-value* corresponding to C_i at level 0 by $dfs\text{-}values^0_{C_i}(x)$. The value of $dfs\text{-}values^0_{C_i}(x)$ is calculated as follows. Let n be the number of direct paths from C_i to x, and let $v_1, \ldots, v_n$ be values corresponding to tight assignments to x with respect to C_i. Then $dfs\text{-}values^0_{C_i}(x) = \min\{v_1 \ldots v_n\}$. The implementation of Phase 2 involves a simple Depth-First Search (DFS) which starts from cutpoints and backtracks on reaching any cutpoint.

Referring to Figure 2, $dfs\text{-}values^0_A(Y) = -1$ and $dfs\text{-}values^0_C(Y) = -100$. Thus, the *dfs-values* for Y are $[-1, -100]$. The other *dfs-values* are shown in Figure 3 in square brackets. The first value is obtained from A and the other, if present, from C.

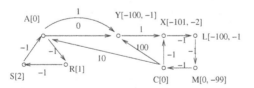

Fig. 3. The *dfs-values* of nodes appear in square brackets. Both cutpoints (A and C) have a path to Y, hence the two *dfs-values*. The final allocated ranges for all nodes are shown in curly brackets.

Phase 3. *The role of Phase 3 is to translate the representative values computed in the first two phases into actual ranges using the ranges allocated to the cutpoints by the recursive call.* In the third phase, we use ranges assigned to cutpoints by the recursive call *Allocate-SCC* (S_C) as the base for shifting the representative values that were computed by the first two phases. The ranges assigned to the cutpoints remain unchanged (none of the three phases modify the ranges assigned to the cutpoints by deeper recursive calls).

For each regular node x we find all the cutpoints $\{C_{1x}, C_{2x}, .., C_{nx}\}$ that can reach it not through other cutpoints. Then $R(x)$ is given by

$$R(x) = \bigcup_{C_{ix}}(\{u + v | u \in R(C_{ix}) \wedge (v \in (cycle\text{-}values^0_{C_{ix}}(x) \cup dfs\text{-}values^0_{C_{ix}}(x)))\})$$

Example 2. Consider once again the graph in Figure 2. Assume that cutpoints have already been assigned the following values: $R(A) = \{-10, -1\}$ and $R(C) = \{0\}$. For node Y, the set $cycle\text{-}values^0(Y)$ is empty and $dfs\text{-}values^0(Y) = \{-1, -100\}$. The cutpoints that can reach Y are A and C. So the range associated with Y is the union of $\{-100\}$ (the values from C) and $\{-11, -2\}$ (the values from A).

The value $u+v \in R(x)$ such that $u \in R(C_{ix})$ and v is a *dfs-value* or a *cycle-value* is said to correspond to *level* u at C_{ix}.

Phase 4. We now add one more value, called the *virtual dfs-value*, to each regular node. The need to have an additional value is explained as follows. Given a satisfiable subgraph $S' \subseteq G$, the values assigned in the previous phases can be used for a node x only if it can be reached from a cutpoint. For the case where x is not reachable from any cutpoint in S' we need to have an extra value.

We allocate *virtual dfs-values* by starting from the highest value at each cutpoint, and going *backward* along the edges until we reach another cutpoint. We assign tight values along each *reverse* path with respect to the starting cutpoint. At the end, for each node x we pick the maximum value among all the values assigned by different paths and make it the *virtual dfs-value*.

From now on, by *dfs-values* of a node x we will mean all the *dfs-values* corresponding to all levels and cutpoints. We use the term *cycle-values* in a similar way. Considering the graph in Figure 2, the final set of values assigned to all nodes is shown in Figure 4. Underlined numbers are those that were allocated in Phase 4.

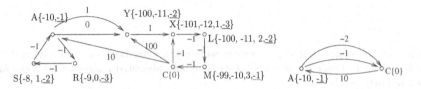

Fig. 4. The final allocated ranges for all nodes are shown in curly brackets. The right figure shows the ranges allocated for the Cutpoint-Graph, which are preserved in higher recursion levels, as can be seen on the left graph. Underlined numbers are allocated in Phase 4.

4   Correctness of the Algorithm

Assuming that *Allocate-SCC* is correct, the correctness of *Allocate-Graph* is easy to see: *Allocate-Graph* simply shifts the ranges allocated to SCCs and assigns a single value to nodes between them so that all the inequality constraints between the SCCs are satisfied. From now on we will focus on proving the correctness of *Allocate-SCC* (the proofs of most of the lemmas in this section appear in the full version of this article [12], and are omitted here due to lack of space). We will prove that the procedure terminates and that the ranges it allocates are adequate.

Termination of *Allocate-SCC* is guaranteed by Lemma 1 because it implies that the number of nodes decreases as we go from S to S_C. This ensures that the size of the considered SCC decreases in successive recursive calls until it is called with a single node and returns.

We now have to show that *Allocate-SCC* allocates adequate ranges. Assume that S is an SCC and *Allocate-SCC* uses a set of cutpoints C in allocating ranges to S. Given a satisfiable subgraph $S' \subset S$, we describe an *assignment procedure* that assigns values to its nodes from the ranges allocated to it by *Allocate-SCC*, which satisfy all of the predicates represented by S'. The assignment procedure and the proof of correctness are explained using an *augmented* graph of S', denoted by S'_{Aug}. Essentially the augmented graph reflects the tightest constraints in the original graph between nodes in S'. Clearly if we satisfy tighter constraints than we can satisfy the original set of constraints in S'.

Building the Augmented Graph. We construct the augmented graph as follows. Find all paths P in S' starting from some cutpoint C_i and ending at a regular node x such that:

- The path P does not occur as part of any non-positive cycle in S
- If nodes in P are given corresponding *dfs-values*$^0_{C_i}$ values then it is not tight with respect to value 0 at cutpoint C_i.

For each such path we add an edge from C_i to x with a weight equal to $-(dfs\text{-}values^0_{C_i}(x))$ (the negation of the level 0 *dfs-value* of x corresponding to C_i). Note that such an edge need not be a part of the graph G. By the following lemma, if S' is satisfiable then the augmented graph S'_{Aug} is satisfiable as well.

Lemma 2. *If S' is a satisfiable subgraph of S then the graph S'_{Aug} as constructed above is satisfiable as well. Further, any assignment that satisfies S'_{Aug} satisfies S'.*

Example 3. Suppose we are given a graph S' as shown in Figure 5 (refer only to the solid edges). S' is a satisfiable subgraph of the graph shown in Figure 2. The *dfs-value* of X and Y corresponding to level 0 and cutpoint A are -1 and -2 respectively (shown in square brackets). In S', the path $A \rightarrow Y \rightarrow X$ is not tight with respect to these values. We therefore augment S' by adding two edges: one

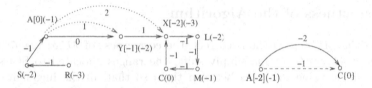

Fig. 5. The graph S' (solid edges), and its augmentation (adding the dotted edges) S'_{Aug} for the first and second recursion levels. The augmented graph can be assigned tight *dfs-values*. The values assigned by the assignment procedure (see Section 4.1) are shown in parenthesis.

```
Input: Augmented satisfiable subgraph S'_Aug
Output: A satisfying assignment to S'_Aug from the ranges allocated by
Allocate-SCC.
```

1. For each regular node x find all cutpoints $\{C_{1x} \ldots C_{mx}\}$ in S'_{Aug} that can reach it directly, not through any other cutpoint.
2. For each cutpoint C_{ix} find all direct paths P to x, and for each such path find tight values assuming the value of cutpoint C_{ix} is as assigned by the previous recursive call.
3. Find the minimum among all these tight values corresponding to all cutpoints in $\{C_{1x} \ldots C_{mx}\}$ and assign it to x.
4. For nodes that cannot be reached from any point in C' assign them their *virtual dfs-values* (see end of Section 3.2).

Fig. 6. The assignment procedure DFS-Assign, which demonstrates how to assign values to a given satisfiable subgraph S' from the ranges allocated by *Allocate-SCC*.

from A to Y with weight 1 and one from A to X with weight 2, both depicted as dotted edges in the graph. These edges reflect the tightest constraints between A, Y and X.

4.1   The Assignment Procedure

The assignment procedure assigns values to S'_{Aug} that satisfy its predicates. By Lemma 2 these values satisfy S' as well. The assignment procedure is recursive: we first handle the graph $S'_{\{C',Aug\}}$, the cutpoint graph of S'_{Aug}, where C' is a set of cutpoints of S'_{Aug} and $C' \subseteq C$. The base case of the recursion corresponds to a graph with a single node to which we assign the value 0. Assume that we have already assigned values, recursively, to nodes in C'. Now we assign values to all the regular nodes in S'_{Aug}, by starting at cutpoints (with the values assigned to them by the deeper recursion calls) and doing a DFS-like search. This procedure is shown below in Figure 6.

Referring to Figure 5, the values assigned by DFS-Assign are shown in parenthesis beside each node. At the end of this procedure each node in S' is assigned a single value such that all predicates in S' are satisfied (yet to be proved).

Then we have the following lemma:

Lemma 3. *Assuming that the assignment procedure assigns satisfying values to a cutpoint graph $S'_{\{C',Aug\}}$ from the appropriate ranges, it does so for S'_{Aug} as well from the ranges allocated by Allocate-SCC.*

4.2   The Ranges Allocated by Allocate-SCC Are Adequate

Our goal is to prove that *Allocate-SCC* assigns adequate ranges to the nodes of any given SCC S. We will use the following lemma

Lemma 4. *Assuming Allocate-SCC assigns adequate ranges to S_C, it assigns adequate ranges to all nodes of S.*

This lemma follows directly from Lemma 3. Now we prove the main theorem.

Theorem 1. *Allocate-SCC assigns adequate ranges to nodes of any given SCC S*

Proof. The termination of *Allocate-SCC* follows from Lemma 1. We prove the correctness of *Allocate-SCC* by induction on the number of cutpoints present in the given SCC. The base case is an SCC with one node for which the theorem holds trivially. For the inductive step, it is shown in Lemma 4 that if we can assign adequate ranges to the Cutpoint-graph S_C then the four phases assign adequate ranges to all nodes of the SCC. Thus it follows that for any SCC S *Allocate-SCC* assigns adequate values to the nodes.   □

5   Experimental Results

We now present results of running *Allocate-Graph* on different benchmarks. The results are summarized in the table below.

Example	SMOD	UCLID	SEP	Example	SMOD	UCLID	SEP
bf12.ucl	12	101	28	code27s.smv	85	104	94
bf13.ucl	15	170	48	code32s.smv	114	109	120
bf14.ucl	21	158	33	code37s.smv	57	71	90
bf6.ucl	105	481	127	code38s.smv	32	34	106
bf17.ucl	176	1714	482	code43s.smv	361	555	424
bf18.ucl	280	2102	603	code44s.smv	69	140	84
BurchDill	250	291	336	code46s.smv	264	287	225

The examples beginning with *bf* were derived from software verification problems. The examples beginning with *code* have been used in [6].

We compare our approach against two other methods. The first method, named UCLID, is the standard implementation from UCLID [4], which is based on giving a full range of $1 \ldots n + maxC$, as described in the Introduction ($maxC$ being the sum of all constants). The other method, named SEP was presented in [10] and is discussed in the Introduction as well. The table shows the number of

Boolean variables that are required to encode the ranges assigned by the three different algorithms (given a set of n values the number of Boolean variables required to encode them is logarithmic in n).

As we can see from the results above, our method is clearly superior to the other two methods. We outperform UCLID by nearly 10 times on large examples (bf17.ucl and bf18.ucl). Compared to SEP we outperform it on the big examples by a factor of nearly 3.

On graphs which are densely connected and have small edge weights our algorithm does not do as well as UCLID. For such graphs, the ideal ranges seem to be dependent on the number of variables and relatively independent of the edges. Our algorithm on the other hand is heavily dependent on the edge structure in determining the values and as the edges to nodes ratio increases, the number of values assigned by our algorithm tends to increase as well. Hence on dense graphs, our algorithm ends up assigning too many values.

6   Conclusion and Future Work

We have presented a technique for allocating small adequate ranges for variables in a Separation Logic formula based on analyzing the corresponding *inequalities graph*. The state-space spawned by these small ranges can be then explored by standard SAT or BDD solvers. Experimental results show that our decision procedure can lead to exponential reduction in the state-space to be explored. A number of optimizations for making the decision procedure faster and reduce the ranges further were not presented here due to lack of space. The tool that we have developed, SMOD, is available for research purposes from [1].

As future work, the most important question still needs to be answered is whether it is possible to find a polynomial algorithm for range allocation. Although we did not experience long run-times in all the experiments that we conducted, this can become a bottleneck in the presence of many non-positive cycles in the inequalities graph.

Acknowledgment

We would like to thank Shuvendu Lahiri for helping us by integrating our tool into UCLID and much more.

References

1. www.cs.cmu.edu/~nishants/smod.tar.gz
2. W. Ackermann. *Solvable cases of the Decision Problem*. Studies in Logic and the Foundations of Mathematics. North-Holland, Amsterdam, 1954.
3. G. Audemard, P. Bertoli, A. Cimatti, A. Kornilowicz, and R. Sebastiani. A SAT based approach for solving formulas over boolean and linear mathematical propositions. In *Proc. 18th International Conference on Automated Deduction (CADE'02)*, 2002.

4. R. E. Bryant, S. K. Lahiri, and S. A. Seshia. Modeling and verifying systems using a logic of counter arithmetic with lambda expressions and uninterpreted functions. In E. Brinksma and K.G. Larsen, editors, *Proc. 14th Intl. Conference on Computer Aided Verification (CAV'02)*, volume 2404 of *LNCS*, pages 78–91, Copenhagen, Denmark, July 2002. Springer-Verlag.
5. D. S. Hochbaum, editor. *approximation-algorithms for NP-hard problems*. PWS Publishing Company, 1997.
6. A. Pnueli, Y. Rodeh, O. Strichman, and M. Siegel. The small model property: How small can it be? *Information and computation*, 178(1):279–293, October 2002.
7. V. Pratt. Two easy theories whose combination is hard. Technical report, Massachusetts Institute of Technology, 1977. Cambridge, Mass.
8. R. Shostak. Deciding combinations of theories. *J. ACM*, 31(1):1–12, 1984.
9. O. Strichman. On solving Presburger and linear arithmetic with SAT. In *Formal Methods in Computer-Aided Design (FMCAD 2002)*, pages 160 – 170, Portland, Oregon, Nov 2002.
10. O. Strichman, S.A. Seshia, and R.E. Bryant. Deciding separation formulas with SAT. In E. Brinksma and K.G. Larsen, editors, *Proc. 14th Intl. Conference on Computer Aided Verification (CAV'02)*, volume 2404 of *LNCS*, pages 209–222, Copenhagen, Denmark, July 2002. Springer-Verlag.
11. A. Stump, C. Barrett, and D. Dill. CVC: a cooperating validity checker. In *Proc. 14th Intl. Conference on Computer Aided Verification (CAV'02)*, 2002.
12. M. Talupur, N. Sinha, O. Strichman, and A. Pnueli. Range allocation for separation logic (Full version). Technical Report TR-04-iem/ise-1, Technion, Industrial Engineering and Management, 2004.

An Experimental Evaluation
of Ground Decision Procedures*

Leonardo de Moura and Harald Rueß

SRI International, Computer Science Laboratory
333 Ravenswood Avenue, Menlo Park, CA 94025, USA
Phone: +1 650 859-6136, Fax: +1 650 859-2844
{demoura,ruess}@csl.sri.com

Abstract. There is a large variety of algorithms for ground decision procedures, but their differences, in particular in terms of experimental performance, are not well studied. We compare the behavior of ground decision procedures by comparing the performance of a variety of technologies on benchmark suites with differing characteristics. Based on these experimental results, we discuss relative strengths and shortcomings of different systems.

1 Introduction

Decision procedures are an enabling technology for a growing number of applications of automated deduction in hardware and software verification, planning, bounded model checking, and other search problems. In solving these problems, decision procedures are used to decide the validity of propositional constraints such as

$$z = f(x - y) \wedge x = z + y \rightarrow -y = -(x - f(f(z))).$$

This formula is in the combination of linear arithmetic and an uninterpreted function symbol f. Since all variables are considered to be universally quantified, they can be treated as (Skolem) constants, and hence we say that the formula is *ground*.

Solving propositional formulas with thousands of variables and hundreds of thousands of literals, as required by many applications, is a challenging problem. Over the last couple of years, many different algorithms, heuristics, and tools have been developed in addressing this challenge. Most of these approaches either use extensions of binary decision diagrams [1], or an equisatisfiable reduction of propositional constraint formulas to propositional logic, which is solved using a Davis-Putnam [2] search procedure. With the notable exception of Simplify [3] there is a lack of systematic benchmarking for most implemented systems. Moreover, their differences, especially in terms of experimental performance, are not well studied.

Ultimately, it is our goal to develop comprehensive maps of the behavior of ground decision procedures by comparing the performance of a variety of technologies on

---

* Funded by SRI International, by NSF Grants CCR-0082560, EIA-0224465, and CCR-0326540, DARPA/AFRL-WPAFB Contract F33615-01-C-1908, and NASA Contract B0906005.

R. Alur and D.A. Peled (Eds.): CAV 2004, LNCS 3114, pp. 162–174, 2004.

benchmark suites with differing characteristics, and the study in this paper is an essential first step towards this goal of comprehensive benchmarking. We have been collecting a number of existing benchmarks for ground decision procedures and applied them to CVC and CVC Lite [4], ICS [5], UCLID [6], MathSAT [7], Simplify [3], and SVC [8] systems. This required developing translators from the various benchmark formats to the input languages of the systems under consideration. For the diversity of the algorithms underlying ground decision procedures, we only measure runtimes. We analyze the computational characteristics of each system on each of the benchmarks, and expose specific strengths and weaknesses of the systems under consideration.

Since such an endeavor should ultimately develop into a cooperative ongoing activity across the field, our main emphasis in conducting these experiments is not only on reproducibility but also on reusability and extensibility of our experimental setup. In particular, all benchmarks and all translators we developed for converting input formats, and all experimental results are publicly available at http://www.csl.sri.com/users/demoura/gdp-benchmarks.html.

This paper is structured as follows. In Section 2 we include a brief overview of the landscape of different methods for ground decision procedures, and in Section 3 we describe the decision procedures, benchmarks, and our experimental setup. Section 4 contains our experimental results by pairwise comparing the behavior of decision procedures on each benchmark set, and in Section 5 and 6 we summarize some general observations from these experiments and provide final conclusions.

2   Ground Decision Procedures

We consider *ground decision procedures* (GDP) for deciding propositional satisfiability for formulas with literals drawn from a given constraint theory $\mathcal{T}$. GDPs are usually obtained as extensions of decision procedures for the satisfiability problem of conjunctions of constraints in $\mathcal{T}$. For example, satisfiability for a conjunction of equations and disequations over uninterpreted terms ($\mathcal{U}$) is decidable in $O(n \log(n))$ using congruence closure [9]. Conjunctions of constraints in rational linear arithmetic are solvable in polynomial time, although many algorithms such as Simplex have exponential worst-case behavior. In the theory $\mathcal{D}$ of *difference logic*, arithmetic constraints are restricted to constraints of the form $x - y \leq c$ with c a constant. An $O(n^3)$ algorithm for the conjunction of such constraints is obtained by searching, using the Bellman-Ford algorithm, for negative-weight cycles in the graph with variables as nodes and an edge of weight c from x to y for each such constraints. For individual theories $\mathcal{T}_i$ with decidable satisfiability problems, the union of all $\mathcal{T}_i$'s is often decided using a Nelson-Oppen [10] or a Shostak-like [11, 12] combination algorithm.

Given a procedure for deciding satisfiability of conjunctions of constraints in $\mathcal{T}$ it is straightforward to decide propositional combinations of constraints in $\mathcal{T}$ by transforming the formula into disjunctive normal form, but this is often prohibitively expensive. Better alternatives are to extend binary decision diagrams to include constraints instead of variables (e.g. difference decision diagrams), or to reduce the propositional constraint problem to a purely propositional problem by encoding the semantics of constraints in terms of added propositional constraints (see, for example, Theorem 1 in [13]). Algo-

Table 1. Command line options used to execute GDPs.

ICS	`ulimit -s 30000; ics problem-name.ics`
UCLID	`uclid problem-name.ucl sat 0 zchaff`
CVC	`cvc +sat < problem-name.cvc`
CVC Lite	`cvcl +sat fast < problem-name.cvc`
SVC	`svc problem-name.svc`
Simplify	`Simplify problem-name.smp`
Math-SAT	`mathsat_linux problem-name.ms -bj math -heuristic SatzHeur`

rithms based on this latter approach are characterized by the eagerness or laziness with which constraints are added.

In *eager* approaches to constructing a GDP from a decision procedure for $\mathcal{T}$, propositional constraints formulas are transformed into equisatisfiable propositional formulas. In this way, Ackermann [14] obtains a GDP for the theory $\mathcal{U}$ by adding all possible instances of the congruence axiom and renaming uninterpreted subterms with fresh variables. In the worst case, the number of such axioms is proportional to the square of the length of the given formula. Other theories such as S-expressions or arrays can be encoded using the reductions given by Nelson and Oppen [10]. Variations of Ackermann's trick have been used, for example, by Shostak [15] for arithmetic reasoning in the presence of uninterpreted function symbols, and various reductions of the satisfiability problem of Boolean formulas over the theory of equality with uninterpreted function symbols to propositional SAT problems have recently been described [16], [17], [18]. In a similar vein, an eager reduction to propositional logic works for constraints in difference logic [19].

In contrast, *lazy* approaches introduce part of the semantics of constraints on demand [13], [20], [7], [21]. Let ϕ be the formula whose satisfiability is being checked, and let L be an injective map from fresh propositional variables to the atomic subformulas of ϕ such that $L^{-1}[\phi]$ is a propositional formula. We can use a propositional SAT solver to check that $L^{-1}[\phi]$ is satisfiable, but the resulting truth assignment, say $l_1 \wedge \ldots \wedge l_n$, might be spurious, that is $L[l_1 \wedge \ldots \wedge l_n]$ might not be ground-satisfiable. If that is the case, we can repeat the search with the added *lemma* clause $(\neg l_1 \vee \ldots \vee \neg l_n)$ and invoke the SAT solver on $(\neg l_1 \vee \ldots \vee \neg l_n) \wedge L^{-1}[\phi]$. This ensures that the next satisfying assignment returned is different from the previous assignment that was found to be ground-unsatisfiable. In such an *offline* integration, a SAT solver and a constraint solver can be used as black boxes. In contrast, in an *online* integration the search for satisfying assignments of the SAT solver is synchronized with constructing a corresponding logical context of the theory-specific constraint solver. In this way, inconsistencies detected by the constraint solver may trigger backtracking in the search for satisfying propositional assignments. An effective *online* integration can not be obtained with a black-box decision procedures but requires the constraint solver to process constraints *incrementally* and to be *backtrackable* in that not only the current logical context is maintained but also contexts corresponding to backtracking points in the search for satisfying assignments. The basic refinement loop in the *lazy* integration is usually accelerated by considering negations of minimal inconsistent sets of constraints or "good" over-approximations thereof. These so-called *explanations* are either obtained from an explicitly generated proof object or by tracking dependencies of facts generated during constraint solver runs.

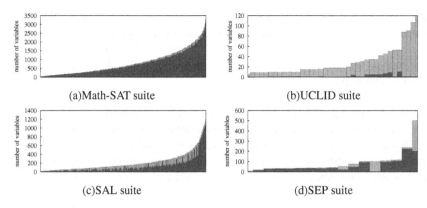

(a)Math-SAT suite   (b)UCLID suite

(c)SAL suite   (d)SEP suite

Fig. 1. Benchmark suites with number of boolean (dark gray) and non-boolean (light gray) variables in each problem.

3   Experimental Setup

We describe the setup of our experiments including the participating systems, the benchmarks and their main characteristics, and the organization of the experiments itself. This setup has been chosen before conducting any experiments.

3.1   Systems

The systems participating in this study implement a wide range of different satisfiability techniques as described in Section 2. All these GDPs are freely available and distributed[1], and in each case we have been using the latest version (as of January 10, 2004). We provide short descriptions in alphabetical order.

The Cooperating Validity Checker. (CVC 1.0a, http://verify.stanford.edu/CVC/) [4] is a GDP for the combination of theories including linear real arithmetic $\mathcal{A}$, uninterpreted function symbols $\mathcal{U}$, functional arrays, and inductive datatypes. Propositional reasoning is obtained by means of a lazy, online integration of the zChaff SAT solver and a constraint solver based on a Shostak-like [11] combination, and explanations are obtained as axioms of proof trees. We also consider the successor system CVC Lite (version 1.0.1, http://chicory.stanford.edu/CVCL/), whose architecture is similar to the one of CVC.

The Integrated Canonizer and Solver. (ICS 2.0, http://ics.csl.sri.com) [5] is a GDP for the combination of theories including linear real arithmetic $\mathcal{A}$, uninterpreted function symbols $\mathcal{U}$, functional arrays, S-expressions, products and coproducts, and bitvectors. It realizes a lazy, online integration of a non-clausal SAT solver with an incremental, backtrackable constraint engine based on a Shostak [11] combination. Explanations are generated and maintained using a simple tracking mechanism.

---

[1] http://www.qpq.org/

UCLID. (version 1.0, http://www-2.cs.cmu.edu/~uclid/) is a GDP for the combination of difference logic and uninterpreted function symbols. It uses an eager transformation to SAT problems, which are solved using zChaff [6]. The use of other theories such as lambda expressions and arrays is restricted in order to eliminate them in preprocessing steps.

Math-SAT. [7] (http://dit.unitn.it/~rseba/Mathsat.html) is a GDP for linear arithmetic based on a black-box constraint solver, which is used to detect inconsistencies in constraints corresponding to partial Boolean assignments in an offline manner. The constraint engine uses a Bellman-Ford algorithm for difference logic constraints and a Simplex algorithm for more general constraints.

Simplify. [3] (http://research.compaq.com/SRC/esc/Simplify.html) is a GDP for linear arithmetic $\mathcal{A}$, uninterpreted functions $\mathcal{U}$, and arrays based on the Nelson-Oppen combination. Simplify uses SAT solving techniques, which do not incorporate many efficiency improvements found in modern SAT solvers. However, Simplify goes beyond the other systems considered here in that it includes heuristic extensions for quantifier reasoning, but this feature is not tested here.

Stanford Validity Checker. (SVC 1.1, http://chicory.stanford.edu/SVC/) [8] decides propositional formulas with uninterpreted function symbols $\mathcal{U}$, rational linear arithmetic $\mathcal{A}$, arrays, and bitvectors. The combination of constraints is decided using a Shostak-style combination extended with binary decision diagrams.

3.2 Benchmark Suites

We have included in this study freely distributed benchmark suites for GDPs with constraints in $\mathcal{A}$ and $\mathcal{U}$ and combinations thereof. These problems range from standard timed automata examples to equivalence checking for microprocessors and the study of fault-tolerant algorithms. For the time being we do not separate satisfiable and unsatisfiable instances. Since some of the benchmarks are distributed in clausal and other in non-clausal form, it is difficult to provide measures on the difficulty of these problems, but Figure 1 contains the number of variables for each benchmark problem. The dark gray bars represents the number of boolean and the light gray bars the number of non-boolean variables.

The Math-SAT Benchmark Suite.
(http://dit.unitn.it/~rseba/Mathsat.html) is composed of timed automata verification problems. The problems are distributed only in clausal normal form and arithmetic is restricted to coefficients in $\{-1, 0, 1\}$. This benchmark format also includes extra-logical *search hints* for the Math-SAT system. This suite comprises 280 problems, 159 of which are in the difference logic fragment. The size of the ASCII representation of these problems ranges from 4Kb to 26Mb. As can be seen in Figure 1(a) most of the variables are boolean[2].

---

[2] We suspect that many boolean variables have been introduced through conversion to CNF.

Table 2. Classification.

Benchmark suite	Sat	Unsat	Unsolved
Math-Sat	37	224	19
UCLID	0	36	2
SAL	21	167	29
SEP	9	8	0

Table 3. Number of timeouts and aborts for each system.

		ICS	UCLID	CVC	CVC Lite	SVC	Simplify	Math-SAT
Math-SAT	timeout	0	3	0	19	50	91	52
suite	aborts	22	21	58	61	39	0	0
UCLID	timeout	4	2	0	9	5	24	n/a
suite	aborts	4	0	14	9	0	0	n/a
SAL	timeout	1	36	1	115	87	99	n/a
suite	aborts	29	4	64	7	4	4	n/a
SEP	timeout	0	0	0	1	1	0	n/a
suite	aborts	0	1	1	1	0	0	n/a

The UCLID Benchmark Suite. (http://www-2.cs.cmu.edu/~uclid) is derived from processor and cache coherence protocol verifications. This suite is distributed in the SVC input format. In particular, propositional structures are non-clausal and constraints include uninterpreted functions $\mathcal{U}$ and difference constraints $\mathcal{D}$. Altogether there are 38 problems, the size of the ASCII representation ranges from 4Kb to 450Kb, and the majority of the literals are non-boolean (Figure 1(b)).

The SAL Benchmark Suite. (http://www.csl.sri.com/users/demoura/gdp-benchmarks.html) is derived from bounded model checking of timed automata and linear hybrid systems, and from test-case generation for embedded controllers. The problems are represented in non-clausal form, and constraints are in full linear arithmetic. This suite contains 217 problems, 110 of which are in the difference logic fragment, the size of the ASCII representation of these problems ranges from 1Kb to 300Kb. Most of the boolean variables are used to encode control flow (Figure 1(c)).

The SEP Benchmark Suite. (http://iew3.technion.ac.il/~ofers/smtlib-local/index.html) is derived from symbolic simulation of hardware designs, timed automata systems, and scheduling problems. The problems are represented in non-clausal form, and constraints in difference logic. This suite includes only 17 problems, the size of the ASCII representation of these problems ranges from 1.5Kb to 450Kb.

We developed various translators from the input format used in each benchmark suite to the input format accepted by each GDP described on the previous section, but Math-SAT. We did not implement a translator to the Math-SAT format because it only accepts formulas in the CNF format, and a translation to CNF would destroy the structural information contained in the original formulas. In addition, no specifics are provided for generating hints for Math-SAT. In developing these translators, we have been careful to preserve the structural information, and we used all the information available to use available language features useful for the underlying search mechanisms[3]. The

---

[3] We have also been contemplating a malicious approach for producing worst-possible translations, but decided against it in such an early stage of benchmarking.

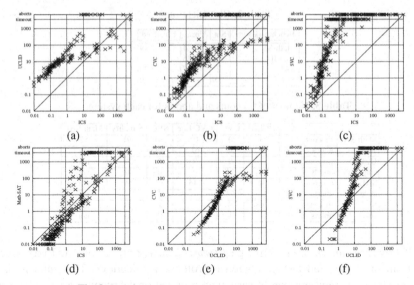

Fig. 2. Runtimes (in seconds) on Math-SAT benchmarks.

Math-SAT *search hints*, however, are ignored in the translation, since this extra-logical information is meaningless for all the other tools.

3.3   Setup

All experiments were performed on machines with 1GHz Pentium III processor 256Kb of cache and 512Mb of RAM, running Red Hat Linux 7.3. Although these machines are now outdated, we were able to set aside 4 machines with identical configuration for our experiments, thereby avoiding error-prone adjustment of performance numbers. We considered an instance of a GDP to *timeout* if it took more than 3600 secs. Each GDP was constrained to 450Mb of RAM for the data area, and 40Mb of RAM for the stack area. We say a GDP *aborts* when it runs out of memory or crashes for other reasons. With these timing and memory constraints running all benchmarks suites requires more than 30 CPU days.

For the diversity of the input languages and the algorithms underlying the GDPs, we do not include any machine-independent and implementation-independent measures. Instead, we restrict ourselves to reporting the user time of each process as reported by Unix. In this way, we are measuring only the systems as implemented, and observations from these experiments about the underlying algorithms can only be made rather indirectly.

With the notable exception of CVC Lite, all GDPs under consideration were obtained in binary format from their respective web sites. The CVC Lite binary was obtained using g++ 3.2.1 and configured in optimized mode. Table 1 contains the command line options used to execute each GDP[4].

---

[4] In [20] the depth first search heuristic (option -dfs) is reported to produce the best overall results for CVC, but we did not use it because this flag causes CVC to produce many incorrect results.

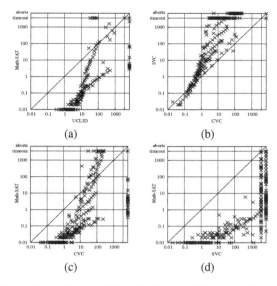

Fig. 3. Runtimes (in seconds) on the Math-SAT benchmarks (cont.).

4   Experimental Results

Table 2 shows the number of satisfiable and unsatisfiable problems[5] for each benchmark, and a problem has been classified "Unsolved" when none of the GDPs could solve it within the time and memory requirements. The scatter graphs in

- Figures 2 and 3 include the results of running CVC, ICS, UCLID, MathSAT, and SVC on the Math-SAT benchmarks,
- Figure 4 contains the runtimes of CVC, ICS, SVC, UCLID on the UCLID benchmarks, and
- Figure 5 reports on our results of running CVC, ICS, SVC, and UCLID on the SAL benchmarks

using the experimental setup as described in Section 3. Points above (below) the diagonal correspond to examples where the system on the x (y) axis is faster than the other; points one division above are an order of magnitude faster; a scatter that is shallower (steeper) than the diagonal indicates the performance of the system on the x (y) axis deteriorates relative to the other as problem size increases; points on the right (top) edge indicate the x (y) axis system timed out or aborted. Multiplicities of dots for timeouts and aborts are resolved in Table 3.

For lack of space, the plots for Simplify and CVC Lite are not included here. Simplify performed poorly in all benchmarks except SEP, and does not seem to be competitive with newer GDP implementations. In the case of CVC Lite, its predecessor system CVC demonstrated over-all superior behavior. Also, the SEP suite did not

---

[5] For validity checkers, satisfiable and unsatisfiable should be read as invalid and valid instances respectively.

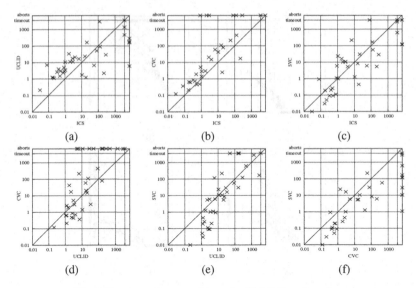

Fig. 4. Runtimes (in seconds) on the UCLID benchmarks.

prove to distinguish well between various systems, as all but one problem could be solved by all systems in a fraction of a second. All these omitted plots are available at http://www.csl.sri.com/users/demoura/gdp-benchmarks.html.

Figures 2 and 3 compare ICS, UCLID, CVC, SVC and Math-SAT on the Math-SAT suite. The plots comparing UCLID contain only the problems in the difference logic fragment supported by UCLID. The results show that the overall performance of ICS is better than those of UCLID, CVC and SVC on most problems of this suite.

With the exception of Math-SAT (which was applied only to its own benchmark set), every other system failed on at least several problems – mainly due to exhaustion of the memory limit. Also, the Math-SAT problems proved to be a non-trivial test on parsers as SVC's parser crashed on several bigger problems (see Table 1). The performance of SVC is affected by the size of the problems and the CNF format used (Figure 3(d)) on this suite, since its search heuristics are heavily dependent on the propositional structure of the formula. On the other hand, the performance of the non-clausal SAT solver of ICS is not quite as heavily impacted by this special format. In fact, ICS is the only GDP which solves all problems solved by Math-SAT (Figure 2(d)), and it also solved several problems not solved by Math-SAT, even though *search hints* were used by Math-SAT. UCLID performs better than CVC and SVC on most of the bigger problems (Figures 2(e) and 2(f)).

Figure 4 compares ICS, UCLID, CVC, and SVC on the UCLID benchmarks. What is surprising here is that SVC is competitive with UCLID on UCLID's own benchmarks (Figure 4(e)). Also, the overall performance of SVC is superior to its predecessor CVC system (Figure 4(f)). ICS does not perform particularly well on this benchmark set in that it exhausts the given memory limit for many of the larger examples.

Figure 5 compares ICS, UCLID, CVC, and SVC on the SAL benchmarks. ICS performs better than UCLID on all examples (Figure 5(a)), and its overall performance

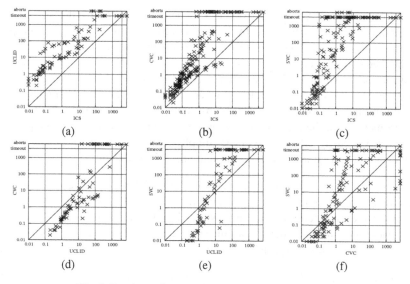

Fig. 5. Runtimes (in seconds) on the SAL benchmarks.

is better than CVC (Figure 5(b)). ICS, UCLID and CVC fail on several problems due lack of memory. Although the overall performance of CVC seems better than UCLID, the latter managed to solve several problems where CVC failed (Figure 5(d)).

5   Observations and Research Questions

As has been mentioned in Section 3, the results produced in our experiments measure mainly implementations of GDPs. Nevertheless, we try to formulate some more general observations about algorithmic strengths and weaknesses from these experiments, which should be helpful in studying and improving GDPs.

Insufficient Constraint Propagation in Lazy Integrations. The eager UCLID system usually outperforms lazy systems such as ICS, CVC, and Math-SAT on problems which require extensive constraint propagation. This seems to be due to the fact that the underlying lazy integration algorithms only propagate inconsistencies detected by the constraint solver, but they do not propagate constraints implied by the current logical context. Suppose a hypothetical problem which contains the atoms $\{x = y, y = z, x = z\}$, and during the search the atoms $x = y$ and $y = z$ are assigned to true, then the atom $x = z$ could be assigned to true by constraint propagation (transitivity), but none of the existing lazy provers propagate this inference. In contrast, these kinds of propagations are performed in eager integrations, since the unit-clause rule of Davis-Putnam like SAT solvers assumes the job of propagating constraints.

Arithmetical Constraints in the Eager Approach. On arithmetic-intensive problems, UCLID usually performs worse than other GDPs with dedicated arithmetic constraint solvers. In particular, UCLID's performance is heavily affected by the size of constants. One of the approaches used by UCLID to reduce difference logic to propositional logic [19] constructs a graph where each node represents an integer variable, and a weighted edge represents a difference constraint. Starting from this graph, a clause is created for each negative cycle. We believe several irrelevant clauses are generated in this process. We say a clause is irrelevant when it cannot be falsified during the search due to, for instance, the presence of other constraints. In several examples, UCLID consumed all memory in the translation to propositional logic. For instance, the problem abz5-900 was easily solved by ICS and Simplify using less than 40Mb, but UCLID consumed all memory during the translation to propositional logic.

Performance vs. Expressiveness. The version of UCLID we have been using is restricted to separation logic, but other systems with support for full arithmetic seem to be competitive even when problems are restricted to this domain. The goal should be a fully general system that reliably does the special cases (restricted theories, bounded instances) at least as well as specialized systems.

Blind Search Problem in Lazy Solvers. The problems in the UCLID suite are mainly composed of non-boolean variables (Figure 1), so almost all atoms are constraints, and the lazy constraint solvers introduce a fresh boolean variable for each distinct constraint. This process produces an underconstrained formula which contains several propositional variables which occurs only once. Thus, the begin of the search is completely chaotic, and arbitrary, since from the point of view of the SAT solving engine any assignment will satisfy the apparently easy and underconstrained formula. We say the SAT engine starts an almost *blind search*, where the successful search heuristics developed by the SAT community are hardly useful. Our hypothesis is corroborated by the Math-SAT and SAL suites, where several boolean variables are used to encode the control flow and finite domains. In this case, although the SAT engine does not know the hidden relationships between the freshly added boolean variables, it is guided by the control flow exposed by the boolean variables. This hypothesis also helps explaining why SVC performs better than ICS and CVC on the UCLID suite, simply because SVC uses specialized heuristics based on the structure of the formula.

Memory Usage. Math-SAT and Simplify are the systems using the least amount of memory. In contrast, CVC often aborts by running out of memory instead of running up its time limits. A similar phenomenon can be observed with ICS. We have traced this deficiency back to imprecise generation of explanations for pruning Boolean assignments. For instance, union-find structures are commonly to represent conjunctions of equalities, but a naive logging mechanism of dependencies might already produce extraneous *explanations* [22]. Better tradeoffs between the accuracy of the generated explanations and the cost for computing them are needed. Another problem in systems such as ICS and CVC is the maintenance of information to perform backtracking. Math-SAT is a non-backtrackable system, so it does not suffer from this problem, at the cost of having to restart from scratch every time an inconsistency is detected.

Loss of Structural Information. When developing the translators for these experiments, we noticed that the performance of most solvers heavily depends on the way problems are encoded. For instance, the repetitive application of the transformation $F[t] \implies F[x] \wedge x = t$ with t a term occurring in F, and x a fresh variable, transforms many easy problems into very hard problems for UCLID, CVC and CVC Lite.

6 Conclusions

Our performance study demonstrates that recently developed translation-based GDPs – eager or lazy – well advance the state-of-the-art. However, this study also exposes some specific weaknesses for each of the GDP tools under consideration. Handling of arithmetic needs to be improved for eager systems, whereas lazy systems can be considerably improved by a tighter integration of constraint propagation, specialized search heuristics, and the generation of more precise explanations. A main impediment for future improvements in the field of GDPs, however, is not necessarily a lack of new algorithms in the field, but rather the limited availability of meaningful benchmarks. Ideally, these benchmarks are distributed in a form close to the problem description (e.g. not necessarily in clausal normal form). A collaborative effort across the field of GDPs is needed here [23].

References

1. Bryant, R.E.: Graph-based algorithms for boolean function manipulation. IEEE Transactions in Computers **8** (1986) 677–691
2. Davis, M., Putnam, H.: A computing procedure for quantification theory. Journal of the ACM **7** (1960) 201–215
3. Detlefs, D., Nelson, G., Saxe, J.B.: Simplify: A theorem prover for program checking. Technical Report HPL-2003-148, HP Labs (2003)
4. Stump, A., Barrett, C.W., Dill, D.L.: CVC: a cooperating validity checker. In: Proc. of CAV'02. Volume 2404 of LNCS. (2002)
5. Filliâtre, J.C., Owre, S., Rueß, H., Shankar, N.: ICS: Integrated Canonization and Solving. In: Proc. of CAV'01. Volume 2102 of LNCS. (2001)
6. Bryant, R.E., Lahiri, S.K., Seshia, S.A.: Modeling and verifying systems using a logic of counter arithmetic with lambda expressions and uninterpreted functions. In: Proc. of CAV'02. Volume 2404 of LNCS. (2002)
7. Audemard, G., Bertoli, P., Cimatti, A., Kornilowicz, A., Sebastiani, R.: A SAT based approach for solving formulas over boolean and linear mathematical propositions. In: Proc. of CADE'02. (2002)
8. Barrett, C., Dill, D., Levitt, J.: Validity checking for combinations of theories with equality. LNCS **1166** (1996) 187–201
9. Downey, P.J., Sethi, R., Tarjan, R.E.: Variations on the common subexpressions problem. Journal of the ACM **27** (1980) 758–771
10. Nelson, G., Oppen, D.C.: Simplification by cooperating decision procedures. ACM Transactions on Programming Languages and Systems **1** (1979) 245–257
11. Shostak, R.E.: Deciding combinations of theories. Journal of the ACM **31** (1984) 1–12
12. Shankar, N., Rueß, H.: Combining Shostak theories. In: Proc. of RTA'02. Volume 2378 of LNCS. (2002)
13. de Moura, L., Rueß, H., Sorea, M.: Lazy theorem proving for bounded model checking over infinite domains. In: Proc. of CADE'02. Volume 2392 of LNCS. (2002)

14. Ackermann, W.: Solvable cases of the decision problem. Studies in Logic and the Foundation of Mathematics (1954)
15. Shostak, R.E.: Deciding linear inequalities by computing loop residues. Journal of the ACM **28** (1981) 769–779
16. Goel, A., Sajid, K., Zhou, H., Aziz, A.: BDD based procedures for a theory of equality with uninterpreted functions. LNCS **1427** (1998) 244–255
17. Pnueli, A., Rodeh, Y., Shtrichman, O., Siegel, M.: Deciding equality formulas by small domains instantiations. LNCS **1633** (1999) 455–469
18. Bryant, R.E., German, S., Velev, M.N.: Exploiting positive equality in a logic of equality with uninterpreted functions. LNCS **1633** (1999) 470–482
19. Strichman, O., Seshia, S.A., Bryant, R.E.: Reducing linear inequalities to propositional formulas. In: Proc. of CAV'02. Volume 2404 of LNCS. (2002)
20. Barrett, C.W., Dill, D.L., Stump, A.: Checking satisfiability of first-order formulas by incremental translation to SAT. In: Proc. of CAV'02. Volume 2404 of LNCS. (2002)
21. Joshi, R., Ou, X., Saxe, J.B., Flanagan, C.: Theorem proving using lazy proof explication. In: Proc. of CAV'03. Volume 2725 of LNCS. (2003)
22. de Moura, L., Rueß, H., Shankar, N.: Justifying Equality. Submitted for publication, http://www.csl.sri.com/users/ruess/papers/PDPAR04/index.html (2004)
23. Ranise, S., Tinelli, C.: The smt-lib format: An initial proposal. In: Proceedings of the 1st International Workshop on Pragmatics of Decision Procedures in Automated Reasoning (PDPAR'03), Miami, Florida. (2003) 94–111

DPLL(T): Fast Decision Procedures

Harald Ganzinger[1], George Hagen[2], Robert Nieuwenhuis[3],
Albert Oliveras[3], and Cesare Tinelli[2]

[1] MPI für Informatik, Saarbrücken, Germany
www.mpi-sb.mpg.de/~hg
[2] Dept. of Computer Science, University of Iowa*
www.cs.uiowa.edu/~{ghagen,tinelli}
[3] Tech. Univ. of Catalonia, Barcelona**
www.lsi.upc.es/~{roberto,oliveras}

Abstract. The logic of equality with uninterpreted functions (EUF) and its extensions have been widely applied to processor verification, by means of a large variety of progressively more sophisticated (*lazy* or *eager*) translations into propositional SAT. Here we propose a new approach, namely a general DPLL(X) engine, whose parameter X can be instantiated with a specialized solver $Solver_T$ for a given theory T, thus producing a system DPLL(T). We describe this DPLL(T) scheme, the interface between DPLL(X) and $Solver_T$, the architecture of DPLL(X), and our solver for EUF, which includes incremental and backtrackable congruence closure algorithms for dealing with the built-in equality and the integer successor and predecessor symbols. Experiments with a first implementation indicate that our technique already outperforms the previous methods on most benchmarks, and scales up very well.

1 Introduction

The logic of equality with uninterpreted functions (EUF) [BD94] and its extensions has been widely used for processor verification (see, e.g., [BD94,BGV01] [BLS02b,VB03]).

For deciding validity – or, dually, unsatisfiability – of formulas in this kind of logics, during the last five years many successively more sophisticated techniques have been developed, most of which can be classified as being *eager* or *lazy*. In the eager approaches the input formula is translated, in a single satisfiability-preserving step, into a propositional CNF, which is checked by a SAT solver for satisfiability. The lazy approaches [ACG00,dMR02,ABC+02,BDS02,FJOS03] instead abstract each atom of the input formula by a distinct propositional variable, use a SAT solver to find a propositional model of the formula, and then check that model against the theory. Models that are incompatible with

---

* Work partially supported by NSF Grant No. 237422.
** Work partially supported by the Spanish CICYT project Maverish ref. TIC2001-2476 and by a FPU grant, ref. AP2002-3533, from the Spanish Secretaría de Estado de Educación y Universidades.

R. Alur and D.A. Peled (Eds.): CAV 2004, LNCS 3114, pp. 175–188, 2004.

the theory are discarded from later consideration by adding a proper *lemma* to the original formula. This process is repeated until a model compatible with the theory is found or all possible propositional models have been explored. Also less lazy variants exist (e.g., in CVC, [BDS02]), in which (partial) propositional models are checked incrementally against the theory while they are built by the SAT solver; however, from partial models that are consistent with the theory no information is derived, contrary to what is proposed here. The main advantage of such lazy approaches is their flexibility, since they can relatively easily combine new decision procedures for different logics with existing SAT solvers.

For the logic of EUF the eager approaches are in general faster than the lazy ones, probably because the theory information is used to *prune* the search, rather than to validate it *a posteriori*. Among the eager approaches for EUF, two different encodings into propositional logic are at present predominant. The first one, known as the *EIJ* (or *per-constraint*) encoding, abstracts each equality atom $t_i=t_j$ by a propositional variable e_{ij} and takes care of the equality by imposing additional transitivity constraints [BV02,SSB02]. A drawback of this technique is that when the number of transitivity constraints is too large, the exponential blowup in the formula may make it too hard for the SAT-solver. The second one, known as the small domain (SD) encoding [PRSS99,BLS02b], is essentially an $O(n \, log \, n)$-size encoding that gets transitivity for free, at the expense of a certain loss of structure, by translating equalities into formulas instead of into single propositional variables. In order to get the best of both encodings, two different *hybrid* approaches were presented in [BLS02a] and [SLB03], based on an analysis of the input problem that estimates properties such as the number of transitivity constraints.

In this paper we introduce the first (to our knowledge) technique that is not based on such lazy or eager translations into SAT. Building on independent previous work by some of the authors [Tin02,NO03], we propose a new approach based on a general engine for propositional solving, DPLL(X), parametrized by a solver for a theory of interest. A system DPLL(T) for deciding the satisfiability of CNF formulas in a theory T is produced by instantiating the parameter X with a module $Solver_T$ that can handle conjunctions of literals in T. For instance, in the case of the pure EUF logic, T is just the theory of equality.

The basic idea is similar to the $CLP(X)$ scheme for constraint logic programming: provide a clean and modular, but at the same time efficient, integration of specialized theory solvers within a general purpose engine, in our case one based on the Davis-Putnam-Logemann-Loveland procedure [DP60,DLL62]. In [Tin02] a DPLL(T) scheme was already given in a more high-level abstract form, as a sequent-style calculus. Although no detailed interface was defined there between the DPLL(X) engine and the theory solver, several optimization strategies were already discussed. The framework given here can be seen as a concrete realization of the calculus in [Tin02], except that, contrary to [Tin02], we do not expect $Solver_T$ to give always complete answers. Relaxing that requirement does not affect completeness, but turns out to be crucial for efficiency, at least in the EUF case. A DPLL(X) scheme was introduced and informally described in [NO03].

There, however, emphasis was placed on the development of new congruence closure algorithms to be used in the theory solver for the EUF logic.

The concrete DPLL(T) scheme and its architecture and implementation presented here combine the advantages of the eager and lazy approaches. On the one hand, experiments reveal that, as soon as the theory predicates start playing a significant role in the formula, our initial implementation of DPLL(T) already outperforms all other approaches. On the other hand, our approach is similar in flexibility to the lazy approaches: more general logics can be dealt with by simply plugging in other solvers into our general DPLL(X) engine, provided that these solvers conform to a minimal interface, described later.

This paper is structured as follows. In Section 2 we describe in detail the DPLL(T) scheme and the kind of logics it can be applied to, discussing the advantages and disadvantages of the small interface. The architecture of our current DPLL(X) implementation is given in Section 3. Section 4 describes our solver for EUF, which includes incremental congruence closure algorithms that deal with the built-in equality and the integer successor and predecessor symbols, as well as with backtracking. Finally, Section 5 gives experimental results of our preliminary implementation of DPLL(T) for EUF, and Section 6 concludes and outlines a number of promising research directions for future work, in particular for instantiating the DPLL(X) engine with solvers for other theories.

2   From DPLL to DPLL(T)

In this section we describe the main characteristics of the DPLL(T) scheme. Any DPLL(T) system consists of two parts: the global DPLL(X) module and a solver $Solver_T$ for the given theory T. The DPLL(X) part is a general DPLL engine that is independent of any particular theory T. Here we will use as examples three possible instances for the theory part T: the ones for propositional logic, pure EUF, and EUF with successors and predecessors.

2.1   The Logics under Consideration

In this paper we will consider the satisfiability problem of formulas in CNF, that is, of a given set S (a conjunction) of clauses. By a clause we mean a disjunction of literals, each literal l being of the form A or $\neg A$, where A is an atom drawn from a set $\mathcal{A}$. What $\mathcal{A}$ is depends on the theory T under consideration.

An *interpretation* I is a function $I \colon \mathcal{A} \to \{0, 1\}$. We write $I \models l$ if the literal l *is true in* I, that is, if l is a positive atom A with $I(A) = 1$ or l is a negated atom $\neg A$ with $I(A) = 0$. For each theory T, we will consider only T-*interpretations*, that is, interpretations that *agree* with the axioms of T, in a sense that will be made precise below for the theories considered here. An interpretation (resp. T-interpretation) I is a *model* (resp. T-*model*) of a clause set S if in each clause of S there is at least one literal l that is true in I. The aim of this work is to design algorithms for deciding whether a clause set S has a T-model, and exhibiting such a model whenever it exists. For all logics under consideration in this paper, this problem is easily shown to be NP-complete.

Propositional Logic. The atoms are just propositional symbols of a set $\mathcal{P}$, and the interpretations under consideration are unrestricted, i.e, any truth assignment $I: \mathcal{P} \to \{0, 1\}$ is admitted: the theory T is empty in this case.

Pure EUF. An atom is either of the form $P(t_1, \ldots, t_n)$ where P is an n-ary symbol of a set of fixed-arity predicate symbols $\mathcal{P}$, or an equation of the form $s{=}t$, where s, t and $t_1, \ldots, t_n$ are terms built over a set of fixed-arity function symbols. All constants (0-ary symbols) are terms, and $f(s_1, \ldots, s_n)$ is a term whenever f is a non-constant n-ary symbol and $s_1, \ldots, s_n$ are terms[1]. In the following, lowercase (possibly indexed) s, t, and u always denote terms, and literals $\neg s{=}t$ are usually written as $s \neq t$. In pure EUF the theory T expresses that '=' is a congruence, i.e., it is reflexive (R), symmetric (S), transitive (T), and monotonic (M); hence the only admissible interpretations I are the ones satisfying the conditions below for all terms s, t, s_i, and t_i:

R: $I \models s{=}s$
S: $I \models s{=}t$ if $I \models t{=}s$
T: $I \models s{=}t$ if $I \models s{=}u$ and $I \models u{=}t$ for some term u
M1: $I \models f(s_1 \ldots s_n){=}f(t_1 \ldots t_n)$ if $I \models s_i{=}t_i$ for all i in $1..n$
M2: $I \models P(s_1 \ldots s_n)$ if $I \models P(t_1 \ldots t_n)$ and $I \models s_i{=}t_i$ for all i in $1..n$

EUF with Successors and Predecessors. This subset of the CLU logic from [BLS02b] is the extension of EUF with two distinguished unary function symbols, *Succ* and *Pred*. Besides the congruence axioms for '=', the interpretations I must also satisfy the following for all terms t:

$$I \models Succ(Pred(t)){=}t \qquad I \models Pred(Succ(t)){=}t \qquad \forall n > 0,\ I \models Succ^n(t) \neq t$$

where $Succ^n(t)$ denotes the term $Succ(\ldots Succ(t)\ldots)$ headed with n *Succ* symbols applied to t; hence the last axiom scheme denotes an infinite set of axioms. Note that $I \models Pred^n(t) \neq t$ is a consequence of the above.

2.2   DPLL(X): The General DPLL Part of DPLL(T)

The DPLL(X) part of a DPLL(T) system is the one that does not depend on the concrete theory T. It can be like any DPLL procedure, with basically all its usual features such as heuristics for selecting the next decision literal, unit propagation procedures, conflict analysis and clause learning, or its policy for doing restarts. Like in the propositional case, it always considers atoms as purely syntactic objects. The only substantial difference with a standard propositional DPLL procedure is that the DPLL(X) engine relies on a *theory solver* for T, denoted here by $Solver_T$, for managing all information about the current interpretation I.

---

[1] Here we do not consider any *if-then-else* constructs, since they do not increase the expressive power of the logics and are eliminated, in linear time, in a structure-preserving preprocessing phase, which moreover preserves conjunctive normal forms. Each occurrence of a (sub)term *if-then-else*(F, s, t) is replaced by a new constant symbol v, and $(\neg F \vee v = s) \wedge (F \vee v = t)$ is added to the formula. Boolean *if-then-else*(A, B, C) constructs are simply considered as $(\neg A \vee B) \wedge (A \vee C)$.

Another difference is that it does not use certain optimization for SAT solvers, such as the *pure literal* rule, which as already pointed out in [BDS02,Tin02], among others, is in general not sound in the presence of a theory T.

2.3 The *Solver$_T$* Part of DPLL(T)

Solver$_T$ knows what the real atoms $\mathcal{A}$ are, and knows about the theory T under consideration. It maintains a *partial* interpretation I: one that is defined only for some literals of the set $\mathcal{L}$ of all literals occurring in the problem input to the DPLL(T) prover. In the following, the literals of $\mathcal{L}$ are called $\mathcal{L}$-literals. Inside *Solver$_T$*, I is seen as a stack of literals, which is possible because I can equivalently be considered as the set of all $\mathcal{L}$-literals that are true in I. In the following, this stack will be called the I-stack. We say that a literal l is a *T-consequence* of I, denoted $I \models_T l$, if l is true in all total T-interpretations extending I. It is assumed that for every $\mathcal{L}$-literal l the solver is able to decide whether $I \models_T l$ or not. Essentially, *Solver$_T$* is an abstract data type with the following five simple operations, which are all is needed for the interface between DPLL(X) and *Solver$_T$*:

Initialize($\mathcal{L}$: Literal set). This procedure initializes *Solver$_T$* with $\mathcal{L}$. It also initializes the I-stack to the empty stack.

SetTrue(l: $\mathcal{L}$-literal): $\mathcal{L}$-literal set. This function raises an "inconsistency" exception if $I \models_T \neg l$ with the current I-stack. Otherwise it pushes l onto the I-stack, and returns a set of $\mathcal{L}$-literals that have become a T-consequence of I only *after* extending I with l.
For example, in the EUF case, if $I \models a=b$ and $I \models d=c$, one of the literals returned by SetTrue($d=b$) can be $f(a,a)=f(b,c)$, if this is an $\mathcal{L}$-literal.
For efficiency reasons, the returned set can be incomplete; for example, in EUF, with SetTrue($f(a) \neq f(b)$) it may be expensive to detect and return all consequences $a' \neq b'$ where $I \models a=a'$ and $I \models b=b'$ (see also Section 4).

IsTrue?(l: $\mathcal{L}$-literal): Boolean. This function returns **true** if $I \models_T l$, and **false** otherwise. Note that the latter can be either because $I \models_T \neg l$, or because neither $I \models_T l$ nor $I \models_T \neg l$.

Backtrack(n: Natural). This procedure pops n literals from the I-stack. Note that n is expected to be no bigger than the size of the I-stack.

Explanation(l: $\mathcal{L}$-literal): $\mathcal{L}$-literal set. This function returns a subset J of I such that $J \models_T l$, for a given literal l such that l was returned as a T-consequence of a SetTrue(l') operation and no backtracking popping off this l' has taken place since then.
Intuitively, these conditions ensure that the "proof" of $I \models_T l$ that was found when l' was asserted is still valid. Note that several such J may exist; for example, in EUF, both $\{\, a \neq b,\ b=c \,\}$ and $\{\, a \neq d,\ d=c \,\}$ may be correct explanations for the literal $a \neq c$.

This operation is used by DPLL(X) for conflict analysis and clause learning. In our implementation it is used specifically to build an implication graph similar to those built by modern SAT solvers. For this application, it is also required that all literals in J are in the I-stack at heights lower than or equal to the height of the literal l' (i.e., no other "later" proof is returned; see Section 3 for an example).

We point out that the solver is independent from the characteristics of the DPLL(X) procedure that will use it. For example, it does not know about decision levels, unit propagation, or related features. In fact, a solver with this interface could be used as well in the context of non-DPLL systems, such as the lazy (or lemmas-on-demand) approaches, or even in resolution-based systems. Note that something like the Explanation operation is needed as well to produce the lemmas in such lazy approaches, and in general, in any deduction system that has to produce proof objects.

These five operations constitute in some sense a minimal set of operations for the exchange of information between the two main components of a DPLL(T) system. Having only these operations provides a high degree of modularity and independence between the global DPLL(X) engine and the theory solver $Solver_T$.

Our current DPLL(T) implementation has a DPLL(X) engine built in house to use the operations above. However, because of the simplicity and modularity of the solver interface, we believe that developers of state-of-the-art SAT solvers would need relatively little work to turn their solvers into DPLL(X) engines.

Although our implementation already performs very well for EUF, a tighter interconnection by means of more operations might enhance its performance. This could be achieved for example by having more fine-tuned theory-specific heuristics for choosing the next decision literal (see Section 6). However, possible efficiency gains would come at the expense of less modularity, and hence require more implementation work, especially when developing solvers for new theories.

3   Our Architecture for DPLL(X)

The current modular design is the result of developments and experiments with our own DPLL(X) implementation (in C). The current system has a clear Chaff-like flavor, mirroring Chaff's features as described in [MMZ+01,ZMMM01], with a 2-watched literal implementation for efficient unit propagation, and the VSIDS heuristic for selecting the next decision literal, in combination with restarts and the 1UIP learning scheme. Most of Chaff's features lift from DPLL to DPLL(X) without major modifications, so here we only point out some differences.

One difference arises in unit clause detection. In the propositional case, when a literal l becomes true, $\neg l$ is the only literal that becomes false before unit propagation is applied to the clause set, so new unit clauses can only come from clauses containing $\neg l$. In DPLL(T), on the other hand, additional literals can be set to false as a consequence of the assertions made to the theory solver. This possibility considerably increases the extent of unit propagations in DPLL(T) and, correspondingly reduces the size of the search space for the DPLL(X) engine. For example, in the EUF case, if $a \neq c \lor P$ is in the clause set and $I \models_T a = b$,

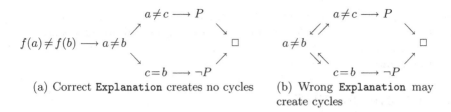

(a) Correct **Explanation** creates no cycles

(b) Wrong **Explanation** may create cycles

Fig. 1. Creation of undesirable cycles in the implication graph.

then setting a literal such as $b{=}c$ to true will make $a{\neq}c$ false and so produce P as a new unit consequence. We point out that this fact will be discovered by the DPLL(X) engine only if the set returned by the call **SetTrue**($b{=}c$) does in fact contain $a \neq c$ which, depending on the theory solver implementation, might or might not be the case. In any case, failing to return $a \neq c$ does not affect the completeness of the overall DPLL(T) system, only the extent of unit propagation.

Another source of incomplete unit clause detection is that two different literals may in fact be equivalent in the current state of the interpretation: again in the EUF case, if in $Solver_T$ we have $I \models_T a{=}b$, and there is a two-literal clause $a{=}c \lor b{=}c$, then the unit consequence $a{=}c$ (or, equivalently, $b{=}c$) will not be detected.

Concerning conflict analysis, the construction of the implication graph is more complex in DPLL(T) than in Chaff. In the latter, a node labeled with a literal l with antecedents nodes $l_1, \ldots, l_n$ is always due to a clause $\neg l_1 \lor \ldots \lor \neg l_n \lor l$ on which unit propagation has taken place. Hence, to build the implication graph it suffices to have, together with each such l, a pointer to its associated clause. In DPLL(T), an implication graph can contain, in addition to nodes like the above, also nodes l that are a T-consequence of their antecedents $l_1, \ldots, l_n$. Such nodes l are those returned by **SetTrue** calls to $Solver_T$, and can be recognized as such since they have no pointer to an associated clause. Their antecedents can be obtained from the solver itself by calling **Explanation**(l). For example, a run of the DPLL(X) algorithm on the clauses:

$$f(a){\neq}f(b) \lor d{\neq}e \qquad a{=}b \lor a{\neq}c \qquad a{=}b \lor c{=}b \qquad a{=}c \lor P \qquad c{\neq}b \lor \neg P$$

can be as follows:

1. **SetTrue**($f(a){\neq}f(b)$). Decision. **SetTrue** returns $a{\neq}b$, a T-consequence.
2. **SetTrue**($a{\neq}c$). Unit propagation of $a{\neq}b$ on $a{=}b \lor a{\neq}c$.
3. **SetTrue**($c{=}b$). Unit propagation of $a{\neq}b$ on $a{=}b \lor c{=}b$.
4. **SetTrue**(P). Unit propagation of $a{\neq}c$ on $a{=}c \lor P$.
5. **SetTrue**($\neg P$). Unit propagation of $c{=}b$ on $c{\neq}b \lor \neg P$. Conflict!

The implication graph is built backwards from P and $\neg P$. When $a{\neq}b$ is reached, **Explanation**($a{\neq}b$) is called, and indeed one possible explanation is $f(a){\neq}f(b)$. This process results in the graph depicted in Figure 1(a). Note that $\{a{\neq}c, c{=}b\}$

also has $a \neq b$ as a T-consequence, but using that set would lead to the graph in Figure 1(b), which has cycles. To avoid cycles, it is enough for Explanation(l) to return explanations that are "older" than l, as precised in the definition of Explanation.

4   A Solver for EUF

A key ingredient for a solver for EUF is an algorithm for congruence closure. Now, the $O(n \; log \; n)$ DST congruence closure algorithm given in [DST80] (see also [NO80]) needs a relatively expensive initial transformation to directed acyclic graphs of outdegree 2. In [NO03] we proposed to replace this transformation by another one, at the formula representation level: we *Currify*, like in the implementation of functional languages; as a result, there will be only one binary "apply" function symbol (denoted here by a dot ".") and constants. For example, Currifying $f(a, g(b), b)$ gives $\cdot(\cdot(\cdot(f, a), \cdot(g, b)), b)$. Furthermore, like in the abstract congruence closure approaches (cf. [Kap97,BT00]), we introduce new constant symbols c for giving names to non-constant subterms t; such t are then replaced everywhere by c, and the equation $t = c$ is added. Then, in combination with Currification, one can obtain the same efficiency as in more sophisticated DAG implementations by appropriately indexing the new constants like c, which play the role of the pointers to the (shared) subterms like t in the DAG approaches. For example, we flatten the equation $\cdot(\cdot(\cdot(f, a), \cdot(g, b)), b) = b$ by replacing it by the four equations $\cdot(f, a) = c$, $\cdot(g, b) = d$, $\cdot(c, d) = e$, and $\cdot(e, b) = b$.

These two (structure-preserving) transformations are done in linear time *once and for all* on the input formula given to our DPLL(T) procedure. As a consequence, since all compound terms (atoms) occuring in the EUF formula have gotten a "name", i.e., they are equal to some constant, all equality atoms in the EUF formula are in fact equations between constants. Furthermore, the congruence closure algorithm of $Solver_T$ only needs to infer consequences from a fixed, static set of equations E of the form $\cdot(a, b) = c$, where a, b and c are constants (note that the $\cdot$ symbol does not occur outside E). This makes our (DST-like) algorithm surprisingly simple and clean, and hence easier to extend. Our implementation of [NO03] also runs in $O(n \; log \; n)$ time, but of course it can be much faster than algorithms for arbitrary terms[2]. Once the closure is computed, deciding whether two constants a and b belong to the same class, i.e., all positive IsTrue?($a = b$) operations, can be done in constant time.

The data structures for congruence closure are:

1. *Pending unions*: a list of pairs of constants yet to be merged.
2. The *Representative* table: an array indexed by constants, containing for each constant its current representative (this can also be seen as a union-find data structure with *eager path compression*).
3. The *Class lists*: for each representative, the list of all constants in its class.

---

[2] In fact, it is about 50 times faster than earlier implementations such as [TV01] on the benchmarks of [TV01].

4. The *Lookup table*: for each input term $\cdot(a, b)$, a call *Lookup(Representative(a)*, *Representative(b))* returns in constant time a constant c such that $\cdot(a, b)$ is equivalent to c, and returns $\perp$ if there is no such c.
5. The *Use lists*: for each representative a, the list of input equations $\cdot(b, c)=d$ such that a is the representative of b or c (or of both).

Each iteration of the algorithm roughly amounts to picking a pending union, and then using the lookup table and the use lists for efficiently detecting new pairs of constants to be merged. We refer to [NO03] for a detailed description and analysis of the algorithm, as well as for its extension to successor and predecessor symbols, which is also $O(n \ log \ n)$.

We now briefly describe the other data structures and algorithms for the $Solver_T$ operations, following a notation where unprimed constants a, b, c are always representatives of primed ones a', b', c'; symbols d and e can be representatives or not.

The Literal Lists and Their Use for SetTrue. Upon its initialization, $Solver_T$ builds, once and for all, for each constant d, a *positive literal list* containing all positive DPLL(X) literals of the form $d = e$, i.e., all positive literals containing d that have been communicated to $Solver_T$ in the Initialize operation. Analogously, there is also a *negative literal list* for each d.

If a positive SetTrue, and its subsequent congruence closure, produces a union such that a class with former representative a is now represented by a different b, then, for each a' in the class list of a, the positive literal list of a' is traversed and all $a'=b'$ in this list are returned as T-consequences. Also the negative literal list of all such a' is traversed, returning those $a' \neq c'$ such that $a \neq c$ is stored in *Diseq*, a hash table containing all currently true disequalities between representatives; analogously also the negative literal list of all b' is traversed.

After a SetTrue operation of a negative equation with representative form $a \neq b$, the negative literal list of all a' is traversed (or equivalently, the one of all b', if this is expected to be less work), returning all $a' \neq b'$.

Backtracking. This is dealt with by means of a mixed policy: unions between constants are stacked in order to be undone. The *Diseq* hash table and the *Lookup* data structure (another hash table) are not restored under backtracking but instead have time stamps (the I-stack height combined with a global counter).

Explanations. A newly derived positive equality is a T-consequence of a set of positive SetTrue operations and of the equations inside the congruence closure module. Negative equations are also T-consequences of such positive equalities, but in addition they are always caused as well by a single negative SetTrue.

Hence, for retrieving the explanations for DPLL(X) literals, we need to be able to proceed "backwards" in our data structures until the set of initial SetTrue operations is reached. At each congruence propagation deriving $d=e$ as a consequence of $\cdot(a', b')=d$ and $\cdot(a'', b'')=e$, (pointers to) these two equations are kept, allowing one to continue backwards with the explanations of $a'=a''$ and $b'=b''$. In addition, there is a method for efficiently extracting from a (slightly extended) union-find data structure the list of unions explaining a certain equality.

Finally, for explaining a negative equality $d_1 \neq e_1$, there is an additional table for retrieving the single negative $\texttt{SetTrue}(d_2 \neq e_2)$ operation that caused it; the remaining part of the explanation can then be found backwards, as the union of the explanations of $d_1 = d_2$ and $e_1 = e_2$.

5   Experimental Results

Experiments have been done with all 54 available benchmarks (generated from verification problems) that can be handled in EUF with successors and predecessors. Most of them were provided by the UCLID group at CMU[3]. All benchmarks are in SVC format [BDL96] (see [BLS02a] for more details on them).

The table below contains (in its second column) the translation times for the four eager approaches described in Section 1: SD and EIJ [VB03], and the two hybrid methods Hybrid1 [BLS02a] and Hybrid2 [SLB03]. All translations were done using the state-of-the-art translator provided within the UCLID 1.0 tool. Furthermore, for two major SAT solvers, zChaff [MMZ+01] (version 2003.12.04) and BerkMin [GN02] (its recent version 561) the running times on the translated formulas are given. For a fair comparison with our system, the times for the zChaff and BerkMin runs *include* the translation times as well, since those translations are not mere formats conversions but the result of sophisticated algorithms for reducing the size and the search space of the propositional formula produced. The choice of zChaff and BerkMin is motivated by the fact that our current DPLL(X) engine is modeled after zChaff and that BerkMin is presently considered one of the best SAT solvers overall. The first table has an extra column with the running times of SVC (version 1.1) as well.

Results are in seconds and are aggregated per family of benchmarks, with times greater than 100s rounded to whole numbers[4]. All experiments were run on a 2GHz 512MB Pentium-IV under Linux, with the same settings for each benchmark except for the "Two queues" benchmarks where our system had learning turned off. Each benchmark was run for 6000 seconds. An annotation of the form (n t) or (n m) in a column indicates respectively that the system timed out or ran out of memory on n benchmarks. Each timeout or memory out is counted as 6000s.

We point out that our current DPLL(X) implementation is far less tightly coded than zChaff, and is more than one order of magnitude slower than zChaff on propositional problems, even when the overhead due to the calls to $Solver_T$ is eliminated. Considering that BerkMin consistently dominates zChaff on all the benchmark families, it is remarkable that our system performs better than the UCLID+BerkMin combination on the great majority of the families. In fact, there is no unique translation-based approach that outperforms DPLL(T) on more than two benchmark families. Furthermore, DPLL(T) is faster than SVC on all benchmarks, and so also faster than the lazy approach-based systems CVC [BDS02] and Verifun [FJOS03] which, as shown in [FJOS03], are outperformed

---

[3] We are grateful to Shuvendu Lahiri and Sanjit Seshia for their kind assistance.

[4] Individual results for each benchmark can be found at www.lsi.upc.es/~oliveras, together with all the benchmarks and an executable of our system.

by SVC. We see this as strong initial evidence that DPLL(T) is qualitatively superior to existing approaches for deciding satisfiability modulo theories[5].

Benchmark family	SD	BerkMin	Chaff	DPLL(T)	SVC
Buggy Cache	2.3	**2.4**	3.4	6.7	(1t) 6000
Code Validation Suite	16.2	44.9	43.9	**3.7**	56.9
DLX processor	3.9	10.2	13.3	**1.2**	16.9
Elf processor	34.1	5882	(1t) 6104	575	(1t) 6078
Out of order proc.(rf)	27.1	(2t) 18211	(3t) 19213	**6385**	(2t) 12666
Out of order proc.(tag)	54.3	**247**	1457	1979	(4t) 28788
Load-Store processor	22.2	51.4	239	**30.3**	(3t) 18476
Cache Coherence Prot.	20.4	4151	(1t) 9634	**3601**	(4t) 26112
Two queues	5.1	407	1148	**73.6**	1872

Benchmark family	EIJ	BerkMin	Chaff	DPLL(T)
Buggy Cache	6.3	**6.4**	9.3	6.7
Code Validation Suite	40.7	41	41.8	**3.7**
DLX processor	13	13.9	14.4	**1.2**
Elf processor	(2m) 20.1	(2m) 12021	(2m) 12021	**575**
Out of order proc.(rf)	70.6	(1t) 7453	(2t) 13926	**6385**
Out of order proc.(tag)	210	**510**	837	1979
Load-Store processor	(1m) 32	(1m) 6034	(1m) 6037	**30.3**
Cache Coherence Prot.	(3m) 102	(3m) 18257	(3m) 18437	**3601**
Two queues	(3m) 19.4	(3m) 18028	(3m) 18034	**73.6**

Benchmark family	Hybrid 1	BerkMin	Chaff	DPLL(T)
Buggy Cache	6.2	**6.4**	9.2	6.7
Code Validation Suite	13.2	13.5	13.5	**3.7**
DLX processor	13.1	14.1	15.2	**1.2**
Elf processor	187	941	1646	**575**
Out of order proc.(rf)	65.3	(1t) 7524	(2t) 13009	**6385**
Out of order proc.(tag)	175	**612**	799	1979
Load-Store processor	64.1	79.6	88.4	**30.3**
Cache Coherence Prot.	(3m) 102	(3m) 18257	(3m) 18438	**3601**
Two queues	(3m) 19.5	(3m) 18019	(3m) 18028	**73.6**

Benchmark family	Hybrid 2	BerkMin	Chaff	DPLL(T)
Buggy Cache	3	**3.2**	3.7	6.7
Code Validation Suite	27.7	28	28.6	**3.7**
DLX processor	11.3	12.9	14.3	**1.2**
Elf processor	47.2	3182	5467	**575**
Out of order proc.(rf)	53	(1t) 10626	(2t) 13913	**6385**
Out of order proc.(tag)	140	6918	(2t) 12173	**1979**
Load-Store processor	40.1	45.47	47.71	**30.3**
Cache Coherence Prot.	37.3	**209**	690	3601
Two queues	5.7	793	1832	**73.6**

---

[5] This evidence was confirmed recently by further experiments (also reported in detail at www.lsi.upc.es/~oliveras) showing that DPLL(T)'s perfomance dominates that of ICS 2.0 as well on the benchmarks listed here.

186 Harald Ganzinger et al.

As expected, translation-based methods will normally outperform DPLL(T) for problems where the theory T plays a very small role. But this is no longer the case when theory predicates start playing a significant role, as in the families Code Validation, Elf and OOO processors (rf), and Two queues. This phenomenon becomes dramatic for instance in benchmarks from group theory[6].

6 Conclusions and Future Work

We have presented a new approach for checking satisfiability in the EUF logic. This approach is based on a general framework and architecture in which a generic DPLL-style propositional solver, DPLL(X), is coupled with a specialized solver $Solver_T$ for a given theory T of interest. The architecture is highly modular, allowing any theory solver conforming to a simple, minimal interface to be plugged in into the DPLL(X) engine. The fundamental advantage with respect to previous approaches is that the theory solver is not only used to *validate* the choices made by the SAT engine, as done for instance in CVC, but also to propagate the entailed literals returned by SetTrue, using information from *consistent* partial models, considerably reducing the search space of the SAT engine. Initial results indicate that in the EUF case this leads to significant speed-ups in overall performance.

More work needs to be done on our implementation. Aspects such as lemma management, decision heuristics and restarting policies are still immature, More accurate theory-dependent heuristics need to be explored. Also minimal-model-preserving optimizations should be worked out; for instance, the notion of P-terms [BGV01] has its counterpart in our framework, and so could be used.

Finally, other future work of course concerns the development of new theory solvers, or the conversion of existing ones (e.g., those used in CVC), into theory solvers conforming to our interface: solvers for EUF with associativity and transitivity (AC) properties for certain symbols, EUFM (EUF+memories) [BD94], Separation Logic [SLB03], or the full *CLU* logic [BLS02b].

References

[ABC+02] G. Audemard, P. Bertoli, A. Cimatti, A. Kornilowicz, and R. Sebastiani. A SAT based approach for solving formulas over boolean and linear mathematical propositions. In *CADE-18*, LNCS 2392, pages 195–210, 2002.

[ACG00] A. Armando, C. Castellini, and E. Giunchiglia. SAT-based procedures for temporal reasoning. In *Procs. of the 5th European Conference on Planning*, LNCS 1809, pages 97–108. Springer, 2000.

[BD94] J. R. Burch and D. L. Dill. Automatic verification of pipelined microprocessor control. In *Procs. 6th Int. Conf. Computer Aided Verification (CAV)*, LNCS 818, pages 68–80, 1994.

[BDL96] C. Barrett, D. L. Dill, and J. Levitt. Validity checking for combinations of theories with equality. In *Procs. 1st Intl. Conference on Formal Methods in Computer Aided Design*, LNCS 1166, pages 187–201, 1996.

---

[6] See again www.lsi.upc.es/~oliveras for details.

[BDS02]   C. Barrett, D. Dill, and A. Stump. Checking satisfiability of first-order formulas by incremental translation into sat. In *Procs. 14th Intl. Conf. on Computer Aided Verification (CAV)*, LNCS 2404, 2002.

[BGV01]   R. E. Bryant, S. German, and M. N. Velev. Processor verification using efficient reductions of the logic of uninterpreted functions to propositional logic. *ACM Trans. Computational Logic*, 2(1):93–134, 2001.

[BLS02a]   R. E. Bryant, S. Lahiri, and S. Seshia. Deciding CLU logic formulas via boolean and pseudo-boolean en codings. In *Procs. 1st Int. Workshop on Constraints in Formal Verification*, 2002.

[BLS02b]   R. E. Bryant, S. Lahiri, and S. Seshia. Modeling and verifying systems using a logic of counter arithmetic with lambda expressions and uninterpreted functions. In *Procs. of CAV'02*, LNCS 2404, 2002.

[BT00]   L. Bachmair and A. Tiwari. Abstract congruence closure and specializations. In *Conf. Autom. Deduction, CADE*, LNAI 1831, pages 64–78, 2000.

[BV02]   R. E. Bryant and M. N. Velev. Boolean satisfiability with transitivity constraints. *ACM Trans. Computational Logic*, 3(4):604–627, 2002.

[DLL62]   M. Davis, G. Logemann, and D. Loveland. A machine program for theorem-proving. *CACM*, 5(7):394–397, 1962.

[dMR02]   L. de Moura and H. Rueß. Lemmas on demand for satisfiability solvers. In *Procs. 5th Int. Symp. on the Theory and Applications of Satisfiability Testing, SAT'02*, pages 244–251, 2002.

[DP60]   M. Davis and H. Putnam. A computing procedure for quantification theory. *Journal of the ACM*, 7:201–215, 1960.

[DST80]   P. J. Downey, R. Sethi, and R. E. Tarjan. Variations on the common subexpressions problem. *JACM* 27(4):758–771, 1980.

[FJOS03]   C. Flanagan, R. Joshi, X. Ou, and J. B. Saxe. Theorem proving using lazy proof explanation. In *Procs. 15th Int. Conf. on Computer Aided Verification (CAV)*, LNCS 2725, 2003.

[GN02]   E. Goldberg and Y. Novikov. BerkMin: A fast and robust SAT-solver. In *Design, Automation, and Test in Europe (DATE '02)*, pages 142–149, 2002.

[Kap97]   D. Kapur. Shostak's congruence closure as completion. In *Procs. 8th Int. Conf. on Rewriting Techniques and Applications*, LNCS 1232, 1997.

[MMZ+01]   M. W. Moskewicz, C. F. Madigan, Y. Zhao, L. Zhang, and S. Malik. Chaff: Engineering an Efficient SAT Solver. In *Proc. 38th Design Automation Conference (DAC'01)*, 2001.

[NO80]   G. Nelson and D. C. Oppen. Fast decision procedures bases on congruence closure. *JACM*, 27(2):356–364, 1980.

[NO03]   R. Nieuwenhuis and A. Oliveras. Congruence closure with integer offsets. In *10th Int. Conf. Logic for Programming, Artif. Intell. and Reasoning (LPAR)*, LNAI 2850, pages 78–90, 2003.

[PRSS99]   A. Pnueli, Y. Rodeh, O. Shtrichman, and M. Siegel. Deciding equality formulas by small domains instantiations. In *Procs. 11th Int. Conf. on Computer Aided Verification (CAV)*, LNCS 1633, pages 455–469, 1999.

[SLB03]   S. Seshia, S. Lahiri, and R. Bryant. A hybrid SAT-based decision procedure for separation logic with uninterpreted functions. In *Procs. 40th Design Automation Conference (DAC)*, pages 425–430, 2003.

[SSB02]   O. Strichman, S. A. Seshia, and R. E. Bryant. Deciding separation formulas with SAT. In *Procs. 14th Intl. Conference on Computer Aided Verification (CAV)*, LNCS 2404, pages 209–222, 2002.

[Tin02]   C. Tinelli. A DPLL-based calculus for ground satisfiability modulo theories. In *Procs. 8th European Conf. on Logics in Artificial Intelligence*,
LNAI 2424, pages 308–319, 2002.

[TV01]   A. Tiwari and L. Vigneron. Implementation of Abstract Congruence Closure, 2001. At www.csl.sri.com/users/tiwari.

[VB03]   M, N. Velev and R. E. Bryant. Effective use of Boolean satisfiability procedures in the formal verification of superscalar and VLIW microprocessors.
Journal of Symbolic Computation, 35(2):73–106, 2003.

[ZMMM01] L. Zhang, C. F. Madigan, M. W. Moskewicz, and S. Malik. Efficient
conflict driven learning in a Boolean satisfiability solver. In *Int. Conf. on
Computer-Aided Design (ICCAD'01)*, pages 279–285, 2001.

Verifying ω-Regular Properties of Markov Chains

Doron Bustan[1], Sasha Rubin[2], and Moshe Y. Vardi[1]

[1] Rice University*
[2] The University of Auckland**

Abstract. In this work we focus on model checking of probabilistic models. Probabilistic models are widely used to describe randomized protocols. A Markov chain induces a probability measure on sets of computations. The notion of correctness now becomes probabilistic. We solve here the general problem of linear-time probabilistic model checking with respect to ω-regular specifications. As specification formalism, we use alternating Büchi infinite-word automata, which have emerged recently as a generic specification formalism for developing model checking algorithms. Thus, the problem we solve is: given a Markov chain $\mathcal{M}$ and automaton $\mathcal{A}$, check whether the probability induced by $\mathcal{M}$ of $L(\mathcal{A})$ is one (or compute the probability precisely). We show that these problem can be solved within the same complexity bounds as model checking of Markov chains with respect to LTL formulas. Thus, the additional expressive power comes at no penalty.

1 Introduction

In model checking, we model a system as a transition system $\mathcal{M}$ and a specification as a temporal formula ψ. Then, using formal methods, we check whether $\mathcal{M}$ satisfies ψ [7]. One of the most significant developments in this area is the discovery of algorithmic methods for verifying temporal logic properties of *finite-state* systems [23,18,6,33]. This derives its significance both from the fact that many synchronization and communication protocols can be modelled as finite-state programs, as well as from the great ease of use of fully algorithmic methods. Looking at model-checking algorithms more closely, we can classify these algorithms according to two criteria. The first criterion is the type of model that we use – nondeterministic or probabilistic. The second criterion is the specification language.

For nondeterministic models and linear temporal logic (LTL), a close and fruitful connection with the theory of automata over infinite words has been developed [32–34]. The basic idea is to associate with each LTL formula a nondeterministic Büchi automaton over infinite words (NBW) that accepts exactly all the computations that satisfy the formula. This enables the reduction of various decision problems, such as satisfiability and model checking, to known automata-theoretic problems, yielding clean and asymptotically optimal algorithms. Furthermore, these reductions are very helpful for

* Supported in part by NSF grants CCR-9988322, CCR-0124077, CCR-0311326, IIS-9908435, IIS-9978135, and EIA-0086264, by BSF grant 9800096, and by a grant from the Intel Corporation.
** For a full version with proofs, see www.cs.rice.edu/~vardi/papers.

implementing temporal-logic based verification algorithms, cf. [14]. This connection to automata theory can also be extended to languages beyond LTL, such as ETL [34] and μTL [30].

In this paper we focus on model checking of probabilistic models. Probabilistic models are widely used to describe randomized protocols, which are often used in distributed protocols [5], communication protocols [8], robotics [27], and more. We use Markov chains as our probabilistic model, cf. [29]. A Markov chain induces a probability measure on sets of computations. The notion of correctness now becomes probabilistic: we say here that a program is correct if the probability that a computation satisfies the specification is one (we also discuss a quantitative notion of correctness, where we compute the probability that a computation satisfies the specification). Early approaches for probabilistic model checking of LTL formulas [19, 29] required determinization of NBW, which involves an additional exponential blow-up over the construction of automata from formulas [24], requiring exponential space complexity, unlike the polynomial space complexity of standard model-checking algorithms for LTL, cf. [28].

The exponential gap for probabilistic model checking was bridged in [9, 10], who provided a polynomial-space algorithm, matching the lower bound of [26]. The algorithm in [9, 10] is specialized to LTL (and ETL) specifications, and proceeds by induction on the structure of the formula. An automata-theoretic account of this algorithm was given in [11]. It is shown there that LTL formulas can be translated to a special type of NBW, which they call *separated automata*. (An NBW is separated if every two states that are located in the same strongly connected component have disjoint languages). As with the standard translation of LTL formulas to NBW, the translation to separated automata is exponential. It is then shown in [11] how to model check Markov chains, in nondeterministic logarithmic space, with respect to separated NBW as complemented specification. This yields a polynomial space upper bound for probabilistic model checking of LTL formulas.

The automata-theoretic framework in [11] is very specifically tailored to LTL. As mentioned earlier contrast, the automata-theoretic framework for model checking nondeterministic models is quite general and can also handle more expressive specification languages such as ETL and μTL. This is not a mere theoretical issue. There has been a major recent emphasis on the development of industrial specification languages. These efforts resulted in a several languages [17, 21, 4, 2], culminating in an industrial standard, PSL 1.01 (www.accellera.com). Most of the new languages have the full power of NBW, i.e., they can express all ω-regular languages. Thus, they are strictly more expressive than LTL [35], and, thus, not covered by the framework of [9–11].

In this paper we solve the general problem of probabilistic model checking with respect to ω-regular specifications. As specification formalism, we use alternating Büchi infinite-word automata (ABW); see discussion below. Thus, the problem we solve is: Given a Markov chain $\mathcal{M}$ and an ABW $\mathcal{A}$, check whether the probability induced by $\mathcal{M}$ of $L(\mathcal{A})$ is one (i.e., whether $P_{\mathcal{M}}(L(\mathcal{A})) = 1$). (A more refined problem is to calculate the probability precisely, see the full version.)

The motivation for using ABWs as a specification formalism is derived from recent developments in the area of linear specification languages. First, ABWs have been used as an intermediate formalism between LTL formulas and nondeterministic Büchi word automata (NBW). As shown in [12, 13], one can exploit the linear translation from LTL formulas to ABWs ([31]) for an early minimization, before the exponential translation to NBW. Second, not only can logics such as ETL and μTL be easily translated to ABW, but also most of the new industrial languages can be translated to ABW. Furthermore, for some of them efficient such translations are known (cf. [1]). Thus, ABW can serve as a generic specification formalism for developing model checking algorithms. Note that applying the techniques of [9, 10] to ABW specifications requires converting them first to NBW at an exponential cost, which we succeed here in avoiding.

We present here an algorithm for model checking of Markov chains, using ABWs as specifications. The space complexity of the algorithm is polylogarithmic in $\mathcal{M}$ and polynomial in $\mathcal{A}$. The linear translation of LTL to ABW implies that this complexity matches the lower bound for this problem.

As in [10,11], our algorithm uses the subset construction to capture the language of every subset of states of $\mathcal{A}$ (an infinite word w is in the language of a set Q of states if $w \in L(s)$ for every state $s \in Q$ and $w \notin L(s)$ for every $s \notin Q$). While for LTL, a straightforward subset construction suffices, this is not the case for ABW. A key technical innovation of this paper is our use of *two* nondeterministic structures that correspond to the alternating automaton $\mathcal{A}$ to capture the language of every set of automaton states. The first nondeterministic structure is an NBW $\mathcal{A}_f$ called the *full automaton*, and the second a "slim" version of the full automaton without accepting conditions, which we call the *local transition system* T_A. Every state q of $\mathcal{A}_f$ and T_A corresponds to a set Q of states in $\mathcal{A}$. While is possible, however, that a several states of $\mathcal{A}_f$ correspond to the same set of states of $\mathcal{A}$, every state of T_A corresponds to a unique set of states of $\mathcal{A}$. The model-checking algorithm make use of the products G and G_f of the Markov chain M with T_A and $\mathcal{A}_f$, respectively.

2 Preliminaries

2.1 Automata

Definition 1. *A nondeterministic Büchi word automaton (NBW) is* $\mathcal{A} = \langle \Sigma, S, S_0, \delta, F \rangle$, *where* Σ *is a finite alphabet,* S *is a finite set of states,* $\delta : S \times \Sigma \to 2^S$ *is a transition function,* $S_0 \subseteq S$ *is a set of initial states, and* $F \subseteq S$ *is a set of accepting states.*

Let $w = w_0, w_1, \ldots$ be an infinite word over Σ. For $i \in \mathbb{N}$, let $w^i = w_i, w_{i+1}, \ldots$ denote the suffix of w from its i'th letter. A sequence $\rho = s_0, s_1, \ldots$ in S^ω is a *run* of $\mathcal{A}$ over an infinite word $w \in \Sigma^\omega$, if $s_0 \in S_0$ and for every $i > 0$ we have $s_{i+1} \in \delta(s_i, w_i)$. We use $inf(\rho)$ to denote the set of states that appear infinitely often in ρ. A run ρ of $\mathcal{A}$ is *accepting* if $inf(\rho) \cap F \neq \emptyset$. An NBW $\mathcal{A}$ accepts a word w if $\mathcal{A}$ has an accepting run over w. We use $L(\mathcal{A})$ to denote the set of words that are accepted by $\mathcal{A}$. For $s \in S$, we denote by $\mathcal{A}^{(s)}$ the automaton $\mathcal{A}$ with a single initial state s. We write $L(s)$ (the language of s) for $L(\mathcal{A}^{(s)})$ when $\mathcal{A}$ is clear from the context.

Before we define an alternating Büchi word automaton, we need the following definition. For a given set X, let $\mathcal{B}^+(X)$ be the set of positive Boolean formulas over X (i.e., Boolean formulas built from elements in X using $\wedge$ and $\vee$), where we also allow the formulas **true** and **false**. Let $Y \subseteq X$. We say that Y *satisfies* a formula $\theta \in \mathcal{B}^+(X)$

if the truth assignment that assigns *true* to the members of Y and assigns *false* to the members of $X \setminus Y$ satisfies θ. A tree is a set $X \subseteq \mathbb{N}^*$, such that for $x \in \mathbb{N}^*$ and $n \in \mathbb{N}$, if $xn \in X$ then $x \in X$. We denote the length of x by $|x|$.

An *alternating Büchi word automaton* (ABW) is $\mathcal{A} = \langle \Sigma, S, s^0, \delta, F \rangle$, where Σ, S, and F are as in NBW, $s^0 \in S$ is a single initial state, and $\delta : S \times \Sigma \to \mathcal{B}^+(S)$ is a transition function. A run of $\mathcal{A}$ on an infinite word $w = w_0, w_1, \ldots$ is a (possibly infinite) S-labelled tree τ such that $\tau(\varepsilon) = s^0$ and the following holds: if $|x| = i$, $\tau(x) = s$, and $\delta(s, w_i) = \theta$, then x has k children $x_1, \ldots, x_k$, for some $k \leq |S|$, and $\{\tau(x1), \ldots, \tau(xk)\}$ satisfies θ. The run τ is *accepting* if every infinite branch in τ includes infinitely many labels in F. Note that the run can also have finite branches; if $|x| = i$, $\tau(x) = s$, and $\delta(s, a_i) = \mathbf{true}$, then x need not have children.

An *alternating weak word automaton* (AWW) is an ABW such that for every strongly connected component C of the automaton, either $C \subseteq F$ or $C \cap F = \emptyset$. Given two AWW $\mathcal{A}_1$ and $\mathcal{A}_2$, we can construct AWW for $\Sigma^\omega \setminus L(\mathcal{A}_1)$, $L(\mathcal{A}_1) \cap L(\mathcal{A}_2)$, and $L(\mathcal{A}_1) \cup L(\mathcal{A}_2)$, which are linear in their size, relative to $\mathcal{A}_1$ and $\mathcal{A}_2$ [22].

Lemma 1. [16] *Let $\mathcal{A}$ be an ABW. Then there exists an AWW $\mathcal{A}_w$ such that $L(\mathcal{A}) = L(\mathcal{A}_w)$ and the size of $\mathcal{A}_w$ is quadratic in the size of $\mathcal{A}$. Furthermore, $\mathcal{A}_w$ can be constructed in time quadratic in the size of $\mathcal{A}$.*

2.2   Markov Chains

We model probabilistic systems by finite *Markov chains*. The basic intuition is that transitions between states are governed by some probability distribution.

Definition 2. *A Markov chain is a tuple $\mathcal{M} = \langle X, P_T, P_I \rangle$ such that X is a set of states, $P_T : (X \times X) \to [0, 1]$ is a transition probability distribution that assigns to every transition (x_1, x_2) its probability. P_T satisfies that for every $x_1 \in X$ we have $\sum_{x_2 \in X} P_T(x_1, x_2) = 1$. $P_I : X \to [0, 1]$ is an initial probability distribution that satisfies $\sum_{x \in X} P_I(x) = 1$.*

We denote by $\mathcal{M}^{(x)}$ the Markov chain $\mathcal{M}$ with P_I that maps x to 1. Sometimes we consider a Markov chain as a graph $\langle X, E \rangle$ where $(x_1, x_2) \in E$ iff $P_T(x_1, x_2) > 0$. For an alphabet $\Sigma = 2^{AP}$, let $V : X \to \Sigma$ be a labelling function, then each path ρ in X^* or in X^ω in $\mathcal{M}$ is mapped by V to a word w in Σ^* or in Σ^ω respectively. For simplicity we assume that $\Sigma = X$ and that $V(x) = x$ for every $x \in X$, this simplification does not change the complexity of verifying the Markov chain [10]. Note, that every infinite path of $\mathcal{M}$ is a word in X^ω but the converse does not necessarily hold. The probability space on the set of pathes of $\mathcal{M}$ is defined as in [29].

The following property of Markov chains is called *ergodicity* and is proved in [15]. Let $\mathcal{M}$ be a Markov chain, then a path of $\mathcal{M}$, with probability one, enters a bottom strongly connected component (BSCC) K of $\mathcal{M}$, and contains every finite path in K infinitely often. In other words, let L_e be the set of infinite words of $\mathcal{M}$ such that every word w in L_e has a suffix that is contained in a BSCC K of $\mathcal{M}$, and contains every finite path in K infinitely often. Then, $P_M(L_e) = 1$.

3   The Full Automaton and the Local Transition System

In this section we capture the behavior of an AWW $\mathcal{A}$ using two nondeterminstic systems. First we define the full automaton, which captures the languages of subsets of the states of $\mathcal{A}$. Then we define the local transition system, which captures the local relations between subsets of states of $\mathcal{A}$.

3.1   The Full Automaton

Given a AWW $\mathcal{A} = \langle \Sigma, S, \delta, F \rangle$ (we ignore its initial state), we define its dual AWW $\hat{\mathcal{A}} = \langle \Sigma, S, \hat{\delta}, \hat{F} \rangle$, where the Boolean formula $\hat{\delta}(s, \sigma)$ is obtained from $\delta(s, \sigma)$ by replacing every **true** with **false** and vice versa, and every $\vee$ with $\wedge$ and vice versa, in addition we define $\hat{F} = S \setminus F$. It is easy to see that $\hat{\mathcal{A}}$ is an AWW.

Lemma 2. [22] *Let $\mathcal{A}$ be an AWW and $\hat{\mathcal{A}}$ be its dual AWW. For every state s we have that $L(\mathcal{A}^{(s)}) = \Sigma^{\omega} \setminus L(\hat{\mathcal{A}}^{(s)})$.*

Given an AWW $\mathcal{A}$ and its dual AWW $\hat{\mathcal{A}}$ we define the state space of the full automaton as a subset of $2^S \times 2^S \times 2^S \times 2^S$. We start with the following definition.

Definition 3. *A tuple (Q_1, Q_2, Q_3, Q_4) is consistent if $Q_2 = S \setminus Q_1$, $Q_3 \subseteq Q_1 \setminus F$, and $Q_4 \subseteq Q_2 \setminus \hat{F}$.*

Definition 4. *Given an AWW $\mathcal{A} = \langle \Sigma, S, \delta, F \rangle$ we define its* full automaton *as the NBW $\mathcal{A}_f = \langle \Sigma, S_f, \delta_f, F_f \rangle$ where*

- S_f *is the set of consistent tuples over $2^S \times 2^S \times 2^S \times 2^S$.*
- *A state (Q'_1, Q'_2, Q'_3, Q'_4) is in $\delta_f((Q_1, Q_2, Q_3, Q_4), \sigma)$ if $Q'_1 \models \wedge_{s \in Q_1} \delta(s, \sigma)$, $Q'_2 \models \wedge_{s \in Q_2} \hat{\delta}(s, \sigma)$, and either:*
  1. *$Q_3 = Q_4 = \emptyset$, $Q'_3 = Q'_1 \setminus F$, and $Q'_4 = Q'_2 \setminus \hat{F}$*
  2. *$Q_3 \neq \emptyset$ or $Q_4 \neq \emptyset$, there exists $Y_3 \subseteq Q'_1$ such that $Y_3 \models \wedge_{s \in Q_3} \delta(s, \sigma)$ and $Q'_3 = Y_3 \setminus F$, and there exists $Y_4 \subseteq Q'_2$ such that $Y_4 \models \wedge_{s \in Q_4} \hat{\delta}(s, \sigma)$ and $Q'_4 = Y_4 \setminus \hat{F}$*
- $F_f = \{(Q_1, Q_2, Q_3, Q_4) \in S_f | Q_3 = Q_4 = \emptyset)\}$

Theorem 1. *Let $\mathcal{A}$ be an AWW and let $\mathcal{A}_f$ be its full automaton, let $Q \subseteq S$ be a set of states, then for every state (Q_1, Q_2, Q_3, Q_4) such that $Q_1 = Q$ we have that*

$$\bigcap_{s \in Q} L(\mathcal{A}^{(s)}) \bigcap_{s \notin Q} \overline{L(\mathcal{A}^{(s)})} = L(\mathcal{A}_f^{(Q_1, Q_2, Q_3, Q_4)})$$

We now present more properties of the full automaton. We use these properties later.

Definition 5. *Let $\mathcal{A}$ be an ABW and let w be an infinite word. We define the* type *of w w.r.t. $\mathcal{A}$ as the set $type_{\mathcal{A}}(w) = \{s | \mathcal{A}^{(s)} \text{ accepts } w\}$.*

The following lemma is a direct consequence of Theorem 1.

Lemma 3. *Let $\mathcal{A}_f$ be full automaton, and let (Q_1, Q_2, Q_3, Q_4) and (Q'_1, Q'_2, Q'_3, Q'_4) be states of $\mathcal{A}_f$. Then,*

– If $Q_1 = Q'_1$ then $L(\mathcal{A}_f^{(Q_1,Q_2,Q_3,Q_4)}) = L(\mathcal{A}_f^{(Q'_1,Q'_2,Q'_3,Q'_4)})$.
– If $Q_1 \neq Q'_1$ then $L(\mathcal{A}_f^{(Q_1,Q_2,Q_3,Q_4)}) \cap L(\mathcal{A}_f^{(Q'_1,Q'_2,Q'_3,Q'_4)}) = \emptyset$.

Lemma 3 and Theorem 1 imply that the first element Q_1 of the states of $\mathcal{A}_f$ characterizes a distinct language.

Definition 6. *The language of Q_1 is defined as $L(Q_1) = L(\mathcal{A}_f^{(Q_1,S\setminus Q_1,\emptyset,\emptyset)})$.*

3.2 The Local Transition System

As observed above, it is sufficient to look at Q_1 in order to determine the language of a state of $\mathcal{A}_f$. Recall that $L(Q_1) = L(\mathcal{A}^{(Q_1,S\setminus Q_1,\emptyset,\emptyset)})$. We observe that if there exists a transition $((Q_1, Q_2, Q_3, Q_4), \sigma, (Q'_1, Q'_2, Q'_3, Q'_4))$ in δ_f, then for every state of the form (Q_1, Q_2, Y_3, Y_4) there exists a state (Q'_1, Q'_2, Y'_3, Y'_4) such that the transition $((Q_1, Q_2, Y_3, Y_4), \sigma, (Q'_1, Q'_2, Y'_3, Y'_4))$ is in δ_f.

These observations imply that there are some local relationships between the languages of the states of $\mathcal{A}_f$. Indeed, if a word w is in $L((Q'_1, Q'_2, Q'_3, Q'_4))$ then for the word $\sigma \cdot w$ that is in $L((Q_1, Q_2, Q_3, Q_4))$, there exists a state of the form (Q'_1, Q'_2, Y'_3, Y'_4) that is in $\delta_f((Q_1, Q_2, Q_3, Q_4), \sigma)$. Thus, we can say that there exists a transition on σ from $L(Q_1)$ to $L(Q'_1)$. The local transition system captures these relationships.

Definition 7. *Given an AWW $\mathcal{A} = \langle \Sigma, S, \delta, F \rangle$ we define its* local transition system *as $T_\mathcal{A} = \langle \Sigma, S_T, \delta_T \rangle$ where*

– S_T *is the set of subsets of S and δ_T is a function from S_T to 2^{S_T}.*
– *A state Q' is in $\delta_T(Q, \sigma)$ if $Q' \models \wedge_{s\in Q}\delta(s, \sigma)$ and $(S \setminus Q') \models \wedge_{s\notin Q}\hat{\delta}(s, \sigma)$.*

Example 1. We now present an example of a full automaton and a local transition system. The example is presented at Figure 1. For simplicity we use a deterministic automaton $\mathcal{A}$. The figure shows $\mathcal{A}$'s dual automaton $\hat{\mathcal{A}}$, the full automaton $\mathcal{A}_f$, and the local transition system $T_\mathcal{A}$. Note that $\hat{\mathcal{A}}$ has $\hat{F} = S$, thus for every state (Q_1, Q_2, Q_3, Q_4) of $\mathcal{A}_f$, we have $Q_4 = \emptyset$. For this reason, and since Q_2 is always equal to $S \setminus Q_1$, we only write the sets Q_1 and Q_3 inside the states. □

The definitions of the full automaton and the local transition system implies the following lemma:

Lemma 4. *Let $\mathcal{A}$ be an AWW and let $\mathcal{A}_f$ and $T_\mathcal{A}$ be its full automaton and local transition system respectively. Let (Q_1, Q_2, Q_3, Q_4) be a state of $\mathcal{A}_f$, and let σ be a letter in Σ. Then, for every state Q'_1 we have that Q'_1 is in $\delta_T(Q_1, \sigma)$ iff there exists a state of the form (Q'_1, Q'_2, Q'_3, Q'_4) in $\delta_f((Q_1, Q_2, Q_3, Q_4), \sigma)$.*

The proof of Lemma 4 is straightforward from the definitions of $\mathcal{A}_f$ and $T_\mathcal{A}$. In particular for every state (Q_1, Q_2, Q_3, Q_4) and infinite word w we have that $\mathcal{A}^{(Q_1,Q_2,Q_3,Q_4)}$ has a run on w iff $T_\mathcal{A}^{(Q_1)}$ has a run on w. However, we do not define accepting conditions for the local transition system. Thus, it is possible that $T_\mathcal{A}^{(Q_1)}$ has a run on w, but $\mathcal{A}_f^{(Q_1,Q_2,Q_3,Q_4)}$ does not have an accepting run on w.

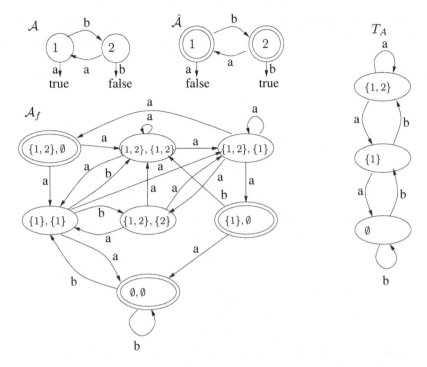

Fig. 1. An example of a full automaton $\mathcal{A}_f$ and a local transition system T_A.

Lemma 5. *Let T_A be a local transition system, and let Q, Q' and Q'' be states of T_A. Let σ be a letter in Σ. If $Q'' \in \delta_T(Q', \sigma)$ and $Q'' \in \delta_T(Q, \sigma)$, then $Q = Q'$.*

When a transition system satisfies the property shown in Lemma 5, we say that the transition system is *reverse deterministic*.

4   Verifying Markov Chains

In this section we construct a product $G_{\mathcal{M},\mathcal{A}}$ of the Markov chain $\mathcal{M}$ and the local transition system T_A. We show that the problem of checking whether $P_{\mathcal{M}}(L(\mathcal{A})) = 1$, can be reduced to checking for a state (x, Q) of G whether the probability of $L(Q) \cap x \cdot \Sigma^\omega$ is positive. Then, we show how to use the full automaton to solve this problem.

Definition 8. *Let $\mathcal{A}$ be an AWW, T_A be $\mathcal{A}$'s local transition system, and $\mathcal{M}$ be a Markov chain. We define the graph $G_{\mathcal{M},\mathcal{A}}$ as having vertex set (x, Q) such that x is a state of $\mathcal{M}$ and Q is a state of T_A. An edge $(x, Q) \rightarrow (x', Q')$ is included in $G_{\mathcal{M},\mathcal{A}}$ if $\mathcal{M}$ has a transition $x \rightarrow x'$ and (Q, x, Q') is a transition in T_A.*

When $\mathcal{A}$ and $\mathcal{M}$ are clear from the context, we write G instead of $G_{\mathcal{M},\mathcal{A}}$. Lemma 5 implies that for every three states (x, Q), (x', Q'), and (x'', Q''), if there is a transition from (x, Q) to (x'', Q'') and there is a transition from (x', Q') to (x'', Q''), then $x \neq x'$. We say that G is *reverse deterministic*.

Example 2. We present in Figure 2 two Markov chains $\mathcal{M}_1$ and $\mathcal{M}_2$. We assume that the initial probability for each state in the Markov chains is $\frac{1}{2}$. The figure also presents the products G_1 and G_2 of $\mathcal{M}_1$ and $\mathcal{M}_2$ respectively, with the local transition system T_A from Example 1. □

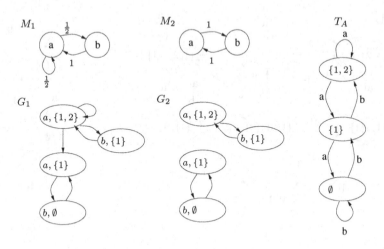

Fig. 2. Two Markov chains $\mathcal{M}_1$ and $\mathcal{M}_2$, and the graphs they impose G_1 and G_2.

Every infinite path in G projected on the first component gives a path in $\mathcal{M}$. Conversely, every path of $\mathcal{M}$ is the projection of at least one path in G. In fact, let $w = x_0 \cdot x_1 \cdots$ be a path of $\mathcal{M}$. For each j, let Q_j be the type of the suffix $x_j \cdot x_{j+1} x_{j+2} \cdots$. Then for each j there is a transition (Q_j, x_j, Q_{j+1}) in δ_T and thus an edge $(x_j, Q_j) \to (x_{j+1}, Q_{j+1})$ in G. We call this path the *augmented path* corresponding to w.

Definition 9. *For a state (x, Q) of G we denote by $P(x, Q)$ the probability that a path that starts in state x has type Q, namely $P(x, Q) = P_M(\mathcal{M}^{(x)}$ has type $Q)$. We call (x, Q) probable if $P(x, Q) > 0$.*

The importance of the probable states is demonstrated in the following two lemmas.

Lemma 6. $P_M(L(Q)) = \sum_{x \in X} P_I(x) \cdot P(x, Q)$.

Let x be a state of a Markov chain with $P_I(x) > 0$. Then for every state (x, Q) we have that if (x, Q) is probable, then $P_M(L(Q)) > 0$. Thus we conclude Lemma 7.

Lemma 7. *Let s be a state of an AWW $\mathcal{A}$ and let $\mathcal{M}$ be a Markov chain. Then, $P_M(L(s)) < 1$ iff there exists a state x of $\mathcal{M}$ and a set $Q \subseteq S$ such that $P_I(x) > 0$, $s \notin Q$ and the state (x, Q) is probable.*

Thus, in order to determine whether $P_M(L(s_0)) = 1$, it is enough to determine the probable states of G. In the rest of this section we show how to identify the probable states. We define H as the restriction of G to the probable states.

Example 3. Look again at Figure 2. It is easy to see that given that a path of $\mathcal{M}_1$ starts at state a, the path is of the form $a((ba)+a)^\omega$ with probability 1. $a((ba)+a)^\omega$ is contained in $L(\{1,2\}) \cup \{(ab)^\omega\}$, since $P_{\mathcal{M}_1}((ab)^\omega) = 0$, we have $P(a, \{1,2\}) = 1$. Similarly, a path of $\mathcal{M}_1$ that starts at b is with probability one in $L(\{1\})$, thus, $P(b, \{1\}) = 1$. This implies that in G_1, H is the subgraph induced by the states $(a, \{1,2\})$ and $(b, \{1\})$. On the other hand, looking at $\mathcal{M}_2$, we see that a path that starts at a is of the form $(ab)^\omega$ and a path that starts at b is of the form $(ba)^\omega$. Thus, in G_2, H is the subgraph induced by the states $(a, \{1\})$ and $(b, \emptyset)$. $\square$

We start with the following observation. Partition the language $L(Q)$ according to the first letter of a word and the type of the suffix that starts from the second letter. Then, for every state (x, Q) of G we have $P(x, Q) = \sum_{(x,Q) \to (x',Q')} P_T(x, x') \cdot P(x', Q')$. Note that if $(x, Q) \to (x', Q')$ is an edge of G, then $P_T(x, x') > 0$ and thus $P(x, Q) \geq P_T(x, x') \cdot P(x', Q')$. Hence, if (x', Q') is probable then all its ancestors are probable. This implies that it is sufficient to identify the BSCCs of H and then to construct the set of probable states using backward reachability.

Let C be an SCC of G. If it contains some probable state (x, Q), then since all the states in C are ancestors of (x, Q), all states in C are probable. That is, either C is an SCC of H or $C \cap H = \emptyset$. Recall that every path in C projects to a path in $\mathcal{M}$. So the set of first components of all members of C are in the same SCC, say K, of $\mathcal{M}$, which is the SCC of $\mathcal{M}$ containing x. We say that C *corresponds* to K. Note that distinct SCC's of G may correspond to the same K.

Theorem 2 characterizes the SCCs of G which are the BSCCs of H. Before we present the theorem we need the following notation. For a tuple $E = \langle E_1, E_2, \ldots E_n \rangle$, we define $\pi_i(E) = E_i$ to be the i'th element in E. This notation is extended naturally to sequences of tuples.

Definition 10. *A finite path ρ_G in G is* fulfilling *if there exists a path ρ_f in $\mathcal{A}_f$ such that $\pi_2(\rho_G) = \pi_1(\rho_f)$, the first state of ρ_f is of the form $(Q_1, Q_2, (Q_1 \setminus F), (Q_2 \setminus \hat{F}))$, and the last state of ρ_f is of the form $(Q_1', Q_2', \emptyset, \emptyset)$.*

Theorem 2. *Let C be an SCC of G. Then C is a BSCC of H iff it satisfies the following conditions:*

1. *C corresponds to a BSCC K of $\mathcal{M}$.*
2. *Every finite path of K is a projection of a path in C.*
3. *C contains a fulfilling path.*

5   Algorithms

In Figure 3 we present the algorithm that determines for an AWW $\mathcal{A}$ and a Markov chain $\mathcal{M}$ whether $P_M(L(\mathcal{A})) = 1$. An extension for exact probability is presented in full version. Theorem 2 implies that the algorithm mark the BSCCs of H. Thus, B is the set of probable states. Lemma 7 implies that the algorithm returns **true** iff $P_M(L(\mathcal{A})) = 1$. Finding SCCs in G that correspond to BSCCs in $\mathcal{M}$, and doing backward reachability can be done in time linear in the size of G. The most complex part of the algorithm is to identify, SCCs C of G that satisfy:

```
Inputs: Markov chain M = ⟨X, P_I, P_T⟩, AWW A = ⟨Σ, S, s_0, δ, F⟩.
Construct the full automaton A_f of A.
Construct the local transition system T_A and the graph G.
Mark all SCCs C of G that satisfy:
    1. C corresponds to a BSCC K of M.
    2. Every finite path of K is a projection of a path in C.
    3. C contains a fulfilling path.
Construct the set B of all states of G from which the marked
SCCs are reachable.
return true iff for every state (x, Q) ∈ B, if P_I(x) > 0, then s_0 ∈ Q.
```

Fig. 3. The model-checking algorithm.

1. C corresponds to a BSCC K of $\mathcal{M}$.
2. Every finite path of K is a projection of a path in C.
3. C contains a fulfilling path.

The following lemma is proved in [10]. The only property of G that they use is that G is reverse deterministic.

Lemma 8. *Let C be an SCC of G that corresponds to an SCC K of $\mathcal{M}$. Then the following are equivalent:*

1. Every finite path in K is a projection of a path in C.
2. No other SCC of G corresponding to K is an ancestor of C.

Lemma 8 implies that the second task is equivalent to checking whether there is no ancestor SCC of C that corresponds to K. This check can be easily done while scanning the SCCs of G.

Example 4. In G_1 at Figure 2 there are two SCC's that correspond to the single BSCC of $\mathcal{M}_1$. The SCC of $(a, \{1, 2\})$ and $(b, \{1\})$ does not have ancestors and contains the fulfilling path $(a, \{1, 2\}), (a, \{1, 2\}), (a, \{1, 2\})$ that corresponds to the path $(\{1, 2\}, \{1, 2\}), (\{1, 2\}, \{1\}), (\{1, 2\}, \emptyset)$ in $\mathcal{A}_f$, thus, this SCC is the BSCC of H. In G_2 there are two SCCs that correspond to the single BSCC of $\mathcal{M}_2$ and neither of them have an ancestor. However, only the SCC of $(a, \{1\})$ and $(b, \emptyset)$ has a fulfilling path, thus it is the BSCC of H.□

We now explain how to check whether an SCC C of G contains a fulfilling path. We construct the product $G_f = \mathcal{M} \times \mathcal{A}_f$, similarly to the construction of G.

Definition 11. *Let $\mathcal{A}$ be an AWW, $\mathcal{A}_f$ be $\mathcal{A}$'s full automaton, and $\mathcal{M}$ be a Markov chain. We define the full graph G_f as having vertex set $(x, (Q_1, Q_2, Q_3, Q_4))$ such that x is a state of $\mathcal{M}$ and (Q_1, Q_2, Q_3, Q_4) is a state of $\mathcal{A}_f$. An edge $(x, (Q_1, Q_2, Q_3, Q_4)) \rightarrow (x', (Q_1', Q_2', Q_3', Q_4'))$ is included in G_f if $\mathcal{M}$ has a transition $x \rightarrow x'$ and (Q_1', Q_2', Q_3', Q_4') is in $\delta_f((Q_1, Q_2, Q_3, Q_4), x)$.*

Lemma 9. *An SCC C of G contains a fulfilling path iff there exists a path $(x_0, (Q_1^0, Q_2^0, Q_3^0, Q_4^0)), (x_1, (Q_1^1, Q_2^1, Q_3^1, Q_4^1)), \ldots, (x_n, (Q_1^n, Q_2^n, \emptyset, \emptyset))$ in G_f such that the path $(x_0, Q_1^0), (x_1, Q_1^1), \ldots (x_n, Q_1^n)$ is contained in C, $Q_3^0 = Q_1^0 \setminus F$, and $Q_4^0 = Q_2^0 \setminus \hat{F}$.*

Complexity. Finding SCCs in G that correspond to BSCCs in $\mathcal{M}$, and doing backward reachability can be done in linear time and polylogarithmic space in $|G|$. Constructing BSCCs of $\mathcal{M}$ can be done in time linear in $|\mathcal{M}|$, identifying SCCs of G that correspond to these BSCC can be done in time linear in $|G|$. Marking SCCs that do not have ancestors that correspond to the same BSCC in $\mathcal{M}$ can also be done in time linear in $|G|$. Checking that an SCC of G contains a fulfilling path can be done in time linear in $|G_f|$, simply by scanning G_f and G in parallel, thus, the algorithm can be implemented in time linear in $|\mathcal{M} \times \mathcal{A}_f|$. Since the size of $\mathcal{A}_f$ is $2^{O(|\mathcal{A}|)}$, we have that the time complexity of the algorithm is $|\mathcal{M}| \cdot 2^{O(|\mathcal{A}|)}$.

As for space complexity we show that algorithm works in space polynomial in $|\mathcal{A}|$ and polylogarithmic in $|\mathcal{M}|$. We rewrite the conditions of Theorem 2, Lemma 7, and Lemma 8 as follows: $P_M(L(\mathcal{A})) < 1$ iff there exists a probable state (x_0, Q_0) such that $s_0 \notin Q$ and $P_I(x_0) > 0$. This is true iff (x_0, Q_0) reaches a state (x, Q) that is in a BSCC of H, $s_0 \notin Q_0$, and $P_I(x_0) > 0$. That is

1. (x, Q) is reachable from a state (x_0, Q_0) such that $P_I(x_0) > 0$ and $s_0 \notin Q_0$.
2. x is in a BSCC of $\mathcal{M}$ (Theorem 2, (1)). This condition is equivalent to the following: for every state x' of $\mathcal{M}$ we have that if there exists a path in $\mathcal{M}$ from x to x' then there exists a path from x' to x.
3. No other SCC of G that corresponds to the SCC of x in $\mathcal{M}$ is the ancestor of the SCC of (x, Q) (Lemma 8). This condition is equivalent to the following: for every state (x', Q'), if there exists a path from (x', Q') to (x, Q), then either there exists a path from (x, Q) to (x', Q'), or there is no path from x to x'.
4. The SCC of (x, Q) contains a fulfilling path (Theorem 2, (3)). By Lemma 9 this condition is equivalent to the following: there exists a path in G_f from a state $(x', (Q_1', Q_2', Q_1' \setminus F, Q_2' \setminus \hat{F}))$ to a state $(x'', (Q_1'', Q_2'', \emptyset, \emptyset))$ such that the projection of the path on G is contained in the SCC of (x, Q). This condition is equivalent to: there is a path from a state $(x', (Q_1', Q_2', Q_1' \setminus F, Q_2' \setminus \hat{F}))$ to a state $(x'', (Q_1'', Q_2'', \emptyset, \emptyset))$ in G_f and there are paths from (x, Q) to (x'', Q_1''), from (x'', Q_1'') to (x', Q'), and from $((x', Q')$ to (x, Q) in G.

In [25] it is shown that checking whether there is a path from one state to another in a graph with n states requires $log^2(n)$ space. This implies that the conditions above can be checked in space $O(log^2(|G_f|)) = log^2(|\mathcal{M}| \cdot 2^{O(|\mathcal{A}|)}) = O(log^2(|\mathcal{M}|) + log(|\mathcal{M}|) \cdot |\mathcal{A}| + |\mathcal{A}|^2) = O(log^2(|\mathcal{M}|) + |\mathcal{A}|^2)$.

6 Concluding Remarks

We presented here an optimal solution to the general problem of linear-time probabilistic model checking with respect to ω-regular specifications, expressed by alternating automata. Beyond the interest in the problem itself, our solution is interesting from a theoretical perspective, since the concept of full automaton may have other applications. More work is needed in reducing our result to practice. One direction is to extend the *ProbaTaf* system, which currently handles LTL specifications of Markov chain [11], to ABW specifications. Another, is to combine the symbolic approach to alternating automata [20] with the symbolic approach to probabilistic model checking [3].

References

1. R. Armoni, D. Bustan, O. Kupferman, and M. Y. Vardi. Resets vs. aborts in linear temporal logic. In *Int'l Conf. on Tools and Algorithms for Construction and Analysis of Systems*, pages 65 – 80, 2003.
2. R. Armoni, L. Fix, R. Gerth, B. Ginsburg, T. Kanza, A. Landver, S. Mador-Haim, A. Tiemeyer, E. Singerman, M.Y. Vardi, and Y. Zbar. The ForSpec temporal language: A new temporal property-specification language. In *Proc. 8th Int'l Conf. on Tools and Algorithms for the Construction and Analysis of Systems (TACAS'02)*, LNCS 2280, pages 296–311, 2002.
3. C. Baier, E.M. Clarke, V. Hartonas-Garmhausen, M.Z. Kwiatkowska, and M. Ryan. Symbolic model checking for probabilistic processes. In *Automata, Languages and Programming, 24th Inte.l Colloq.*, LNCS 1256, pages 430–440, 1997.
4. I. Beer, S. Ben-David, C. Eisner, D. Fisman, A. Gringauze, and Y. Rodeh. The temporal logic sugar. In *Proc. Conf. on Computer-Aided Verification*, LNCS 2102, pages 363–367, 2001.
5. P. Berman and J.A Garay. Randomized distributed agreement revisited. In *Proceedings of the 23rd Inte'l Symp. on Fault-Tolerant Computing (FTCS '93)*, pages 412–421, 1993.
6. E.M. Clarke, E.A. Emerson, and A.P. Sistla. Automatic verification of finite-state concurrent systems using temporal logic specifications. *ACM Trans. on Programming Languages and Systems*, 8(2):244–263, 1986.
7. E.M. Clarke, O. Grumberg, and D. Peled. *Model Checking*. MIT Press, 1999.
8. R. Cole, B.M. Maggs, F. M. auf der Heide, A. Richa M. Mitzenmacher, K. Schroder, R. Sitaraman, and B. Vocking. Randomized protocols for low-congestion circuit routing in multistage interconnection networks. In *30th ACM Symp. on Theo. of Comp. (STOC)*, pages 378–388, 1998.
9. C. Courcoubetis and M. Yannakakis. Markov decision processes and regular events. In *Proc. 17th Int'l Coll. on Automata Languages and Programming*, volume 443, pages 336–349. LNCS, 1990.
10. C. Courcoubetis and M. Yannakakis. The complexity of probabilistic verification. *Journal of the ACM*, 42(4):857–907, 1995.
11. J. M. Couvreur, N. Saheb, and G. Sutre. An optimal automata approach to LTL model checking of probabilistic systems. In *Proc. 10th Int. Conf. Logic for Programming, Artificial Intelligence, and Reasoning (LPAR'2003), Almaty, Kazakhstan, Sep. 2003*, volume 2850 of *Lecture Notes in Artificial Intelligence*. Springer, 2003.
12. C. Fritz and T. Wilke. State space reductions for alternating Büchi automata: Quotienting by simulation equivalences. In *FST TCS 2002: Foundations of Software Technology and Theoretical Computer Science: 22nd Conf.*, volume 2556 of *LNCS*, pages 157–168, 2002.
13. P. Gastin and D. Oddoux. Fast LTL to Büchi automata translation. In *Computer Aided Verification, Proc. 13th Inte'l Conf.*, volume 2102 of *LNCS*, pages 53–65, 2001.
14. G.J. Holzmann. The model checker SPIN. *IEEE Trans. on Software Engineering*, 23(5):279–295, May 1997. Special issue on Formal Methods in Software Practice.
15. J.G. Kemeny, J.L. Snell, and A.W. Knapp. *Denumerable Markov Chains*. Springer-Verlag, 1976.
16. O. Kupferman and M.Y. Vardi. Weak alternating automata are not that weak. In *Proc. 5th Israeli Symp. on Theory of Computing and Systems*, pages 147–158. IEEE Computer Society Press, 1997.
17. R.P. Kurshan. *FormalCheck User's Manual*. Cadence Design, Inc., 1998.
18. O. Lichtenstein and A. Pnueli. Checking that finite state concurrent programs satisfy their linear specification. In *Proc. 12th ACM Symp. on Principles of Programming Languages*, pages 97–107, 1985.

19. O. Lichtenstein, A. Pnueli, and L. Zuck. The glory of the past. In *Logics of Programs*, volume 193 of *Lecture Notes in Computer Science*, pages 196–218, Brooklyn, June 1985. Springer-Verlag.

20. S. Merz. Weak alternating automata in Isabelle/HOL. In J. Harrison and M. Aagaard, editors, *Theorem Proving in Higher Order Logics: 13th International Conference*, volume 1869 of *Lecture Notes in Computer Science*, pages 423–440. Springer-Verlag, 2000.

21. M.J. Morley. Semantics of temporal *e*. In T. F. Melham and F.G. Moller, editors, Banff'99 *Higher Order Workshop (Formal Methods in Computation)*. University of Glasgow, Department of Computing Science Technic al Report, 1999.

22. D.E. Muller, A. Saoudi, and P.E. Schupp. Alternating automata, the weak monadic theory of the tree and its complexity. In *Proc. 13th Intel Colloq. on Automata, Languages and Programming*, volume 226 of *LNCS*, 1986.

23. J.P. Queille and J. Sifakis. Specification and verification of concurrent systems in Cesar. In *Proc. 5th Inte'l Symp. on Programming*, volume 137 of *LNCS*, pages 337–351, 1981.

24. S. Safra. On the complexity of ω-automata. In *Proc. 29th IEEE Symp. on Foundations of Computer Science*, pages 319–327, White Plains, October 1988.

25. W.J. Savitch. Relationship between nondeterministic and deterministic tape complexities. *Journal on Computer and System Sciences*, 4:177–192, 1970.

26. A.P. Sistla and E.M. Clarke. The complexity of propositional linear temporal logic. *J. ACM*, 32:733–749, 1985.

27. S. Thrun. Probabilistic algorithms in robotics. *AI Magazine*, 21(4):93–109, 2000.

28. M. Y. Vardi. Probabilistic linear-time model checking: An overview of the automata-theoretic approach. In *Formal Methods for Real-Time and Probabilistic Systems: 5th Inte'l AMAST Workshop*, volume 1601 of *LNCS*, pages 265–276, 1999.

29. M.Y. Vardi. Automatic verification of probabilistic concurrent finite-state programs. In *Proc. 26th IEEE Symp. on Foundations of Computer Science*, pages 327–338, Portland, October 1985.

30. M.Y. Vardi. A temporal fixpoint calculus. In *Proc. 15th ACM Symp. on Principles of Programming Languages*, pages 250–259, San Diego, January 1988.

31. M.Y. Vardi. Nontraditional applications of automata theory. In *Proc. Inte'l Symp. on Theoretical Aspects of Computer Software*, volume 789, pages 575–597. LNCS, 1994.

32. M.Y. Vardi. An automata-theoretic approach to linear temporal logic. In *Logics for Concurrency: Structure versus Automata*, volume 1043 of *LNCS*, pages 238–266, 1996.

33. M.Y. Vardi and P. Wolper. An automata-theoretic approach to automatic program verification. In *Proc. 1st Symp. on Logic in Computer Science*, pages 332–344, Cambridge, June 1986.

34. M.Y. Vardi and P. Wolper. Reasoning about infinite computations. *Information and Computation*, 115(1):1–37, November 1994.

35. P. Wolper. Temporal logic can be more expressive. *Information and Control*, 56(1–2):72–99, 1983.

Statistical Model Checking
of Black-Box Probabilistic Systems

Koushik Sen, Mahesh Viswanathan, and Gul Agha

Department of Computer Science
University of Illinois at Urbana-Champaign
{ksen,vmahesh,agha}@uiuc.edu

Abstract. We propose a new statistical approach to analyzing stochastic systems against specifications given in a sublogic of continuous stochastic logic (CSL). Unlike past numerical and statistical analysis methods, we assume that the system under investigation is an *unknown, deployed black-box* that can be passively observed to obtain sample traces, but cannot be controlled. Given a set of executions (obtained by Monte Carlo simulation) and a property, our algorithm checks, based on statistical hypothesis testing, whether the sample provides evidence to conclude the satisfaction or violation of a property, and computes a quantitative measure (p-value of the tests) of confidence in its answer; if the sample does not provide statistical evidence to conclude the satisfaction or violation of the property, the algorithm may respond with a "don't know" answer. We implemented our algorithm in a Java-based prototype tool called VESTA, and experimented with the tool using case studies analyzed in [15]. Our empirical results show that our approach may, at least in some cases, be faster than previous analysis methods.

1 Introduction

Stochastic models and temporal logics such as continuous stochastic logic (CSL) [1, 3] are widely used to model practical systems and analyze their performance and reliability. There are two primary approaches to analyzing the stochastic behavior of such systems: *numerical* and *statistical*. In the numerical approach, the formal model of the system is *model checked* for correctness with respect to the specification using symbolic and numerical methods. Model checkers for different classes of stochastic processes and specification logics have been developed [8, 14, 13, 4, 5, 2, 6]. Although the numerical approach is highly accurate, it suffers from being computation intensive. An alternate method, proposed by Younes and Simmons [16], is based on Monte Carlo simulation and sequential hypothesis testing. Being statistical in nature, this approach is less accurate and only provides probabilistic guarantees of correctness. The approach does not assume knowledge of a specific formal model for the system being analyzed, and therefore can be potentially applied to analyzing complex dynamical systems such as generalized semi-Markov processes (GSMPs), for which symbolic

R. Alur and D.A. Peled (Eds.): CAV 2004, LNCS 3114, pp. 202–215, 2004.

and numerical methods are impractical. However, the Younes and Simmons' approach assumes that the system is controllable (not black-box) and can be used to generate sample executions from any state on need basis.

Both the numerical and the current statistical methods suffer from several serious drawbacks when it comes to analyzing practical systems. First, modern day systems are large heterogeneous, and assembled by integrating equipment and software from diverse vendors, making the construction of a formal model of the entire system often impossible and thus limiting the feasibility of numerical and symbolic methods. Second, for large network systems, meaningful experiments may involve dozens or even thousands of routers and hosts, which would mean that the system needs to be deployed before reasonable performance measures can be obtained. However, once they are deployed, such systems cannot be controlled to generate traces from any state, making it impossible to generate execution samples on a need basis as is required by the Younes *et. al*'s statistical approach.

Despite the success of current analysis methods [10, 13, 12, 15, 8], there is therefore a need to develop methods to analyze stochastic processes that can be applied to deployed, unknown "black-box" systems (systems from which traces cannot be generated from any state on need) [1]. In this paper we address these concerns by proposing a new statistical approach to model checking. Like in Younes *et. al*'s approach, discrete event simulation methods are used to obtain a set of sample executions; however, unlike their method we assume no control over the set of samples we obtain. We then test these samples using various statistical tests determined by the property to be verified. Since we assume that the samples are generated before testing, our algorithm relies on statistical hypothesis testing, rather than sequential hypothesis testing. Our inability to generate samples of our choosing and at the time of our choosing ensures that our approach differs from the previous statistical approach in one significant way: unlike the previous approach where the model checker's answer can be guaranteed to be correct within the required error bounds, we instead compute a quantitative measure of confidence (the p-value, in statistical testing terminology [11]) in the model checker's answer. Our algorithm computes the satisfaction of the desired formula by recursively determining the satisfaction of its subformulas (and the confidence of such an answer) in the "states" present in the sample. This presents a technical challenge because our algorithm, being statistical in nature, may be uncertain about the satisfaction of some formulas based on the given samples. The algorithm needs to compute useful answers (as far as possible) even in the presence of uncertain answers about the satisfaction of subformulas. We overcome this challenge by interpreting such "don't know" answers in an adversarial fashion. Our algorithm, thus checks if the sample provides evidence

---

[1] We assume that the samples generated from the system by discrete event simulation have information about the "system state". We, however, make no assumptions about the transition structure of the underlying system, nor do we assume knowledge about the transition probabilities; the system under investigation is black-box in this sense.

for the satisfaction or violation of a property and the confidence with which such an assertion holds, or gives up and says "don't know." The algorithm that we propose suffers from one drawback when compared with the previous statistical approach. Since we analyze a fixed sample, we will get useful answers only when there are sufficient samples for each "relevant state." Therefore our method is likely to work well only when a finite set of samples is enough to provide sufficient information about relevant states. Examples of systems we can successfully analyze are Continuous-time Markov Chains (CTMCs) or systems whose relevant states are discrete, while we are unlikely to succeed for GSMPs in general.

A closely related approach to analyzing stochastic systems based on Monte Carlo simulation is by Herault et. al. [7], which can model-check discrete-time Markov chains against properties expressed in an expressively weak logic ("positive LTL").

We have implemented the whole procedure in Java as a prototype tool, called VESTA (VErification based on STatistical Analysis)[2]. We have experimented with VESTA by applying it to some examples that have been previously analyzed in [15] and the results are encouraging. However, we suspect that VESTA would require a lot more space, because it stores the entire collection of samples it is analyzing. Even though space was not a problem for the examples we tried, we suspect that it may become an issue later.

The rest of the paper is organized as follows. Section 2 defines the class of systems we analyze and the logic we use. In Section 3, we present our algorithm based on statistical hypothesis testing in detail. Details about VESTA and our case studies are presented in Section 4. In Section 5, we conclude and present possible directions for future research.

2 Preliminaries

2.1 Sample Execution Paths

The verification method presented here can be independent of the system model as long as we can generate sample execution paths of the system; the model and its definition are very similar to [16]. We will assume that the system being analyzed is some discrete event system that occupies some state $s \in S$, where S is the set of states of the system. The states in S that can effect the satisfaction of a property of our interest are called the "relevant states." Note that the number of relevant states may be quite small compared to the whole state space of the system. For example, for a formula $\phi_1 \mathcal{U}^{\leq t} \phi_2$ the states that can be reached within time t are relevant. We assume that each relevant state can be uniquely identified and that information about a state's identity is available in the executions. Since samples are generated before running our analysis algorithm, we require that a Monte Carlo simulation is likely to generate a sample that has enough "information" about the relevant states; if not our algorithm is likely to say that it cannot infer anything about the satisfaction of the property.

---

[2] Available from http://osl.cs.uiuc.edu/~ksen/vesta/

We assume that there is a labeling function L that assigns to each state a set of atomic propositions (from among those appearing in the property of interest) that hold in that state; thus $L : S \rightarrow 2^{AP}$, where AP is a set of relevant atomic propositions. The system remains in a state s until an event occurs, and then proceeds instantaneously to a state s'. An execution path that appears in our sample is thus a sequence

$$\pi = s_0 \xrightarrow{t_0} s_1 \xrightarrow{t_1} s_2 \xrightarrow{t_2} \cdots$$

where s_0 is the unique initial state of the system, s_i is the state of the system after the ith event and t_i is the time spent in state s_i. If the kth state of this sequence is absorbing, then $s_i = s_k$ and $t_i = \infty$ for all $i \geq k$.

We denote the ith state in an execution π by $\pi[i] = s_i$ and the time spent in the ith state by $\delta(\pi, i)$. The time at which the execution enters state $\pi[i + 1]$ is given by $\tau(\pi, i + 1) = \sum_{j=0}^{j=i} \delta(\pi, j)$. The state of the execution at time t (if the sum of sojourn times in all states in the path exceeds t), denoted by $\pi(t)$, is the smallest i such that $t \leq \tau(\pi, i + 1)$. We let $Path(s)$ be the set of executions starting at state s. We assume $Path(s)$ is a measurable set (in an appropriate σ-field) and has an associated probability measure.

2.2   Continuous Stochastic Logic

Continuous stochastic logic (CSL) is introduced in [1] as a logic to express probabilistic properties of continuous time Markov chains (CTMCs). In this paper we adopt a sublogic of CSL (excluding unbounded untils and stationary state operators) as in [16]. This logic excludes the steady-state probabilistic operators and the unbounded until operators. We next present the syntax and the semantics of the logic.

CSL Syntax

$$\phi ::= true \mid a \in AP \mid \neg\phi \mid \phi \wedge \phi \mid \mathcal{P}_{\bowtie p}(\psi)$$
$$\psi ::= \phi \, \mathcal{U}^{\leq t} \phi \mid \mathbf{X}\phi$$

where AP is the set of atomic propositions, $\bowtie \in \{<, \leq, >, \geq\}$, $p \in [0, 1]$, and $t \in \mathbb{R}_{\geq 0}$. Here ϕ represents a *state* formula and ψ represents a *path* formula. The notion that a state s (or a path π) *satisfies* a formula ϕ is denoted by $s \models \phi$ (or $\pi \models \phi$), and is defined inductively as follows:

CSL Semantics

$s \models true$

$s \models \neg\phi$ iff $s \not\models \phi$

$s \models \mathcal{P}_{\bowtie p}(\psi)$ iff $Prob\{\pi \in Path(s) \mid \pi \models \psi\} \bowtie p$

$\pi \models \mathbf{X}\phi$ iff $\tau(\pi, 1) < \infty$ and $\pi[1] \models \phi$

$\pi \models \phi_1 \, \mathcal{U}^{\leq t} \phi_2$ iff $\exists x \in [0, t]. \, (\pi(x) \models \phi_2$ and $\forall y \in [0, x). \, \pi(y) \models \phi_1)$

$s \models a$ iff $a \in AP(s)$

$s \models \phi_1 \wedge \phi_2$ iff $s \models \phi_1$ and $s \models \phi_2$

A formula $\mathcal{P}_{\bowtie p}(\psi)$ is satisfied by a state s if $Prob[\text{path starting at } s \text{ satisfies } \psi] \bowtie p$. To define probability that a path satisfies ψ we need to define a σ-algebra over the set of paths starting at s and a probability measure on the corresponding measurable space in a way similar to [5]. The path formula $\mathbf{X}\phi$ holds over a path if ϕ holds at the second state on the path. The formula $\phi_1 \mathcal{U}^{\leq t}\phi_2$ is true over a path π if ϕ_2 holds in some state along π at a time $x \in [0, t]$, and ϕ holds along all prior states along π. This can also be recursively defined as follows:

$$Sat(s_i \xrightarrow{t_i} \pi_{i+1}, \phi_1 \mathcal{U}^{\leq t}\phi_2)$$
$$= (t \geq 0) \wedge (Sat(s_i, \phi_2) \vee (Sat(s_i, \phi_1) \wedge Sat(\pi_{i+1}, \phi_1 \mathcal{U}^{\leq t - t_i}\phi_2))) \quad (1)$$

where $Sat(s, \phi)$ (or $Sat(\pi, \psi)$) are the propositions that $s \models \phi$ (or $\pi \models \psi$). This definition will be used later to describe the algorithm for verification of $\phi_1 \mathcal{U}^{\leq t}\phi_2$ formula.

3   Algorithm

In what follows we say that $s \models_{\mathcal{A}} \phi$ if and only if our algorithm (denoted by $\mathcal{A}$) says that ϕ holds at state s. Since the algorithm is statistical, the decision made by the algorithm provides *evidence* about the actual fact. In our approach, we bound the strength of this evidence quantitatively by a number in $[0, 1]$ which gives the probability of making the decision given that the decision is actually incorrect. In statistics, this is called the p-value of the testing method. We denote it by α [3] and write $s \models \phi$ if the state s actually satisfies ϕ.

We assume that we are given a set of finite executions. The length of a finite execution path must be large enough so that all the bounded until formulas can be evaluated on that path. Given a set of sample execution paths starting at the initial state and a formula ϕ, the algorithm works recursively as follows:

```
verifyAtState(φ, s){
    if cache contains (φ, s) return cache(φ, s);
    else if φ = true then (z, α) ← (1, 0.0);
    else if φ = a ∈ AP then (z, α) ← verifyAtomic(a, s);
    else if φ = ¬φ' then (z, α) ← verifyNot(¬φ', s);
    else if φ = φ₁ ∧ φ₂ then (z, α) ← verifyAnd(φ₁ ∧ φ₂, s);
    else if φ = P◁▷ₚ(ψ) then (z, α) ← verifyProb(P◁▷ₚ(ψ), s);
    store (s, φ) ↦ (z, α) in cache;
    return (z, α);
}
```

where *verifyAtState* returns a pair having 0, 1, or *undecided* corresponding to the cases $s \models_{\mathcal{A}} \phi$, $s \not\models_{\mathcal{A}} \phi$, or $\mathcal{A}$ *cannot decide* respectively, as the first component, and p-value for this decision as the second component. To verify a system we check if the given formula holds at the initial state. Once computed, we store the decision of the algorithm for ϕ at state s in a cache to avoid recomputation. The result of our hypothesis testing can be shown to hold in presence of caching. This results in a significantly faster running time and a reduction in the sample set size. In the remainder of this section we define the various procedures *verifyAtomic*, *verifyAnd*, *verifyNot*, and *verifyProb* recursively.

The key idea of the algorithm is to statistically verify the probabilistic operator. We present the corresponding procedure *verifyProb* below.

---

[3] This should not be confused with the Type I error which is also denoted by α.

3.1 Probabilistic Operator

We use statistical hypothesis testing [11] to verify a probabilistic property $\phi = \mathcal{P}_{\bowtie p}(\psi)$ at a given state s. Without loss of generality we show our procedure for $\phi = \mathcal{P}_{\geq p}(\psi)$. This is because, for the purpose of statistical analysis, $\mathcal{P}_{< p}(\psi)$ is essentially the same as $\neg \mathcal{P}_{\geq 1-p}(\psi)$ and $<$ (or $>$) is in effect the same as $\leq$ (or $\geq$). Let p' be the probability that ψ holds over paths starting at s. We say that $s \models \mathcal{P}_{\geq p}(\psi)$ if and only if $p' \geq p$ and $s \not\models \mathcal{P}_{\geq p}(\psi)$ if and only if $p' < p$. We want to decide either $s \models \mathcal{P}_{\geq p}(\psi)$ or $s \not\models \mathcal{P}_{\geq p}(\psi)$. Accordingly we set up two experiments. In the first experiment, we use sample execution paths starting at s to test the *null hypothesis* $H_0 \colon p' < p$ against the *alternative hypothesis* $H_1 \colon p' \geq p$. In the second experiment, we test the *null hypothesis* $H_0 \colon p' \geq p$ against the *alternative hypothesis* $H_1 \colon p' < p$ [4].

Let the number of sample execution paths having a state s somewhere in the path be n. We can treat the portion of all these paths starting at s (suffix) as samples from $Path(s)$. Let $X_1, X_2, \ldots, X_n$ be a random sample having Bernoulli distribution with unknown parameter $p' \in [0, 1]$ i.e. for each $i \in [1, n]$, $Prob[X_i = 1] = p'$. Then the sum $Y = X_1 + X_2 + \ldots + X_n$ has binomial distribution with parameters n and p'. We say that x_i, an observation of the random variable X_i, is 1 if the ith sample execution path satisfies ψ and 0 otherwise. In the first experiment, we reject $H_0 \colon p' < p$ and say $s \models_{\mathcal{A}} \mathcal{P}_{\geq p}(\psi)$ if $\frac{\sum x_i}{n} \geq p$ and calculate the p-value as $\alpha = Prob[s \models_{\mathcal{A}} \phi \mid s \not\models \phi] = Prob[Y \geq \sum x_i \mid p' < p]$. Note we do not know p'. Therefore, to calculate α we use p which is an upper bound for p'. If we are not able to reject H_0 in the first experiment then we do the second experiment. In the second experiment, we reject $H_0 \colon p' \geq p$ and say $s \not\models_{\mathcal{A}} \mathcal{P}_{\geq p}(\psi)$ if $\frac{\sum x_i}{n} < p$ and calculate the p-value as $\alpha = Prob[s \not\models_{\mathcal{A}} \phi \mid s \models \phi] = Prob[Y < \sum x_i \mid p' \geq p]$. Thus, a smaller α represents a greater confidence in the decision of the algorithm $\mathcal{A}$.

3.2 Nested Probabilistic Operators

The above procedure for hypothesis testing works if the truth value of ψ over an execution path determined by the algorithm is the same as the actual truth value. However, in the presence of nested probabilistic operators in ψ, $\mathcal{A}$ cannot determine the satisfaction of ψ over a sample path exactly. Therefore, in this situation we need to modify the hypothesis test so that we can use the inexact truth values of ψ over the sample paths.

Let the random variable X be 1 if a sample execution path π actually satisfies ψ in the system and 0 otherwise. Let the random variable Z be 1 for a sample execution path π if $\pi \models_{\mathcal{A}} \psi$ and 0 otherwise. In our procedure we cannot get samples from the random variable X; instead our samples come from the random variable Z. Let X and Z have Bernoulli distributions with parameters p'

---

[4] While handling nested probabilistic operators, these experiments will no longer be symmetric. Moreover, setting up these two experiments is an alternate way of getting at a conservative estimate of what Type II error (β value) may be.

and p'' respectively. Let $Z_1, Z_2, \ldots, Z_n$ be a random sample from the Bernoulli distribution with unknown parameter $p'' \in [0, 1]$. We say that z_i, an observation of the random variable Z_i, is 1 if *the algorithm says* that the ith sample execution path satisfies ψ and 0 otherwise.

For the formula $\phi = \mathcal{P}_{\geq p}(\psi)$ we calculate regions of indifference, denoted by the fractions δ_1 and δ_2, based on the algorithm's decision for the satisfaction of ψ over the different sample paths. Depending on the values of δ_1 and δ_2 we set up the two experiments. In the first experiment, we test the null hypothesis $H_0 : p'' \leq p + \delta_1$ against the alternative hypothesis $H_1 : p'' > p + \delta_1$. If we get $\frac{\sum z_i}{n} > p + \delta_1$ we reject H_0 and say $s \models_{\mathcal{A}} \mathcal{P}_{\geq p}(\psi)$ with p-value $\alpha = Prob[s \models_{\mathcal{A}} \phi \mid s \not\models \phi] = Prob[\sum Z_i > \sum z_i \mid p'' \leq p + \delta_1]$. If we fail to reject H_0 we go for the second experiment, in which the null hypothesis $H_0 : p'' \geq p - \delta_2$ against the alternative hypothesis $H_1 : p'' < p - \delta_2$. We reject H_0 and say that $s \not\models_{\mathcal{A}} \mathcal{P}_{\geq p}(\psi)$ if $\frac{\sum z_i}{n} < p - \delta_2$ and calculate the p-value as $\alpha = Prob[s \not\models_{\mathcal{A}} \phi \mid s \models \phi] = Prob[\sum Z_i < \sum z_i \mid p'' \geq p - \delta_2]$. Otherwise, we say the algorithm cannot decide.

We now show how to calculate δ_1 and δ_2. Using the samples from Z we can estimate p''. However, we need an estimation for p' in order to decide whether $\phi = \mathcal{P}_{\geq p}(\psi)$ holds in state s or not. To get an estimate for p' we note that the random variables X and Z are related as follows:

$$Prob[Z = 0 \mid X = 1] \leq \alpha' \qquad Prob[Z = 1 \mid X = 0] \leq \alpha'$$

where α' is the p-value calculated while verifying the formula ψ. By elementary probability theory, we have

$$Prob[Z = 1] = Prob[Z = 1 \mid X = 0]Prob[X = 0] + Prob[Z = 1 \mid X = 1]Prob[X = 1]$$

Therefore, we can approximate $p'' = Prob[Z = 1]$ as follows:

$$Prob[Z = 1] \leq \alpha'(1 - p') + 1.p' = p' + (1 - p')\alpha'$$
$$Prob[Z = 1] \geq Prob[Z = 1 \mid X = 1]Prob[X = 1] \geq (1 - \alpha')p' = p' - \alpha'p'$$

This gives the following range in which p'' lies:

$$p' - \alpha'p' \leq p'' \leq p' + (1 - p')\alpha'$$

Hence, $Prob[\sum Z_i > \sum z_i \mid p' \leq p] \leq Prob[\sum Z_i > \sum z_i \mid p' = p] \leq Prob[\sum Z_i > \sum z_i \mid p'' = p - \alpha'p]$ which gives $\delta_2 = \alpha'p$. Similarly, we get $\delta_1 = (1 - p)\alpha'$.

Note that the p-value obtained while verifying ψ over different sample paths are different. We take the worst or the maximum of all such p-values as α'. Moreover, since $\mathcal{A}$ can say *true*, *false*, or *cannot decide*, note that the $\mathcal{A}$ may not have a definite *true* or *false* answer along certain sample paths. For such paths the algorithm will assume the worst possible answer in the two experiments. For the first experiment, where we check whether $\frac{\sum z_i}{n} > p + \delta_1$, we take the answers for the sample paths for which $\mathcal{A}$ cannot decide as *false* and the p-value as 0. For the second experiment we consider the answer for the undecided paths to be *true* and the p-value as 0. This allows us to obtain useful answers even when the sample does not have enough statistical evidence for the satisfaction of a subformula.

Thus we can define the procedure $verifyProb(\mathcal{P}_{\geq p}(\psi), s)$ as follows:

$verifyProb(\mathcal{P}_{\geq p}(\psi), s)\{$
    $zsum_{min} \leftarrow 0;\ zsum_{max} \leftarrow 0;\ \alpha' \leftarrow 0.0;\ n \leftarrow 0;$
    for each sample path π starting at $s\{$
        $(z, \alpha'') \leftarrow verifyPath(\psi, \pi);$
        if $z =undecided$ **then** $\{zsum_{min} \leftarrow zsum_{min} + 1;\ zsum_{max} \leftarrow zsum_{max} + 0;\}$
        else $\{zsum_{min} \leftarrow zsum_{min} + z;\ zsum_{max} \leftarrow zsum_{max} + z;\}$
        $\alpha' \leftarrow max(\alpha', \alpha'');\ n \leftarrow n + 1;$
    $\}$
    if $zsum_{max}/n > p + (1 - p)\alpha'$ **then**
        return $(1, Prob[\sum Z_i > zsum_{max} \mid p'' = p + (1 - p)\alpha']);$
    else if $zsum_{min}/n < p - p\alpha'$ **then**
        return $(0, Prob[\sum Z_i < zsum_{min} \mid p'' = p - p\alpha']);$
    else return $(undecided, 0.0);$
$\}$

One can calculate $Prob[\sum Z_i > zsum_{max} \mid p'' = p+(1-p)\alpha']$ (or $Prob[\sum Z_i > zsum_{min} \mid p'' = p - p\alpha'])$ by noting that $\sum Z_i$ has binomial distribution with parameters $p + (1 - p)\alpha'$ (or $p - p\alpha'$) and n.

3.3 Negation

For the verification of a formula $\neg\phi$ at a state s, we recursively verify ϕ at state s. If $s \models_{\mathcal{A}} \phi$ with p-value α we say that $s \not\models_{\mathcal{A}} \neg\phi$ with p-value $Prob[s \not\models_{\mathcal{A}} \neg\phi \mid s \models \neg\phi] = Prob[s \models_{\mathcal{A}} \phi \mid s \not\models \phi] = \alpha$. Similarly, if $s \not\models_{\mathcal{A}} \phi$ with p-value α then $s \models_{\mathcal{A}} \neg\phi$ with p-value α. Otherwise, if $\mathcal{A}$ cannot answer the satisfaction of ϕ at s, we say that $\mathcal{A}$ cannot answer the satisfaction of $\neg\phi$ at s. Thus we can define *verifyNot* as follows:

$verifyNot(\neg\phi', s)\{$
    $(z, \alpha) \leftarrow verifyAtState(\phi', s);$
    if $z =undecided$ **then return** $(undecided, 0.0);$ **else return** $(1 - z, \alpha);$
$\}$

3.4 Conjunction

To verify a formula $\phi = \phi_1 \wedge \phi_2$ at a state s, we verify ϕ_1 and ϕ_2 at the state s separately. Depending on the outcome of the verification of ϕ_1 and ϕ_2, $\mathcal{A}$ decides for ϕ as follows:

1. If $s \models_{\mathcal{A}} \phi_1$ and $s \models_{\mathcal{A}} \phi_2$ with p-values α_1 and α_2 respectively, then $s \models_{\mathcal{A}} \phi$. The p-value for this decision is $Prob[s \models_{\mathcal{A}} \phi_1 \wedge \phi_2 \mid s \not\models \phi_1 \wedge \phi_2]$. Note that $s \not\models \phi_1 \wedge \phi_2$ holds in three cases, namely 1) $s \not\models \phi_1$ and $s \models \phi_2$, 2) $s \models \phi_1$ and $s \not\models \phi_2$, and 3) $s \not\models \phi_1$ and $s \not\models \phi_2$. Thus, the p-value for the decision of $s \models_{\mathcal{A}} \phi$ can be taken as the maximum of the p-values in the above three cases which is $max(\alpha_1, \alpha_2)$.

2. If $s \not\models_{\mathcal{A}} \phi_1$ (or $s \not\models_{\mathcal{A}} \phi_2$) and either $s \models_{\mathcal{A}} \phi_2$ or $\mathcal{A}$ cannot decide ϕ_2 at s (or either $s \models_{\mathcal{A}} \phi_1$ or $\mathcal{A}$ cannot decide ϕ_1 at s), then $s \not\models_{\mathcal{A}} \phi$ and the p-value is $Prob[s \not\models_{\mathcal{A}} \phi_1 \wedge \phi_2 \mid s \models \phi_1 \text{ and } s \models \phi_2] = \alpha_1 + \alpha_2$ (or $\alpha_2 + \alpha_1$).

3. If $s \not\models_{\mathcal{A}} \phi_1$ and $s \not\models_{\mathcal{A}} \phi_2$ then $s \not\models_{\mathcal{A}} \phi_1 \wedge \phi_2$. The p-value for this decision is $Prob[s \not\models_{\mathcal{A}} \phi_1 \wedge \phi_2 \mid s \models \phi_1 \text{ and } s \models \phi_2] \leq \alpha_1 + \alpha_2$.

4. Otherwise, $\mathcal{A}$ cannot decide ϕ.

Thus we can define the procedure *verifyAnd* as follows:

```
verifyAnd(φ₁ ∧ φ₂, s){
    (z₁, α₁) ← verifyAtState(φ₁, s); (z₂, α₂) ← verifyAtState(φ₂, s);
    if z₁ = 1 and z₂ = 1 then return (1, max(α₁, α₂));
    else if z₁ = 0 and z₂ ≠ 0 then return (0, α₁ + α₂);
    else if z₁ ≠ 0 and z₂ = 0 then return (0, α₁ + α₂);
    else if z₁ = 0 and z₂ = 0 then return (0, α₁ + α₂);
    else return (undecided, 0.0);
}
```

3.5 Atomic Proposition

In this simplest case, given $\phi = a$ and a state s, $\mathcal{A}$ checks if $s \models_{\mathcal{A}} a$ or not by checking if $a \in AP(s)$ or not. If $a \in AP(s)$ then $s \models_{\mathcal{A}} \phi$ with p-value 0. Otherwise, $s \not\models_{\mathcal{A}} \phi$ with p-value 0.

```
verifyAtomic(a, s){
    if a ∈ AP(s) then return (1, 0.0); else return (0, 0.0);
}
```

3.6 Next

To verify a path formula $\psi = \mathbf{X}\phi$ over a path π, $\mathcal{A}$ verifies ϕ at the state $\pi[1]$. If $\pi[1] \models_{\mathcal{A}} \phi$ with p-value α then $\pi \models_{\mathcal{A}} \psi$ with p-value α. Otherwise, if $\pi[1] \not\models_{\mathcal{A}} \phi$ with p-value α then $\pi \not\models_{\mathcal{A}} \psi$ with the same p-value. Thus we can define *verifyPath* for $\mathbf{X}\phi$ as follows:

```
verifyPath(Xφ, π){
    return verifyAtState(φ, π[1]);
}
```

3.7 Until

Let $\psi = \phi_1 \mathcal{U}^{\leq t} \phi_2$ be an until formula that we want to verify over the path π. We can recursively evaluate the truth value of the formula over the path π by following the recursive definition given by Equation 1. Given the truth value and the p-value for the formula $\phi_1 \mathcal{U}^{\leq t'-t_i}\phi_2$ over the suffix π_{i+1}, we can calculate the truth value of $\phi_1 \mathcal{U}^{\leq t'}\phi_2$ over the path π_i by applying the decision procedure for conjunction and negation. Observe that the recursive formulation in Equation 1 can be unrolled to obtain an equation purely in terms of conjuction and negation (and without any until formulas); it is this "unrolled" version that is used in the implementation for efficiency reasons.

4 Implementation and Performance

We have implemented the above algorithm as part of a prototype Java tool called VeSTA. We successfully used the tool to verify several programs having a CTMC model[5]. The performance of the verification procedure depends on the number of samples required to reach a decision with sufficiently small p-value. To get a smaller p-value the number of samples needs to be increased. We need a lot of samples only when the actual probability of a path from a state s satisfying a formula ψ is very close to the threshold p in a formula $\mathcal{P}_{\bowtie p}(\psi)$ whose satisfaction we are checking at s.

To evaluate the performance and effectiveness of our implementation we did a few case studies. We mostly took the stochastic systems used for case studies in [15]. The experiments were done on a 1.2 GHz Mobile Pentium III laptop running Windows 2000 with 512 MB memory[6]. We did not take into account the time required for generating samples: we assumed that such samples come from a running system. However, this time, as observed in some of our experiments, is considerably less than the actual time needed for the analysis. We generated samples of length sufficient to evaluate all the time-bounded until formulas. In all of our case studies we checked the satisfaction of a given formula at the initial state. We give a brief description of our case studies below followed by our results and conclusions. The details for the case studies can be obtained from http://osl.cs.uiuc.edu/~ksen/vesta/.

Grid World: We choose this case study to illustrate the performance of our tool in the presence of nested probabilistic operators. It consists of an $n \times n$ grid with a robot located at the bottom-left corner and a janitor located at the top-right corner of the grid. The robot first moves along the bottom edge of a cell square and then along the right edge. The time taken by the robot to move from one square to another is exponentially distributed. The janitor also moves randomly over the grid. However, either the robot or the janitor cannot move to a square that is already occupied by the other. The robot also randomly sends a signal to the base station. The underlying model for this example is a CTMC. The aim of the robot is to reach the top-right corner in time T_1 units with probability at least 0.9, while maintaining a minimum 0.5 probability of communica-

---

[5] We selected systems with CTMC model so that we can compare our results with that of existing tools.

[6] [15] used a 500 MHz Pentium III. However, our performance gain due to the use of faster processor is more than offset by the use of Java instead of C.

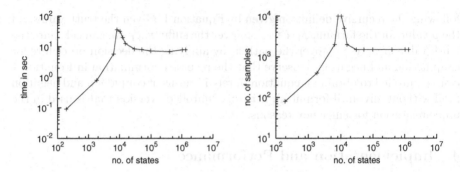

Fig. 1. Grid world: verification time and number of samples versus number of states.

tion with the base station with periodicity less than T_2 units of time. This can be specified using the CSL formula $\mathcal{P}_{\geq 0.9}(\mathcal{P}_{\geq 0.5}(true\,\mathcal{U}^{\leq T_2}\,communicate)\mathcal{U}^{\leq T_1}\,goal)$.

We verified the CSL property for Grid World with $n \in [1, 100]$. The property holds only for $n \in [1, 13]$. The state space of the program is $\Theta(n^3)$. In Fig.1 we plot the results of our experiment. The graph shows that for n closer to 13 the running time and the number of samples required increases considerably to get a respectable p-value of around 10^{-8}. This is because at $n = 13$ the probability that $\mathcal{P}_{\geq 0.5}(true\,\mathcal{U}^{\leq T_2}\,communicate)\,\mathcal{U}^{\leq T_1}\,goal$ holds over an execution path becomes very close to 0.9. We found that our graphs are similar to [15].

Cyclic Polling System: This case study is based on a cyclic server polling system, taken from [12]. The model is represented as a CTMC. We use N to denote the number of stations handled by the polling server. Each station has a single-message buffer and they are cyclically attended by the server. The server serves the station i if there is a message in the buffer of i and then moves on to poll the station $(i+1)$ modulo N. Otherwise, the server starts polling the station $i+1$ modulo N. The polling and service times are exponentially distributed. The state space of the system is $\Theta(N.2^N)$. We verified the property that "once a job arrives at the first station, it will be polled within T time units with probability at least 0.5." The property is verified at the state in which all the stations have one message in their message buffer and the server is serving station 1. In CSL the property can be written as $(m_1 = 1) \rightarrow \mathcal{P}_{\geq 0.5}(true\,\mathcal{U}^{\leq T}(s = 1 \wedge a = 0))$, where $m_1 = 1$ means there is one message at station 1, and $s = 1 \wedge a = 0$ means that the server is polling station 1.

Tandem Queuing Network: This case study is based on a simple tandem queuing network studied in [9]. The model is represented as a CTMC which consists of a M/Cox$_2$/1-queue sequentially composed with a M/M/1-queue. We use N to denote the capacity of the queues. The state space is $\Theta(N^2)$. We verified the CSL property $\mathcal{P}_{<0.5}(true\,\mathcal{U}^{\leq T}\,full)$ which states that the probability of the queuing network becoming full within T time units is less than 0.5.

The results of the above two case studies is plotted in Fig. 2. The characteristics of the graphs for both the examples are similar to that in [15]. However, while achieving a level of confidence around 10^{-8}, the running time of our tool

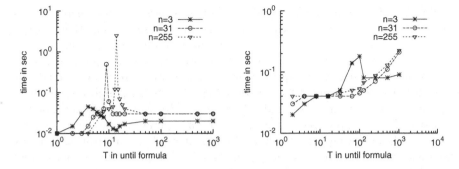

Fig. 2. Polling System and Tandem Queuing Network: Running time versus the parameter T in CSL formula.

for these cases is faster than the running time of the tool described in [15]. It is important to observe that, unlike the work of [15], VESTA cannot guarantee that the error of it's probabilistic answer is bounded; the p-value computed depends on the specific sample.

We could not compare the number of samples for these case studies as they are not available from [15]; theoretically sequential hypothesis testing should require a smaller sample size than simple hypothesis testing to achieve the same level of confidence. While in our case studies we never faced a memory problem, we suspect that this may be a problem in very big case studies. We observed that, although the state space of a system may be large, the number of states that appeared in the samples may be considerably smaller. This gives us hope that our approach may work as well for very large-scale systems.

5   Conclusion and Future Work

We have presented a new statistical approach to verifying stochastic systems based on Monte Carlo simulation and statistical hypothesis testing. The main difference between our approach and previous statistical approaches is that we assume that the system under investigation is not under our control. This means that our algorithm computes on a fixed set of executions and cannot obtain samples as needed. As a consequence, the algorithm needs to check for the satisfaction of a property and compute the p-value of its tests. Since the sample may not provide sufficient statistical evidence to conclude the satisfaction or violation of a property, one technical challenge is to provide useful answers despite insufficient statistical evidence for the satisfaction of subformulas. We implemented our approach in Java and our experimental case studies have demonstrated that the running time of our tool is faster than previous methods for analyzing stochastic systems in at least some cases; this suggests that our method may be a feasible alternative.

Another important challenge is the amount of memory needed. Since we store all the sample executions, our method is memory intensive, and though we did not suffer from memory problems on the examples studied here, we suspect that it will be an issue when analyzing larger case studies. Hence, there is a need to design efficient data structures and methods to store and compute with a large set of sample executions. We suspect statistical hypothesis testing approaches (as opposed to sequential hypothesis testing approaches) might be extendible to check liveness for certain types of systems, possibly by extracting some additional information about the traces. Note that liveness properties are particularly complicated by the fact that the operators may be nested. We are currently exploring that direction. Finally, it would be interesting to apply statistical methods to analyze properties described in probabilistic logics other than CSL.

Acknowledgments

The work is supported in part by the DARPA IPTO TASK Award F30602-00-2-0586, the DARPA IXO NEST Award F33615-01-C-1907, the DARPA/AFOSR MURI Award F49620-02-1-0325, the ONR Grant N00014-02-1-0715, and the Motorola Grant MOTOROLA RPS #23 ANT. We would also like to acknowledge the contribution of Jose Meseguer to this research. Our work has benefitted considerably from stimulating discussions with him and from our many years of collaboration on probabilistic rewriting theories. We would like to thank Reza Ziaie for reviewing a previous version of this paper and giving us valuable feedback.

References

1. A. Aziz, K. Sanwal, V. Singhal, and R. K. Brayton. Verifying continuous-time Markov chains. In *8th International Conference on Computer Aided Verification (CAV'96)*, volume 1102, pages 269–276. Springer, 1996.
2. R. Alur, C. Courcoubetis, and D. Dill. Model-checking for probabilistic real-time systems (extended abstract). In *Proceedings of the 18th International Colloquium on Automata, Languages and Programming (ICALP'91)*, volume 510 of *LNCS*, pages 115–126. Springer, 1991.
3. A. Aziz, K. Sanwal, V. Singhal, and R. Brayton. Model-checking continuous-time Markov chains. *ACM Transactions on Computational Logic*, 1(1):162–170, 2000.
4. C. Baier, E. M. Clarke, V. Hartonas-Garmhausen, M. Z. Kwiatkowska, and M. Ryan. Symbolic model checking for probabilistic processes. In *Proceedings of the 24th International Colloquium on Automata, Languages and Programming (ICALP'97)*, volume 1256 of *LNCS*, pages 430–440. Springer, 1997.
5. C. Baier, J. P. Katoen, and H. Hermanns. Approximate symbolic model checking of continuous-time markov chains. In *International Conference on Concurrency Theory*, volume 1664 of *LNCS*, pages 146–161. Springer, August 1999.
6. A. Bianco and L. de Alfaro. Model checking of probabilistic and nondeterministic systems. In *Proceedings of 15th Conference on the Foundations of Software Technology and Theoretical Computer Science (FSTTCS'95)*, volume 1026 of *LNCS*.

7. T. Herault, R. Lassaigne, F. Magniette, and S. Peyronnet. Approximate Probabilistic Model Checking. In *Proceedings of Fifth International Conference on Verification, Model Checking and Abstract Interpretation (VMCAI'04)*, volume 2937 of *LNCS*, pages 73–84. Springer, 2004.

8. H. Hermanns, J. P. Katoen, J. Meyer-Kayser, and M. Siegle. A Markov chain model checker. In *Tools and Algorithms for Construction and Analysis of Systems (TACAS'00)*, pages 347–362, 2000.

9. H. Hermanns, J. Meyer-Kayser, and M. Siegle. Multi-terminal binary decision diagrams to represent and analyse continuous-time markov chains. In *Proceedings of 3rd International Workshop on the Numerical Solution of Markov Chains (NSMC'99)*, 1999.

10. J. Hillston. *A Compositional Approach to Performance Modelling*. Cambridge University Press, 1996.

11. R. V. Hogg and A. T. Craig. *Introduction to Mathematical Statistics*. Macmillan, New York, NY, USA, fourth edition, 1978.

12. O. C. Ibe and K. S. Trivedi. Stochastic petri net models of polling systems. *IEEE Journal on Selected Areas in Communications*, 8(9):1649–1657, 1990.

13. M. Z. Kwiatkowska, G. Norman, and D. Parker. Prism: Probabilistic symbolic model checker, 2002.

14. M. Z. Kwiatkowska, G. Norman, R. Segala, and J. Sproston. Verifying quantitative properties of continuous probabilistic timed automata. In *International Conference on Concurrency Theory (CONCUR'00)*, volume 1877 of *LNCS*, pages 123–137. Springer, 2000.

15. H. L. S. Younes, M. Kwiatkowska, G. Norman, and D. Parker. Numerical vs. statistical probabilistic model checking: An empirical study. In *10th International Conference on Tools and Algorithms for the Construction and Analysis of Systems (TACAS'04)*. Springer, 2004.

16. H. L. S. Younes and R. G. Simmons. Probabilistic verification of discrete event systems using acceptance sampling. In *14th International Conference on Computer Aided Verification (CAV'02)*, volume 2404 of *LNCS*, pages 223–235. Springer, 2002.

Compositional Specification
and Model Checking in GSTE

Jin Yang and Carl-Johan H. Seger

Strategic CAD Labs, Intel Corp.
{jin.yang,carl.seger}@intel.com

Abstract. We propose a compositional specification and verification approach based on GSTE (Generalized Symbolic Trajectory Evaluation). There are two main contributions. First, we propose a specification language that allows concurrent properties be described succinctly in a compositional algebraic manner. Second, we show a precise model checking solution for a compositional specification through automata construction, but much more importantly and practically, we develop an efficient model checking algorithm for directly verifying the compositional specification. At the end, we show the result of our approach in the verification of a micro-instruction scheduler in a state-of-the-art microprocessor.

1 Introduction

GSTE is a symbolic model checking solution that combines the high capacity and ease of use of STE with the expressive power (Ω-regular languages) of classic symbolic model checking [7, 22, 23]. It has been successfully applied to the formal verification of complex Intel designs with tens of thousands of state elements [22, 5, 21].

The specification language in GSTE is called *assertion graphs*, an operational formalism based on a special form of regular automata with assertion letters (antecedent and consequent pairs) as its input alphabet. Each word in the language of an assertion graph provides both a sequential stimuli for simulating the system and the expected sequential responses. The sequential nature of an assertion graph, however, hinders its ability to succinctly describe the concurrent behavior of a circuit.

In this paper, we present a compositional approach based on GSTE to overcome the limitation. First, we propose a specification language that allows the concurrent behavior of a system to be specified succinctly in a compositional manner. Such a composition is logical and does not rely on a deep understanding of the implementation details of the system. The language is an extension of the GSTE specification language with a new meet operator and is expressed in the form of Process Algebra [13, 19, 10]. Second, although we show that the compositional specification can be precisely model checked, we develop a much more efficient and practical solution to directly verify the compositional specification. The solution extends the GSTE model checking algorithm [22] with the ability to walk through the syntactical structure of the specification and establish a simulation relation from the language elements of the specification to the sets of states in the circuit. This avoids the exponentially expensive global assertion graph construction.

R. Alur and D.A. Peled (Eds.): CAV 2004, LNCS 3114, pp. 216–228, 2004.

There have been extensive studies on concurrent system specification and verification, most notably along the lines of hierarchical state machines (e.g. Statecharts) [9, 14, 4, 3, 2] and Process Algebra [19, 13, 10, 6]. However, most of these approaches have mainly focused on specification formalisms, correctness of specifications, and modular refinement strategies. None has provided an efficient and practical model checking solution to verify a concurrent specification against an implementation. Relying on model checking the global transition system for the specification is prohibitively expensive.

In recent years, the assume-guarantee based compositional approach has been gaining popularity [20, 19, 15, 8, 16–18, 11, 12], driven by the need to deal with the capacity limitation of symbolic model checking. In this framework, a circuit under verification is described as a parallel composition of finite state components, and the correctness of the circuit is described as a collection of local properties, each of which specifies the correctness of one component assuming that the correctness of the interfacing components. This approach achieves verification efficiency by model checking each local property against its component separately, and then establishing the global correctness using an inductive assume-guarantee reasoning. A main drawback of the approach, however, is that the specification is heavily implementation-dependent, requiring the deep understanding of how these components interact with each other. Therefore, it is rather manual, labor-intensive and sensitive to the changes in the implementation.

We firmly believe that a practical approach must contain two ingredients, a formal language to support succinct concurrent specifications, and an efficient solution (such as model checking) to verify such a specification against a complex implementation. Our GSTE based approach addresses both. The rest of the paper is organized as follows. In Section 2, we define assertion languages for GSTE and their trace semantics. In Section 3, we introduce the new binary *meet* operator $\sqcap$ for assertion languages. In Section 4, we present the compositional specification language for GSTE in a form of algebraic equations [13, 19, 10], and show that this language is well defined. We also prove a regularity result for a compositional specification, i.e., the limit of a repeated application of $\sqcap$ to any assertion language in the specification is regular. Since the limit is trace equivalent to the original language, this gives us a way to precisely model check the compositional specification using the GSTE model checking algorithm in [22, 23]. However, the construction of the regular automaton for the limit may cause an exponential blow-up in the size of the specification. Therefore in Section 5, we develop a GSTE model checking algorithm for directly verifying a compositional specification. In Section 6, we briefly discuss the result of the compositional GSTE approach in the verification of a micro-instruction scheduler from an Intel microprocessor design.

2   Assertion Languages

For the entire scope of the paper, we assume a finite, non-empty alphabet $\mathcal{D}$ called the *domain*. An ω-*trace* (or simply *trace*), denoted by $\tau = d_1 d_2 \ldots$, is any ω-word in $\mathcal{D}^\omega$. For a circuit under verification, the domain $\mathcal{D}$ is the set of all states in the circuit, and a trace is simply any infinite sequence of states.

We define the *assertion alphabet* Σ over domain $\mathcal{D}$ as the tuple $\Sigma = \mathbb{P}(\mathcal{D}) \times \mathbb{P}(\mathcal{D})$ where $\mathbb{P}(\mathcal{D})$ denotes the power set of $\mathcal{D}$. We call any letter in Σ an *assertion letter*, any word in Σ^* an *assertion word*, and any language in $\mathbb{P}(\Sigma^*)$ an *assertion language*.

Given an assertion letter $\sigma = (\mathcal{A}, \mathcal{B})$, $\mathcal{A}$ and $\mathcal{B}$ are called the *antecedent* and the *consequent* of the letter, denoted by $ant(\sigma) = \mathcal{A}$ and $cons(\sigma) = \mathcal{B}$. The antecedent and consequent functions are point-wise generalized to an assertion word w in Σ^*, i.e., $ant(w)$ and $cons(w)$ as defined by

$$\forall 1 \leq i \leq |w|, ant(w)[i] = ant(w[i]), cons(w)[i] = cons(w[i]).$$

Assertion graphs defined in [22, 23] are basically regular automata (or ω-regular automata if an additional fairness condition is specified) for generating regular assertion languages. We shall use the following simple *voting machine* example throughout the paper to illustrate various concepts in the paper.

Example 1. (Voting Machine) A voting machine (VM) consists of three voting stations (Figure 1). Each voting station receives a single vote through $vin[i]$ ($1 \leq i \leq 3$). Once all stations have received their votes, the VM conducts a poll among the three stations and produces a final voting result *vout*. It then clears all voting stations to accept a new round of votes. Output signal $av[i]$ tells if the i-th voting station is available. Signal *reset* resets the VM to its initial state. For simplicity, we ignore the content of a vote and that of the final result, and just care about control/status signals.

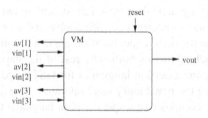

Fig. 1. Voting Machine (VM)

The domain D for the VM is the set of values for the external signals. For instance,

$$[reset = 0, vin[1] = 1, av[1] = 1, vin[2] = 0, av[2] = 0, vin[3] = 0, av[1] = 1, vout = 0]$$

is a value in D. We use state predicates over D to represent sets of values in D, for instance, $vin[1] \vee \neg vin[2]$ represents all values in D where either $vin[1] = 1$ or $vin[2] = 0$. The assertion word for the VM

$$((reset, true), (vin[1] \wedge \neg vin[2] \wedge \neg vin[3], true), (vin[2] \wedge vin[3], true), (true, vout))$$

says that after reset, if vote $vin[1]$ comes in followed by votes $vin[2]$ and $vin[3]$, then the VM produces the final result in the next time. □

Note that the specification in Figure 1 does not address how the system is implemented. As we shall show later in the paper, our compositional approach allows one to state the correctness of the system succinctly without the worry of implementation details. It empowers the model checking algorithm to connect the specification with the implementation of the system.

An assertion language is in some sense an operational specification formalism, where each assertion word in the language provides both a sequential stimuli for simulating the system and the expected sequential responses. Many or even an infinite number of words may be needed to cover all possible behaviors of the system. An assertion graph in [22, 23] is a way to use a labeled finite graph to capture theses words. However, it can still be quite a cumbersome way to describe a system with inherent concurrency. For instance, there are $1 + 3 \times 2! + 3! = 13$ different orders for the three votes to arrive to the VM, each of which must be captured by a path in the assertion graph for the VM, although the specification does not care about in which particular order the votes arrive. The compositional extension in this paper addresses this issue.

In the following, we define the semantics of an assertion language. We say a trace τ over $\mathcal{D}$ *satisfies* a word π over $\mathbb{P}(\mathcal{D})$, denoted by $\tau \models \pi$, iff $\forall 1 \leq i \leq |\pi|,\ \tau[i] \in \pi[i]$. We say τ *satisfies* an assertion word w in Σ^*, iff $\tau \models ant(w) \Rightarrow \tau \models cons(w)$. The *trace language* of an assertion word w, denoted $\Omega(w)$, is the set of all traces satisfying w, i.e.,

$$\Omega(w) = \{\tau \in \mathcal{D}^\omega \mid \tau \models w\}. \tag{1}$$

The *trace language* of an assertion language L, denoted by $\Omega(L)$, is the *intersection* of the trace languages of the assertion words in L, i.e.,

$$\Omega(L) = \cap_{w \in L}\Omega(w). \tag{2}$$

This is the same as the semantics for assertion graphs in [22, 23]. Because of the $\forall$-semantics, the union $\cup$ of two assertion languages becomes stronger and yields fewer traces, in contrast to the traditional wisdom. The $\forall$-semantics is the basis for efficient GSTE model checking. The following theorem shows that a language with fewer assertion words yields more traces.

Theorem 1. $L_1 \subseteq L_2 \Rightarrow \Omega(L_1) \supseteq \Omega(L_2)$.

3 The Meet Operator

To facilitate compositional specifications, we introduce a *meet* operator $\sqcap : \Sigma \times \Sigma \to \Sigma$ that takes two assertion letters $\sigma_1, \sigma_2 \in \Sigma$ and produces another assertion letter such that

$$ant(\sigma_1 \sqcap \sigma_2) = ant(\sigma_1) \cap ant(\sigma_2), \text{ and } cons(\sigma_1 \sqcap \sigma_2) = cons(\sigma_1) \cap cons(\sigma_2). \tag{3}$$

The meet operator is applied point-wise to two words $w_1, w_2 \in \Sigma^*$ of the same length, denoted by $w_1 \sqcap w_2$, such that

$$w_1 \sqcap w_2 = \begin{cases} \varepsilon & \text{if } w_1 = w_2 = \varepsilon \\ (w_1' \sqcap w_2') \cdot (\sigma_1 \sqcap \sigma_2) & \text{if } w_1 = w_1' \cdot \sigma_1 \text{ and } w_2 = w_w' \cdot \sigma_2, \end{cases} \tag{4}$$

where $\cdot$ is the language concatenation operator. It is not difficult to show that the operator is associative, commutative and idempotent. Finally, the meet operator is generalized to two languages $L_1, L_2 \in \mathbb{P}(\Sigma^*)$:

$$L_1 \sqcap L_2 = \{w_1 \sqcap w_2 \mid w_1 \in L_1, w_2 \in L_2, |w_1| = |w_2|\}. \tag{5}$$

Example 2. Consider the VM specification in Example 1. Language $(1 \leq i \leq 3)$

$$\mathcal{V}[i] = (reset, true) \cdot (\neg vin[i], true)^* \cdot (vin[i], true) \cdot (\neg vin[i], true)^*$$

describes the first vote at the i-th station. The meet $\mathcal{V}_1 \sqcap \mathcal{V}_2 \sqcap \mathcal{V}_3$ succinctly describes all possible sequences of getting the first three votes without the explicit enumeration. $\square$

In the following, we define a repeated application of $\sqcap$ over a language L, $\sqcap^k L$, as

$$\sqcap^k L = \begin{cases} L & \text{if } k = 0 \\ (\sqcap^{k-1} L) \sqcap L & \text{if } k > 0. \end{cases} \tag{6}$$

We can show that although the resulting meet language may produce new words, it is trace equivalent to the original language.

Lemma 1. *For all $k \geq 0$,*

1. $\sqcap^k L \subseteq \sqcap^{k+1} L$,
2. $\Omega(\sqcap^k L) = \Omega(\sqcap^{k+1} L)$.

Now consider the limit $\bigcup_{m \geq 0} \sqcap^m L$ for the ascending chain $(\sqcap^0 L, \sqcap^1 L, \sqcap^2 L, \ldots)$.

Theorem 2.

1. *(Containment)* $L \subseteq \bigcup_{m \geq 0} \sqcap^m L$,
2. *(Trace Equivalence)* $\Omega(L) = \Omega(\bigcup_{m \geq 0} \sqcap^m L)$.

The proof directly follows Lemma 1 by a transitivity argument. This result is important in establishing a regularity result for a compositional specification in Section 4.

4   Compositional Specification

We define a *compositional specification* $C(\Pi)$ as a set of algebraic equations over a set of assertion languages

$$\Pi = \{\mathcal{L}_0\} \cup \{\mathcal{L}_1, \ldots, \mathcal{L}_{h-1}\} \cup \{\mathcal{L}_h, \ldots, \mathcal{L}_{l-1}\} \cup \{\mathcal{L}_l, \ldots, \mathcal{L}_{n-1}\},$$

in which each equation is of the form

1. (Initialization)
$$\mathcal{L}_0 = \varepsilon \cup \mathcal{L}_0 \cdot \sigma_0, \tag{7}$$

where $\sigma_0 = (\mathcal{D}, \mathcal{D})$, or
2. (Prefix)
$$\mathcal{L}_i = \mathcal{L}_j \cdot \sigma_j, \tag{8}$$

for each $1 \leq i < h$ where $0 \leq j < n$ and $\sigma_j \in \Sigma$, or
3. (Summation)
$$\mathcal{L}_i = \mathcal{L}_{i_1} \cup \ldots \cup \mathcal{L}_{i_{k_i}}, \tag{9}$$

for each $h \leq i < l$ where $1 \leq i_j < h$ for $1 \leq j \leq k_i$, or

4. (Meet)
$$\mathcal{L}_i = \mathcal{L}_{i_1} \sqcap \ldots \sqcap \mathcal{L}_{i_{k_i}},\tag{10}$$

for each $l \leq i < n$ where $q \leq i_j < l$ for $1 \leq j \leq k_i$,

where ε denotes the singleton language with the empty word $\{\varepsilon\}$ and $\cdot$ denotes the concatenation of a letter to the end of each word in a language.

This style of compositional definition is similar to Milner's CCS (*Calculus of Communicating Systems*) [19] with three differences: a special initialization equation, the meet operator in place of the parallel composition operator $\mid$, and (3) the trace semantics of assertion languages. Note also that this style is a generalization of assertion graphs in [22, 23]. In fact, without any meet composition, it corresponds to an assertion graph where (1) the initial language corresponds to the initial vertex with a self-loop, (2) a prefix language corresponds to an edge, and (3) a summation language corresponds to a vertex in the graph.

Example 3. The specification of the VM in Figure 1 is captured by the following set of algebraic equations, shortened by use a mixture of language and regular expressions.

1. (Ready) Station i ($1 \leq i \leq 3$) is in its *Ready*[i] state after being reset or polled.

$$Ready[i] = (\ (true,true)^* \cdot (reset, av[i]) \cup Poll \cdot (reset \vee \neg vin[i], av[i]) \ )$$
$$\cdot (reset \vee \neg vin[i], av[i])^*.$$

2. (Voting) Station i ($1 \leq i \leq 3$) is accepting a vote.

$$Voting[i] = Ready[i] \cdot (\neg reset \wedge vin[i], av[i]).$$

3. (Vote) Station i ($1 \leq i \leq 3$) has got a vote.

$$Voted[i] = Voting[i] \cup (Voted[i] \sqcap Wait) \cdot (\neg reset, \neg av[i]).$$

4. (Wait) At least one voting station is in its *Ready* state.

$$Wait = \cup_{i=1}^{3} Ready[i].$$

5. (Poll) Every station is in its *Voted* state and one station is accepting a vote.

$$Poll = (\sqcap_{i=1}^{3} Voted[i]) \sqcap (\cup_{i=1}^{3} Voting[i]).$$

6. (Output) The VM outputs the polling result.

$$Output = Wait \cdot (true, \neg vout) \cup Poll \cdot (true, vout).$$

$\square$

Note that this specification is not a conjunction of simple independent properties. Rather it is a network of semantically inter-dependent "communicating" properties. The following theorem shows that this set of equations is well defined in the algebraic sense.

Theorem 3. *The set of equations $C(\Pi)$ has a unique language solution.*

The proof is based on Tarski's fix-point theorem and an induction on the length of the words in the languages in the equations. We omit the proof due to the page limitation. In the following, we show that the limit of $\sqcap^m L_i$ to each language L_i in the compositional specification is regular. This is significant based on Theorem 2, as it gives us a way to precisely model check the specification by constructing an assertion graph for the language and verifying the graph using the GSTE model checking algorithm in [22, 23]. To make the argument simple, we break each $\cup$ and $\sqcap$ composition into a series of pairwise compositions by introducing intermediate languages.

Lemma 2.

1. $\bigcup_{m\geq 0} \sqcap^m (L \cdot \sigma) = (\bigcup_{m\geq 0} \sqcap^m L) \cdot \sigma.$
2. $\bigcup_{m\geq 0} \sqcap^m (L_1 \sqcap L_2) = (\bigcup_{m\geq 0} \sqcap^m L_1) \sqcap (\bigcup_{m\geq 0} \sqcap^m L_2).$
3. $\bigcup_{m\geq 0} \sqcap^m (L_1 \cup L_2) = (\bigcup_{m\geq 0} \sqcap^m L_1) \cup (\bigcup_{m\geq 0} \sqcap^m L_2) \cup (\bigcup_{m\geq 0} \sqcap^m L_1)$
   $\sqcap (\bigcup_{m\geq 0} \sqcap^m L_2).$

The proof of the lemma is done by distributing $\sqcap$ over $\cdot$ and $\cup$, and then using the language containment argument. We omit the proof due to the page limitation.

Theorem 4. $\bigcup_{m\geq 0} \sqcap^m L_i$ *is regular for every language* L_i $(0 \leq i < n)$ *in* Π.

Proof. Consider the power set of the limit languages $\mathbb{P}(\bigcup_{m\geq 0} \sqcap^m L_i \mid L_i \in \Pi)$. Based on Lemma 2, each language in the power set can be expanded algebraically into either a prefix composition of another language, or a summation composition of some other languages in the set. Without the meet, the construction of a regular automaton for each language in the set is straight forward. Since $\bigcup_{m\geq 0} \sqcap^m L_i$ is in the set, the claim holds.

$\square$

5   Direct Model Checking of Compositional Specification

Although model checking any language in the compositional specification can be done through the construction of the regular automaton for the meet limit of the language, such a construction is likely to cause an exponential blow-up in the specification size. To avoid the problem, we develop a GSTE model checking algorithm that directly walks through the syntactical structure of the specification and establishes a simulation relation from the language elements in the specification to the sets of states in the circuit.

We first define a *model* over $\mathcal{D}$ as a triple $M = (\mathcal{S}, \mathcal{R}, L)$ where

1. $\mathcal{S}$ is a finite set of *states*,
2. $\mathcal{R} \subseteq \mathcal{S} \times \mathcal{S}$ is a *state transition relation* over $\mathcal{S}$ such that for every state $s \in \mathcal{S}$, there is a state $s' \in \mathcal{S}$ satisfying $(s, s') \in \mathcal{R}$,
3. $L: \mathcal{S} \to \mathcal{D}$ is a *labeling* function that labels each state $s \in \mathcal{S}$ with a value $d \in \mathcal{D}$.

M induces a monotonic *post-image* transformation function $post_M : \mathbb{P}(S) \to \mathbb{P}(S)$:

$$post_M(S') = \{s' \mid \exists s \in S', (s, s') \in \mathcal{R}\}, \tag{11}$$

for all $S' \in \mathbb{P}(S)$. We drop the subscript M when it is understood. A model is a Kripke structure without the initial state. To follow the STE convention, we assume that every state in M is an initial state. We extend L to state sets and define its inverse function L^-

$$L(S') = \{L(s) \mid s \in S'\}, \text{ and } L^-(D') = \{s \in S \mid L(s) \in D'\} \tag{12}$$

for all $S' \in \mathbb{P}(S)$ and $D' \in \mathbb{P}(D)$.

A *run* of the model is any mapping function $\gamma: \mathbb{N} \rightarrow S$ such that for all $i \geq 0$, $(\gamma(i), \gamma(i+1)) \in \mathcal{R}$. The trace generated by γ, denoted by $L(\gamma)$, is the point-wise application of L over γ, i.e., $L(\gamma)(i) = L(\gamma(i))$ for all $i \geq 0$. The *trace language* of the model, denoted by $\Omega(M)$, is the set of all traces generated by the runs of the model, i.e., $\Omega(M) = \{L(\gamma) \mid \gamma \text{ is a run of } M\}$.

We say that the model M *satisfies* an assertion language L, denoted by $M \models L$, if

$$\Omega(M) \subseteq \Omega(L). \tag{13}$$

M *satisfies* the set of equations $C(\Pi)$, denoted by $M \models C(\Pi)$, if $M \models L_i$ for all $L_i \in \Pi$.

The key idea of the model checking algorithm is to compute a simulation relation for each language in Π on M. A *simulation relation* is a mapping from each language L_i ($0 \leq i < n$) to a state set $\mathcal{T}_i \in \mathbb{P}(S)$, such that for every state $s \in S$, $s \in \mathcal{T}_i$ if there is a word $w \in L_i$ and a run γ in M such that

$$(1) \ L(\gamma) \models ant(w), \text{ and } (2) \ s = \gamma(|w|). \tag{14}$$

The simulation relation captures, for each language, the end of any run in the model satisfying the antecedent sequence of a word in the language. It has nothing to do with consequents. The importance of the simulation relation is stated in the following lemma.

Lemma 3. $M \models C(\Pi)$, *if for every prefix language* $L_i = L_j \cdot \sigma_j$, $\mathcal{T}_i \subseteq cons(\sigma_j)$.

Proof. First we prove that $M \models L_i$ for every prefix language. Assume $M \not\models L_i$. Then by (13) and (1), there is run γ of M and a word $w = w' \cdot \sigma_j$ in L_i such that (1) $L(\gamma) \models ant(w)$, but (2) $L(\gamma(|w|) \notin cons(\sigma_j)$. By (14), $\gamma(|w|)$ is in $\mathcal{T}_i$, and thus $L(\mathcal{T}_i) \not\subseteq cons(\sigma_j)$. Further, $M \models L_0$ since $L_0 = (\mathcal{D}, \mathcal{D})^*$. Based on this result, It also becomes obvious that $M \models L_i$ for every $\cup$-composition L_i ($h \leq i < l$) by (2). Finally, consider a $\sqcap$-composition $L_i = L_{i_1} \sqcap \ldots \sqcap L_{i_{k_i}}$. Consider a trace τ in $\Omega(M)$. Let $w = w_1 \sqcap \ldots \sqcap w_{k_i}$ be a word in L_i. By (13), we have $\tau \models ant(w_j) \Rightarrow \tau \models cons(w_j)$ for all $1 \leq j \leq k_i$. Now let us assume $\tau \models ant(w)$. Then by (4), $\tau \models ant(w_j)$ and therefore $\tau \models cons(w_j)$ for $1 \leq j \leq k_i$. Thus, $\tau \models cons(w)$. Therefore, $\tau \in \Omega(L_i)$ by (5) and thus $M \models L_i$. $\square$

We now show how to iteratively compute a simulation relation for the specification based on its structure. Let $\mathcal{S}_n$ to denote the *n*-ary state set tuple $(\mathcal{S}_0, \mathcal{S}_1, \ldots, \mathcal{S}_{n-1})$. We define a partial order relation $\preceq: \mathcal{S}_n \preceq \mathcal{S}'_n$, iff $\forall 0 \leq i < n, \mathcal{S}_i \subseteq \mathcal{S}'_i$. $(\mathbb{P}(S) \times \ldots \times \mathbb{P}(S), \preceq)$ forms a finite c.p.o. with the bottom element being $\emptyset_n = (\emptyset, \ldots, \emptyset)$.

We define an update function for *n*-ary state set tuples on model M

$$Y(\mathcal{S}_n) = (Y_0(\mathcal{S}_n), Y_1(\mathcal{S}_n), \ldots, Y_{n-1}(\mathcal{S}_n)) \tag{15}$$

where

1. (Initialization) $L_0 = \varepsilon \cup L_0 \cdot \sigma_0$:

$$Y_0(\mathcal{S}_n) = S, \tag{16}$$

2. (Prefix) $\mathcal{L}_i = \mathcal{L}_j \cdot \sigma_j$ for $1 \le i < h$:

$$Y_i(S_n) = \begin{cases} L^-(ant(\sigma_j)) & \text{if } L_j = L_0 \\ post(S_j) \cap L^-(ant(\sigma_j)) & \text{otherwise,} \end{cases} \tag{17}$$

3. (Summation) $\mathcal{L}_i = \mathcal{L}_{i_1} \cup \ldots \cup \mathcal{L}_{i_{k_i}}$ for $h \le i < l$:

$$Y_i(S_n) = \cup_{j=1}^{k_i} S_{i_j}, \tag{18}$$

4. (Meet) $\mathcal{L}_i = \mathcal{L}_{i_1} \cap \ldots \cap \mathcal{L}_{i_{k_i}}$ for $l \le i < n$:

$$Y_i(S_n) = \cap_{j=1}^{k_i} S_{i_j}. \tag{19}$$

It can be shown that Y is monotonic, and the sequence $(Y^0(\emptyset_n), Y^1(\emptyset_n), Y^2(\emptyset_n), \ldots)$ is an ascending chain with a least fixpoint, i.e., $\exists M \ge 0, \forall k \ge M, Y^k(\emptyset_n) = Y^M(\emptyset_n)$.

Lemma 4. $Y^M(\emptyset_n)$ *is a simulation relation for* $C(\Pi)$ *on* M.

The proof is based on an induction on the length of words leading to a state in the simulation relation, and is omitted due to the page limitation. Based on this result, we develop a GSTE model checking algorithm for the compositional specification in Figure 2. The following correctness result holds.

Algorithm: $cGSTE(C(\Pi), post)$
1. $\mathcal{T}_0 := S$, $\mathcal{T}_i := \emptyset$ for all $1 \le i \le n$;
2. $active := \{\mathcal{L}_i \mid \mathcal{L}_i = \mathcal{L}_0 \cdot \sigma_j\}$;
3. **while** $active \ne \emptyset$
4. $\mathcal{L}_i := pickOne(active)$;
5.   **case** $\mathcal{L}_i = \mathcal{L}_0 \cdot \sigma_j$: $new := L^-(ant(\sigma_j))$;
6. $\mathcal{L}_i = \mathcal{L}_j \cdot \sigma_j$: $new := post(\mathcal{T}_j) \cap L^-(ant(\sigma_j))$;
7. $\mathcal{T}_i = \mathcal{L}_{i_1} \cup \ldots \cup \mathcal{L}_{i_{k_i}}$: $new := \cup_{j=1}^{k_i} \mathcal{T}_{i_j}$;
8.   **else**: $new := \cap_{j=1}^{k_i} \mathcal{T}_{i_j}$;
9.   **endcase**
10.   **if** $new \ne \mathcal{T}_i$
11.   add to $active$ every $\mathcal{L}_k$ having $\mathcal{L}_i$ in its definition;
12. $\mathcal{T}_i := new$;
13. **endwhile**
14. **if** $\mathcal{T}_i \not\subseteq cons(\sigma_j)$ for some $\mathcal{L}_i = \mathcal{L}_j \cdot \sigma_j$
15.   return($false$);
16. return($true$);
end.

Fig. 2. cGSTE

Theorem 5. $M \models C(\Pi)$, *if* $cGSTE(C(\Pi), M)$ *returns true.*

The algorithm initially sets the simulation relation to the empty set for every language except for $\mathcal{L}_0$, which is set to S. It then iteratively updates the simulation relation for a language by locally propagating the simulation relations for the languages in its definition. It does so until no change can be made to any simulation relation. By avoiding the construction of a "global" automaton which may cause an exponential blow-up in the specification size, it becomes conservative but gains great efficiency.

To show the advantage of our approach over the assume-guarantee based compositional approach, we continue on the VM in Example 1. Figure 3 shows two different implementations of the VM. Implementation (1) is partitioned into four modules, one for each station and one for the final polling. Each station i tracks its own voting status in $v[i]$. Implementation (2) bundles all the signals from and to the three stations into 3-bit vectors, and the vector $av[1:3]$ tracks the availability status of each station. Assume that clr (set) sets the register to 0 (1) for the current and next steps.

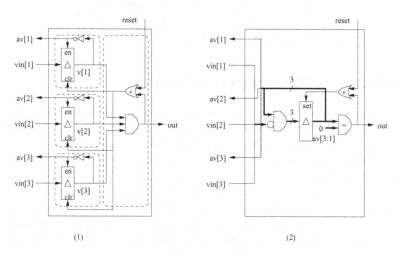

Fig. 3. Two VM Implementations

The assume-guarantee based approach is heavily implementation dependent and requires a clear understanding of the implementation details of the VM. For instance, given implementation (1), the overall specification may be decomposed into four local properties for the four modules, linking together through the interface behaviors of the voting status signals $v[1]$, $v[2]$ and $v[3]$. The property for the polling module may say, among other things, that if $v[i]$ is high for all $1 \leq i \leq 3$, then $out = 1$. The correctness of the decomposition also needs to be justified. Further, the change of the implementation could require an entirely different decomposition. For instance, the decomposition for implementation (2) would be bit-slicing based and relies on behaviors of the availability signals $av[3:1]$ to glue local properties together. It is conceivable that such a manual approach will be labor-intensive and difficult to get it right for complex designs.

On the contrary, our compositional specification is implementation independent. The languages in the specification can be viewed as a logical decomposition of the specification with no mentioning of the internal signal behaviors. Our model checking algorithm automatically computes the mapping from the end behavior specified by each language to the set of corresponding circuit states for any given implementation. Table 1 summarises the final simulation relations for $Ready[i]$, $Voting[i]$ and $Voted[i]$ computed by the algorithm on the two implementations. Based on this, the simulation relation for *Poll* on implementation (1) is $\neg clr \wedge (\wedge_{i=1}^{3}(vin[i] \vee v[i])) \wedge (\vee_{i=1}^{3}(vin[i] \wedge \neg v[i]))$, which allows one to conclude that the implmentation will indeed satisfy $out = 1$ at the next step. Finally, we point out that the quaternary simulation aspect of GSTE allows our algorithm to focus only the relevant part of the model at each iteration step and store the simulation relations efficiently in an abstract form. We will not talk about it in the paper due to the page limitation.

Table 1. Final Simulation Relations for the VM

Language	Implementation (1)	Implementation (2)
$Ready[i]$	$(clr \vee \neg vin[i]) \wedge \neg v[i]$	$(set \vee \neg vin[i]) \wedge av[i]$
$Voting[i]$	$\neg clr \wedge vin[i] \wedge \neg v[i]$	$\neg set \wedge vin[i] \wedge av[i]$
$Voted[i]$	$\neg clr \wedge (vin[i] \vee v[i])$	$\neg set \wedge (vin[i] \vee \neg av[i])$

6   Verification of Micro-instruction Scheduler

The compositional GSTE has been implemented as a part of the GSTE verification system inside the Intel *Forte* environment ([1]). In this section, we discuss the verification of a micro-instruction (uop) scheduler in the original Intel®Pentium® 4 Microprocessor Scheduler/Scoreboard unit (SSU) (see Figure 4) as described in [5, 21]. The scheduler can hold and schedule up to 10 micro-instructions. The correctness property for the scheduler is that "when the resource is available, the oldest ready uop in the scheduler will be sent out." Even a much weaker version of the property, on the priority matrix module only stating "a uop would be scheduled if there are ready uops", had been quite difficult to prove previously using a state-of-the-art in-house symbolic model checker based on an assume-guarantee based approach. The logic involved created significant tool capacity problems, and required that the high level property be decomposed into literally hundreds of small local properties. Creating and proving this decomposition was done manually, and required a significant amount of time. Its maintenance and regression has been costly as the design changed.

Using the compositional GSTE approach, we were able to specify the entire correctness property succinctly in a compositional manner at the unit level, and verify it very efficiently using the compositional model checking algorithm. The compositional specification was developed in a top-down fashion. The top level property is

$$Prop = OldestReadyUop[i] \cdot (\neg stop, sched[i])$$

which simply says that if $uop[i]$ ($0 \leq i < 10$) is the oldest ready uop, then schedule it at the next step if the resource is available. We then expand the property $OldestReadyUop[i]$:

$$OldestReadyUop[i] = Ready[i] \sqcap (\sqcap_{j \neq i}(NotReady[j] \cup EnqueuedEarlier[i, j]))$$

which simply defines the oldest ready uop as the uop that is ready and was enqueued to the scheduler earlier than any other ready uop. We keep expanding the properties until they are described in terms of input/output signal behaviors.

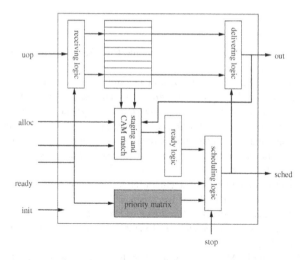

Fig. 4. Intel® Pentium® 4 Microprocessor SSU Scheduler

A recent rerun of the verification was done on a computer with 1.5 GHz Intel® Pentium® 4 processor with 1 GB memory. It was done on the original SSU circuit with no prior abstraction, which contains 718 latches, 361 inputs, and 17367 gates. The verification was done in 122 seconds using only 36MB memory. Most of the memory was used for storing the circuit. The tremendous verification efficiency benefits from the specification driven state space exploration strategy of the GSTE algorithm and the extended quaternary circuit abstraction technique [22]. Because of these, the verification complexity largely depends on the complexity of the specification to be verified rather than that of the circuit under verification, and is very scalable when the number of uops handled by the scheduler increases.

Finally, we would like to point out that compositional GSTE has been in active use in Intel and been successfully applied to the verification of several large-scale complex circuits in microprocessor designs.

7   Conclusion

In this paper, we presented a practical compositional extension to GSTE. For future work, we would like to extend the terminal condition and the fairness condition [23] to compositional GSTE, and apply the abstraction/refinement methodology in [22] to the compositional framework.

Acknowledgment

We would like to thank Ching-Tsun Chou, John O'Leary, Andreas Tiemeyer, Roope Kaivola, Ed Smith and reviewers for valuable feedbacks.

References

1. M. Aagaard, R. Jones, T. Melham, J. O'Leary, and C.-J. Seger. A methodology for large-scale hardware verification. In *FMCAD'2000*, November 2000.
2. R. Alur and R. Grosu. Modular refinement of hierarchical state machines. In *Proc. of the 27th ACM Symposium on Principles of Programming Languages*, pages 390–402, 2000.
3. R. Alur, R. Grosu, and M. McDougall. Efficient reachability analysis of hierarchic reactive machines. In *Computer-Aided Verification (LNCS1855*, pages 280–295, 2000.
4. R. Alur, S. Kannan, and M. Yannakakis. Communicating hierarchical state machines. In *Proc. of the 26th International Colloquium on Automata, Languages, and Programming (LNCS1644)*, pages 169–178, 1999.
5. B. Bentley. High level validation of next generation micro-processors. In *IEEE International High-Level Design, Validation, and Test Workshop*, 2002.
6. J. Bergstra, A. Ponse, and S. Smolka. *Handbook of Process Algebra*. Elsevier, 2001.
7. C.-T. Chou. The mathematical foundation of symbolic trajectory evaluation. In *Computer Aided Verification*, July 1999.
8. E. Clarke, D. Long, and K. McMillan. A language for compositional specification and verification of finite state hardware controllers. *Proc. of the IEEE*, 79(9):1283–92, Sept. 1991.
9. D. Harel. A visual formalism for complex systems. *Science of Computer Programming*, 8(3):231–274, June 1987.
10. M. Hennessy. *Algebraic Theory of Processes*. MIT Press, 1988.
11. T. Henzinger, S. Qadeer, and K. Rajamani. You assume, we guaranee: Methodology and case studies. In *Computer Aided Verification (LNCS 1427)*, pages 440–451, 1998.
12. T. Henzinger, S. Qadeer, K. Rajamani, and S. Tasiran. An assume-guarantee rule for checking simulation. *ACM Trans. on Programming Languages and Systems*, 24:51–64, 2002.
13. C. Hoare. *Communicating Sequential Processes*. Prentice Hall, 1985.
14. F. Jahanian and A. Mok. Modechart: A specification language for real-time systems. *IEEE Trans. on Software Engineering*, 20(2):933–947, Dec. 1994.
15. B. Josko. Verifying the correctness of aadl-modules using model checking. In *Proc. of the REX Workshop on Stepwise Refinement of Distributed Systems, Models, Formalisms, Correctness (LNCS430)*. Springer, 1989.
16. D. Long. *Model Checking, Abstraction, and Compositional Reasoning*. PhD thesis, Computer Science Department, Carnegie Mellon University, 1993.
17. K. McMillan. A compositional rule for hardware design refinement. In *Computer Aided Verification*, June 1997.
18. K. McMillan. Verification of an implementation of tomasulo's algorithm by compositional model checking. In *Computer Aided Verification*, June 1998.
19. R. Milner. *Communication and Concurrency*. Prentice Hall, 1989.
20. A. Pnueli. In transition from global to modular temporal reasoning about programs. In *Logics and Models of Concurrent Systems*, volume NATO ASI 13. Springer, 1997.
21. T. Schubert. High-level formal verification of next generation micro-processors. In *40th ACM/IEEE Design Automation Conference*, 2003.
22. J. Yang and C.-J. Seger. Generalized symbolic trajectory evaluation – abstraction in action. In *FMCAD'2002*, pages 70–87, November 2002.
23. J. Yang and C.-J. Seger. Introduction to generalized symbolic trajectory evaluation. *IEEE Trans. on VLSI Systems*, 11(3):345–353, June 2003.

GSTE Is Partitioned Model Checking

Roberto Sebastiani[1,*], Eli Singerman[2], Stefano Tonetta[1], and Moshe Y. Vardi[3,**]

[1] DIT, Università di Trento
{rseba,stonetta}@dit.unitn.it
[2] Intel Israel Design Center
eli.singerman@intel.com
[3] Dept. of Computer Science, Rice University
vardi@cs.rice.edu

Abstract. Verifying whether an ω-regular property is satisfied by a finite-state system is a core problem in model checking. Standard techniques build an automaton with the complementary language, compute its product with the system, and then check for emptiness. Generalized symbolic trajectory evaluation (GSTE) has been recently proposed as an alternative approach, extending the computationally efficient symbolic trajectory evaluation (STE) to general ω-regular properties. In this paper, we show that the GSTE algorithms are essentially a partitioned version of standard symbolic model-checking (SMC) algorithms, where the partitioning is driven by the property under verification. We export this technique of property-driven partitioning to SMC and show that it typically does speed up SMC algorithms.

1 Introduction

Verifying whether an ω-regular property is satisfied by a finite-state system is a core problem in Model Checking (MC) [23,31]. Standard MC techniques build a complementary *Büchi automaton* (BA), whose language contains all violations of the desired property. They then compute the product of this automaton with the system, and then check for emptiness [30,23]. To check emptiness, one has to compute the set of *fair states*, i.e., those states of the product automaton that are extensible to a fair path. This computation can be performed in linear time by using a depth-first search [10]. The main obstacle to this procedure is *state-space explosion*, i.e., the product is usually too big to be handled. Symbolic model checking (SMC) [3] tackles this problem by representing the product automaton symbolically, usually by means of BDDs. Most symbolic model checkers compute the fair states by means of some variant of the doubly-nested-fixpoint Emerson-Lei algorithm (EL) [13].

Another approach to formal verification is that of Symbolic Trajectory Evaluation (STE) [28], in which one tries to show that the system satisfies the desired prop-

---

* Sponsored by the CALCULEMUS! IHP-RTN EC project, code HPRN-CT-2000-00102, by a MIUR COFIN02 project, code 2002097822_003, and by a grant from the Intel Corporation.

** Supported in part by NSF grants CCR-9988322, CCR-0124077, CCR-0311326, IIS-9908435, IIS-9978135, EIA-0086264, and ANI-0216467 by BSF grant 9800096, and by a grant from the Intel Corporation.

R. Alur and D.A. Peled (Eds.): CAV 2004, LNCS 3114, pp. 229–241, 2004.

erty by using symbolic simulation and quaternary symbolic abstraction. This often enables quick response time, but is restricted to very simple properties, constructed from Boolean implication assertions by means of conjunction and the temporal next-time operator [5]. Recently, GSTE [33] has been proposed as an extension of STE that can handle all ω-regular properties. In this framework, properties are specified by means of *Assertion Graphs* (AG). The GSTE algorithm augments symbolic simulation with a fixpoint iteration. Recent work on GSTE, e.g., in [34], has described various case studies and has focused mainly on abstraction in GSTE. The fundamental relation between GSTE and SMC, however, has not been completely clarified. The basic relationship between AGs and BAs is sketched in [21], but the algorithmic relationship between GSTE and SMC has not been studied.

In this work, we analyze the property-specification language and the checking algorithm used by GSTE and compare them to those used in SMC. (We do not deal with abstraction, which is an orthogonal issue.) We first fill in details not given in [21] to show that assertion graphs are essentially *universal* ω-automata [24], which require all runs to be accepting. Universal automata enjoy the advantage of easy complementation; in fact, they can be viewed as nondeterministic automata for the complementary property. Formally, given a BA, one can easily construct an AG for the complementary language, and vice versa. This permits us to do a direct comparison between the algorithms underlying GSTE and SMC.

We then point out that the GSTE algorithms are essentially a partitioned version of the standard SMC algorithms. SMC algorithms operate on subsets of the product state space $S \times V$, where S is the state space of the system and V is the state space of complementary automaton. We show that GSTE operates on partitioned subsets of the product state space. The partitioning is driven by the automaton state space. The GSTE analog of a subset $Q \subseteq S \times V$ is the partition $\{Q_v : v \in V\}$, where $Q_v = \{s : (s,v) \in Q\}$. The GSTE algorithms are in essence an adaptation of the standard SMC algorithms to the partitioned state space. Thus, rather than operate on a BDD representing a subset P of the product state space, GSTE operates on an array of BDDs, representing a partitioning of P. We refer to such partitioning as *property-driven partitioning*.

Finally, we proceed to explore the benefits of property-driven partitioning in the framework of SMC. We use NuSMV [6] as our experimental platform in the context of LTL model checking. We added to NuSMV the capability of property-driven partitioned SMC, both for safety LTL properties and for full LTL properties, and compared the performance of SMC with partitioned SMC. We find that property-driven partitioning is an effective technique for SMC, as partitioned SMC is typically faster than SMC. The major factor seems to be the reduction in the number of BDD variables, which results in smaller BDDs. The reduced BDD size more than compensates for the additional algorithmic overhead for handling a partitioned state space.

Partitioning techniques have often been proposed in order to tackle the state space explosion problem. (We refer here to *disjunctive* partitioning, rather than to the orthogonal technique of *conjunctive* partitioning, which is used to represent large transition relations.) Static partitioning techniques, which require an analysis of the state space, have been discussed, e.g., in [25]. Dynamic partitioning techniques, which are driven by heuristics to reduce BDD size, have been discussed, e.g., in [4]. Partitioning has been used in [19] to develop a distributed approach to SMC.

Property-driven partitioning is orthogonal to previous partitioning techniques. Unlike dynamic partitioning techniques, no expensive BDD-splitting heuristics are required. Unlike previous static partitioning techniques, property-driven partitioning is fully automated and no analysis of the system state space is needed. The technique is also of interest because it represents a novel approach to automata-theoretic verification. So far, automata-theoretic verification means that either both system and property automaton state spaces are represent explicitly (e.g. in SPIN [20]) or symbolically (in NuSMV [6] or in Cadence SMV www-cad.eecs.berkeley.edu/~kenmcmil/smv/). Just like GSTE, property-driven partitioning enables a hybrid approach, in which the property automaton, whose state space is often quite manageable, is represented explicitly, while the system, whose state space is typically exceedingly large is represented symbolically. Other hybrid approaches have been described in [1, 7, 18], but ours is the first work to evaluate a hybrid approach in the context of general model checking.

The paper begins with an overview of the basic notions of SMC [9] and GSTE [33] in Section 2: first, BAs and AGs are defined in a new perspective that clarifies the common underlying structure; we then describe SMC and GSTE model checking procedures. In Section 3, first, we prove that AGs and BAs are equivalent; then, we analyze the checking algorithms of GSTE and show that it is a partitioned version of standard SMC algorithms. In Section 4, we export property-driven partitioning to SMC and we report on the comparison of SMC with partitioned SMC in the framework of NuSMV. We conclude in Section 5 with a discussion of future research directions.

2   Büchi Automata and Assertion Graphs

In this section, we introduce the specification languages and the checking algorithms used by SMC [9] and GSTE [33]. In SMC, we can specify properties by means of BAs, while GSTE uses AGs. Both the languages have a finite and a fair semantics. The finite semantics is checked with a fixpoint computation, while the fair one requires a doubly-nested fixpoint computation.

We define a system M as a tuple $\langle S, S_I, T \rangle$, where S is the set of states, $S_I \subseteq S$ is the set of initial states, $T \subseteq S \times S$ is the transition relation. We use capital letters such as $Y, Z, ..$ to denote subsets of S. We define functions $post, pre : 2^S \longrightarrow 2^S$ such that $post(Y) = \{s' \in S \mid (s, s') \in T, s \in Y\}$ and $pre(Y) = \{s' \in S \mid (s', s) \in T, s \in Y\}$. A finite (resp., infinite) trace in M is a finite (resp., infinite) sequence σ of states such that $\sigma[i+1] \in post(\sigma[i])$ for all $1 \leq i < |\sigma|$ (resp., $i \geq 1$). A trace σ is initial iff $\sigma(1) \in S_I$. We define $L_f(M)$ as the set of all initial finite traces of M and $L(M)$ as the set of all initial infinite traces.

In the following, we propose a new representation for BAs and AGs: both can be seen as an extension of Fair Graphs (FG). This is the structure which AGs and BAs have in common. As we shall see, while an AG is an FG with two labeling functions, a BA is an FG with just one labeling function. We use labels on vertices rather than on edges (as in GSTE [33]). This does not affect the generality of our framework and allows for an easier comparison between GSTE and SMC as well as an experimental evaluation in the framework of NuSMV. Moreover, labels are defined as sets of systems states. (In practice, labels are given as predicates on system states; a predicate describes the sets of states that satisfy it.)

2.1 Fair Graphs, Büchi Automata and Assertion Graphs

Fair Graphs are essentially graphs with the addition of a fairness condition.

Definition 1. *A Fair Graph G is a tuple $\langle V, V_I, E, \mathcal{F} \rangle$ where V is the set of vertices, $V_I \subseteq V$ is the set of initial vertices, $E \subseteq V \times V$ is a total relation representing the set of edges, and $\mathcal{F} = \{F_1, ..., F_n\}$, with $F_j \subseteq V$ for $1 \le j \le n$, is the set of fair sets.*

A finite (resp., infinite) path in G is a finite (resp., infinite) sequence ρ of vertices such that $(\rho[i], \rho[i+1]) \in E$ for all $1 \le i < |\rho|$ (resp., $i \ge 1$). ρ is initial iff $\rho[1] \in V_I$. ρ is fair iff it visits every set $F \in \mathcal{F}$ infinitely often. We define $L_f(G)$ as the set of all finite initial paths of G and $L(G)$ as the set of all fair initial paths.

For every $v \in V$ we define the set of successor vertices $E(v) = \{v' \in V \mid (v, v') \in E\}$ and the set of predecessor vertices $E^-(v) = \{v' \in V \mid (v', v) \in E\}$. (The operators E and E^- are analogous to *post* and *pre*. They are used for clarity of notation.)

A labeling function is a function $\gamma : V \longrightarrow 2^S$. Given a set of vertices $V' \subseteq V$, we define the restriction $\gamma_{|V'}$ of γ to V' as follows: $\gamma_{|V'}(v) = \gamma(v)$ if $v \in V'$, and $\gamma_{|V'}(v) = \emptyset$ otherwise. Typically, we use α, β, γ to denote labeling functions. Notice that a labeling function γ can be considered and represented as a set of subsets of S: $\{\gamma(v)\}_{v \in V}$. With abuse of notation, given two labeling functions α and γ, we will write $\alpha \subseteq \gamma$ (resp., $\alpha \cap \gamma$, $\alpha \cup \gamma$) to mean, for all $v \in V$, $\alpha(v) \subseteq \gamma(v)$ (resp., $\alpha(v) \cap \gamma(v)$, $\alpha(v) \cup \gamma(v)$).

Definition 2. *Given a trace σ in M, a path ρ in G of the same length l (resp., both infinite) and a function $\gamma : V \longrightarrow 2^S$, we say that σ satisfies ρ under γ (denoted $\sigma \models_\gamma \rho$) iff $\sigma[i] \in \gamma(\rho[i])$ for all $1 \le i \le l$ (resp., $i \ge 1$).*

A Büchi automaton (BA) is essentially an FG with the addition of a labeling function. A trace is accepted by a BA iff it satisfies the labeling function along at least one path of the FG. In the following, BAs express complementary properties, that is, their language contains all violations of the desired property.

Formally, a Büchi Automaton B is a tuple $\langle G, L \rangle$ where $G = \langle V, V_I, E, \mathcal{F} \rangle$ is a fair graph, and $L : V \longrightarrow 2^S$ is the labeling function. We define the set $L_f(B)$ (resp., $L(B)$) as the set of finite (resp., infinite) traces of M accepted by B:

Definition 3.
- finite semantics: if $\mathcal{F} = \{F\}$, $L_f(B) = \{\sigma \in L_f(M) \mid$ *there exists a finite path* $\rho \in L_f(G)$ *with* $|\sigma| = |\rho| = l$, $\rho[l] \in F$ *and* $\sigma \models_L \rho\}$;
- fair semantics: $L(B) = \{\sigma \in L(M) \mid$ *there exists a fair path* $\rho \in L(G)$ *with* $\sigma \models_L \rho\}$.

Since BAs have the complementary language of the specification, the model checking problem consists in verifying whether $L_f(B) = \emptyset$, in the case of finite semantics, $L(B) = \emptyset$, in the case of fair semantics.

An assertion graph (AG) is essentially an FG with the addition of two labeling functions: the antecedent and the consequent. An AG accepts a trace iff, along all paths, either the trace does not satisfy the antecedent or if it satisfies the consequent.

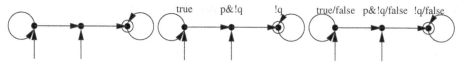

Fig. 1. FG example   **Fig. 2.** BA example   **Fig. 3.** AG example

Formally, an Assertion Graph A is a tuple $\langle G, ant, cons \rangle$ where $G = \langle V, V_I, E, \mathcal{F} \rangle$ is a fair graph, $ant : V \longrightarrow 2^S$ is the antecedent function, and $cons : V \longrightarrow 2^S$ is the consequent function. Given a trace σ in M and a path ρ in G of the same length, we say that σ satisfies ρ in A (denoted $\sigma \models_A \rho$) iff $\sigma \models_{ant} \rho \Rightarrow \sigma \models_{cons} \rho$. We define the set $L_f(A)$ (resp., $L(A)$) as the set of finite (resp., infinite) traces of M accepted by A:

Definition 4.
- finite semantics: *if* $\mathcal{F} = \{F\}$, $L_f(A) = \{\sigma \in L_f(M) \mid \text{for all finite path } \rho \in L_f(G),$ *if* $|\sigma| = |\rho| = l$ *and* $\rho[l] \in F$, *then* $\sigma \models_A \rho\}$;
- fair semantics: $L(A) = \{\sigma \in L(M) \mid \text{for all fair path } \rho \in L(G), \sigma \models_A \rho\}$.

The model checking problem for AGs consists in verifying whether $L_f(M) \subseteq L_f(A)$, in the case of finite semantics, $L(M) \subseteq L(A)$, in the case of fair semantics.

Example 1. An example of FG is depicted in Fig. 1. The vertices are represented by points, the edges by arrows. An arrow without starting vertex point to a vertex to indicate that it is initial. For simplicity, in the example we have only one fair set. The circle around the rightmost vertex means that it belongs to this fair set.

Examples of BA and AG are depicted resp. in Fig. 2 and 3. They have the same underlying FG. In the AG, the labels are represented in the format $ant/cons$. p and q are propositional properties. With the fair semantics, the AG corresponds to the LTL property $G(p \rightarrow Fq)$, while the BA has the complementary language. $\square$

2.2 SMC Algorithms

Given a system $M = \langle S, S_I, T \rangle$ and a BA $B = \langle \langle V, V_I, E, \mathcal{F} \rangle, \mathcal{L} \rangle$, SMC first computes the product P between B and M. Then, in the case of finite semantics, it finds the set of vertices reachable from the initial vertices and check if it intersects a certain set of vertices F_P in P; in the case of fair semantics it finds the set of fair vertices, i.e., those which are extensible to fair paths, and it checks if it intersects the set of initial vertices.

The product between M and B is a BA defined as follows: $P := \langle \langle V_P, I_P, E_P, \mathcal{F}_P \rangle, \mathcal{L}_P \rangle$ where $V_P = \{(s,v) \mid s \in M, v \in V, s \in \mathcal{L}(v)\}$, $I_P = \{(s,v) \in V_P \mid s \in S_I, v \in V_I\}$, $E_P = \{((s,v),(s',v')) \mid (s,v) \in V_P, (s',v') \in V_P, (s,s') \in T, (v,v') \in E\}$, $\mathcal{F}_P = \{F_{P1}, ..., F_{Pn}\}$ where $F_{Pj} = \{(s,v) \in V_P \mid v \in F_j\}$, $\mathcal{L}_P(s,v) = \{s\}$.

In the case of finite semantics $\mathcal{F} = \{F\}$, so that $\mathcal{F}_P = \{F_P\}$, where $F_P = \{(s,v) \in V_P \mid v \in F\}$. Then, it is easy to see that $L_f(P) = L_f(B)$. Moreover, every finite path of P corresponds to a finite trace of M accepted by B. Thus, to verify that $L_f(P) = \emptyset$, we can just compute the set of reachable vertices and check that it does not intersect F_P. Usually, this set is found with a traversal algorithm like the one described in Fig. 4.

Algorithm *traversal(P)*

1. $R := I_P$
2. $N := I_P$
3. **repeat**
4. $Z := \mathbf{EY}[N]$
5. $N := Z \backslash R$
6. $R := R \cup Z$
7. **until** $N = \emptyset$
8. **return** R

Algorithm *fairstates(P)*

1. $Y := \top$
2. **repeat**
3. $Y' := Y$
4.   **for** $F_P \in \mathcal{F}_P$
5. $Z := \mathbf{E}[YU(Y \wedge F_P)]$
6. $Y := Y \wedge \mathbf{EX}[Z]$
7. **until** $Y' = Y$
8. **return** Y

Fig. 4.   **Fig. 5.**

Similarly, in the case of fair semantics, it is easy to see that $L(P) = L(B)$. Moreover, every fair path of P corresponds to an infinite trace of M accepted by B. Thus, to verify that $L(P) = \emptyset$ we can just compute the set of fair vertices and check that it does not intersect I_P. The standard algorithm to compute the set of fair vertices is the Emerson-Lei algorithm (EL) described in Fig. 5 [13]. SMC tools typically implement a variant of this doubly-nested fixpoint computation.

2.3 GSTE Algorithms

The algorithm used by GSTE to check the AG in the different semantics is described in Fig. 6. The function $GSTE\_fairstates$ of line 2 is called only in the case of fair semantics and it is described in Fig. 7. $GSTE\_fairstates$ restricts the antecedent function to the states of the system that are extensible to fair paths. In the lines 3-9 of Fig. 6, α is defined iteratively until a fixpoint is reached. First, α is initialized to be the restriction of *ant* to the set of initial vertices and to the set of initial states. Then, at every iteration, a state s is added to $\alpha(v)$ iff $s \in ant(v)$ and there exists a state $s' \in \alpha(v')$ such that s is reachable from s' in one step and v is reachable from v' in one step. When the fixpoint is reached, $\alpha(v)$ contains s iff there exists an initial path ρ of the assertion graph and an initial trace σ of the system of the same length l such that $\rho[l] = v$, $\sigma[l] = s$ and $\sigma \models_{ant} \rho$.

With an analogous fixpoint computation (lines 6-10), $GSTE\_fairstates$ finds a function α such that $\alpha(v)$ contains s iff there exist a path ρ of the assertion graph and a trace σ of the system of the same length l such that $\rho[l] \in F$, $\rho[1] = v$, $\sigma[1] = s$ and $\sigma \models_{ant} \rho$. This computation is applied for every $F \in \mathcal{F}$ and it is nested in a second fixpoint computation: at every iteration the antecedent function is updated with α until a fixpoint is reached. At the end of the outer loop, $ant(v)$ contains s iff there exist a fair path ρ of the assertion graph and an infinite trace σ of the system such that $\sigma \models_{ant} \rho$.

3   GSTE vs. SMC

In this section, we clarify the relationship between GSTE and SMC. First, we show that AGs and BAs are equivalent. Then, we show GSTE algorithm is essentially a "partitioned" version of the SMC algorithm.

We now show that, given a BA B, one can easily find an AG A with the complementary language and vice versa. This means that, given a specification φ, one can choose either GSTE or SMC techniques to check φ, no matters whether φ is an AG or a BA.

Algorithm *GSTE(M,A)*
1. **if** fair semantics
2.   **then** $A := GSTE\_fairstates(M,A)$
3. $\alpha := ant_{|_{V_I}}$
4. **for** $v \in V$ $\alpha(v) := \alpha(v) \cap S_I$
5. **repeat**
6. $\alpha' := \alpha$
7.   **for** $v \in V$ $\alpha(v) :=$
8. $\alpha'(v) \cup \bigcup_{v' \in E^-(v)} post(\alpha'(v')) \cap ant(v)$
9. **until** $\alpha' = \alpha$
10. **if** fair semantics
11.   **then return** $\alpha \subseteq cons$
12.   **else return** $\alpha_{|_F} \subseteq cons$

Fig. 6.

Algorithm *GSTE_fairstates(M,A)*
1. **repeat**
2. $ant' := ant$
3.   **for** $F \in \mathcal{F}$
4.   **for** $v \in V$ $\alpha(v) :=$
5. $\bigcup_{v' \in E(v), v' \in F} pre(ant(v')) \cap ant(v)$
6.   **repeat**
7. $\alpha' := \alpha$
8.   **for** $v \in V$ $\alpha(v) :=$
9. $\alpha'(v) \cup \bigcup_{v' \in E(v)} pre(\alpha'(v')) \cap ant(v)$
10.   **until** $\alpha' = \alpha$
11. $ant := \alpha$
12. **until** $ant' = ant$
13. **return** A

Fig. 7.

Moreover, since BAs are nondeterministic (i.e., existential) automata, AGs are revealed to be their dual, which are universal automata.

The following four theorems establish the relationship between AGs and BAs[1]. First, the following two theorems show how to express AGs as BAs.

Theorem 1. *Let $A = \langle G, ant, cons \rangle$ be an AG where $G = \langle V, V_I, E, \mathcal{F} \rangle$ and $\mathcal{F} = \{F\}$. Let B be the BA $\langle G', \mathcal{L} \rangle$, where $G' = \langle V', V'_I, E', \mathcal{F}' \rangle$ s.t. $V' = V \times \{0,1,2\}$, $V'_I = V_I \times \{0,1\}$, $E' = \{((v_1, k_1), (v_2, k_2)) \mid (v_1, v_2) \in E, k_2 \in \{0,1\}$ if $k_1 = 0$, and $k_2 = 2$ otherwise$\}$, $\mathcal{F}' = \{F \times \{1,2\}\}$, $\mathcal{L}((v,k)) = ant(v)$ if $k \in \{0,2\}$, and $\mathcal{L}((v,k)) = ant(v) \cap (S \backslash cons(v))$ if $k = 1$. Then $L_f(B) = L_f(M) \backslash L_f(A)$*

Theorem 2. *Let $A = \langle G, ant, cons \rangle$ be an AG where $G = \langle V, V_I, E, \mathcal{F} \rangle$ and $\mathcal{F} = \{F_1, ..., F_n\}$. Let B be the BA $\langle G', \mathcal{L} \rangle$, where $G' = \langle V', V'_I, E', \mathcal{F}' \rangle$ s.t. $V' = V \times \{0,1,2\}$, $V'_I = V_I \times \{0,1\}$, $E' = \{((v_1, k_1), (v_2, k_2)) \mid (v_1, v_2) \in E, k_2 \in \{0,1\}$ if $k_1 = 0$, and $k_2 = 2$ otherwise$\}$, $\mathcal{F}' = \{F_1 \times \{2\}, ..., F_n \times \{2\}\}$, $\mathcal{L}((v,k)) = ant(v)$ if $k \in \{0,2\}$, and $\mathcal{L}((v,k)) = ant(v) \cap (S \backslash cons(v))$ if $k = 1$. Then $L(B) = L(M) \backslash L(A)$*

The following two theorems show how to express BAs as AGs.

Theorem 3. *Let $B = \langle G, \mathcal{L} \rangle$ be a BA where $G = \langle V, V_I, E, \mathcal{F} \rangle$ and $\mathcal{F} = \{F\}$. Let A be the AG $\langle G, ant, cons \rangle$, where $ant = \mathcal{L}$, $cons(v) = \emptyset$ for all $v \in V$. Then $L_f(B) = L_f(M) \backslash L_f(A)$*

Theorem 4. *Let $B = \langle G, \mathcal{L} \rangle$ be a BA where $G = \langle V, V_I, E, \mathcal{F} \rangle$. Let A be the AG $\langle G, ant, cons \rangle$, where $ant = \mathcal{L}$, $cons(v) = \emptyset$ for all $v \in V$. Then $L(B) = L(M) \backslash L(A)$*

We now compare the algorithms used by GSTE and SMC. In particular, we show that the former is essentially a "partitioned" version of the latter.

---

[1] A longer version of the paper, containing the proofs of the theorems and a more extensive bibliography , can be downloaded at www.science.unitn.it/~stonetta/partitioning.html.

In Section 2, we saw how SMC solves the model checking problem for a BA B: it builds the product automaton P between M and B and it verifies that the language of P is empty. GSTE follows an analogous procedure for checking an AG A: it actually computes the product between M and B_{ant}, where B_{ant} is a BA with the same underlying graph G of A and the labeling function equal to ant. The only difference between SMC and GSTE is that the latter operates on partitioned subsets of the product state space. The partitioning is driven by the automaton state space and we refer to such partitioning as *property-driven partitioning*. The GSTE analog of a subset $Q \subseteq S_P$ is the partition $\{Q_v : v \in V\}$, where $Q_v = \{s : (s,v) \in S_P\}$. Indeed, every labeling function γ can be seen as a division of the model into sets of states, one for every vertex v of the graph, which is exactly the set $\gamma(v)$. If $\gamma \subseteq ant$, then γ turns out to represent a set $S_\gamma \subseteq S_P$ of states in the product defined as follows: $S_\gamma = \{(s,v) | s \in \gamma(v)\}$

One can see that the lines 3-9 of the algorithm in Fig. 6 computes the reachable states of S_P. In fact, we could rewrite lines 6-8 in terms of CTL formulas as $\alpha = \alpha \cup \mathbf{EY}[\alpha]$. Thus, at the end of the loop, $\alpha(v) = \{s | (s,v)$ is reachable in $S_P\}$. This computation is actually a partitioned version of the one of Fig. 4 with the difference that SMC applies the post-image only to the new states added in the previous iteration, while GSTE applies the post-image to the whole set of reached states.

In the case of fair semantics the computation of reachable states is preceded by a pruning of the product: $GSTE\_fairstates$ finds all vertices of S_P such that they are extensible to fair paths. To compare this procedure with EL, we rewrite the operations of $GSTE\_fairstates$ in terms of CTL formulas. At the lines 4-5 of the algorithm in Fig. 7, $GSTE\_fairstates$ actually computes the preimage of $ant_{|F}$ (seen as a set of states in S_P). So, we can rewrite these lines as $\alpha = \mathbf{EX}[(ant_{|F})]$. Furthermore, the lines 7-9 are the same as $\alpha = \alpha \cup (ant \cap \mathbf{EX}[(\alpha)])$ so that one can see the loop of lines 6-10 as $\alpha = \mathbf{E}[(ant)\mathbf{U}(\alpha)]$. This reachability computation is nested in a second fixpoint computation, so that it becomes evident that $GSTE\_fairstates$ is a variant of the EL algorithm of Fig. 5.

4   SMC vs. Property-Driven Partitioned SMC

In Section 3, we saw that GSTE is a partitioned version of SMC. We can also apply property-driven partitioning to standard SMC algorithms. In particular, there are two algorithms to be partitioned: *traversal* and *fairstates* (Fig. 4 and 5). We partitioned both of them, by using NuSMV as platform. This choice is motivated by the fact that NuSMV implements symbolic model checking for LTL, its source is open, and its code is well-documented and easy to modify.

The "translated" algorithms are shown is Fig. 8 and Fig. 9. Both are based on backward reachability and respect the structure of NuSMV's implementation (e.g., the order of fair sets is irrelevant). The difference with the non-partitioned versions is that while *traversal* and *fairstates* operate on a single set of states in the product automaton, *partitioned_traversal* and *partitioned_fairstates* operate on an array of sets of states of the system (one set for every vertex of the BA). Thus, every variable in the algorithms of Fig. 8 and 9 can be considered as a labeling function. For every set $Y \subseteq S$ of states and labeling L, we define the labeling function $par_L(Y)$ such that: $par_L(Y)(v) = Y \cap L(v)$ for all $v \in V$. The initial states of the product are given by $par_L(S_I)_{|V_I}$. Given a fair set

Algorithm *partitioned_traversal(M, B)*

1. $\alpha := par_L(S)_{|F}$
2. $\beta := \alpha$
3. **repeat**
4. $\gamma := \mathbf{EX}[\beta]$
5. $\beta = \gamma \backslash \alpha$
6. $\alpha := \alpha \cup \gamma$
7. **until** $\beta = \emptyset$
8. **return** α

Fig. 8.

Algorithm *partitioned_fairstates(M, B)*

1. $\alpha := \top$;
2. **repeat**
3. $\alpha' := \alpha$;
4. $\beta := \top$;
5. **for** $F \in \mathcal{F}$
6. $\beta := \beta \cap \mathbf{E}[\alpha \mathbf{U}(\alpha \cap par_L(S)_{|F})]$;
7. $\alpha := \alpha \cap \beta$;
8. $\alpha := \alpha \cap \mathbf{EX}[\alpha]$;
9. **until** $\alpha' = \alpha$
10. **return** α

Fig. 9.

F of the BA, the correspondent set in the product is given by $par_L(S)_{|F}$. The backward image of a labeling function α is given by $\mathbf{EX}[(\alpha)](v) = \bigcup_{v' \in E(v)} pre(\alpha(v')) \cap L(v)$.

We investigated if property-driven partitioning is effective for symbolic model checking. In particular, we applied such technique to LTL model checking. In fact, it is well known that, given a formula φ expressed by an LTL formula, we can find a BA with the same language. The standard LTL symbolic model checkers translate the negation of the specification into a *BA*, they add the latter to the model and check for emptiness. The goal of our experiments was to compare the performance of partitioned and non-partitioned SMC algorithms. Thus, we did not try to optimize the algorithms implemented in NuSMV, but to apply to them property-driven partitioning. The question we wanted to answer is whether the reduction in BDD size more than compensates for the algorithmic overhead involved in handling a partitioned state-space. This provides also an indirect comparison between GSTE and standard SMC techniques.

To verify an LTL formula φ, NuSMV calls ltl2smv, which translates $\neg\varphi$ into a symbolically represented BA with fairness constraints $\mathcal{F}$. Then, the function $\mathbf{E}_{\mathcal{F}}\mathbf{G}[true]$ checks if the language of the product is empty. Since NuSMV does not apply any particular technique when φ is a safety formula [22], we enhanced the tool with the option -safety: when φ contains only the temporal connectives X, G, and V, it constructs a predicate F on the automaton states (representing accepting states for the complementary property) and calls the function $\mathbf{E}[true\mathbf{U}F]$. In the following, we refer to this procedure and to the standard NuSMV's procedure as ''NuSMV -safety'' and ''NuSMV'' respectively. We implemented the partitioned versions of both and we refer to latter ones as ''NuSMV -safety -partitioned'' and ''NuSMV -partitioned'' respectively. The BA is built automatically by ltl2smv in the case of non-partitioned algorithms while it is constructed by hand (in these experiments) in the case of partitioned algorithms.

We run our tests on three examples of SMV models (for the SMV code, we refer the reader to www.science.unitn.it/~stonetta/partitioning.html). For every example, we chose two properties true in the model (one safety and one liveness property, see Tab. 1) and two properties that failed (again one safety and one liveness property, see Tab. 2). The first example is a dining-philosophers protocol [12]. Concurrency is modeled with the interleaving semantics. Typically, a philosopher iterates through a sequence of four states: she thinks, tries to pick up the chopsticks, eats and, finally, she

Table 1. Satisfied properties

	Safety	Liveness
Dining	$G((p \wedge r \wedge X(r) \wedge XX(r) \wedge XXX(r)) \rightarrow XXXX(e))$	$(\bigwedge_{1 \leq i \leq N} GFr_i) \rightarrow (GFs)$
Mutex	$G((t_1 \wedge \bigwedge_{2 \leq i \leq N} \neg t_i) \rightarrow Xc)$	$G(\bigwedge_{1 \leq i \leq N} t_i \rightarrow Fc_i)$
Life	$G(b \rightarrow Xc)$	$G((G!b) \rightarrow FG(d))$

Table 2. Failed properties

	Safety	Liveness
Dining	$G((p \wedge r \wedge X(r) \wedge XX(r) \wedge XXX(r)) \rightarrow XXXX(\neg e))$	$(GFr_1) \rightarrow (GFe_1)$
Mutex	$G((t_1 \wedge \bigwedge_{2 \leq i \leq N} \neg t_i) \rightarrow X \neg c)$	$F(t_1 \rightarrow G \neg c_1)$
Life	$G(b \rightarrow X \neg c)$	$F((G!b) \wedge GF(!d))$

puts down the chopsticks. When a deadlock condition happens, a philosopher puts the chopsticks down. The safety property true in this example is the following: if a philosopher is thinking and both her chopsticks are free and she is scheduled for 4 four steps in a row, then she will start eating. From this property, we deduce an analogous one which fails: with the same premises, after 4 steps the philosopher does not eat. The satisfied liveness property states that if every philosopher is scheduled infinitely often, then somebody eats infinitely often (at least one philosopher does not starve). In contrast, the following liveness property does not hold in the example: if a philosopher is scheduled infinitely often, then she eats infinitely often.

The second example is a mutual-exclusion protocol: N processes non-deterministically try to access the critical session. The access is controlled by the main module, which guarantees that a process does not wait forever. The true safety property says that, if a process is the only one that is waiting, then it accesses the critical session in one step. If we change this property by writing that the process does not access the critical session in one step, we obtain the safety property that fails. The satisfied liveness property asserts that, if a process is trying, sooner or later it will access the critical session. We chose the negation of this property as an example of liveness property that fails.

Finally, the third example is a variant of the game of life: at the beginning there is only one creature; every creature has a maximum life set to 100, but it can die non-deterministically in every moment; when the age is between 15 and 65, a creature can bear a child, which is born in the next step; at most N creatures can be born; when all the creatures are dead the game is reset. The true safety property states that, if a creature is bearing a child, then the number of born creatures increases; the failed property states that the number decreases. The true liveness property asserts the following: if no creature will be born anymore, then, after a certain point in the future (likely after a reset), the number of alive creatures will be equal to one forever. The negation of this property corresponds exactly to the liveness property which failed.

We run NuSMV on the Rice Terascale Cluster (RTC), a 1 TeraFLOP Linux cluster based on Intel Itanium 2 Processors. A timeout has been fixed to 172800 sec. (2 days). The results are shown in Fig. 10 and 11. The execution time has been plotted in log scale against the number N of processes in the model. Every example takes a column of plots. On the first row, we have the safety properties and on the second one the

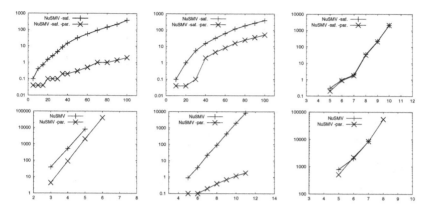

Fig. 10. Satisfied properties of Tab. 1. X axis: number of processes. Y axis: time. First row: performances of ''NuSMV -safety -partitioned'' and ''NuSMV -safety'' on safety properties. Second row: performances of ''NuSMV -partitioned'' and ''NuSMV'' on liveness properties. 1st column: dining-philosophers. 2nd column: mutex. 3rd column: life

liveness properties. Comparing the partitioned version with the non-partitioned one in the case of satisfied properties (Fig. 10), we notice that, in the first two columns (dining philosophers and mutual exclusion), the former outperforms the latter. Moreover, in the case of the safety property for dining philosophers and the liveness property for mutual exclusion, the gap is exponential, i.e. the difference between the two execution times grows exponentially with the size of the model. In the third column (life), NuSMV does not seem to get relevant benefit from the property-driven partitioning (even if you should notice that, in the last point of the liveness case, NuSMV runs out of time). Similarly, in the case of failed properties, the partitioned version outperforms always the non-partitioned one (see Fig. 11). Moreover, in the case of liveness properties, the improvement is exponential for all the three examples.

5   Conclusions

Our contributions in this work are two-fold. First, we elucidate the relationship between GSTE and SMC. We show that assertion graphs are simply universal automata, or, viewed dually, are nondeterministic automata for the complementary properties. Furthermore, GSTE algorithms are essentially a partitioned version of standard SMC algorithms, where the partitioning is static and is driven by the property under verification. Second, we exported the technique of property-driven partitioning to SMC and showed its effectiveness in the framework of NuSMV.

This opens us several directions for future work. First, we need to combine the tool with an automated generator of explicit BAs for LTL formulas and evaluate property-driven partitioning for more complex LTL properties. Second, it requires revisiting the issue of translating LTL formulas to BAs. Previous translations have focused on making the BA smaller (cf. [16, 11, 29, 15]) or more deterministic [27]. The relative merit of the two approaches has to be investigated in the context of property-partitioned SMC.

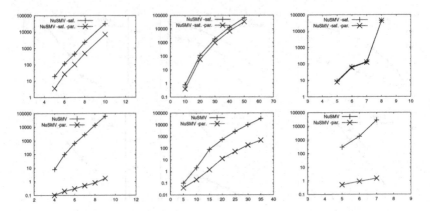

Fig. 11. Same pattern as in Fig. 10 but with the failed properties of Tab. 2

Third, it requires revisiting the issue of symbolic fair-cycle detection. Previous works have compared various variations of the EL algorithm, as well as non-EL algorithms, cf. [2, 26, 14]. This has to be re-evaluated for property-partitioned SMC. Finally, a major topic of research in the last few years has been that of property-driven abstraction in model checking, [8, 17]. The combination of this technique with property-driven partitioning is also worth of investigation, which could benefit from the study of abstraction in GSTE [34, 32].

References

1. A. Biere, E. M. Clarke, and Y. Zhu. Multiple State and Single State Tableaux for Combining Local and Global Model Checking. In *Correct System Design*, pages 163–179, 1999.
2. R. Bloem, H.N. Gabow, and F. Somenzi. An algorithm for strongly connected component analysis in $n \log n$ symbolic steps. In *Formal Methods in Computer Aided Design*, 2000.
3. J.R. Burch, E.M. Clarke, K.L. McMillan, D.L. Dill, and L.J. Hwang. Symbolic Model Mhecking: 10^{20} States and Beyond. *Information and Computation*, 98(2), 1992.
4. G. Cabodi, P. Camurati, L. Lavagno, and S. Quer. Disjunctive Partitioning and Partial Iterative Squaring: An Effective Approach for Symbolic Traversal of Large Circuits. In *Design Automation Conf.*, 1997.
5. C.-T. Chou. The Mathematical Foundation of Symbolic Trajectory Evaluation. In *Computer-Aided Verification*. Springer, 1999.
6. A. Cimatti, E.M. Clarke, F. Giunchiglia, and M. Roveri. NUSMV: a new Symbolic Model Verifier. In *Proc. of the 11th Conf. on Computer-Aided Verification*, 1999.
7. A. Cimatti, M. Roveri, and P. Bertoli. Searching Powerset Automata by Combining Explicit-State and Symbolic Model Checking. In *TACAS'01*, 2001.
8. E.M. Clarke, O. Grumberg, S. Jha, Y. Lu, and H. Veith. Counterexample-Guided Abstraction Refinement. In *Computer Aided Verification*, 2000.
9. E.M. Clarke, O. Grumberg, and D. Peled. *Model Checking*. MIT Press, 1999.
10. C. Courcoubetis, M.Y. Vardi, P. Wolper, and M. Yannakakis. Memory-Efficient Algorithms for the Verification of Temporal Properties. *Formal Methods in System Design*, 1(2/3), 1992.
11. N. Daniele, F. Guinchiglia, and M.Y. Vardi. Improved automata generation for linear temporal logic. In *Computer Aided Verification, Proc. 11th International Conf.*, 1999.

12. E.W. Dijksta. *Hierarchical ordering of sequential processes, Operating systems techniques.* Academic Press, 1972.
13. E.A. Emerson and C.L. Lei. Efficient Model Checking in Fragments of the Propositional μ–Calculus. In *Symp. on Logic in Computer Science*, 1986.
14. K. Fisler, R. Fraer, G. Kamhi, M.Y. Vardi, and Z. Yang. Is there a best symbolic cycle-detection algorithm? In *Tools and algorithms for the construction and analysis of systems,* 2001.
15. C. Fritz. Constructing Büchi Automata from Linear Temporal Logic Using Simulation Relations for Alternating Büchi Automata. In *Implementation and Application of Automata,* 2003.
16. R. Gerth, D. Peled, M. Vardi, and P. Wolper. Simple on-the-fly automatic verification of linear temporal logic. In *Protocol Specification, Testing and Verification,* 1995.
17. S.G. Govindaraju and D.L. Dill. Counterexample-guided Choice of Projections in Approximate Symbolic Model Checking. In *Proc. of ICCAD 2000,* 2000.
18. T. A. Henzinger, O. Kupferman, and S. Qadeer. From Pre-Historic to Post-Modern Symbolic Model Checking. *Form. Methods Syst. Des.,* 23(3), 2003.
19. T. Heyman, D. Geist, O. Grumberg, and A. Schuster. A Scalable Parallel Algorithm for Reachability Analysis of Very Large Circuits. In *Formal Methods in System Design,* 2002.
20. G.J. Holzmann. *The SPIN model checker: Primer and reference manual.* Addison Wesley, 2003.
21. A.J. Hu, J. Casas, and J. Yang. Reasoning about GSTE Assertion Graphs. In *Correct Hardware Design and Verification Methods.* Springer, 2003.
22. O. Kupferman and M.Y. Vardi. Model checking of safety properties. *Formal methods in System Design,* 19(3), 2001.
23. R.P. Kurshan. *Computer Aided Verification of Coordinating Processes.* Princeton Univ. Press, 1994.
24. Z. Manna and A. Pnueli. Specification and Verification of Concurrent Programs by $\forall$-automata. In *Proc. 14th ACM Symp. on Principles of Programming,* 1987.
25. A. Narayan, J. Jain, M. Fujita, and A. Sangiovanni-Vincentelli. Partitioned ROBDDs-a Compact, Canonical and Efficiently Manipulable Representation for Boolean Functions. In *Inter. Conf. on Computer-aided design,* 1996.
26. K. Ravi, R. Bloem, and F. Somenzi. A Comparative Study of Symbolic Algorithms for the Computation of Fair Cycles. In *Formal Methods in Computer-Aided Design,* 2000.
27. R. Sebastiani and S. Tonetta. "More Deterministic" vs. "Smaller" Buechi Automata for Efficient LTL Model Checking. In *Correct Hardware Design and Verification Methods,* 2003.
28. C.-J.H. Seger and R.E. Bryant. Formal Verification by Symbolic Evaluation of Partially-Ordered Trajectories. *Formal Methods in System Design: An Inter. Journal,* 6(2), 1995.
29. F. Somenzi and R. Bloem. Efficient Büchi Automata from LTL Formulae. In *Proc CAV'00,* volume 1855 of *LNCS.* Springer, 2000.
30. M.Y. Vardi and P. Wolper. An Automata-Theoretic Approach to Automatic Program Verification. In *Proc. 1st Symp. on Logic in Computer Science,* 1986.
31. M.Y. Vardi and P. Wolper. Reasoning about Infinite Computations. *Information and Computation,* 115(1), 1994.
32. J. Yang and A. Goel. GSTE through a Case Study. In *Proc. of the 2002 IEEE/ACM Inter. Conf. on Computer-Aided Design.* ACM Press, 2002.
33. J. Yang and C.-J.H. Seger. Generalized Symbolic Trajectory Evaluation, 2000. Intel SCL Technical Report, under revision for Journal Publication.
34. J. Yang and C.-J.H. Seger. Generalized Symbolic Trajectory Evaluation - Abstraction in Action. In *Formal Methods in Computer-Aided Design,* 2002.

Stuck-Free Conformance

Cédric Fournet, Tony Hoare, Sriram K. Rajamani, and Jakob Rehof

Microsoft Research
{fournet,thoare,sriram,rehof}@microsoft.com

Abstract. We present a novel refinement relation (stuck-free conformance) for CCS processes, which satisfies the substitutability property: If I conforms to S, and P is any environment such that $P \mid S$ is stuck-free, then $P \mid I$ is stuck-free. Stuck-freedom is related to the CSP notion of deadlock, but it is more discriminative by taking orphan messages in asynchronous systems into account. We prove that conformance is a pre-congruence on CCS processes, thereby supporting modular refinement. We distinguish conformance from the related preorders, stable failures refinement in CSP and refusal preorder in CCS. We have implemented conformance checking in a new software model checker, ZING, and we report on how we used it to find errors in distributed programs.

1 Introduction

We are interested in checking that message-passing programs are *stuck-free* [12]. Stuck-freedom formalizes the property that a communicating system cannot deadlock waiting for messages that are never sent or send messages that are never received. In this paper we extend [12] by generalizing the theory of conformance and by reporting on its application in model checking distributed programs. In our example application, programmers write *contracts*, which are interfaces that specify the externally visible message-passing behavior of the program. Contracts can be as rich as CCS processes. Stuck-freedom is ensured by checking that an implementation *conforms* to its contract using a model checker.

Checking stuck-freedom by exploring the state space of the entire system quickly leads to state explosion, because the state space grows exponentially in the number of concurrent processes; and it requires that the entire system is available for analysis, which is especially unrealistic for distributed systems. We therefore wish to check stuck-freedom compositionally. If I is an implementation of a component and C is its contract, we use the notation $I \leq C$ to denote that I conforms to C. For our compositional approach to be sound with respect to stuck-freedom, the conformance relation $\leq$ needs to obey the following *substitutability* property: If $I \leq C$ and P is any environment such that $P \mid C$ is stuck-free, then $P \mid I$ is stuck-free as well ($P \mid C$ denotes the parallel composition of P and C). Substitutability means that the contract of a component can be safely used instead of the component in invocation contexts, and hence it helps model checking to scale.

Our notion of conformance is a novel process preorder that preserves *stuckness*. Stuckness can be directly observed in any labeled transition system in

R. Alur and D.A. Peled (Eds.): CAV 2004, LNCS 3114, pp. 242–254, 2004.

which visible actions as well as stability (the inability to perform hidden actions) can be observed. In our applications this is important, because we want to analyze a system by executing a model of it and observing what happens. Stuckness is more discriminative than CSP deadlock or unspecified reception [10], since stuckness encompasses any "left-over" action on a channel name. In addition to deadlock, this includes orphan messages that are never consumed in asynchronous systems and directly models important failure conditions in software such as unhandled exception messages.

This paper makes the following contributions:

- We define a notion of conformance based on standard CCS transition semantics and prove that it is a precongruence (i.e., it is preserved by all CCS contexts) satisfying the substitutability property for stuck-freedom. We distinguish conformance from the most closely related known preorders, CSP stable failures refinement [3, 6, 13] and CCS refusal preorder [11].
- We have implemented a conformance checker in our software model checker, ZING. The implementation technique is quite general and can be used to adapt existing model checkers for software to do conformance checking. ZING processes can be regarded as CCS processes, and hence our conformance theory applies to the ZING conformance checker. We have applied ZING to check contract conformance in a non-trivial distributed application, leading to the discovery of several bugs in the application.

This paper significantly extends the work reported in [12], which proposes a conformance relation satisfying the substitutability property. The conformance relation of [12] is limited in several respects. First, conformance in [12] is defined by reference to the syntactic form of processes[1], which precludes a purely observational implementation of conformance checking by recording actions generated by transitions. Second, the relation in [12] is not a precongruence, because the syntactic constraints are not preserved under arbitrary CCS contexts. As a consequence, natural and useful algebraic laws fail, including the desirable modular principle, that $P_1 \leq Q_1$ and $P_2 \leq Q_2$ implies $P_1 \mid P_2 \leq Q_1 \mid Q_2$. Third, the theory in [12] is complicated by using a non-standard action[2] to treat nondeterminism. This paper provides a substantial generalization of conformance that is purely observational, is based on the standard CCS transition system, and gives a unified treatment of nondeterminism, hiding, and stability in terms of hidden actions (τ). It can be implemented in a model checker by observing visible actions and stability, and it can be compared to other semantic refinement relations. In addition to proving substitutability, we prove that our generalized conformance relation is a precongruence, thereby supporting modular refinement. Finally, we have applied this theory by implementing it in a software model checker and applying it to contract checking for distributed programs.

---

[1] For example, some cases in the conformance definition of [12] apply only to processes of the form $P \# Q$ or $P + Q$. Other similar syntactic dependencies of this nature is present in [12] as well.

[2] The action is named ϵ in [12].

The remainder of this paper is organized as follows. In Section 2 we discuss refinement relations in the CSP and CCS traditions that are most closely related to stuck-free conformance. In Section 3 we present our theory of conformance. In order to keep the paper within limits, we have left out all proofs in the presentation of our conformance theory. Fully detailed proofs can be found in our technical report [5]. In Section 4 we describe the application of the ZING conformance checker to find errors in distributed programs, and Section 5 concludes.

2   Related Work

Our notion of conformance is modeled on stable failures refinement in CSP [3, 6, 13] and is inspired by the success of the refinement checker FDR [13]. Our process model combines the operational semantics of CCS with a notion of refusals similar to but distinct from the CSP notion. The definition of conformance relies on simulation and applies directly to any labeled transition system in which visible actions and stability can be observed. As is discussed in Section 3.3, substitutability with respect to stuck-freedom is not satisfied, if stable failures refinement is adopted directly into CCS. The reason is that stuck-freedom is a different and more discriminative notion than the CSP concept of deadlock. In order to accomodate this difference, our conformance relation is based on the idea of *ready refusals*, which requires a process to be ready to accept certain actions while (at the same time) refusing others.

Stuck-free conformance is also related to the refusals preorder for CCS as developed in Iain Phillips' theory of refusal testing [11]. Refusal preorder allows the observation of actions that happen after refusals and can therefore express readiness conditions in combination with refusals. However, as discussed in Section 3.4, stuck-free conformance is a strictly larger precongruence than refusal preorder.

The notion of 2/3 bisimulation, presented by Larsen and Skou [7] bears some resemblance to conformance. However, Larsen and Skou do not treat hiding and internal actions (τ-actions), and therefore the problems of stability do not arise there. Our theory of conformance gives a unified treatment of internal actions, non-determinism, and stability, which are essential in our applications.

Alternating simulation [1] has been used to relate interfaces to implementations in [4]. As discussed in [12], alternating simulation does not satisfy substitutability for stuck-freedom.

3   Conformance Theory

In this section we give necessary background on CCS [8, 9], we define our notions of stuck-freedom and conformance, and we prove that conformance is a precongruence (Theorem 1) and that it satisfies the substitutability property (Theorem 2).

3.1   CCS Processes

We assume a denumerable set of names $\mathcal{N} = \{a, b, c, \ldots\}$. The set $\mathcal{L} \stackrel{\Delta}{=} \mathcal{N} \cup \{\bar{a} \mid a \in \mathcal{N}\}$ is called the set of *labels*. The set $\mathcal{A} \stackrel{\Delta}{=} \mathcal{L} \cup \{\tau\}$ is called the set of *actions*.

We let α range over $\mathcal{A}$ and we let λ range over $\mathcal{L}$, and we write $\bar{\bar{a}} = a$. For a subset X of $\mathcal{L}$ we write $\bar{X} = \{\bar{a} \mid a \in X\}$. CCS processes, ranged over by P, are defined by:

$$P ::= \mathbf{0} \mid A\langle a_1, \ldots, a_n \rangle \mid G_1 + \ldots + G_n \mid (P|Q) \mid (\nu\, a)P$$
$$G ::= \alpha.P$$

Here, A ranges over process names, with defining equations $A \stackrel{\Delta}{=} P$. We say that the name a is bound in $(\nu\, a)P$. The free names of P, denoted $\mathrm{fn}(P)$, are the names in P that are not bound.

Definition 1 (Structural congruence, $\equiv$). *Structural congruence, $\equiv$, is the least congruence relation on terms closed under the following rules, together with change of bound names and variables (alpha-conversion) and reordering of terms in a summation:*

1. $P|\mathbf{0} \equiv P$, $P|Q \equiv Q|P$, $P|(Q|R) \equiv (P|Q)|R$
2. $(\nu\, a)(P|Q) \equiv P|(\nu\, a)Q$, *if* $a \notin \mathrm{fn}(P)$
3. $(\nu\, a)\mathbf{0} \equiv \mathbf{0}$, $(\nu\, ab)P \equiv (\nu\, ba)P$, $(\nu a)(\nu b)P \equiv (\nu b)(\nu a)P$

The operational semantics of CCS is given by the labeled transition system shown in Definition 2. This system is exactly the one given by Milner [9], except that we have added rule [CONG], as is standard in recent presentations of CCS. In rule [SUM] below, M ranges over a summation.

Definition 2 (Labeled transition).

$$M + \alpha.P \xrightarrow{\alpha} P \quad [\text{SUM}] \qquad \frac{P \xrightarrow{\lambda} P' \quad Q \xrightarrow{\bar{\lambda}} Q'}{P|Q \xrightarrow{\tau} P'|Q'} \quad [\text{REACT}]$$

$$\frac{P \xrightarrow{\alpha} P'}{P|Q \xrightarrow{\alpha} P'|Q} \quad [\text{PAR-L}] \qquad \frac{P \equiv P' \quad P' \xrightarrow{\alpha} Q' \quad Q' \equiv Q}{P \xrightarrow{\alpha} Q} \quad [\text{CONG}]$$

$$\frac{P \xrightarrow{\alpha} P' \quad \alpha \notin \{a, \bar{a}\}}{(\nu\, a)P \xrightarrow{\alpha} (\nu\, a)P'} \quad [\text{RES}]$$

$$\frac{P_A[\tilde{b}/\tilde{a}] \xrightarrow{\alpha} P' \quad A(a) \stackrel{\Delta}{=} P_A}{A\langle \tilde{b} \rangle \xrightarrow{\alpha} P'} \quad [\text{IDENT}]$$

We let $P \# Q \stackrel{\Delta}{=} \tau.P + \tau.Q$. The difference between $a.P \# b.Q$ and $a.P + b.Q$ is important. The former represents *internal choice*, where the process chooses to transition to $a.P$ or $b.Q$, whereas the latter represents *external choice* [6], where the environment controls whether the process moves to P or Q by offering $\bar{a}$ or $\bar{b}$. The distinction between internal and external choice is crucial in our notion of conformance.

Asynchronous actions are modeled as actions with no sequential continuation in CCS. Hence, asynchronous actions are "spawned", as in $a \mid P$, where a happens asynchonously.

Notation. We write $\tilde{a}$ and $\tilde{\alpha}$ for (possibly empty) sequences of names and actions. For $\tilde{\alpha} = \alpha_0 \ldots \alpha_{n-1}$ we write $P \xrightarrow{\tilde{\alpha}} P'$, if there exist $P_0, P_1, \ldots, P_n$ such that $P \equiv P_0$, $P' \equiv P_n$ and for $0 \le i < n$, we have $P_i \xrightarrow{\alpha_i} P_{i+1}$. We use the notation $P \xrightarrow{\tau^*\lambda} P'$, where $(\tau^*\lambda) \in \{\lambda, \tau\lambda, \tau\tau\lambda, \ldots\}$. We write $P \longrightarrow P'$ if there exists $\tilde{\alpha}$ such that $P \xrightarrow{\tilde{\alpha}} P'$; $P \xrightarrow{\tilde{\alpha}}$ means there exists P' such that $P \xrightarrow{\tilde{\alpha}} P'$; $P \longrightarrow$ means that $P \xrightarrow{\tilde{\alpha}}$ for some $\tilde{\alpha}$. P is *stable* if P can make no hidden actions, i.e., $P \xnrightarrow{\tau}$, and P is an *end-state* if P can make no action at all, i.e., $P \not\longrightarrow$. Finally, we use the shorthand notation $\lambda \tilde{\in} \tilde{a}$ to mean that either λ or $\bar{\lambda}$ is among the labels appearing in $\tilde{a}$.

3.2 Stuck-Freedom, Ready Refusal, and Conformance

If two processes, P and Q, communicate via local names in $\tilde{a}$, we can write the system as $(\nu\tilde{a})(P|Q)$. Since $\tilde{a}$ are names local to P and Q, no further environment can interact on $\tilde{a}$, and therefore it makes sense to test whether the interaction of P and Q on $\tilde{a}$ succeeds completely. Informally, we call a process *stuck* on $\tilde{a}$ if it cannot make any progress, and some part of it is ready to communicate on a name in $\tilde{a}$: the communication on $\tilde{a}$ has not succeeded, because it did not finish. In our applications, P is typically a model of a program that has a local connection $\tilde{a}$ to a process whose specification (contract) is Q. We wish to check that the interaction between P and the implementation represented by Q is *stuck-free*, i.e., it cannot get stuck. Stuck-freedom is a safety property and can be checked by a reachability analysis of the system $P \mid Q$. The following definitions make the notions of stuckness and stuck-freedom precise.

Definition 3 (Stuck process). *A process P is called* stuck on $\tilde{a}$, *if $(\nu\tilde{a})P$ is an end-state, and $P \xrightarrow{\lambda}$ for some $\lambda \tilde{\in} \tilde{a}$. We refer to such λ as a residual action.*

Definition 4 (Stuck-free processes). *A process P is called* stuck-free on $\tilde{a}$ *if there is no P' and $\tilde{\alpha}$ such that $P \xrightarrow{\tilde{\alpha}} P'$ with $\tilde{\alpha} \cap \tilde{a} = \emptyset$, and P' is stuck on $\tilde{a}$.*

In the situation mentioned above we apply Definition 4 by searching for a transition $P \mid Q \xrightarrow{\tilde{\alpha}} P' \mid Q'$ such that $\tilde{\alpha} \cap \tilde{a} = \emptyset$ and $P' \mid Q'$ is stuck on $\tilde{a}$. The restriction $(\nu\tilde{a})$ in Definition 3 and the condition $\tilde{\alpha} \cap \tilde{a} = \emptyset$ in Definition 4 enforce that only internal reactions (τ-actions) can happen on names in $\tilde{a}$, consistently with $\tilde{a}$ being local. Since $P' \mid Q' \xrightarrow{\lambda}$ for some $\lambda \tilde{\in} \tilde{a}$, the interaction between P and Q ends with a residual action, λ, that cannot be matched by any co-action, $\bar{\lambda}$. If λ models an input action, then a component is waiting to receive a message that never arrives, and if λ models a send action, then a component is sending a message that is never consumed. An example of the latter is a remote exception message that is not handled. Such situations are important indicators of problems in many asynchronous applications. Section 4 has examples of how we have used Definition 4 in checking conformance of actual systems.

We seek a conformance relation, $\le$, such that $S \le Q$ guarantees the substitutability property, that if $P \mid Q$ is stuck-free, then $P \mid S$ is stuck-free, on any selected names $\tilde{a}$. In the example scenario, this means that it is *safe* to check stuck-freedom of the system $P \mid Q$, where the implementation S is represented by its contract Q. To achieve this goal, the relation $\leq$ must be such that, if $S \leq Q$, then Q gets stuck on $\tilde{a}$ in any context at least as often as S does. This requirement implies that Q may not promise to offer actions that are not actually delivered by S and can be elegantly captured by the notion of refusal in CSP [6]. However, it turns out that the refusal requirement alone is not sufficient, because it does not rule out all cases of residual actions. This motivates the following definitions, where refusals are strengthened to *ready refusals*.

Let $init(P) = \{\alpha \mid P \xrightarrow{\alpha}\}$, and let $\mathcal{L}^{(1)}$ denote the singleton sets of $\mathcal{L}$ together with the empty set, $\mathcal{L}^{(1)} = \{\{\lambda\} \mid \lambda \in \mathcal{L}\} \cup \{\emptyset\}$.

Definition 5 (Refusal). *If X is a subset of $\mathcal{L}$, we say that P refuses X if and only if P is stable and $\mathrm{init}(P) \cap \bar{X} = \emptyset$. We say that P can refuse X if and only if there exists P' such that $P \xrightarrow{\tau^*} P'$ and P' refuses X.*

Definition 6 (Readiness). *If $Y \in \mathcal{L}^{(1)}$, we say that P is ready on Y, if and only if P is stable and $\lambda \in Y$ implies $P \xrightarrow{\lambda}$. Notice that any stable process is trivially ready on $\emptyset$.*

Definition 7 (Ready Refusal). *If $X \subseteq \mathcal{L}$ and $Y \in \mathcal{L}^{(1)}$, we say that P can refuse X while ready on Y if and only if P can refuse X from a state that is ready on Y, i.e., there exists P' such that $P \xrightarrow{\tau^*} P'$, P' refuses X, and P' is ready on Y.*

Notice that ready sets are defined in terms of actions (Definition 6) but refusals are defined in terms of co-actions (Definition 5). Initially, this can be a bit confusing. For example, the process a refuses $\{a\}$ and is ready on $\{a\}$.

Definition 8 (Conformance Relation). *A binary relation $\mathcal{R}$ on processes is called a conformance relation if and only if, whenever $P \, \mathcal{R} \, Q$, then the following conditions hold:*

C1. If $P \xrightarrow{\tau^*\lambda} P'$ then there exists Q' such that $Q \xrightarrow{\tau^*\lambda} Q'$ and $P' \, \mathcal{R} \, Q'$.
C2. If P can refuse X while ready on Y, then Q can refuse X while ready on Y.

Condition [C2] in Definition 8 may appear surprising. It is further motivated and discussed below, including Section 3.3 and Section 3.4.
If $\mathcal{R}_1$ and $\mathcal{R}_2$ are binary relations on processes, we define their composition, denoted $\mathcal{R}_1 \circ \mathcal{R}_2$, by

$$\mathcal{R}_1 \circ \mathcal{R}_2 = \{(P,Q) \mid \exists R. \ (P,R) \in \mathcal{R}_1 \ \wedge \ (R,Q) \in \mathcal{R}_2\}$$

Lemma 1. *Let $\{\mathcal{R}_i\}_{i \in I}$ be a family of conformance relations. Then*

1. *The relation $\cup_{i \in I} \mathcal{R}_i$ is a conformance relation*
2. *For any $i, j \in I$, the relation $\mathcal{R}_i \circ \mathcal{R}_j$ is a conformance relation*
3. *The identity relation on processes is a conformance relation*

Lemma 1.1 shows that we can define $\leq$ as the largest conformance relation by taking the union of all conformance relations, in the way that is standard for CCS bisimulation and simulation [8].

Definition 9 (Conformance, $\leq$). *The largest conformance relation is referred to as* conformance *and is denoted $\leq$. We write $P \leq Q$ for $(P, Q) \in \leq$, and we say that P conforms to Q.*

Condition [C2] of Definition 8 ensures that, if $P \leq Q$, then Q gets stuck on a name a as often as P does. In Definition 8 it is very important that the readiness constraint is only imposed one name at a time, by the fact that the ready sets Y are at most singleton sets (choosing $Y = \emptyset$ yields the standard refusals condition with no readiness constraint, as a special case.) This allows a specification to be more nondeterministic than its refinements, because the specification may resolve its nondeterminism differently for each name. For example, we have $a + b \leq a\#b$. Considered over the alphabet of names $\{a, b\}$, the process $a + b$ refuses $\{a, b\}$ and is ready on both $\{a\}$ and on $\{b\}$. The process $a\#b$ refuses $\{a, b, \bar{b}\}$ from the state a, and it refuses $\{a, \bar{a}, b\}$ from the state b. From the state a, it is ready on $\{a\}$, and from the state b it is ready on $\{b\}$. Therefore, condition [C2] is satisfied. The reader may wish to verify a few more interesting examples:

$$a \mid b \ \leq \ (a.b)\#(b.a), \quad (a.b)\#(b.a) \ \not\leq \ a \mid b, \quad a \mid b \ \cong \ a.b + b.a$$

where we write $P \cong Q$ if and only if $P \leq Q$ and $Q \leq P$. We also remark that $\equiv \ \subseteq \ \leq$, by rule [CONG] (further algebraic properties of conformance can be found in [5].)

Proposition 1. *The conformance relation $\leq$ is reflexive and transitive.*

The following theorems state our main theoretical results, precongruence (the operators of CCS are monotonic with respect to conformance, Theorem 1) and substitutability (specifications can safely be substituted for processes that conform to them, Theorem 2). Full proofs are given in [5]. Let C range over CCS contexts, which are process expressions with a "hole" (written $[]$) in them:

$$C ::= [] \ \mid \ (P \mid []) \ \mid \ ([] \mid P) \ \mid \ (\alpha.[] + M) \ \mid \ ((\nu a) \, [])$$

We write $C[Q]$ to denote the process expression that arises by substituting Q for the hole in C.

Theorem 1 (Precongruence). $P \leq Q$ *implies* $C[P] \leq C[Q]$.

Theorem 2 (Substitutability). *Assume* $P \leq Q$. *Then* $C[Q]$ *stuck-free on* $\tilde{a}$ *implies* $C[P]$ *stuck-free on* $\tilde{a}$.

The following two sections imply that conformance is finer than stable failures refinement in CSP (when conformance is defined in terms of traces or, alternatively, when stable failures refinement is defined in terms of transitions) and coarser than refusal preorder in CCS. In this sense, conformance is in between.

3.3   Conformance and Stable Failures Refinement

Condition [C2] in the definition of conformance is adapted from the theory of stable failures refinement in CSP [6, 13], which is based on the concepts of traces and refusals. In the stable failures model, a process P is represented by the set of its *failures*. A failure of P is a pair $(\tilde{\lambda}, X)$ where $\tilde{\lambda}$ is a finite trace of P and X is *refusal set*, i.e., a set of events P can refuse from a stable state after $\tilde{\lambda}$. Process P failure-refines process Q if the traces of P are contained in the traces of Q and the failures of P are contained in the failures of Q.

In our conformance definition we use refusals, but using the stronger ready refusals in condition [C2]. This is motivated by the requirement that conformance should be substitutable with respect to stuck-freedom. As an example, consider the two processes P and Q defined by

$$P = a.0 \quad \text{and} \quad Q = a.0 + \tau.0$$

Considered as processes over the label set $\{a, \bar{a}\}$, the failures[3] of P are: $\{(\langle\rangle, \{a\}), (\langle a\rangle, \{a, \bar{a}\})\}$, and the failures of Q are: $\{(\langle\rangle, \{a, \bar{a}\}), (\langle a\rangle, \{a, \bar{a}\})\}$. It follows that P failure-refines Q. However, P is stuck on a, but Q cannot get stuck, since its only stable derivative is 0, which is not a stuck process. Hence, even though P failure-refines Q, stuck-freedom of Q does not imply stuck-freedom of P. In contrast, the readiness constraint in condition [C2] in our definition of conformance entails that $P \not\preceq Q$, because P can perform action a from a stable state (P itself), whereas Q can only perform action a from an unstable state (Q itself).

The natural trace model corresponding to stuck-free conformance modifies the stable failures model to use ready refusals in its failures, so that a failure is now a pair $(\tilde{\lambda}, R)$ where $R = (X, Y)$ is a ready refusal consisting of a refusal set $X \subseteq \mathcal{L}$ and a ready set $Y \in \mathcal{L}^{(1)}$.

The differences between stable failures refinement in CSP and stuck-free conformance results from differences between stuckness and CSP deadlock. In CSP, deadlock is indicated by the absence of a special, successful termination event, $\sqrt{}$. Stuckness is directly observable on states in a labeled transition system and is more discriminative than CSP deadlock.

3.4   Conformance and Refusal Preorder

Our notion of conformance bears resemblance to the *refusal preorder* as defined in Iain Phillips' theory of refusal testing [11]. In the refusal preorder, we can observe what happens after a refusal (or a deadlock) by turning refusal sets into observations. Following [2], we can define refusal preorder by adding the transition rule

$$P \xrightarrow{X} P, \quad \text{provided } P \text{ refuses } X$$

for $X \subseteq \mathcal{L}$. For $\rho \in \wp(\mathcal{L}) \cup \mathcal{L}$, we write $P \overset{\rho}{\Longrightarrow} P'$ if and only if $P \xrightarrow{\tau^*} P_1 \xrightarrow{\rho} P_2 \xrightarrow{\tau^*} P'$. We lift to vectors $\tilde{\rho}$ in the usual way. We then define failure traces,

---

[3] We express failures in terms of maximal refusal sets and use $\langle \ldots \rangle$ for sequences.

$f\text{-}traces(P) = \{\tilde{\rho} \in (\wp(\mathcal{L}) \cup \mathcal{L})^* \mid P \overset{\tilde{\rho}}{\Longrightarrow}\}$. The refusal preorder, denoted $\leq_{rf}$, is defined by setting $P \leq_{rf} Q$ if and only if $f\text{-}traces(P) \subseteq f\text{-}traces(Q)$. This definition captures simultaneous refusal- and readiness-properties. For example, with $\mathcal{L} = \{a, \bar{a}\}$, we have $a \overset{\{a\}}{\longrightarrow} a \overset{a}{\longrightarrow} \mathbf{0}$ which shows that a is a stable state from which the set $\{a\}$ is refused and the label a is offered. It is interesting to observe that we have $a \not\leq_{rf} a + \tau.\mathbf{0}$, because the transition $a \overset{\{a\}}{\longrightarrow} a \overset{a}{\longrightarrow} \mathbf{0}$ cannot be matched by $a + \tau.\mathbf{0}$. Indeed, the refusal preorder is strong enough to guarantee substitutability for stuck-freedom. However, it is more restrictive than conformance. Consider the processes P and Q defined by

$$P = (a + b.c)\#(c + b.a)$$
$$Q = (a + b.a)\#(c + b.c)$$

It can be checked from the definitions (or see details in [5]) that $P \leq Q$ but $P \not\leq_{rf} Q$. The reason we have $P \leq Q$ is that Q is allowed to choose *different* derivatives as witnesses of condition [C1] and [C2]. Condition [C1] is witnessed by the derivative $(c + b.c)$ of Q, and [C2] is witnessed by the derivative $(a + b.a)$ of Q.

4   Application

Based on the theory presented in Section 3, we have implemented a conformance checker that can be used to analyze asynchronous programs written in common programming languages. Such languages (e.g., C, Java, C#) have several features (such as procedure calls, pointers, shared memory, exceptions, and objects) that are cumbersome to model directly in CCS. Our conformance checker accepts a language ZING, which supports such features directly without the need for complicated encodings. The operational semantics of ZING is given as a labeled transition system. All statements except the send and receive statements are modeled as transitions labeled with τ actions. Transitions from send and receive statements are labeled with the corresponding channel names (ignoring the data values that are sent or received). Note that Definition 8 of conformance makes no reference to the syntax of CCS, and is purely based on the semantics of the labeled transition system. Thus we can define conformance between two ZING processes using Definition 8 directly.

We have applied our conformance checker to check contracts of distributed programs. We next describe how the conformance checks were done and the errors that we found.

Our example application is a distributed program for managing inventory and ordering processes for a bookstore. Contracts are specified as communicating state machines. We used the ZING conformance checker to check that implementations conform to their contract specifications and that implementations do not get stuck with contracts specifying other components that they use.

The structure of the system is shown in Figure 1 (top). It contains five components, ShoppingCartImpl, InventoryImpl, OrderImpl, PublicInventoryImpl

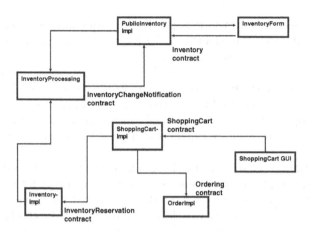

```
Contract ShoppingCart =
    AddItem?. ShoppingCart
 + RemoveItem?. ShoppingCart
 + CheckOut?. AcknowledgeOrder!
 + Cancel?. AcknowledgeOrder!


Contract InventoryReservation =
      ReserveInventory?. InventoryReservation
  +  UnreserveInventory?. InventoryReservation
  +  CommitReservation?. Acknowledgement!
  +  CancelReservation?. Acknowledgement!
  +  Timeout
```

Fig. 1. Structure of the Bookstore System (top) and two contracts (bottom)

and InventoryProcessing, and, in addition, two user interface processes. There is an arrow from component A to component B, if A *uses* (is a client of) B. Each of the five components has an associated contract, which is a specification of the publically visible behavior of the component. In Figure 1 (top) each contract is named in association with the component it specifies. Two of the contracts are shown in Figure 1 (bottom). A contract specifies a communicating state machine over a set of message types. For example, the Shoppingcart contract specifies that the component will repeatedly input messages of type AddItem or RemoveItem until either a CheckOut message or a Cancel message is received (we use the notation T? for input and T! for output, where T is a message type.) The Timeout event used in the InventoryReservation contract is a special event. Timeouts can be attached to input constructs in the implementation language.

The implementation code for a component is placed in a declaration that states the contract it is supposed to implement, as in:

$$\text{ShoppingCartImpl} \leq \text{ShoppingCart}$$

By relying on the contracts it is possible to automatically translate an implementation into a ZING model that *substitutes contracts for the components it uses.* In doing so, we rely on Theorem 2.

In addition to checking conformance between a component and its contract, we always perform a *stuckness test* that checks for stuck states in the interaction between a component and the contracts it uses. This is necessary, since, for example, a component might have a trivial contract and yet get stuck with components it uses. Such cases are caught and flagged by our conformance checker as well.

The conformance analysis of the Bookstore system was done by compiling each component implementation and its associated contract into ZING, resulting in two ZING processes, which were then compared using our conformance checker. The conformance check was done compositionally, by checking one component implementation at a time against its contract specification, substituting contracts to represent the components that are *used*. The entire process is fully automatic. Our conformance analysis detected a number of serious errors including a deadlock, which are briefly described below. In the list below we indicate which contract was checked, and which condition ([C1] or [C2]) of Definition 8 was violated; we also indicate failure of the stuckness test referred to above. We emphasize that these errors were not found before we checked the code[4].

(1) InventoryReservation. *Missing timeout specification ([C2]).* The contract failed to specify that the component could timeout on its event loop. This resulted in a ready refusals failure identified by the conformance checker, because the component would refuse all requests after timing out. The contract was corrected by adding a Timeout case. A Timeout event is modeled as an internal (τ) action, and when attached to an input a it is represented by ZING as $a + \tau.0$ (assuming here that nothing happens after the timeout).

(2) InventoryReservation. *Repeated input not specified ([C1]).* After correction of the previous error, the conformance checker reported a simulation failure. The problem was that the contract specified that the component takes message CommitReservation only once, terminating the event loop of the component. However, the implementation did not terminate its loop on receipt of CommitReservation as it should, and the implementation was corrected.

(3) ShoppingCart. *Stuckness.* Figure 1 shows the contract ShoppingCart and the corrected InventoryReservation. The implementation uses the components InventoryImpl and OrderImpl. The conformance check finds that the implementation gets stuck with the InventoryReservation contract in a situation where the implementation receives a CheckOut message, then goes on to send a CommitReservation message to the InventoryImpl and then waits to receive an Acknowledgement. This receive deadlocks, if the InventoryImpl has timed out. In other situations, the timeout causes stuckness by residual messages sent from the ShoppingCartImpl. The implementation was corrected.

---

[4] The code had not been thoroughly tested. Notice, however, that several of the errors would typically not be found by testing.

(4) **Inventory**. *Input not implemented in component ([C2])*. An input specified in the contract **Inventory** but not implemented resulted in a refusals failure. The implementation was corrected.

(5) **InventoryChangeNotification**. *Inputs unavailable after receipt of a particular message ([C2])*. In one particular state, on receipt of message **Done** in its event loop, the imlmentation **PublicInventoryImpl** would exit its event loop without terminating its communication with a publish-subscribe system in the **InventoryProcessing** component, whereas the contract does not reflect this possibility. Messages for that system could therefore be lost, and the implementation was corrected.

5   Conclusion

We have presented a novel refinement relation for CCS and demonstrated that it is suitable for compositional checking of stuck-freedom of communicating processes. Conformance has the advantage of being directly applicable to a labeled transition system in which visible actions and stability can be observed. Stuckness is more discriminative than CSP deadlock by taking orphan messages into account, which is useful for checking asynchronous processes. We proved that conformance is a precongruence on CCS processes satisfying substitutability, and we distinguished it from related process preorders. We have built a conformance checker for ZING, an expressive modeling language, and have applied it to a distributed system.

Acknowledgments

We are grateful to Robin Milner for encouraging comments on a draft of this paper, and to Ranko Lazic for an inspiring conversation. We thank the participants of workshops arranged by Tony Hoare at Microsoft Research, Cambridge in June 2002 (Ernie Cohen, Paul Gardiner, Andy Gordon, Robin Milner, and Bill Roscoe) and at the Computing Laboratory, Oxford University, in November 2003 (Christie Bolton, Michael Goldsmith, Ranko Lazic, and Gavin Lowe). We also wish to thank Tony Andrews, Microsoft, for his work on the design and implementation of ZING.

References

1. R. Alur, T. A. Henzinger, O. Kupferman, and M. Y. Vardi. Alternating refinement relations. In *CONCUR 98: Concurrency Theory*, LNCS 1466, pages 163–178. Springer-Verlag, 1998.
2. E. Brinksma, L. Heerink, and J. Tretmans. Developments in testing transition systems. In *Testing of Communicating Systems*, IFIP TC6 10th International Workshop on Testing of Communicating Systems, pages 143 – 166. Chapman & Hall, 1997.

3. S.D. Brookes, C.A.R. Hoare, and A.W. Roscoe. A theory of communicating sequential processes. *Journal of the ACM*, 31(3):560–599, 1984.
4. L. de Alfaro and T. A. Henzinger. Interface theories for component-based design. In *EMSOFT 01: Embedded Software*, LNCS, pages 148–165. Springer-Verlag, 2001.
5. C. Fournet, C.A.R. Hoare, S.K. Rajamani, and J. Rehof. Stuck-free conformance theory for CCS. Technical report, Microsoft Research, 2004.
6. C. A. R. Hoare. *Communicating Sequential Processes*. Prentice Hall, 1985.
7. K.G. Larsen and A. Skou. Bisimulation through probabilistic testing. In *POPL 89: ACM Principles of Programming Languages*, pages 344–352. ACM, 1989.
8. R. Milner. *Communication and Concurrency*. Prentice Hall, 1989.
9. R. Milner. *Communicating and Mobile Systems: the π-Calculus*. Cambridge University Press, 1999.
10. W. Peng and S. Puroshothaman. Towards dataflow analysis of communicating finite state machines. In *PODC 89*, pages 45–58. ACM, 1989.
11. I. Phillips. Refusal testing. *Theoretical Computer Science*, 50(2):241 – 284, 1987.
12. S. K. Rajamani and J. Rehof. Conformance checking for models of asynchronous message passing software. In *CAV 02: Computer-Aided Verification*, LNCS 2404, pages 166–179. Springer-Verlag, 2002.
13. A. W. Roscoe. *The Theory and Practice of Concurrency*. Prentice Hall, 1998.

Symbolic Simulation, Model Checking and Abstraction with Partially Ordered Boolean Functional Vectors*

Amit Goel[1] and Randal E. Bryant[2]

[1] Dept. of ECE, Carnegie Mellon University
agoel@ece.cmu.edu
[2] Computer Science Dept., Carnegie Mellon University
Randy.Bryant@cs.cmu.edu

Abstract. Boolean Functional Vectors (BFVs) are a symbolic representation for sets of bit-vectors that can be exponentially more compact than the corresponding characteristic functions with BDDs. Additionally, BFVs are the natural representation of bit-vector sets for Symbolic Simulation. Recently, we developed set manipulation algorithms for canonical BFVs by interpreting them as totally ordered selections. In this paper we generalize BFVs by defining them with respect to a partial order. We show that partially ordered BFVs can serve as abstractions for bit-vector sets and can be used to compute over-approximations in reachability analysis. In the special case when the underlying graph of the partial order is a forest, we can efficiently compute an abstract interpretation in a symbolic simulation framework. We present circuit examples where we leverage the exponential gap in the representations and inherent structure in the state-space to demonstrate the usefulness of Partially Ordered Boolean Functional Vectors.

1 Introduction

Symbolic Model Checking and related state-space exploration techniques usually represent sets of states with a characteristic function, often using BDDs to encode the characteristic function. A characteristic function is essentially a test for membership, returning a one if and only if the input is in the set. Alternatively, bit-vector sets can be represented symbolically by Boolean Functional Vectors (BFVs) [4] which map bit-vectors to bit-vectors; the set represented is the range of this mapping. Hence, characteristic functions serve as set acceptors while Boolean Functional Vectors are set generators.

We are interested in the Boolean Functional Vector representation for two main reasons:

- They can be exponentially more compact than the corresponding characteristic function when using BDDs as the underlying representation.

---

* This work was supported in part by the MARCO/DARPA Gigascale Systems Research Center. Their support is gratefully acknowledged.

R. Alur and D.A. Peled (Eds.): CAV 2004, LNCS 3114, pp. 255–267, 2004.

- Boolean Functional Vectors are the natural representation for Symbolic Simulation.

However, there are two drawbacks that have prevented the representation from being used more often. Firstly, the representation is not canonical, *per se*. Secondly, until recently there were no set manipulation algorithms for this representation.

The representation can be made canonical by placing certain restrictions on the representation [4, 10]. Recently, we presented algorithms for set union, intersection and projection based on our interpretation of the canonical BFV as an ordered selection [5], thus enabling Symbolic Simulation based Model Checking.

In this paper, we generalize the framework by defining Boolean Functional Vectors with respect to a *partial order*. We show that Partially Ordered Boolean Functional Vectors serve as abstractions for bit-vector sets. If the underlying graph of the partial order is a forest, the partially ordered BFVs form a lattice and the abstraction defines a Galois connection between the BFV space and the concrete space of bit-vector sets.

The partial order allows us to selectively constrain some variables with respect to each other while ignoring constraints between unrelated variables. This is in contrast to most other approaches to abstraction where some of the variables are discarded and all constraints between the remaining variables are retained.

We present algorithms for (abstract) set manipulation and show how to use these algorithms for image computation. When the underlying graph is a forest, our method is a complete abstract interpretation. We then present two examples where we leverage the exponential gap between BFVs and characteristic functions as well as inherent structure in the state-space to enable efficient verification.

1.1 Related Work

Boolean Functional Vectors were originally used in [4] for image computation where symbolic simulation was used for next state computation but all other set manipulation operations were performed by first converting to characteristic functions, performing the necessary operations and converting back to Boolean Functional Vectors for the next iteration. The canonical BFVs were described in [4, 10]. An efficient algorithm to obtain a BFV from a characteristic function (parameterization) was presented in [1].

The most prominent use of Boolean Functional Vectors is in Symbolic Trajectory Evaluation (STE) [2] which is a symbolic simulation based bounded model checking approach. In [3], Chou developed a framework for symbolic ternary simulation based abstract interpretation. STE has recently been extended to Generalized Symbolic Trajectory Evaluation (GSTE) [11] to enable model checking of all ω-regular properties. This was made possible by using a *reparameterization* algorithm to convert a given BFV into a canonical BFV. This algorithm, presented in [12], can be seen as a special case of the projection algorithm presented here. GSTE also uses a *ternary abstraction* in which each state element is classified as concrete or ternary. A choice for a concrete element is represented by a state variable whereas a choice for a ternary element is represented by the ternary value X. In this scheme, all relations between concrete values are captured and the ternary variables can only be constrained by the concrete values. No relations between ternary values are captured. The abstraction by partial order BFVs presented here subsumes ternary abstraction. We can model the ternary abstraction by a partial order in which the concrete variables are related to each other, all concrete variables precede all ternary variables, and the ternary variables are unrelated to each other.

The conjunctive canonical decomposition [7] is a symbolic representation closely related to Boolean Functional Vectors. This correspondence was explored in our earlier work [5]. The theory we develop here can be applied, with suitable modifications, to conjunctive decompositions as well.

In [6], the authors perform abstraction using overlapping projections. These projections correspond to the chains in our partial orders. The difference is primarily this: with overlapping projections, there is a set constraint for each projection while with partially ordered BFVs, there is an evaluation function for each state element. With overlapping projections, the constraints between variables occurring together in multiple projections will be repeated in each of these projections. With partially ordered BFVs, each variable is constrained only once.

1.2   Preliminaries

An n-length bit-vector $\vec{X}$ is a mapping from the set of indices $\mathcal{I} = \{1, \ldots, n\}$ to the set of Boolean values $\mathcal{B} = \{0, 1\}$. The set of all n-length bit vectors is noted $[\mathcal{I} \mapsto \mathcal{B}]$. Let $\preceq$ be a partial order on $\mathcal{I}$ and $\prec$ the associated strict order. The set of ancestors for index i is given by $ancestors(i) = \{j | j \prec i\}$.

Let $\prec_{min}$ be the minimum relation whose transitive, reflexive closure is $\preceq$. When the graph $(\mathcal{I}, \prec_{min})$ is a forest, we say that i is a root if it has no ancestors, and we define $parent(i)$ when i is not a root by $parent(i) \prec_{min} i$. The set of children of an index is then given by $children(i) = \{j | i = parent(j)\}$.

In the following, $\vec{V} = \langle v_1, \ldots, v_n \rangle$ represents a vector of Boolean variables, $\vec{X}$ and $\vec{Y}$ represent bit-vectors and $\vec{F}, \vec{G}$ and $\vec{H}$ represent Boolean Functional Vectors.

2   Partially Ordered Boolean Functional Vectors

Definition 1. *An $(\mathcal{I}, \preceq)$-BFV is a vector of Boolean functions $\vec{F} = \langle f_1, \ldots, f_n \rangle$ such that for all indices i:*

$$f_i(\vec{V}) = f_i^1(\vec{V}) + f_i^c(\vec{V}) \cdot v_i$$

where f_i^1 and f_i^c are mutually exclusive Boolean functions of the ancestors of i:

$$f_i^1(\vec{X}) \cdot f_i^c(\vec{X}) = 0$$
$$(\forall j \in ancestors(i).f_j(\vec{X}) = f_j(\vec{Y})) \Rightarrow (f_i^1(\vec{X}) = f_i^1(\vec{Y})) \wedge (f_i^c(\vec{X}) = f_i^c(\vec{Y}))$$

for all $\vec{X}, \vec{Y} \in [\mathcal{I} \mapsto \mathcal{B}]$.

An $(\mathcal{I}, \preceq)$-BFV is to be interpreted as an ordered selection. The variable v_i represents an input *choice* for the i-th bit while f_i is the corresponding *selection*. The definition requires that the selection for the i-th bit is constrained only by the selections for its ancestors. We will refer to f_i^1 and f_i^c as the *forced-to-one* and *free-choice* conditions for the i-th bit. Additionally, we define the *forced-to-zero* condition $f_i^0 = \neg(f_i^1 + f_i^c)$.

Definition 2. *We define the space $\mathcal{F}_{(\mathcal{I}, \preceq)}$ to include all $(\mathcal{I}, \preceq)$-BFVs and extend it to $\mathcal{F}_{(\mathcal{I}, \preceq)}^{\perp}$ by including a bottom element to represent the empty set:*

$$\mathcal{F}_{(\mathcal{I}, \preceq)} = \{\vec{F} | \vec{F} \text{ is an } (\mathcal{I}, \preceq)\text{-BFV}\}$$
$$\mathcal{F}_{(\mathcal{I}, \preceq)}^{\perp} = \mathcal{F}_{(\mathcal{I}, \preceq)} \cup \{\perp\}$$

We now define a concretization function which maps an $(\mathcal{I}, \preceq)$-BFV to its range and the bottom element to the empty set.

Definition 3. *The concretization function $\gamma : \mathcal{F}_{(\mathcal{I}, \preceq)}^{\perp} \mapsto \mathcal{P}([\mathcal{I} \mapsto \mathcal{B}])$ is given by:*

$$\gamma(\perp) = \emptyset$$
$$\gamma(\vec{F}) = \{\vec{X} \in [\mathcal{I} \mapsto \mathcal{B}] | \exists \vec{Y} \in [\mathcal{I} \mapsto \mathcal{B}].\vec{F}(\vec{Y}) = \vec{X}\} \text{ for all } \vec{F} \in \mathcal{F}_{(\mathcal{I}, \preceq)}$$

We say that $\vec{F}$ abstracts a bit vector set S if $\gamma(\vec{F}) \supseteq S$ and that $\vec{F}$ represents S if $\gamma(\vec{F}) = S$. Not all bit-vector sets S can be represented in $\mathcal{F}_{(\mathcal{I}, \preceq)}^{\perp}$ but our definition ensures that if there is a representation for S, then it is unique. Additionally, vectors in the range of an $(\mathcal{I}, \preceq)$-BFV are mapped to themselves:

Theorem 1. *Given $\vec{F}, \vec{G} \in \mathcal{F}_{(\mathcal{I}, \preceq)}$ and $\vec{X} \in [\mathcal{I} \mapsto \mathcal{B}]$:*

$$\gamma(\vec{F}) = \gamma(\vec{G}) \Leftrightarrow \forall \vec{X} \in [\mathcal{I} \mapsto \mathcal{B}].F(\vec{X}) = G(\vec{X})$$
$$\vec{X} \in \gamma(\vec{F}) \Leftrightarrow \vec{F}(\vec{X}) = \vec{X}$$

The above theorem gives us a procedure to obtain the characteristic function $\chi_{\gamma(\vec{F})}$ for a set from its BFV $\vec{F}$. Recall that $\chi_{\gamma(\vec{F})}(\vec{X}) = 1$ if and only if $\vec{X} \in \gamma(\vec{F})$. From Theorem 1 it follows that $\chi_{\gamma(\vec{F})}(\vec{X}) = 1$ if and only if $F(\vec{X}) = \vec{X}$. Hence, we can derive:

$$\chi_{\gamma(\vec{F})}(\vec{V}) = \prod_{i \in \mathcal{I}} v_i \leftrightarrow f_i(\vec{V})$$

We observe that $\langle v_1 \leftrightarrow f_i, \ldots, v_n \leftrightarrow f_n \rangle$ is a canonical conjunctive decomposition [7] for $\gamma(\vec{F})$. The theory we develop in this paper for Boolean Functional Vectors applies, with suitable modifications, to conjunctive decompositions as well.

We now define a partial ordering $\sqsubseteq$ on $\mathcal{F}_{(\mathcal{I}, \preceq)}^{\perp}$ by lifting the subset ordering $\subseteq$ on bit-vector sets.

Definition 4. *The partial ordering $\sqsubseteq$ is defined on $\mathcal{F}_{(\mathcal{I}, \preceq)}^{\perp}$ by:*

$$\vec{F} \sqsubseteq \vec{G} \Leftrightarrow \gamma(\vec{F}) \subseteq \gamma(\vec{G})$$

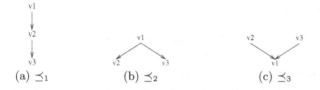

Fig. 1. Partial Orders used in Example 1

Example 1. Given $S = \{000, 100, 111\}$, $\mathcal{I} = 1, 2, 3$ and $\vec{V} = \langle v_1, v_2, v_3 \rangle$, let $\preceq_1$, $\preceq_2$ and $\preceq_3$ be the reflexive transitive closures of the partial orders depicted in Figures 1(a),1(b) and 1(c) respectively.

The $(\mathcal{I}, \preceq_1)$-BFV $\vec{F}_1 = \langle v_1, v_1 \cdot v_2, v_1 \cdot v_2 \rangle$ represents S, i.e., $\gamma(\vec{F}_1) = S$.

The $(\mathcal{I}, \preceq_2)$-BFV $\vec{F}_2 = \langle v_1, v_1 \cdot v_2, v_1 \cdot v_3 \rangle$ abstracts S. We have $\gamma(\vec{F}_2) = \{000, 100, 101, 110, 111\}$ which is a superset of S. Moreover, $\vec{F}_2$ is the minimum abstraction for S in $\mathcal{F}^{\perp}_{(\mathcal{I}, \preceq)}$.

The $(\mathcal{I}, \preceq_3)$-BFVs $\vec{G} = \langle (v_2 \cdot v_3) + (\neg v_2 \cdot \neg v_3) \cdot v_1, v_2, v_3 \rangle$ and $\vec{H} = \langle (v_2 + v_3) + (\neg v_2 \cdot \neg v_3) \cdot v_1, v_2, v_3 \rangle$ abstract S, since $\gamma(\vec{G}) = \{000, 001, 010, 100, 111\}$ and $\gamma(\vec{H}) = \{000, 101, 110, 100, 111\}$. Note that $\vec{G}$ and $\vec{H}$ are unrelated minimal abstractions.

Lemma 1. *If $(\mathcal{I}, \prec_{min})$ is a forest then there is a minimum abstraction $\alpha(S)$ in $\mathcal{F}^{\perp}_{(\mathcal{I}, \preceq)}$ for every set $S \subseteq \mathcal{P}([\mathcal{I} \mapsto \mathcal{B}])$.*

Theorem 2. *If $(\mathcal{I}, \prec_{min})$ is a forest then:*

1. *$(\mathcal{F}^{\perp}_{(\mathcal{I}, \preceq)}, \sqsubseteq)$ forms a complete lattice. For $\vec{F}, \vec{G} \in \mathcal{F}^{\perp}_{(\mathcal{I}, \preceq)}$, the least upper bound and greatest lower bound are given by:*

$$\vec{F} \sqcup \vec{G} = \alpha(\gamma(\vec{F}) \cup \gamma(\vec{G}))$$
$$\vec{F} \sqcap \vec{G} = \alpha(\gamma(\vec{F}) \cap \gamma(\vec{G}))$$

2. *The pair of adjoined functions (α, γ) forms a Galois connection between the concrete space $(\mathcal{P}([\mathcal{I} \mapsto \mathcal{B}]), \subseteq)$ and the abstract space $(\mathcal{F}^{\perp}_{(\mathcal{I}, \preceq)}, \sqsubseteq)$. For all $S \in \mathcal{P}([\mathcal{I} \mapsto \mathcal{B}])$ and $\vec{F} \in \mathcal{F}^{\perp}_{(\mathcal{I}, \preceq)}$:*

$$S \subseteq \gamma(\alpha(S))$$
$$\vec{F} = \alpha(\gamma(\vec{F}))$$

Note that concretization does not lose any information. Furthermore, if $(\mathcal{I}, \preceq)$ is a total order, then the abstract space $\mathcal{F}^{\perp}_{(\mathcal{I}, \preceq)}$ is isomorphic to the concrete space $\mathcal{P}([\mathcal{I} \mapsto \mathcal{B}])$ and no information is lost in abstraction, either:

Theorem 3. *If $\mathcal{F}^{\perp}_{(\mathcal{I}, \preceq)}$ is totally ordered, then for all $S \in \mathcal{P}([\mathcal{I} \mapsto \mathcal{B}])$:*

$$S = \gamma(\alpha(S))$$

3   Algorithms

In this section, we assume that $(\mathcal{I}, \prec_{min})$ is a forest and present algorithms for computing the least upper bound and greatest lower bound of $(\mathcal{I}, \preceq)$-BFVs $\vec{F}$ and $\vec{G}$ to give us abstractions for set union and intersection respectively. We also present an algorithm to compute the minimum abstraction for projection.

The set union and intersection algorithms are modified from [5] to take into account that $\preceq$ is not necessarily a total order. The algorithm for projection is new and is more efficient than computing the union of the cofactors because of fewer intermediate computations.

The algorithms presented here can be modified for the case when $(\mathcal{I}, \prec_{min})$ is not a forest. The modifications are required to account for cases when there are conflicting constraints from unrelated ancestors for the selection of a bit. In such a case, we could obtain a minimal abstraction by choosing the constraint from one of these ancestors, or an upper bound of these minimal abstraction by ignoring all constraints in case of a conflict.

3.1   Set Union

In selecting a vector from the union of two sets, we could select the vector from either of the operands. If we select the bits one at a time (in an order consistent with $\preceq$), initially we can make a selection from either set. In this scenario, the bit being selected is forced-to-zero(one) if and only if it is forced-to-zero(one) in both sets. We can continue to select from either set, until we commit ourselves to one of the operands. This happens when the bit being selected is forced-to-zero(one) in one of the operand sets and we select the opposite value. From then on, we can exclude the operand set that disagrees with our selection.

Given $(\mathcal{I}, \preceq)$-BFVs $\vec{F}$ and $\vec{G}$, we define conditions f_i^x and g_i^x to indicate when $\vec{F}$ and $\vec{G}$ can be excluded from the selection for the union. If i is a root, then:

$$f_i^x = 0$$
$$g_i^x = 0$$

Otherwise, let $j = parent(i)$:

$$f_i^x = f_j^x + f_j^0 \cdot h_j + f_j^1 \cdot \neg h_j$$
$$g_i^x = g_j^x + g_j^0 \cdot h_j + g_j^1 \cdot \neg h_j$$

We now define $\vec{H}$ so that bit i is forced-to-zero(one) in the union if and only if it is forced-to-zero(one) in the non-excluded sets:

$$h_i^0 = f_i^0 \cdot g_i^0 + f_i^0 \cdot g_i^x + f_i^x \cdot g_i^0$$
$$h_i^1 = f_i^1 \cdot g_i^1 + f_i^1 \cdot g_i^x + f_i^x \cdot g_i^1$$

Theorem 4. *Given $(\mathcal{I}, \preceq)$-BFVs $\vec{F}$ and $\vec{G}$, let $\vec{H}$ be defined as above. Then:*

$$\vec{H} = \vec{F} \sqcup \vec{G}$$

From Theorems 2 and 4, it follows that our algorithm computes an over-approximation of the corresponding set union, i.e., $\gamma(\vec{H}) \supseteq \gamma(\vec{F}) \cup \gamma(\vec{G})$.

3.2 Set Intersection

A vector can be selected from the intersection of two sets only if it can be selected in both sets. Hence, we can make selections for bits only if both operands agree on the selection. The selection is forced-to-zero(one) in the intersection if it is forced-to-zero(one) in either operand. We must be careful, however, to avoid conflicts that can occur when, for some bit, the selection in one operand is forced-to-zero while the selection is forced-to-one in the other operand because of the selections made for the ancestors of the bit in question.

Given $(\mathcal{I}, \preceq)$-BFVs $\vec{F}$ and $\vec{G}$, we define elimination conditions e_i to indicate conflicting selections while computing the intersection:

$$e_i = \sum_{j \in children(i)} (f_j^0 \cdot g_j^1 + f_j^1 \cdot g_j^0 + \forall v_j.e_j)$$

If there is no possible selection for some bit, then the intersection is empty:

$$(\exists i.e_i = 1) \Rightarrow H = \bot$$

Otherwise, we obtain a vector $\vec{K}$ by eliminating the conflicts:

$$k_i^0 = f_i^0 + g_i^0 + e_{i|v_i \leftarrow 1}$$
$$k_i^1 = f_i^1 + g_i^1 + e_{i|v_i \leftarrow 0}$$

We then obtain $\vec{H}$ by normalizing $\vec{K}$ by propagating the selection constraints (introduced by the elimination) downstream:

$$h_i^0 = k_{i|v_j \leftarrow h_j, \forall j \in ancestors(i)}^0$$
$$h_i^1 = k_{i|v_j \leftarrow h_j, \forall j \in ancestors(i)}^1$$

Theorem 5. *Given $(\mathcal{I}, \preceq)$-BFVs $\vec{F}$ and $\vec{G}$, define $\vec{H}$ as above. Then:*

$$\vec{H} = \vec{F} \sqcap \vec{G}$$

As with set union, it follows from Theorems 5 and 2 that $\vec{H}$ is an over-approximation of the corresponding set intersection, i.e., $\gamma(\vec{H}) \supseteq \gamma(\vec{F}) \cap \gamma(\vec{G})$.

3.3 Projection

Given $\mathcal{I}' \subseteq \mathcal{I}$, the (existential) projection of a set $S \in \mathcal{P}([\mathcal{I} \mapsto \mathcal{B}])$ on $\mathcal{I}'$ is:

$$proj_{\mathcal{I}'}(S) = \{\vec{X} \in [\mathcal{I}' \mapsto \mathcal{B}] | \exists \vec{Y} \in S. \forall i \in \mathcal{I}'. \vec{Y}(i) = \vec{X}(i)\}$$

In selecting a vector for the projection, we can select an $\vec{X} \in [\mathcal{I}' \mapsto \mathcal{B}]$ as long as there is some selection for the bits in $(\mathcal{I} \setminus \mathcal{I}')$ that can extend $\vec{X}$ to some vector $\vec{Y}$ in S. The projection loses information about the relation between the bits retained and the bits projected out. We capture this information with the

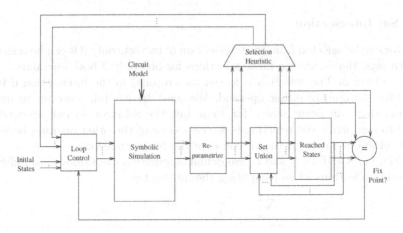

Fig. 2. Symbolic Reachability Analysis using Symbolic Simulation with Boolean Functional Vectors

don't-care conditions f_i^{dc}. If i is a root, then $f_i^{dc} = \mathbf{0}$. Otherwise, let $j = parent(i)$ in:

$$
\begin{aligned}
f_i^{dc} &= f_j^{dc} && \text{if } j \notin \mathcal{I}', \\
&= f_j^{dc} + f_j^0 \cdot h_j + f_j^1 \cdot \neg h_j && \text{otherwise.}
\end{aligned}
$$

The abstract projection $\vec{H}$ is now defined so that a bit is forced-to-zero(one) if and only if it is forced-to-zero(one) in the care space irrespective of the values of the projected out bits. Let $V'' = \{v_i | i \in (\mathcal{I} \setminus \mathcal{I}')\}$. Then, for $i \in \mathcal{I}'$:

$$
\begin{aligned}
h_i^0 &= \forall V''.(f_i^0 + f_i^{dc}) \\
h_i^1 &= \forall V''.(f_i^1 + f_i^{dc})
\end{aligned}
$$

Theorem 6. *Given an $(\mathcal{I}, \preceq)$-BFV $\vec{F}$ and $\mathcal{I}' \subseteq \mathcal{I}$, let $\vec{H}$ be defined as above. Then:*

$$
\vec{H} = \alpha(proj_{\mathcal{I}'}(\gamma(\vec{F})))
$$

4   Symbolic Simulation, Model Checking and Abstraction

Using the algorithms from the previous section, we can perform the computations necessary for symbolic model checking using Boolean Functional Vectors. We can compute the image (or pre-image) of a given set of states relative to a transition relation by computing the relational cross product which involves intersection and projection. The fix-point iterations also require set union and an equality check to determine the fix point. If the model is a circuit, however, forward image computation can be performed by symbolic simulation, making it unnecessary to compute the transition relation and its intersection with the current set of states for forward reachability analysis (Figure 2).

Consider a circuit with state elements $\vec{S} = \langle s_1, \ldots, s_j \rangle$ and transition functions $\vec{\Delta} = \langle \delta_1, \ldots, \delta_n \rangle$, we associate the choice variables $\vec{V} = \langle v_1, \ldots, v_n \rangle$ with

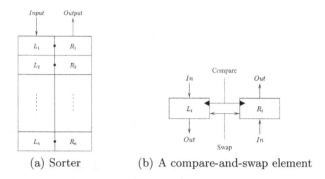

(a) Sorter   (b) A compare-and-swap element

Fig. 3. An Up/Down Sorter

$\vec{S}$. Given an $(\mathcal{I}, \preceq)$-BFV for a set of current states $\vec{F}$, we can simulate the circuit with the state variables set to $\vec{F}$ to obtain the next state vector $\vec{G} = \langle \delta_1(\vec{F}), \ldots, \delta_n(\vec{F}) \rangle$. We can then *reparameterize* G using the *next-state* variables $\vec{V}' = \langle v_{n+1}, \ldots, v_{2n} \rangle$ to obtain a canonical abstraction $\vec{H}$. Note that the range of $\vec{G}$ is the exact image of the set of states we simulated with. The abstraction occurs during reparameterization and is determined by the partial order $\preceq$.

$\vec{H}$ is obtained by projecting out the current state bits from the extended $(\mathcal{I}_{2n}, \preceq_{2n})$-BFV $\langle v_1, \ldots, v_n, g_1, \ldots, g_n \rangle$ over $(\mathcal{I}_{2n}, \preceq_{2n})$ where $\mathcal{I}_{2n} = \{1, \ldots, 2n\}$ and $\preceq_{2n}$ is obtained by extending $\preceq$ to $\mathcal{I}_{2n}$ by requiring that all present state bits precede all next state bits. In practice, we project out one variable at a time, heuristically choosing a 'low-cost' variable. This allows us to optimize the projection algorithm by only modifying (and computing constraints for) the components that are dependent on the variable being projected out, thus avoiding the generation of the monolithic relation between the non-canonical $\vec{G}$ and the canonical $\vec{H}$.

We note that symbolic simulation followed by re-parameterization computes a complete *abstract interpretation* of the circuit transition function [3] when $(\mathcal{I}, \prec_{min})$ is a forest.

4.1 Example: Up/Down Sorter

Consider the Up/Down Sorter [9] of Figure 3. It has $2n$ words, each m bits wide, arranged in two columns. Initially, all the words are set to 0. On any cycle, we may either insert a word at *Input* or extract the maximum word in the sorter from *Output*. The operation of the sorter may be viewed as a two step process: an insert or extract followed by a compare and swap. If we are inserting a word, then in the first step, all words in the left column are pushed down, with L_1 getting *Input*. For a read operation, in the first step all words in the right column are pushed one up, with R_n getting 0 and the value in R_1 read out at *Output*. In the second step, adjacent words are compared and if the entry in the left column is greater than the corresponding entry in the right column, the two are swapped.

1. Insert:

$$(L'_1 \leftarrow Input) \wedge (\forall 1 \leq i < n.L'_{i+1} \leftarrow L_i)$$

or Read:

$$(Output \leftarrow R_1) \wedge (\forall 1 \leq i < n.R'_i \leftarrow R_{i+1}) \wedge (R'_n \leftarrow 0)$$

2. Compare and Swap:

$$\forall 1 \leq i \leq n.(L'_i, R'_i) \leftarrow \text{if } (L_i > R_i) \text{ then } (R_i, L_i)$$
$$\text{else } (L_i, R_i)$$

The sorter works by maintaining the right column in sorted order so that $R_1 \geq R_2 \geq \cdots \geq R_n$. Additionally, the right entry is always greater than or equal to the corresponding left entry, i.e., $R_i \geq L_i$ for all $1 \leq i \leq n$. These two invariants guarantee that R_1 is the maximum entry in the sorter.

The basic data structure is a sorted array (the right column) which is hard to represent as a characteristic function with BDDs. Let r_i^j represent the j-th bit of the i-th word of the right column. If we choose a word-based BDD variable order, i.e., $\langle r_1^1, r_1^2, \ldots, r_1^m, \ldots, r_n^1, \ldots, r_n^m \rangle$, then the BDD for the characteristic function is exponential in m. On the other hand, if we choose the bit-sliced order $\langle r_1^1, r_2^1, \ldots, r_n^1, \ldots, r_1^m, \ldots, r_n^m \rangle$, then the representation is exponential in n. If $m = n$, then we conjecture that the BDD for the characteristic function is exponential in n, irrespective of the variable order used.

The sorted array can be efficiently represented by a Boolean Functional Vector using BDDs, by organizing the words as a balanced binary search tree, e.g., Figure 4, and using a bit-sliced BDD variable order. The words are constrained only by the values of their ancestors. The relation between the unrelated words is captured implicitly by transitivity through common ancestors. The largest BDDs are for the m-th bits of the leaves. These are linear in m and exponential in the depth of the tree, hence linear in n. Since there are $n \cdot m$ functions in the Boolean Functional Vector, one for each bit of each entry, the bound for the overall representation is quadratic in n and m.

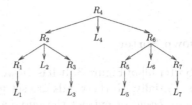

Fig. 4. Partial Order on Words for an Up-Down Sorter with $n = 7$

Figure 5 plots the sizes of the Boolean Functional Vector (using the binary tree layout) and characteristic function representations (using the linear and bit-sliced BDD variable orders) for the reachable states of an up-down sorter with a depth of n ($2n$ entries), each n bits wide ($m = n$).

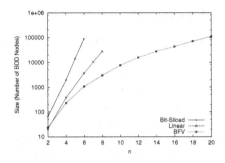

Fig. 5. Size of BDD representations for Up-Down Sorters with with $n = m$

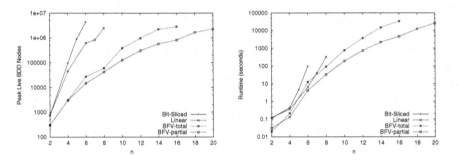

Fig. 6. Symbolic Reachability Analysis for Up-Down Sorters with $n = m$

The partial order in this case is accurate enough to represent the actual state-space of the sorter so that there is no information lost in the abstraction. The ordering constraints between entries unrelated by the partial order are captured by implicit transitivity through their common ancestor. Hence, the use of the partial order does not affect the size of the state-space; any linear extension of the partial order (e.g. the DFS order) would give the same size for the final state-space. However, the partial order is useful during reachability analysis since it prevents the computation of unnecessary constraints.

Figure 6 shows the peak live node count and runtime for reachability analysis, starting from a state with all entries set to 0. The experiments were performed on a Sun-Fire 280R (SUN UltraSPARC-III+ 1015 MHz CPU) with the memory limit set to 1 GB and the time limit set to 10 hours. The experiments with the characteristic function representation were performed using VIS with the MLP heuristics [8]. The current-state and next-state variables are interleaved in the BDD variable order. As expected, there is an exponential gap between the Boolean Functional Vector and characteristic function based approaches. Note that there is a significant performance improvement obtained by using the partial order BFVs instead of the totally ordered BFVs. The largest experiment with partially ordered BFVs ($n = 20$) had 800 state bits, all of which are relevant to the property, i.e. the global sorted order.

4.2   Example: FIFO Equivalence

Consider the two implementations of a FIFO queue shown in Figure 7. In the shift register, new entries are inserted at the front of the queue, the other entries shifting over by one. In the ring buffer, the new entries are inserted at the *head* pointer. In both implementations, the oldest entries are read out at the *tail* pointer. We can check the equivalence of the two implementations by performing reachability analysis on the product machine.

Given the value for the *head* pointer, there is a correspondence between the entries in the two queues. In general, though, we cannot fix such a correspondence since the *head* pointer can change. The BDD for the characteristic function of the reachable state-space is provably exponential in n, irrespective of the variable order. In [7], McMillan showed that there is a canonical conjunctive decomposition for this state-space that is quadratic in n. The basic observation is that the entries are *conditionally independent* since we can fix the correspondence once the value of the control signals is known. The conjunctive decomposition factors out the conditionally independent variables into separate components. The same observations essentially apply to the Boolean Functional Vector representation.

We can take this further by realizing that the entries in any one of the queues are not correlated. The correlation we are interested in is between entries in the shift register and the corresponding entries (given the control signals) in the ring buffer. Hence, we can use a partial order such as the one in Figure 7(c). We obtain approximately a 3X improvement in runtime with the partially ordered BFVs as compared to the totally ordered BFVs for all values of n tried.

5   Conclusions and Future Work

We have developed a general framework for symbolic simulation, model checking and abstraction using partially ordered Boolean Functional Vectors. Our examples demonstrated that this framework can allow us to efficiently verify some circuits where characteristic functions would fail. The most important future work from a practical point of view is the development of an automated abstraction-refinement framework and a dynamic reordering procedure for BFV components to work in tandem with BDD variable reordering.

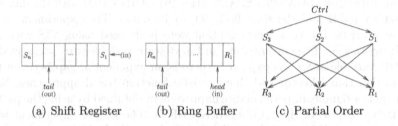

(a) Shift Register   (b) Ring Buffer   (c) Partial Order

Fig. 7. Equivalence Checking for two Implementations of a FIFO

References

1. Mark D. Aagaard, Robert B. Jones, and Carl-Johan H. Seger. Formal Verification Using Parametric Representations of Boolean Constraints. In *Proceedings of the 36th Design Automation Conference (DAC' 99)*, pages 402–407, 1999.
2. Randal E. Bryant, Derek L. Beatty, and Carl-Johan H. Seger. Formal hardware verification by symbolic ternary trajectory evaluation. In *Proceedings of the 28th Design Automation Conference (DAC'91)*, pages 397–402, 1991.
3. Ching-Tsun Chou. The Mathematical Foundation of Symbolic Trajectory Evaluation. In *Proceedings of the 11th International Conference on Computer Aided Verification (CAV'99)*, pages 196–207, 1999.
4. O. Coudert, C. Berthet, and J. C. Madre. Verification of Sequential Machines using Boolean Functional Vectors. In *Proceedings of the IFIP International Workshop on Applied Formal Methods for Correct VLSI Design*, pages 179–196, 1989.
5. Amit Goel and Randal E. Bryant. Set Manipulation with Boolean Functional Vectors for Symbolic Reachability Analysis. In *2003 Design Automation and Test in Europe(DATE'03)*, pages 816–821, 2003.
6. Shankar G. Govindaraju, David L. Dill, Alan J. Hu, and Mark A. Horowitz. Approximate Reachability with BDDs using Overlapping Projections. In *Proceedings of the 35th Design Automation Conference (DAC'98)*, pages 451–456, 1998.
7. Kenneth L. McMillan. A Conjunctively Decomposed Boolean Representation for Symbolic Model Checking. In *Proceedings of the 8th International Conference on Computer Aided Verification (CAV'96)*, pages 13–24, 1996.
8. In-Ho Moon, Gary D. Hachtel, and Fabio Somezni. Border-Block Triangular Form and Conjunction Schedule in Image Computation. In *3rd Internation Conference on Formal Methods in Computer Aided Design (FMCAD'00)*, pages 73–90, 2000.
9. Simon W. Moore and Brian T. Graham. Tagged up/down sorter – A hardware priority queue. *The Computer Journal*, 38(9):695–703, 1995.
10. H. J. Touati, H. Savoj, B. Lin, R. K. Brayton, and A. Sangiovanni-Vincentelli. Implicit State Enumeration of Finite State Machines Using BDDs. In *Proceedings of the IEEE International Conference on Computer-Aided Design(ICCAD'90)*, pages 130–133, 1990.
11. Jin Yang and Carl-Johan H. Seger. Introduction to Generalized Symbolic Trajectory Evaluation. In *Proceedings of the IEEE International Conference on Computer Design(ICCD'01)*, pages 360–367, 2001.
12. Jin Yang and Carl-Johan H. Seger. Generalized Symbolic Trajectory Evaluation - Abstraction in Action. In *Formal Methods in Computer-Aided Design (FMCAD'02)*, pages 70–87, 2002.

Functional Dependency
for Verification Reduction*

Jie-Hong R. Jiang and Robert K. Brayton

Department of Electrical Engineering and Computer Sciences
University of California, Berkeley

Abstract. The existence of functional dependency among the state variables of a state transition system was identified as a common cause of inefficient BDD representation in formal verification. Eliminating such dependency from the system compacts the state space and may significantly reduce the verification cost. Despite the importance, how to detect functional dependency *without or before knowing the reachable state set* remains a challenge. This paper tackles this problem by unifying two closely related, but scattered, studies — detecting signal correspondence and exploiting functional dependency. The prior work on either subject turns out to be a special case of our formulation. Unlike previous approaches, we detect dependency directly from transition functions rather than from reached state sets. Thus, reachability analysis is not a necessity for exploiting dependency. In addition, our procedure can be integrated into reachability analysis as an on-the-fly reduction. Preliminary experiments demonstrate promising results of extracting functional dependency without reachability analysis. Dependencies that were underivable before, due to the limitation of reachability analysis on large transition systems, can now be computed efficiently. For the application to verification, reachability analysis is shown to have substantial reduction in both memory and time consumptions.

1 Introduction

Reduction [12] is an important technique in extending the capacity of formal verification. This paper is concerned with property-preserving reduction [7], where the reduced model satisfies a property if and only if the original model does. In particular, we focus on reachability-preserving reduction for safety property verification using functional dependency.

The existence of dependency among state variables frequently occurs in state transition systems at both high-level specifications and gate-level implementations [17]. As identified in [11], such dependency may cause inefficient BDD [6] representation in formal verification. Moreover, it can be used in logic minimization [13,17]. Its detection, thus, has potential impact on formal verification and logic synthesis, and has attracted extensive research in both domains (e.g., see

---

* This work was supported in part by NSF grant CCR-0312676, California Micro program, and our industrial sponsors, Fujitsu, Intel and Synplicity.

R. Alur and D.A. Peled (Eds.): CAV 2004, LNCS 3114, pp. 268–280, 2004.

[2, 13, 11, 8, 17]). The essence of all prior efforts [2, 13, 8, 17] can be traced back to *functional deduction* [5], where variable dependency is drawn from a single characteristic function. Thus, as a common path, the variable dependency was derived from the characteristic function of a reached state set. However, state transition systems of practical applications are often too complex to compute their reachable states, even though these systems might be substantially reduced only after variable dependency is known. An improvement was proposed in [8] to exploit the dependency from the currently reached state set in every iteration of a reachability analysis. The computation, however, may still be too expensive and may simplify subsequent iterations very little.

To avoid such difficulty, we take a different path to exploit the dependency. The observation is that the dependency among state variables originates from the dependency among transition functions[1]. In consideration of efficiency, some variable dependency can better be concluded directly from the transition functions rather than from the characteristic function of a reached state set. Therefore, the computation requires only *local* image computation. As the derived dependency is an invariant, it can be used by any BDD- or SAT-based model checking procedure to reduce the verification complexity. Since not all dependency can be discovered this way due to the imperfect information about state reachability, this method itself is an approximative approach. To complete the approximative computation, our procedure can be embedded into reachability analysis as an on-the-fly detection. Reachability analysis is thus conducted on a reduced model in each iteration. Our formulation leads to a unification of two closely related, but scattered, studies on detecting signal correspondence [10, 9] and exploiting functional dependency [11, 8].

2 Preliminaries and Notations

As a notational convention, a vector (or, an ordered set) $v = \langle v_1, \ldots, v_n \rangle$ is specified in a bold-faced letter while its unordered version is written as $\{v\} = \{v_1, \ldots, v_n\}$. In this case, n is the cardinality (size) of both v and $\{v\}$, i.e., $|v| = |\{v\}| = n$. Also, when a vector v is partitioned into k sub-vectors $v_1, \ldots, v_k$, the convention $\langle v_1; \ldots; v_k \rangle$ denotes that $v_1, \ldots, v_k$ are combined into one vector with a proper reordering of elements to recover the ordering of v.

This paper assumes, without loss of generality, that multi-valued functions are replaced with vectors of Boolean functions. The image of a Boolean functional vector ψ over a subset C of its domain is denoted as $Image(\psi, C)$; the range of ψ is denoted as $Range(\psi)$. Let $\psi : \mathbb{B}^n \to \mathbb{B}$ be a Boolean function over variables $x_1, \ldots, x_n$. The **support set** of ψ is $Supp(\psi) = \{x_i \mid (\psi|_{x_i=0} \text{ XOR } \psi|_{x_i=1}) \neq \text{FALSE}\}$. For a characteristic function $F(x)$ over the set $\{x\}$ of Boolean

---

[1] As state transition systems are often compactly representable in transition functions but not in transition relations, this paper assumes that transition functions are the underlying representation of state transition systems. Consequently, our formulation is not directly applicable to nondeterministic transition systems. The corresponding extension can apply the MOCB technique proposed in [11].

variables, its **projection** on $\{y\} \subseteq \{x\}$ is defined as $F[\{y\}/\{x\}] = \exists x_i \in \{x\}\backslash\{y\}.F(x)$. Also, we denote the identity function and its complement as $\Im$ and $\Im^\dagger$, respectively.

A state transition system $\mathcal{M}$ is a six-tuple $(S, I, \Sigma, \Omega, \delta, \lambda)$, where S is a finite set of states, $I \subseteq S$ is the set of initial states, Σ and Ω are the sets of input and output alphabets, respectively, and $\delta : \Sigma \times S \to S$ (resp. $\lambda : \Sigma \times S \to \Omega$) is the transition function (resp. output function). As symbols and functions are in binary representations in this paper, $\mathcal{M}$ will be specified, instead, with a five-tuple $(I, r, s, \delta, \lambda)$, where r (resp. s) is the vector of Boolean variables that encodes the input alphabets (resp. states).

3   Functional Dependency

We formulate functional dependency for state transition systems in two steps. First, **combinational dependency** among a collection of functions is defined. Second, the formulation is extended to **sequential dependency**.

3.1   Combinational Dependency

Given two Boolean functional vectors $\phi : \mathbb{B}^l \to \mathbb{B}^m$ and $\varphi : \mathbb{B}^l \to \mathbb{B}^n$ over the same domain, we are interested in rewriting ϕ in terms of a function of φ. The condition when such a rewrite is feasible can be captured by a refinement relation, $\sqsubseteq \subseteq (\mathbb{B}^l \to \mathbb{B}^m) \times (\mathbb{B}^l \to \mathbb{B}^n)$, defined as follows.

Definition 1. *Given two Boolean functional vectors* $\phi : \mathbb{B}^l \to \mathbb{B}^m$ *and* $\varphi : \mathbb{B}^l \to \mathbb{B}^n$, φ **refines** ϕ *in* $C \subseteq \mathbb{B}^l$, *denoted as* $\phi \sqsubseteq_C \varphi$, *if* $\phi(a) \neq \phi(b)$ *implies* $\varphi(a) \neq \varphi(b)$ *for all* $a, b \in C$.

In other words, φ refines ϕ in C if and only if φ is more distinguishing than ϕ in C. (As the orderings within ϕ and φ are not a prerequisite, our definition of refinement relation applies to two unordered sets of functions as well.) In the sequel, the subscription C will be omitted from the refinement relation $\sqsubseteq$ when C is the universe of the domain. Based on the above definition, the following proposition forms the foundation of our later development.

Proposition 1. *Given* $\phi : \mathbb{B}^l \to \mathbb{B}^m$ *and* $\varphi : \mathbb{B}^l \to \mathbb{B}^n$, *there exists a functional vector* $\theta : \mathbb{B}^n \to \mathbb{B}^m$ *such that* $\phi = \theta \circ \varphi = \theta(\varphi(\cdot))$ *over* $C \subseteq \mathbb{B}^l$ *if and only if* $\phi \sqsubseteq_C \varphi$. *Moreover,* θ *is unique when restricting its domain to the range of* φ.

For $\phi = \theta \circ \varphi$, we call $\phi_1, \ldots, \phi_m \in \phi$ the **functional dependents** (or, briefly, dependents), $\varphi_1, \ldots, \varphi_n \in \varphi$ the **functional independents** (or, briefly, independents), and $\theta_1, \ldots, \theta_n \in \theta$ the **dependency functions**.

Problem Formulation. The problem of detecting (combinational) functional dependency can be formulated as follows. Given a collection of Boolean functions ψ, we are asked to partition ψ into two parts ϕ and φ such that $\phi = \theta(\varphi)$. Hence, the triple (ϕ, φ, θ) characterizes the functional dependency of ψ. We call such a triple a **dependency triplet**. Suppose φ cannot be further reduced in (ϕ, φ, θ) by recognizing more functional dependents from φ with all possible modifications of θ. That is, $|\varphi|$ is minimized; equivalently, $|\phi|$ is maximized. Then the triplet maximally characterizes the functional dependency of ψ. In this paper, we are interested in computing maximal functional dependency. (Although finding a maximum dependency might be helpful, it is computationally much harder than finding a maximal one as it is the supremum over the set of maximal ones.)

The Computation. In the discussion below, when we mention Boolean functional vectors $\phi(x)$ and $\varphi(x)$, we shall assume that $\phi : \mathbb{B}^l \to \mathbb{B}^m$ and $\varphi : \mathbb{B}^l \to \mathbb{B}^n$ with variable vector $x : \mathbb{B}^l$. Notice that $Supp(\phi)$ and $Supp(\varphi)$ are subsets of $\{x\}$. The following properties are useful in computing dependency.

Theorem 1. *Given functional vectors ϕ and φ, $\phi \sqsubseteq \varphi$ only if $Supp(\phi) \subseteq Supp(\varphi)$.*

Corollary 1. *Given a collection of Boolean functions $\psi_1(x), \ldots, \psi_k(x)$, if, for any $x_i \in \{x\}$, ψ_j is the only function such that $x_i \in Supp(\psi_j)$, then ψ_j is a functional independent.*

With the support set information, Theorem 1 and Corollary 1 can be used as a fast screening in finding combinational dependency.

Theorem 2. *Given functional vectors ϕ and φ, $\phi \sqsubseteq \varphi$ if and only if $|Range(\varphi)| = |Range(\langle \phi, \varphi \rangle)|$.*

Theorem 3. *Let $\theta_i \in \theta$ be the corresponding dependency function of a dependent $\phi_i \in \phi$. Let $\Theta_i^0 = \{\varphi(x)|\phi_i(x) = 0\}$ and $\Theta_i^1 = \{\varphi(x)|\phi_i(x) = 1\}$. Then $\phi_i \sqsubseteq \varphi$ if and only if $\Theta_i^0 \cap \Theta_i^1 = \emptyset$. Also, θ_i has Θ_i^0, Θ_i^1, and $\mathbb{B}^n \backslash \{\Theta_i^0 \cup \Theta_i^1\}$ as its off-set, on-set, and don't-care set, respectively. That is, $\theta_i(\varphi(x)) = \phi_i(x)$ for all valuations of x.*

From Theorem 2, we know that the set $\{\varphi\}$ of functional independents is as distinguishing as the entire set $\{\phi\} \cup \{\varphi\}$ of functions. Theorem 3, on the other hand, shows a way of computing dependency functions.

Given a collection $\{\psi\}$ of Boolean functions, its maximal dependency can be computed with the procedure outlined in Figure 1. First, by Theorem 2, for each function $\psi_i \in \{\psi\}$ we obtain the minimal subsets of $\{\psi\}$ which refine ψ_i. Let the minimal refining subsets for ψ_i be $E_i^1, \ldots, E_i^k$. (Notice that $k \geq 1$ since ψ_i refines itself and, thus, $\{\psi_i\}$ is one of the subsets.) The calculation can be done with *local* image computation because by Theorem 1 and Corollary 1 we only need to consider subsets of functions in $\{\psi\}$ which overlap with ψ_i in support sets. Second, we heuristically derive a minimal set of functional independents that refines all the functions of $\{\psi\}$. Equivalently, for each ψ_i, some $E_i^{j_i}$ is selected such that the cardinality of $\bigcup_{i=1}^{|\psi|} E_i^{j_i}$ is minimized. This union set forms the basis of representing all other functions. That is, functions in the union set are the functional independents; others are the functional dependents. Finally, by Theorem 3, dependency functions are obtained with respect to the selected basis.

CombinationalDependency
   input: a collection $\{\psi\}$ of Boolean functions
   output: a dependency triplet (ϕ, φ, θ)
   begin
   01   for each $\psi_i \in \{\psi\}$
   02   derive minimal refining sets $E_1^i, \ldots, E_k^i$
   03   select a minimal basis $\{\varphi\}$ that refines all $\psi_i \in \{\psi\}$
   04   compute the dependency functions $\{\theta\}$ for $\{\phi\} = \{\psi\} \backslash \{\varphi\}$
   05   **return** (ϕ, φ, θ)
   end

Fig. 1. Algorithm: CombinationalDependency.

A Digression. There were other variant definitions of dependency (see [15] for more examples). The functional dependency defined in [5] (Section 6.9), which follows [15], is too weak to be applicable in our application. We, thus, resort to a stronger definition. As noted below, our definition turns out to be consistent with *functional deduction* (see [5], Chapter 8), which is concerned with the variable dependency in a single characteristic function.

We relate our formulation to functional deduction as follows. In functional deduction, variable dependency is drawn from a single characteristic function. Thus, to exploit the dependency among a collection of functions $\psi(x)$, a single relation $\Psi(x, y) = \bigwedge_i (y_i \equiv \psi_i(x))$ should be built, where y_i's are newly introduced Boolean variables. In addition, to derive dependency solely among $\{y\}$, input variables $\{x\}$ should be enforced in the *eliminable subset* [5]. With the foregoing transformation, variable dependency in functional deduction coincides with our defined functional dependency. A similar result of Theorem 3 was known in the context of functional deduction. Compared to the relational-oriented functional deduction, our formulation can be understood as more functional-oriented, which is computationally more practical.

3.2   Sequential Dependency

Given a state transition system $\mathcal{M} = (I, r, s, \delta, \lambda)$, we consider the detection of functional dependency among the set $\{\delta\}$ of transition functions. More precisely, detecting the sequential dependency of $\mathcal{M}$ is equivalent to finding θ such that δ is partitioned into two vectors: the dependents δ_ϕ, and the independents δ_φ. Let $\{s\} = \{s_\phi\} \cup \{s_\varphi\}$ be such that the valuations of s_ϕ and s_φ are updated by δ_ϕ and δ_φ, respectively. Then θ specifies the dependency of $\mathcal{M}$ by $s_\phi = \theta(s_\varphi)$ and $\delta_\phi = \theta(\delta_\varphi)$, i.e., $\delta_\phi(r, \langle \theta(s_\varphi); s_\varphi \rangle) = \theta \circ \delta_\varphi(r, \langle \theta(s_\varphi); s_\varphi \rangle)$.

Sequential dependency is more relaxed than its combinational counterpart because of the reachability nature of $\mathcal{M}$. The derivation of θ shall involve a fixed-point computation, and can be obtained in two different ways, the greatest fixed-point (gfp) and the least fixed-point (lfp) approaches, with different optimality and complexity. Our discussions start from the easier gfp computation, and continue with the more complicated lfp one. The optimality, on the other hand, is usually improved from the gfp to the lfp computation.

Remark 1. We mention a technicality regarding the set I of initial states. In general, the combinational dependency among transition functions may not hold for the states in I because I may contain dangling states. (A state is called **dangling** if it has no predecessor states. Otherwise, it is **non-dangling**.) To overcome this difficulty, a new set I' of initial states is defined. Let I' be the set of states which are one-step reachable from I. Now, since all states in I' are non-dangling, the calculated dependency holds for I'. On the other hand, the set of reachable states from I is identical to that from I' except for some states in I. In the verification of safety properties, such a substitution is legitimate as long as states in I satisfy the underlying property to be verified. In our discussion, unless otherwise noted, we shall assume that the set of initial states consists of only non-dangling states.

The Greatest Fixed-Point Calculation. In the gfp calculation, state variables are treated functionally independent of each other initially. Their dependency is then discovered iteratively. Combinational dependency among transition functions is computed in each iteration. The resultant dependency functions are substituted backward in the subsequent iteration for the state variables of their corresponding functional dependents. Thereby, the transition functions and previously derived dependency functions are updated. More precisely, let $\theta^{(i)}$ be the set of derived dependency functions for $\delta^{(i)}$ at the ith iteration. For j from $i-1$ to 1, the set $\theta^{(j)}(s_\varphi^{(i-1)})$ of dependency functions is updated in order with $\theta^{(j)}(s_\varphi^{(i)}) = \theta^{(j)}(\langle\theta^{(j+1)}(s_\varphi^{(i)});\ldots;\theta^{(i)}(s_\varphi^{(i)}); s_\varphi^{(i)}\rangle)$. After the updates of $\theta^{(j)}$'s, $\delta^{(i+1)}$ is set to be $\delta_\varphi^{(i)}(r, \langle\theta^{(1)}(s_\varphi^{(i)});\ldots;\theta^{(i)}(s_\varphi^{(i)}); s_\varphi^{(i)}\rangle)$, where $\{\delta_\varphi^{(i)}\} \subseteq \{\delta\}$ corresponds to the functional independents of $\delta^{(i)}$. At the $(i+1)$st iteration, the combinational dependency among $\delta^{(i+1)}$ is computed. The iteration terminates when the size of the set of functional independents cannot be reduced further. The termination is guaranteed since $|\delta^{(i)}|$ decreases monotonically. In the end of the computation, the final θ is simply the collection of $\theta^{(i)}$'s, and the final set of functional independents is $\delta_\varphi^{(k)}$, where k is the last iteration. The computation is summarized in Figure 2, where the procedure *CombinationalDependencyRestore* is similar to *CombinationalDependency* with a slight difference. It computes the dependency among the set of functions given in the first argument in the same way as *CombinationalDependency*. However, the returned functional dependents and independents are the corresponding functions given in the second argument instead of those in the first argument.

Notice that the final result of the gfp calculation may not be unique since, in each iteration, there are several possible choices of maximal functional dependency. As one choice has been made, it fixes the dependency functions for state variables that are declared as dependents. Thereafter, the dependency becomes an invariant throughout the computation since the derivation is valid for the entire set of non-dangling states. For the same reason, the gfp calculation may be too conservative. Moreover, the optimality of the gfp calculation is limited because the state variables are initially treated functionally independent of each other. This limitation becomes apparent especially when the dependency to be

SequentialDependencyGfp
    input: a state transition system $\mathcal{M} = (I, r, s, \delta, \lambda)$
    output: a dependency triplet $(\delta_\phi, \delta_\varphi, \theta)$ for δ
    begin
    01    $i := 0$; $\delta^{(1)} := \delta$
    02   **repeat**
    03   **if** $i \geq 2$
    04   **for** j from $i - 1$ to 1
    05                $\theta^{(j)}(s_\varphi^{(i)}) := \theta^{(j)}((\langle\theta^{(j+1)}(s_\varphi^{(i)}); \ldots; \theta^{(i)}(s_\varphi^{(i)}); s_\varphi^{(i)}\rangle)$
    06   **if** $i \geq 1$
    07            $\delta^{(i+1)}(r, s_\varphi^{(i)}) := \delta_\varphi^{(i)}(r, \langle\theta^{(1)}(s_\varphi^{(i)}); \ldots; \theta^{(i)}(s_\varphi^{(i)}); s_\varphi^{(i)}\rangle)$
    08        $i := i + 1$
    09        $(\delta_\phi^{(i)}, \delta_\varphi^{(i)}, \theta^{(i)}) := CombinationalDependencyRestore(\delta^{(i)}, \delta)$
    10   **until** $|\delta^{(i)}| = |\delta_\varphi^{(i)}|$
    11   **return** $(\langle\delta_\phi^{(1)}; \ldots; \delta_\phi^{(i-1)}\rangle, \delta_\varphi^{(i-1)}, \langle\theta^{(1)}; \ldots; \theta^{(i-1)}\rangle)$
    end

Fig. 2. Algorithm: SequentialDependencyGfp.

discovered is between two state transition systems (e.g., in equivalence check-ing). To discover more dependency, we need to adopt a least fixed-point strategy and refine the dependency iteratively.

The Least Fixed-Point Calculation. In the lfp calculation, unlike the gfp one, the initial dependency among state variables is exploited maximally based on the set of initial states. The dependency is then strengthened iteratively until a fixed point has been reached. The set of functional independents tend to increase during the iterations, in contrast to the decrease in the gfp calculation.

Consider the computation of initial dependency. For the simplest case, when $|I| = 1$, any state variable s_φ can be selected as the basis. Any other variable is replaced with either $\Im(s_\varphi)$ or $\Im^\dagger(s_\varphi)$, depending on whether its initial value equals that of s_φ or not. For arbitrary I, the initial variable dependency can be derived using functional deduction on the characteristic function of I. (As noted in Remark 1, excluding dangling states from I reveals more dependency.)

For the iterative computation, transition functions are updated in every it-eration by eliminating dependent state variables with the latest dependency functions. Combinational dependency is then obtained for the new set of tran-sition functions. Unlike the gfp iterations, the obtained functional dependency in the ith iteration may not be an invariant for the following iterations because the derived dependency may be valid only in the state subspace spanned by $\{s_\varphi^{(i-1)}\}$. As the state subspace changes over the iterations due to different selec-tions of independent state variables, the dependency may need to be rectified. Notice that the set of functional independents may not increase monotonically during the iterations. This non-convergent phenomenon is due to the existence of the don't-care choices of $\theta^{(i)}$ in addition to the imperfect information about the currently reachable state set. Therefore, additional requirements need to be

SequentialDependencyLfp
  input: a state transition system $\mathcal{M} = (I, r, s, \delta, \lambda)$
  output: a dependency triplet $(\delta_\phi, \delta_\varphi, \theta)$ for δ
  begin
  01   $i := 0;\ (s_\phi^{(0)}, s_\varphi^{(0)}, \theta^{(0)}) := InitialDependency(I)$
  02   **repeat**
  03     $i := i + 1$
  04     $\delta^{(i)} := \delta(r, \langle \theta^{(i-1)}(s_\varphi^{(i-1)}); s_\varphi^{(i-1)} \rangle)$
  05     $(\delta_\phi^{(i)}, \delta_\varphi^{(i)}, \theta^{(i)}) := CombinationalDependencyReuse(\delta^{(i)}, \theta^{(i-1)})$
  06   **until** $\theta^{(i)} = \theta^{(i-1)}$
  07   **return** $(\delta_\phi^{(i)}, \delta_\varphi^{(i)}, \theta^{(i)})$
  end

Fig. 3. Algorithm: SequentialDependencyLfp.

imposed to guarantee termination. Here we request that, after a certain number of iterations, the set of independent state variables increase monotonically until $\theta^{(i)}$ can be reused in the next iteration, that is, the fixed point is reached. The algorithm is outlined in Figure 3. To simplify the presentation, it contains only the iterations where $\{s_\varphi^{(i)}\}$ increases monotonically. Procedure *CombinationalDependencyReuse* is the same as *CombinationalDependency* except that it tries to maximally reuse the dependency functions provided in its second argument.

In theory, the optimality of the lfp calculation lies somewhere between that of the gfp calculation and that of the most general computation with reachability analysis. Since not all dependency in $\mathcal{M}$ can be detected by the lfp procedure due to the imperfect information about the reachable states, the algorithm is incomplete in detecting dependency. To make it complete, reachability analysis should be incorporated. We postpone this integration to the next section and phrase it in the context of verification reduction.

Remark 2. Notice that when $\theta^{(i)}$'s are restricted to consisting of only identity functions and/or complementary identity ones, refinement relation $\sqsubseteq$ among transition functions reduces to an equivalence relation; the lfp calculation of sequential dependency reduces to the detection of equivalent state variables. Hence, detecting signal correspondence [9] is a special case of our formulation.

4   Verification Reduction

Here we focus on the reduction for safety property verification, where reachability analysis is the core computation. The verification problem asks if a state transition system $\mathcal{M} = (I, r, s, \delta, \lambda)$ satisfies a safety property P, denoted as $\mathcal{M} \models P$, for all of its reachable states.

Suppose that $(\delta_\phi, \delta_\varphi, \theta)$ is a dependency triplet of δ; let s_ϕ and s_φ be the corresponding state variables of δ_ϕ and δ_φ, respectively. To represent the reachable state set, either s or s_φ can be selected as the basis. Essentially, $R(s) = Expand(R^\perp(s_\varphi), (s_\phi, s_\varphi, \theta)) = R^\perp(s_\varphi) \wedge \bigwedge_i (s_{\phi i} \equiv \theta_i(s_\varphi))$, where R and $R^\perp$ are the characteristic functions representing the reachable state sets in

ComputeReachWithDependencyReduction
    input: a state transition system $\mathcal{M} = (I, r, s, \delta, \lambda)$
    output: the set R of reachable states of $\mathcal{M}$
    begin
    01   $i := 0;\ (s_\phi^{(0)}, s_\varphi^{(0)}, \theta^{(0)}) := \textit{InitialDependency}(I)$
    02   $I^{\perp_0} := I[\{s_\varphi^{(0)}\}/\{s\}]$
    03   $R^{\perp_0} := I^{\perp_0};\ F^{\perp_0} := I^{\perp_0}$
    04   **repeat**
    05     $i := i + 1$
    06     $\delta^{(i)} := \delta(r, \langle \theta^{(i-1)}(s_\varphi^{(i-1)}); s_\varphi^{(i-1)} \rangle)$
    07     $(\delta_\phi^{(i)}, \delta_\varphi^{(i)}, \theta^{(i)}) := \textit{CombinationalDependencyReach}(\delta^{(i)}, \theta^{(i-1)}, R^{\perp_{i-1}})$
    08     $T^{\perp_i} := \textit{Image}(\delta_\varphi^{(i)}, F^{\perp_{i-1}})$
    09     $s_\nu := s_\varphi^{(i)} \backslash s_\varphi^{(i-1)};\ \theta_\nu := s_\nu$'s corresponding functions in $\theta^{(i-1)}$
    10     $R^{\perp_{i-1}} := \textit{Expand}(R^{\perp_{i-1}}, (s_\nu, s_\varphi^{(i-1)}, \theta_\nu))$
    11     $R^{\perp_{i-1}} := R^{\perp_{i-1}}[\{s_\varphi^{(i)}\}/\{s_\varphi^{(i)} \cup s_\varphi^{(i-1)}\}]$
    12     $F^{\perp_i} := \text{simplify } T^{\perp_i} \text{ with } R^{\perp_{i-1}} \text{ as don't care}$
    13     $R^{\perp_i} := R^{\perp_{i-1}} \cup T^{\perp_i}$
    14   **until** $R^{\perp_i} = R^{\perp_{i-1}}$
    15   **return** $\textit{Expand}(R^{\perp_i}, (s_\phi^{(i)}, s_\varphi^{(i)}, \theta^{(i)}))$
    end

Fig. 4. Algorithm: ComputeReachWithDependencyReduction.

the total space and, respectively, in the reduced space spanned by s_φ. Let $P(s)$ denote the states that satisfy P. Checking whether $R(s) \Rightarrow P(s)$ is equivalent to checking whether $R^\perp(s_\varphi) \Rightarrow P^\perp(s_\varphi)$, where $P^\perp(s_\varphi) = P(\langle \theta(s_\varphi); s_\varphi \rangle)$. Hence, the verification problem can be carried out solely over the reduced space. As noted in Remark 1, the set I of initial states might require special handling.

For given dependency, reachability analysis can be carried out solely upon the reduced basis. The validity of the given dependency can be tested in every iteration of the reachability analysis as was done in [11]. Below we concentrate on the cases where dependency is not given. We show how the detection of functional dependency can be embedded into and simplify the reachability analysis.

To analyze the reachability of a transition system with unknown dependency, two approaches can be taken. One is to find the sequential dependency with the forementioned gfp and/or lfp calculation, and then perform reachability analysis on the reduced state space based on the obtained dependency. The other is to embed the dependency detection into the reachability analysis as an on-the-fly reduction. Since the former is straightforward, we only detail the latter. Figure 4 sketches the algorithm. Procedure *CombinationalDependencyReach* is similar to *CombinationalDependencyReuse* with two exceptions: First, the derived dependency is with respect to the reached state set provided in the third argument. Second, the set of independent state variables needs not increase monotonically since the termination condition has been taken care of by the reached state sets. In each iteration of the state traversal, the previously reached state set R is adjusted (by the expansion and projection operations) to a new basis according to the derived dependency triplet.

5   Experimental Results

The forementioned algorithms have been implemented in the VIS [4] environment. Experiments were conducted on a Sun machine with a 900-MHz CPU and 2-Gb memory. Three sets of experiments have results shown in Tables 1, 2, and 3, respectively. Table 1 demonstrates the relative power of exploiting dependency by the detection of signal correspondence, the gfp, and lfp calculations of sequential dependency. Table 2 compares their applicabilities in the equivalence checking problem. Finally, Table 3 shows how reachability analysis can benefit from our computation of functional dependency. In the experiments, all the approaches under comparison use the same BDD ordering. In addition, no reordering is invoked.

Table 1. Comparisons of Capabilities of Discovering Dependency.

Circuit	State Var.	Signal Corr. [9]				Seq. Dep. Gfp				Seq. Dep. Lfp			
		indp.	iter.	mem. (Mb)	time (sec)	indp.	iter.	mem. (Mb)	time (sec)	indp.	iter.	mem. (Mb)	time (sec)
s298-rt	34 (14)	31	5	10	0.3	**23**	2	23	1.6	24	10	41	6.2
s499-rt	41 (22)	41	21	13	1.6	**29**	1	23	11.6	**29**	22	23	8.2
s510-rt	34 (6)	32	4	13	0.4	**21**	2	51	17.5	23	6	58	81.1
s526n-rt	64 (21)	55	4	13	1.0	**37**	2	60	104.2	40	14	58	26.8
s635-rt	51 (32)	50	16	13	0.6	**34**	2	13	2.8	**34**	33	21	7.4
s838.1-rt	73 (32)	48	20	13	1.5	**33**	1	22	3.7	**33**	46	21	18.3
s991-rt	42 (19)	24	2	13	0.5	21	2	21	1.4	**20**	2	21	1.4
mult16a-rt	106 (16)	66	6	13	0.9	75	2	13	1.0	**61**	8	13	4.6
tbk-rt	49 (5)	49	2	49	6.8	**13**	4	62	264.1	21	3	59	48.4
s3271	116	**114**	6	29	2.1	116	0	29	3.0	**114**	6	45	12.6
s4863	104	81	3	47	4.7	81	1	69	178.7	**75**	3	47	14.5
s5378	179	163	12	37	6.5	155	2	51	15.9	**154**	14	51	43.1
s9234.1	211	188	18	99	79.5	189	2	97	250.2	**184**	38	99	967.6
s13207	669	303	16	138	95.6	460	5	111	384.6	**263**	37	100	836.0
s15850	597	431	24	142	221.7	569	3	134	1487.1	**315**	32	142	1441.0
s35932	1728	**1472**	31	281	599.8	1728	0	146	34091.5	–	–	–	> 10^5
s38584	1452	869	17	303	525.5	1440	1	155	4103.3	**849**	25	303	22001.1
8085	193	91	15	65	28.9	193	0	70	42.4	**79**	17	63	64.3

Compared in Table 1 are three approaches: the computation of signal correspondence [9], the gfp, and lfp calculations of sequential dependency. The first two columns list the benchmark circuits and their sizes in state variables. The original sizes of retimed circuits (for timing optimization) are listed in the following parentheses. For each compared approach, four columns in order list the sizes of the computed independent state variables, the required numbers of iterations, memory usage, and CPU time. Among these three approaches, the minimum sizes of independent variables are highlighted in bold. It is evident from Table 1 that the lfp calculation of sequential dependency subsumes the detection of signal correspondence in both generality and optimality. On the other hand, the powers of the lfp and gfp calculations are incomparable in practice. They have different directions of approximating reachable state sets. For the gfp calculation, the unreachable state set is gradually pruned each time dependency functions are substituted backward. For the lfp one, the reachable state set grows with the iterative computation. It turns out that the gfp computation is very effective in exploiting dependency for retimed circuits. For instance, in circuit tbk-rt, 13 variables are identified as independents by the gfp calculation, compared to 24 by the lfp one. In general, the gfp computation uses much fewer iterations than the other two approaches. In contrast, the lfp calculation outperforms the other two approaches in circuits not retimed. The table also reveals that all the approaches do not suffer from memory explosion. Rather, the time consumption may be a concern in the gfp and lfp calculations of sequential dependency. This is understandable because testing the refinement relation is more general and complicated than testing the equivalence relation used in the detection of signal correspondence. Fortunately, the tradeoff between quality and time can be easily controlled, for example, by imposing k-substitutability, which uses up to k functions to substitute a dependent function. With our formulation, dependencies that were underivable before, due to the limitation of reachability analysis on large transition systems, can now be computed efficiently.

Table 2. Comparisons of Capabilities of Checking Equivalence.

Circuit	State Var.	Signal Corr. [9]				Seq. Dep. Gfp				Seq. Dep. Lfp			
		indp.	iter.	mem. (Mb)	time (sec)	indp.	iter.	mem. (Mb)	time (sec)	indp.	iter.	mem. (Mb)	time (sec)
s298	14+34	39	5	10	0.5	37	2	21	1.5	**30**	13	31	4.4
s499	22+41	63	21	14	3.1	43	2	38	7.3	**42**	22	45	23.6
s510	6+34	38	4	13	0.6	**27**	2	50	25.9	29	5	36	39.8
s526n	21+64	69	8	13	2.4	58	2	59	121.9	**50**	12	58	31.8
s635	32+51	66	31	13	7.8	66	1	21	1.4	**51**	33	25	9.1
s838.1	32+73	78	31	25	16.8	65	2	48	4.2	**59**	47	37	22.5
s991	19+42	42	2	22	1.5	40	2	38	2.5	**39**	3	41	5.4
mult16a	16+106	82	6	14	4.6	91	2	14	1.7	**77**	8	26	5.1
tbk	5+49	54	2	44	5.5	**17**	4	61	175.6	25	3	59	86.4

With similar layout to Table 1, Table 2 compares the applicabilities of these three approaches to the equivalence checking problem. Here a product machine is built upon a circuit and its retimed version. As noted earlier, the gfp calculation itself cannot prove the equivalence between two systems. It, essentially, computes the dependency inside each individual system, but not the interdependency between them. On the other hand, the detection of signal correspondence can rarely prove equivalence unless the two systems under comparison are almost functionally identical. In contrast, the lfp calculation of sequential dependency can easily prove the equivalence between two systems where one is forwardly retimed from the other, and vice versa. Arbitrary retiming, however, may cause a failure, although in principle there always exists a lfp calculation that can conclude the equivalence. In Table 2, since the retiming operations on the retimed circuits involve both forward and backward moves, none of the approaches can directly conclude the equivalences. However, as can be seen, the lfp calculation can compactly condense the product machines.

Although detecting dependency can reduce state space, it is not clear if the BDD sizes for the dependency functions and the rewritten transition functions are small enough to benefit reachability analysis. In Table 3, we justify that it indeed can improve the analysis. Some hard instances for state traversal are

Table 3. Comparisons of Capabilities of Analyzing Reachability.

Circuit	Iter.	R.A. w/o Dep. Reduction				R.A. w Dep. Reduction			
		peak (bdd nodes)	reached (bdd nodes)	mem. (Mb)	time (sec)	peak (bdd nodes)	reached (bdd nodes)	mem. (Mb)	time (sec)
s3271	4	28819301	16158242	620	2784.1	18843837	10746053	415	1082.6
s4863	2	18527781	248885	365	404.8	549006	8772	67	13.1
s5378	2	–	–	> 2000	–	1151439	113522	70	21.5
s15850	15	29842889	9961945	653	21337.4	17667076	6356714	463	8175.0
8085	50	16663749	1701604	390	24280.2	7830602	1338322	212	4640.1

studied. We compare reachability analyses without and with on-the-fly reduction using functional dependency. In the comparison, both analyses have the same implementation except switching off and on the reduction option. The second column of Table 3 shows the steps for (partial) state traversal. For each reachability analysis, four columns in order shows the peak number of live BDD nodes, the size of the BDD representing the final reached state set, memory usage, and CPU time. It is apparent that, with the help of functional dependency, the reachability analysis yields substantial savings in both memory and time consumptions, compared to the analysis without reduction.

6   Comparisons with Related Work

Among previous studies [11, 8] on exploiting functional dependency, the one closest to ours is [8] while functional dependency in [11] is assumed to be given. The method proposed in [8] is similar to our reachability analysis with on-the-fly reduction. However, several differences need to be addressed. First, previous dependency was drawn entirely from the currently reached state set (using functional deduction) rather than from the transition functions. Thus, in each iteration of their reachability analysis, image computation need to be done before the detection of new functional dependency. The image computation rarely benefits from functional dependency. In contrast, our approach is more effective because the dependency is discovered before the image computation, which is performed on the reduced basis. Second, as previous dependency was obtained from a currently reached state set, not from transition functions, it is not as robust as ours to remain valid through the following iterations. Third, the prior method cannot compute functional dependency without reachability analysis while our formulation can be used as a stand-alone technique. Also, we identify a new initial set of non-dangling states. It uncovers more dependency to be exploited.

For related work specific to sequential equivalence checking, we mention [16, 1, 18, 9]. Among them, the work of [9] is the most relevant to ours; it is a special case of our lfp calculation as noted in Remark 2. While these prior efforts focus on equivalence checking, ours is more general for safety property checking.

7   Conclusions and Future Work

We formulate the dependency among a collection of functions based on a refinement relation. When applied to state transition systems, it allows the detection of functional dependency without knowing reached state sets. With an integration into a reachability analysis, it can be used as a complete verification procedure with the power of on-the-fly reduction. Our formulation unifies the work of [9] and [8] in the verification framework. In application to the equivalence checking problem, our method bridges the complexity gap between combinational and sequential equivalence checking. Preliminary experiments show promising results in detecting dependency and verification reduction.

As a future research direction, our results might be reformulated in a SAT-solving framework. A path similar to that of [3], where van Eijk's algorithm was adjusted, could be taken to prove safety properties by strengthened induction. Because our approach may impose more invariants than just signal correspondence, we believe that SAT-based verification can benefit from our results.

References

1. P. Ashar, A. Gupta, and S. Malik. Using complete-1-distinguishability for FSM equivalence checking. In *Proc. ICCAD*, pages 346–353, 1996.
2. C. Berthet, O. Coudert, and J.-C. Madre. New ideas on symbolic manipulations of finite state machines. In *Proc. ICCD*, pages 224–227, 1990.
3. P. Bjesse and K. Claessen. SAT-based verification without state space traversal. In *Proc. FMCAD*, pages 372–389, 2000.
4. R. K. Brayton, et al. VIS: a system for verification and synthesis. In *Proc. CAV*, pages 428–432, 1996.
5. F. M. Brown. *Boolean Reasoning: The Logic of Boolean Equations*. Dover Publications, 2003.
6. R. E. Bryant. Graph-based algorithms for Boolean function manipulation. *IEEE Trans. Computers*, pages 677–691, August 1986.
7. E. M. Clarke, O. Grumberg, and D. A. Peled. *Model Checking*. MIT Press, 1999.
8. C. A. J. van Eijk and J. A. G. Jess. Exploiting functional dependencies in finite state machine verification. In *Proc. European Design & Test Conf.*, pages 9–14, 1996.
9. C. A. J. van Eijk. Sequential equivalence checking based on structural similarities. *IEEE Trans. Computer-Aided Design*, pages 814–819, July 2000.
10. T. Filkorn. Symbolische methoden für die verifikation endlicher zustandssysteme. Ph.D. thesis. Institut für Informatik der Technischen Universität München, 1992.
11. A. J. Hu and D. L. Dill. Reducing BDD size by exploiting functional dependencies. In *Proc. DAC*, pages 266–271, 1993.
12. R. P. Kurshan. *Computer-Aided Verification of Coordinating Processes*. Princeton University Press, 1994.
13. B. Lin and A. R. Newton. Exact redundant state registers removal based on binary decision diagrams. In *Proc. Int'l Conf. VLSI*, pages 277–286, 1991.
14. C. E. Leiserson and J. B. Saxe. Optimizing synchronous systems. *J. VLSI Computer Syst.*, vol. 1, no. 1, pp. 41–67, 1983.
15. E. Marczewski. Independence in algebras of sets and Boolean algebra. *Fundamenta Mathematicae*, vol. 48, pages 135–145, 1960.
16. S. Quer, G. Cabodi, P. Camurati, L. Lavagno, and R. Brayton. Verification of similar FSMs by mixing incremental re-encoding, reachability analysis, and combinational check. *Formal Methods in System Design*, vol. 17, pages 107–134, 2000.
17. E. Sentovich, H. Toma, and G. Berry. Latch optimization in circuits generated from high-level descriptions. In *Proc. ICCAD*, pages 428–435, 1996.
18. D. Stoffel and W. Kunz. Record & play: A structural fixed point iteration for sequential circuit verification. In *Proc. ICCAD*, pages 394–399, 1997.

Verification via Structure Simulation

Niel Immerman[1,*], Alexander Rabinovich[2], Thomas W. Reps[3,**],
Mooly Sagiv[2,**], and Great Yorsh[2,***]

[1] Dept. of Comp. Sci., Univ. of Massachusetts
immerman@cs.umass.edu
[2] School of Comp. Sci., Tel Aviv Univ.
{rabinoa,msagiv,gretay}@post.tau.ac.il
[3] Comp. Sci. Dept., Univ. of Wisconsin
reps@cs.wisc.edu

Abstract. This paper shows how to harness decision procedures to automatically verify safety properties of imperative programs that perform dynamic storage allocation and destructive updating of structure fields. Decidable logics that can express reachability properties are used to state properties of linked data structures, while guaranteeing that the verification method always terminates. The main technical contribution is a method of structure simulation in which a set of *original* structures that we wish to model, e.g., doubly linked lists, nested linked lists, binary trees, etc., are mapped to a set of *tractable* structures that can be reasoned about using decidable logics. Decidable logics that can express reachability are rather limited in the data structures that they can directly model. For instance, our examples use the logic *MSO-E*, which can only model function graphs; however, the simulation technique provides an indirect way to model additional data structures.

1 Introduction

In this paper, we explore the extent to which decidable logics can help us check properties of programs that perform dynamic storage allocation and destructive updating of structure fields. One of our key contributions is a method of structure simulation in which a set of *original* structures that we wish to model, e.g., doubly linked lists, nested linked lists, binary trees, etc., are mapped to a set of *tractable* structures that can be reasoned about using decidable logics.

1.1 Motivation

Automatically proving safety and liveness properties of sequential and concurrent programs that permit dynamic storage allocation and low-level pointer manipulations is challenging. Dynamic allocation causes the state space to be infinite. Also, abstract-datatype operations are implemented using loops, procedure calls, and sequences of

---

* Supported by NSF grant CCR-0207373 and a Guggenheim fellowship.
** Supported by ONR contract N00014-01-1-0796 and the von Humboldt Foundation.
*** Supported by the Israel Science Foundation.

R. Alur and D.A. Peled (Eds.): CAV 2004, LNCS 3114, pp. 281–294, 2004.

low-level pointer manipulations; consequently, it is hard to prove that a data-structure invariant is reestablished once a sequence of operations is finished [7].

Reachability is crucial for reasoning about linked data structures. For example, to verify that a memory configuration contains no garbage elements, we must show that every element is reachable from some program variable. Specifying such properties presents a challenge because it requires a logic with the ability to quantify over unbounded resources and to express reachability properties. Even simple decidable fragments of first-order logic become undecidable when reachability is added [9]. The reader may wonder how undecidable logics can be useful for automatic verification.

1.2   An Overview of the Approach

In this section, we illustrate the simulation technique by showing its applicability to semi-automatic Hoare-style verification. The technique can also be applied to improve the precision of operations used in abstract interpretation [14].

Hoare-Style Verification: Recall that in Hoare-style verification, a programmer expresses partial-correctness requirements of the form $\{pre\}st\{post\}$, where pre and $post$ are logical formulas that express the pre- and post-condition of statement st. To handle loops, it is necessary that loop invariants be provided (also specified as logical formulas). From these annotations, a formula φ is generated, called the *verification condition* of the program; φ is valid if and only if the program is partially correct.

In this paper, we allow pre-conditions, post-conditions, and loop invariants to be specified in FO(TC): first-order formulas with transitive closure. The generated verification condition is also an FO(TC) formula. The logic FO(TC) is natural because it can express pointer dereferencing and dynamic creation of objects and threads. However, validity in this logic is undecidable, and therefore the validity of a program's verification condition cannot be checked directly.

Restricting the Set of Reachable Program States: To perform verification automatically, we will restrict the set of program states sufficiently to make the validity problem for FO(TC) decidable. More precisely, for every program and class of data structures of interest, we choose a designated set of structures C, such that the problem of checking whether a general FO(TC) formula holds for all structures in C is decidable. In other words, we work with FO(TC) formulas, for which the validity problem is undecidable in general, but by restricting our attention to the class of structures in C, we change the problem into one that is decidable.

Simulation Invariants: Because C is defined per class of data structures and per program, we cannot assume that the set C is defined *a priori*. Instead, we assume that the class C is also definable by an FO(TC) formula, i.e., there exists a formula SI such that $\mathcal{A} \in C$ iff $\mathcal{A} \models SI$. SI is called the *simulation invariant*, and is similar to a data-structure invariant or a class invariant. This formula can usually be defined once the data structure that we wish to model is known.

From a logical perspective, restricting attention to structures satisfying SI allows us to check if an $FO(TC)$ property φ holds in all structures in C by showing the validity of

$$SI \Rightarrow \varphi \tag{1}$$

First-Order Reductions: Instead of implementing a decision procedure that is parametric in SI for validity of formulas of the form Eq. (1), we provide a way to translate these formulas automatically into another decidable logic, with an existing decision procedure. We define admissibility conditions that guarantee that an $FO(TC)$ formula of the form Eq. (1) is valid if and only if the corresponding formula in the decidable logic is valid. This allows us to use existing decision procedures to determine the validity of verification conditions. In the paper, we illustrate the method using the decidable logic *MSO-E*, i.e., weak monadic second-order logic on function graphs. $FO(TC)$ formulas over a restricted set of graphs – but including possibly cyclic graphs, and graphs containing nodes that have in-degree greater than one – are translated into *MSO-E* formulas on function graphs. This opens up the possibility to apply *MSO-E* to a larger set of graphs.

Handling Low-Level Mutations: Destructive updates of pointer-valued structure fields might cause the simulation invariant to be violated. Therefore, the verification condition must also check whether the simulation invariant is maintained. For example, we change the requirement for a statement from $\{pre\} st \{post\}$ to $\{pre \wedge SI\} st \{post \wedge SI\}$. This guarantees that the method will never miss an error: it will either detect an error in the specification, or a violation of the simulation invariant by some operation.

Even correct programs can temporarily violate a *data-structure invariant*. That is, a violation of the data-structure invariant need not indicate an error. For example, it is possible to rotate an acyclic singly-linked list by first creating a cycle, and later breaking the cycle. This complicates the task of defining *simulation invariants*. In particular, the user needs to allow simulation invariant SI to be less restrictive than the data-structure invariant for the data-structure of interest. Still, we believe that this approach can handle realistic programs that manipulate their data structures in a limited way, e.g., when the number of mutated pointer fields is limited. The programmer can specify an SI that allows sufficient flexibility, and assert that the data-structure invariant is reestablished at certain ("stable") states.

1.3   Main Results

The contributions of this paper can be summarized as follows:

- We state the precise requirements that allow the method to be applied to verify properties of imperative programs written in a programming language with pointers and destructive updates (Section 2.2 ; for proofs see the full version of the paper).
- We show that programs that manipulate commonly used data structures, such as singly-linked (including cyclic and shared) lists, doubly-linked lists, and trees with unbounded branching, satisfy the above requirements (Section 2.3). (We note that for structures that are already tractable, such as singly linked lists, simple trees, etc., our methods work trivially.)

- In Section 3.1, we show how to use our method for Hoare-style verification. We assume that the programmer specifies loop invariants and pre- and post- conditions for procedures.
- In Section 3.2, we show how to use our method for automatic verification using abstract interpretation. This eliminates the need to provide loop invariants, but may only establish weaker safety properties than those proved by Hoare-style verification. This fills in the missing piece of the algorithm presented in [14], which requires a decidable logic to compute the *best* abstract transformer automatically. This allows us to apply the algorithm from [14] to imperative programs that perform destructive updates. We have implemented this using TVLA and MONA.

2   Simulation

In this section, we define the notation used, and describe the simulation methodology in detail.

2.1   Notation

For any vocabulary τ, let $\mathcal{L}(\tau)$ denote a logic with vocabulary τ. In our examples, $\mathcal{L}(\tau)$ is first-order logic with transitive closure. We allow arbitrary uses of a binary transitive closure operator, TC; $\mathrm{TC}_{u,u'}[\varphi]$ denotes the reflexive, transitive closure of binary relation $\varphi(u, u')$ [8]. We omit the subscript from $\mathrm{TC}_{u,u'}$ whenever it is clear from the context. In principle, however, we could use other logics, such as second-order logic. Let STRUCT$[\tau]$ denote the set of finite structures over vocabulary τ. We denote the set of structures that satisfy a closed formula φ by $[\![\varphi]\!] \subseteq$ STRUCT$[\tau]$.

Let Org be a class of *original* structures. Let $\tau_{Org} = \{R_1^{a_1}, \ldots R_k^{a_k}\}$ be the vocabulary of Org, where the arity of the relation symbol R_i is a_i. Note that τ_{Org} may be arbitrarily rich. Org is a subset of STRUCT$[\tau_{Org}]$. Not all structures of Org can be simulated. We assume that the user provides a *simulation invariant*, SI, that defines the subclass $[\![SI]\!]$ of Org to be simulated. SI is a global invariant that must hold throughout the program.

Example 1. Let Org be the set of forests of binary trees, represented as logical structures over $\tau_{Org} = \{l^2, r^2\}$ where the two binary relations l and r denote pointers to the left and right subtree. SI, shown in the third column of Table 1, specifies that l and r are partial functions, and forbids structures with shared nodes or cycles created by l and r pointers. It is clear that all forests of binary trees satisfy this requirement. A structure in τ_{Org} satisfies SI if and only if it represents a forest of binary trees.

We use this example of binary trees throughout the section to demonstrate our method. We use the notation $TREE\{l, r\}$ (and other similar notation in Section 2.3), in the same manner as a data-type in a programming language, and not a specific object of the tree data-type.

Let Rep be the set of *representation* structures, and let $\mathcal{D}$ be a decidable logic over Rep. That is, we have an algorithm that halts on all inputs and tells us for every formula $\psi \in \mathcal{D}$ whether ψ holds for all structures in Rep.

In our examples, *Rep* will always be a set of (finite) function graphs, i.e., every vertex has at most one edge leaving it. Let τ_{Rep} denote the vocabulary of *Rep*. We illustrate our method by fixing $\mathcal{D}$ to be *MSO-E*, which is weak monadic second-order logic on function graphs. The vocabulary τ_{Rep} includes one binary relation symbol, E, which must be interpreted by a relation that is a partial function. Arbitrary unary relation symbols and constant symbols may be included. Reachability is expressible in *MSO-E* using second-order quantification. *MSO-E* is decidable by reduction to the monadic second-order theory of one unary function [11].

In addition to the simulation invariant, *SI*, we assume that the user provides a *representation invariant*, *RI*, that defines the subclass $[\![RI]\!]$ of *Rep*.

2.2   Simulation Methodology

We define a first-order mapping, $\eta : \text{STRUCT}[\tau_{Rep}] \to \text{STRUCT}[\tau_{Org}]$.

Definition 1. (First-order mapping η) *Let $\mathcal{A} \in \text{STRUCT}[\tau_{Rep}]$ be a structure with universe $|\mathcal{A}|$. For each relation symbol $R_i \in \tau_{Org}$ of arity a_i, η provides a formula $\delta[R_i](v_1, \ldots v_{a_i}) \in \mathcal{L}(\tau_{Rep})$. The structure $\eta(\mathcal{A})$ has the same universe as $\mathcal{A}$[1]. The relation symbol R_i is interpreted in $\eta(\mathcal{A})$ as follows:*

$$R_i^{\eta(\mathcal{A})} \quad = \quad \left\{ \langle e_1, \ldots, e_{a_i} \rangle \in |\mathcal{A}|^{a_i} \mid \mathcal{A} \models \delta[R_i](e_1, \ldots, e_{a_i}) \right\} .$$

Example 2. The second column of Table 1 lists the δ formulas for the main original data structures that we consider. The representation of the $TREE\{l, r\}$ example uses $\tau_{Rep} = \{E^2, L^1, R^1\}$. For example, $\delta[l](v_1, v_2)$ is the formula $E(v_2, v_1) \wedge L(v_2)$. Intuitively, the simulation reverses the l- and r-edges (recording them as E-edges), and marks each node that was a target of an l-edge or r-edge with L or R, respectively.

The first-order mapping on structures, η, defines a dual, first-order translation on formulas in the opposite direction, $\overline{\eta} : \mathcal{L}(\tau_{Org}) \to \mathcal{L}(\tau_{Rep})$.

Definition 2. (First-order translation $\overline{\eta}$) *For any formula $\varphi \in \mathcal{L}(\tau_{Org})$, $\overline{\eta}(\varphi) \in \mathcal{L}(\tau_{Rep})$ is the result of replacing each occurrence in φ of $R_i(t_1, \ldots, t_{a_i})$, by the formula $\delta[R_i](t_1, \ldots, t_{a_i})$.*

It follows immediately that for all $\mathcal{A} \in \text{STRUCT}[\tau_{Rep}]$ and $\varphi \in \mathcal{L}(\tau_{Org})$,

$$\mathcal{A} \models \overline{\eta}(\varphi) \quad \Leftrightarrow \quad \eta(\mathcal{A}) \models \varphi . \tag{2}$$

Definition 2 and Eq. (2) follow from [8, Proposition 3.5] which can be easily extended to handle the transitive-closure operator allowed in $\mathcal{L}(\tau_{Org})$.

See Figure 1 for a sketch of the mapping η from *Rep* to *Org* and the corresponding dual $\overline{\eta}$ from $\mathcal{L}(\tau_{Org}) \to \mathcal{L}(\tau_{Rep})$. To guarantee that queries over the original structures can be precisely answered in the representation, the following restrictions are imposed on η, *SI*, and *RI*.

---

[1] For simplicity, we make this same-universe assumption in this paper. Actually first-order mappings may change the size of the universe by any polynomial function [8].

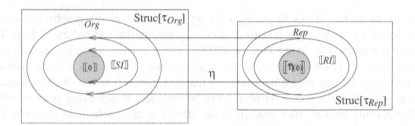

Fig. 1. *SI* defines a class of structures that can be mapped to *Rep*.

Definition 3. (Admissibility requirement) *Given a first-order mapping*
$\eta: STRUCT[\tau_{Rep}] \to STRUCT[\tau_{Org}]$, *a simulation invariant SI such that* $[\![SI]\!] \subseteq Org$,
and a representation invariant RI such that $[\![RI]\!] \subseteq Rep$, *we say that* $\langle \eta, SI, RI \rangle$ *is*
admissible if the following properties hold:

Well-Definedness of η. *For all* $S_r \in Rep$ *such that* $S_r \models RI$, $\eta(S_r) \models SI$
Ontoness of η. *For all* $S_o \in Org$ *such that* $S_o \models SI$, *there exists a structure* $S_r \in Rep$
  such that $S_r \models RI$ *and* $\eta(S_r) = S_o$.

In fact, for all examples shown in Table 1, we do not provide *RI* explicitly, but
define it to be $\bar{\eta}(SI)$. The following lemma provides a sufficient condition for admissibility of $\langle \eta, SI, \bar{\eta}(SI) \rangle$.

Lemma 1. *If for all* $S_o \in Org$ *such that* $S_o \models SI$, *there exists* $S_r \in Rep$ *such that*
$\eta(S_r) = S_o$, *then* $\langle \eta, SI, \bar{\eta}(SI) \rangle$ *is admissible.*

Admissibility guarantees that each query in the original language is translated by $\bar{\eta}$ to
a query in the representation language, where it can be answered using the decision
procedure:

Theorem 1. (Simulation Theorem) *Assume that* $\langle \eta, SI, RI \rangle$ *defines an admissible*
simulation. Then for any $\varphi \in \mathcal{L}(\tau_{Org})$, $SI \Rightarrow \varphi$ *holds in Org iff* $RI \Rightarrow \bar{\eta}(\varphi)$ *holds in*
Rep.

Corollary 1. *Assume that (i)* $\langle \eta, SI, RI \rangle$ *defines an admissible simulation, (ii) for all*
$\varphi \in \mathcal{L}(\tau_{Org})$, $RI \Rightarrow \bar{\eta}(\varphi) \in \mathcal{D}$, *and (iii)* $\mathcal{D}$ *is decidable over Rep. Then there exists an*
algorithm that for any $\varphi \in \mathcal{L}(\tau_{Org})$, *checks whether* $SI \Rightarrow \varphi$ *holds in Org.*

A simpler way to express condition (i) is with the equation, $[\![SI]\!] = \eta([\![RI]\!])$. We
show that condition (i) holds for all examples in Section 2.3. From Definition 2 and
Eq. (2), it immediately follows that $\bar{\eta}(\mathcal{L}(\tau_{Org})) \subseteq \mathcal{L}(\tau_{Rep})$, which in turn is contained
in monadic second-order logic over one binary relation E (not necessarily interpreted
as a partial function). Because in all of our examples *RI* ensures that E is a partial
function, $RI \Rightarrow \bar{\eta}(\mathcal{L}(\tau_{Org}))$ is in *MSO-E*. Thus, condition (ii) holds for all of the
examples that we consider. This allows us to use a decision procedure for *MSO-E* in our
examples, to check validity of FO(TC) formulas over $[\![SI]\!]$. Instead of implementing a
decision procedure for *MSO-E*, we have implemented a translation of *MSO-E* formulas

into *WS2S* (using the simulation method, as described in the full paper), and used an existing decision procedure MONA [5] for *WS2S* logic.

Remark. If the decidable logic $\mathcal{D}$ places a syntactic restriction on formulas, as is the case for $\exists \forall (\text{DTC}[E])$ [9], then condition (ii) of Corollary 1 may not be satisfied. In such cases, it may be possible to replace $\bar{\eta}$ (Definition 2) with an algorithm (or a set of heuristics) that generates a formula $\psi \in \mathcal{D}$ that is equivalent to $RI \Rightarrow \bar{\eta}(\varphi)$ over *Rep*. From our experience, the main difficulty is to ensure that $\neg RI$ is in $\mathcal{D}$. This problem can be addressed by choosing a stronger representation invariant RI with $[\![RI]\!] \subseteq [\![\bar{\eta}(SI)]\!]$, such that $RI \in \mathcal{D}$, and a corresponding simulation invariant SI' (stronger than the original SI), and proving admissibility directly from Definition 3, rather than by Lemma 1.

2.3 Simulating Commonly Used Data Structures

We distinguish between families of data structures according to the field-pointers in use and their intended meaning. Table 1 shows the simulation-specific definitions required for each family of data structures: (i) the translation $\bar{\eta}$; and (ii) the invariant SI.

Table 1. Commonly used data structures and their simulations. The formula $func[f]$ for some field-pointer f is defined by $\forall v, v_1, v_2 : f(v, v_1) \wedge f(v, v_2) \Rightarrow v_1 = v_2$; it ensures that f is interpreted as a partial function; the formula $uns[\psi(v_1, v_2)]$ for some formula ψ is defined by $\forall v, v_1, v_2 : \psi(v_1, v) \wedge \psi(v_2, v) \Rightarrow v_1 = v_2$; the formula $acyc[\psi(v_1, v_2)]$ for some formula ψ is defined by $\forall v_1, v_2 : \psi(v_1, v_2) \Rightarrow \neg TC[\psi](v_2, v_1)$. The formula $unique[p]$ for some unary predicate p is defined by $\forall v_1, v_2 : p(v_1) \wedge p(v_2) \Rightarrow v_1 = v_2$.

Data Structure	Translation ($\bar{\eta}$)	Simulation Invariant (SI)
$SLL\{n\}$	$n(v_1, v_2) \mapsto E(v_1, v_2)$	$func[n]$
$TREE\{l, r\}$	$l(v_1, v_2) \mapsto E(v_2, v_1) \wedge L(v_2)$ $r(v_1, v_2) \mapsto E(v_2, v_1) \wedge R(v_2)$	$func[l] \wedge func[r]$ $\wedge uns[l(v_1, v_2) \vee r(v_1, v_2)]$ $\wedge acyc[l(v_1, v_2) \vee r(v_1, v_2)]$
$UBTREE\{s\}$	$s(v_1, v_2) \mapsto E(v_2, v_1)$	$uns[s] \wedge acyc[s]$
$DLL\{f, b\}$	$f(v_1, v_2) \mapsto E(v_1, v_2)$ $b(v_1, v_2) \mapsto E(v_2, v_1) \wedge B(v_1)$	$\forall v_1, v_2 : b(v_1, v_2) \Rightarrow f(v_2, v_1)$ $\wedge func[f] \wedge func[b] \wedge uns[f]$
$DLL\{f, b\}$ b points to one of $\{p_1, \ldots, p_k\}$	$f(v_1, v_2) \mapsto E(v_1, v_2)$ $b(v_1, v_2) \mapsto f(v_2, v_1) \wedge B(v_1)$ $\vee \bigvee_{i=1,\ldots,k} p_i(v_2) \wedge B_{p_i}(v_1)$	$\forall v_1, v_2 : b(v_1, v_2) \Rightarrow$ $(f(v_2, v_1) \vee \bigvee_{i=1,\ldots,k} p_i(v_2))$ $\wedge func[f] \wedge func[b] \wedge uns[f]$ $\wedge uns[b] \wedge \bigwedge_{i=1,\ldots,k} unique[p_i]$
$DLL\{f, b\}$ b defined by $\varphi(v_1, v_2)$	$f(v_1, v_2) \mapsto E(v_1, v_2)$ $b(v_1, v_2) \mapsto f(v_2, v_1) \wedge B(v_1)$ $\vee B_\varphi(v_1) \wedge \varphi(v_1, v_2)$	$\forall v_1, v_2 : b(v_1, v_2) \Rightarrow$ $(f(v_2, v_1) \vee \varphi(v_1, v_2)) \wedge func[f]$ $\wedge func[b] \wedge uns[f] \wedge uns[b]$

The vocabulary τ_{Org} contains binary predicates that represent field-pointers and unary predicates that represent pointer variables and properties of elements. The names of binary predicates are specific to each example; unary predicates are usually named x, y, p_i. A formula in $\mathcal{D}$ over the vocabulary τ_{Rep} can use all unary predicates from τ_{Org} and additional simulation-specific unary predicates.

SLL{n}. A singly linked list, where n denotes the field-pointer to the next element in the list. *Rep* is the set of all function graphs over τ_{Rep}. The translation $\bar{\eta}$ and the mapping η are identity functions. Because n represents a field-pointer that can point to at most one memory location, SI requires that n be interpreted as a partial function. This simulation invariant allows us to handle any singly-linked list, including cyclic and/or shared lists.

TREE$\{l, r\}$. The standard tree data-structure was explained earlier.

UBTREE$\{s\}$. A tree with unbounded branching, where $s(v_1, v_2)$ is a successor relation: v_2 is a successor of v_1 in the tree. Rep is the set of acyclic function graphs over τ_{Rep}. The simulation simply reverses the edges.

DLL$\{f, b\}$. A doubly linked list, where f and b denote the forward and backward field-pointers. At this point, we refer only to the first simulation of DLL in Table 1; the purpose of other simulations is explained in Section 3.4. τ_{Rep} includes one simulation-specific unary predicate B. $[\![RI]\!]$ is the set of all function graphs over τ_{Rep} such that a graph node labeled with B must not be shared i.e., it may have at most one incoming E-edge.

The simulation invariant ensures that the backward pointer can only point to its f-predecessor (if an element does not have an f-predecessor, its backward pointer must be NULL). The translation represents the binary relation $b(v_1, v_2)$ with a unary predicate $B(v_1)$, which denotes the presence (or absence) of the backward pointer from element v_1.

The full version of the paper contains more complex simulations of generalized trees and undirected graphs.

3   Applications

In this section, we provide motivation for potential applications.

Meaning of Program Statements. We assume that the meaning of every atomic program statement st is expressed as a formula transformer, $wp_{st} \colon \mathcal{L}(\tau) \to \mathcal{L}(\tau)$, which expresses the weakest precondition required for st to produce structures that satisfy a given formula; i.e., for every $\varphi \in \mathcal{L}(\tau)$, the input structure before st satisfies $wp_{st}(\varphi)$ if and only if the resultant structure produced by st satisfies φ.

3.1   Hoare-Style Verification

In Hoare-style verification, the programmer expresses partial-correctness requirements of the form $\{pre\}st\{post\}$, where pre and $post$ are logical formulas in $\mathcal{L}(\tau)$ that express the pre- and post-condition of a statement st. To handle loops, it is required that loop invariants be provided (also specified as logical formulas in $\mathcal{L}(\tau)$).

In conventional Hoare-style verification, the partial correctness of a statement st is ensured by the validity of the formula $pre \Rightarrow wp_{st}(post)$. In our approach, the partial correctness of st is ensured by the validity of the formula $SI \wedge pre \Rightarrow wp_{st}(post \wedge SI)$. The presence of SI on the left-hand side corresponds to an assumption that we are only interested in states in which SI holds; the presence of SI on the right-hand side – within the operator wp_{st} – ensures that the execution of st yields a state in which SI again holds. (This means that the verification system will report an error if execution of st can cause either *post* to be violated or the global invariant SI to be violated.) The partial correctness of sequential composition, conditional statements, and loop invariants is expressed by similar extensions to the standard Hoare-style approach.

3.2 Abstract Interpretation

The abstract-interpretation technique [2] allows conservative automatic verification of partial correctness to be conducted by identifying sound over-approximations to loop invariants. An iterative computation is carried out to determine an appropriate abstract value for each program point. The result at each program point is an abstract value that summarizes the sets of reachable concrete states at that point.

In abstract interpretation we usually assume that the set of potential abstract values forms a lattice A. Also, concrete states can be represented as logical structures over vocabulary τ. We introduce a non-standard requirement that all concrete states manipulated by a correct program satisfy SI. Thus, the abstract-interpretation system needs to issue a warning if this requirement is violated. We formalize this restriction of concrete states to $[\![SI]\!]$ as follows:

A concretization function $\gamma \colon A \to 2^{[\![SI]\!]}$ yields the set of concrete states that an abstract element represents. Similarly, the abstraction function $\alpha \colon 2^{[\![SI]\!]} \to A$ yields the abstract value that represents a set of concrete states. The partial order on A (denoted by $\sqsubseteq$) satisfies $a \sqsubseteq a' \iff \gamma(a) \subseteq \gamma(a')$.

An element $a \in A$ is a **lower bound** of a set $X \subseteq A$ if, for every $x \in X$, $a \sqsubseteq x$. The lattice is closed under a **meet operator**, denoted by $\sqcap$, which yields the greatest lower bound with respect to $\sqsubseteq$; i.e., for every set $X \subseteq A$, $\sqcap X$ is a lower bound of X, and for every lower bound a of X, $a \sqsubseteq \sqcap X$. The concretization and the abstraction functions form a Galois connection between $2^{[\![SI]\!]}$ and A; i.e., for all $a \in A$ and $X \subseteq [\![SI]\!]$, $\alpha(X) \sqsubseteq a \iff X \subseteq \gamma(a)$. An additional assumption that we place on A is that the concretization can be expressed in $\mathcal{L}(\tau)$; i.e., for every $a \in A$, there exists a formula in $\mathcal{L}(\tau)$, denoted by $\widehat{\gamma}(a)$, that exactly represents a: $s \in [\![\widehat{\gamma}(a)]\!]$ if and only if $s \in \gamma(a)$. The tightest over-approximation in A of the set of concrete states specified by a formula φ (denoted by $\widehat{\alpha}(\varphi)$) can be computed by

$$\widehat{\alpha}(\varphi) \stackrel{\text{def}}{=} \sqcap \{a \,|\, (SI \wedge \varphi) \Rightarrow \widehat{\gamma}(a)\}. \tag{3}$$

The following lemma states that $\widehat{\alpha}$ is indeed the tightest over-approximation:

Lemma 2. *For every formula φ, $\widehat{\alpha}(\varphi) = \alpha([\![\varphi]\!])$.*

Now consider a statement st and an abstract value a that denotes the set of states before st. First, as in Section 3.1, we need to ensure that the global invariant SI is maintained by checking the validity of

$$(SI \wedge \widehat{\gamma}(a)) \Rightarrow wp_{st}(SI). \tag{4}$$

This requirement is non-standard in abstract interpretation, and reflects the fact that states violating SI are ignored. Thus, the abstract-interpretation system needs to issue a warning when this condition is violated.

We can also compute the (most-precise) effect in A of a statement st on an abstract input value $a \in A$ as the tightest over-approximation to the strongest post-condition of st:

$$best[st](a) \stackrel{\text{def}}{=} \sqcap\{a' | (SI \wedge \widehat{\gamma}(a)) \Rightarrow wp_{st}(\widehat{\gamma}(a') \wedge SI)\} \tag{5}$$

Not surprisingly, the formulas for abstract interpretation given above are similar to the formulas for Hoare-style verification given in Section 3.1.

In certain circumstances, $\widehat{\gamma}$ and validity checkers automatically yield algorithms for $\widehat{\alpha}(\varphi)$ (Eq. (3)), for checking that a statement st maintains SI (Eq. (4)), and for the abstract interpretation of a given statement in the most precise way (Eq. (5)). In particular, when the abstract domain A is a finite lattice, Eqns. (3), (4), and (5) can be used in a brute-force way (by generating a validity query for all elements in the domain). For more elaborate algorithms that handle finite-height lattices of infinite cardinality, the reader is referred to [12, 14].

3.3 Summary

We now summarize the steps that a user of our approach has to go through to carry out a verification. The user must provide the inputs listed below. The first two inputs are standard for many verification methods. The other inputs are interdependent, as explained later.

1. A scheme for encoding the program's possible memory configurations as logical structures over vocabulary τ_{Org}.
2. A description in $\mathcal{L}(\tau_{Org})$ of the weakest precondition for each statement.
3. A decidable logic $\mathcal{D}$ over Rep.
4. The first-order mapping η.
5. A simulation invariant SI in $\mathcal{L}(\tau_{Org})$.
6. A representation invariant RI in $\mathcal{D}$.

Also, the user must ensure that (i) $\langle \eta, SI, RI \rangle$ is admissible, and (ii) the initial program state satisfies SI.

We have implemented our approach as part of the TVLA system – a parametric system for performing abstract interpretation. The *simulation package* is initialized by reading the definition of τ_{Org}, τ_{Rep}, SI, and tr in FO(TC) from a file provided by the user of TVLA. Currently, it uses *WS2S* as $\mathcal{D}$ and binary trees as Rep, but it could easily be configured to use other decidable logics. The package takes formula $\varphi \in$ FO(TC) and returns a translation into *WS2S*, computed by substitution. We have also implemented a *SymbolicChecker* that interfaces to the MONA tool. SymbolicChecker takes a formula $\varphi \in WS2S$, and checks whether the formula is valid. We have used SymbolicChecker to perform abstract interpretation of sample programs.

3.4 An Example of a Simulation Invariant That Supports Low-Level Heap Mutations

In this section, we show an example program that temporarily violates a data-structure invariant, and show how to gradually generalize the simulation invariant to cope with the low-level mutations in this program.

Table 2. (a) a data type of colored doubly linked lists: each list node is marked with either RED or BLACK. (b) a program that divides a colored doubly linked list into two disjoint lists, pointed to by dllR and dllB, each of which contains nodes of one color only.

``/* dll.h */

enum Color
    {RED, BLACK};

typedef struct node {
    struct node *f, *b;
    enum Color c;
} *DLL;``` | ```/* divide.c */
DLL *dllR, *dllB;
void divide (DLL *x) {
    DLL *t;
    dllB = dllR = NULL;
    while (x != null) {
        if (x->c == RED) {
            x->b = dllR; dllR = x;
        } else {
            x->b = dllB; dllB = x;
        }
        x = x->f;
    }
    if (dllR != NULL) {
        while(dllR->b != NULL) {
            t = dllR; dllR = dllR->b; dllR->f = t;
        }
    }
    if (dllB != NULL) {
        while(dllB->b != NULL) {
            t = dllB; dllB = dllB->b; dllB->f = t;
}}}``` |
| (a) | (b) |

Consider the data-type in Table 2(a) that defines a doubly-linked list with an additional bit for each element, represented by the unary predicates $RED(v)$ and $BLACK(v)$. The program divide (x) in Table 2(b) takes as input a doubly-linked list pointed to by x that may contain both red and black elements. We can verify that this program arranges the elements reachable from x into two disjoint doubly-linked lists pointed to by dllR and dllB, each of which contains elements of only one color. To automatically verify this property using one of the verification methods described above, we need to provide an appropriate simulation invariant.

Basic Simulation. The basic simulation of $DLL\{f, b\}$ in Table 1 defines simulation invariant SI_1. Consider the statement x->b = dllR from the divide (x) program. The weakest precondition of x->b = dllR with the basic simulation invariant SI_1 is $wp_1 \stackrel{\text{def}}{=} \forall v_1, v_2 : x(v_1) \wedge dllR(v_2) \Rightarrow f(v_1, v_2)$. If a structure satisfies wp_1, then the result of applying x->b = dllR satisfies SI_1. However, one of the structures that arises in divide (x) before the statement x->b = dllR does not satisfy wp_1. This means that a result of applying this statement, the structure shown on the left of Fig. 2(b), does not satisfy SI_1. The reason is that the backward pointer from the second element does not point to the predecessor of this element, while SI_1 allows only mutations that result in a structure where the backward pointer is either NULL or points to its f-predecessor. The backward pointer to the element pointed to by dllR cannot be recorded using only the $B(v)$ predicate, provided by the basic simulation.

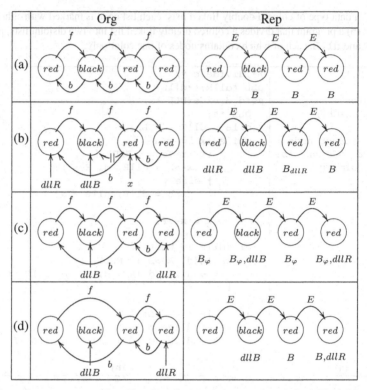

Fig. 2. Example structures produced by the `divide(x)` operation on Red-Black List from Table 2, are shown on the left. The corresponding representation structures are on the right. (a) initial structure and its basic simulation; (b) the structure after two iterations of the first while loop, and its k-bounded simulation with the set of unary predicates $\{dllR, dllB\}$; the symbol $\parallel$ on the edge in the Org structure indicates the edge deleted by `x->b = dllR`; (c) the structure at the end of the first loop and its formula-based simulation, as is defined in Eq. (6); (d) the result of `divide(x)` is two disjoint doubly linked lists that can be represented correctly using the basic simulation.

k-Bounded Simulation. The second simulation of $DLL\{f, b\}$ in Table 1 defines simulation invariant SI_2. The weakest precondition of `x->b = dllR` and SI_2 is $wp_2 \stackrel{\text{def}}{=} \forall v_1, v_2 : x(v_1) \wedge dllR(v_2) \Rightarrow f(v_1, v_2) \vee dllR(v_2) \vee dllB(v_2)$. We can show that every structure that satisfies SI_2 remains in SI_2 after `x->b = dllR`, because SI_2 is less restrictive than SI_1, i.e., $[\![SI_1]\!] \subseteq [\![SI_2]\!]$. It allows mutations that redirect the backward pointer to an element pointed to by one of the variables $p_1, \ldots, p_k$. Each p_i is unique, that is, it may point to at most one element. The translation represents $b(v_1, v_2)$ using unary predicates $B_{p_1}(v), \ldots, B_{p_k}(v)$ in addition to $B(v)$. $B_{p_i}(v)$ indicates that there is a backward pointer from the element v to the element pointed to by p_i. For example, in `divide(x)` these variables are `dllR` and `dllB`. The representation structure on the right of Fig. 2(b) uses predicate B_{dllR} to correctly capture the result of the `x->b = dllR` operation.

The subsequent operation `dllR = x` in program `divide(x)` moves `dllR` forward in the list. The weakest precondition of `dllR = x` and SI_2 does not hold for the structure in Fig. 2(b), the statement dllR = x makes the previous use of B_{dllR} undefined, and SI_2 enables the mutation only for structures in which dllR and x point to the same element, or no backward pointer is directed to the element pointed to by dllR, except maybe the backward pointer from its f-successor (which can be captured by $B(v)$).

Simulation with b-Field Defined by a Formula φ. The third simulation of $DLL\{f, b\}$ in Table 1 defines simulation invariant SI_3. SI_3 defines the backward pointer either by a formula $\varphi(v_1, v_2) \in MSO\text{-}E$ or by its predecessor. The translation represents $b(v_1, v_2)$ using a unary predicate $B_\varphi(v)$ (in addition to $B(v)$), to indicate that the backward pointer from the element represented by v_1 points to some element represented by v_2 such that $\varphi(v_1, v_2)$ holds. In the example, $\varphi(v_1, v_2)$ is defined by

$$\varphi(v_1, v_2) \stackrel{\text{def}}{=} \varphi_{RED}(v_1, v_2) \vee \varphi_{BLACK}(v_1, v_2) \tag{6}$$

where $\varphi_c(v_1, v_2)$ for $c \in \{RED, BLACK\}$ is defined by

$$\varphi_c(v_1, v_2) \stackrel{\text{def}}{=} c(v_2) \wedge \forall v : TC[f](v_2, v) \wedge TC[f](v, v_1) \wedge (v \neq v_2) \wedge (v \neq v_1) \Rightarrow \neg c(v)$$

It guarantees that v_1 is the first element of color c reachable from v_2 using f-edges. This simulation can capture all intermediate structures that may occur in divide(x), some of which are shown in Fig. 2(c).

To summarize, the *high-level* operation divide(x) preserves the data-structure invariant: if the input is a doubly-linked list that satisfies the basic simulation invariant SI_1 in Table 1, then the result satisfies SI_1 as well. The problem is that the implementation of divide(x) performs *low-level* mutations that may temporarily violate the invariant (and restore it later). In this case, the mutation operation cannot be simulated correctly with the basic invariant SI_1, but only with SI_3.

4 Related Work

4.1 Decidable Logics for Expressing Data-Structure Properties

Two other decidable logics have been successfully used to define properties of linked data structures: *WS2S* has been used in [3, 10] to define properties of heap-allocated data structures, and to conduct Hoare-style verification using programmer-supplied loop invariants in the PALE system [10].

A decidable logic called L_r (for "logic of reachability expressions") was defined in [1]. L_r is rich enough to express the shape descriptors studied in [13] and the path matrices introduced in [4]. Also, in contrast to *WS2S*, *MSO-E* and $\exists\forall(DTC[E])$ [9], L_r can describe certain families of *arbitrary* stores – not just trees or structures with one binary predicate. However, the expressive power of L_r is rather limited because it does not allow properties of memory locations to be described. For instance, it cannot express many of the families of structures that are captured by the shape descriptors that arise during a run of TVLA. L_r cannot be used to define doubly linked lists because L_r provides no way to specify the existence of cycles starting at arbitrary memory locations.

4.2 Simulating Stores

The idea of simulating low-level mutations is related to representation simulation (Milner, 1971) and data-structure refinement (Hoare [6]). In [6], the simulation invariant is defined over the representation structures; it denotes the set of representation structures for which η is well-defined. This method has the obvious advantage of specifying the formulas directly, without the need for translation, whereas our method requires translation, which may not be defined for some formulas and some logics.

PALE [10] uses a hard-coded mapping of linked data-structures into *WS2S*, and uses MONA decision procedures. The simulation technique can be used to extend the applicability of *WS2S* to more general sets of stores than those handled in [10], for example, cyclic shared singly-linked lists, as described in Section 2.3, and also to simulate generalized trees and undirected graphs.

5 Conclusion

In this paper, we have described a technique that can increase the applicability of decision procedures to larger classes of graph structures. We allow graph mutations to be described using arbitrary first-order formulas that can model deterministic programming-language statements, including destructive updates.

We have implemented an interface between TVLA and MONA using simulation. This allows us to apply the simulation method as described in Section 3.2, thus, enabling precise abstract interpretation.

References

1. M. Benedikt, T. Reps, and M. Sagiv. A decidable logic for describing linked data structures. In *European Symp. On Programming*, pages 2–19, March 1999.
2. P. Cousot and R. Cousot. Systematic design of program analysis frameworks. In *Symp. on Princ. of Prog. Lang.*, pages 269–282, New York, NY, 1979. ACM Press.
3. J. Elgaard, A. Møller, and M.I. Schwartzbach. Compile-time debugging of C programs working on trees. In *European Symp. On Programming*, pages 119–134, 2000.
4. L. Hendren. *Parallelizing Programs with Recursive Data Structures*. PhD thesis, Cornell Univ., Ithaca, NY, Jan 1990.
5. J.G. Henriksen, J. Jensen, M. Jørgensen, N. Klarlund, B. Paige, T. Rauhe, and A. Sandholm. Mona: Monadic second-order logic in practice. In *TACAS*, 1995.
6. C.A.R. Hoare. Proof of correctness of data representations. *Acta Inf.*, 1:271–281, 1972.
7. C.A.R. Hoare. Recursive data structures. *Int. J. of Comp. and Inf. Sci.*, 4(2):105–132, 1975.
8. N. Immerman. *Descriptive Complexity*. Springer-Verlag, 1999.
9. N. Immerman, A. Rabinovich, T. Reps, M. Sagiv, and G. Yorsh. The boundery between decidability and undecidability of transitive closure logics. Submitted for publication, 2004.
10. A. Møller and M.I. Schwartzbach. The pointer assertion logic engine. In *SIGPLAN Conf. on Prog. Lang. Design and Impl.*, pages 221–231, 2001.
11. M. Rabin. Decidability of second-order theories and automata on infinite trees. *Trans. Amer. Math. Soc.*, 141:1–35, 1969.
12. T. Reps, M. Sagiv, and G. Yorsh. Symbolic implementation of the best transformer. In *Proc. VMCAI*, 2004.
13. M. Sagiv, T. Reps, and R. Wilhelm. Solving shape-analysis problems in languages with destructive updating. *Trans. on Prog. Lang. and Syst.*, 20(1):1–50, January 1998.
14. G. Yorsh, T. Reps, and M. Sagiv. Symbolically computing most-precise abstract operations for shape analysis. In *TACAS*, pages 530–545, 2004.

Symbolic Parametric Safety Analysis
of Linear Hybrid Systems
with BDD-Like Data-Structures*

Farn Wang

Dept. of Electrical Engineering, National Taiwan University
1, Sec. 4, Roosevelt Rd., Taipei, Taiwan 106, ROC
Phone: +886-2-23635251 ext. 435; Fax: +886-2-23671909
farn@cc.ee.ntu.edu.tw
http://cc.ee.ntu.edu.tw/~farn

Model-checker/simulator red 5.3 is available at http://cc.ee.ntu.edu.tw/~val

Abstract. We introduce a new BDD-like data structure called *Hybrid-Restriction Diagrams (HRDs)*, for the representation and manipulation of linear hybrid automata (LHA) state-spaces, and present algorithms for weakest precondition calculations. This permits us to reason about the valuations of parameters that make safety properties satisfied. Advantages of our approach include the ability to represent discrete state information and concave polyhedra in a unified scheme as well as to save both memory consumptions and manipulation times, when processing the same substructures in state-space representations. Our experimental results document its efficiency in practice.

Keywords: data-structures, BDD, hybrid automata, verification, model-checking

1 Introduction

Linear hybrid automata (LHA) are state-transition systems equipped with continuous variables that can change values with different rates [6]. They are important to computing and society because of their extensive modeling capability. In practice, such models are usually presented with symbolic constants, called *parameters*, whose values may engender different behaviors of the models. Setting and calibrating these parameters is a crucial task for the engineers developing hybrid systems. *Parametric safety analysis (PSA)* of LHA can generate a symbolic characterization of the parameters' valuations, called *solutions*, that make a model satisfy a *safety property*. Such a symbolic characterization, once constructed, sheds important feedback information to engineers and can be used

---

* The work is partially supported by NSC, Taiwan, ROC under grants NSC 92-2213-E-002-103 and NSC 92-2213-E-002-104. We would like to thank the TReX team, especially Mihaela Sighireanu and Aurore Collomb-Annichini, for kindly implementing a TReX version without the reduce package for us.

R. Alur and D.A. Peled (Eds.): CAV 2004, LNCS 3114, pp. 295–307, 2004.

repeatedly in the synthesis and verification of implementations of the corresponding model.

Although, the emptiness problem of PSA solution spaces is undecidable in general [7], people have constructed experimental tools for the verification of LHA [1,3,4,6] based on the following three reasons. First, the verification problem is by itself interesting and challenging. Second, it may happen that there exist techniques and strategies which can solve many typical examples. Third, there is still an urgent need in industry for such tools to help engineers with fast prototyping of their compelx designs.

Because LHA necessarily involves continuous variables, it is helpful and more efficient to represent and manipulate their state-space symbolically. Others have developed separate representation schemes for the discrete part and continuous part of LHA [1,3,4,6]. According to previous experiences [9,11,17–19], it can be more efficient to have a unified data-structure for both the discrete part and the continuous part. Moreover, the schemes used in [1,3,4,6] only represent convex polyhedra in LHA state-space (concave polyhedra have to be represented as sets of convex ones) and suffer from the limitation to share common representation structures in different convex polyhedra.

In this work, we extend BDD [9,11] for the representation and manipulation of LHA state-spaces. A BDD [11] is an acyclic graph, with a single source and two sinks for *true* and *false* respectively. Each internal node is labeled with a Boolean *decision atom* and has a *true*-child and a *false*-child. A BDD works as a *decision diagram* for state-space membership. Any sequence of decision atoms labeled on a path in a BDD must follow a predefined total ordering.

The term *BDD-like data-structure* is coined in [19] to call the many BDD extensions in the literature. BDD-like data-structures have the advantage of data-sharing in both representation and manipulation and have shown great success in VLSI verification industry. The same structure following two decision path prefixes will only be represented once. Also, a pattern of operand substructures will only be manipulated once. The manipulation result will be saved and returned immediately the next time when the same pattern is encountered. These features of BDD-technology lead to not only savings in memory consumptions but also speed-up in manipulations.

One of the major difficulties to use BDD-like data-structures to analyze LHAs comes from the unboundedness of the dense variable value ranges and the unboundedness of linear constraints. To explain one of the major contribution of this work, we need to discuss the following issue first. In the research of BDD-like data-structures, there are two classes of variables: *system variables* and *decision atoms* [19]. System variables are those used in the input behavior descriptions. Decision atoms are those labeled on each BDD nodes. For discrete systems, these two classes are the same. But for dense-time systems, decision atoms can be different from state variables. For example, in CDD (Clock-Difference Diagram) [10] and CRD (Clock-Restriction Diagram) [19], decision atoms are of the form $x - x'$ where x and x' are system variables of type clock. Previous work on BDD-like data-structures are based on the assumption that decision atom domains are of finite sizes. Thus we need new techniques to extend BDD-like data-structures to represent and manipulate state-spaces of LHAs. Our innovations include using constraints, like $-3A + x - 4y$ (where A, x, y are dense system variables), as the decision atoms and using total dense orderings among these atoms. In this way, we devise HRD (Hybrid-Restriction Diagram) and successfully extend BDD-technology to models with unbounded domains of decision atoms.

In total, we defined three total dense orderings for HRD decision atoms (section 5). We also present algorithms for set-oriented operations (section 6) and symbolic weakest precondition calculation (section 7), and a procedure for symbolic parametric safety analysis (section 7). We have also developed a technique, which prunes state-space exploration based on parameter space characterization and enhances the performance of our tool by orders of magnitude (section 8). Desirably, this technique does not sacrifice the precision of parametric safety analysis. Especially, for one benchmark in our experiments (see section 9), the state-space exploration does not converge without this technique! To our knowledge, nobody else has come up with a similar technique. Finally, we have implemented our ideas in our tool red 5.0 and reported our experiments to see how the three dense-orderings perform and how our implementation performs in comparison with HyTech 2.4.5 [13] and TReX 1.3 [1,3].

2   Related Work

People have used convex subspaces, called *convex polyhedra*, as basic unit for symbolic manipulation. A convex polyhedron characterizes a state-space of an LHA and can be symbolically represented by a set of constraints like $a_1x_1 + \ldots + a_nx_n \sim c$ [4–6]. Two commonly used representations for convex polyhedra in HyTech are polyhedras and frames in dense state-space [13]. These two representations neither are BDD-like nor can represent concave state-spaces. Data-sharing among convex polyhedra is difficult.

In 1993 [22], Wang, Mok, and Emerson discussed how to use BDD with decision atoms like $x_i + c \leq x_j + d$ to model-check timed automata. In the last several years, people have explored in this approach in the hope of duplicating the success of BDD techniques [9,11] in hardware verification for the verification of timed automata [2,8,10,14–19]. Especially, our HRD can be seen as variation of CDD [10] and extension of CRD [17,18] for timed systems. In [10], CDD only served as a recording device in that reachable state-space representations were analyzed using DBM [12] and then converted to CDD. In [19–21], a full set of verification algorithms (including forward/backward reachability analysis, normalization, and full TCTL model-checking procedures) for CRD were reported.

For parametric safety analysis, Annichini et al have extended DBM [12] to PDBM for parametric safety analysis of timed automata [1,3] and implemented a tool called *TReX*, which also supports verification with lossy channels.

3   Parametric Safety Analysis of Linear Hybrid Automata

A *linear hybrid automaton (LHA)* [6] is a finite-state automaton equipped with a finite set of dense system variables which can hold real-values. At any moment,

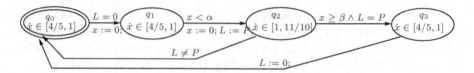

Fig. 1. Fischer's timed mutual exclusion algorithm in LHA

the LHA can stay in only one *mode* (or *control location*). In its operation, one of the transitions can be triggered when the corresponding triggering condition is satisfied. Upon being triggered, the LHA instantaneously transits from one mode to another and sets some dense variables to values in certain ranges. In between transitions, all dense variables increase their readings at rates determined by the current mode. Since LHA has been well-studied in the literature, we leave its definition in our full version report. In figure 1, we have drawn a version of the Fischer's mutual exclusion algorithm for a process. There are two parameters α and β that control the behavior of the processes. In each mode, local clock x increases its reading according to a rate in $[4/5, 1]$ or $[1, 11/10]$.

Our verification framework is called *parametric safety analysis (PSA) problem*. Such a problem instance, denoted $PSA(A, \eta)$, consists of an LHA A and a safety state-predicate η and asks for a symbolic characterization of all parameter valuations, called *solutions*, that make all reachable states satisfy η. The general parametric safety analysis problem can be proved incomputable with a straightforward adaptation of the undecidability proof in [7].

4   HRD (Hybrid-Restriction Diagram)

For efficiency of manipulation, we have the following requirements on constraints used to represent a *convex polyhedron*. Given a constraint like $\sum_i a_i x_i \sim c$, (1) a_i's are integers such that $\gcd\{a_i \mid 1 \leq i \leq n; a_i \neq 0\} = 1$, (2) $x_1, \ldots, x_n$ are system variables, (3) $\sim \in \{ \text{"}\leq\text{"}, \text{"}<\text{"}\}$, and (4) c is either a rational number or ∞ such that when $c = \infty$, $\sim = \text{"}<\text{"}$. We shall call "$\sum_i a_i x_i$" an *LH-expression* and "$(\sim, c)$" an *LH-upperbound*. Formally, a convex polyhedron can be defined as a mapping from the set of LH-expressions to the set of LH-upperbounds. For a given X, the set of all LH-expressions and the set of convex polyhedra are both infinite. For any two $(\sim, c)$ and $(\sim', c')$, $(\sim, c)$ is *more restrictive than* $(\sim', c')$, denoted $(\sim, c) \sqsubseteq (\sim', c')$, iff $c < c'$ or $(c = c' \wedge \sim = \text{"}<\text{"} \wedge \sim' = \text{"}\leq\text{"})$.

To construct BDD-like data-structures, three fundamental issues have to be solved. The first is the domain of the decision atoms; the second is the range of the arc labels from BDD nodes; and the third is the evaluation ordering among the decision atoms. For modularity of presentation, we shall leave the discussion of the evaluation orderings to section 5. In this section, we shall assume that we are given a decision atom evaluation ordering.

We decide to follow an approach similar to the one adopted in [19]. That is, the decision atoms of HRD are LH-expressions and the arcs are labeled with LH-upperbounds. A node label $\sum_i a_i x_i$ with a corresponding outgoing arc label

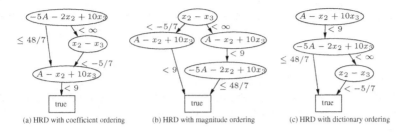

| (a) HRD with coefficient ordering | (b) HRD with magnitude ordering | (c) HRD with dictionary ordering |

Fig. 2. Examples of HRD

$(\sim, c)$ constitute the constraint of $\sum_i a_i x_i \sim c$. A source-to-sink path in an HRD thus represents the conjunction of constituent constraints along the path. Figure 2(a) is an HRD example for the concave space of

$$(x_2 - x_3 \leq -5/7 \vee -5A - 2x_2 + 10x_3 \leq 48/7) \wedge A - x_2 + 10x_3 < 9$$

assuming that $-5A - 2x_2 + 10x_3$ precedes $x_2 - x_3$ (in symbols $-5A - 2x_2 + 10x_3 \prec x_2 - x_3$) and $x_2 - x_3$ precedes $A - x_2 + 10x_3$ in the given evaluation ordering. In this example, the system variables are A, x_2, x_3 while the decision atoms are $x_2 - x_3$, $-5A - 2x_2 + 10x_3$, and $A - x_2 + 10x_3$.

Definition 1. *HRD (Hybrid-Restriction Diagram)* Given a dense variable set $X = \{x_1, \ldots, x_n\}$ and an evaluation ordering $\prec$ among normalized LH-expressions of X, an *HRD* is either *true* or a tuple $(v, (\beta_1, D_1), \ldots, (\beta_m, D_m))$ such that

- v is a normalized LH-expression;
- for each $1 \leq i \leq m$, β_i is an LH-upperbound s.t. $(<, \infty) \neq \beta_1 \sqsubset \beta_2 \sqsubset \ldots \sqsubset \beta_m$; and
- for each $1 \leq i \leq m$, D_i is an HRD such that if $D_i = (v_i, \ldots)$, then $v \prec v_i$.

For completeness, we use "()" to represent the HRD for *false*. ∎

In our algorithms, *false* does not participate in comparison of evaluation orderings among decision atoms. Also, note that in figure 2, for each arc label $(\sim, c)$, we simply put down $\sim c$ for convenience.

5 Three Dense Orderings among Decision Atoms

In the definition of a dense-ordering among decision atoms (i.e., LH-expressions), special care must be taken to facilitate efficient manipulation of HRDs. Here we use the experience reported in [19] and present three heuristics in designing the orderings among LH-expressions. The three heuristics are presented in sequence proportional to their respective importances.

HEURISTICS I: It is desirable to place a pair of converse LH-expressions next to one another so that simple inconsistencies can be easily detected. That is, LH-expressions $\sum_i a_i x_i$ and $\sum_i -a_i x_i$ are better placed next to one another in the ordering. With this arrangement, inconsistencies like $-x_1 + 3x_2 \leq -5 \wedge x_1 - 3x_2 < 0$ can be checked by comparing adjacent nodes in HRD paths. To fulfill this requirement, when comparing the precedence between LH-expressions in a given ordering, we shall first toggle the signs of coefficients of an LH-expression if its first nonzero coefficient is positive. If two LH-expressions are identical after the necessary toggling, then we compare the signs of their first nonzero coefficients to decide the precedence between the two.

With this heuristics, from now on, we shall only focus on the orderings among LH-expressions whose first nonzero coefficients are negative.

HEURISTICS II: According to the literature, it is important to place strongly correlated LH-expressions close together in the evaluation orderings. Usually, instead of a single global LHA, we are given a set of communicating LHAs, each representing a process. Thus it is desirable to place LH-expressions for the same process close to each other in the orderings. Our second heuristics respects this experience. Given a system with m processes with respective local dense variables, we shall partition the LH-expressions into $m + 1$ groups: $G_0, G_1, \ldots, G_m$. G_0 contains all LH-expressions without local variables (i.e., coefficients for local variables are all zero). For each $p > 0$, G_p contains all LH-expressions with a nonzero coefficient for a local variable of process p and only zero coefficients for local variables of processes $p+1, \ldots, m$. Then our second heuristics requires that for all $0 \leq p < m$, LH-expressions in G_p precede those in $G_{p+1}, \ldots, G_m$.

HEURISTICS III: If the precedence between two LH-expressions cannot be determined with heuristics I and II, then the following third heuristics comes to play. The design of this heuristics is a challenge since each of $G_0, \ldots, G_m$ can be of infinite size. Traditionally, BDD-like data-structures have been used with finite decision atom domains. Carefully examining the BDD manipulation procedures, we found that the sizes of the domains do not matter. What really matters is the ordering among all decision atoms so that we know which atoms is to be decided next along a decision path. Thus, we invent to use the following three dense-orderings among LH-expressions.

Dictionary Ordering: We can represent each LH-expression as a string, assuming that the ordering among $x_1, \ldots, x_n$ is fixed and no blanks are used in the string. Then we can use dictionary ordering and ASCII ordering to decide the precedence among LH-expressions. For the LH-expressions in figure 2, we then have $-5A - 2x_2 + 10x_3 \prec A - x_2 + 10x_3 \prec x_2 - x_3$ since '$-$' precedes 'A' and 'A' precedes 'x' in ASCII. The corresponding HRD in dictionary ordering is in figure 2(c). One interesting feature of this ordering is that it has the potential to be extended to nonlinear hybrid constraints. For example, we may say $\cos(x_1) + x_2^3 \prec x_2^2 - x_2x_3$ in dictionary ordering since 'c' precedes 'x' in ASCII.

Coefficient Ordering: Assume that the ordering of the dense variables is fixed as $x_1, \ldots, x_m$. In this ordering, the precedence between two LH-expressions is determined by iteratively comparing the coefficients of dense variables $x_1, \ldots, x_n$ in sequence. For the LH-expressions in figure 2, we then have $-5A - 2x_2 + 10x_3 \prec x_2 - x_3 \prec A - x_2 + 10x_3$. The HRD in this ordering is in figure 2(a).

Magnitude Ordering: This ordering is similar to the last one. Instead of comparing coefficients, we compare the absolute values of coefficients. We iteratively

- first compare the absolute values of coefficients of x_i, and
- if they are equal, then compare the signs of coefficients of x_i.

For the LH-expressions in figure 2, $x_2 - x_3 \prec A - x_2 + 10x_3 \prec -5A - 2x_2 + 10x_3$ in this magnitude ordering. The corresponding HRD is in figure 2(b).

6   Set-Oriented Operations

Please be reminded that an HRD records a set of convex polyhedra. For convenience of discussion, given an HRD, we may just represent it as the set of convex polyhedra recorded in it. Definitions of set-union ($\cup$), set-intersection ($\cap$), and set-exclusion ($-$) of two convex polyhedra sets respectively represented by two HRDs are straightforward. For example, given HRDs $D_1 : \{\zeta_1, \zeta_2\}$ and $D_2 : \{\zeta_2, \zeta_3\}$, $D_1 \cap D_2$ is the HRD for $\{\zeta_2\}$; $D_1 \cup D_2$ is for $\{\zeta_1, \zeta_2, \zeta_3\}$; and $D_1 - D_2$ is for $\{\zeta_1\}$. The complexities of the three manipulations are all $O(|D_1| \cdot |D_2|)$.

Given two convex polyhedra ζ_1 and ζ_2, $\zeta_1 \wedge \zeta_2$ is a new convex polyhedron representing the space-intersection of ζ_1 and ζ_2. Formally speaking, for decision atom $\sum_i a_i x_i$, $\zeta_1 \wedge \zeta_2(\sum_i a_i x_i) = \zeta_1(\sum_i a_i x_i)$ if $\zeta_1(\sum_i a_i x_i) \sqsubseteq \zeta_2(\sum_i a_i x_i)$; or $\zeta_2(\sum_i a_i x_i)$ otherwise. Space-intersection ($\wedge$) of two HRDs D_1 and D_2, in symbols $D_1 \wedge D_2$, is a new HRD for $\{\zeta_1 \wedge \zeta_2 \mid \zeta_1 \in D_1; \zeta_2 \in D_2\}$. Our current algorithm of the manipulation has complexity $O(|D_1|^2 |D_2|^2)$.

Given an evaluation ordering, we can write HRD-manipulation algorithms pretty much as usual [9, 11, 15, 19]. For convenience of presentation, we may represent an HRD $(u, (\beta_1, B_1), \ldots, (\beta_n, B_n))$ symbolically as $(u, (\beta_i, B_i)_{1 \leq i \leq n})$. A union operation $\mathtt{union}(B, D)$ can then be implemented as follows.

---

set Ψ; /* database for the recording of already-processed cases */
$\mathtt{union}(B, D)$ {
    if $B = \mathit{false}$, return D; else if $D = \mathit{false}$, return B;
    $\Psi := \emptyset$; return $\mathtt{rec\_union}(B, D)$;
}

$\mathtt{rec\_union}(B, D)$ where $B = (u, (\beta_i, B_i)_{1 \leq i \leq n})$, $D = (v, (\alpha_j, D_j)_{1 \leq j \leq m})$ {
    if B is true or D is true, return true; else if $\exists F, (B, D, F) \in \Psi$, return F;   (1)
    else if $u \prec v$, construct $F := (u, (\beta_i, \mathtt{rec\_union}(B_i, D))_{1 \leq i \leq n})$;
    else if $v \prec u$, construct $F := (v, (\alpha_j, \mathtt{rec\_union}(B, D_j))_{1 \leq j \leq m})$;
    else {
        $i := n; j := m; F := \mathit{false}$;
        while $i \geq 1$ and $j \geq 1$, do {
            if $\beta_i = \alpha_j$, { $F := F \cup (u, (\beta_i, \mathtt{rec\_union}(B_i, D_j)))$; $i--; j--;$ }
            else if $\beta_i \sqsubset \alpha_j$, { $F := F \cup (u, (\alpha_j, D_j))$; $j := j - 1;$ }
            else if $\alpha_j \sqsubset \beta_i$, { $F := F \cup (u, (\beta_i, B_i))$; $i := i - 1;$ }
        }
        if $i \geq 1$, $F := F \cup (u, (\beta_1, B_1)_{1 \leq h \leq i})$;
        if $j \geq 1$, $F := F \cup (u, (\alpha_1, D_1)_{1 \leq k \leq j})$;
    }
    $\Psi := \Psi \cup \{(B, D, F)\}$; return F; . . . . (2)
}

Note in statement (1), we take advantage of the data-sharing capability of HRDs so that we do not process the same substructure twice. Set Ψ is maintained in statement (2) to record the processing result the first time the substructure is encountered. The algorithms for $\cap$ and $-$ are pretty much the same. The one for space intersection $\wedge$ is much more involved and is not discussed here.

7   Weakest Preconditon Calculation and Symbolic PSA

Our tool red 5.0 runs a backward reachability analysis by default. Suppose we are given an LHA A. There are two basic procedures in this analysis procedure. The first, $\mathtt{xtion}(D, e)$, computes the weakest precondition from state-space represented by HRD D through discrete transition e from mode q to q'. Assume that the variables that get assigned in e are $y_1, \ldots, y_k$ and there is no variable that gets assigned twice in e. The characterization of $\mathtt{xtion}(D, e)$ is

$$\mu(q) \wedge \tau(e) \wedge \exists y_1 \ldots \exists y_k (D \wedge \wedge_{1 \leq i \leq k} y_i \in \pi(e, y_i))\ ^1$$

Assume that $\mathtt{delta\_exp}(D)$ is the same as D except that all dense variables x are replaced by $x + \delta_x$ respectively. Here δ_x represents the value-change of variable x in time-passage. For example, $\mathtt{delta\_exp}(2x_1 - 3x_2 \leq 3/5) = 2x_1 + 2\delta_{x_1} - 3x_2 - 3\delta_{x_2} \leq 3/5$.

Assume that for each dense variable x, $\gamma(q, x)$ specifies the rate interval of x in q. The second basic procedure, $\mathtt{time}(D, q)$, computes the weakest precondition from D through time passage in mode q. It is characterized as

$$\mu(q) \wedge \exists \delta_{x_1} \exists \delta_{x_2} \ldots \exists \delta_{x_n} \exists \delta \left(\begin{array}{c} \delta \geq 0 \wedge \mathtt{delta\_exp}(D) \\ \wedge \wedge_{1 \leq i \leq n; \gamma(q, x_i) = \langle d_i, d_i' \rangle} \delta_{x_i} \in \langle d_i \delta, d_i' \delta \rangle \end{array} \right)$$

One basic building block of both $\mathtt{xtion}()$ and $\mathtt{time}()$ is for the evaluation of $\exists x(D(x))$ and is implemented as follows.

$$\exists x(D(x)) \equiv \mathtt{var\_del}(\mathtt{xtivity}(D, x), \{x\}).$$

Procedure $\mathtt{var\_del}(D, X')$ eliminates all constraints in D involving variables in set X'. Procedure $\mathtt{xtivity}(D, x)$ adds to a path every constraint that can be transitively deduced from two peer constraints involving x in the same path in D. The algorithm of $\mathtt{xtivity}()$ is as follows.

```
set R, S;
xtivity(D, x) { R := ∅; return rec_xtivity(D); }
rec_xtivity(D) {
    if D is true or false, return D; else if ∃(D, D') ∈ R, return D';
    else /* assume D = (ax + ε, (β₁, D₁), ..., (βₘ, Dₘ)) */ {
        S := ∅; D' := ⋃₁≤ᵢ≤ₘ ax + εβᵢ ∧ rec_xtivity_given(Dᵢ, ax + ε, βᵢ);
        R := R ∪ {(D, D')}; return D';
    }
}
```

---

^{1} $y \in [d, d'] \equiv d \leq y \leq d'$. $y \in (d, d'] \equiv d < y \leq d'$. $y \in [d, d') \equiv d \leq y < d'$. $y \in (d, d') \equiv d < y < d'$.

```
rec_xtivity_given(D, ax + ε, β) {
    if D is true or false, return D; else if ∃(D, D') ∈ S, return D'; ........... (3)
    else /* assume D = (bx + ε', (β₁, D₁), ..., (βₘ, Dₘ)) */ {
        if ab < 0,
```

$$D' := \bigcup_{1 \le i \le m} \left(\begin{array}{l} bx + \epsilon'\beta_i \wedge \texttt{rec\_xtivity\_given}(D_i, ax + \epsilon, \beta) \\ \wedge\ |b|\epsilon/\gcd(a,b) + |a|\epsilon'/\gcd(a,b)((|b|\beta + |a|\beta_i)/\gcd(a,b)) \end{array} \right);$$

```
        else D' := ⋃₁≤ᵢ≤ₘ bx + ε'βᵢ ∧ rec_xtivity_given(Dᵢ, ax + ε, β);
        S := S ∪ {(D, D')}; return D'; ..................................... (4)
    }
} /*
```
$(|b|\beta + |a|\beta_i)/\gcd(a,b)$ is a shorthand for the new upperbound obtained from the xtivity of $ax + \epsilon\beta$ and $bx + \epsilon'\beta_i$. */

Thus we preserve all constraints transitively deducible from a dense variable before it is eliminated from a predicate. This guarantees that no information will be unintentionally lost after the variable elimination.

Note that in our algorithm, we do not enumerate all paths in HRD to carry out this least fixpoint evaluation. Instead, in statement (3), our algorithm follows the traditional BDD programming style which takes advantage of the data-sharing capability of BDD-like data-structures. Thus our algorithm does not explode due to the combinatorial complexity of path counts in HRD. This can be justified by the performance of our implementation reported in section 9.

Assume that the transition set is E and the unsafe states are in mode q_f. With the two basic procedures, then the backward reachable state-space from the unsafe states in $\neg\eta$ (represented as an HRD) can be characterized by

$$\texttt{lfp}Z. \left(\texttt{time}(\neg\eta, q_f) \cup \bigcup_{e=(q,q')\in E} \texttt{time}(\texttt{xtion}(Z, e), q) \right)$$

Here $\texttt{lfp}Z.F(Z)$ is the least fixpoint of function $F()$ and is very commonly used in the reachable state-space representation of discrete and dense-time systems. After the fixpoint is successfully constructed, we conjunct it with the initial condition and then eliminate all variables except those parameters (geometrically speaking, projecting the reachable state-space to the dimensions of the parameters). Suppose the set of dense parameters is H. The characterization of unsafe parameter valuations is thus

$$\texttt{var\_del}(I \wedge \texttt{lfp}Z.(\texttt{time}(\neg\eta, q_f) \cup \bigcup_{e=(q,q')\in E} \texttt{time}(\texttt{xtion}(Z, e), q)), X - H)$$

The solution space is characterized by the complement of this final result.

In our experience, normalizing convex polyhedron representations in HRDs may consume most of the resources. At this moment, our implementation does not enforce a normal form. We only try to eliminate some redundancies that can be derived from two peer constraints in the same convex polyhedron.

Polyhedron containment checking in an HRD is also important in controlling the size of the HRD. Specifically, we want to check if a path in the HRD specifies a polyhedra that is subsumed by another path's HRD. In [19], a sufficient condition called SCR (Straightforward Containment Requirement) was presented for the containment checking of zones. We have adapted SCR for HRDs. Specifically, given $D = (v, (\alpha_j, D_j)_{1 \le j \le m})$, $\texttt{SCR}(D) = (v, (\alpha_j, D_j - \bigcup_{j < k \le m} D_k)_{1 \le j \le m})$.

Lemma 1. *Given any HRD D, D and* SCR(D) *characterize the same real space.* ∎

In our current implementation, when we need to eliminate polyhedras contained by peer polyhedras in an HRD, we perform SCR to each node in the HRD in a bottom-up fashion.

8   Pruning Strategy Based on Parameter Space Construction (PSPSC)

We have also experimented with techniques to improve the efficiency of parametric safety analysis. One such technique, called *PSPSC*, is avoiding new state-space exploration if the exploration does not contribute to new parametric solutions. A constraint is *static* iff all its dense variables are parameters. Static constraints do not change their truth values. Once a static constraint is derived in a convex polyhedron, its truth value will be honored in all weakest preconditions derived from this convex polyhedron. All states backwardly reachable from a convex polyhedron must also satisfy the static constraints required in the polyhedron. Thus if we know that static parameter valuation $\mathcal{H}$ is already in the parametric solution space, then we really do not need to explore those states whose parameter valuations fall in H.

With PSPSC, our new parametric safety analysis procedure is as follows.

```
PSA_with_PSPSC(A, η) {
    D̄ := time(¬η, q_f); D := false; P := var_del(D, X − H);
    while D̄ ≠ false, do {
        D := D ∪ D̄; D̄ := ⋃_{e=(q,q′)∈E} time(xtion(D̄, e), q);
        D̄ := D̄ ∧ (¬P) ∧ (¬D); ..............................................(5)
        P := P ∪ var_del(I ∧ D̄, X − H);
    }
    return ¬P;
}
```

In the procedure, we use variable P to symbolically accumulate the parametric evaluations leading to the unsafe states in the least fixpoint iterations. In statement (5), we check and eliminate in $\bar{D}$ those state descriptions which cannot possibly contribute to new parametric evaluations by conjuncting $\bar{D}$ with $\neg P$.

One nice feature of PSPSC is that it does not sacrifice the precision of our parametric safety analysis.

Lemma 2. $\mathcal{H}$ *is a* parametric solution *to* A *and* η *iff* $\mathcal{H}$ *satisfies the return result of* PSA_with_PSPSC(A, η).

Proof: Note that the intersection at line (5) in procedure PSA_with_PSPSC() only stops the further exploration of those states that do not contribute to new parameter-spaces. Those parameter-spaces pruned in line (5) do not contribute

Table 1. Comparison with HyTech w.r.t. number of processes

direction	benchmarks	rates used	m	HyTech 2.4.5	red 5.0 (backward)			
					dictionary	coefficient	magnitude	coefficient
						no PSPSC		PSPSC
backward	Fischer's mutual exclusion (m processes)	[4/5, 1]	2	0.23s	0.10s/17k	0.11s/17k	0.11s/17k	0.07s/16k
		[1, 11/10]	3	2.40s	1.83s/81k	1.75s/74k	1.23s/59k	0.70s/44k
			4	28.04s	20.29s/320k	23.85s/269k	12.38s/215k	5.14s/163k
			5	O/M	278.8s/1420k	354.1s/1149k	162.0s/1034k	31.36s/474k
			6	O/M	2846s/5848k	9923s/8796k	1485s/4000k	168.6s/1170k
	GRC (gate +controller +m trains)	[0, 0], [1, 1]	2	O/M	0.79s/103k	0.68s/101k	0.68s/101k	0.76s/94k
		[9, 10]	3	O/M	11.48s/806k	8.85s/616k	8.84s/616k	11.48s/530k
		[−10, −9]	4	O/M	248.5s/6046k	184.9s/4249k	186.1s/4249k	252.5s/2820k
			5	O/M	6095s/37093k	4883s/25841k	4900s/25841k	6527s/19234k
	reactor (controller +m rods)	[1, 1]	2	0.056s	0.08s/19k	0.07s/19k	0.06s/19k	0.05s/15k
			3	0.33s	0.41s/51k	0.38s/52k	0.37s/52k	0.22s/41k
			4	2.61s	3.10s/187k	2.69s/186k	2.71s/186k	1.42s/155k
			5	31.29s	41.47s/1042k	37.03s/1039k	36.89s/1039k	18.67s/884k
			6	647.8s	951.5s/8228k	866.9s/8191k	839.3s/8191k	461.8s/6941k
	CSMA/CD (bus +m senders)	[1, 1]	2	O/M	0.98s/42k*	1.47s/125k	0.57s/34k	0.56s/33k
			3	O/M	O/M	5076s/2407k*	121.5s/807k	0.66s/105k
			4	O/M	O/M	O/M	O/M	2.47s/378k
			5	O/M	O/M	O/M	O/M	9.77s/1192k
			6	O/M	O/M	O/M	O/M	40.58s/3513k
forward	Fischer's mutual	same as above	2	0.34s	0.10s/20k	0.10s/20k	0.10s/19k	0.08s/18k
			3	37.89s	O/M	22.10s/561k	19.18s/654k	5.59s/538k
	GRC	same as above	2	3.29s	2.29s/192k	1.41s/95k	1.43s/95k	0.44s/84k
			3	O/M	O/M	O/M	O/M	6.35s/418k
	reactor	[1, 1]	2	O/M	O/M	O/M	O/M	O/M
	CSMA/CD	[1, 1]	2	0.19s	0.19s/29k	0.17s/29k	0.17s/29k	0.25s/33k
			3	2.63s	1.81s/102k	1.64s/101k	1.62s/101k	2.61s/106k
			4	68.75s	20.07s/370k	17.49s/378k	17.52s/378k	27.03s/378k
			5	O/M	268.0s/1905k	240.3s/1906k	242.2s/1906k	331.9s/1910k
			6	O/M	3889s/11725k	3123s/11525k	3155s/11525k	4163s/11552k

s: seconds; k: kilobytes of memory in data-structure; O/M: Out of memory;

because they are already contained in the known parameter constraints P and along each exploration path, the parameter constraints only get restricter. ∎

PSPSC can help in pruning the space of exploration in big chunks. But in the worst case, PSPSC does not guarantee the exploration will terminate. In section 9, we shall report the performance of this technique. Especially, for one benchmark, the state-space exploration cannot converge without PSPSC.

9   Implementation and Experiments

We have implemented our ideas in our tool **red** which has been previously reported in [15–19] for the verification of timed automata. We have also carried out experiments and compared with HyTech 2.4.5 [13] and TReX 1.3 [1,3]. Details about the benchmarks can be found in our full version report. Experiments are conducted on a Pentium 4M 1.6GHz/256MB running LINUX.

Comparison with HyTech 2.4.5: We compare performance in both forward and backward reachability analyses. The performance data of HyTech 2.4.5 and **red** 5.0 with dictionary ordering (no PSPSC), coefficient ordering (no PSPSC), magnitude ordering (PSPSC), and coefficient ordering with PSPSC is reported in table 1. The experiment, although not extensive, does show signs that HRD-technology (with or without PSPSC) can compete with the technology used

Table 2. Performance comparison with TReX w.r.t. number of processes

benchmarks	concurrency	Forward			Backward		
		TReX 1.3	red 5.0 magnitude	red 5.0 coeff.+PSPSC	TReX 1.3	red 5.0 magnitude	red 5.0 coeff.+PSPSC
Fischer's mutual exclusion (m	2 procs	1.12s	0.07s/17k	0.07s/15k	8.96s	0.08s/13k	0.04s/13k
	3 procs	O/M	1.86s/137k	0.78s/79k	N/A	0.66s/43k	0.49s/43k
	4 procs	O/M	197.9s/2714k	16.92s/539k	N/A	5.81s/180k	3.58s/158k
	5 procs	O/M	N/A	752.7s/5254k	N/A	59.27s/945k	24.71s/658k
	6 procs	O/M	N/A	N/A	N/A	567.1s/4341k	170.3s/2798k
reactor (m rods)	2 rods	O/M	O/M	O/M	N/A	0.06s/19k	0.05s/15k
	3 rods	O/M	O/M	O/M	N/A	0.37s/52k	0.22s/41k
	4 rods	O/M	O/M	O/M	N/A	2.71s/186k	1.42s/155k
	5 rods	O/M	O/M	O/M	N/A	36.89s/1039k	18.67s/884k
	6 rods	O/M	O/M	O/M	N/A	839.3s/8191k	461.8s/6941k

s: seconds; k: kilobytes of memory in data-structure;
O/M: Out of memory; N/A: not available;

in HyTech 2.4.5. For all the benchmarks, HRD-technology demonstrates better scalability w.r.t. concurrency complexity.

Finally, PSPSC cuts down the time and memory needed for parametric safety analysis. Especially, in forward analysis of the general railroad benchmark with three trains, without PSPSC, the state-space exploration fails to converge. This shows very good promise of this technique.

Comparison with TReX 1.3: Since TReX 1.3 only supports the verification of systems with clocks, parameters, and lossy channels, we choose the following two benchmarks. The first is Fischer's protocol with all clocks in the uniform rate of 1. The second is the Nuclear Reactor Controller. The performance data is shown in table 2 for both forward and backward analysis.

Two additional options of **red** 5.0 were chosen: coefficient evaluation ordering with PSPSC and magnitude evaluation ordering without. We marked N/A (not available) with higher concurrencies when we feel that too much time (like more than 1 hour) or too much memory (20MB) has been consumed in early fixpoint iterations. Although the data set is still small and incomplete, but we feel that the HRD-technology shows promise in the table.

References

1. A. Annichini, E. Asarin, A. Bouajjani. Symbolic Techniques for Parametric Reasoning about Counter and Clock Systems. CAV'2000, LNCS 1855, Springer-Verlag.
2. E. Asarin, M. Bozga, A. Kerbrat, O. Maler, A. Pnueli, A. Rasse. Data-Structures for the Verification of Timed Automatas. Proceedings, HART'97, LNCS 1201.
3. A. Annichini, A. Bouajjani, M. Sighireanu. TReX: A Tool for Reachability Analysis of Complex Systems. CAV'2001, LNCS, Springer-Verlag.
4. R. Alur, C.Courcoubetis, T.A. Henzinger, P.-H. Ho. Hybrid Automata: an Algorithmic Approach to the Specification and Verification of Hybrid Systems. Proceedings of HYBRID'93, LNCS 736, Springer-Verlag, 1993.
5. R. Alur, C. Courcoubetis, N. Halbwachs, T.A. Henzinger, P.-H. Ho, X. Nicollin, A. Olivero, J. Sifakis, S. Yovine. The Algorithmic Analysis of Hybrid Systems. Theoretical Computer Science 138(1995) 3-34, Elsevier Science B.V.

6. R. Alur, T.A. Henzinger, P.-H. Ho. Automatic Symbolic Verification of Embedded Systems. in Proceedings of 1993 IEEE Real-Time System Symposium.
7. R. Alur, T.A. Henzinger, M.Y. Vardi. Parametric Real-Time Reasoning, in Proceedings, 25th ACM STOC, pp. 592-601.
8. F. Balarin. Approximate Reachability Analysis of Timed Automata. IEEE RTSS, 1996.
9. J.R. Burch, E.M. Clarke, K.L. McMillan, D.L.Dill, L.J. Hwang. Symbolic Model Checking: 10^{20} States and Beyond. IEEE LICS, 1990.
10. G. Behrmann, K.G. Larsen, J. Pearson, C. Weise, Wang Yi. Efficient Timed Reachability Analysis Using Clock Difference Diagrams. CAV'99, July, Trento, Italy, LNCS 1633, Springer-Verlag.
11. R.E. Bryant. Graph-based Algorithms for Boolean Function Manipulation, IEEE Trans. Comput., C-35(8), 1986.
12. D.L. Dill. Timing Assumptions and Verification of Finite-state Concurrent Systems. CAV'89, LNCS 407, Springer-Verlag.
13. T.A. Henzinger, P.-H. Ho, H. Wong-Toi. HyTech: The Next Generation. in Proceedings of 1995 IEEE Real-Time System Symposium.
14. J. Moller, J. Lichtenberg, H.R. Andersen, H. Hulgaard. Difference Decision Diagrams. In proceedings of Annual Conference of the European Association for Computer Science Logic (CSL), Sept. 1999, Madreid, Spain.
15. F. Wang. Efficient Data-Structure for Fully Symbolic Verification of Real-Time Software Systems. TACAS'2000; LNCS 1785, Springer-Verlag.
16. F. Wang. Region Encoding Diagram for Fully Symbolic Verification of Real-Time Systems. The 24th COMPSAC, Oct. 2000, Taipei, Taiwan, ROC, IEEE press.
17. F. Wang. RED: Model-checker for Timed Automata with Clock-Restriction Diagram. Workshop on Real-Time Tools, Aug. 2001, Technical Report 2001-014, ISSN 1404-3203, Dept. of Information Technology, Uppsala University.
18. F. Wang. Symbolic Verification of Complex Real-Time Systems with Clock-Restriction Diagram. FORTE'2001, Kluwer; August 2001, Cheju Island, Korea.
19. F. Wang. Efficient Verification of Timed Automata with BDD-like Data-Structures, to appear in special issue of STTT (Software Tools for Technology Transfer, Springer-Verlag) for VMCAI'2003, LNCS 2575, Springer-Verlag.
20. F. Wang. Model-Checking Distributed Real-Time Systems with States, Events, and Multiple Fairness Assumptions. 10th AMAST, LNCS, Springer-Verlag.
21. F. Wang, G.-D. Hwang, F. Yu. TCTL Inevitability Analysis of Dense-Time Systems. 8th CIAA, LNCS 2759, Springer-Verlag.
22. F. Wang, A. Mok, E.A. Emerson. Symbolic Model-Checking for Distributed Real-Time Systems. 1st FME, April 1993, Denmark; LNCS 670, Springer-Verlag.
23. H. Wong-Toi. Symbolic Approximations for Verifying Real-Time Systems. Ph.D. thesis, Stanford University, 1995.

Abstraction-Based Satisfiability Solving of Presburger Arithmetic*

Daniel Kroening[1], Joël Ouaknine[1], Sanjit A. Seshia[1], and Ofer Strichman[2]

[1] Computer Science Department, Carnegie Mellon University
5000 Forbes Ave., Pittsburgh PA 15213, USA
{kroening,ouaknine,sanjit}@cs.cmu.edu
[2] Faculty of Industrial Engineering, the Technion
Haifa 32000, Israel
ofers@ie.technion.ac.il

Abstract. We present a new abstraction-based framework for deciding satisfiability of quantifier-free Presburger arithmetic formulas. Given a Presburger formula ϕ, our algorithm invokes a SAT solver to produce proofs of unsatisfiability of approximations of ϕ. These proofs are in turn used to generate abstractions of ϕ as inputs to a theorem prover. The SAT-encodings of the approximations of ϕ are obtained by instantiating the variables of the formula over finite domains. The satisfying integer assignments provided by the theorem prover are then used to selectively increase domain sizes and generate fresh SAT-encodings of ϕ. The efficiency of this approach derives from the ability of SAT solvers to extract small unsatisfiable cores, leading to small abstracted formulas. We present experimental results which suggest that our algorithm is considerably more efficient than directly invoking the theorem prover on the original formula.

1 Introduction

Decision procedures for arithmetic over the integers have many applications in formal verification. For instance, the quantifier-free fragment of Presburger arithmetic has been used in infinite-state model checking [9], symbolic timing verification [2], and RTL-datapath analysis [8]. Unfortunately, the satisfiability problem for quantifier-free Presburger arithmetic is known to be NP-complete [25]. Consequently, efficient techniques and tools for solving such problems are very valuable.

In this paper, we present an abstraction-based algorithm for the satisfiability solving of quantifier-free Presburger formulas (QFP formulas for short).

* This research is supported by the Semiconductor Research Corporation (SRC) under contract no. 99-TJ-684, the National Science Foundation (NSF) under grants no. CCR-9803774 and CCR-0121547, the Office of Naval Research (ONR) and the Naval Research Laboratory (NRL) under contract no. N00014-01-1-0796, and the Army Research Office (ARO) under contract no. DAAD19-01-1-0485.

Presburger arithmetic is the first-order theory of linear arithmetic over the non-negative integers. It was shown to be decidable in [27], although the best-known decision algorithms have complexity triply exponential in the size of the formula [29]. For many applications, however, the quantifier-free fragment of Presburger arithmetic suffices.

The algorithm we propose receives as input a QFP formula and attempts to satisfy it over a small range of integers, through a Boolean encoding of the formula and interaction with a SAT solver. In case the Boolean formula is found to be unsatisfiable, the SAT solver is able to supply us with a proof of this fact, in the form of a (small) unsatisfiable core. This in turn can be used to pinpoint the linear arithmetic constraints of the original QFP formula that cannot be satisfied over our bounded domain. This (likewise small) set of linear constraints represents an abstraction of the original QFP formula: whenever these constraints cannot be satisfied over the whole of the non-negative integers, the original formula is unsatisfiable as well. The advantage of this operation is that it is generally much easier to solve the abstracted formula than the original one. We can do so by using any of the existing decision procedures for Presburger arithmetic. The abstracted formula may however be satisfiable; in that case, we increase the size of our bounded integer domain to accommodate the satisfying integer assignment supplied by the decision procedure. We then repeat the whole process until the original formula is shown to be either satisfiable or unsatisfiable.

Note that while the domain over which we work (the integers) is infinite, termination is guaranteed provided the inner Presburger decision procedure we use is itself complete.

Our implementation of this algorithm uses the SAT solvers zChaff [32] and SMVSAT[1], as well as the commercial constraint-solving package CPLEX [17]. Our experimental results, which include both random formulas as well as industrial benchmarks, suggest that our algorithm is considerably more efficient than directly invoking our inner CPLEX-based Presburger decision procedure on its own.

Related Work. There currently exist a number of algorithms and tools for solving QFP, some of which we discuss in Section 2. We refer the reader to the excellent surveys [18, 14] for a more detailed presentation of the matter. While no single technique is found to dominate all others, Ganesh *et al.* [14] report that ILP-based methods perform best in most contexts. To the best of our knowledge, however, no existing tools make use of the sort of abstractions that we have just described.

McMillan and Amla [23] use a related technique to accelerate model checking algorithms over finite Kripke structures. More precisely, they invoke a bounded model checker to decide which state variables should be made visible in order to generate a 'good' abstraction for the next iteration of model checking. Our approach differs from theirs in several respects: we work over an infinite domain, we use a Presburger decision procedure instead of a model checker, and we seek to eliminate constraints rather than variables.

---

[1] We thank Ken McMillan for providing us with this proof-generating SAT solver.

Henzinger *et al.* [15] use a theorem prover to refute counterexamples generated by predicate abstraction in software verification. When the counterexample is shown to be spurious, the proof is 'mined' for new predicates to use in predicate abstraction. Although similar in spirit, this approach differs significantly from ours in both the domain of application and the techniques used.

Our framework also bears certain similarities with automated counterexample-guided abstraction refinement [20]. Chauhan *et al.* [10], for example, use a SAT solver to derive an abstraction sufficient to refute a given abstract counterexample in model checking. The successive abstractions they obtain, however, are cumulative, in that state variables made visible at some point are never subsequently re-hidden. In contrast, our approach generates a fresh abstraction every time.

2 Preliminaries

2.1 Boolean Satisfiability

We begin by recalling some well-known facts concerning (propositional) Boolean formulas and Boolean satisfiability.

Let $b_1, b_2, \ldots$ be Boolean variables. A *literal* is either a b_i or its negation. A *(Boolean) clause* is a disjunction of zero or more literals—by convention, the empty clause is equivalent to *False*.

Let ϕ be a Boolean formula with free variables $b_1, \ldots, b_n$. It is possible to manufacture a Boolean formula $\mathsf{cnf}(\phi)$ with free variables $b_1, \ldots, b_{n+p}$ (where the $b_{n+1}, \ldots, b_{n+p}$ are fresh Boolean variables), such that

- $\mathsf{cnf}(\phi)$ is in conjunctive normal form (CNF): $\mathsf{cnf}(\phi) = \bigwedge_{j=1}^{m} B_j$, where each B_j is a Boolean clause,
- $\mathsf{cnf}(\phi)$ is satisfiable iff ϕ is satisfiable; more precisely, $\exists b_{n+1}, \ldots, b_{n+p} . \mathsf{cnf}(\phi)$ is tautologically equivalent to ϕ, and
- The number of variables and the size of $\mathsf{cnf}(\phi)$ are both linear in the size of ϕ.

Linear-time algorithms for computing $\mathsf{cnf}(\phi)$ are well-known; see, for instance, [26].

A SAT solver is an algorithm which determines, given a Boolean formula ϕ in CNF, whether ϕ is satisfiable. In the affirmative case, the SAT solver will produce a satisfying assignment for ϕ. If, on the other hand, ϕ is unsatisfiable, the SAT solver can be required to produce a *proof of unsatisfiability* [33, 23]. Such a proof in turns yields an *unsatisfiable core*, i.e., an unsatisfiable subset of clauses of ϕ. In practice, SAT solvers tend to generate small unsatisfiable cores. The SAT solvers we have used in our experiments are zChaff [32] and SMVSAT.

2.2 Presburger Arithmetic

Presburger arithmetic can be defined as the first-order theory of the structure $\langle \mathbb{N}, 0, 1, \leqslant, + \rangle$, where $\mathbb{N}$ denotes the set of non-negative integers. In this paper, we focus on the *quantifier-free* fragment of Presburger arithmetic.

More precisely, let $x_1, x_2, \ldots$ be variables ranging over non-negative integers. A *linear constraint* is any expression of the form

$$\sum_{i=1}^{n} a_i x_i \sim c \; ,$$

where each a_i and c are integer constants (i.e., $a_i, c \in \mathbb{Z}$), and $\sim$ is a comparison operator ($\sim \; \in \{<, \leqslant, >, \geqslant, =\}$). *Quantifier-free Presburger formula* (henceforth *QFP formulas*) are Boolean combinations of linear constraints:

Definition 1. *The collection of QFP formulas is defined inductively as follows:*

- *Any linear constraint is a QFP formula, and*
- *If ϕ_1 and ϕ_2 are QFP formulas, then so are $\neg\phi_1$, $\phi_1 \wedge \phi_2$, and $\phi_1 \vee \phi_2$.*

Remark 1. Note that an integer variable x can easily be represented in Presburger arithmetic by two non-negative variables: $x = x_+ - x_-$. It is equally straightforward to encode Boolean variables as equalities of the form $x = 1$, together with constraints of the form $x \leqslant 1$ conjoined at the outermost level.

We are interested in the *satisfaction problem* for QFP formulas: given a QFP formula ϕ, is there an assignment of non-negative integers to the variables of ϕ under which ϕ evaluates to *True*?

Ganesh *et al.* [14] present a comprehensive survey of decision procedures for satisfiability solving of QFP formulas. The abstraction-based algorithm we describe in Section 3 can be used in conjunction with any such decision procedure; it is however desirable that the procedure also generate satisfying integer assignments. We briefly describe in the next two paragraphs how we use the commercial package CPLEX [17], together with the SAT solver zChaff, to achieve this[2]. Put succinctly, our decision procedure iteratively refines Boolean encodings of the QFP formula based on satisfying assignments from zChaff that are inconsistent with the linear arithmetic. This technique is known as 'lazy explication of axioms', and was originally proposed by the authors of the tools ICS [16, 12], CVC [11, 4, 6], Math-SAT [22, 3], and Verifun [13].

CPLEX uses integer linear programming techniques (and in particular the simplex algorithm) to decide whether a *conjunction* of linear arithmetic constraints is satisfiable. When such a conjunction is satisfiable, CPLEX also generates a satisfying integer assignment.

Our CPLEX-based QFP solver is implemented as follows. Given a QFP formula ϕ, we first extract a 'Boolean skeleton' ϕ_{bool} from ϕ, by simply replacing each linear constraint in ϕ with a fresh Boolean variable. We then invoke zChaff to determine whether ϕ_{bool} is satisfiable. If it is not, then ϕ cannot possibly be satisfiable either, and we terminate. Otherwise, we take the satisfying assignment (say $\bar{b}$) provided by zChaff and form a corresponding conjunction of linear constraints, which we then submit to CPLEX. If CPLEX is able to find a satisfying

---

[2] We also experimented with the tool LP_SOLVE [21] but encountered difficulties with certain formulas, for which LP_SOLVE appears to be unsound.

assignment for this conjunction of linear constraints, then this assignment also satisfies ϕ, and we are done. Otherwise, we augment the Boolean formula ϕ_{bool} with a 'blocking' clause ruling out the Boolean assignment $\bar{b}$ produced earlier by zChaff. We then repeat the procedure with the new Boolean formula until the satisfiability of ϕ is established or refuted.

In the remainder of this paper, let us refer to our implementation of the above algorithm as 'PresSolver'.

Remark 2. Among other existing QFP solvers, let us mention (i) the OMEGA tool[3] [28], which converts a QFP formula into disjunctive normal form and then applies an extension of the Fourier-Motzkin linear programming algorithm on each disjunct; (ii) the automata-based tool LASH [31]; and (iii) the previously mentioned ILP-based tools LP_SOLVE, ICS, and CVC[4].

Our abstraction-based framework can be used in conjunction with any of these decision procedures, and indeed we intend to carry out a number of experiments with them in the near future. We have so far mostly worked with the commercial package CPLEX mainly because of its high reliability, completeness over the integers, and efficiency. While ICS and CVC are not at present complete over the integers, and are therefore unsuitable for our purposes, their implementors inform us that they are planning to release complete versions of these tools in the near future.

3   Abstraction-Based Presburger Satisfiability Solving

We now present the main contribution of this paper, a SAT-based algorithm that generates increasingly precise *abstractions* of QFP formulas. Our abstractions are obtained by eliminating linear constraints from QFP formulas in a conservative manner. The choice of which constraints to eliminate is guided by an iterative interaction with a SAT solver.

Let ϕ be a QFP formula. If we view the linear constraints occurring in ϕ as atomic propositions, we can convert ϕ into a satisfaction-equivalent QFP formula ϕ' in CNF by invoking the procedure described in Section 2.1. Note that ϕ' may require the introduction of fresh Boolean variables; as discussed in Remark 1, these are modeled as new constrained integer variables. For the remainder of this section, let us therefore assume without loss of generality that the QFP formula ϕ is given to us in CNF.

Write $\phi = \bigwedge_{j=1}^{m} C_j$, with each C_j a (Presburger) clause. (A Presburger clause is a disjunction of linear constraints.) Let $x_1, \ldots, x_n$ be the collection of variables appearing in ϕ. Suppose we are given a function *size* which assigns to each variable x_i a positive integer $size(x_i)$. Intuitively, $size(x_i)$ denotes the maximum number of bits allowed in the binary representation of x_i; put another way, $size(x_i)$ implicitly represents the constraint $x_i < 2^{size(x_i)}$.

---

[3] In fact, the OMEGA tool handles the full first-order theory of Presburger arithmetic, not just its quantifier-free fragment.

[4] We note that while much of the work on ILP has in fact focused on *0-1 ILP* (see, e.g., [5]), the latter is less useful here because of the presence of unbounded variables.

Let C_j^{size} stand for the formula $C_j \wedge \bigwedge_{i \in J_j} x_i < 2^{size(x_i)}$, where J_j is the set of indices of the variables that appear in C_j. We can encode C_j^{size} as an equivalent *Boolean* formula $\mathsf{bool}(C_j^{size})$, as follows. For each variable x_i appearing in C_j, allocate $size(x_i)$ Boolean variables, one for each of the bits allowed in the binary representation of x_i. The linear constraints in C_j are then encoded as Boolean formulas on these Boolean variables. Note that the encoding uses exact (i.e., arbitrary-precision) bit-vector arithmetic.

Next, let $B_j^{size} \;\hat{=}\; \mathsf{cnf}(\mathsf{bool}(C_j^{size}))$ denote the CNF representation of this Boolean formula, ensuring in the process that all newly introduced auxiliary Boolean variables are fresh. Write

$$\phi^{size} \;\hat{=}\; \bigwedge_{j=1}^{m} C_j^{size} \qquad \text{and} \qquad \mathsf{cbe}(\phi^{size}) \;\hat{=}\; \bigwedge_{j=1}^{m} B_j^{size} \;.$$

(Here cbe stands for 'CNF Boolean Encoding'.) The two main points are:

- The QFP formula ϕ^{size} is satisfiable iff the Boolean formula $\mathsf{cbe}(\phi^{size})$ is satisfiable, and
- Any satisfying assignment for ϕ^{size} is also a satisfying assignment for ϕ.

Observe that since each B_j^{size} is a conjunction of Boolean clauses, $\mathsf{cbe}(\phi^{size})$ is itself in CNF; let us therefore write $\mathsf{cbe}(\phi^{size}) = \bigwedge_{k=1}^{p} A_k$. Note that it is straightforward when building $\mathsf{cbe}(\phi^{size})$ to maintain a table recording, for each clause A_k of $\mathsf{cbe}(\phi^{size})$, its 'origin' $\mathsf{orig}(A_k) = C_j$ in ϕ. While it is possible for several Presburger clauses to yield a common Boolean clause A_k, $\mathsf{orig}(A_k)$ only records one of them. It is clear that, whenever $\mathsf{orig}(A_k) = C_j$, any satisfying integer assignment for C_j^{size} yields a corresponding satisfying Boolean assignment for A_k.

We now come to the crux of the paper, our abstraction-based algorithm for solving QFP formulas, which we call 'ASAP' (Abstraction-based Satisfiability Algorithm for Presburger). ASAP takes as input a QFP formula ϕ in CNF with free variables $x_1, \ldots, x_n$, and either outputs a satisfying assignment of non-negative integers to these variables, or declares ϕ to be unsatisfiable. ASAP repeatedly invokes as subroutines both a SAT solver (SMVSAT) and a quantifier-free Presburger arithmetic decision procedure (PresSolver, which itself is based on CPLEX and zChaff).

ASAP first attempts to satisfy an over-constrained version of ϕ in which the integer variables are only allowed to range over a bounded domain. This is achieved by encoding the over-constrained QFP formula as a Boolean formula, which is then given as input to SMVSAT. If a satisfiable assignment is found, then ϕ is clearly also satisfiable, and an integer witness is easily extracted from the satisfying Boolean assignment produced by SMVSAT. Otherwise, SMVSAT returns an unsatisfiable core, which is in turn used to pinpoint a subset of the clauses of ϕ as unsatisfiable over the chosen bounded domain. The conjunction of these clauses is clearly a conservative abstraction of ϕ, in that if it is unsatisfiable then so is ϕ. We therefore run PresSolver on this abstracted QFP formula. If it is found to be satisfiable, we increase the size of our bounded domain to accommodate the satisfying assignment supplied by PresSolver, and repeat the whole process. We continue until a conclusive judgment on the satisfiability of ϕ is obtained.

Section 4 presents experimental evidence which suggests that ASAP is considerably more efficient than PresSolver on its own. ASAP is described in pseudocode in Figure 1.

Algorithm ASAP
Input: QFP formula ϕ in CNF with free variables $x_1, \ldots, x_n$
Output: satisfying assignment for ϕ or 'UNSAT'

```
let size(x_i) = 1 for each i
repeat forever
    run SMVSAT on cbe(φ^size)
    if cbe(φ^size) is satisfiable then
        return(corresponding satisfying assignment for φ^size)
    else
        let ⋀_{k∈K} A_k be an unsatisfiable core of cbe(φ^size)
        let ψ = ⋀_{k∈K} orig(A_k)
        run PresSolver on ψ
        if ψ is unsatisfiable then
            return('UNSAT')
        else
            let v_1, ..., v_n be a satisfying assignment for ψ
            let size(x_i) = max(⌈log_2(v_i)⌉, size(x_i)) for each i
endrepeat
```

Fig. 1. ASAP: an abstraction-based Presburger satisfiability solving algorithm

Theorem 1. *The algorithm ASAP described in Figure 1 is correct and always terminates.*

Proof. We first examine the issue of correctness. Observe that ψ is less constrained a QFP formula than ϕ, in that it contains only a subset of the clauses of ϕ. Thus if ψ is unsatisfiable, then so is ϕ. On the other hand, suppose that ASAP terminates with an assignment $\overline{v}$ of non-negative integers to the variables. $\overline{v}$ is a satisfying assignment for ϕ^{size}, for some instance of $size$. But since any satisfying assignment for ϕ^{size} is automatically a satisfying assignment for ϕ, $\overline{v}$ is indeed a satisfying assignment for ϕ, as required.

We now claim that, in any execution of ASAP, we never see two identical instances of the QFP formula ψ. Since ψ is always a conjunction of a subset of the clauses of ϕ, it only has finitely many possible instantiations, which immediately entails the termination of the algorithm.

It remains to establish our claim. Suppose, on the contrary, that two identical instances of ψ are observed in a given execution of ASAP. The first time around, an unsatisfiable core $\bigwedge_{k\in K} A_k$ of cbe(ϕ^{size}) is obtained, and the function $size$ is then subsequently increased to $size'$ to accommodate a satisfying integer assignment $\overline{v}$ for ψ. In other words, $\psi = \bigwedge_{k\in K} \text{orig}(A_k)$ and $\psi^{size'}[\overline{v}]$ evaluates to

True. (Here $\psi^{size'}$ denotes the QFP formula ψ conjoined with linear constraints of the form $x_i < 2^{size'}$.)

Some iterations later, we encounter a second unsatisfiable core $\bigwedge_{l \in L} A_l$ of $\mathsf{cbe}(\phi^{size''})$ such that $\psi = \bigwedge_{l \in L} \mathsf{orig}(A_l)$. Writing $C_{j(l)} \widehat{=} \mathsf{orig}(A_l)$, we have that $C_{j(l)}^{size'}[\overline{v}]$ evaluates to true for every $l \in L$, since $\overline{v}$ is a satisfying assignment for $\psi^{size'}$. Since each iteration of the repeat loop increases (pointwise) the function *size*, we conclude that $size'' \geqslant size'$, and therefore that $C_{j(l)}^{size''}[\overline{v}]$ also evaluates to true for every $l \in L$. Let $\overline{b}$ be the Boolean assignment to the bit-variables prescribed by $size''$ corresponding to the integer assignment $\overline{v}$. We immediately get that $A_l[\overline{b}]$ evaluates to *True* for each $l \in L$, and therefore that $\bigwedge_{l \in L} A_l$ is satisfiable, contradicting our earlier hypothesis. □

Remark 3. We record the following observations concerning ASAP:

– Any ILP-based solver, such as PresSolver, offers the option of generating satisfying integer assignments that moreover minimize some linear 'objective function' $f(x_1, \ldots, x_n)$. In the case at hand, it is desirable that satisfying assignments be as compact as possible; more precisely, they should ideally minimize the number of new bits that are required for their representation. A simple linear function which approximates this requirement is $f(x_1, \ldots, x_n) \widehat{=} \sum_{i=1}^{n} x_i$, and in fact that is the function that PresSolver uses. Note that while minimizing the number of bits subsequently leads to easier queries for the SAT solver, the minimization requirement is an additional burden for the ILP-based Presburger solver.
– Note that, while our inner Presburger decision procedure PresSolver generates satisfying integer assignments, many theorem proving tools do not. Nonetheless, we could still use a pure decision procedure in ASAP by simply requiring, on every iteration, that the function *size* be increased by 1 for each of its arguments.
– An examination of the proof of termination reveals that the number of iterations of the main loop of our algorithm is bounded by the number of different subsets of clauses of the original Presburger formula ϕ, a quantity which is exponential in the size of ϕ. One can in fact guarantee at most a *polynomial* number of iterations, by invoking the fact that, if ϕ admits a solution at all, ϕ admits a solution in which each variable is assigned a value that can be represented with polynomially many bits [7, 19]. Since each iteration of the main loop increases the number of bits used by at least one, at most polynomially many iterations are required to reach this bound. Note nonetheless that since a SAT solver is invoked each time, the overall worst-case time complexity of ASAP remains exponential.

4   Implementation and Experimental Results

We implemented our tool ASAP within the UCLID verification system [30], which is implemented in Moscow ML [24], a dialect of Standard ML. In implementing ASAP, we used PresSolver as a decision procedure for QFP formulas, and SMVSAT as a proof-generating SAT solver. SMVSAT outputs a proof as a set of resolution steps. The set of all original (i.e., not introduced by resolution) clauses that appear in this proof constitute the unsatisfiable core. ASAP interacts with PresSolver and SMVSAT using a file-based interface. The total running time for ASAP is the cumulative time spent in generating input for SMVSAT and PresSolver, in running SMVSAT and PresSolver, and in analyzing their output.

We performed an experimental evaluation to investigate whether using PresSolver within ASAP could achieve a significant speed-up over directly using PresSolver on the input formula. We used two benchmark sets of QFP formulas in CNF: randomly generated formulas, and formulas generated in real-world software verification problems.

The experiments were performed on a Linux workstation with an AMD Athlon 1.5 GHz dual-processor CPU, with 3 GB of RAM. Both ASAP and PresSolver are single-threaded.

4.1   Results on Random Benchmarks

We ran both ASAP and PresSolver on a set of 45 randomly generated formulas with a timeout of 1200 seconds. The formulas included both unsatisfiable and satisfiable instances. We generated the formulas recursively as follows: for each node, we randomly select either a boolean operator ($\wedge$, $\vee$, $\neg$) or a relational operator ($=$, $<$, etc.). In case of a relation, we generate a linear constraint, randomly selecting the coefficients of the variables and the constant term from the range $[0, 100]$. The number of variables is fixed, but the number of linear constraints can vary, allowing us to generate over-constrained formulas that have a reasonable likelihood of being unsatisfiable. The depth of nesting of Boolean operators in the formula is bounded, eventually forcing the selection of a relational operator.

Figure 2 compares, for each formula, the total run-time of ASAP with the run-time of PresSolver. In the plot, the x-coordinate of each point is the time taken by ASAP, and the y-coordinate is the time taken by PresSolver. We also plot the diagonal line $y = x$: points above the diagonal correspond to benchmarks on which ASAP outperforms PresSolver, while points below it correspond to benchmarks on which ASAP is outperformed.

The results show that ASAP outperforms PresSolver on most of the benchmarks, completing on all benchmarks within a minute while PresSolver times out on 6 benchmarks. On larger benchmarks for which PresSolver terminates, we notice that ASAP performs an order of magnitude better; the speed-up is more than a factor of 100 on some benchmarks. PresSolver outperforms ASAP on some smaller formulas, but ASAP completes within 4 seconds on all of these; the reason for PresSolver's superior performance on these is simply because the original formulas themselves are fairly small (about 80 clauses), so that ASAP's extra overhead is comparatively more costly.

We also investigated how the maximum size of any abstracted formula ψ, measured in terms of number of CNF clauses, compares with that of the original

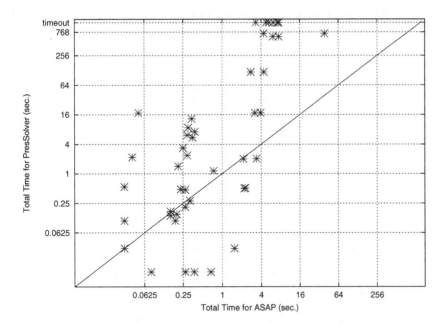

Fig. 2. Comparing ASAP against PresSolver on random benchmarks. The timeout was 1200 seconds. Note the log scale on both axes

formula ϕ. This was done by computing the ratio of the number of clauses in ψ with the number of clauses in ϕ. We found the smallest such ratio to be 0.009, where the original formulas has 648 clauses and the largest abstraction contains just 6. The largest ratio was 0.206, with 354 clauses in the original formula, and 73 in the largest abstraction. This reduction is the main reason for the speed-ups achieved over directly using PresSolver on ϕ.

4.2   Results on Software Verification Benchmarks

We now report on the second set of experiments performed on formulas generated from software verification. We used a suite of formulas generated in the WiSA project[5] in checking for format string vulnerabilities. The benchmarks include 20 formulas, both satisfiable and unsatisfiable, in an extension of QFP with uninterpreted functions. Uninterpreted functions were first eliminated using Ackermann's technique [1], and both ASAP and PresSolver were run on the resulting QFP formula. Each generated QFP formula is an arbitrary Boolean combination of linear constraints. The number of variables in the formulas ranges from 33 to 43, the number of linear constraints ranges between 197 and 267, and the total number of clauses ranges between 695 and 1054.

PresSolver was unable to solve any of these formulas within a timeout of one hour. On the other hand, ASAP was able to complete on all but one benchmark

---

[5] http://www.cs.wisc.edu/wisa

Table 1. ASAP results on WiSA benchmarks. A "*" indicates that ASAP timed out after 1 hour. (PresSolver timed out on all instances.)

Benchmark	ASAP Time		Max. Ratio
	PresSolver Time	Total Time	$\#(\psi$ clauses)
	(sec.)	(sec.)	$\#(\phi$ clauses)
s-5-3	199.70	230.44	0.139
s-5-5	239.48	262.00	0.142
s-5-6	193.53	215.56	0.148
s-5-7	274.08	303.45	0.142
s-6-5	286.88	310.05	0.125
s-6-6	261.93	292.05	0.132
xs-5-2	408.56	434.16	0.120
xs-5-3	596.82	631.77	0.122
xs-5-5	970.01	994.11	0.124
xs-5-6	934.18	959.76	0.126
xs-5-7	978.83	1008.53	0.124
xs-5-9	126.44	150.90	0.155
xs-5-10	127.93	155.01	0.155
xs-5-11	1034.01	1062.88	0.161
xs-6-2	648.44	683.79	0.103
xs-6-5	1051.57	1116.78	0.106
xs-6-6	1008.85	1043.09	0.110
xs-6-9	132.04	158.97	0.135
xs-6-10	184.51	220.18	0.135
xs-6-11	*	*	–

within the timeout. Table 1 shows the results of running ASAP on the WiSA benchmarks. We give the total time taken by ASAP and the time taken by PresSolver on abstractions generated by ASAP, summed over all invocations of PresSolver. We notice that on all benchmarks, the time taken by PresSolver is the bottleneck for ASAP, accounting for over 90% of the total time on most benchmarks. ASAP takes on the order of a few minutes to solve each formula. SMVSAT took less than 5 seconds on each occasion, with the remaining time spent in generating encodings and parsing output from SMVSAT and PresSolver.

The abstractions generated by ASAP were fairly compact. The last column in Table 1 shows the ratio of the number of clauses in the largest abstraction ψ generated by ASAP to the number of clauses in the original formula ϕ. We see that this ratio is roughly between 10 and 15 percent. Again, the compactness of the abstraction is the main reason why ASAP is able to solve these formulas, while PresSolver is unable to complete on any. Finally, we note that the number of iterations taken by ASAP ranged between 19 and 28.

5　Conclusion

We have presented a novel abstraction-based approach to the satisfiability solving of quantifier-free Presburger formulas. Our experimental results, over both random formulas as well as industrial benchmarks, indicate that embedding a theorem prover for QFP formulas within our framework can achieve significant speed-ups over directly using the prover on the input formula.

In the future, we would like to experiment with a number of other Presburger solvers, and in particular ICS and CVC. While these tools are at present incomplete over the integers, and hence not suitable for our purposes, their implementors inform us that new releases will remedy this, something we look forward to.

Another research direction would be to investigate whether the abstraction-based methodology presented here could be applied to other (higher-order?) logics and theories, possibly over different domains such as bit vectors, real numbers, etc.

Acknowledgments

We thank Vinod Ganapathy and Somesh Jha for providing us with benchmark formulas.

References

1. W. Ackermann. *Solvable Cases of the Decision Problem.* North-Holland, 1954.
2. T. Amon, G. Borriello, T. Hu, and J. Liu. Symbolic timing verification of timing diagrams using Presburger formulas. In *Proceedings of DAC 97*, pages 226–231, 1997.
3. G. Audemard, P. Bertoli, A. Cimatti, A. Kornilowicz, and R. Sebastiani. A SAT based approach for solving formulas over boolean and linear mathematical propositions. In *Proceedings of CADE 02*, pages 195–210, 2002.
4. C. Barrett, D. Dill, and A. Stump. Checking satisfiability of first-order formulas by incremental translation to SAT. In *Proceedings of CAV 02*, volume 2404, pages 236–249. Springer LNCS, 2002.
5. P. Barth. *Logic-Based 0-1 Constraint Programming.* Kluwer, 1995.
6. S. Berezin, V. Ganesh, and D. L. Dill. An online proof-producing decision procedure for mixed-integer linear arithmetic. In *Proceedings of TACAS 03*, volume 2619, pages 521–536. Springer LNCS, 2003.
7. I. Borosh and L. B. Treybig. Bounds on positive integral solutions of linear diophantine equations. *Proceedings of the American Mathematical Society*, 55(2):299–304, 1976.
8. R. Brinkmann and R. Drechsler. RTL-datapath verification using integer linear programming. In *Proceedings of VLSI Design*, pages 741–746, 2002.
9. T. Bultan, R. Gerber, and W. Pugh. Symbolic model checking of infinite state systems using Presburger arithmetic. In *Proceedings of CAV 97*, volume 1254, pages 400–411. Springer LNCS, 1997.
10. P. Chauhan, E. M. Clarke, J. H. Kukula, S. Sapra, H. Veith, and D. Wang. Automated abstraction refinement for model checking large state spaces using SAT based conflict analysis. In *FMCAD 02*, pages 33–51, 2002.
11. CVC. http://verify.stanford.edu/CVC/.

12. L. de Moura, H. Rueß, and M. Sorea. Lazy theorem proving for bounded model checking over infinite domains. In *Proceedings of CADE 02*, pages 438–455, 2002.
13. C. Flanagan, R. Joshi, X. Ou, and J. B. Saxe. Theorem proving using lazy proof explication. In *Proceedings of CAV 03*, volume 2725, pages 355–367, 2003.
14. V. Ganesh, S. Berezin, and D. L. Dill. Deciding Presburger arithmetic by model checking and comparisons with other methods. In *Proceedings of FMCAD 02*, volume 2517, pages 171–186. Springer LNCS, 2002.
15. T. A. Henzinger, R. Jhala, R. Majumdar, and G. Sutre. Lazy abstraction. In *Proceedings of POPL 02*, pages 58–70. ACM, 2002.
16. ICS. http://www.icansolve.com.
17. ILOG CPLEX. http://www.ilog.com/products/cplex/.
18. P. Janičić, I. Green, and A. Bundy. A comparison of decision procedures in Presburger arithmetic. Research paper no. 872, Division of Informatics, 1997. University of Edinburgh.
19. R. Kannan and C. L. Monma. On the computational complexity of integer programming problems. In *Optimisation and Operations Research*, volume 157 of *Lecture Notes in Economics and Mathematical Systems*, pages 161–172. Springer-Verlag, 1978.
20. R. Kurshan. *Computer-Aided Verification of Coordinating Processes*. Princeton University Press, 1994.
21. LP_SOLVE. http://www.freshports.org/math/lp_solve/.
22. Math-SAT. http://dit.unitn.it/~rseba/Mathsat.html.
23. K. McMillan and N. Amla. Automatic abstraction without counterexamples. In *Proceedings of TACAS 03*, volume 2619, pages 2–17. Springer LNCS, 2003.
24. Moscow ML. http://www.dina.dk/~sestoft/mosml.html.
25. C. H. Papadimitriou. On the complexity of integer programming. *Journal of the ACM*, 28(4):765–768, 1981.
26. D. A. Plaisted and S. Greenbaum. A structure-preserving clause form translation. *Journal of Symbolic Computation*, 2(3):293–304, 1986.
27. M. Preßburger. Über die Vollständigkeit eines gewissen Systems der Arithmetik ganzer Zahlen, in welchem die Addition als einzige Operation hervortritt. *Comptes-rendus du premier congrès des mathématiciens des pays slaves*, 395:92–101, 1929.
28. W. Pugh. The Omega Test: A fast and practical integer programming algorithm for dependence analysis. In *Supercomputing*, pages 4–13, 1991.
29. R. E. Shostak. A practical decision procedure for arithmetic with function symbols. *Journal of the ACM*, 26(2):351–360, 1979.
30. UCLID. http://www.cs.cmu.edu/~uclid.
31. P. Wolper and B. Boigelot. An automata-theoretic approach to Presburger arithmetic constraints. In *Proceedings of SAS 95*, volume 983, pages 21–32. Springer LNCS, 1995.
32. zChaff. http://www.ee.princeton.edu/~chaff/zchaff.php.
33. L. Zhang and S. Malik. Extracting small unsatisfiable cores from unsatisfiable boolean formulas. In *Proceedings of SAT 03*, 2003.

Widening Arithmetic Automata[*]

Constantinos Bartzis and Tevfik Bultan

Department of Computer Science
University of California
Santa Barbara CA 93106, USA
{bar,bultan}@cs.ucsb.edu

Abstract. Model checking of infinite state systems is undecidable, therefore, there are instances for which fixpoint computations used in infinite state model checkers do not converge. Given a widening operator one can compute an upper approximation of a least fixpoint in finite number of steps even if the least fixpoint is uncomputable. We present a widening operator for automata encoding integer sets. We show how widening can be used to verify safety properties that cannot be verified otherwise. We also show that the dual of the widening operator can be used to detect counter examples for liveness properties. Finally, we show experimentally how the same technique can be used to verify properties of complex infinite state systems efficiently.

1 Introduction

Symbolic verification of large and complex infinite state systems may require an unreasonable number of fixpoint iterations. Furthermore, since the problem of verification of temporal properties of infinite state systems is in general undecidable, the fixpoint computations might not converge at all. To overcome this problem one can use approximations. Abstract interpretation framework [9] provides a technique known as widening, to compute a least fixpoint's upper bound in finite time. Widening has been successfully applied to Polyhedra based verification of systems specified with arithmetic constraints [10, 13, 7]. On the other hand, similar work for the automata encoding of arithmetic constraints has been limited. We present a widening operator for automata encoding of integer sets as described in [3]. We also show how to verify properties of infinite state systems using an approximate fixpoint computation based on our widening technique. Note that, for these properties the exact fixpoint computation does not converge. Finally, we show experimentally how the same technique can be used to improve the efficiency of our infinite state model checking tool, Action Language Verifier (ALV) [8], and compare its performance with BRAIN [15].

Most reachability properties can be formulated as least fixpoints over sets of states. If the state space is infinite, these fixpoints may not be computable. Widening is a well known technique [9, 10] that facilitates the convergence of a fixpoint computation by extrapolating an upper approximation of the exact least

---

[*] This work is supported by NSF grants CCR-9984822 and CCR-0341365.

R. Alur and D.A. Peled (Eds.): CAV 2004, LNCS 3114, pp. 321–333, 2004.

fixpoint. In [10, 12] a widening operator was defined for systems whose transition relation and sets of states can be described by linear arithmetic constraints, symbolically represented as sets of convex Polyhedra. This technique has been successfully used in the analysis of various types of systems such as concurrent systems (by extending it to Presburger arithmetic formulas [7]), synchronous programs and linear hybrid systems [13].

Systems described by Presburger arithmetic formulas can also be symbolically represented by finite automata [6, 16]. Experimental results in [3], indicate that the automata representation often outperforms the polyhedral representation. However, until lately the use of approximation techniques for the automata representation has been limited. In a series of recent papers [14, 5] "Regular Model Checking" (RMC) has been defined as a framework for algorithmic verification of systems with transition relations represented by a regular length-preserving relation on strings. Typical examples of such systems are linear parameterized networks of processes. Widening techniques have been used to compute the set of reachable configurations of such systems in finite time. However, the arithmetic relations considered in [14, 5] are restricted because of the unary encoding used (only addition of constants is allowed). Our goal is to develop a widening technique for automata representing Presburger formulas.

Another way to deal with non-termination of exact infinite state model checking is to compute the reflexive-transitive closure R^* of the transition relation R of the system (or an upper approximation of R^*). Given R^*, one can compute the set of states forward or backward reachable from an initial set of states I with a single image computation. Therefore computing R^* is at least as hard as computing sets of reachable states. In fact, it may be the case that the set of states reachable from I is regular but R^* is not. Nevertheless, ways to approximate R^* for regular transition relations R have been studied in [5, 11, 4]. In particular, in [4] the authors present a generic technique for computing R^* (sometimes precisely) for transition relations representing arithmetic relations. The technique is generic in the sense that it can handle relations that are not in a restricted form. Our technique is also generic but is based on widening instead of iterating relations. As we show in Section 4 our approach can verify some properties of systems with non-regular R^*. The algorithm in [4] is complicated and involves determinization of automata which is potentially an expensive operation even when heuristics are used to improve efficiency. There is no full implementation of this algorithm that allows it to be used for verification applications. As we show in Section 5, our widening technique can be used to verify properties of complex systems efficiently. Finally, note that one can use our widening technique to iterate transducers but the opposite is not true.

The rest of the paper is organized as follows. First we discuss fixpoint computations and how widening technique can be used to help them converge in Section 2. Next, we briefly present the automata representation we are using for integer sets satisfying Presburger formulas in Section 3. In Section 4 we formally define our widening operator for arithmetic automata, prove some interesting properties and illustrate how it can be applied to a set of characteristic systems. Finally in Section 5 we present experimental results that demonstrate how our widening technique can be used to verify properties of complex systems efficiently.

2 Fixpoint Computations and Widening

We consider systems whose states can be described by the values of v integer variables $x_1, \ldots, x_v$. A set of states of the system, $S \subseteq \mathbb{Z}^v$, is a relation on the v integer variables. The transition relation of the system, $R \subseteq \mathbb{Z}^{2v}$, is a relation on the current state and next state variables $x_1, \ldots, x_v, x_1', \ldots, x_v'$. In particular, we consider systems where S and R can be represented as Presburger arithmetic formulas, i.e., $S = \{(x_1, \ldots, x_v) \mid \phi_S(x_1, \ldots, x_v)\}$ and $R = \{(x_1, \ldots, x_v, x_1', \ldots, x_v') \mid \phi_R(x_1, \ldots, x_v, x_1', \ldots, x_v')\}$, where ϕ_S and ϕ_R are Presburger arithmetic formulas. In Section 3, we show how to represent S and R symbolically using finite automata.

We define the pre-condition of S with respect to R, $pre(S, R) \subseteq \mathbb{Z}^v$, as the set of states that can reach some state in S in one step. Similarly we define $post(S, R) \subseteq \mathbb{Z}^v$ as the set of states reachable from some state in S in one step. One can compute $pre(S, R)$ and $post(S, R)$ as follows

$$pre(S, R) = \{(x_1, \ldots, x_v) \mid \exists x_1' \ldots \exists x_v'.(\phi_{S[x_1 \leftarrow x_1', \ldots, x_v \leftarrow x_v']} \wedge \phi_R)$$

$$post(S, R) = \{(x_1, \ldots, x_v) \mid (\exists x_1 \ldots \exists x_v.\phi_S \wedge \phi_R)_{[x_1' \leftarrow x_1, \ldots, x_v' \leftarrow x_v]}\}.$$

where $\psi_{[y \leftarrow z]}$ is the formula generated by substituting z for y in ψ. Hence, to compute $pre(S, R)$ and $post(S, R)$ we need to be able to compute three operations: conjunction, existential variable elimination and renaming. In Section 3, we will show that these operations can be implemented using an automata representation for R and S.

We can formulate the verification problem of invariants based on pre- and post-condition functions as follows. We are given a set of initial states I, a transition relation R, pre- and post-condition functions $pre(S, R)$ and $post(S, R)$, and a property P. To verify the property we have two alternatives. The first is to compute $FR(I)$, the set of states forward reachable from the initial states I, and then check whether

$$FR(I) \subseteq P \tag{1}$$

The second way is to compute $BR(\neg P)$ the set of states backward reachable from the negation of the property and then check that

$$BR(\neg P) \cap I = \emptyset \tag{2}$$

Since the problem is undecidable, we might not be able to compute $FR(I)$ or $BR(\neg P)$ exactly. In that case we can follow a conservative approach by replacing $FR(I)$ and $BR(\neg P)$ by over approximations $FR(I)^+ \supseteq FR(I)$ and $BR(\neg P)^+ \supseteq BR(\neg P)$ in equations 1 and 2 respectively. Note that, we may not be able to verify a property that actually holds when we use approximations. Below we describe how to compute $FR(I)$ and $FR(I)^+$. Computation of $BR(\neg P)$ and $BR(\neg P)^+$ is similar.

The set $FR(I)$ of reachable states from I is the least fixpoint of the functional $\lambda X \, . \, I \cup post(X, R)$. This fixpoint is the limit of the sequence $S_0, S_1, \ldots$, where $S_0 = I$ and $S_{i+1} = S_i \cup post(S_i, R)$. This sequence may not converge. However we can compute an over approximation $FR(I)^+$ which is the limit of a new sequence $S_0', S_1', \ldots$, such that for each i, $S_i \subseteq S_i'$ and the sequence $S_0', S_1', \ldots$ converges after a finite number of iterations. We compute the S_i's by using a widening operator ∇, which satisfies the following property:

$$\text{Given two sets } A \text{ and } B, \ A \cup B \subseteq A \nabla B. \tag{3}$$

Now we can define S_i' as:

$$S_i' = \begin{cases} S_i & \text{if } 0 \le i \le s \\ S_{i-1}' \nabla (S_{i-1}' \cup post(S_{i-1}', R)) & \text{if } i > s \end{cases}$$

where s is the seed of the widening sequence. Experiments show that higher seeds are likely to result in better approximations. The goal is to find a widening operator such that the sequence $S_0', S_1', \ldots$ converges as fast as possible to a fixpoint that is as close as possible to the exact set of reachable states. We present a widening operator for automata representing integer sets.

3 Automata Representation for Integer Sets

The representation of Presburger formulas by finite automata has been studied in [6, 16, 3]. Here we briefly describe finite automata that accept the set of natural number tuples that satisfy a Presburger arithmetic formula on v variables. The representation we discuss below can be extended to integers using 2's complement arithmetic [3]. We present the construction for natural numbers to simplify the presentation. Our implementation of widening technique and our verification tool also handles negative integers.

We encode numbers using their binary representation. A v-tuple of natural numbers $(n_1, n_2, \ldots, n_v)$ is encoded as a word over the alphabet $\{0, 1\}^v$, where the i_{th} letter in the word is $(b_{i1}, b_{i2}, \ldots, b_{iv})$ and b_{ij} is the i_{th} least significant bit of number n_j. Given a Presburger formula ϕ, we construct a finite automaton $FA(\phi) = (K, \Sigma, \delta, e, F)$ that accepts the language $L(\phi)$ over the alphabet $\Sigma = \{0, 1\}^v$, which contains all the encodings of the natural number tuples that satisfy the formula. K is the set of automaton states, Σ is the input alphabet, δ : $K \times \Sigma \to K$ is the transition function, $e \in K$ is the initial state, and $F \subseteq K$ is the set of final or accepting states.

For equalities, $FA(\sum_{i=1}^{v} a_i \cdot x_i = c) = (K, \Sigma, \delta, e, F)$, where

$$K = \{k \mid \sum_{a_i < 0} a_i \le k \le \sum_{a_i > 0} a_i \vee 0 \le k \le -c \vee -c \le k \le 0\} \cup \{sink\},$$

$$\Sigma = \{0, 1\}^v, \quad e = -c, \quad F = \{0\},$$

$$\delta(k, (b_1, \ldots, b_v)) = \begin{cases} (k + \sum_{i=1}^{v} a_i \cdot b_i)/2 & \text{if } k + \sum_{i=1}^{v} a_i \cdot b_i \text{ is even and } k \ne sink \\ sink & \text{otherwise} \end{cases}$$

For inequalities, $\mathrm{FA}(\sum_{i=1}^{v} a_i \cdot x_i < c) = (K, \Sigma, \delta, e, F)$, where

$$K = \{k \mid \sum_{a_i < 0} a_i \le k \le \sum_{a_i > 0} a_i \vee 0 \le k \le -c \vee -c \le k \le 0\}$$

$$\Sigma = \{0,1\}^v, \quad e = -c, \quad F = \{k \mid k \in K \wedge k < 0\},$$

$$\delta(k, (b_1, ..., b_v)) = \lfloor (k + \sum_{i=1}^{v} a_i \cdot b_i)/2 \rfloor.$$

Moreover, conjunction, disjunction and negation of constraints can be implemented by automata intersection, union and complementation, respectively. Finally, if some variable is existentially quantified, we can compute a non-deterministic FA accepting the projection of the initial FA on the remaining variables and then determinize it. The resulting FA may not accept *all* satisfying encodings (with any number of leading zeros). We can overcome this by recursively identifying all rejecting states k such that $\delta(k, (0, 0, ..., 0)) \in F$, and make them accepting. Universal quantification can be similarly implemented by the use of the FA complementation.

4   Widening Arithmetic Automata

Before formally defining a widening operator for arithmetic automata we briefly describe the intuition behind it. Let A and A' be two automata representing two consecutive members of a sequence $A_0, A_1, \ldots$, whose limit A_∞ is the exact least fixpoint we are trying to compute. Since A_∞ is the union of all A_is, it can be seen as a product automaton with each state being a tuple (of possibly infinite size) containing a state from each A_i. First, consider a string w and assume that after consuming w A, A' and A_∞ move to state k, k' and k_∞ respectively. Then k_∞ contains k and k'. Second, consider states k and k' of A and A' respectively, such that the languages accepted from k and k' are the same. Then again there exists a state k_∞ of A_∞ that contains both k and k'. For either scenario, our widening method, given A and A' as an input, produces an automaton that accepts both languages of A and A' and in which k and k' are merged in a single state.

Given two finite automata $A = (K, \Sigma, \delta, e, F)$ and $A' = (K', \Sigma, \delta', e', F')$ we define the binary relation $\equiv_\nabla$ on $K \cup K'$ as follows. Given $k \in K$ and $k' \in K'$, we say that $k \equiv_\nabla k'$ and $k' \equiv_\nabla k$ if and only if

$$\forall w \in \Sigma^*.\ \delta^*(k, w) \in F \Leftrightarrow \delta'^*(k', w) \in F' \qquad (4)$$

$$\text{or} \quad k, k' \ne sink \wedge \exists w \in \Sigma^*.\ \delta^*(e, w) = k \wedge \delta'^*(e', w) = k', \qquad (5)$$

where $\delta^*(k, w)$ is defined as the state A reaches after consuming w starting from state k. In other words, condition 4 states that $k \equiv_\nabla k'$ if the languages accepted by A from k and by A' from k' are the same. Condition 5 states that $k \equiv_\nabla k'$ if for some word w, A ends up in state k and A' ends up in state k' after consuming w. For $k_1 \in K$ and $k_2 \in K$ we say that $k_1 \equiv_\nabla k_2$ if and only if

$$\exists k' \in K'.\ k_1 \equiv_\nabla k' \wedge k_2 \equiv_\nabla k' \quad \vee \quad \exists k \in K.\ k_1 \equiv_\nabla k \wedge k_2 \equiv_\nabla k \qquad (6)$$

Similarly we can define $k_1' \equiv_\nabla k_2'$ for $k_1' \in K'$ and $k_2' \in K'$.

It is easy to prove that $\equiv_\nabla$ is an equivalence relation. Call C the set of equivalence classes of $\equiv_\nabla$. We define $A\nabla A' = (K'', \Sigma, \delta'', e'', F'')$ by:

$$K'' = C$$
$$\delta''(c_i, \sigma) = c_j \text{ s.t. } (\forall k \in c_i \cap K.\ \delta(k, \sigma) \in c_j \vee \delta(k, \sigma) = sink) \wedge$$
$$(\forall k' \in c_i \cap K'.\ \delta'(k', \sigma) \in c_j \vee \delta'(k', \sigma) = sink)$$
$$e'' = c \text{ s.t. } e \in c \wedge e' \in c$$
$$F'' = \{c_1, c_2, ..., c_n\} \text{ s.t. } \forall c_i, \exists k \in F \cup F'.\ k \in c_i$$

In other words, the set of states of $A\nabla A'$ is the set C of equivalence classes of $\equiv_\nabla$. Transitions are defined from the transitions of A and A'. The initial state is the class containing the initial states e and e'. The set of final states is the set of classes that contain some of the final states in F and F'. The following Theorem states that ∇ satisfies condition (3).

Definition 1. *Given an automaton $A = (K, \Sigma, \delta, e, F)$ and a state $k \in K$, we define $L(k)$ to be the language accepted by the automaton $(K, \Sigma, \delta, k, F)$. Also $L(A) = L(e)$.*

Theorem 1. *Given two automata A and A', $L(A) \cup L(A') \subseteq L(A\nabla A')$.*

Proof. Essentially we want to prove that given $w \in \Sigma^*$ such that w is accepted by A or A' then w is also accepted by $A\nabla A'$. Without loss of generality we may assume that w is accepted by A. Let $w = \sigma_0\sigma_1\ldots\sigma_n$. Then there is a sequence of non-sink states $k_0, k_1, \ldots, k_{n+1}$ such that $k_0 = e$, $\delta(k_i, \sigma_i) = k_{i+1}$ and $k_{n+1} \in F$. From the definition of $A\nabla A' = (K'', \Sigma, \delta'', e'', F'')$ it follows that there exists a sequence $c_0, c_1, \ldots, c_{n+1}$ such that $c_0 = e''$, $\delta''(c_i, \sigma_i) = c_{i+1}$ and $k_i \in c_i$ for all $0 \le i \le n + 1$. Since $k_{n+1} \in c_{n+1}$ and $k_{n+1} \in F$ it follows that $c_{n+1} \in F''$ and thus w is accepted by $A\nabla A'$.

According to the original definition [9], a widening operator has to guarantee convergence. Our widening operator does not guarantee convergence. Nevertheless, we can force it to converge by a slight modification. If we discard the condition $k, k' \neq sink$ from equation 5, for each state in one automaton there exists an equivalent state in the other. Thus, the produced automaton has at most as many states as the smaller operand. As a result, the automata in the sequence can not increase in size. There are finitely many automata with a given number of states and a fixed alphabet. On the other hand, the size of the set of states represented by the automata in the sequence is monotonically increasing, otherwise we would have reached a fixpoint. Consequently, the sequence will converge. One can deploy this technique when the number of iterations has become too high. However, we decided not to use it in our implementation (see Section 5), because in most of the cases this modification in the widening operator makes the approximation too coarse to prove any property.

On the other hand, in the sequel we show that for a class of systems, if the approximate computation converges, it computes the exact set of reachable states.

Definition 2. *An automaton $A_1 = (K_1, \Sigma, \delta_1, e_1, F_1)$ is called weakly equivalent to automaton $A_2 = (K_2, \Sigma, \delta_2, e_2, F_2)$ iff there exists a total function $f : K_1 \setminus \{sink\} \to K_2$ such that $\delta_1(k, \sigma) = sink$ or $f(\delta_1(k, \sigma)) = \delta_2(f(k), \sigma)$ for all $k \in K_1 \setminus \{sink\}$ and $\sigma \in \Sigma$. Furthermore, $f(e_1) = e_2$ and for all $k_1 \in F_1$, $f(k_1) \in F_2$.*

Lemma 1. *If automaton $A_1 = (K_1, \Sigma, \delta_1, e_1, F_1)$ is weakly equivalent to automaton $A_2 = (K_2, \Sigma, \delta_2, e_2, F_2)$ then state $k_1 \in K_1 \setminus \{sink\}$ is mapped to state $k_2 \in K_2$ iff for all $w \in \Sigma^*$, $\delta_1^*(e_1, w) = k_1 \Rightarrow \delta_2^*(e_2, w) = k_2$.*

Lemma 2. *If automaton $A_1 = (K_1, \Sigma, \delta_1, e_1, F_1)$ is weakly equivalent to automaton $A_2 = (K_2, \Sigma, \delta_2, e_2, F_2)$ then, if state $k_1 \in K_1$ is mapped to state $k_2 \in K_2$ then $L(k_1) \subseteq L(k_2)$.*

The proofs of Lemma 1 and Lemma 2 are trivial and have been omitted.

Definition 3. *An automaton $A = (K, \Sigma, \delta, e, F)$ is called state-disjoint iff $L(k_1) \cap L(k_2) = \emptyset$ for all $k_1 \neq k_2 \in K$.*

Lemma 3. *Consider a transition system and an approximate sequence S_0', $S_1', \ldots$ as defined in Section 2. If $\lambda X . I \cup post(X, R)$ has a least fixpoint represented by a state-disjoint automaton A_∞ and the automaton A_i representing S_i', $i \geq s$ is weakly equivalent to A_∞, then the automaton A_{i+1} representing S_{i+1}' is also weakly equivalent to A_∞.*

Proof. Let A_i' represent $S_i' \cup post(S_i', R)$. Then $A_{i+1} = A_i \nabla A_i'$. Let $A_i = (K, \Sigma, \delta, e, F)$, $A_i' = (K', \Sigma, \delta', e', F')$ and $A_\infty = (K_\infty, \Sigma, \delta_\infty, e_\infty, F_\infty)$. Note that by Lemma 2 and the monotonicity of $\lambda X . I \cup post(X, R)$, $L(A_i) \subseteq L(A_i') \subseteq L(A_\infty)$. Hence, the states of A_{i+1} are of two kinds: classes of $\equiv_\nabla$ that contain states from both A_i and A_i' and singleton classes containing one state from A_i'. Recall that A_i is weakly equivalent to A_∞ with respect to a function f.

First we show that for any two distinct states k_1, k_2 of A_i that belong to the same class, $f(k_1) = f(k_2)$. States k_1 and k_2 are in the same class iff they are both $\equiv_\nabla$ to some state k' of A_i'. This can happen in two ways. First, assume that there exist $w_1, w_2 \in \Sigma^*$ such that $\delta^*(e, w_1) = k_1$, $\delta^*(e, w_2) = k_2$, $\delta'^*(e', w_1) = k'$ and $\delta'^*(e', w_2) = k'$. Then by Lemma 1, $\delta_\infty^*(e_\infty, w_1) = f(k_1)$ and $\delta_\infty^*(e_\infty, w_2) = f(k_2)$. Since $L(A_i) \subseteq L(A_i') \subseteq L(A_\infty)$, $\emptyset \neq L(k_1) \cup L(k_2) \subseteq L(k') \subseteq L(f(k_1)) \cap L(f(k_2))$. Since A_∞ is state-disjoint, we conclude that $f(k_1) = f(k_2)$. Second, assume that $L(k') = L(k_2)$ and for some $w \in \Sigma^*$, $\delta^*(e, w) = k_1$ and $\delta'^*(e', w) = k'$. Using similar arguments we conclude that $\emptyset \neq L(k_1) \subseteq L(k') = L(k_2) \subseteq L(f(k_1)) \cap L(f(k_2))$ and therefore $f(k_1) = f(k_2)$.

Now we can prove that A_i' is weakly equivalent to A_∞. To do so, we define a function $f' : K' \to K_\infty$ according to Definition 2. Given any state $k' \in K'$ such that $k' \equiv_\nabla k$ for some $k \in K$ (i.e., k' belongs to a non-singleton class), we define $f'(k') = f(k)$. Now we can show that all transitions from k' conform to Definition 2. First we consider transitions to states in non-singleton classes. If $L(k') = L(k)$ then for all $\sigma \in \Sigma$, $L(\delta'(k', \sigma)) = L(\delta(k, \sigma))$. Consequently, $\delta'(k', \sigma) \equiv_\nabla \delta(k, \sigma)$ and thus $f'(\delta'(k', \sigma)) = f(\delta(k, \sigma)) = \delta_\infty(f(k), \sigma) = \delta_\infty(f'(k'), \sigma)$. Now if $L(k') \neq L(k)$, then there exists $w \in \Sigma^*$ such that $\delta^*(e, w) = $

k and $\delta'^*(e', w) = k'$. Then $\delta^*(e, w.\sigma) = \delta(k, \sigma)$ and $\delta'^*(e', w.\sigma) = \delta'(k', \sigma)$, thus $\delta(k, \sigma) \equiv_\nabla \delta'(k', \sigma)$ and again we can conclude that $f'(\delta'(k', \sigma)) = \delta_\infty(f'(k'), \sigma)$. Now let us consider transitions going to singleton states, for which f' has not been defined yet. Assume $\delta'(k', \sigma)$ is such a state. We define $f'(\delta'(k', \sigma)) = \delta_\infty(f'(k'), \sigma)$. Now we need to prove that there is no state $k'' \in K'$ that belongs to a non-singleton class and symbol $\sigma' \in \Sigma$ such that $\delta'(k'', \sigma') = \delta'(k', \sigma)$ and $f'(\delta'(k'', \sigma')) \neq \delta_\infty(f'(k''), \sigma')$. If that were the case, we can show that $L(\delta_\infty(f'(k'), \sigma))$ would intersect $L(\delta_\infty(f'(k''), \sigma'))$, which contradicts the hypothesis. Proceeding in the same manner we can show that f' can be defined for the rest of the states, so that A'_i is weakly equivalent to A_∞. Finally, A_{i+1} is weakly equivalent to A_∞, since it is constructed by merging states of A'_i that have the same f'.

Theorem 2. *Consider a transition system and an approximate sequence $S'_0, S'_1, \dots$ as defined in Section 2. If $\lambda X \,.\, I \cup post(X, R)$ has a least fixpoint represented by a state-disjoint automaton A_∞ and the automaton A_s representing S'_s is weakly equivalent to A_∞, then if the sequence converges, it will converge to the exact least fixpoint.*

Proof. Automaton A_s, i.e., the last automaton that has been computed without widening, is weakly equivalent to A_∞. By Lemma 3, all A_i, $i > s$, are also weakly equivalent to A_∞. Since $L(A_0) \subseteq L(A_1) \subseteq \dots \subseteq L(A_\infty)$, the limit of the sequence is $L(A_\infty)$, which represents the least fixpoint of $\lambda X \,.\, I \cup post(X, R)$.

Corollary 1. *Consider a transition system with one integer variable x that is initially set to 0 and is increased by a constant c at each step. Then the approximate fixpoint corresponds to the exact set of reachable states.*

Proof. Clearly all reachable states satisfy $\exists y \geq 0 \,.\, x = c \cdot y$. If c is odd, the automaton A_∞ representing this constraint has states $0, 1, \dots, c-1$, where $L(n)$ contains all non-negative integers for which the remainder of division with c is n. State 0 is the initial and only accepting state. Also $\delta(0, 0) = 0$. Clearly $L(n) \cap L(m) = \emptyset$ whenever $n \neq m$, therefore A_∞ is state-disjoint. Moreover, the automaton A_0 representing the initial state $x = 0$ has only one accepting and initial state that loops 0 and sends 1 to $sink$. Obviously A_0 is weakly equivalent to A_∞ and hence the hypothesis of Theorem 2 holds. Consequently, the exact set of reachable states will be computed. If c is even, it can be written as $c = 2^n \cdot d$, where d is odd. Then every number divisible by c consists of a prefix of n zeros and a suffix that is divisible by d. Following similar arguments as before we can conclude that the hypothesis of Theorem 2 holds, if the widening seed is 1.

Note that the class of systems that satisfy the hypothesis of Theorem 2 is quite large. Corollary 1 is just an example of such a system. Figure 1 illustrates an example fixpoint computation for the system described in Corollary 1, when $c = 3$. The first column shows the automata representing the approximate fixpoint iterate S_i, the second column shows the automata representing $S'_i = S_i \cup post(S_i)$ and the third column shows the equivalence classes on the states of S'_i. For each i, $S_{i+1} = S_i \nabla S'_i$.

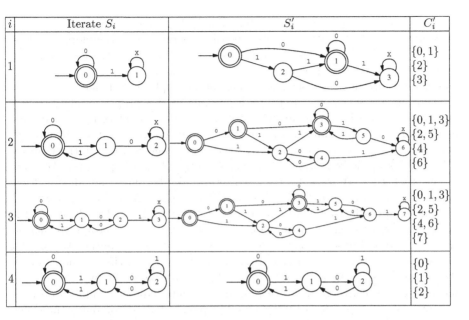

Fig. 1. Example fixpoint computation for increment by 3

```
module square()                        module con_decr()
  integer y,z;                           integer x,y;
  parameterized integer x;               initial: x>=0 && y>=0;
  initial: y=0 && z=x;                   con_decr: y>0 => (x'=x-1 && y'=y-1);
  square: z>0 && z'=z-1 && y'=y+x;       spec: AF([x=0])
  spec: AG([z=0 => ((x<=3 => y<=9) &&  endmodule
  (x=4 => y=16) && (x>=5 => y>=25))])
endmodule
```

Fig. 2. Example specifications of transition systems

Our second example, shown in Figure 2 as module **square**, is a transition system that computes the square of an integer parameter x by iteratively adding x to a variable y that is initially set to 0. Variable z is used to count the iterations. The set of reachable states of the system contains exactly those states where $y = (x - z) \cdot x$ and is obviously non-regular. Hence, no forward fixpoint computation is expected to converge since the fixpoint cannot be represented in a finite way. Also, the closure of the transition relation of the system is not regular and thus cannot be computed exactly. On the other hand, there are meaningful properties, like the one shown in Figure 2, which can be verified using a backward fixpoint computation. The exact computation does not converge. However our algorithm terminates after 10 iterations and indeed verifies the property.

Finally, the third example illustrates the use of the collapse operator $\bar{\nabla}$, the dual of the widening operator ∇. The collapse operator should satisfy the condition that given two sets A and B, $A \cap B \supseteq A \bar{\nabla} B$. Given a widening operator ∇, one can trivially define a collapse operator as: $A \bar{\nabla} B = \neg(\neg A \nabla \neg B)$. For other representations for integer sets (e.g. Polyhedra [7], or composite disjunctive representations [17]), negation is an expensive operation and therefore this definition is not efficient. However, for deterministic automata, negation has linear complexity in the number of states (it suffices to make accepting states rejecting and vice versa), thus the above definition can be implemented efficiently.

The collapse operator is useful in disproving liveness properties and producing counter examples for them, whenever the exact fixpoint computation does not converge. As an example, consider the system shown in Figure 2 as module con_decr. There are two non-negative variables x and y with arbitrary initial values. We keep decrementing them concurrently while y is positive. We want to check whether $AF(x = 0)$ i.e., x will eventually become 0 for all execution paths. It is easy to see that this does not hold when $x > y$. The exact backward fixpoint computation for $AF(x = 0)$ does not converge. If we stop the computation after a fixed number of iterations, we can obtain an under-approximation of $AF(x = 0)$ and observe that it does not include the set of initial states, thus the property might not hold. To prove that, we need to verify the negation of the initial property, namely $EG(x \neq 0)$. Once again the exact fixpoint computation does not converge. However, an approximate fixpoint computation that uses our collapse operator converges in 3 steps and indeed computes the exact set of states that violate $AF(x = 0)$, namely those states where $x > y$. Note that since the sequence of fixpoint iterates for EG is decreasing, we cannot use widening.

5 Experiments

Widening can be used for two purposes: 1) As we explained above, it can be used when the exact fixpoint computations do not converge; 2) It can be used to speed up fixpoint computations that would otherwise converge but only after a large number of iterations. To demonstrate this fact we repeated the experiments in [2] using widening as well.

We integrated the construction algorithms in [2, 3] as well as the approximate fixpoint computation algorithms based on the widening technique presented earlier to an infinite state CTL model checker called Action Language Verifier (ALV) [8] built on top of the Composite Symbolic Library [17]. In our experiments we compare the running times of the exact and approximate forward and backward fixpoint algorithms. For the same experiments we also present the running time of BRAIN [15]. BRAIN is a reachability analysis tool, that 1) uses Hilbert's basis as symbolic representation for integer sets, and 2) computes the exact backward fixpoint iterations. There is no approximation operation in BRAIN for the fixpoint computations which do not converge.

We experimented with a set of examples taken from the BRAIN distribution available at: http://www.cs.man.ac.uk/~voronkov/BRAIN/ and the ALV distribution available at: http://www.cs.ucsb.edu/~bultan/composite/. We obtained the experimental results on a SUN ULTRA 10 work station with 768 Mbytes of memory, running SunOs 5.7. The results are presented in Table 1. For the approximate fixpoint computations we also report the seed used for widen-

Table 1. Experimental results. Time measurements appear in seconds

Problem Instance	BRAIN	ALV					
		exact forward	exact backward	approximate forward	seed	approximate backward	seed
CSM4	3.76	∞	99.35	0.21	0	79.29	5
CSM6	25.01	∞	540.88	0.21	0	482.11	7
CSM8	128.54	∞	1772.85	0.21	0	3782.51	9
CSM10	494.03	∞	4809.13	0.21	0	↑	11
CSM12	1644.33	∞	9676.81	0.20	0	↑	13
CSMinv10	0.93	∞	0.58	0.18	0	0.61	4
CSMinv20	3.57	∞	0.90	0.18	0	0.79	4
CSMinv30	9.59	∞	1.09	0.19	0	1.01	4
CSMinv40	20.71	∞	1.20	0.19	0	1.08	4
CSMinv50	38.58	∞	1.45	0.19	0	1.36	4
bigjava	11244.60	∞	↑	↑	0	↑	0
bigjavainv	2641.05	2.85	82.33	9.78	0	43.17	10
bigjavainv1	30615.20	8.57	1160.09	8.32	0	26.13	1
consistencyprot	1.09	∞	24.28	0.34	0	26.85	7
consistencyprotinv	7.75	1.16	59.38	1.14	0	11.55	1
consistencyprotinv1	0.05	∞	0.16	0.20	0	0.17	4
consprod	11346.40	1.85	↑	1.39	0	↑	4
consprodinv	1.27	∞	0.66	139.17	0	0.54	5
ticket2	⋆	0.13	∞	0.12	0	0.13	0
ticket3	⋆	0.45	∞	0.45	0	0.56	0
ticket4	⋆	2.93	∞	2.89	0	6.77	0
coherence	⋆	∞	∞	0.23	0	0.13	0
bakery3	0.35	∞	0.38	7.95	0	0.44	4
bakery4	14.82	∞	9.83	1681.85	0	10.09	5
bakery5	1107.75	∞	577.45	↑	0	582.43	6

ing. Entries of ↑ mean that the computation was aborted because it did not finish in 5 hours or the memory limit was exceeded. Entries of ∞ mean that the exact fixpoint computation does not converge. Finally, ⋆ means that we are checking a liveness property that cannot be handled by BRAIN. Problem instances can be categorized in three groups:

1. Pure integer problems (CSM, bigjava, consistencyprot and consprod)
2. Integer problems with invariants (those with the suffix inv)
3. Problems with both boolean and integer variables (ticket, coherence, bakery)

The problems with invariants are obtained from the original problems by conjoining the transition relation with a set of invariants. A typical invariant has the form $x_1 + ... + x_k < m$, where m is a natural number. Such invariants essentially bound the variables $x_1, ..., x_k$ to a finite region.

We analyzed each of the problem instances with three different configurations of ALV using two exact fixpoint computation algorithms (forward and backward) and two approximate fixpoint computation algorithms based on our widening technique. For each problem we chose a widening seed that makes our approximation precise enough to allow us to verify the properties. For the forward case, the lowest possible value for the seed, 0, is adequate. However, for the backward case we had to set the seed higher to achieve the required precision. In this sense our technique is not fully automatic. Nevertheless, one could automate the choice of widening seed by iteratively trying all possible values, starting from 0, until the property is verified.

For almost all problem instances, one of the configurations of ALV (depending on the choice of exact or approximate algorithm, forward or backward fixpoint, and the value of the widening seed) is faster than BRAIN. Note that according to [15] BRAIN outperforms other infinite state model checkers: Hytech, DMC and a version of ALV that uses a Polyhedral representation for arithmetic sets. The only two exceptions are consistencyprotinv1, for which the difference of performance is very small, and bigjava, for which ALV runs out of memory.

Among all fixpoint computation algorithms used in ALV, the approximate forward algorithm is the faster for most of the problems with the approximate backward algorithm coming second. This indicates that the use of widening can speed up fixpoint computations significantly even when the exact computations converge. We believe that the fact that the forward algorithm is usually faster than the backward algorithm is due to the specifics of each problem instance and is not a general rule. A characteristic example is consprod and consprodinv. Another observation is that while the approximate backward algorithm performs well for the invariant versions of the problem instances, it usually performs poorly for the non-invariant versions. This does not happen with the forward algorithm. An explanation to this fact is that each of the forward fixpoint iterates naturally satisfies the invariants. However, this is not true for the backward fixpoint iterates, whose size is reduced when intersected with the invariants.

The problem instances ticket2, ticket3, ticket4 and coherence could not be solved by any exact backward algorithm. For ALV, the exact backward fixpoint computation diverges whereas the forward fixpoint computation converges. BRAIN cannot handle liveness properties as the ones specified in ticket and coherence. On the other hand, both approximate algorithms were able to verify the properties. Furthermore, while the exact forward fixpoint computation diverges for most of the problem instances, the approximate one converges relatively fast for almost all of these problem instances. This shows that in practice our widening technique can be successfully applied to non-trivial systems, whereas in [4] only very simple systems are considered. A problem of special interest is bakery. Our exact backward fixpoint computation always converges and scales better than BRAIN, whereas the exact forward fixpoint computation always diverges. Widening does not help much for this problem. The approximate forward fixpoint computation does not scale well. The approximate backward fixpoint computation is precise enough only when widening is used in the last iteration and thus it takes a little longer than the exact computation to finish.

Finally, we repeated all experiments using another version of ALV in which integer sets are symbolically represented as polyhedra and manipulated by the Omega Library [1]. This version uses an extension of Halbwachs' widening algorithm [10] to Presburger arithmetic [7]. For the ticket, coherence and bakery problems, we could verify the properties using both forward and backward approximate fixpoint computations but the running times are much higher than those for the automata version. For the CSM problem instances, the approximate forward fixpoint computed was not precise enough to verify the properties immediately. Due to internal limitations of the Omega Library we could not get results for the rest of the problem instances.

References

1. The Omega project. http://www.cs.umd.edu/projects/omega/
2. Constantinos Bartzis and Tevfik Bultan. Efficient image computation in infinite state model checking. In *Proceedings of the 15th International Conference on Computer Aided Verification (CAV 2003)*, volume 2725 of *Lecture Notes in Computer Science*, pages 249–261. Springer, 2003.
3. Constantinos Bartzis and Tevfik Bultan. Efficient symbolic representations for arithmetic constraints in verification. *International Journal of Foundations of Computer Science*, 14(4):605–624, 2003.
4. Bernard Boigelot, Axel Legay, and Pierre Wolper. Iterating transducers in the large. In *Proceedings of the 15th International Conference on Computer Aided Verification*, volume 2725 of *LNCS*, pages 223–235. Springer, 2003.
5. Ahmed Bouajjani, Bengt Jonsson, Marcus Nilsson, and Tayssir Touili. Regular model checking. In *Computer Aided Verification*, pages 403–418, 2000.
6. A. Boudet and H. Comon. Diophantine equations, Presburger arithmetic and finite automata. In *Proceedings of the 21st International Colloquium on Trees in Algebra and Programming*, volume 1059 of *LNCS*, pages 30–43. Springer-Verlag, April 1996.
7. T. Bultan, R. Gerber, and W. Pugh. Model-checking concurrent systems with unbounded integer variables: Symbolic representations, approximations, and experimental results. *ACM Transactions on Programming Languages and Systems*, 21(4):747–789, July 1999.
8. T. Bultan and T. Yavuz-Kahveci. Action language verifier. In *Proceedings of the 16th IEEE International Conference on Automated Software Engineering*, 2001.
9. P. Cousot and R. Cousot. Abstract interpretation: A unified lattice model for static analysis of programs by construction or approximation of fixpoints. In *Proceedings of the 4th Annual ACM Symposium on Principles of Programming Languages*, pages 238–252, 1977.
10. P. Cousot and N. Halbwachs. Automatic discovery of linear restraints among variables of a program. In *Proceedings of the 5th Annual ACM Symposium on Principles of Programming*, pages 84–97, 1978.
11. Denis Dams, Yassine Lakhnech, and Martin Steffen. Iterating transducers. In *Computer Aided Verification'01*, 2001.
12. N. Halbwachs. *Détermination automatique de relations linéaires vérifiées par les variables d'un programme*. PhD thesis, University of Grenoble, March 1979.
13. N. Halbwachs, Y. E. Proy, and P. Roumanoff. Verification of real-time systems using linear relation analysis. *Formal Methods in System Design*, 11(2):157–185, August 1997.
14. Bengt Jonsson and Marcus Nilsson. Transitive closures of regular relations for verifying infinite-state systems. In *Tools and Algorithms for Construction and Analysis of Systems*, pages 220–234, 2000.
15. Tatiana Rybina and Andrei Voronkov. Using canonical representations of solutions to speed up infinite-state model checking. In *Proceedings of the 14th International Conference on Computer Aided Verification*, pages 400–411, 2002.
16. P. Wolper and B. Boigelot. On the construction of automata from linear arithmetic constraints. In *Proceedings of the 6th Conference on Tools and Algorithms for the Construction and Analysis of Systems*, LNCS, pages 1–19. Springer, April 2000.
17. T. Yavuz-Kahveci, M. Tuncer, and T. Bultan. Composite symbolic library. In *Proceedings of the 7th International Conference on Tools and Algorithms for the Construction and Analysis of Systems*, volume 2031 of *Lecture Notes in Computer Science*, pages 335–344. Springer-Verlag, April 2001.

Why Model Checking
Can Improve WCET Analysis

Alexander Metzner

Safety critical Embedded Systems group
Department of Computer Science
Carl von Ossietzky University Oldenburg
metzner@informatik.uni-oldenburg.de

Abstract. Calculating predictions for an upper bound of the execution time of real-time tasks in embedded systems is a necessary step in designing such systems. There exist successful analysis methods, based on abstract interpretation and integer linear programming (ILP) for that problem. In [12] it is stated, that model checking *is not adequate* for this task. The approach presented in this paper shows that model checking *is adequate* and, furthermore, can improve the results. This is done by defining an automaton based semantic for control flow graphs of programs for abstract and concrete instruction cache analysis. A binary search based bunch of model checker runs is used to calculate the upper bound of execution time.

1   Introduction

Schedulability analysis is one of the key factors in the design of a hard real-time system, that has to fulfill timing constraints stemming from the interaction with a physical environment. Particularly, in safety critical systems, as used in the domains of automotive, avionics or power-plant electronics, the guarantee to meet given deadlines is a stringent property of the system. To prove this property, common schedulability analysis methods[6] need an upper bound for the execution time of programs, so-called worst case execution time (WCET). This bound has to be safe and accurate: it will never under-estimating the real behaviour. Furthermore it should be as close as possible to the real maximal execution time of the program. Deriving such execution time bounds from software is a challenging task, since modern processor and cache architectures have to be taken into account. The dynamics of programs, ie. which paths through a program are valid or not, also influence the WCET, independent from the architecture. Therefore, usually the analysis of WCET is separated into two tasks, namely the low level analysis (dealing with architectural features) and the high-level analysis (dealing with program paths)[11]. In this paper, we focus on the first one, but give some hints how possibly to combine this with a high-level analysis.

There exist several approaches to tackle the low-level analysis with respect to caches and pipelines. In general, the low level analysis consists of two sub-problems. Firstly, the timing behaviour of instructions of a program must be

R. Alur and D.A. Peled (Eds.): CAV 2004, LNCS 3114, pp. 334–347, 2004.
© Springer-Verlag Berlin Heidelberg 2004

predicted. Secondly, the longest path through the program must be calculated by using the predicted instruction timing. In [10] an abstract cache behaviour classification is defined, that statically predicts the worst case behaviour of each memory reference. [11] derives a similar classification of memory accesses using an abstract interpretation for cache behaviour prediction and integer linear programming for finding the longest path by a method called implicit path enumeration[7]. Only ILP is used in [8] for pipeline and simple cache analysis, whereas [3] uses data-flow analysis methods for pipeline and cache analysis.

Both tasks, the behaviour prediction and the longest path finding problem, can be solved by a model checker[9]. Since a model checker traverses the entire state space of a model and therefore returns a concrete path in the program, better results can be obtained than all mentioned approaches above, because of their abstract nature. However, [12] claims model checking to be an inadequate technique for this analysis task. The approach presented in this paper will show, that model checking *can* be used for WCET analysis and furthermore it could be a benefit to use it. In order to prove this, we have implemented an experimental framework for an instruction cache analysis within the OFFIS verification environment[1] based on the VIS model checker[4].

2   Basic Modelling

Calculations of the WCET for programs are performed on the control flow graph. In this section we define the construction of the control flow graph of a program from the program code. Further, we define an automaton based representation of the control flow graph that is used in the next chapter to build the semantics for WCET analysis.

The starting point of a WCET analysis in a low level manner are executables, object code or assembler code. Our approach analyses timing behaviour of a program at assembler code level. For effectiveness reasons, the control flow graph is built from blocks of assembler instructions instead of single instructions. The idea is, to merge strongly connected instructions to so called basic blocks[10], that consists of the longest sequence of instructions with only one entry and one exit.

Definition 1 (Basic Block).
A basic block is constructed from a control flow of an assembler program by merging sequential instructions to blocks of instructions. Only the first instruction of a block may be target of a jump and the last instruction must be a jump or the last instruction of the program. There are no other jumps within this block.

Definition 2 (Basic Block Graph (BBG)).
A basic block graph is a tuple $\mathcal{B} = (BB, T_\mathcal{B}, \mathcal{L})$ with:

- *BB set of basic blocks of a program*
- *$T_\mathcal{B} \subseteq BB \times BB$ transition relation according to the control flow*

– $\mathcal{L} \subseteq BB \times BB \times \mathbb{N}_0 \times \mathbb{N}^+$ *the labelling relation for loops (minimal and maximal iteration count)*

For each basic block $b_i \in BB$ that is a head of a loop the following attributes are defined:

- $backjump : BB \rightarrow 2^{BB}$: *All source basic blocks that jump backwards to b_i*
- $exits : BB \rightarrow 2^{BB}$: *All basic blocks which are outside the loop headed by b_i and which are targets of basic blocks inside the loop*
- $cost : BB \rightarrow \mathbb{N}_0$ *the number of processor cycles of an execution of each basic block in the worst case*

Note, that the assembler instructions of each basic block are considered in the *cost* attribute. The attribute *backjump* denotes all basic blocks that lead to a further iteration of loops, whereas *exits* denotes all blocks that finish the loop. The labelling relation must be defined by the user or a high level analysis in order to avoid unbounded loops and defines the possible interval of iterations for each loop. It has to be defined for each backjump basic block to the loop head.

For simplicity reasons, we restrict our analysis to the prediction of instruction cache related timing, so an analysis of the pipeline behaviour with respect to timing is assumed to be given with the *cost* attribute. (Below, we will give a hint, how the integration of pipeline analysis is possible, too).

The basic block graph can be statically derived from the assembler program and represents a control flow graph of the program. In order to calculate a safe upper bound of the execution time by using model checking techniques, we represent the basic block graph by a finite state machine, that contains all possible paths through the program.

Definition 3 (Basic Block Automaton (BBA)).
The Basic Block Automaton is a tuple $BBA = (s_0, S_T, S, \mathcal{I}, V, T)$ with:

- S *the set of states*
- $s_0 \in S$ *the initial state*
- $S_T \subseteq S$ *the set of termination states*
- $\mathcal{I}$ *the set of inputs (used to resolve non-determinism)*
- V *the set of variables (used for loop counters, cache contents and consumed time)*
- $T \subseteq S \cup \{\bot\} \times S$ *the transition relation. The $\bot$ element is used to define the init transition.*

For each transition $t \in T$ the following functions are defined:

- $guard : T \rightarrow BEXPR^{V \cup \mathcal{I}}$ *a guarding condition of type boolean expression*
- $action : T \rightarrow 2^{ASSIGN_V}$ *with $ASSIGN_V = \{v := e \mid v \in V \wedge e \in EXPR^{V \cup \mathcal{I}}\}$ an action on each transition to conditionally update the system variables. EXPR is defined as usual, with the notation of $c?e_1 : e_2$ for conditional expressions.*

We will define the semantics of a BBG in terms of a BBA. The main idea is to represent all paths through a BBG by an automaton that jumps each step from basic block to basic block. A sequence of states represents a path in the BBG. On each step the emerging costs of the successor state are added to a global variable, which contains the consumed time (from the init state to the actual state), ie. the runtime on the actual path. In the next chapter we will show for two different kinds of semantics, how this is done with respect to the cache architecture and the BBG.

3   Two Different Semantics for BB Graphs

The well known method from [11] to calculate safe and accurate WCETs uses a mixture of abstract interpretation (AI) for cache behaviour classification and integer linear programming to derive the worst case path through a BBG. To handle this problem by model checking, one can think of mainly two different approaches: First, model checking can replace the integer linear programming in order to solve only the subtask of finding the longest path. Secondly, it can replace both subtasks, the path finding as well as the prediction of cache behaviour, to solve the entire problem. Changing only the method of critical path finding will not lead to more accurate WCETs with respect to ILP, but it will help to avoid ILP specific problems. In section 3.1 the semantic of this approach is described.

On the other hand, employing the model checker for precise cache behaviour prediction can improve the results due to the avoidance of over-approximations of the abstraction methods of AI. We describe the semantics for precise cache behaviour prediction in section 3.2.

3.1   Model Checking for Path Finding

If the task for model checking is reduced to finding the longest path in a BBG, we have to assume a pre-calculated prediction of the behaviour of cache accesses. This is done by the prediction of the worst case hit/miss behaviour and is derived statically by an implementation of the abstract interpretation formalisation found eg. in [11]. The idea is to collect abstract states of the cache contents in order to compute an over-approximation of timing. In the next section, when we show why model checking can lead to more accurate results, this method will be explained in more detail. Here we are only interested in the classification for all memory accesses. Each memory access is predicted to behave like *always-miss (am)*, *always-hit (ah)* or *first-miss (fm)*. Memory accesses of type "am" will produce a cache miss each time. "fm" means that only the first access leads to a cache miss, all further accesses will produces cache hits. Finally, "ah" indicates a cache hit for every access to this memory location.

Since the approach presented in this paper is restricted to the behaviour of instruction caches, this analysis is performed for each instruction in a basic block b_i. For efficiency reasons, the cache behaviour prediction of instructions within one basic block are merged and the syntax of a BB is extended by the two mappings (all accesses that are not handled by these two mappings are treated as always hit):

- $get\_am : BB \to \mathbb{N}_0$ number of always miss in a BB
- $get\_fm : BB \to \mathbb{N}_0$ number of first miss in a BB

Exploiting this knowledge we can abstract from the concrete cache architecture. We only have to consider the penalty of cache hits and misses (in processor cycles). For pipeline architectures we assume, that each instruction can be executed within one cycle, including the hit penalty of the instruction memory access (pipelined RISC concept).

The main idea of the semantic for path finding is to sum up the emerging costs (in processor cycles) of all basic blocks on a concrete path through the BBA in a variable *cycles*. This is performed at the transitions to each block. The addend is constant for the fixed costs of instruction execution in the pipeline and the cache accesses that are predicted as "am" and "ah". In order to handle the category first-miss, we have to introduce one boolean variable f_{b_i} for each basic block b_i, if there exist "fm" accesses within this block. The content of the f_{b_i} variable indicates, whether this is the first time of access or a subsequent one. Consequently, the cost that has to be added to *cycles* on entering b_i contains the miss and the hit penalty, respectively.

In order to resolve the non-determinism that occurs in each branch in the BBG (conditional jumps in the assembler program are the source of these non-determinism, because at this low level analysis we do not care about the conditions in the source program), an input n_{cond} is required. Since an input, determining the chosen path of a branch, is independent from all other branches in each step, one input n_{cond} is sufficient for this task.

Loop iteration bounds are used to avoid unbounded unrolling of loops. As always the case in real-time systems, software with divergent loops is not allowed and for the worst case analysis we need the interval of loop iterations for each loop.

Therefore, for each loop a local loop counter l_{b_i} is inserted, that contains the actual number of loop unrolls for the current path. Figure 1 shows the transformation from a loop in the BBG to the BBA. For each transition to a loop head, that is not a backward jump from within the loop, the loop counter is initialised with 0. On each

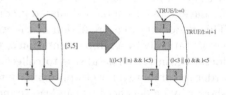

Fig. 1. Semantic transformation of loops

backward jump towards the loop head, the loop counter is incremented to indicate a new iteration. Exiting the loop is performed by taking a transition to a basic block outside the loop, which we called exit block. The path to an exit block always uses branching blocks[1], thus the transformation has to follow the rule of

---

[1] Otherwise it would be no exit block, because if a block within a loop has only one successor, this target block must be within the loop, too.

introducing an input variable n_{cond}. However, this alone would allow unbounded loop iterations, hence we have to take the iteration bounds into account. This is done by an extended guard at the transition of branching blocks, that leads to a loop exit $(\neg((l_{b_i} < m_d \vee n_{cond}) \wedge l_{b_i} < m_u))$. Exiting the loop by using the input variable n_{cond} is only possible, if the number of iterations is greater than the minimal iteration count (m_d) and is enforced if the maximal iteration count (m_u) is exceeded (see figure 1)[2]. This leads to the following definition:

Definition 4 (BBA semantics of a BBG).

The semantics $BBA = (s_0, S_T, S, \mathcal{I}, V, T)$ *of a given basic block graph* $\mathcal{B} = (BB, T_{\mathcal{B}}, \mathcal{L})$ *is defined by the following rules:*
Let $S_{head} = \{b \mid b \in S \wedge \exists b_i \in BB, \exists l = (b_i, b, \cdot, \cdot) \in \mathcal{L}\}$ *be the set of all loop heads within* $\mathcal{B}$.

- $S = BB$
- $s_0 = b$ *with* $\exists b_i \in BB, t_{\mathcal{B}} \in T_{\mathcal{B}} : t_{\mathcal{B}} = (b, b_i) \wedge \forall b_j \in BB : \nexists t_{\mathcal{B}} \in T_{\mathcal{B}} : t_{\mathcal{B}} = (b_j, b)$
- $S_T = \{b \mid b \in BB \wedge \forall b_i \in BB : \nexists t_{\mathcal{B}} \in T_{\mathcal{B}} : t_{\mathcal{B}} = (b, b_i)\}$
- $\mathcal{I} = \{n_{cond}\}$ *with* $n_{cond} \in BOOL$
- $V = \{cycles\} \cup \{l_{b_j} \mid b_j \in S_{head}\} \cup \{f_{b_j} \mid b_j \in BB : get\_fm(b_j) > 0\}$
- $T = T_{\mathcal{B}} \cup \{t_{init}\}$ *with* $t_{init} = (\bot, s_0)$

With a transition $t = (b_1, b_2) \in T$ *it holds:*

$$
guard(t) = \begin{cases}
n_{cond} \in \mathcal{I} & \text{if } \exists b_i \neq b_2 \in BB, \exists t_i = (b1, b_i) \in T_{\mathcal{B}} \\
& \wedge\ guard(t_i) = \neg n_{cond} \wedge b_i \notin S_{head} \\[4pt]
\neg n_{cond} \in \mathcal{I} & \text{if } \exists b_i \neq b_2 \in BB, \exists t_i = (b1, b_i) \in T_{\mathcal{B}} \\
& \wedge\ guard(t_i) = n_{cond} \wedge b_i \notin S_{head} \\[4pt]
\begin{aligned}
&\neg((l_{b_i} < m_d \vee n_{cond}) \\
&\quad \wedge l_{b_i} < m_u) \\
&\text{with } l_{b_i} \in V \wedge n_{cond} \in \mathcal{I}
\end{aligned}
& \begin{aligned}
&\text{if } \exists b_i \in S_{head} : b_2 \in exits(b_i) \\
&\quad \wedge \exists \lambda = (\cdot, b_i, m_d, m_u) \in \mathcal{L}
\end{aligned} \\[4pt]
\begin{aligned}
&(l_{b_i} < m_d \vee n_{cond}) \\
&\quad \wedge l_{b_i} < m_u \\
&\text{with } l_{b_i} \in V \wedge n_{cond} \in \mathcal{I}
\end{aligned}
& \begin{aligned}
&\text{if } \exists b_i \in S_{head}, \exists b_j \in BB, \\
&\quad \exists t_j \in T_{\mathcal{B}}, \exists \lambda \in \mathcal{L} : \\
&\quad b_j \neq b_2 \wedge b_j \in exits(b_i) \\
&\quad \wedge t_j = (b_1, b_j) \\
&\quad \wedge \lambda = (\cdot, b_i, m_d, m_u)
\end{aligned} \\[4pt]
TRUE & else
\end{cases}
$$

---

[2] Using the first exit in case of bound exceeding is a structural property of assembler code for loops that is constructed by common compilers.

For each basic block b_j let $c_{am}(b_j) = get\_am(b_j) \times MISS\_PENALTY$ be the cost of a cache miss of type "am". Let $c_{fm} = get\_fm(b_j) \times MISS\_PENALTY$ the similar attribute for "fm" classified misses. Let $action_n$ (assignment for cache and pipeline costs) be defined as follows:

$$action_n(t) = \begin{cases} \{cycles := cost(s_0) + c_{am}(s_0) + c_{fm}(s_0)\} \\ \cup\{f_{b_j} := FALSE \mid \forall f_{b_j} \in V : b_j \neq s_0\} \\ \cup\{f_{s_0} := TRUE\} & \text{if } t = t_{init} \\ \{cycles := cost(b_2) + c_{am}(b_2) \\ \qquad\qquad + (f_{b_2})?c_{fm}(b_2) : 0\} \\ \cup\{f_{b_2} := TRUE\} & \text{if } get\_fm(b_2) > 0 \\ & \qquad \wedge \ t \neq t_{init} \\ \{cycles := cycles + cost(b_2) + c_{am}(b_2)\} & else \end{cases}$$

To avoid unbound unrolling of loops, $action_l$ is defined:

$$action_l(t) = \begin{cases} \{l_{b_2} := 0\} & \text{if } b_2 \in S_{head} \wedge b_1 \notin backjump(b_2) \\ \{l_{b_2} := l_{b_2} + 1\} & \text{if } b_2 \in S_{head} \wedge b_1 \in backjump(b_2) \\ \emptyset & else \end{cases}$$

With this two parts, the action function can be constructed by

$$action(t) = action_n(t) \cup action_l(t)$$

This BBA of a given BBG can now be translated to a model for a model checker. What we can do with model checking techniques, is the proof of $M_{BBA} \models \mathbf{EF}(\phi_N)$, where ϕ_N is the state formula:

$$\phi_N = \left(\bigvee_{t:b_t \in S_T} b_t \right) \wedge cycles > N$$

The target of this proof is a path to one of the termination blocks whose cost (in processor cycles) is greater than N. Since searching for WCET is an optimisation problem with the objective function of $max(cycles)$, we must execute a bunch of model check runs to converge to the real WCET. This is performed in a binary search manner and we do an update on N each run: If $M_{BBA} \models \mathbf{EF}(\phi_N)$ fails, the value of N has to be decreased, otherwise it has to be increased[3]. If we have found a proof for $M_{BBA} \models \mathbf{EF}(\phi_{N_i-1})$ and the proof of $M_{BBA} \models \mathbf{EF}(\phi_{N_i})$ fails, we have reached the maximum for the variable $cycles$ and thus we have found, that the WCET equals N_i.

3.2   Model Checking for Cache Behaviour Prediction

As mentioned above, the former approach can compete with other techniques, like ILP based methods presented in [11]; it shows that with model checking techniques a low level analysis of WCET is possible as well. Furthermore, the

---

[3] Note, that with very slightly changes the BCET can easily be analysed with the same technique.

ILP method is known to suffer from numerical instabilities that can produce non-valid solutions. In contrast, model checking based techniques by construction do not suffer from problems like this and always calculate valid solutions.

To get some improvements on WCET analysis, we try to transfer the prediction of cache accesses from the statical way to the dynamic way under the control of a model check run. This increases complexity, but, however, we can avoid too pessimistic over-approximations of the static analysis.

Static analysis, such as AI based methods, do not consider concrete paths through a program but work with abstract ones. The prerequisite for this abstraction is a safe over-approximation of the cache behaviour. Since model checking considers a concrete path, at some points in a control flow graph the pessimistic prediction

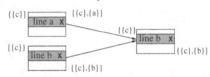

Fig. 2. Merging paths in an abstract cache behaviour analysis. Crosses mark cache miss prediction.

of abstract cache behaviour can be improved. These points are basic blocks, that are targets of more than one predecessor block. Regarding the abstract cache behaviour, the abstract analysis method is not able to determine, which predecessor is used (because this is only known in a concrete path). Therefore, at these points so-called *join*-functions merge all possible paths in a safe way with respect to WCET.

For example, in figure 2 the lower block loads a cache line, that is used in the successor block, but the upper block does not use this line. In order to give safe predictions, the *join-function* does some kind of set intersection of abstract cache states with the result, that in an "am" or "fm" analysis this cache accesses in both blocks leads to a cache miss for cache line b. This also holds, if the concrete path uses the block that pre-loads cache line b.

To overcome this drawback, we give in this section a BBA based semantic for BBGs with dynamic cache analysis. We will reuse parts of the above defined semantic, namely most of the construction rules and the whole *guard* function. To model the cache behaviour of concrete paths, we introduce new variables to represent the contents of the lines of an instruction cache with given size, associativity and other parameters.

In order to model dynamic cache contents on a concrete path, the whole cache memory must be taken into account. Each access to instruction memory is deterministically mapped into one set of the cache and belongs to a so called "program line" [10]. Program lines are the set of instruction memory locations in a program that are mapped to the same cache set with

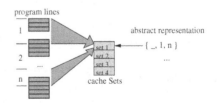

Fig. 3. Abstract cache content representation.

the same tag (see figure 3). If we assume a critical word first loading strategy (modern processors usually implement this strategy), only the first access of instructions within one program line to a cache set leads to a miss. Hence, we can abstract without loss of precision from collecting each memory location access by collecting only the program lines. While traversing a concrete path, we collect the program lines per cache line and set, that are loaded, and we delete the program lines that are replaced (depending on the replacement strategy). This is performed in the sequence of memory accesses on the concrete path. Therefore, the definition of a basic block graph is extended by the set of program lines of each BB:

$pl : BB \to 2^{\mathbb{N}^+}$ denotes all program lines of a basic block

$set : N^+ \to \mathbb{N}^+$ gives the cache set that belongs to program line p

Note, that we assume implicitly, that the size of the cache is sufficient to record all program lines of a basic block[4]. With this additional information we can now define the BBA-based semantic for a basic block graph with cache behaviour prediction.

Definition 5 (BBA semantic of BBG with cache behaviour prediction).
The semantics $BBA = (s_0, S_T, S, \mathcal{I}, V, T)$ of a given basic block graph $\mathcal{B} = (BB, T_{\mathcal{B}}, \mathcal{L})$ is defined by the following rules:

- *Let $S_{head}, s_0, S_T, \mathcal{I}, T$ be defined as in definition 4.*
- *$V = \{cycles\} \cup \{l_{b_j} \mid b_j \in S_{head}\} \cup \{IC_{g,h} \mid IC_{g,h} \in \mathbb{N} \cup \{\bot\} \wedge g \in \{1, \dots, SETS\} \wedge h \in \{1, \dots, A\}\}$ with SETS is the number of cache sets, A is the associativity of the cache and $\bot$ denotes an invalid cache line*
- *Let $guard(t)$ and $action_l(t)$ be defined as in definition 4*

Let the cost of memory accesses of a basic block b on a cache with associativity A be defined as

$$c_{cache}(b) = \sum_{p \in pl(b)} \left(\bigvee_{i=\{1,\dots,A\}} (IC_{set(p),i} = p) \right) ?0 : MISS\_PENALTY$$

and the cost of entering the first basic block by transition t_{init} as

$$c_{init} = \sum_{p \in pl(s_0)} MISS\_PENALTY$$

With $t = (b_1, b_2) \in T$, the assignments for cache and pipeline costs are defined:

$$action_n(t) = \begin{cases} \{cycles := cost(s_0) + c_{init}\} & \text{if } t = t_{init} \\ \{cycles := cycles + cost(b_2) + c_{cache}(b_2)\} & \text{else} \end{cases}$$

The assignments for dynamic cache prediction $action_c$ is defined with

$$hit(p) = \bigvee_{i=\{1,\dots,A\}} (IC_{set(p),i} = p)$$

---

[4] This is the standard case in modern processors, since basic blocks are typically small.

$$action_c(t) = \begin{cases} \{IC_{p,a} := \bot \mid p \in \{1, \ldots, SETS\} \backslash \{set(pl(s_0))\} \\ \qquad \land \ a \in \{1, \ldots, A\}\} \ \cup \\ \bigcup_{p \in pl(s_0)} \{(hit(p))?AGE(p) : LOAD(p)\} & \text{if } t = t_{init} \\ \bigcup_{p \in pl(b_2)} \{(hit(p))?AGE(p) : LOAD(p)\} & \text{else} \end{cases}$$

With these three parts, the action function can be constructed by

$$action(t) = action_n(t) \cup action_l(t) \cup action_c(t)$$

The concrete cache contents (ie. the program line actually stored in the cache lines) are represented in $(SETS \cdot A)$ $IC_{s,a}$ variables, that are updated on each memory reference. The cost of an access depends on the hit/miss state and is calculated by checking whether the program lines of the target block are within the cache variables or not. In the init transition a completely invalidated cache is assumed (worst case scenario).

The real cache behaviour of loading lines is hidden by the $AGE(p)$ and $LOAD(p)$ macros, because they depend on the used cache architecture. For a two-way associative cache ($A = 2$) with the popular LRU strategy, $AGE(p)$ and $LOAD(p)$ are defined with $s = set(p)$ (the $:=:$ notation denotes swapping the contents):

$$AGE(p) \equiv (IC_{s,2} = p)?IC_{s,2} :=: IC_{s,1} \ : \ < null >$$

$$LOAD(p) \equiv IC_{s,2} := IC_{s,1} \ ; \ IC_{s,1} := p$$

For higher degrees of the associativity this is a bit more complex, but the basic scheme is the same, even if we have more complicated and less predictable (in an abstract analysis) replacement schemes, like the pseudo-LRU used in the Embedded Pentium[5].

4   Evaluation and Discussion

For an evaluation of the two described approaches, first, the design-flow and construction of the model from an assembler program is described. A very short sketch of our model checking environment is given, too. Using this framework, the result of an evaluation of three example case studies will be demonstrated and discussed. As mentioned above, we restrict the evaluation on the behaviour of an instruction cache and assume a "perfect" pipelined RISC architecture with a priori generated costs of one cycle per instruction.

4.1   Design-Flow

Starting point of the analysis is a C program with user annotations to bound the number of loop iterations. This is transfered to assembly language whereby the annotations are preserved. From this assembler program, we build the basic block graph and generate the BBA, which itself is a C program that represents the given semantic as a finite state machine. This is the base for the use of the

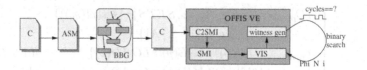

Fig. 4. The design-flow of WCET analysis using model checking techniques provided by the OFFIS verification environment.

OFFIS verification environment[1], in which the C program is transformed[2] to an input language for the model checker core. As model checker engine we use the VIS[4]. Figure 4 gives an overview over our design-flow for WCET analysis.

For the inquiry whether $M \models \mathbf{EF}(\phi_N)$, we use the *drive to property* checking of the OFFIS VE (technically an invariance check) and produce a witness in case of a result of true. The witness contains the value of the *cycles* variable for the concrete path to one of the termination basic blocks. The result is used to increase or decrease the bound N, until we reach the termination point, where it holds $M_{BBA} \models \mathbf{EF}(\phi_{N_i-1}) \wedge M_{BBA} \not\models \mathbf{EF}(\phi_{N_i})$.

4.2 Experimental Results

For evaluation of our approach we take three case studies as inputs for the above described design-flow to calculate the WCET. The case studies are derived from running projects and are located in the domain of embedded systems, partly implemented with typical CASE tools of an embedded systems development process (see table 1 for details).

Table 1. Case studies with number of instructions, description and source of the code.

case study	instructions	comment
robot	~ 250	control of a LEGO mindstorm to find a light source and react on collisions, hand written C code
collision	~ 1100	collision detection and avoidance for a satellite control unit, derived C code from STATEMATE specification
flight	~ 2500	flight control unit to compensate side drift, generated C code from SCADE

As cache parameters we choose an instruction cache of 128 sets with 8 instructions (4 bytes per instruction) per line and an associativity of two (altogether a cache size of 8KB; the size is typical for processors used in todays embedded systems). The evaluation machine was a SUN BLADE 2000 (900 MHz UltraSparc III processor, 2 GB main memory) and the results are summarised in the table 2 below. The times in *time(A)* and *time(C)* are the time to find the WCET, including witness generation. As mentioned above, the results of *WCET(A)* are identical to the WCET the approach in [12] would calculate. Hence we can directly compare [12] and the results from *WCET(C)* to highlight the improvement of our approach. The time of one single model check run ranges from 8 seconds for *robot* to 21 seconds for *flight* with abstract cache analysis and from 13 seconds for *robot* to 315 seconds for *flight* with concrete cache analysis. However, the results have shown, that WCET analysis with model checking techniques is possible and can partly improve the results of the abstract analysis on case studies, that are typical in their size and complexity for tasks in embedded systems.

To limit the number of iterations in the binary search procedure for the abstract cache analysis, we determine an interval, that was derived at the lower bound by a reachability analysis[5] and on the upper bound by a rule of thumb. For the concrete cache analysis we use the result of the abstract analysis and the number of joins to decrease the number of iterations (shown by *iter. (A/C)* in table 2).

Table 2. Evaluation of the three benchmarks with results and runtime for the abstract and the concrete cache behaviour analysis and maximal iterations of the binary search. The letter A denotes the abstract, C the concrete cache analysis. *bits* denotes the state bits of the problem.

case study	WCET(A)	bits(A)	WCET(C)	bits(C)	time(A)	time(C)	iter. (A/C)
robot	387	35	376	75	0:46 min	0:36 min	9/4
collision	502	38	478	135	2:00 min	4:56 min	10/5
flight	1782	40	1749	362	2:16 min	15:24 min	11/4

4.3   Discussion and Perspectives

As mentioned in the last chapter, the improvement of the concrete cache analysis compared to abstract cache analysis is founded in the more accurate cache behaviour prediction at merging points in the control flow graph. Analysing the number of these points can give a good hint whether a concrete cache analysis could be profitable or not. In our case studies, we determine that 33% to 50% of the joins lead to additional cache miss predictions in the abstract cache analysis with respect to the concrete one. As a whole this results in an improvement of 1.5% to 5% of the predicted WCET, if only instruction caches are taken into consideration.

The investigation of concrete paths increases the complexity, as shown by *bits* in table 2. The used operations (addition and comparison with constants) are not expected to lead to state explosion problems. Thus the main factor for complexity are the $IC_{s,a}$ variables which depend on the cache architecture and the size of the program. Since we are dealing with tasks (parts of functions), program sizes greater than the flight examle are quite unusual. Furthermore,

---

[5] The reachability analysis checks for the reachability of one termination block and returns a witness for the *cycles* variable within a few seconds on each of the models.

cache lines, that are not used, are sliced from the BBA during construction. This could also be possible for the associativity: For cache lines that are known to store only one program line there is no need for more than one cache line in the BBA, thus we can assume for this lines an associativity of one). This is currently not implemented but would decrease the number of state bits.

Regarding pipeline analysis, there occurs the same problem at merging points, since without a concrete path the analysis method cannot determine which of the predecessor blocks is on the path. Hence there is an over-approximation by taking the maximal delay, too. The consequences to the accuracy of the execution time computation are hard to predict, because this deeply depends on the used processor architecture. In well balanced pipelines there are no great differences in the delay of two predecessor blocks, but in pipelines with instructions of various execution time intervals there can possibly be ten's of cycles difference (for example using floating point execution units is very popular but yields exactly this problem). We conjecture, that with modern processor architectures the improvement of a concrete analysis could reach the same magnitude as for the cache analysis. Note, that for the pipeline analysis we do not need a pipeline behaviour analysis under control of the model checker. A pre-analysis can provide path specific delays for each basic block that can be integrated in the BBA in a similar way as we do this for caches at the moment. Thus, the complexity of the problem should not grow dramatically. If we take the same for data caches into account, the use of model checking can reach an improvement of about 10% in average.

More over, the described technique will allow for a more accurate path validation of WCET analysis by combining it with a high level analysis. In a high level analysis, for example, the mutual exclusiveness of parts of the paths can be proven. This can simply be exploited in our analysis by introducing new inputs n_i at the branching blocks instead of the one input used now. By formulating an assumption over these inputs, the impossible paths through the control flow graph can be avoided and a more accurate WCET prediction can be achieved.

5   Conclusion

As a conclusion, our experimental environment for WCET analysis using model checking techniques and the evaluations with some typical embedded systems examples have shown, that this approach not only is able to produce valid execution times, but also can improve the results of the analysis with respect to the well known abstract analysis. Furthermore, for the abstract cache analysis, our approach always produces correct runtime predictions, different from the ILP approach that sometimes suffer from numerical instabilities.

Altogether we have shown, that model checking can be used quite well to solve the problem of determining execution time bounds. The application in a verification framework for the development of embedded systems opens a wide area of coupling the WCET analysis directly to the design in a CASE tool and promises further use cases, for example the combination with property checking for a high level path analysis, that can support the low level analysis, or the combination with automatic code generators.

References

1. T. Bienmüller, W. Damm, and H. Wittke. The STATEMATE Verification Environment – Making it real. In *12th international Conference on Computer Aided Verification*, number 1855 in LNCS, 2000.
2. W. Damm, C. Schulte, M. Segelken, H. Wittke, U. Higgen, and M. Eckrich. Formale Verifikation von ASCET Modellen im Rahmen der Entwicklung der Aktivlenkung. *Lecture Notes in Informatics*, P-34, 2003.
3. S.-S. Lim et al. An accurate worst case timing analysis for RISC processors. *Software Engineering*, 21(7):593–604, 1995.
4. The VIS Group. VIS : A System for Verification and Synthesis. In *8th international Conference on Computer Aided Verification*, number 1102 in LNCS, 1996.
5. Intel Corp. *Intel Embedded Pentium Processor Family Dev. Manual*, 1998.
6. M. Joseph, editor. *Real-time Systems Specification, Verification and Analysis*. Prentice Hall International, London, 1996.
7. Y. Li and S. Malik. Performance analysis of embedded software using implicit path enumeration. In *Workshop on Languages, Compilers and Tools for Real-Time Systems*, pages 88–98, 1995.
8. Y. Li, S. Malik, and A. Wolfe. Efficient microarchitecture modeling and path analysis for real-time software. In *IEEE Real-Time Systems Symposium*, 1995.
9. K. McMillan. *Symbolic Model Checking*. Kluwer Academic Publishers, 1993.
10. F. Mueller. *Static Cache Simulation and its Applications*. PhD thesis, Dept. of CS, Florida State University, 1994.
11. H. Theiling, C. Ferdinand, and R. Wilhelm. Fast and precise WCET prediction by separated cache and path analyses. *Real-Time Systems*, 18(2/3):157–179, 2000.
12. R. Wilhelm. Why AI + ILP is good for WCET, but MC is not, nor ILP alone. *Lecture Notes in Computer Science*, 2937, 2003.

Regular Model Checking for LTL(MSO)*

Parosh Aziz Abdulla, Bengt Jonsson, Marcus Nilsson,
Julien d'Orso, and Mayank Saksena

Dept. of Information Technology, P.O. Box 337, S-751 05 Uppsala, Sweden
{parosh,bengt,marcusn,juldor,mayanks}@it.uu.se

Abstract. Regular model checking is a form of symbolic model checking for parameterized and infinite-state systems whose states can be represented as words of arbitrary length over a finite alphabet, in which regular sets of words are used to represent sets of states. We present *LTL(MSO)*, a combination of the logics MSO and LTL as a natural logic for expressing temporal properties to be verified in regular model checking. *LTL(MSO)* is a two-dimensional modal logic, where MSO is used for specifying properties of system states and transitions, and LTL is used for specifying temporal properties. In addition, the first-order quantification in MSO can be used to express properties parameterized on a position or process. We give a technique for model checking *LTL(MSO)*, which is adapted from the automata-theoretic approach: a formula is translated to a (Büchi) transducer with a regular set of accepting states, and regular model checking techniques are used to search for models. We have implemented the technique and show its application to a number of parameterized algorithms from the literature.

1   Introduction

Regular model checking is a framework for algorithmic symbolic verification of parameterized and infinite-state systems [BLW03,KMM$^+$01,WB98,BJNT00]. It considers systems whose states can be represented as finite words of arbitrary length over a finite alphabet, including array or ring-formed parameterized systems with an arbitrary number of finite-state processes, and systems that operate on queues, stacks, integers, and other linear unbounded data structures. In a system description, the set of initial states is represented as a regular set of strings, and the transition relation is given as a finite regular length-preserving transducer. Previous work on regular model checking [JN00,BJNT00,AJNd02] has developed methods for computing the set of reachable states of a system description, as well as the set of reachable loops, obtained from the transitive closure of the transition relation. In general, this problem is undecidable, but decidable results for certain classes have been obtained [JN00].

---

* This work was supported in part by the European Commission (FET project AD-VANCE, contract No IST-1999-29082), and by the the Swedish Research Council (http://www.vr.se/).

R. Alur and D.A. Peled (Eds.): CAV 2004, LNCS 3114, pp. 348–360, 2004.
© Springer-Verlag Berlin Heidelberg 2004

The techniques for computing reachable states and reachable loops can in principle be used to verify both safety and liveness properties of parameterized system descriptions, but do not provide a convenient approach for checking arbitrary temporal logic properties of parameterized and infinite-state systems. Significant ingenuity is required in order to manually transform the verification of a temporal property of a parameterized system into a property of reachable states and transitive closures, in particular if the verification uses fairness properties that are parameterized on system components [BJNT00,PS00]. It would be desirable to have a framework, analogous to the automata-theoretic approach in finite-state model checking [VW86], where the property of verifying a temporal property is automatically transformed into a problem of checking emptiness for a Büchi automaton.

In this paper, we address this problem by presenting an extension of the automata-theoretic approach [VW86] to the setting of regular model checking. We present a logic for expressing system models and temporal properties, which is a combination of the logics MSO over finite words and LTL. We use MSO for specifying sets of states and transition relations and LTL for specifying temporal constraints. The result is a two-dimensional modal logic, where MSO is used in the "space" (system state) dimension and LTL is used in the "time" dimension. Models of the logic are infinite sequences of (constant-length) words, representing computations of the specified system. We can then specify a verification problem as the conjunction of a system specification and a negation of the property to be verified.

Following the automata-theoretic approach, we present an automated translation from the translation from a formula φ in $LTL(MSO)$ to a *Büchi transducer*, consisting of a regular set I of initial states, a regular length-preserving transducer T, and a regular set F of accepting states. Accepting runs of the Büchi transducer are infinite sequences of words, where the first word is in I, consecutive words satisfy T, and infinitely many words are in F. Thus, φ is satisfiable if and only if the Büchi transducer has an accepting run. Since T is length-preserving, the existence of an accepting run can be checked by searching for a reachable loop which contains a state in F.

A nice feature of our combination of MSO with LTL is that we get the power to express parameterized temporal properties for free: MSO offers variables to represent positions and quantify over them, which can be interleaved with temporal operators. As a concrete example, for a parameterized mutual exclusion algorithm, a typical property one would want to express is the following.

> If all processes satisfy a weak fairness requirement, then each process that is interested in entering its critical section will eventually do so.

If the number of processes is fixed, the terms like *"each process"* can be replaced by explicit conjunctions to obtain a standard model checking problem in propositional temporal logic. However, in regular model checking the number of processes is arbitrary. Fortunately, our logic gives quantification for free, so we can express this property directly, by a formula like

$$\forall i.[\Box\Diamond(\text{blocked}(i) \lor \text{progressing}(i))] \longrightarrow \forall i.[\Box(\text{trying}(i) \to \Diamond\text{critical}(i))]$$

where i ranges over positions in the state, and each position represents a process. In this formula, we apply LTL operators ($\Box$ and $\Diamond$) to formulas with the MSO variable i, and later use MSO quantification over i to express parameterized properties. In our logic $LTL(MSO)$, temporal operators can be applied to formulas with at most one free first-order variable and no free second-order variables. This restriction allows to express parameterized temporal properties (e.g., fairness constraints) of individual processes in a parameterized system, as well as temporal properties of pairs of adjacent processes (in positions i and $i+1$ using one free variable i).

A further nice property of adapting the automata-theoretic approach is that our transformation results in a uniform problem of checking for accepting runs, for which we can develop techniques that are more uniform than those presented in previous work [JN00,BJNT00,AJNd02]. We have extended our tool for regular model checking [AJNd03] to check whether Büchi transducers have accepting runs. This is done in two steps. First, the set of reachable states are computed as $Inv = I \circ T^*$. Secondly, loops are found by identifying identical pairs in $(F \cap T \cap Inv) \circ T^*$. This computation is more uniform and more efficient than the approach to verification of temporal logic properties outlined in [BJNT00], which builds on computation of the transitive closure T^+ of the transducer relation. We have verified safety properties with the tool for many of the examples in our previous work, as well as liveness properties for some of the examples.

As special cases, when the formula contains no temporal operators, our method specializes into a decision procedure for MSO similar to that of MONA [HJJ+96], and when the formula contains no quantifiers our method specializes to ordinary LTL model checking.

The remainder of the paper is structured as follows. In the next section, we present the logic $LTL(MSO)$. Section 3 illustrates how it can be used to model and specify parameterized algorithms. The model checking technique, including the translation to Büchi transducer is presented and proven correct in Section 4. New techniques and evaluations of our extended implementation are presented in Section 5.

Related Work. In addition to the work on regular model checking, cited earlier, there is a large body of research on the problem of model checking parameterized systems of *identical* processes, in which there is no ordering between processes, and hence the system state can be represented as a multiset of process states (e.g., [BLS01,Del00,EK03,EK00,GS92]). This problem is substantially simpler, since ordering between processes need not be considered. Emerson and Namjoshi [EN95] give a technique for verifying a restricted class of parameterized token-passing algorithms by reducing an arbitrary ring to a small fixed-size ring under certain conditions. These restrictions are substantially stronger than in our framework. Sistla [Sis97] uses Büchi automata over two dimensional languages (reminding of transducers) to specify network invariants when verifying systems by induction over their linear process structure. It is unclear what class of systems can be handled automatically by this technique.

The problem of checking liveness properties of array-shaped parameterized systems was considered by Pnueli and Shahar [PS00], who presented a technique for computing the transitive closure of a restricted class of transition relations. They also first manually employ abstractions to make the implementation terminate.

Pnueli, Xu, and Zuck [PXZ02] present an interesting use of specialized abstractions in order to prove absence of starvation properties for Szymanski's algorithm and the Bakery algorithm. The abstractions keep track of the number of processes with certain properties, and generate a finite-state system, which can be model-checked. The presented abstraction is specialized to prove non-starvation, and loses much information so that e.g., safety properties can no longer be checked.

Our logic *LTL(MSO)* applied to words is related to existential monadic second-order logic (EMSO) on grids to define picture languages accepted by *tiling systems* (see e.g. [GR97]). Indeed, transducers over words can be considered as *tiling systems* where each transition represents a *tile*. Thus, it is expected that our logic *LTL(MSO)* is equivalent to EMSO on grids. However, the two logics come from different motivations. While EMSO on grids is used to reason about *pictures*, our logic is used to reason about *parameterized structures over time*. When applied to the word structure, the two logics coincide.

2   The Logic *LTL(MSO)*

We present the syntax and semantics of *LTL(MSO)*. This logic combines the operators of MSO and LTL, under the restriction that temporal operators can be applied to formulas with at most one free first-order (MSO) variable and no free second-order variables. In this paper, we restrict the presentation to the temporal operators □ (always) and ◇ (eventually), but this is not a fundamental restriction.

Syntax. We denote *first-order variables* Var_{FO} by lowercase letters $i, j, k, \ldots$, *second-order variables* Var_{SO} by uppercase letters $I, J, K, \ldots$ and *configuration variables* V by lowercase letters $x, y, z, \ldots$

$\varphi ::= i \in I \mid I \subseteq J \mid i = j + 1 \mid x[i] \mid x'[i]$	Atomic MSO formulas
$true \mid false$	Boolean constants
$\varphi \sim \varphi, \sim \in \{\wedge, \vee, \rightarrow, \leftrightarrow\} \mid \neg\varphi$	Propositional connectives
$\exists i\varphi \mid \forall i\varphi \mid \exists I\varphi \mid \forall I\varphi$	MSO Quantification
$\Box\varphi \mid \Diamond\varphi$	Temporal operators

No negation should have any temporal operator within its scope, which is why we provide dual versions of each operator. We further require that in every subformula of the form $\Box\varphi$ or $\Diamond\varphi$, there is at most one free first-order variable (and no free second-order variables). More operators on first-order variables, such as $<, \leq, =$, can be expressed in MSO using standard encodings.

Semantics. Closed $LTL(MSO)$ formulas are interpreted over *matrices* M over 2^V of dimension $\infty \times n$ where $n \in \mathbf{Z}_+$ is a parameter that can take an arbitrary positive integer value. We call the vertical (first) dimension *time*, and the horizontal (second) dimension *space*. Let $\mathbf{Z}_n = \{0, 1, \ldots, n-1\}$. The element $M(t, i) \in 2^V$ for $t \in \mathbf{N}$ and $i \in \mathbf{Z}_n$ represents the system configuration at time t of position (or subsystem) i, which assigns truth values to the configuration variables V. Thus, each row $M(t, 0) \cdots M(t, n)$ represents the system configuration at time t.

In general, a formula φ depends on its free first- and second-order variables, which are interpreted in the space dimension, and on a time point t. A model $\mathcal{M}$ for an arbitrary $LTL(MSO)$-formula ϕ is a triple $(M, \mathcal{I}, t)$, where $M : (\mathbf{N} \times \mathbf{Z}_n) \to 2^V$ is a matrix over 2^V, where $\mathcal{I}$ is a valuation $\mathcal{I} \colon \mathrm{Var}_{FO} \to \mathbf{Z}_n$ and $\mathcal{I} \colon \mathrm{Var}_{SO} \to 2^{\mathbf{Z}_n}$ of first-order and second-order variables, and where t is a time point $t \in \mathbf{N}$. Satisfaction of formulas is defined as follows.

$$
\begin{aligned}
(M, \mathcal{I}, t) &\not\models false \\
(M, \mathcal{I}, t) &\models true \\
i \in I \quad &\text{iff } \mathcal{I}(i) \in \mathcal{I}(I) \\
I \subseteq J \quad &\text{iff } \mathcal{I}(I) \subseteq \mathcal{I}(J) \\
i = j + 1 \quad &\text{iff } \mathcal{I}(i) = \mathcal{I}(j) + 1 \\
x[i] \quad &\text{iff } x \in M(t, \mathcal{I}(i)) \\
x'[i] \quad &\text{iff } x \in M(t+1, \mathcal{I}(i)) \\
\varphi_1 \wedge \varphi_2 \quad &\text{iff } (M, \mathcal{I}, t) \models \varphi_1 \text{ and } (M, \mathcal{I}, t) \models \varphi_2 \\
\varphi_1 \vee \varphi_2 \quad &\text{iff } (M, \mathcal{I}, t) \models \varphi_1 \text{ or } (M, \mathcal{I}, t) \models \varphi_2 \\
\varphi_1 \to \varphi_2 \quad &\text{iff } (M, \mathcal{I}, t) \models \varphi_1 \text{ implies } (M, \mathcal{I}, t) \models \varphi_2 \\
\varphi_1 \leftrightarrow \varphi_2 \quad &\text{iff } (M, \mathcal{I}, t) \models \varphi_1 \text{ if and only if } (M, \mathcal{I}, t) \models \varphi_2 \\
\neg \varphi \quad &\text{iff } (M, \mathcal{I}, t) \not\models \varphi \\
\exists i \varphi \quad &\text{iff } \exists m \in \mathbf{Z}_n \ (M, \mathcal{I}[i \mapsto m], t) \models \varphi \\
\forall i \varphi \quad &\text{iff } \forall m \in \mathbf{Z}_n \ (M, \mathcal{I}[i \mapsto m], t) \models \varphi \\
\exists I \varphi \quad &\text{iff } \exists S \in 2^{\mathbf{Z}_n} \ (M, \mathcal{I}[I \mapsto S], t) \models \varphi \\
\forall I \varphi \quad &\text{iff } \forall S \in 2^{\mathbf{Z}_n} \ (M, \mathcal{I}[I \mapsto S], t) \models \varphi \\
\Box \varphi \quad &\text{iff } \forall t' \geq t \ (M, \mathcal{I}, t') \models \varphi \\
\Diamond \varphi \quad &\text{iff } \exists t' \geq t \ (M, \mathcal{I}, t') \models \varphi
\end{aligned}
$$

where $\mathcal{I}[i \mapsto m]$ is the valuation which sends i to m and otherwise acts as $\mathcal{I}$, and $\mathcal{I}[I \mapsto S]$ is defined analogously.

3   Modeling in $LTL(MSO)$

In this section, we discuss how to model systems and set up a verification problem in $LTL(MSO)$.

A system model consists of a set of initial states, a transition relation, and possibly fairness properties. Let a *state formula* be a formula without temporal operators or primed configuration variables. Following the style of TLA [Lam91], the initial states are specified by a state formula φ_I, the transition relation by a formula φ_T over unprimed and primed configuration variables without temporal operators, and fairness properties by a formula φ_{fair}. A *property* is given as a formula φ; for instance, an invariant property is of the form $\Box\varphi_{Inv}$ for a state formula φ_{Inv}. To check whether the system model satisfies the property φ, we search for models of the formula

$$\varphi_I \;\wedge\; \Box\varphi_T \;\wedge\; \varphi_{fair} \;\wedge\; \neg\varphi \;.$$

If φ is a safety property, the fairness properties φ_{fair} are not necessary, and can be omitted.

There are several forms of fairness properties. Process fairness can be expressed as

$$\varphi_{fair} = \forall i \Box\Diamond(\mathcal{A}(i) \;\vee\; \neg\text{enabled}(\mathcal{A}(i)))$$

where $\mathcal{A}(i)$ represents all actions of process i, and enabled($\mathcal{A}(i)$) represents the set of states where the action $\mathcal{A}(i)$ can be taken, obtained using an existential quantification of the primed configuration variables in $\mathcal{A}(i)$.

Example. To illustration modeling in $LTL(MSO)$, we take the Bakery algorithm for mutual exclusion. This algorithm synchronizes entries into critical section for an arbitrary number of processes, using a mechanism with integer-numbered "tickets". A process which wants to get into the critical section receives a ticket which is the maximum of all the outstanding tickets plus one. When a process has the lowest outstanding ticket, it enters the critical section and drops the ticket when leaving. Below is a pseudo-code description of the algorithm, in which the ticket of process p is represented by the variable $ticket_p$, whose value is initially 0.

Idle:	$ticket_p := 1 + \max_q ticket_q$
Waiting:	**await** $\forall q \neq p : (ticket_p < ticket_q \;\vee\; ticket_q = 0)$
Critical:	$ticket_p := 0$

Fig. 1. Bakery Algorithm

To model the Bakery Algorithm in $LTL(MSO)$, we change the perspective; rather than modeling the vector of process states, we let a configuration represent the states of the sequence of ticket numbers, using the configuration variable q. For each i, the value of $q[i]$ is

- $\bot$ if there is no process that has ticket $i + 1$, and
- W if some process with ticket $i + 1$ is waiting, and
- C if some process with ticket $i + 1$ is in critical

Note that we do not model tickets with number 0, since this is the ticket number of all "inactive" processes. For brevity, we implicitly use the invariant that each positive ticket number can be held by at most one process. This invariant can be verified separately, or not be assumed (e.g., by adding one more value of $q[i]$ representing that several process have this ticket number).

The initial state and transition relation of the Bakery Algorithm can then be specified by the following formulas.

$$
\begin{aligned}
\textbf{initial} \quad &= \quad \forall i \; q[i] = \bot \\
\textbf{ticket}(i) \quad &= \quad q[i] = \bot \;\wedge\; q'[i] = W \;\wedge\; (\forall j > i \; q[j] = \bot) \;\wedge \\
&\qquad (i \neq 0 \;\rightarrow\; q[i-1] \neq \bot) \\
\textbf{enter}(i) \quad &= \quad q[i] = W \;\wedge\; q'[i] = C \;\wedge\; (\forall j < i \; q[j] = \bot) \\
\textbf{exit}(i) \quad &= \quad q[i] = C \;\wedge\; q'[i] = \bot \\
\textbf{copy}(i) \quad &= \quad q[i] = q'[i] \\
\textbf{actions}(i) \quad &= \quad (\textbf{ticket}(i) \;\vee\; \textbf{enter}(i) \;\vee\; \textbf{exit}(i)) \;\wedge\; (\forall j \neq i \; \textbf{copy}(j)) \\
\textbf{sys} \quad &= \quad \textbf{initial} \;\wedge\; \Box((\exists i \; \textbf{actions}(i)) \;\vee\; \forall i \; \textbf{copy}(i))
\end{aligned}
$$

Mutual exclusion can be specified by the formula

$$
\textbf{mutex} \quad = \quad \Box \neg (\exists i \exists j \; i \neq j \;\wedge\; q[i] = C \;\wedge\; q[j] = C)
$$

In order to specify non-starvation, we add a fairness constraint for the actions $\textbf{enter}(i)$ and $\textbf{exit}(i)$. We add no fairness constraint for $\textbf{ticket}(i)$, since the arrival of new processes should not be controlled by the algorithm itself.

$$
\begin{aligned}
\textbf{fairactions}(i) \quad &= \quad (\textbf{enter}(i) \;\vee\; \textbf{exit}(i)) \;\wedge\; (\forall j \neq i \; \textbf{copy}(j)) \\
\textbf{fairness} \quad &= \quad \forall i \; \Box\Diamond(\textbf{fairactions}(i) \;\vee\; \neg\text{enabled}(\textbf{fairactions}(i))) \\
\textbf{non-starvation} \quad &= \quad \forall i \; \Box \; (q[i] = W \;\rightarrow\; \Diamond q[i] = C)
\end{aligned}
$$

To check that the algorithm satisfies mutual exclusion and non-starvation, we should check that the formulas

$$
\begin{aligned}
&\textbf{sys} \;\wedge\; \neg\textbf{mutex} \\
&\textbf{sys} \;\wedge\; \textbf{fairness} \;\wedge\; \neg\textbf{non-starvation}
\end{aligned}
$$

do not have any models. The property that models are of arbitrary but fixed size implies that we actually verify the algorithm under the assumption that there is an arbitrarily chosen upper bound on ticket numbers. For safety properties, this is not a limitation since violations will be finite sequences of computation steps, but for fairness properties it can play a role. For the Bakery Algorithm, it can be seen that an arbitrary upper limit on ticket numbers does not affect non-starvation for waiting processes, but in general one must be aware of this modeling constraint.

4   Translating $LTL(MSO)$ to Büchi Transducers

In this section, we describe how to transform a formula in $LTL(MSO)$ into a Büchi transducer, consisting of a regular set I of initial states, a regular length-preserving transducer T, and a regular set F of accepting states. In this section, we will represent such a Büchi transducer by the $LTL(MSO)$ formula $\phi_I \wedge \Box \phi_T \wedge \Box\Diamond\phi_F$, where ϕ_I and ϕ_F are MSO formulas denoting the regular sets of initial and accepting states, and ϕ_T is an MSO formula over primed and unprimed configuration variables denoting the regular transition relation. The accepting runs of the Büchi transducer accept exactly the models of the temporal formula, so in the following we will consider $\phi_I \wedge \Box\phi_T \wedge \Box\Diamond\phi_F$ to be a Büchi transducer where I, T, and F are regular transducers expressed in MSO.

The idea of the construction is similar to that of the standard translation of propositional temporal logic to Büchi Automata [VW86]: the semantics of temporal operators is translated to additional state information in the Büchi automaton. In our case the operators are translated to new configuration variables that represent the values of certain temporal subformulas of ϕ. The semantics of these subformulas is represented by constraints on the values of the new configuration variables.

We assume that ϕ is in negative normal form. Define a *core subformula* of ϕ as a subformula of ϕ which has a temporal operator as its main connective. For each core subformula ψ of ϕ, we introduce an auxiliary configuration variable x_ψ. Intuitively, the value of x_ψ at time point t and space position i should represent the value of ψ at that entry in the matrix. For each core subformula $\Diamond\psi$ where the main connective is $\Diamond$ we introduce an auxiliary configuration variable $y_{\Diamond\psi}$ (called an *eventuality variable*). Intuitively, if the variable $y_{\Diamond\psi}$ is true, then the formula ψ should be true at some future time point.

Using the auxiliary configuration variables, the value of any subformula ψ can be represented by a formula in MSO over the extended set of configuration variables. Let us define this formula $\langle\!\langle \psi \rangle\!\rangle$ as follows:

$$
\begin{aligned}
\langle\!\langle \phi \rangle\!\rangle &= \phi \text{ for } \phi \text{ in MSO} \\
\langle\!\langle \psi_1 \wedge \psi_2 \rangle\!\rangle &= \langle\!\langle \psi_1 \rangle\!\rangle \wedge \langle\!\langle \psi_2 \rangle\!\rangle \\
\langle\!\langle \psi_1 \vee \psi_2 \rangle\!\rangle &= \langle\!\langle \psi_1 \rangle\!\rangle \vee \langle\!\langle \psi_2 \rangle\!\rangle \\
\langle\!\langle \exists i\psi \rangle\!\rangle &= \exists i \langle\!\langle \psi \rangle\!\rangle \\
\langle\!\langle \forall i\psi \rangle\!\rangle &= \forall i \langle\!\langle \psi \rangle\!\rangle \\
\langle\!\langle \exists I\psi \rangle\!\rangle &= \exists I \langle\!\langle \psi \rangle\!\rangle \\
\langle\!\langle \forall I\psi \rangle\!\rangle &= \forall I \langle\!\langle \psi \rangle\!\rangle \\
\langle\!\langle \Box\psi \rangle\!\rangle &= x_{\Box\psi} \\
\langle\!\langle \Diamond\psi \rangle\!\rangle &= x_{\Diamond\psi}
\end{aligned}
$$

Let **localconstr**(ϕ) define the conjunction of a set of constraints on the auxiliary variables, called *local constraints*, as defined below.

(a) For each auxiliary variable of form x_ψ, where i is the (possibly) free first-order variable in ψ, define its constraint as follows.

$$
\forall i. \left(x_{\Box\psi_1}[i] \leftrightarrow \langle\!\langle \psi_1 \rangle\!\rangle[i] \wedge x'_{\Box\psi_1}[i] \right) \qquad \text{when } \psi \text{ is } \Box\psi_1
$$

$$
\forall i. \left(x_{\Diamond\psi_1}[i] \leftrightarrow \langle\!\langle \psi_1 \rangle\!\rangle[i] \vee x'_{\Diamond\psi_1}[i] \right) \qquad \text{when } \psi \text{ is } \Diamond\psi_1
$$

(b) Let $y_{\Diamond\psi_1}, \ldots, y_{\Diamond\psi_k}$ be the set of eventuality variables. We define their local constraint as:

$$
\bigwedge_{m=1}^{k} \forall i. \left(y_{\Diamond\psi_m}[i] \wedge \neg y'_{\Diamond\psi_m}[i] \longrightarrow \langle\!\langle \psi_m \rangle\!\rangle[i] \right)
$$

Furthermore, we require that all eventuality variables are false infinitely often and that they load new eventualities: let **evconstr**(ϕ) define the conjunction of a set of constraints on the auxiliary variables, called *eventuality constraint*, defined below.

$$\bigwedge_{m=1}^{k} \forall i. \left(\neg y_{\Diamond\psi_m}[i] \wedge (y'_{\Diamond\psi_m}[i] \leftrightarrow x'_{\Diamond\psi_m}[i]) \right)$$

The goal of this section is to prove that for each formula ϕ there is a model M such that $(M, \mathcal{I}, t) \models \phi$ iff there is a model M' such that $(M', \mathcal{I}, t) \models \langle\langle\phi\rangle\rangle \wedge \Box\textbf{localconstr}(\phi) \wedge \Box\Diamond\textbf{evconstr}(\phi)$ where M' differs from M only on the auxiliary variables. By its form, the latter formula can be regarded as a Büchi transducer, and so we have translated ϕ into an equivalent Büchi transducer. We first prove the following lemma.

Lemma 1. *If* $(M', \mathcal{I}, t) \models \Box\textbf{localconstr}(\phi) \wedge \Box\Diamond\textbf{evconstr}(\phi)$, *then for all auxiliary variables of* ϕ *we have*

(a) $(M', \mathcal{I}, t) \models \forall i. x_{\Box\psi}[i] \longrightarrow \Box\langle\langle\psi\rangle\rangle$
(b) $(M', \mathcal{I}, t) \models \forall i. x_{\Diamond\psi}[i] \longrightarrow \Diamond\langle\langle\psi\rangle\rangle \vee \Diamond y_{\Diamond\psi}[i]$
(c) $(M', \mathcal{I}, t) \models \forall i. y_{\Diamond\psi}[i] \longrightarrow \Diamond\langle\langle\psi\rangle\rangle$

Proof. (a) Let $(M', \mathcal{I}', t) \models x_{\Box\psi}[i]$ for some $\mathcal{I}' = \mathcal{I}[i \mapsto m]$. Since $(M', \mathcal{I}, t) \models \Box\textbf{localconstr}(\phi)$, we have

$$(M', \mathcal{I}', t) \models \Box \left(x_{\Box\psi}[i] \leftrightarrow \langle\langle\psi\rangle\rangle[i] \wedge x'_{\Box\psi}[i] \right)$$

It follows that $(M', \mathcal{I}', t') \models \langle\langle\psi\rangle\rangle[i]$ for every $t' \geq t$.
(b) Let $(M', \mathcal{I}', t) \models x_{\Diamond\psi}[i]$ for some $\mathcal{I}' = \mathcal{I}[i \mapsto m]$. Since $(M', \mathcal{I}, t) \models \Box\textbf{constr}(\phi) \wedge \Box\Diamond\textbf{evconstr}(\phi)$, we have
 - $(M', \mathcal{I}', t) \models \Box \left(x_{\Diamond\psi}[i] \leftrightarrow \langle\langle\psi\rangle\rangle[i] \vee x'_{\Diamond\psi}[i] \right)$.
 - $(M', \mathcal{I}', t') \models y'_{\Diamond\psi}[i] \leftrightarrow x'_{\Diamond\psi}[i]$ for some $t' \geq t$
If $(M', \mathcal{I}', t'') \models \langle\langle\psi(i)\rangle\rangle$ for some $t'' \geq t$ we are done, suppose that no such t'' exists. Then it follows that $(M', \mathcal{I}', t') \models y'_{\Diamond\psi}[i]$ and thus $(M', \mathcal{I}', t'+1) \models y_{\Diamond\psi}[i]$.
(c) Let $(M', \mathcal{I}', t) \models y_{\Diamond\psi}[i]$ for some $\mathcal{I}' = \mathcal{I}[i \mapsto m]$, and let $t' > t$ be the earliest point in time when

$$(M', \mathcal{I}', t') \models \neg y_{\Diamond\psi}[i]$$

Then we have

$$(M', \mathcal{I}', t' - 1) \models y_{\Diamond\psi}[i] \wedge \neg y'_{\Diamond\psi}[i]$$

and by the eventuality constraint of $y_{\Diamond\psi}$ we get

$$(M', \mathcal{I}', t' - 1) \models \langle\langle\psi\rangle\rangle(i)$$

Since $t' - 1 \geq t$ we conclude that

$$(M', \mathcal{I}', t) \models \Diamond\langle\langle\psi(i)\rangle\rangle$$

Theorem 1. *For each subformula ψ of ϕ, interpretation I and timepoint t we have there is a model M such that $(M, \mathcal{I}, t) \models \psi$ iff there is a model M' such that $(M', \mathcal{I}, t) \models \langle\!\langle \psi \rangle\!\rangle \wedge \Box\textbf{localconstr}(\phi) \wedge \Box\Diamond\textbf{evconstr}(\phi)$ where M differs from M' only in the auxiliary variables of ϕ.*

Proof. $\Longrightarrow$: This case is rather straight-forward. Define $M^\phi(i)$ by letting $x_{\psi(i)}$ be true at point $M^\phi(t, i)$ iff $(M, \mathcal{I}, t) \models \psi(i)$. Then the local constraints follow by the definitions of the temporal operators. The values of variables $y_{\Diamond\psi(i)}$ are then defined in a way that satisfies the eventuality constraint:

- at time t, all variables $y_{\Diamond\psi}[i]$ are set to false;
- if all $y_{\Diamond\psi}[i]$ are false at time t', then set the value of each $y_{\Diamond\psi}[i]$ at time $t'+1$ to the value of corresponding $x_{\Diamond\psi}[i]$ at time $t' + 1$;
- if variable $y_{\Diamond\psi}[i]$ is true at time t', and $\langle\!\langle \psi(i) \rangle\!\rangle$ holds, then set $y_{\Diamond\psi}[i]$ to false at time $t' + 1$.

$\Longleftarrow$: Let $(M', \mathcal{I}, t) \models \langle\!\langle \psi \rangle\!\rangle \wedge \Box\textbf{localconstr}(\phi) \wedge \Box\Diamond\textbf{evconstr}(\phi)$. We prove by induction over the structure of ψ.

$\psi \in MSO$: Since $\langle\!\langle \psi \rangle\!\rangle = \psi$, we get $(M', \mathcal{I}, t) \models \psi$.

$\psi = \exists i \psi_0$: We get $(M', \mathcal{I}, t) \models \exists i \langle\!\langle \psi_0 \rangle\!\rangle$ and by semantics $(M', \mathcal{I}[i \mapsto m], t) \models \langle\!\langle \psi_0 \rangle\!\rangle$ for some $m \in \mathbf{Z}$. Since $\Box\textbf{localconstr}(\phi) \wedge \Box\Diamond\textbf{evconstr}(\phi)$ is a closed formula and thus does not depend on i, it follows that $(M', \mathcal{I}[i \mapsto m], t) \models \Box\textbf{localconstr}(\phi) \wedge \Box\Diamond\textbf{evconstr}(\phi)$. By induction there is some M that differs from M' only in the auxiliary variables of ψ_0 such that $(M, \mathcal{I}[i \mapsto m], t) \models \psi_0$. By semantics we get $(M, \mathcal{I}, t) \models \exists i \psi_0$.

$\psi = \{\exists I \psi_0, \forall i \psi_0, \forall I \psi_0\}$ Similar to $\psi = \exists i \psi_0$.

$\psi = \Box\psi_0$: We get $(M', \mathcal{I}, t) \models x_{\Box\psi_0}$. By Lemma 1 it follows that $(M', \mathcal{I}, t) \models \Box\langle\!\langle \psi_0 \rangle\!\rangle$. Then by semantics for all $t' \geq t$, we have $(M', \mathcal{I}, t') \models \langle\!\langle \psi_0 \rangle\!\rangle$ and then by induction there is some M that differs from M' only in the auxiliary variables of ψ_0 such that $(M, \mathcal{I}, t') \models \psi_0$. Since this holds for all $t' \geq t$ we have by semantics that $(M, \mathcal{I}, t) \models \Box\psi_0$.

$\psi = \Diamond\psi_0$: We get $(M', \mathcal{I}, t) \models x_{\Diamond\psi_0}$. By Lemma 1 it follows that $(M', \mathcal{I}, t) \models \Diamond\langle\!\langle \psi_0 \rangle\!\rangle \vee \Diamond y_{\Diamond\psi_0}$. We have $(M', \mathcal{I}, t') \models \langle\!\langle \psi_0 \rangle\!\rangle$ for some $t' \geq t$ in both cases as follows. In the case $(M', \mathcal{I}, t) \models \Diamond y_{\Diamond\psi_0}$ holds, it follows by Lemma 1, and in the case $(M', \mathcal{I}, t) \models \Diamond\langle\!\langle \psi_0 \rangle\!\rangle$ holds it follows from semantics. Then by induction there is some M that differs from M' only in the auxiliary variables of ψ_0 such that $(M, \mathcal{I}, t') \models \psi_0$. Since $t' \geq t$ we have by semantics that $(M, \mathcal{I}, t) \models \Diamond\psi_0$. $\qquad\Box$

Corollary 1. *For a formula ϕ, interpretation I and timepoint t we have that there is a model M such that $(M, \mathcal{I}, t) \models \phi$ iff there is a model M' such that $(M', \mathcal{I}, t) \models \langle\!\langle \phi \rangle\!\rangle \wedge \Box\textbf{localconstr}(\phi) \wedge \Box\Diamond\textbf{evconstr}(\phi)$ where M differs from M' only in the auxiliary variables of ϕ.*

5 Implementation

The transformation of the previous section results in a formula of the form

$$I \wedge \Box T \wedge \Box\Diamond F$$

where the formulas I, T, and F are in MSO and can be translated into transducers. The transducers can be seen as binary relations on words that are closed under standard operations such as union, intersection and composition. For the sake of presentation, we will assume that I only contains non-primed configuration variables and look at I as a set instead of a binary relation. The general case does not introduce any significant additional problems.

We find models of the formula $I \wedge \Box T \wedge \Box \Diamond F$ as follows.

(a) Compute the set of reachable states as $Inv = I \circ T^*$.
(b) Define T_{Inv} as $\{(w, w') \in T : w \in Inv\}$ and compute the set of loops by finding identical pairs in $(T_{Inv} \cap F) \circ T^*$

We use an optimized version of the above scheme as follows. When computing the invariant $I \circ T^*$ the transition relation T contains local constraints for eventuality variables. For eventualities that hold infinitely often, such local constraints are only needed when checking for loops through F and not when computing the set of reachable states. To simplify the transition relation used when computing the set of reachable states, the formula is transformed into the following form:

$$I \wedge \Box T_0 \wedge \Diamond(F \wedge \Box T \wedge \Box \Diamond F)$$

where T_0 is like T but without the local constraints on eventuality variables for eventualities that hold infinitely often. The final procedure is then as follows.

(a) Compute the set of reachable states $Inv = I \circ T_0^*$.
(b) As before, define T_{Inv} as $\{(w, w') \in T : w \in Inv\}$ and compute the set of loops by finding identical pairs in $(T_{Inv} \cap F) \circ T^*$.

To calculate expressions like $T_1 \circ T_2^*$, we employ a technique for computing arbitrary relational compositions of transducers, expressed as regular expressions, by encoding the states of the automaton recognizing the regular expression in the first position of the word. As an example, the expression $T_1 \circ T_2^*$ corresponds to an automaton with two states q_1, and q_2. We use a transducer accepting the union of $(q_1, q_2) \cdot T_1$ and $(q_2, q_2) \cdot T_2$. Words in the transitive closure of the resulting transducer, of the form $(q_1, q_2) \cdot (w[1], w'[1]) \cdots (w[n], w'[n])$, then represent an element (w, w') in the relation $T_1 \circ T_2^*$.

We have successfully verified safety properties for many of the examples in our previous work, as well as liveness properties for some of the smaller examples. Execution times are given in the table below.

Algorithm	Safety (ms)	Liveness (ms)
Tokenpass	3930	14790
Tokenring	4840	29590
Bakery	4840	23070
Burns	38560	
Dijkstra	593220	
Szymanski	1073200	

We experience high execution times for checking safety properties for some of the algorithms. This is because we use the entire transition as opposed to computing the transitive closure of separate actions and using them for reachability analysis. This reachability analysis does not always terminate, however, since some algorithms require the transitive closure of combinations of actions for the analysis to terminate. Using the entire transition relation is a more general technique, but potentially more costly.

References

[AJNd02]   Parosh Aziz Abdulla, Bengt Jonsson, Marcus Nilsson, and Julien d'Orso. Regular model checking made simple and efficient. In *Proc. CONCUR 2002, 13th Int. Conf. on Concurrency Theory*, volume 2421 of *Lecture Notes in Computer Science*, pages 116–130, 2002.

[AJNd03]   Parosh Aziz Abdulla, Bengt Jonsson, Marcus Nilsson, and Julien d'Orso. Algorithmic improvements in regular model checking. In *Proc. 14th Int. Conf. on Computer Aided Verification*, volume 2725 of *Lecture Notes in Computer Science*, 2003.

[BJNT00]   A. Bouajjani, B. Jonsson, M. Nilsson, and T. Touili. Regular model checking. In Emerson and Sistla, editors, *Proc. 12th Int. Conf. on Computer Aided Verification*, volume 1855 of *Lecture Notes in Computer Science*, pages 403–418. Springer Verlag, 2000.

[BLS01]   K. Baukus, Y. Lakhnech, and K. Stahl. Verification of parameterized networks. *Journal of Universal Computer Science*, 7(2), 2001.

[BLW03]   Bernard Boigelot, Axel Legay, and Pierre Wolper. Iterating transducers in the large. In *Proc. 14th Int. Conf. on Computer Aided Verification*, volume 2725 of *Lecture Notes in Computer Science*, pages 223–235, 2003.

[Del00]   G. Delzanno. Automatic verification of cache coherence protocols. In Emerson and Sistla, editors, *Proc. 12th Int. Conf. on Computer Aided Verification*, volume 1855 of *Lecture Notes in Computer Science*, pages 53–68. Springer Verlag, 2000.

[EK00]   E.A. Emerson and V. Kahlon. Reducing model checking of the many to the few. In *Proc. 17th International Conference on Automated Deduction*, volume 1831 of *Lecture Notes in Computer Science*, pages 236–254. Springer Verlag, 2000.

[EK03]   E.A. Emerson and V. Kahlon. Rapid parameterized model checking of snoopy cache coherence protocols. In *Proc. TACAS '03, 9th Int. Conf. on Tools and Algorithms for the Construction and Analysis of Systems*, 2003.

[EN95]   E.A. Emerson and K.S. Namjoshi. Reasoning about rings. In *Proc. 22th ACM Symp. on Principles of Programming Languages*, 1995.

[GR97]   D. Giammarresi and A. Restivo. Two-dimensional languages. In A. Salomaa and G. Rozenberg, editors, *Handbook of Formal Languages*, volume 3, Beyond Words, pages 215–267. Springer-Verlag, Berlin, 1997.

[GS92]   S. M. German and A. P. Sistla. Reasoning about systems with many processes. *Journal of the ACM*, 39(3):675–735, 1992.

[HJJ+96]   J.G. Henriksen, J. Jensen, M. Jørgensen, N. Klarlund, B. Paige, T. Rauhe, and A. Sandholm. Mona: Monadic second-order logic in practice. In *Proc. TACAS '95, 1th Int. Conf. on Tools and Algorithms for the Construction and Analysis of Systems*, volume 1019 of *Lecture Notes in Computer Science*, 1996.

[JN00]   Bengt Jonsson and Marcus Nilsson. Transitive closures of regular relations for verifying infinite-state systems. In S. Graf and M. Schwartzbach, editors, *Proc. TACAS '00, 6th Int. Conf. on Tools and Algorithms for the Construction and Analysis of Systems*, volume 1785 of *Lecture Notes in Computer Science*, 2000.

[KMM+01] Y. Kesten, O. Maler, M. Marcus, A. Pnueli, and E. Shahar. Symbolic model checking with rich assertional languages. *Theoretical Computer Science*, 256:93–112, 2001.

[Lam91]   L. Lamport. The temporal logic of actions. Technical report, DEC/SRC, 1991.

[PS00]   A. Pnueli and E. Shahar. Liveness and acceleration in parameterized verification. In *Proc. 12th Int. Conf. on Computer Aided Verification*, volume 1855 of *Lecture Notes in Computer Science*, pages 328–343. Springer Verlag, 2000.

[PXZ02]   A. Pnueli, J. Xu, and L. Zuck. Liveness with $(0, 1, \infty)$-counter abstraction. In Brinskma and Larsen, editors, *Proc. 14th Int. Conf. on Computer Aided Verification*, volume 2404 of *Lecture Notes in Computer Science*, pages 107–122. Springer Verlag, 2002.

[Sis97]   A. Prasad Sistla. Parametrized verification of linear networks using automata as invariants. In O. Grumberg, editor, *Proc. 9th Int. Conf. on Computer Aided Verification*, volume 1254 of *Lecture Notes in Computer Science*, pages 412–423, Haifa, Israel, 1997. Springer Verlag.

[VW86]   M. Y. Vardi and P. Wolper. An automata-theoretic approach to automatic program verification. In *Proc. LICS '86, 1st IEEE Int. Symp. on Logic in Computer Science*, pages 332–344, June 1986.

[WB98]   Pierre Wolper and Bernard Boigelot. Verifying systems with infinite but regular state spaces. In *Proc. 10th Int. Conf. on Computer Aided Verification*, volume 1427 of *Lecture Notes in Computer Science*, pages 88–97, Vancouver, July 1998. Springer Verlag.

Image Computation
in Infinite State Model Checking

Alain Finkel[1] and Jérôme Leroux[2]

[1] Laboratoire Spécification et Vérification, CNRS UMR 8643 & ENS de Cachan
61 av. du Président Wilson, 94235 Cachan cedex, France
finkel@lsv.ens-cachan.fr
[2] Departement d'Informatique et de Recherche Opérationnelle
Université de Montréal, Pavillon André-Aisenstadt
CP 6128 succ Centre Ville, H3C 3J7, Montréal, QC Canada
leroujer@iro.umontreal.ca

Abstract. The model checking of a counters system S often reduces to the effective computation of the set of predecessors $\mathrm{Pre}_S^*(X)$ of a set of integer vectors X. Because the exact computation of this set is not possible in general, we are interested in characterizing the minimal Number Decision Diagrams (NDD) [WB00] that represents the set $\mathrm{Pre}^{\leq k}(X)$. In particular, its size is proved to be just polynomially bounded in k when S is a counters system with a finite monoïd [FL02], explaining why there is no exponential blow up in k.

1 Introduction

Model checking infinite-state transition systems S often reduces to the effective computation of the potentially infinite set of predecessors Pre_S^*. More precisely, the safety model checking can be expressed as the following problem:

- Given as inputs an infinite-state transition system S and two possibly infinite sets X_0 and X of respectively initial states and non-safe states, decide if $X_0 \cap \mathrm{Pre}_S^*(X)$ is empty.

Infinite Sets. In order to effectively compute $\mathrm{Pre}_S^*(X)$, one generally needs to find a class of infinite sets which has the following properties: closure under union, closure under Pre_S, membership and inclusion are decidable with a good complexity, and there exists a canonical representation. We are considering the Number Decision Diagrams (NDD) that provides an automata-based symbolic representation of some subsets of $\mathbb{N}^m$.

Infinite-State Transition Systems. We will focus on systems S with m integer variables and more precisely on counters systems with a finite monoïd (also known as finite linear systems [FL02]), a class of systems that contains the reset/transfer Petri Nets [DJS99], generalized broadcast protocols [EN98, Del00], and all the counters automata. As this model is very general and powerful, the

R. Alur and D.A. Peled (Eds.): CAV 2004, LNCS 3114, pp. 361–371, 2004.
© Springer-Verlag Berlin Heidelberg 2004

price to pay is the undecidability of reachability properties and in particular the sequence $(\mathrm{Pre}_S^{\leq k}(X))_k$ does not converge in general.

Our Image Computation Problem. The characterization of the NDD structure that represents $\mathrm{Pre}_S^{\leq k}(X)$ in function of k is an important problem in order to effectively compute the exact limit $\mathrm{Pre}_S^*(X)$ or a "good" over-approximation:

- When there exists an integer k_0 such that $\mathrm{Pre}_S^*(X) = \mathrm{Pre}_S^{\leq k_0}(X)$, the characterization can be useful in order to design an efficient algorithm that incrementally computes these sets. Recall that even if the convergence of $(\mathrm{Pre}_S^{\leq k}(X))_k$ is not guaranteed by the theory, in practice we observe that often, this sequence converges [Del00, BB03] and it often converges quickly [Bra, Bab]. Moreover, as soon as the set X is upward closed and S is a Well Structured Transition System [FS01], the convergence is insured.
- When the sequence $(\mathrm{Pre}_S^{\leq k}(X))_k$ diverges, the characterization can be useful in order to design NDD specialized acceleration operators that computes the exact limit $\mathrm{Pre}_S^*(X)$ [BLW03, FL02] or an over-approximation [BGP99].

Related Works. We use the approach called the *regular model checking*: for channel systems, Semi-Linear Regular Expressions [FPS00] and Constrained Queue-content Decision Diagrams [BH99] have been proposed; for lossy channel systems [ABJ98], the tools LCS (in the more general tool TREX [ABS01] [Tre]) uses the downward-closed regular languages and the corresponding subset of Simple Regular Expressions for sets and it represents them by finite automata to compute Post*; for stack automata, regular expressions or finite automata are sufficient to represent Pre* and Post* [BEF+00]; for Petri nets and parameterized rings, [FO97] uses regular languages and Presburger arithmetics (and acceleration) for sets. For Transfer and Reset Petri nets [DFS98], the tool BABYLON [Bab] utilizes the upward closed sets and represents them by Covering Sharing Trees [DRV01], a variant of BDD; for counters automata, the tool BRAIN [Bra] uses linear sets and represent them by their linear bases and periods; MONA [Mon] [KMS02] and FMONA [BF00] use formula in WS1S to represent sets; the tool CSL-ALV [BGP97] [Alv] uses linear arithmetic constraints for sets and manipulates formula with the OMEGA solver and the automata library of LASH.

For counters systems with a finite monoïd, tools FAST [Fas], [FL02], [BFLP03] and LASH [Las] utilize semi-linear sets and represents them by NDD, moreover, these two tools are able to accelerate loops [Boi03] [FL02]. In [FL04], the NDD $\mathrm{Pre}_S(X)$ is proved to be computable in polynomial time in function of the NDD X for a large class of systems S that contains all the counters system with a finite (or infinite) monoïd. Moreover, the size of the NDD that represents $\mathrm{Pre}_S^{\leq k}(X)$ is proved to be polynomial in k when S and X are "defined in the interval-logic", a restrictive class compared to the sets that can be represented by NDD.

Our Results.

1. We prove that the asymptotic number of states of the minimal NDD that represents $\mathrm{Pre}_S^{\leq k}(X)$ is polynomial in k for any counters systems S with a finite monoïd and for any set X represented by a NDD.

2. We show that the structure of the minimal NDD that represents $\text{Pre}_S^{\leq k}(X)$ is similar to a BDD. That provides a new way for implementing a NDD library using all the BDD techniques for speeding-up the computation like cache-computation, minimization in linear time, Strong canonical form, well-known in the field of BDD [Bry92].

Plan of the Paper. The structure of the minimal NDD that represents a set X is given in section 3. In the next one, the definition of counters systems with a finite monoïd is recall. The structure of the minimal NDD that represents $\text{Pre}_S^{\leq k}(X)$ in function of k, is studied in the last section 5.

2 Preliminaries

The cardinal of a finite set X is written $\text{card}(X)$. The set of rational numbers, non negative rational numbers, integers and positive integers are respectively written $\mathbb{Q}$, $\mathbb{Q}^+$, $\mathbb{Z}$ and $\mathbb{N}$. The set of vectors with $m \geq 1$ components in a set X is written X^m. The i-th component of a vector $x \in X^m$ is written $x_i \in X$; we have $x = (x_1, \ldots, x_m)$. For any vector $v, v' \in \mathbb{Q}^m$ and for any $t \in \mathbb{Q}$, we define $t.v$ and $v + v'$ in $\mathbb{Q}^m$ by $(t.v)_i = t.v_i$ and $(v + v')_i = v_i + v'_i$. For any $x \in \mathbb{Q}^m$, we define $||x||_\infty = \max_i(|x_i|)$.

The set of square matrices of size m in $K \subseteq \mathbb{Q}$ is written $\mathcal{M}_m(K)$. The element $M_{ij} \in K$ is the i-th raw and j-th column of a matrix $M \in \mathcal{M}_m(K)$. The identity matrix is written I_m. The vector $M.x \in \mathbb{Q}^m$ is naturally defined by $(M.x)_i = \sum_{j=1}^m M_{ij}x_j$. The subset $M^{-1}Y \subseteq \mathbb{Q}^m$ is defined by $M^{-1}Y = \{x \in \mathbb{Q}^m; \ M.x \in Y\}$ for any $M \in \mathcal{M}(\mathbb{Q})$ and $X \subseteq \mathbb{Q}^m$. For any $M \in \mathcal{M}_m(\mathbb{Q})$, we define $||M||_\infty = \max_{i,j}(|M_{ij}|)$.

The set of words over a finite alphabet Σ is written Σ^*. The concatenation of two words σ and σ' in Σ^* is written $\sigma.\sigma'$. The empty word in Σ^* is written ϵ. The residue $\sigma^{-1}.\mathcal{L}$ of a language $\mathcal{L} \subseteq \Sigma^*$ by a word $\sigma \in \Sigma^*$ is defined by $\sigma^{-1}.\mathcal{L} = \{w \in \Sigma^*; \ \sigma.w \in \mathcal{L}\}$

A deterministic and complete automaton $\mathcal{A}$ is a tuple $\mathcal{A} = (Q, \Sigma, \delta, q_0, F)$; Q is the finite set of states, Σ is the finite alphabet, $\delta : Q \times \Sigma \to Q$ is the transition relation, $Q_0 \subseteq Q$ is the set of initial states and $F \subseteq Q$ is the set of final states. As usual, we extends δ over $Q \times \Sigma^*$ such that $\delta(q, \sigma.\sigma') = \delta(\delta(q, \sigma), \sigma')$. The language $\mathcal{L}(\mathcal{A}) \subseteq \Sigma^*$ accepted by a deterministic and complete automaton $\mathcal{A}$ is defined by $\mathcal{L}(\mathcal{A}) = \{\sigma \in \Sigma^*; \ \delta(q_0, \sigma) \in F\}$.

3 Number Decision Diagrams

Recall that there exist two natural ways in order to associate to a word σ a vector in $\mathbb{N}^m$ following that the first letter of σ is considered as an "high bit" or a "low bit". In this article, we consider the "low bit" representation (even if the other one, just seems to be symmetrical, results proved in the paper cannot be easily extended to the other one).

Let us consider an integer $r \geq 2$ called the *basis of the decomposition* and an integer $m \geq 1$ called the *dimension of the represented vectors*. A *digit vector* b is an element of the finite alphabet $\Sigma_{rm} = \{0, \ldots, r-1\}^m$. The vector $\rho(\sigma) \in \mathbb{N}^m$ associated to a word $\sigma = b_1 \ldots b_n$ of $n \geq 1$ digit vectors $b_i \in \Sigma_{rm}$ is defined by $\rho(\sigma) = \sum_{i=1}^{n} r^{i-1}.b_i$. We naturally define $\rho(\epsilon) = (0, \ldots, 0)$.

Definition 1 ([WB00], [BC96]). *A Number Decision Diagram (NDD) $\mathcal{A}$ is a finite deterministic and complete automaton over the alphabet Σ_{rm} such that:*

$$\rho^{-1}(\rho(\mathcal{L}(\mathcal{A}))) = \mathcal{L}(\mathcal{A})$$

The subset $X = \rho(\mathcal{L}(\mathcal{A})) \subseteq \mathbb{N}^m$ is called *the set represented* by the NDD $\mathcal{A}$. Such a subset X is said *NDD-definable*.

Remark 1. Thanks to the condition $\rho^{-1}(\rho(\mathcal{L}(\mathcal{A}))) = \mathcal{L}(\mathcal{A})$, the set $\mathbb{N}^m \backslash X$ is represented by the NDD $\mathcal{A} = (Q, \Sigma_{rm}, \delta, q_0, Q \backslash F)$. Recall that from any deterministic and complete binary automaton $\mathcal{A}$, we can efficiently computes a NDD $\mathcal{A}'$ such that $\rho(\mathcal{L}(\mathcal{A})) = \rho(\mathcal{L}(\mathcal{A}'))$ [KMS02, Ler03].

Remark 2. Any Presburger definable set (a set defined by a formula in the first order logic $\langle \mathbb{N}, +, \leq \rangle$) [BC96, WB00], or any semi-linear set (a set equal to a finite union of sets of the form $x_0 + \sum_{p \in P} \mathbb{N}.p$ where $x_0 \in \mathbb{N}^m$ and P is a finite subset of $\mathbb{N}^m$) [GS66, Reu89] can be effectively represented by a NDD. Moreover, recall that a set is NDD-definable if and only if it is definable by a formula in the first order logic $\langle \mathbb{N}, +, \leq, V_r \rangle$ where V_r is the valuation function in base r defined by $y = V_r(x)$ if and only if y is the greatest power of r that divides x [BHMV94].

In the remaining of this section, we characterize the minimal NDD that represents a subset X.

The equality $\rho(\sigma.\sigma') = \rho(\sigma) + r^{|\sigma|}.\rho(\sigma')$ shows that the function $\gamma_\sigma : \mathbb{N}^m \rightarrow \mathbb{N}^m$ defined by $\gamma_\sigma(x) = \rho(\sigma) + r^{|\sigma|}.x$ plays an important role. We are going to prove that X is NDD-definable if and only if the following set $Q(X)$ is finite:

$$Q(X) = \{\gamma_\sigma^{-1}(X); \ \sigma \in \Sigma_{rm}^*\}$$

Remark that for any digit vector $b \in \Sigma_{rm}$ and for any $q \in Q(X)$, the set $\gamma_b^{-1}(q)$ remains in $Q(X)$. Hence, if $Q(X)$ is finite, we can easily associate to a set X a deterministic and complete automaton $\mathcal{A}(X)$.

Definition 2. *Let $X \subseteq \mathbb{N}^m$ be such that $Q(X) = \{\gamma_\sigma^{-1}(X); \ \sigma \in \Sigma_{rm}^*\}$ is finite. The deterministic and complete automaton $\mathcal{A}(X)$ is defined by:*

$$\begin{cases} \mathcal{A}(X) = (Q(X), \Sigma_{rm}, \delta, q_0, F) \\ \delta(q, b) = \gamma_b^{-1}(q) \\ q_0 = X \\ F = \{q \in Q(X); \ (0, \ldots, 0) \in q\} \end{cases}$$

We are going to prove that $\mathcal{A}(X)$ is the unique minimal NDD that represents X.

Lemma 1. *For any $X \subseteq \mathbb{N}^m$ and $\sigma \in \Sigma_{rm}^*$, we have $\sigma^{-1}.\rho^{-1}(X) = \rho^{-1}(\gamma_\sigma^{-1}(X))$.*

Proof. We have $w \in \sigma^{-1}.\rho^{-1}(X)$ iff $\sigma.w \in \rho^{-1}(X)$ iff $\rho(\sigma.w) \in X$ iff $\gamma_\sigma(\rho(w)) \in X$ iff $\rho(w) \in \gamma_\sigma^{-1}(X)$ iff $w \in \rho^{-1}(\gamma_\sigma^{-1}(X))$. $\qquad\square$

The following theorem is really important because it proves that the structure of the minimal NDD that represents a set X can be obtained just by studying the sets $\gamma_\sigma^{-1}(X)$.

Theorem 1. *A set $X \subseteq \mathbb{N}^m$ is NDD-definable if and only if $Q(X)$ is finite. Moreover, in this case, $\mathcal{A}(X)$ is the unique minimal NDD that represents X.*

Proof. Assume that $Q(X)$ is a finite set. We are going to show that $\mathcal{A}(X)$ is a NDD that represents X by proving $\mathcal{L}(\mathcal{A}(X)) = \rho^{-1}(X)$. By definition of $\mathcal{A}(X)$, we have $\sigma \in \mathcal{L}(\mathcal{A}(X))$ iff $(0, \ldots, 0) \in \gamma_\sigma^{-1}(X)$. Therefore $\sigma \in \mathcal{L}(\mathcal{A}(X))$ iff $\rho(\sigma) = \gamma_\sigma((0, \ldots, 0)) \in X$. Hence, we have proved that $\mathcal{L}(\mathcal{A}(X)) = \rho^{-1}(X)$. In particular $\rho(\mathcal{L}(\mathcal{A}(X))) = X$ and $\rho^{-1}(\rho(\mathcal{L}(\mathcal{A}(X)))) = \mathcal{L}(\mathcal{A}(X))$. We have proved that $\mathcal{A}(X)$ is an NDD that represents X.

Now, assume that X is NDD-definable and let us prove that $Q(X)$ is finite. There exists a NDD $\mathcal{A}$ such that X is represented by $\mathcal{A}$. Let $\mathcal{L}$ be the regular language accepted by $\mathcal{A}$. As $\mathcal{A}$ is an NDD that represents X, we have $\rho^{-1}(\rho(\mathcal{L})) = \mathcal{L}$ and $\rho(\mathcal{L}) = X$. We deduce $\mathcal{L} = \rho^{-1}(X)$. As the minimal deterministic and complete automaton that recognizes $\mathcal{L}$ is unique, there exists a unique minimal automaton that represents X. Recall that the set of states of this minimal automaton is given by $\{\sigma^{-1}.\mathcal{L}; \ \sigma \in \Sigma_{rm}^*\}$. From lemma 1, we deduce that $Q(X) = \{\rho(\sigma^{-1}.\mathcal{L}); \ \sigma \in \Sigma_{rm}^*\}$. Therefore, $Q(X)$ is finite and by uniqueness of the minimal automaton, $\mathcal{A}(X)$ is the unique minimal NDD that represents X. $\qquad\square$

4   Counters Automata with Finite Monoïd

The class of counters automata with finite monoïd finite (a.k.a finite linear systems [FL02]) is a natural extension of some classes of models like Reset/Transfer Petri Nets [DJS99], counter automata or broadcast protocols [EN98, Del00]. Recall that this class is also used as the input model of the accelerated symbolic model checker FAST [BFLP03].

Let us first provide the definition of a counters system.

Definition 3. *A NDD-linear function f is a tuple $f = (D, M, v)$ such that $D \subseteq \mathbb{N}^m$ is NDD-definable, $M \in \mathcal{M}_m(\mathbb{Z})$ and $v \in \mathbb{Z}^m$.*

Without any ambiguity, we also denote by f the function $f : D \to \mathbb{N}^m$ defined by $f(x) = M.x + v$ for any $x \in D$. The composition of two NDD-linear functions is naturally defined by $(D_1, M_1, v_1) \circ (D_2, M_2, v_2) = (D_2 \cap M_2^{-1}(D_1 - v_2), M_1.M_2, M_1.v_2 + v_1)$.

Definition 4. *A counters system S (a.k.a linear system [FL02]) is a tuple $S = (\Sigma, f_\Sigma)$ where Σ is a finite set of actions and $f_\Sigma = \{f_a; \ a \in \Sigma\}$ is a finite set of NDD-linear functions.*

For any word $\sigma = b_1 \ldots b_n$ of $n \geq 1$ actions $b_i \in \Sigma$, the NDD-linear function f_σ is defined as $f_\sigma = f_{b_n} \circ \cdots f_{b_1}$. The NDD-linear function f_ϵ is defined by $f_\epsilon = (\mathbb{N}^m, I, (0, \ldots, 0))$. We denote by $(D_\sigma, M_\sigma, v_\sigma)$ the NDD-linear function f_σ. Like in [FL02], we define the monoïd of S.

Definition 5 ([FL02]). *The monoïd multiplicatively generated by the square matrices M_a is called the monoïd of S and written $\mathfrak{M}_S = \{M_\sigma; \ \sigma \in \Sigma^*\}$.*

Definition 6. *A counters system S such that $\mathfrak{M}_S$ is finite is called a counter system with a finite monoïd (a.k.a a finite linear system [FL02]).*

Remark 3. The class of counters systems with a finite monoïd enjoys good properties that allow to easily *accelerate* the computation of the reachability set [FL02, Boi03, Ler03].

Finally, let us recall the definition of the set of immediate predecessors.

Definition 7. *Let S be a counters system. The set $\mathrm{Pre}_S(X)$ of immediate predecessors of a set X is defined by $\mathrm{Pre}_S(X) = \bigcup_{a \in \Sigma} f_a^{-1}(X)$.*

5   Structure of the Minimal NDD $\mathcal{A}(\mathrm{Pre}_S^{\leq k}(X))$

In [FL04], we have proved that for any counters system S, we can effectively computes in polynomial time a NDD that represents $\mathrm{Pre}_S(X)$ from any NDD that represents X. This result provides an exponential time algorithm for computing the minimal NDD $\mathcal{A}(\mathrm{Pre}_S^{\leq k}(X))$ in function of k. In fact, assume that each step of the computation multiplies the number of states of the NDD just by 2, then after k steps, the number of states of the NDD is multiplied by 2^k. However, in practice, such an exponential blow up does not appear.

To explain this experimental result, we are going to study the structure of the minimal NDD $\mathcal{A}(\mathrm{Pre}_S^{\leq k}(X))$ in function of $k \geq 0$. We prove an *unexpected result*: the NDD has a "BDD-like" structure and its number of states is polynomial in k for any counter systems S with a finite monoïd and for any set X NDD-definable. We first prove a technical lemma.

Lemma 2. *Let $X \subseteq \mathbb{N}^m$ be a NDD-definable set, $M \in \mathfrak{M}(\mathbb{Z})$ and $\alpha \in \mathbb{Q}^+$. There exists a finite class $\mathcal{C}_{X,M,\alpha}$ such that for any $v \in \mathbb{Z}^m$ and for any $w \in \Sigma_{rm}^*$, we have:*

$$||v||_\infty \leq \alpha . r^{|w|} \implies \gamma_w^{-1}(\mathbb{N}^m \cap M^{-1}(X - v)) \in \mathcal{C}_{X,M,\alpha}$$

Proof. Let $v \in \mathbb{Z}^m$ and $w \in \Sigma_{rm}^*$ such that $||v||_\infty \leq \alpha . r^{|w|}$. We have:

$$\gamma_w^{-1}(\mathbb{N}^m \cap M^{-1}(X - v)) = \mathbb{N}^m \cap \left[\frac{1}{r^{|w|}}(\mathbb{N}^m \cap M^{-1}(X - v) - \rho(w)) \right]$$

$$= \mathbb{N}^m \cap \left[M^{-1}(\frac{1}{r^{|w|}}(X - v - M.\rho(w))) \right]$$

From the equality $X = \bigcup_{w_0 \in \Sigma_{rm}^{|w|}} \gamma_{w_0}(\gamma_{w_0}^{-1}(X))$, we deduce:

$$\gamma_w^{-1}(\mathbb{N}^m \cap M^{-1}(X - v))$$

$$= \bigcup_{w_0 \in \Sigma_{rm}^{|w|}} \left(\mathbb{N}^m \cap M^{-1}\left(\gamma_{w_0}^{-1}(X) + \frac{\rho(w_0) - v - M.\rho(w)}{r^{|w|}}\right)\right)$$

Let $B = \{z \in \mathbb{Z}^m;\ ||z||_\infty \le 1 + \alpha + m.||M||_\infty\}$ and let us prove that for any $w_0 \in \Sigma_{rm}^{|w|}$, if $\mathbb{N}^m \cap M^{-1}\left(\gamma_{w_0}^{-1}(X) + \frac{\rho(w_0) - v - M.\rho(w)}{r^{|w|}}\right) \ne \emptyset$ then $\frac{\rho(w_0) - v - M.\rho(w)}{r^{|w|}} \in B$.
In fact, in this case, there exists $x_0 \in \gamma_{w_0}^{-1}(X)$ such that $x_0 + \frac{\rho(w_0) - v - M.\rho(w)}{r^{|w|}} \in M.\mathbb{N}^m \subseteq \mathbb{Z}^m$. Therefore $\frac{\rho(w_0) - v - M.\rho(w)}{r^{|w|}} \in \mathbb{Z}^m$. Moreover, we have the following inequality:

$$\left\|\frac{\rho(w_0) - v - M.\rho(w)}{r^{|w|}}\right\|_\infty \le \frac{(r^{|w|} - 1) + \alpha.r^{|w|} + m.||M||_\infty.(r^{|w|} - 1)}{r^{|w|}}$$

$$\le 1 + \alpha + m.||M||_\infty$$

Now, just remark that the following finite class $\mathcal{C}_{X,M,\alpha}$ satisfies the lemma:

$$\mathcal{C}_{X,M,\alpha} = \left\{ \bigcup_{(q,b) \in F} \mathbb{N}^m \cap M^{-1}(q + b);\ F \subseteq Q(X) \times B \right\}$$

$\square$

Theorem 2. *Let S be a counters system with a finite monoïd and X be a NDD-definable set. There exists a finite class $\mathcal{C}_{S,X}$ of subsets of $\mathbb{N}^m$ such that for any $w \in \Sigma_{rm}^*$ and for any $\mathcal{L} \subseteq \Sigma^{\le r^{|w|}}$, we have:*

$$\gamma_w^{-1}\left(\bigcup_{\sigma \in \mathcal{L}} f_\sigma^{-1}(X) \right) \in \mathcal{C}_{S,X}$$

Proof. Let $\alpha = \max_{(M,a) \in \mathcal{M}_S \times \Sigma} ||M.v_a||_\infty$. We define the function $g_\sigma : \mathbb{Q}^m \to \mathbb{Q}^m$ by $g_\sigma(x) = M_\sigma.x + v_\sigma$ for any $x \in \mathbb{Q}^m$, $\sigma \in \Sigma^*$.
   Let $\sigma = a_1 \dots a_n$ be a word of $n \ge 1$ actions in Σ and $w \in \Sigma_{rm}^*$ be a word of vector digits such that $|\sigma| \le r^{|w|}$. The sequence of prefixes $(\sigma_i)_{0 \le i \le n}$ of σ is defined by $\sigma_i = a_1 \dots a_i$. The set $I(M, a, \sigma) = \{i \in \{1, \dots, n\};\ (M_{\sigma_i}, v_{\sigma_i}) = (M, v)\}$ where $(M, a) \in \mathcal{M}_S \times \Sigma$ is useful to compute the set $\gamma_w^{-1}(f_\sigma^{-1}(X))$ as it is shown by the following equality:

$$\gamma_w^{-1}(f_\sigma^{-1}(X)) = \gamma_w^{-1}\left(g_{\sigma_0}^{-1}(D_{a_1}) \cap \dots \cap g_{\sigma_{n-1}}^{-1}(D_{a_n}) \cap g_{\sigma_n}^{-1}(X)\right)$$

$$= \bigcap_{(M,a) \in \mathcal{M}_S \times \Sigma} \bigcap_{i \in I(M,a,\sigma)} \gamma_w^{-1}\left(\mathbb{N}^m \cap M^{-1}(D_a - v_{\sigma_i})\right)$$

$$\cap \gamma_w^{-1}(\mathbb{N}^m \cap M_{\sigma_n}^{-1}(X - v_{\sigma_n}))$$

Let $\mathcal{C}_{X,M,\alpha}$ and $\mathcal{C}_{D_a,M,\alpha}$ be some finite classes satisfying lemma 2 for any $(M,a) \in \mathcal{M}_S \times \Sigma$. From $v_{\sigma_i} = \sum_{j=1}^{i} M_{\sigma_j}.v_{a_j}$, we deduce $||v_{\sigma_i}||_\infty \leq \alpha.i \leq \alpha.|\sigma| \leq \alpha.r^{|w|}$. Therefore, we have proved that $\gamma_w^{-1}(f_\sigma^{-1}(X))$ is in the following finite class $\mathcal{C}_{S,X}^0$:

$$\mathcal{C}_{S,X}^0 = \left\{ \bigcap_{Y \in F} Y \cap X'; \ X' \in \bigcup_{M \in \mathcal{M}_S} \mathcal{C}_{X,M,\alpha}; \ F \subseteq \bigcup_{(M,a) \in \mathcal{M}_S \times \Sigma} \mathcal{C}_{D_a,M,\alpha} \right\}$$

Now, let $\mathcal{C}_{S,X}$ be the set of all finite unions of elements in $\mathcal{C}_{S,X}^0$. From the equality $\gamma_w^{-1}(\bigcup_{\sigma \in \mathcal{L}} f_\sigma^{-1}(X)) = \bigcup_{\sigma \in \mathcal{L}} \gamma_w^{-1}(f_\sigma^{-1}(X))$, we deduce that $\gamma_w^{-1}(\bigcup_{\sigma \in \mathcal{L}} f_\sigma^{-1}(X)) \in \mathcal{C}_{S,X}$ for any $\mathcal{L} \subseteq \Sigma^{\leq r^{|w|}}$. □

We can deduce many interesting results from the previous theorem. The first *unexpected one* is about the asymptotic number of states of the minimal NDD $\mathcal{A}(\text{Pre}_S^{\leq k}(X))$ in function of k.

Corollary 1. *Let S be a counters system with a finite monoïd and X be a NDD-definable set. There exists a constant $c_{S,X}$ such that the number of states of the minimal NDD that represents $\text{Pre}_S^{\leq k}(X)$ is bounded $k^m + c_{S,X}$.*

Proof. Let $\mathcal{C}_{S,X}$ be a class of finite subsets of $\mathbb{N}^m$ satisfying theorem 2 and let $X_k = \text{Pre}_S^{\leq k}(X)$. From $X_k = \bigcup_{\sigma \in \Sigma^{\leq k}} f_\sigma^{-1}(X)$, we deduce that for any $w \in \Sigma_{r^m}^*$ such that $k \leq r^{|w|}$, we have $\gamma_w^{-1}(X_k) \in \mathcal{C}_{S,X}$. From theorem 1 we deduce that the set of states $Q(X_k)$ of the minimal NDD that represents X_k satisfies $Q(X_k) \subseteq \mathcal{C}_{S,X} \cup \{\gamma_w^{-1}(X_k); \ r^{|w|} < k\}$. From $\text{card}(\{\gamma_w^{-1}(X_k); \ r^{|w|} < k\}) \leq k^m$, we deduce that the cardinal of $Q(X_k)$ is bounded by $k^m + \text{card}(\mathcal{C}_{S,X})$. □

The previous corollary proves an experimental result : the number of counters m is an exponential limitation for the effective computation of $\mathcal{A}(\text{Pre}_S^{\leq k}(X))$ for large value of k. However, it explains why there is no exponential blow up in k.

Now, let us study precisely the structure of $\mathcal{A}(\text{Pre}_S^{\leq k}(X))$.

Definition 8. *A state q of a NDD $\mathcal{A}$ is said acyclic if the number of paths $q_0 \rightarrow q$ is finite.*

Corollary 2. *Let S be a counters system with a finite monoïd and let X be a NDD-definable set. The number of non acyclic states of the minimal NDD $\mathcal{A}(\text{Pre}_S^{\leq k}(X))$ is bounded independently of k.*

Proof. Let $\mathcal{C}_{S,X}$ be a class of finite subsets of $\mathbb{N}^m$ satisfying theorem 2 and let $X_k = \text{Pre}_S^{\leq k}(X)$. We are going to prove that for any non acyclic state q of $\mathcal{A}(X_k)$, we have $q \in \mathcal{C}_{S,X}$. As the number of paths $q_0 \rightarrow q$ is infinite, there exists a path $q_0 \xrightarrow{\sigma} q$ such that $r^{|\sigma|} \geq k$. In this case $\gamma_\sigma^{-1}(X_k) \in \mathcal{C}_{S,X}$. From $q = \gamma_\sigma^{-1}(X_k)$, we deduce $q \in \mathcal{C}_{S,X}$. Therefore, the number of non acyclic states of $\mathcal{A}(X_k)$ is bounded by $\text{card}(\mathcal{C}_{S,X})$. □

Remark 4. The cardinal of the set $\mathcal{C}_{S,X}$ is used in the two corollaries. From the proof of lemma 2 and the proof of theorem 2, this cardinal can be easily bounded by an elementary function in the size of S, $\mathcal{A}(X)$ and in the size of the monoïd $\mathcal{M}_S$. From [MS77], we deduce that $\mathcal{M}_S$ has a size elementary in the size of S when matrices M_a are in $\mathcal{M}_m(\mathbb{N})$. Therefore, in this case, the cardinal of $\mathcal{C}_{S,X}$ is elementary in the size of S and $\mathcal{A}(X)$. When matrices M_a are in $\mathcal{M}_m(\mathbb{Z})$, the elementary size of the monoïd is an open problem to the best of our knowledge.

We can easily extend the previous corollary in order to show that the structure of the minimal NDD that represents $\mathrm{Pre}_S^{\leq k}(X)$ corresponds to a BDD [Bry92] "concatenated" with a NDD that does not depends on k. This final result shows a new way for implementing a NDD library using all the BDD techniques for speeding-up the computation like cache-computation, minimization in linear time and strong canonical form, well-known in the field of BDD. Our symbolic model-checker FAST [Fas], will be available with this new library as soon as possible.

References

[ABJ98]   Parosh Aziz Abdulla, Ahmed Bouajjani, and Bengt Jonsson. On-the-fly analysis of systems with unbounded, lossy FIFO channels. In *Proc. 10th Int. Conf. Computer Aided Verification (CAV'98), Vancouver, BC, Canada, June-July 1998*, volume 1427 of *Lecture Notes in Computer Science*, pages 305–318. Springer, 1998.

[ABS01]   Aurore Annichini, Ahmed Bouajjani, and Mihaela Sighireanu. TReX: A tool for reachability analysis of complex systems. In *Proc. 13th Int. Conf. Computer Aided Verification (CAV'2001), Paris, France, July 2001*, volume 2102 of *Lecture Notes in Computer Science*, pages 368–372. Springer, 2001.

[Alv]   ALV homepage. http://www.cs.ucsb.edu/~bultan/composite/.

[Bab]   BABYLON homepage.
            http://www.ulb.ac.be/di/ssd/lvbegin/CST/-index.html.

[BB03]   Constantinos Bartziz and Tevfik Bultan. Efficient image computation in infinite state model checking. In *Proc. 15th Int. Conf. Computer Aided Verification (CAV'2003), Boulder, CO, USA, July 2003*, volume 2725 of *Lecture Notes in Computer Science*, pages 249–261. Springer, 2003.

[BC96]   Alexandre Boudet and Hubert Comon. Diophantine equations, Presburger arithmetic and finite automata. In *Proc. 21st Int. Coll. on Trees in Algebra and Programming (CAAP'96), Linköping, Sweden, Apr. 1996*, volume 1059 of *Lecture Notes in Computer Science*, pages 30–43. Springer, 1996.

[BEF+00]   A. Bouajjani, J. Esparza, A. Finkel, O. Maler, P. Rossmanith, B. Willems, and P. Wolper. An efficient automata approach to some problems on context-free grammars. *Information Processing Letters*, 74(5–6):221–227, 2000.

[BF00]   J.-P. Bodeveix and M. Filali. FMona: a tool for expressing validation techniques over infinite state systems. In *Proc. 6th Int. Conf. Tools and Algorithms for the Construction and Analysis of Systems (TACAS'2000), Berlin, Germany, Mar.-Apr. 2000*, volume 1785 of *Lecture Notes in Computer Science*, pages 204–219. Springer, 2000.

[BFLP03]   Sébastien Bardin, Alain Finkel, Jérôme Leroux, and Laure Petrucci. FAST: Fast Acceleration of Symbolic Transition systems. In *Proc. 15th Int. Conf. Computer Aided Verification (CAV'2003), Boulder, CO, USA, July 2003*, volume 2725 of *Lecture Notes in Computer Science*, pages 118–121. Springer, 2003.

[BGP97]   Tevfik Bultan, Richard Gerber, and William Pugh. Symbolic model-checking of infinite state systems using Presburger arithmetic. In *Proc. 9th Int. Conf. Computer Aided Verification (CAV'97), Haifa, Israel, June 1997*, volume 1254 of *Lecture Notes in Computer Science*, pages 400–411. Springer, 1997.

[BGP99]   Tevfik Bultan, Richard Gerber, and William Pugh. Model-checking concurrent systems with unbounded integer variables: symbolic representations, approximations, and experimental results. *ACM Transactions on Programming Languages and Systems*, 21(4):747–789, 1999.

[BH99]   Ahmed Bouajjani and Peter Habermehl. Symbolic reachability analysis of FIFO-channel systems with nonregular sets of configurations. *Theoretical Computer Science*, 221(1–2):211–250, 1999.

[BHMV94]   Véronique Bruyère, Georges Hansel, Christian Michaux, and Roger Villemaire. Logic and p-recognizable sets of integers. *Bull. Belg. Math. Soc.*, 1(2):191–238, March 1994.

[BLW03]   Bernard Boigelot, Alexandre Legay, and Pierre Wolper. Iterating transducers in the large. In *Proc. 15th Int. Conf. Computer Aided Verification (CAV'2003), Boulder, CO, USA, July 2003*, volume 2725 of *Lecture Notes in Computer Science*, pages 223–235. Springer, 2003.

[Boi03]   Bernard Boigelot. On iterating linear transformations over recognizable sets of integers. *Theoretical Computer Science*, 309(2):413–468, 2003.

[Bra]   BRAIN homepage.
           http://www.cs.man.ac.uk/~voronkov/BRAIN/index.html.

[Bry92]   Randal E. Bryant. Symbolic boolean manipulation with ordered binary-decision diagrams. *ACM Computing Surveys*, 24(3):293–318, 1992.

[Del00]   Gorgio Delzanno. Automatic verification of parameterized cache coherence protocols. In *Proc. 12th Int. Conf. Computer Aided Verification (CAV'2000), Chicago, IL, USA, July 2000*, volume 1855 of *Lecture Notes in Computer Science*, pages 53–68. Springer, 2000.

[DFS98]   Catherine Dufourd, Alain Finkel, and Philippe Schnoebelen. Reset nets between decidability and undecidability. In *Proc. 25th Int. Coll. Automata, Languages, and Programming (ICALP'98), Aalborg, Denmark, July 1998*, volume 1443 of *Lecture Notes in Computer Science*, pages 103–115. Springer, 1998.

[DJS99]   Catherine Dufourd, Petr Jančar, and Philippe Schnoebelen. Boundedness of Reset P/T nets. In *Proc. 26th Int. Coll. Automata, Languages, and Programming (ICALP'99), Prague, Czech Republic, July 1999*, volume 1644 of *Lecture Notes in Computer Science*, pages 301–310. Springer, 1999.

[DRV01]   Gorgio Delzanno, Jean-Francois Raskin, and Laurent Van Begin. Attacking symbolic state explosion. In *Proc. 13th Int. Conf. Computer Aided Verification (CAV'2001), Paris, France, July 2001*, volume 2102 of *Lecture Notes in Computer Science*, pages 298–310. Springer, 2001.

[EN98]   E. Allen Emerson and Kedar S. Namjoshi. On model checking for non-deterministic infinite-state systems. In *Proc. 13th IEEE Symp. Logic in Computer Science (LICS'98), Indianapolis, IN, USA, June 1998*, pages 70–80. IEEE Comp. Soc. Press, 1998.

[Fas]   FAST homepage. http://www.lsv.ens-cachan.fr/fast/.

[FL02]   Alain Finkel and Jérôme Leroux. How to compose Presburger-accelerations: Applications to broadcast protocols. In *Proc. 22nd Conf. Found. of Software Technology and Theor. Comp. Sci. (FST&TCS'2002), Kanpur, India, Dec. 2002*, volume 2556 of *Lecture Notes in Computer Science*, pages 145–156. Springer, 2002.

[FL04]   Alain Finkel and Jérôme Leroux. Polynomial time image computation with interval-definable counters system. In *SPIN Model Checking and Software Verification, Proc. 11th Int. SPIN Workshop, Barcelona, Spain, Apr. 2004*, volume 2989 of *Lecture Notes in Computer Science*, pages 182–197. Springer, 2004.

[FO97]   Laurent Fribourg and Hans Olsén. Proving safety properties of infinite state systems by compilation into Presburger arithmetic. In *Proc. 8th Int. Conf. Concurrency Theory (CONCUR'97), Warsaw, Poland, Jul. 1997*, volume 1243 of *Lecture Notes in Computer Science*, pages 213–227. Springer, 1997.

[FPS00]   Alain Finkel, S. Purushothaman Iyer, and Grégoire Sutre. Well-abstracted transition systems. In *Proc. 11th Int. Conf. Concurrency Theory (CONCUR'2000), University Park, PA, USA, Aug. 2000*, volume 1877 of *Lecture Notes in Computer Science*, pages 566–580. Springer, 2000.

[FS01]   Alain Finkel and Phillipe Schnoebelen. Well structured transition systems everywhere! *Theoretical Computer Science*, 256(1–2):63–92, 2001.

[GS66]   Seymour Ginsburg and Edwin H. Spanier. Semigroups, Presburger formulas and languages. *Pacific J. Math.*, 16(2):285–296, 1966.

[KMS02]   Nils Klarlund, A. Møller, and M. I. Schwartzbach. MONA implementation secrets. *Int. J. of Foundations Computer Science*, 13(4):571–586, 2002.

[Las]   LASH homepage.
           http://www.montefiore.ulg.ac.be/~boigelot/research/lash/.

[Ler03]   Jérôme Leroux. *Algorithmique de la vérification des systèmes à compteurs. Approximation et accélération. Implémentation de l'outil Fast*. PhD thesis, Ecole Normale Supérieure de Cachan, Laboratoire Spécification et Vérification. CNRS UMR 8643, décembre 2003.

[Mon]   MONA homepage. http://www.brics.dk/mona/index.html.

[MS77]   Arnold Mandel and Imre Simon. On finite semigroups of matrices. *Theoretical Computer Science*, 5(2):101–111, October 1977.

[Reu89]   Christophe Reutenauer. *Aspects Mathématiques des Réseaux de Petri*, chapter 3. Collection Études et Recherches en Informatique. Masson, Paris, 1989.

[Tre]   TREX homepage. http://www.liafa.jussieu.fr/~sighirea/trex/.

[WB00]   Pierre Wolper and Bernard Boigelot. On the construction of automata from linear arithmetic constraints. In *Proc. 6th Int. Conf. Tools and Algorithms for the Construction and Analysis of Systems (TACAS'2000), Berlin, Germany, Mar.-Apr. 2000*, volume 1785 of *Lecture Notes in Computer Science*, pages 1–19. Springer, 2000.

Abstract Regular Model Checking[*]

Ahmed Bouajjani[1], Peter Habermehl[1], and Tomáš Vojnar[2]

[1] LIAFA, University Paris 7, Case 7014, 2, place Jussieu, F-75251 Paris Cedex 05, France
{Ahmed.Bouajjani,Peter.Habermehl}@liafa.jussieu.fr
[2] FIT, Brno University of Technology, Božetěchova 2, CZ-61266, Brno, Czech Republic
vojnar@fit.vutbr.cz

Abstract. We propose *abstract regular model checking* as a new generic technique for verification of parametric and infinite-state systems. The technique combines the two approaches of regular model checking and verification by abstraction. We propose a general framework of the method as well as several concrete ways of abstracting automata or transducers, which we use for modelling systems and encoding sets of their configurations as usual in regular model checking. The abstraction is based on collapsing states of automata (or transducers) and its precision is being incrementally adjusted by analysing spurious counterexamples. We illustrate the technique on verification of a wide range of systems including a novel application of automata-based techniques to an example of systems with dynamic linked data structures.

1 Introduction

Model checking is nowadays widely accepted as a powerful technique for the verification of finite-state systems. However, many real-life systems, especially software systems, exhibit various aspects requiring one to reason about infinite-state models (data manipulation, dynamic creation of objects and threads, etc.). Several approaches extending model checking to be able to deal with them have recently been proposed. One of them is *regular model checking* [22, 30, 12] – a generic, automata-based approach allowing for a uniform modelling and verification of various kinds of infinite-state systems such as pushdown systems, (lossy) FIFO-channel systems, systems with counters, parameterised and dynamic networks of processes, etc.

In regular model checking, configurations of systems are encoded as words over a finite alphabet and transitions are modelled as finite state transducers mapping configurations to configurations. Finite automata can then be naturally used to represent and manipulate (potentially infinite) sets of configurations, and reachability analysis can be performed by computing transitive closures of transducers [21, 15, 3, 9] or images of automata by iteration of transducers [12, 28] – depending on whether dealing with *reachability relations* or *reachability sets* is preferred. To facilitate termination of the computation, which is in general not guaranteed as the problem being solved is undecidable, various acceleration methods are usually used.

---

[*] This work was supported in part by the EU (FET project ADVANCE IST-1999-29082), the French ministry of research (ACI project Securité Informatique), and the Czech Grant Agency (projects GA CR 102/04/0780 and GA CR 102/03/D211).

R. Alur and D.A. Peled (Eds.): CAV 2004, LNCS 3114, pp. 372–386, 2004.

A crucial problem to be faced in regular model checking is the state space explosion in automata (transducer) representations of the sets of configurations (or reachability relations) being examined. One of the sources of this problem is related to the nature of the current regular model checking techniques. Typically, these techniques try to calculate the *exact* reachability sets (or relations) independently of the property being verified. However, it would often be enough to only compute an overapproximation of the reachability set (or relation) sufficiently precise to verify the given property. Indeed, this is the way large (or infinite) state spaces are being successfully handled outside the domain of regular model checking using the so-called *abstract-check-refine* paradigm [20, 26, 14, 16] implemented, e.g., in tools for software model checking like Slam [6], Magic [13], or Blast [19]. All these tools use the method of *predicate abstraction*, where a finite set of boolean predicates is used to abstract a concrete system C into an abstract one A by considering equivalent the configurations of C that satisfy the same predicates. If a property is verified in A, it is guaranteed to hold in C too. If a counterexample is found in A, one can check if it is also a counterexample for C. If not, this *spurious* counterexample can be used to *refine* the abstraction such that the new abstract system A' no longer admits the spurious counterexample. In this way, one can construct finer and finer abstractions until a sufficient precision is achieved and the property is verified, or a real counterexample is found.

In this work, we propose a new approach to regular model checking based on the abstract-check-refine paradigm. Instead of precise acceleration techniques, we use abstract fixpoint computations in some *finite* domain of automata. The abstract fixpoint computations always terminate and provide overapproximations of the reachability sets (relations). To achieve this, we define techniques that systematically map any automaton M to an automaton M' from some finite domain such that M' recognises a superset of the language of M. For the case that the computed overapproximation is too coarse and a spurious counterexample is detected, we provide effective principles allowing the abstraction to be refined such that the new abstract computation does not encounter the same counterexample.

We propose two techniques for abstracting automata. They take into account the structure of the automata and are based on collapsing their states according to some equivalence relation. The first one is inspired by predicate abstraction. However, notice that contrary to classical predicate abstraction, we associate predicates with states of automata representing sets of configurations rather than with the configurations themselves. An abstraction is defined by a set of regular *predicate languages* L_P. We consider a state q of an automaton M to "satisfy" a predicate language L_P if the intersection of L_P with the language $L(M,q)$ accepted from the state q is not empty. Then, two states are equivalent if they satisfy the same predicates. The second abstraction technique is then based on considering two automata states equivalent if their *languages of words up to a certain fixed length* are equal. For both of these two abstraction methods, we provide effective refinement techniques allowing us to discard spurious counterexamples.

We also introduce several natural alternatives to the basic approaches based on backward and/or trace languages of states of automata. For them, it is not always possible to guarantee the exclusion of a spurious counterexample, but according to our experience, they still provide good practical results.

All of our techniques can be applied to dealing with reachability sets (obtained by iterating length-preserving or even general transducers) as well as length-preserving reachability relations.

We have implemented the different abstraction and refinement schemas in a prototype tool and tested them on a number of examples of various types of systems including parametric networks of processes, pushdown systems, counter automata, systems with queues, and – for the first time in the context of regular model checking – an example of dynamic linked data structures. The experiments show that our techniques are quite powerful in all the considered cases and that they are complementary – different techniques turn out to be the most successful in different scenarios. The results are very promising and compare favourably with other existing tools.

Related Work. In addition to what is mentioned above, many other results have been obtained for symbolic model checking of various kinds of infinite state systems, such as pushdown systems [10, 17], systems with counters [5, 18] or queues [4, 2, 11]. These works do not consider abstraction. For parameterised networks of processes, several methods using abstractions have been proposed [7, 24]. Contrary to our approach, these methods do not provide the possibility of refinement of the abstraction. Moreover, they are specialised for parameterised networks whereas our technique is generic.

2   Finite Automata and Transducers

We first provide a simple example that we use to demonstrate the way systems are modelled in (abstract) regular model checking and later to illustrate the verification techniques we propose. Then, we formalise the basic notions of finite automata and transducers and briefly comment on their use in verification by regular model checking.

As a running example, we consider the transducer τ in Fig. 1. It models a simple parameterised system implementing a token passing algorithm. The system consists of a parametric number of processes arranged in an array. Each process either has (T) or does not have (N) the token. Each process can pass the token to its third right neighbour. The transducer includes the identity relation too. In the initial configurations described by the automaton *Init*, the second process has the token, and the number of processes is divisible by three. We want to show that it is not possible to reach any configuration where the last process has the token. This set is described by the automaton *Bad*.

Formally, a *finite automaton* is a 5-tuple $M = (Q, \Sigma, \delta, q_0, F)$ where Q is a finite set of states, Σ a finite alphabet, $\delta \subseteq Q \times \Sigma \times Q$ a set of transitions, $q_0 \in Q$ an initial state and $F \subseteq Q$ a set of final states. The transition relation $\rightarrow \subseteq Q \times \Sigma^* \times Q$ of M is defined as the smallest relation satisfying: (1) $\forall q \in Q : q \xrightarrow{\varepsilon} q$, (2) if $(q, a, q') \in \delta$, then $q \xrightarrow{a} q'$ and (3) if $q \xrightarrow{w} q'$ and $q' \xrightarrow{a} q''$, then $q \xrightarrow{wa} q''$. Given a finite automaton M and an equivalence relation $\sim$ on its states, $M/\sim$ denotes the *quotient automaton* defined in the usual way.

The language recognised by M from a state $q \in Q$ is defined by $L(M, q) = \{w \mid \exists q' \in F : q \xrightarrow{w} q'\}$. The language $L(M)$ is equal to $L(M, q_0)$. A set $L \subseteq \Sigma^*$ is regular iff there exists a finite automaton M such that $L = L(M)$. We also define the backward language $\overleftarrow{L}(M, q) = \{w \mid q_0 \xrightarrow{w} q\}$ and the forward/backward languages of words up to a certain length: $L^{\leq n}(M, q) = \{w \in L(M, q) \mid |w| \leq n\}$ and similarly $\overleftarrow{L}^{\leq n}(M, q)$. We define

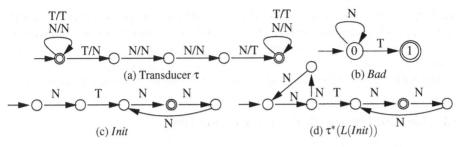

Fig. 1. A transducer modelling a simple token passing, initial, bad and reachable configurations

the forward/backward trace languages of states $T(M,q) = \{w \in \Sigma^* \mid \exists w' \in \Sigma^* : ww' \in L(M,q)\}$ and similarly $\overleftarrow{T}(M,q)$. Finally, we define accordingly forward/backward trace languages $T^{\leq n}(M,q)$ and $\overleftarrow{T}^{\leq n}(M,q)$ of traces up to a certain length.

Let Σ be a finite alphabet and $\Sigma_\varepsilon = \Sigma \cup \{\varepsilon\}$. A *finite transducer* over Σ is a 5-tuple $\tau = (Q, \Sigma_\varepsilon \times \Sigma_\varepsilon, \delta, q_0, F)$ where Q is a finite set of states, $\delta \subseteq Q \times \Sigma_\varepsilon \times \Sigma_\varepsilon \times Q$ a set of transitions, $q_0 \in Q$ an initial state and $F \subseteq Q$ a set of final states. A finite transducer is called a *length-preserving transducer* if its transitions do not contain ε. The transition relation $\rightarrow \subseteq Q \times \Sigma^* \times \Sigma^* \times Q$ is defined as the smallest relation satisfying: (1) $q \xrightarrow{\varepsilon,\varepsilon} q$ for every $q \in Q$, (2) if $(q,a,b,q') \in \delta$, then $q \xrightarrow{a,b} q'$ and (3) if $q \xrightarrow{w,u} q'$ and $q' \xrightarrow{a,b} q''$, then $q \xrightarrow{wa,ub} q''$. Then, by abuse of notation, we identify a transducer τ with the relation $\{(w,u) \mid \exists q' \in F : q_0 \xrightarrow{w,u} q'\}$. For a set $L \subseteq \Sigma^*$ and a relation $R \subseteq \Sigma^* \times \Sigma^*$, we denote $R(L)$ the set $\{w \in \Sigma^* \mid \exists w' \in L : (w',w) \in R\}$. Let $id \subseteq \Sigma^* \times \Sigma^*$ be the identity relation and $\circ$ the composition of relations. We define recursively the relations $\tau^0 = id$, $\tau^{i+1} = \tau \circ \tau^i$ and $\tau^* = \cup_{i=0}^\infty \tau^i$. Below, we suppose $id \subseteq \tau$ meaning that $\tau^i \subseteq \tau^{i+1}$ for all $i \geq 0$.

The properties we want to check are primarily reachability properties. Given a system with a transition relation modelled as a transducer τ, a regular set of initial configurations given by an automaton *Init*, and a set of "bad" configurations given by an automaton *Bad*, we want to check $\tau^*(L(Init)) \cap L(Bad) = \emptyset$. We transform more complicated properties into reachability by composing the appropriate property automaton with the system being checked. In this way, even liveness properties may be handled if the transition relation is instrumented to allow for loop detection as briefly mentioned later. For our running example, $\tau^*(L(Init))$ is shown in Fig. 1(d), and the property of interest clearly holds. Notice, however, that in general, $\tau^*(L(Init))$ is neither guaranteed to be regular nor computable. In the following, the verification task is to find a regular overapproximation $L \supseteq \tau^*(L(Init))$ such that $L \cap L(Bad) = \emptyset$.

3   Abstract Regular Model Checking

In this section, we describe the general approach of abstract regular model checking and propose a common framework for automata abstraction based on collapsing states of the automata. This framework is then instantiated in several concrete ways in the following two sections. We concentrate on the use of abstract regular model checking for dealing with reachability sets. However, the techniques we propose may be applied to dealing with reachability relations too – though in the context of length-preserving transducers only. (Indeed, length-preserving transducers over an alphabet Σ can be seen as finite-state automata over $\Sigma \times \Sigma$.) We illustrate the applicability of the method to dealing with reachability relations by one of the experiments presented in Section 6.

3.1   The Basic Framework of Automata Abstraction

Let Σ be a finite alphabet and $\mathbb{M}_\Sigma$ the set of all finite automata over Σ. By an *automata abstraction function* α, we understand a function that maps every automaton M over Σ to an automaton $\alpha(M)$ whose language is an overapproximation of the one of M, i.e. for some $\mathbb{A}_\Sigma \subseteq \mathbb{M}_\Sigma$, $\alpha : \mathbb{M}_\Sigma \to \mathbb{A}_\Sigma$ such that $\forall M \in \mathbb{M}_\Sigma : L(M) \subseteq L(\alpha(M))$. We call α *finitary* iff its range $\mathbb{A}_\Sigma$ is finite.

Working conveniently on the level of automata, we introduce the *abstract transition function* τ_α for a transition relation expressed as a transducer τ over Σ and an automata abstraction function α as follows: For each automaton $M \in \mathbb{M}_\Sigma$, $\tau_\alpha(M) = \alpha(\hat{\tau}(M))$ where $\hat{\tau}(M)$ is the minimal deterministic automaton of $\tau(L(M))$. Now, we may iteratively compute the sequence $(\tau_\alpha^i(M))_{i \geq 0}$. Since we suppose $id \subseteq \tau$, it is clear that if α is finitary, there exists $k \geq 0$ such that $\tau_\alpha^{k+1}(M) = \tau_\alpha^k(M)$. The definition of α implies $L(\tau_\alpha^k(M)) \supseteq \tau^*(L(M))$. This means that in a finite number of steps, we can compute an overapproximation of the reachability set $\tau^*(L(M))$.

3.2   Refining Automata Abstractions

We call an automata abstraction function α' a *refinement* of α iff $\forall M \in \mathbb{M}_\Sigma : L(\alpha'(M)) \subseteq L(\alpha(M))$. Moreover, we call α' a *true refinement* iff it yields a smaller overapproximation in at least one case – formally, iff $\exists M \in \mathbb{M}_\Sigma : L(\alpha'(M)) \subset L(\alpha(M))$.

A need to refine α arises when a situation depicted in Fig. 2 happens. Suppose we are checking whether no configuration from the set described by some automaton *Bad* is reachable from some given set of initial configurations described by an automaton M_0. We suppose $L(M_0) \cap L(Bad) = \emptyset$ – otherwise the property being checked is broken already by the initial configurations. Let $M_0^\alpha = \alpha(M_0)$ and for each $i > 0$, $M_i = \hat{\tau}(M_{i-1}^\alpha)$ and $M_i^\alpha = \alpha(M_i) = \tau_\alpha(M_{i-1}^\alpha)$. There exist k and l ($0 \leq k < l$) such that: (1) $\forall i : 0 \leq i < l : L(M_i) \cap L(Bad) = \emptyset$. (2) $L(M_l) \cap L(Bad) = L(X_l) \neq \emptyset$. (3) If we define X_i as the minimal deterministic automaton accepting $\tau^{-1}(L(X_{i+1})) \cap L(M_i^\alpha)$ for all i such that $0 \leq i < l$, then $\forall i : k < i < l : L(X_i) \cap L(M_i) \neq \emptyset$ and $L(X_k) \cap L(M_k) = \emptyset$ despite $L(X_k) \neq \emptyset$. Next, we see that either $k = 0$ or $L(X_{k-1}) = \emptyset$, and it is clear that we have encountered a *spurious counterexample*.

Note that when no l can be found such that $L(M_l) \cap L(Bad) \neq \emptyset$, the computation eventually reaches a fixpoint, and the property is proved to hold. On the other hand, if $L(X_0) \cap L(M_0) \neq \emptyset$, we have proved that the property is broken.

The *spurious counterexample may be eliminated* by refining α to α' such that for any automaton M whose language is disjoint with $L(X_k)$, the language of its α'-abstraction will not intersect $L(X_k)$ either. Then, the same faulty reachability computation (i.e. the same sequence of M_i and M_i^α) may not be repeated because we exclude the abstraction

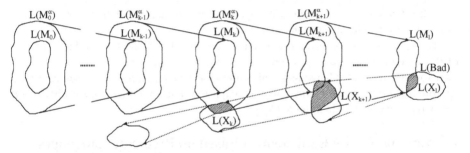

Fig. 2. A spurious counterexample in an abstract regular fixpoint computation

of M_k to M_k^α. Moreover, the reachability of the bad configurations is in general excluded unless there is another reason for it than overapproximating by subsets of $L(X_k)$.

A slightly *weaker way of eliminating the spurious counterexample* consists in refining α to α' such that at least the language of the abstraction of M_k does not intersect with $L(X_k)$. In such a case, it is not excluded that some subset of $L(X_k)$ will again be used for an overapproximation somewhere, but we still exclude a repetition of exactly the same faulty computation. The obtained refinement can be coarser, which may lead to more refinements and a slower computation. On the other hand, the computation may terminate sooner due to quickly jumping to the fixpoint and use less memory due to working with less structured sets of configurations of the systems being verified – the abstraction is prevented from becoming unnecessarily precise in this case. For the latter reason, as illustrated later, one may sometimes successfully use even some more heuristic approaches that guarantee that the spurious counterexample will only eventually be excluded (i.e. after a certain number of refinements) or that do not guarantee the exclusion at all.

An obvious danger of using a heuristic approach that does not guarantee an exclusion of spurious counterexamples is that the computation may easily start looping. Notice, however, that even when we refine automata abstractions such that spurious counterexamples are always excluded, and the computation does not loop, we do not guarantee that it will eventually stop – we may keep refining forever. Indeed, the verification problem we are solving is undecidable in general.

3.3   Abstracting Automata by Collapsing Their States

In the following two sections, we discuss several concrete automata abstraction functions. They are based on automata state equivalence schemas that define for each automaton from $\mathbb{M}_\Sigma$ an equivalence relation on its states. An automaton is then abstracted by collapsing all its states related by this equivalence. We suppose such an equivalence to reflect the fact that the future and/or history of the states to be collapsed is close enough, and the difference may be abstracted away.

Formally, an *automata state equivalence schema* $\mathbb{E}$ assigns an automata state equivalence $\sim_M^\mathbb{E} \subseteq Q \times Q$ to each finite automaton $M = (Q, \Sigma, \delta, q_0, F)$ over Σ. We define the *automata abstraction function* $\alpha_\mathbb{E}$ based on $\mathbb{E}$ such that $\forall M \in \mathbb{M}_\Sigma : \alpha_\mathbb{E}(M) = M / \sim_M^\mathbb{E}$.

We call $\mathbb{E}$ *finitary* iff $\alpha_{\mathbb{E}}$ is finitary. We *refine* $\alpha_{\mathbb{E}}$ by refining $\mathbb{E}$ such that more states are distinguished in at least some automata.

The automata state equivalence schemas presented below are then all based on one of the following two basic principles: (1) comparing states wrt. the intersections of their forward/backward languages with some *predicate languages* (represented by the appropriate *predicate automata*) and (2) comparing states wrt. their forward/backward behaviours up to a certain *bounded length*.

4 Automata State Equivalences Based on Predicate Languages

The two automata state equivalence schemas we introduce in this section – $\mathbb{F}_{\mathcal{P}}$ based on forward languages of states and $\mathbb{B}_{\mathcal{P}}$ based on backward languages – are both defined wrt. a finite set of *predicate automata* $\mathcal{P}$. They compare two states of a given automaton according to the intersections of their forward/backward languages with the languages of the predicates. Below, we first introduce the basic principles of the schemas and then add some implementation and optimisation notes.

4.1 The $\mathbb{F}_{\mathcal{P}}$ Automata State Equivalence Schema

The automata state equivalence schema $\mathbb{F}_{\mathcal{P}}$ defines two states of a given automaton to be equivalent when their languages have a *nonempty intersection with the same predicates* of $\mathcal{P}$. Formally, for an automaton $M = (Q, \Sigma, \delta, q_0, F)$, $\mathbb{F}_{\mathcal{P}}$ defines the state equivalence as the equivalence $\sim_M^{\mathcal{P}}$ such that $\forall q_1, q_2 \in Q : q_1 \sim_M^{\mathcal{P}} q_2 \Leftrightarrow (\forall P \in \mathcal{P} : L(P) \cap L(M, q_1) \neq \emptyset \Leftrightarrow L(P) \cap L(M, q_2) \neq \emptyset)$.

Clearly, as $\mathcal{P}$ is finite and there is only a finite number of subsets of $\mathcal{P}$ representing the predicates with which a given state has a nonempty intersection, $\mathbb{F}_{\mathcal{P}}$ is *finitary*.

For our example from Fig. 1, if we take as $\mathcal{P}$ the automata of the languages of the states of *Bad*, we obtain the automaton in Fig. 3(a) as the abstraction of *Init* from Fig. 1(c). This is because all states of *Init* except the final one become equivalent. Then, the intersection of $\hat{\tau}(\alpha(Init))$ with the bad configurations – shown in Fig. 3(c) – is not empty, and we have to refine the abstraction.

The $\mathbb{F}_{\mathcal{P}}$ schema may be *refined by adding new predicates* into the current set of predicates $\mathcal{P}$. In particular, we can extend $\mathcal{P}$ by automata corresponding to the languages of all the states in X_k from Fig. 2. Theorem 1 proved in the full paper shows that this prevents abstractions of languages disjoint with $L(X_k)$, such as – but not only – $L(M_k)$, from intersecting with $L(X_k)$. Thus, as already mentioned, a repetition of the same faulty computation is excluded, and the set of bad configurations will not be reached unless there is another reason for this than overapproximating by subsets of $L(X_k)$.

Theorem 1. *Let us have any two finite automata* $M = (Q_M, \Sigma, \delta_M, q_0^M, F_M)$ *and* $X = (Q_X, \Sigma, \delta_X, q_0^X, F_X)$ *and a finite set of predicate automata* $\mathcal{P}$ *such that* $\forall q_X \in Q_X : \exists P \in \mathcal{P} : L(X, q_X) = L(P)$. *Then, if* $L(M) \cap L(X) = \emptyset$, $L(\alpha_{\mathbb{F}_{\mathcal{P}}}(M)) \cap L(X) = \emptyset$ *too.*

In our example, we refine the abstraction by extending $\mathcal{P}$ with the automata representing the languages of the states of X_0 from Fig. 3(d). Fig. 3(e) then indicates for each state q of *Init*, the predicates corresponding to the states of *Bad* and X_0 whose languages have a non-empty intersection with the language of q. The first two states of

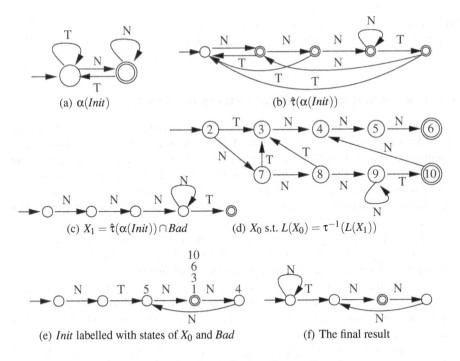

(a) $\alpha(Init)$

(b) $\hat{\tau}(\alpha(Init))$

(c) $X_1 = \hat{\tau}(\alpha(Init)) \cap Bad$

(d) X_0 s.t. $L(X_0) = \tau^{-1}(L(X_1))$

(e) $Init$ labelled with states of X_0 and Bad

(f) The final result

Fig. 3. An example using abstraction based on predicate languages

Init are equivalent and are collapsed to obtain the automaton from Fig. 3(f), which is a fixpoint showing that the property is verified. Notice that it is an overapproximation of the set of reachable configurations from Fig. 1(d).

The price of refining $\mathbb{F}_{\mathcal{P}}$ by adding predicates for all the states in X_k may seem prohibitive, but fortunately this is not the case in practice. As described in Sect. 4.3, we do not have to treat all the new predicates separately. We exploit the fact that they come from one original automaton and share large parts of their structure. In fact, we can work just with the original automaton and each of its states may be considered an initial state of some predicate. This way, adding the original automaton as the only predicate and adding predicates for all of its states becomes roughly equal. Moreover, the refinement may be weakened by taking into account just some states of X_k as discussed in Sect. 4.3.

4.2   The $\mathbb{B}_{\mathcal{P}}$ Automata State Equivalence Schema

The $\mathbb{B}_{\mathcal{P}}$ automata state equivalence schema is an alternative of $\mathbb{F}_{\mathcal{P}}$ based on *backward languages of states* rather than forward. For an automaton $M = (Q, \Sigma, \delta, q_0, F)$, it defines the state equivalence as the equivalence $\overleftarrow{\backsim}_M^{\mathcal{P}}$ such that $\forall q_1, q_2 \in Q : q_1 \overleftarrow{\backsim}_M^{\mathcal{P}} q_2 \Leftrightarrow (\forall P \in \mathcal{P} : L(P) \cap \overleftarrow{L}(M, q_1) \neq \emptyset \Leftrightarrow L(P) \cap \overleftarrow{L}(M, q_2) \neq \emptyset)$.

Clearly, $\mathbb{B}_{\mathcal{P}}$ is *finitary* for the same reason as $\mathbb{F}_{\mathcal{P}}$. It may also be *refined* by extending $\mathcal{P}$ by automata corresponding to the languages of all the states in X_k from Fig. 2. As stated in Theorem 2, the effect is the same as for $\mathbb{F}_{\mathcal{P}}$.

Theorem 2. *Let us have any two finite automata* $M = (Q_M, \Sigma, \delta_M, q_0^M, F_M)$ *and* $X = (Q_X, \Sigma, \delta_X, q_0^X, F_X)$ *and a finite set of predicate automata* $\mathcal{P}$ *such that* $\forall q_X \in Q_X : \exists P \in \mathcal{P} : \overleftarrow{L}(X, q_X) = L(P)$. *Then, if* $L(M) \cap L(X) = \emptyset$, $L(\alpha_{\mathbb{B}_{\mathcal{P}}}(M)) \cap L(X) = \emptyset$ *too.*

4.3   Implementing and Optimising Collapsing Based on $\mathbb{F}_{\mathcal{P}}/\mathbb{B}_{\mathcal{P}}$

The abstraction of an automaton M wrt. the automata state equivalence schema $\mathbb{F}_{\mathcal{P}}$ may be implemented by first labelling states of M by the states of predicate automata in $\mathcal{P}$ with whose languages they have a non-empty intersection and then collapsing the states of M that are labelled by the initial states of the same predicates. (Provided the sets of states of the predicate automata are disjoint.) The labelling can be done in a way similar to constructing a backward synchronous product of M with the particular predicate automata: (1) $\forall P \in \mathcal{P} \ \forall q_F^P \in F_P \ \forall q_F^M \in F_M$: q_F^M is labelled by q_F^P, and (2) $\forall P \in \mathcal{P} \ \forall q_1^P, q_2^P \in Q_P \ \forall q_1^M, q_2^M \in Q_M$: if q_2^M is labelled by q_2^P, and there exists $a \in \Sigma$ such that $q_1^M \xrightarrow{a}_{\delta_M} q_2^M$ and $q_1^P \xrightarrow{a}_{\delta_P} q_2^P$, then q_1^M is labelled with q_1^P. The abstraction of an automaton M wrt. the $\mathbb{B}_{\mathcal{P}}$ schema may be implemented analogously.

If the above construction is used, it is then clear that when *refining* $\mathbb{F}_{\mathcal{P}}/\mathbb{B}_{\mathcal{P}}$, we can just add X_k into $\mathcal{P}$ and modify the construction such that in the collapsing phase, we simply take into account all the labels by states of X_k and do not ignore the (anyway constructed) labels other than $q_0^{X_k}$.

Moreover, we can try to optimise the refinement of $\mathbb{F}_{\mathcal{P}}/\mathbb{B}_{\mathcal{P}}$ by replacing X_k in $\mathcal{P}$ by its *important tail/head part* defined wrt. M_k as the subautomaton of X_k based on the states of X_k that appear in at least one of the labels of M_k wrt. $\mathbb{F}_{\mathcal{P} \cup \{X_k\}}/\mathbb{B}_{\mathcal{P} \cup \{X_k\}}$, respectively. As stated in Theorem 3 (proved in the full paper), the effect of such a refinement corresponds to the weaker way of refining automata abstraction functions described in Section 3.2. This is due to the strong link of the important tail/head part of X_k to M_k wrt. which it is computed. A repetition of the same faulty computation is then excluded, but the obtained abstraction is coarser, which may sometimes speed up the computation as we have already discussed.

Theorem 3. *Let* M *and* X *be any finite automata over* Σ *and* $Y = (Q_Y, \Sigma, \delta_Y, q_0^Y, F_Y)$ *the important tail/head part of* X *wrt.* $\mathbb{F}_{\mathcal{P}}/\mathbb{B}_{\mathcal{P}}$ *and* M. *If* $\mathcal{P}'$ *is such that* $\forall q_Y \in Q_Y \ \exists P \in \mathcal{P}' : L(Y, q_Y)/\overleftarrow{L}(Y, q_Y) = L(P)$ *and* $L(M) \cap L(X) = \emptyset$, $L(\alpha_{\mathbb{F}_{\mathcal{P}'}/\mathbb{B}_{\mathcal{P}'}}(M)) \cap L(X) = \emptyset$.

A further possible heuristic to optimise the refinement of $\mathbb{F}_{\mathcal{P}}/\mathbb{B}_{\mathcal{P}}$ is trying to find just one or two *key states* of the important tail/head part of X_k such that if their languages are considered in addition to $\mathcal{P}$, $L(M_k^\alpha)$ will not intersect $L(X_k)$.

We close the section by noting that in the *initial set of predicates* $\mathcal{P}$ of $\mathbb{F}_{\mathcal{P}}/\mathbb{B}_{\mathcal{P}}$, we may use, e.g., the automata describing the set of bad configurations and/or the set of initial configurations. Further, we may also use the domains or ranges of the transducers encoding the particular transitions in the systems being examined (whose union forms the one-step transition relation τ which we iterate). The meaning of the latter predicates is similar to using guards or actions of transitions in predicate abstraction [8].

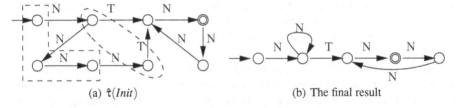

(a) $\hat{\tau}(Init)$ (b) The final result

Fig. 4. An example using abstraction based on languages of words up to length n (for $n = 2$)

5 Automata State Equivalences Based on Finite-Length Languages

We now present the possibility of defining automata state equivalence schemas based on comparing automata states wrt. a certain bounded part of their languages. It is a simple, yet (according to our practical experience) often quite efficient approach. As a basic representative of this kind of schemas, we first present a schema $\mathbb{F}_n^L$ based on forward languages of words of a limited length. Then, we discuss its possible alternatives.

The $\mathbb{F}_n^L$ automata state equivalence schema defines two states of an automaton to be equal if their *languages of words of length up to a certain bound n* are identical. Formally, for an automaton $M = (Q, \Sigma, \delta, q_0, F)$, $\mathbb{F}_n^L$ defines the state equivalence as the equivalence $\sim_M^n$ such that $\forall q_1, q_2 \in Q : q_1 \sim_M^n q_2 \Leftrightarrow L^{\leq n}(M, q_1) = L^{\leq n}(M, q_2)$.

$\mathbb{F}_n^L$ is clearly *finitary*. It may be *refined* by incrementally increasing the bound n on the length of the words considered. This way, as we work with minimal deterministic automata, we may achieve the weaker type of refinement described in Section 3.2. Such an effect is achieved when n is increased to be equal or bigger than the number of states in M_k from Fig. 2 minus one. In a minimal deterministic automaton, this guarantees that all states are distinguishable wrt. $\sim_M^n$, and M_k will not be collapsed at all.

In Fig. 4, we apply $\mathbb{F}_n^L$ to the example from Fig. 1. We choose $n = 2$. In this case, the abstraction of the *Init* automaton is *Init* itself. Fig. 4(a) indicates the states of $\hat{\tau}(Init)$ that have the same languages of words up to size 2 and are therefore equivalent. Collapsing them yields the automaton shown in Fig. 4(b) (after determinisation and minimisation), which is a fixpoint. Notice that it is a different overapproximation of the set of reachable configurations than the one obtained using $\mathbb{F}_{\mathcal{P}}$. If we choose $n = 1$, we obtain a similar result, but we need one refinement step of the above described kind.

Let us, however, note that according to our practical experience, the increment of n by $|Q_M| - 1$ may often be too big. Alternatively, one may use its fraction (e.g., one half), increase n by the number of states in X_k (or its fraction), or increase n just by one. In such cases, an immediate exclusion of the faulty run is not guaranteed, but clearly, such a computation will be *eventually excluded* because n will sooner or later reach the necessary value. The impact of working with abstractions refined in a coarser way is then like in the case of using $\mathbb{F}_{\mathcal{P}}/\mathbb{B}_{\mathcal{P}}$.

Regarding the *initial value of n*, one may use, e.g., the number of states in the automaton describing the set of initial configurations or the set of bad configurations, their fraction, or again just one.

As a natural alternative to dealing with forward languages of words of a limited length, we may also think of *backward languages of words* of a limited length and forward or backward *languages of traces* with a limited length. The automata equivalence schemas $\mathbb{B}_n^L$, $\mathbb{F}_n^T$, and $\mathbb{B}_n^T$ based on them can be formally defined analogously to $\mathbb{F}_n^L$.

Clearly, all these schemas are *finitary*. Moreover, we can *refine* them in a similar way as $\mathbb{F}_n^L$. For $\mathbb{F}_n^T$ and $\mathbb{B}_n^T$, however, no guarantee of excluding a spurious counterexample may be provided. Using $\mathbb{F}_n^T$, e.g., we can never distinguish the last three states of the automaton in Fig. 4(b) – they all have the same trace languages. Thus, we cannot remember that the token cannot get to the last process. Nevertheless, despite this, our practical experience shows the schemas based on traces are quite successful in practice.

6   Experiments

We have implemented the ideas proposed in the paper in a prototype tool written in YAP Prolog using the FSA library [29]. To demonstrate that abstract regular model checking is applicable to verification of a broad variety of systems, we tried to apply the tool to a number of different verification tasks.

6.1   The Types of Systems Verified

Parameterised Networks of Processes. We considered several slightly idealised *mutual exclusion algorithms* for an arbitrary number of processes (namely the Bakery, Burns, Dijkstra, and Szymanski algorithms in versions similar to [23]). In most of these systems, particular processes are finite-state. We encode global configurations of such systems by words whose length corresponds to the number of participating processes, and each letter represents the local state of some process. In the case of the Bakery algorithm where each process contains an unbounded ticket value, this value is not represented directly, but encoded in the ordering of the processes in the word.

We verified the mutual exclusion property of the algorithms, and for the Bakery algorithm, we verified that some process will always eventually get to the critical section (communal liveness) as well as that each individual process will always eventually get there (individual liveness) under suitable fairness assumptions. For checking liveness, we manually composed the appropriate Büchi automata with the system being verified. Loop detection was allowed by working with pairs of configurations consisting of a remembered potential beginning of a loop (fixed at a certain point of time) and the current configuration being further modified. Checking that a loop is closed then consisted in checking that a pair of the same configurations was reached. To encode the pairs of configurations using finite automata, we interleaved their corresponding letters.

Push-Down Systems. We considered a simple system of *recursive procedures* – the plotter example from [17]. We verified a safety part of the original property of interest describing the correct order of plotter instructions to be issued. In this case, we use words to encode the contents of the stack.

Systems with Queues. We experimented with a model of the Alternating Bit Protocol (ABP) for which we checked correctness of the delivery order of the messages. A word encoding a configuration of the protocol contained two letters representing internal states of the communicating processes. Moreover, it contained the contents of the two *lossy communication channels* with a letter corresponding to each message. Let us note that in this case, as well as in the above and below case, general (non-length-preserving) transducers were used to encode transitions of the systems.

Petri Nets, Systems with Counters. We examined a general *Petri net* with inhibitor arcs, which can be considered an example of a system with *unbounded counters* too. In particular, we modelled a Readers/Writers system extended with a possibility of dynamic creation/deletion of processes, for which we verified mutual exclusion between readers and writers and between multiple writers. We considered a correct version of the system as well as a faulty one, in which we omitted one of the Petri net arcs. Markings of places in the Petri net were encoded in unary and the particular values were put in parallel. (Using this encoding, a marking of a net with places p and q, two tokens in p, and four in q would be encoded as $q|q|pq|pq$.) In some other examples of systems with counters (such as the Bakery algorithm for two processes with unbounded counters), we also successfully used a binary encoding of the counters like in NDDs [30].

Dynamic Linked Data Structures. We considered verification of a *procedure for reversing lists* shown in Fig. 5. As according to our knowledge, it is for the first time that regular model checking has been applied to such a task, let us now spend a bit more time with this experiment.

When abstracting the memory manipulated by the procedure, we focus on the cases where in the first n memory cells (we take the biggest n possible) there are at most two linked lists linking consecutive cells, the first list in a descending way and the second one in an ascending way. We represent configurations of the procedure as words over the following alphabet: list items are represented by symbols $\underline{i}$, left/right pointers by $</>$, pointer variables are represented by their names (*list* is shortened to l), and $\underline{o}$ is used to represent the memory outside the list. Moreover, we use symbols $\underline{iv}$ (resp. $\underline{ov}$) to denote that

```
1:  x := 0;
2:  while (list → next) {
3:      y := list → next;
4:      list → next := x;
5:      x := list; list := y;
6:  }
7:  list → next := x;
```

Fig. 5. Reversing a linear list

v points to i (resp. outside the list). We use | to separate the ascending and descending lists. Pointer variables pointing to null are not present in the configuration representations. A typical abstraction of the memory may then look like $\underline{i} < \underline{i} < \underline{i} \mid \underline{il} > \underline{i} \, \underline{ox}$ where the first list contains three items, the second one two, *list* points to the beginning of the second list, x points outside the two lists, and y points to null. Provided such an abstraction is used for the memory contents (prefixed with the current control line), it is not difficult to associate transducers to each command of the procedure. For example, the transducer corresponding to the command *list* → *next* := x at line 4 transforms a typical configuration 4 $\underline{i} < \underline{ix} \mid \underline{il} > \underline{iy} > \underline{i} \, \underline{o}$ to the configuration 5 $\underline{i} < \underline{ix} < \underline{il} \mid \underline{iy} > \underline{i} \, \underline{o}$ (the successor of the item pointed to by l is not anymore the one pointed to by y, but the one pointed to by x). Then, the transducer τ corresponding to the whole procedure is the union of the transducers of all the commands.

If the memory contents does not fit the above described form, we abstract it to a single word with the "don't know" meaning. However, when we start from a configuration like $1 \underline{il} > \underline{i} > \underline{i} \underline{o}$ or $1 \underline{i} < \underline{i} < \underline{il} \underline{o}$, the verification shows that such a situation does not happen. Via a symmetry argument exploiting the fact that the procedure never refers to concrete addresses, the results of the verification may then easily be generalised to lists with items stored at arbitrary memory locations.

By computing an abstraction of the reachability set $\tau^*(Init)$, we checked that the procedure outputs a list. Moreover, by computing an overapproximation of the reachability relation τ^* of the system, we checked that the output list is a reversion of the input one (modulo the fact that we consider a finite number of different items). To speed up the computation, the reachability relation was restricted to the initial configurations, i.e. to $id_{Init} \circ \tau^*$.

6.2   A Summary of the Results

Our method has been quite successful in all the described experiments. The best results (corresponding to a certain automata state equivalence used, its initialisation, and the way of refinement) for the particular examples obtained from our prototype tool were mostly under 1 sec. on an Intel Pentium 4 processor at 1.7 GHz. The only exceptions were checking individual liveness in the Bakery example where we needed about 9 sec., the Readers/Writers example where we needed about 6 sec., and the example of reversing lists where on the level of working with the reachability relation, we needed about 22 sec. (A more detailed description of the results may be found in the full paper.) Taking into account that the tool used was an early prototype written in Prolog, the results are very encouraging. For example, on the same computer, the Uppsala Regular Model Checker [3] in version 0.10 took from about 8 to 11 seconds when applied to the Burns, Szymanski, and Dijkstra examples over whose comparable encoding we needed in the most successful scenarios from 0.06 to 0.73 sec.

The results we obtained from our experiments also showed that apart from cases where the approaches based on languages of words/traces up to a bounded length and the ones based on intersections with predicate languages are roughly equal, there are really cases where either the former or the latter approach is clearly faster. The latter approach is faster, e.g., in the Dijkstra and Readers/Writers examples whereas the former, e.g., in the cases of reversing lists or checking the individual liveness in the Bakery example. This experimentally justifies our interest in both of the techniques.

Let us note that for some of the classes of systems we considered, there exist various special purpose verification approaches, and the appropriate verification problems are sometimes even decidable (as, e.g., for push-down systems [10, 17, 27] or lossy channel systems [4, 2, 1]). However, we wanted to show that our approach is generic and can be uniformly applied to all these systems. Moreover, in the future, with a new version of our tool, we would like to compare the performance of abstract regular model checking with the specialised approaches on large systems. We believe that while we can hardly outperform these algorithms in general, in some cases of systems with complex state spaces, our approach could turn out to be quite competitive due to not working with the exact representation of the state spaces, but their potentially much simpler approximations in which many details not important for the property being checked are ignored.

7 Conclusions

We have proposed a new technique for verification of parameterised and infinite-state systems. The technique called *abstract regular model checking* combines the approach of regular model checking with the abstract-check-refine paradigm. We have described the general framework of the method as well as several concrete strategies for abstracting automata or transducers, which are used in the framework for representing reachability sets and relations, by collapsing their states. As we have illustrated on a number of experiments we did, including a novel application of automata-based techniques to verification of systems with dynamic linked structures, the technique is very broadly applicable. Moreover, compared to the other techniques of regular model checking, it is also quite efficient due to working with approximations of reachability sets or relations with precision found iteratively by eliminating spurious counterexamples and sufficient just to verify the property of interest.

In the future, we plan to implement the techniques we proposed in the paper in a more efficient way and test them on larger examples. An interesting theoretical question is then whether some guarantees of termination can be obtained at least for some classes of systems. Further, the way of dealing with liveness properties within abstract regular model checking can be put on a more systematic basis allowing for a better automation. Similarly, we would like to extend our results on verifying systems with linear (linearisable) dynamic linked data structures and see how automata-based verification techniques compare with static analysis techniques like shape analysis [25]. Finally, we believe that there is a wide space for generalising the method to working with non-regular reachability sets and/or systems with non-linear (tree-like or in general graph-like) structure of states. The latter generalisation is primarily motivated by our interest in verifying multithreaded programs with recursive procedures and/or programs with dynamically allocated memory structures that cannot be easily linearised.

Acknowledgement

We would like to thank Andreas Podelski for fruitful discussions.

References

1. P. Abdulla, A. Annichini, and A. Bouajjani. Symbolic Verification of Lossy Channel Systems: Application to the Bounded Retransmission Protocol. In *Proc. of TACAS*, volume 1579 of *LNCS*. Springer, 1999.
2. P. Abdulla, A. Bouajjani, and B. Jonsson. On-the-fly Analysis of Systems with Unbounded, Lossy Fifo Channels. In *Proc. of CAV'98*, volume 1427 of *LNCS*. Springer, 1998.
3. P.A. Abdulla, J. d'Orso, B. Jonsson, and M. Nilsson. Algorithmic improvements in regular model checking. In *Proc. of CAV'03*, volume 2725 of *LNCS*. Springer, 2003.
4. B. Boigelot and P. Godefroid. Symbolic verification of communication protocols with infinite state spaces using QDDs. In *Proc. of CAV'96*, volume 1102 of *LNCS*. Springer, 1996.
5. B. Boigelot and P. Wolper. Symbolic verification with periodic sets. In *Proc. of CAV'94*, volume 818 of *LNCS*, pages 55–67. Springer, 1994.
6. T. Ball and S. K. Rajamani. The SLAM toolkit. In *Proc. CAV'01*, LNCS. Springer, 2001.

7. K. Baukus, S. Bensalem, Y. Lakhnech, and K. Stahl. Abstracting WS1S systems to verify parameterized networks. In *Proc. of TACAS*, volume 1785 of *LNCS*. Springer, 2000.
8. S. Bensalem, Y. Lakhnech, and S. Owre. Computing abstractions of infinite state systems compositionally and automatically. In *Proc. of CAV'98*, LNCS. Springer, 1998.
9. B. Boigelot, A. Legay, and P. Wolper. Iterating transducers in the large. In *Proc. CAV'03*, volume 2725 of *LNCS*. Springer, 2003.
10. A. Bouajjani, J. Esparza, and O. Maler. Reachability analysis of pushdown automata: Application to model-checking. In *Proc. of CONCUR'97*, LNCS. Springer, 1997.
11. A. Bouajjani and P. Habermehl. Symbolic Reachability Analysis of Fifo-Channel Systems with Nonregular Sets of Configurations. *Theoretical Computer Science*, 221(1-2), 1999.
12. A. Bouajjani, B. Jonsson, M. Nilsson, and T. Touili. Regular model checking. In *Proc. of CAV'00*, volume 1855 of *LNCS*. Springer, 2000.
13. S. Chaki, E. Clarke, A. Groce, J. Ouaknine, O. Strichman, and K. Yorav. Efficient verification of sequential and concurrent c programs. *Formal Methods in System Design*, 2004. To appear.
14. E. M. Clarke, O. Grumberg, S. Jha, Y. Lu, and H. Veith. Counterexample-guided abstraction refinement. In *Proc. CAV'00*, volume 1855 of *LNCS*. Springer, 2000.
15. D. Dams, Y. Lakhnech, and M. Steffen. Iterating transducers. In *Proc. CAV'01*, volume 2102 of *LNCS*. Springer, 2001.
16. S. Das and D.L. Dill. Counter-example based predicate discovery in predicate abstraction. In *Formal Methods in Computer-Aided Design*, 2002.
17. J. Esparza, D. Hansel, P. Rossmanith, and S. Schwoon. Efficient algorithms for model checking pushdown systems. In *Proc. of CAV'00*, volume 1855 of *LNCS*. Springer, 2000.
18. A. Finkel and J. Leroux. How to compose presburger-accelerations: Applications to broadcast protocols. In *Proc. of FST&TCS'02*, volume 2556 of *LNCS*. Springer, 2002.
19. T. A. Henzinger, R. Jhala, R. Majumdar, and G. Sutre. Software verification with Blast. In *Proc. of 10th SPIN Workshop*, volume 2648 of *LNCS*. Springer, 2003.
20. T.A. Henzinger, R. Jhala, R. Majumdar, and G. Sutre. Lazy abstraction. In *Proc. of POPL'02*. ACM Press, 2002.
21. B. Jonsson and M. Nilsson. Transitive closures of regular relations for verifying infinite-state systems. In *Proc. of TACAS'00*, volume 1785 of *LNCS*. Springer, 2000.
22. Y. Kesten, O. Maler, M. Marcus, A. Pnueli, and E. Shahar. Symbolic model checking with rich assertional languages. *Theoretical Computer Science*, 256(1–2), 2001.
23. M. Nilsson. Regular Model Checking. Licentiate Thesis, Uppsala University, Sweden, 2000.
24. A. Pnueli, J. Xu, and L. Zuck. Liveness with (0,1,infinity)-counter abstraction. In *Proc. of CAV'02*, volume 2404 of *LNCS*. Springer, 2002.
25. S. Sagiv, T.W. Reps, and R. Wilhelm. Parametric shape analysis via 3-valued logic. *TOPLAS*, 24(3), 2002.
26. H. Saïdi. Model checking guided abstraction and analysis. In *Proc. of SAS'00*, volume 1824 of *LNCS*. Springer, 2000.
27. Stefan Schwoon. *Model-Checking Pushdown Systems*. PhD thesis, Technische Universität München, 2002.
28. T. Touili. Widening techniques for regular model checking. *ENTCS*, 50, 2001.
29. G. van Noord. FSA6.2, 2004. http://odur.let.rug.nl/~vannoord/Fsa/
30. P. Wolper and B. Boigelot. Verifying systems with infinite but regular state spaces. In *Proc. of CAV'98*, volume 1427, 1998.

Global Model-Checking of Infinite-State Systems

Nir Piterman[1,*] and Moshe Y. Vardi[2,**]

[1] Weizmann Institute of Science, Department of Computer Science, Rehovot 76100, Israel
nir.piterman@weizmann.ac.il
http://www.wisdom.weizmann.ac.il/~nirp
[2] Rice University, Department of Computer Science, Houston, TX 77251-1892, USA
vardi@cs.rice.edu
http://www.cs.rice.edu/~vardi

Abstract. In this paper we extend the automata-theoretic framework for reasoning about infinite-state sequential systems to handle also the global model-checking problem. Our framework is based on the observation that states of such systems, which carry a finite but unbounded amount of information, can be viewed as nodes in an infinite tree, and transitions between states can be simulated by finite-state automata. Checking that the system satisfies a temporal property can then be done by a two-way automaton that navigates through the tree. The framework is known for local model checking. For branching time properties, the framework uses two-way alternating automata. For linear time properties, the framework uses two-way path automata. In order to solve the global model-checking problem we show that for both types of automata, given a regular tree, we can construct a nondeterministic word automaton that accepts all the nodes in the tree from which an accepting run of the automaton can start.

1 Introduction

An important research topic over the past decade has been the application of model checking to infinite-state systems. A major thrust of research in this area is the application of model checking to *infinite-state sequential systems*. These are systems in which a state carries a finite, but unbounded, amount of information, e.g., a pushdown store. The origin of this thrust is the important result by Muller and Schupp that the monadic second-order theory of *context-free graphs* is decidable [MS85]. As the complexity involved in that decidability result is nonelementary, researchers sought decidability results of elementary complexity. This started with Burkart and Steffen, who developed an exponential-time algorithm for model-checking formulas in the *alternation-free μ-calculus* with respect to context-free graphs [BS92]. Researchers then went on to extend this result to the μ-calculus, on one hand, and to more general graphs on the other

* Supported in part by the European Commission (FET project ADVANCE, contract No IST-1999-29082). This work was carried out at the John von Neumann Minerva Center.
** Supported in part by NSF grants CCR-9988322, CCR-0124077, CCR-0311326, IIS-9908435, IIS-9978135, EIA-0086264, and ANI-0216467 by BSF grant 9800096, and by a grant from the Intel Corporation.

R. Alur and D.A. Peled (Eds.): CAV 2004, LNCS 3114, pp. 387–400, 2004.
© Springer-Verlag Berlin Heidelberg 2004

hand, such as *pushdown graphs* [BS95,Wal96], *regular graphs* [BQ96], and *prefix-recognizable graphs* [Cau96]. One of the most powerful results so far is an exponential-time algorithm by Burkart for model checking formulas of the μ-calculus with respect to prefix-recognizable graphs [Bur97][1]. Some of this theory has also been reduced to practice. Pushdown model-checkers such as Mops [CW02], Moped [ES01], and Bebop [BR00] (to name a few) have been developed. Successful applications of these model-checkers to the verification of software are reported, for example, in [CW02].

We usually distinguish between *local* and *global* model-checking. In the first setting we are given a specific state of the system and determine whether it satisfies a given property. In the second setting we compute (a finite representation) of the set of states that satisfy a given property. For many years global model-checking algorithms were the standard; in particular, CTL model checkers [CES86], and symbolic model-checkers [BCM+92] perform global model-checking. While local model checking holds the promise of reduced computational complexity [SW91] and is more natural for explicit LTL model-checking [CVWY92], global model-checking is especially important where the model-checking is only part of the verification process. in [CKKV01] global model-checking is used to supply coverage information, which informs us what parts of the design under verification are relevant to the specified properties. In [LBBO01] an infinite-state system is abstracted into a finite-state system. Global model-checking is performed over the finite-state system and the result is then used to compute invariants for the infinite-state system. In [PRZ01] results of global model-checking over small instances of a parameterized system are generalized to invariants for every value of the system's parameter.

An automata-theoretic framework for reasoning about infinite-state sequential systems was developed in [KV00,KPV02]. The automata-theoretic approach uses the theory of automata as a unifying paradigm for system specification, verification, and synthesis [EJ91,Kur94,VW94]. Automata enable the separation of the logical and the algorithmic aspects of reasoning about systems, yielding clean and asymptotically optimal algorithms. Traditionally automata-theoretic techniques provide algorithms only for local model-checking [CVWY92,KV00,KPV02]. As model-checking in the automata-theoretic approach is reduced to the emptiness of an automaton, it seems that this limitation to local model checking is inherent to the approach. For finite-state systems we can reduce global model-checking to local model-checking by iterating over all the states of the system, which is essentially what happens in symbolic model checking of LTL [BCM+92]. For infinite-state systems, however, such a reduction cannot be applied. In this paper we remove this limitation of automata-theoretic techniques. We show that the automata-theoretic approach to infinite-state sequential systems generalizes nicely to global model-checking. Thus, all the advantages of using automata-theoretic methods, e.g., the ability to handle regular labeling and regular fairness constraints, the ability to handle μ-calculus with backward modalities, and the ability to check realizability [KV00,ATM03], apply also to the more general problem of global model checking.

We use two-way tree alternating automata to reason about properties of infinite-state sequential systems. The idea is based on the observation that states of such systems can

---

[1] The monadic second-order theory and μ-calculus model-checking over *high-order pushdown graphs* is also decidable [KNU03,Cac03]. The complexity of both problems is nonelementary.

be viewed as nodes in an infinite tree, and transitions between states can be simulated by finite-state automata. Checking that the system satisfies a temporal property can then be done by a two-way alternating automaton. Local model checking is then reduced to emptiness or membership problems for two-way tree automata.

In this work, we give a solution to the global model-checking problem. The set of configurations of a prefix-recognizable system satisfying a μ-calculus property can be infinite, but it is regular, so it is finitely represented. We show how to construct a nondeterministic word automaton that accepts all the configurations of the system that satisfy (resp., do not satisfy) a branching-time (resp., linear-time) property. In order to do that, we study the *global membership* problem for two-way alternating parity tree automata and two-way path automata. Given a regular tree, the global membership problem is to find the set of states of the automaton and locations on the tree from which the automaton accepts the tree. We show that in both cases the question is not harder than the simple membership problem (is the tree accepted from the root and the initial state). Our result matches the upper bounds for global model checking established in [EHRS00,EKS01,Cac02]. Our contribution is in showing how this can be done uniformly in an automata-theoretic framework rather than via an eclectic collection of techniques.

2 Preliminaries

Labeled Rewrite Systems. A *labeled transition graph* is $G = \langle \Sigma, S, L, \rho, s_0 \rangle$, where Σ is a finite set of labels, S is a (possibly infinite) set of states, $L : S \to \Sigma$ is a labeling function, $\rho \subseteq S \times S$ is a transition relation, and $s_0 \in S_0$ is an initial state. When $\rho(s, s')$, we say that s' is a *successor* of s, and s is a *predecessor* of s'. For a state $s \in S$, we denote by $G^s = \langle \Sigma, S, L, \rho, s \rangle$, the graph G with s as its initial state. An *s-computation* is an infinite sequence of states $s_0, s_1, \ldots \in S^\omega$ such that $s_0 = s$ and for all $i \geq 0$, we have $\rho(s_i, s_{i+1})$. An *s-computation* $s_0, s_1, \ldots$ induces the *s-trace* $L(s_0) \cdot L(s_1) \cdots \in \Sigma^\omega$. Let $T_s \subseteq \Sigma^\omega$ be the set of all *s-traces*.

A *rewrite system* is $R = \langle \Sigma, V, Q, L, T \rangle$, where Σ is a finite set of labels, V is a finite alphabet, Q is a finite set of states, $L : Q \times V^* \to \Sigma$ is a labeling function that depends only on the first letter of x (Thus, we may write $L : Q \times V \cup \{\epsilon\} \to \Sigma$. Note that the label is defined also for the case that x is the empty word ϵ). The finite set of rewrite rules T is defined below. The set of *configurations* of the system is $Q \times V^*$. Intuitively, the system has finitely many control states and an unbounded store. Thus, in a configuration $(q, x) \in Q \times V^*$ we refer to q as the *control state* and to x as the *store*. We consider here two types of rewrite systems. In a *pushdown* system, each rewrite rule is $\langle q, A, x, q' \rangle \in Q \times V \times V^* \times Q$. Thus, $T \subseteq Q \times V \times V^* \times Q$. In a *prefix-recognizable* system, each rewrite rule is $\langle q, \alpha, \beta, \gamma, q' \rangle \in Q \times reg(V) \times reg(V) \times reg(V) \times Q$, where $reg(V)$ is the set of regular expressions over V. Thus, $T \subseteq Q \times reg(V) \times reg(V) \times reg(V) \times Q$. For a word $w \in V^*$ and a regular expression $r \in reg(V)$ we write $w \in r$ to denote that w is in the language of the regular expression r. We note that the standard definition of prefix-recognizable systems does not include control states. Indeed, a prefix-recognizable system without states can simulate a prefix-recognizable system with states by having the state as the first letter of the unbounded store. We use prefix-recognizable systems with control states for the sake of uniform notation.

The rewrite system R starting in configuration (q_0, x_0) induces the labeled transition graph $G_R^{(q_0, x_0)} = \langle \Sigma, Q \times V^*, L', \rho_R, (q_0, x_0) \rangle$. The states of G_R are the configurations of R and $\langle (q, z), (q', z') \rangle \in \rho_R$ if there is a rewrite rule $t \in T$ leading from configuration (q, z) to configuration (q', z'). Formally, if R is a pushdown system, then $\rho_R((q, A \cdot y), (q', x \cdot y))$ if $\langle q, A, x, q' \rangle \in T$; and if R is a prefix-recognizable system, then $\rho_R((q, x \cdot y), (q', x' \cdot y))$ if there are regular expressions α, β, and γ such that $x \in \alpha$, $y \in \beta$, $x' \in \gamma$, and $\langle q, \alpha, \beta, \gamma, q' \rangle \in T$. Note that in order to apply a rewrite rule in state $(q, z) \in Q \times V^*$ of a pushdown graph, we only need to match the state q and the first letter of z with the second element of a rule. On the other hand, in an application of a rewrite rule in a prefix-recognizable graph, we have to match the state q and we should find a partition of z to a prefix that belongs to the second element of the rule and a suffix that belongs to the third element. A labeled transition graph that is induced by a pushdown system is called a *pushdown graph*. A labeled transition system that is induced by a prefix-recognizable system is called a *prefix-recognizable graph*.

Consider a prefix-recognizable system $R = \langle \Sigma, V, Q, L, T \rangle$. For a rewrite rule $t_i = \langle s, \alpha_i, \beta_i, \gamma_i, s' \rangle \in T$, let $\mathcal{U}_\lambda = \langle V, Q_\lambda, q_\lambda^0, \eta_\lambda, F_\lambda \rangle$, for $\lambda \in \{\alpha_i, \beta_i, \gamma_i\}$, be the non-deterministic automaton for the language of the regular expression λ. We assume that all initial states have no incoming edges and that all accepting states have no outgoing edges. We collect all the states of all the automata for α, β, and γ regular expressions. Formally, $Q_\alpha = \bigcup_{t_i \in T} Q_{\alpha_i}$, $Q_\beta = \bigcup_{t_i \in T} Q_{\beta_i}$, and $Q_\gamma = \bigcup_{t_i \in T} Q_{\gamma_i}$.

We define the *size* $\|T\|$ of T as the space required in order to encode the rewrite rules in T and the labeling function. Thus, in a pushdown system, $\|T\| = \sum_{\langle q, A, x, q' \rangle \in T} |x|$, and in a prefix-recognizable system, $\|T\| = \sum_{\langle q, \alpha, \beta, \gamma, q' \rangle \in T} |\mathcal{U}_\alpha| + |\mathcal{U}_\beta| + |\mathcal{U}_\gamma|$.

We are interested in specifications expressed in the μ-calculus [Koz83] and in LTL [Pnu77]. For introduction to these logics we refer the reader to [Eme97]. We want to model check pushdown and prefix-recognizable systems with respect to specifications in these logics. We differentiate between *local* and *global* model-checking. In *local model-checking*, given a graph G and a specification φ, one has to determine whether G satisfies φ. In *global model-checking* we are interested in the set of configurations s such that G^s satisfies φ. As G is infinite, we hope to find a finite representation for this set. It is known that the set of configurations of a prefix-recognizable system satisfying a monadic second-order formula is regular [Cau96,Rab72], which implies that this also holds for pushdown systems and for μ-calculus and LTL specifications.

In this paper, we extend the automata-theoretic approach to model-checking of sequential infinite state systems [KV00,KPV02] to global model-checking. Our model-checking algorithm returns a nondeterministic finite automaton on words (NFW, for short) recognizing the set of configurations that satisfy (not satisfy, in the case of LTL) the specification. The complexity of our algorithms matches the previously known upper bounds [EHRS00,EKS01,Cac02][2].

Theorem 1. *Global model-checking for a system R and a specification φ is solvable*

- *in time $(\|T\|)^3 \cdot 2^{O(|\varphi|)}$ and space $(\|T\|)^2 \cdot 2^{O(|\varphi|)}$, where R is a pushdown system and φ is an LTL formula.*

---

[2] In order to obtain the stated bound for prefix-recognizable systems and LTL specifications one has to combine the result in [EKS01] with our reduction from prefix-recognizable systems to pushdown systems with regular labeling [KPV02].

- in time $(\|T\|)^3 \cdot 2^{O(|\varphi| \cdot |Q_\beta|)}$ and space $(\|T\|)^2 \cdot 2^{O(|\varphi| \cdot |Q_\beta|)}$, where R is a prefix-recognizable system and φ is an LTL formula.
- in time $2^{O(\|T\| \cdot |\varphi| \cdot k)}$, where R is a prefix-recognizable system and φ is a μ-calculus formula of alternation depth k.

Alternating Two-Way Automata. Given a finite set Υ of directions, an Υ-*tree* is a set $T \subseteq \Upsilon^*$ such that if $v \cdot x \in T$, where $v \in \Upsilon$ and $x \in \Upsilon^*$, then also $x \in T$. The elements of T are called *nodes*, and the empty word ε is the *root* of T. For every $v \in \Upsilon$ and $x \in T$, the node x is the *parent* of $v \cdot x$. Each node $x \neq \varepsilon$ of T has a *direction* in Υ. The direction of the root is the symbol $\bot$ (we assume that $\bot \notin \Upsilon$). The direction of a node $v \cdot x$ is v. We denote by $dir(x)$ the direction of node x. An Υ-tree T is a *full infinite tree* if $T = \Upsilon^*$. A *path* π of a tree T is a set $\pi \subseteq T$ such that $\varepsilon \in \pi$ and for every $x \in \pi$ there exists a unique $v \in \Upsilon$ such that $v \cdot x \in \pi$.

Given two finite sets Υ and Σ, a Σ-*labeled* Υ-*tree* is a pair $\langle T, V \rangle$ where T is an Υ-tree and $V : T \to \Sigma$ maps each node of T to a letter in Σ. When Υ and Σ are not important or clear from the context, we call $\langle T, V \rangle$ a labeled tree.

A tree is *regular* if it is the unwinding of some finite labeled graph. More formally, a *transducer* $\mathcal{D}$ is a tuple $\langle \Upsilon, \Sigma, Q, q_0, \eta, L \rangle$, where Υ is a finite set of directions, Σ is a finite alphabet, Q is a finite set of states, $q_0 \in Q$ is a start state, $\eta : Q \times \Upsilon \to Q$ is a deterministic transition function, and $L : Q \to \Sigma$ is a labeling function. We define $\eta : \Upsilon^* \to Q$ in the standard way: $\eta(\varepsilon) = q_0$ and $\eta(ax) = \eta(\eta(x), a)$. Intuitively, a transducer is a labeled finite graph with a designated start node, where the edges are labeled by Υ and the nodes are labeled by Σ. A Σ-labeled Υ-tree $\langle \Upsilon^*, \tau \rangle$ is regular if there exists a transducer $\mathcal{D} = \langle \Upsilon, \Sigma, Q, q_0, \eta, L \rangle$, such that for every $x \in \Upsilon^*$, we have $\tau(x) = L(\eta(x))$. The size of $\langle \Upsilon^*, \tau \rangle$, denoted $\|\tau\|$, is $|Q|$, the number of states of $\mathcal{D}$.

Alternating automata on infinite trees generalize nondeterministic tree automata and were first introduced in [MS87]. Here we describe alternating *two-way* tree automata. For a finite set X, let $\mathcal{B}^+(X)$ be the set of positive Boolean formulas over X (i.e., Boolean formulas built from elements in X using $\wedge$ and $\vee$), where we also allow the formulas **true** and **false**, and, as usual, $\wedge$ has precedence over $\vee$. For a set $Y \subseteq X$ and a formula $\theta \in \mathcal{B}^+(X)$, we say that Y *satisfies* θ iff assigning **true** to elements in Y and assigning **false** to elements in $X \setminus Y$ makes θ true. For a set Υ of directions, the *extension* of Υ is the set $ext(\Upsilon) = \Upsilon \cup \{\varepsilon, \uparrow\}$ (assuming $\Upsilon \cap \{\varepsilon, \uparrow\} = \emptyset$). An *alternating two-way automaton* over Σ-labeled Υ-trees is $\mathcal{A} = \langle \Sigma, Q, q_0, \delta, F \rangle$, where Σ is the input alphabet, Q is a finite set of states, $q_0 \in Q$ is an initial state, $\delta : Q \times \Sigma \to \mathcal{B}^+(ext(\Upsilon) \times Q)$ is the transition function, and F specifies the acceptance condition.

A run of an alternating automaton $\mathcal{A}$ over a labeled tree $\langle \Upsilon^*, V \rangle$ is a Σ_r-labeled Γ-tree, for some set Γ of directions, where $\Sigma_r = \Upsilon^* \times Q$. The root ε of T_r is labeled by (ε, q_0). The labels of a node and its successors have to satisfy the transition function: Consider $y \in T_r$ with $r(y) = (x, q)$ and $\delta(q, V(x)) = \theta$. Then there is a (possibly empty) set $S \subseteq ext(\Upsilon) \times Q$, such that S satisfies θ, and for all $\langle c, q' \rangle \in S$, there is $\gamma \in \Gamma$ such that $\gamma \cdot y \in T_r$ and the following hold: (a) If $c \in \Upsilon$, then $r(\gamma \cdot y) = (c \cdot x, q')$. (b) If $c = \varepsilon$, then $r(\gamma \cdot y) = (x, q')$. (c) If $c = \uparrow$, then $x = v \cdot z$, for some $v \in \Upsilon$ and $z \in \Upsilon^*$, and $r(\gamma \cdot y) = (z, q')$.

A run $\langle T_r, r \rangle$ is *accepting* if all its infinite paths satisfy the acceptance condition. We consider here *parity* acceptance conditions [EJ91]. A parity condition over a state set Q is a finite sequence $F = \{F_1, F_2, \ldots, F_m\}$ of subsets of Q, where $F_1 \subseteq F_2 \subseteq \ldots \subseteq F_m = Q$. The number m of sets is called the *index* of $\mathcal{A}$. Given a run $\langle T_r, r \rangle$ and an infinite path $\pi \subseteq T_r$, let $inf(\pi) \subseteq Q$ be such that $q \in inf(\pi)$ if and only if there are infinitely many $y \in \pi$ for which $r(y) \in \Upsilon^* \times \{q\}$. That is, $inf(\pi)$ is the set of states that appear infinitely often in π. A path π satisfies the condition F if there is an even i for which $inf(\pi) \cap F_i \neq \emptyset$ and $inf(\pi) \cap F_{i-1} = \emptyset$. An automaton accepts a labeled tree if and only if there exists a run that accepts it. We denote by $\mathcal{L}(\mathcal{A})$ the set of all Σ-labeled trees that $\mathcal{A}$ accepts. The automaton $\mathcal{A}$ is *nonempty* iff $\mathcal{L}(\mathcal{A}) \neq \emptyset$. The Büchi condition $F \subseteq Q$ is equivalent to the parity condition $\langle \emptyset, F, Q \rangle$ [Büc62]. A path π satisfies the Büchi condition F iff $inf(\pi) \cap F \neq \emptyset$.

The size of an automaton is determined by the number of its states and the size of its transition function. The size of the transition function is $|\eta| = \Sigma_{q \in Q} \Sigma_{a \in \Sigma} |\eta(q, a)|$ where, for a formula in $B^+(ext(\Upsilon) \times Q)$ we define $|(\Delta, q)| = |\mathbf{true}| = |\mathbf{false}| = 1$ and $|\theta_1 \vee \theta_2| = |\theta_1 \wedge \theta_2| = |\theta_1| + |\theta_2| + 1$.

We say that $\mathcal{A}$ is one-way if δ is restricted to formulas in $B^+(\Upsilon \times Q)$, it is advancing if δ is restricted to $B^+((\Upsilon \cup \{\varepsilon\}) \times Q)$. We say that $\mathcal{A}$ is nondeterministic if its transitions are of the form $\bigvee_{i \in I} \bigwedge_{v \in \Upsilon}(v, q_v^i))$, in such cases we write $\delta : Q \times \Sigma \to 2^{Q^{|\Upsilon|}}$. In the case that $|\Upsilon| = 1$, $\mathcal{A}$ is a word automaton.

Given an alternating two-way parity tree automaton $\mathcal{A}$ with n states and index k, we can construct an equivalent nondeterministic one-way parity tree automaton whose number of states is exponential in nk and whose index is linear in nk [Var98], and we can check the nonemptiness of $\mathcal{A}$ in time exponential in nk [EJS93]. The *membership problem* of an automaton $\mathcal{A}$ and a regular tree $\langle \Upsilon^*, \tau \rangle$ is to determine whether $\mathcal{A}$ accepts $\langle \Upsilon^*, \tau \rangle$; or equivalently whether $\langle \Upsilon^*, \tau \rangle \in \mathcal{L}(\mathcal{A})$. For $q \in Q$ and $w \in \Upsilon^*$, we say that $\mathcal{A}$ accepts $\langle \Upsilon^*, \tau \rangle$ from (q, w) if there exists an accepting run of $\mathcal{A}$ that starts from state q reading node w (i.e. a run whose root is labeled by (w, q) and satisfies the transition). The *global membership problem* of $\mathcal{A}$ and regular tree $\langle \Upsilon^*, \tau \rangle$ is to determine the set $\{(q, w) \mid \mathcal{A} \text{ accepts } \langle \Upsilon^*, \tau \rangle \text{ from } (q, w)\}$.

We use acronyms in $\{1, 2\} \times \{A, N\} \times \{B, P\} \times \{T, W\}$ to denote the different types of automata. The first symbol stands for the type of movement: 1 for 1-way or advancing automata (we often omit the 1) and 2 for 2-way automata. The second symbol stands for the branching mode: A for alternating and N for nondeterministic. The third symbol stands for the type of acceptance: B for Büchi and P for parity, and the last symbol stands for the object the automaton is reading: W for words and T for trees. For example, a 2APT is a 2-way alternating parity tree automaton and an NBW is a 1-way nondeterministic Büchi word automaton.

Alternating Automata on Labeled Transition Graphs. Consider a labeled transition graph $G = \langle \Sigma, S, L, \rho, s_0 \rangle$. Let $\Delta = \{\varepsilon, \Box, \Diamond\}$. An alternating automaton on labeled transition graphs (*graph automaton*, for short) [Wil99][3] is a tuple $\mathcal{S} = \langle \Sigma, Q, q_0, \delta, F \rangle$, where Σ, Q, q_0, and F are as in alternating two-way automata, and $\delta : Q \times \Sigma \to B^+(\Delta \times Q)$ is the transition function. Intuitively, when $\mathcal{S}$ is in state q and it reads a state s of G, fulfilling an atom $\langle \Diamond, t \rangle$ (or $\Diamond t$, for short) requires $\mathcal{S}$ to send a copy in state t to some successor of s. Similarly, fulfilling an atom $\Box t$ requires $\mathcal{S}$ to send copies

---

[3] See related formalism in [JW95].

in state t to all the successors of s. Thus, graph automata cannot distinguish between the various successors of a state and treat them in an existential or universal way.

Like runs of alternating two-way automata, a run of a graph automaton $\mathcal{S}$ over a labeled transition graph $G = \langle \Sigma, S, L, \rho, s_0 \rangle$ is a Σ_r-labeled Γ-tree $\langle T_r, r \rangle$, where Γ is some set of directions, $\Sigma_r = S \times Q$. The root ε of T_r is labeled by (s_0, q_0). The labels of a node and its successors have to satisfy the transition function: Consider $y \in T_r$ with $r(y) = (s, q)$ and $\delta(q, L(s)) = \theta$. Then there is a (possibly empty) set $S \subseteq \Delta \times Q$, such that S satisfies θ, and for all $\langle c, q' \rangle \in S$, we have: (a) If $c = \varepsilon$, then there is $\gamma \in \Gamma$ such that $\gamma \cdot y \in T_r$ and $r(\gamma \cdot y) = (s, q')$. (b) If $c = \square$, then for every successor s' of s, there is $\gamma \in \Gamma$ such that $\gamma \cdot y \in T_r$ and $r(\gamma \cdot y) = (s', q')$. (c) If $c = \Diamond$, then there is a successor s' of s and $\gamma \in \Gamma$ such that $\gamma \cdot y \in T_r$ and $r(\gamma \cdot y) = (s', q')$. Acceptance is defined as in 2APT runs. The graph G is accepted by $\mathcal{S}$ if there is an accepting run on it. We denote by $\mathcal{L}(\mathcal{S})$ the set of all graphs that $\mathcal{S}$ accepts and by $\mathcal{S}^q = \langle \Sigma, Q, q, \delta, F \rangle$ the automaton $\mathcal{S}$ with q as its initial state.

We use graph automata as our branching time specification language. A labeled transition graph G satisfies a graph automaton $\mathcal{S}$, denoted $G \models \mathcal{S}$, if $\mathcal{S}$ accepts G. Graph automata have the same expressive power as the μ-calculus. Formally, given a μ-calculus formula ψ, of length n and alternation depth k, we can construct a graph parity automaton $\mathcal{S}_\psi$ such that $\mathcal{L}(\mathcal{S}_\psi)$ is exactly the set of graphs satisfying ψ. The automaton $\mathcal{S}_\psi$ has n states and index k [Wil99].

We use NBW as our linear time specification language. A labeled transition graph G satisfies an NBW N, denoted $G \models N$, if $T_{s_0} \cap L(N) \neq \emptyset$ (where s_0 is the initial state of G)[4]. We are especially interested in cases where $\Sigma = 2^{AP}$, for some set AP of atomic propositions AP, and in languages $L \subseteq (2^{AP})^\omega$ definable by NBW or formulas of the linear temporal logic LTL [Pnu77]. For an LTL formula φ, the *language* of φ, denoted $L(\varphi)$, is the set of infinite words that satisfy φ. For every LTL formula φ, we can construct an NBW N_φ with $2^{O(|\varphi|)}$ states such that $L(N_\varphi) = L(\varphi)$ [VW94].

Given a graph G and a specification $\mathcal{S}$, the *global model-checking* problem is to compute the set of configurations s of G such that $G^s \models \mathcal{S}$. Whether we are interested in branching or linear time model-checking is determined by the type of automaton.

3   Global Membership for 2APT

In this section we solve the global membership problem for 2APT. Consider a 2APT $\mathcal{A} = \langle \Sigma, S, s_0, \rho, \alpha \rangle$ and a regular tree $T = \langle \Upsilon^*, \tau \rangle$. Our construction consists of a few stages. First, we modify $\mathcal{A}$ into a 2APT $\mathcal{A}'$ that starts its run from the root of the tree in an idle state. In this idle state it goes to a node in the tree that is marked with a state of $\mathcal{A}$. From that node, the new automaton starts a fresh run of $\mathcal{A}$ from the marked state. We convert $\mathcal{A}'$ into an NPT $\mathcal{P}$ [Var98]. Second, we combine $\mathcal{P}$ with an NBT $\mathcal{D}'$ that accepts only trees that are identical to the regular tree T and in addition have exactly one node marked by some state of $\mathcal{A}$. We check now the emptiness of this automaton $\mathcal{A}''$. From the emptiness information we derive an NFW N that accepts a word $w \in \Upsilon^*$

---

[4] Notice, that our definition dualizes the usual definition for LTL. Here, we say that a linear time specification is satisfied if there exists a trace that satisfies it. Usually, a linear time specification is satisfied if all traces satisfy it.

in state $s \in S$ (i.e. the run ends in state s of $\mathcal{A}$; state s is an accepting state of N) iff $\mathcal{A}$ accepts T from (s, w).

Theorem 2. *Consider a 2APT* $\mathcal{A} = \langle \Sigma, S, s_0, \rho, \alpha \rangle$ *and a regular tree* $T = \langle \Upsilon^*, \tau \rangle$. *We can construct an NFW* $N = \langle \Upsilon, R' \cup S, r_0, \Delta, S \rangle$ *that accepts the word* w *in state* $s \in S$ *iff* $\mathcal{A}$ *accepts* T *from* (s, w). *Let* n *be the number of states of* $\mathcal{A}$ *and* h *its index; the NFW* N *is constructible in time exponential in* nh *and polynomial in* $\|\tau\|$.

Proof. Let $S_+ = S \cup \{\bot\}$ and $\Upsilon = \{v_1, \ldots, v_k\}$. Consider the 2APT $\mathcal{A}' = \langle \Sigma \times S_+, S', s'_0, \rho', \alpha' \rangle$ where $S' = S \cup \{s'_0\}$, s'_0 is a new initial state, α' is identical to α except having s'_0 belonging to some odd set of α', and ρ' is defined as follows.

$$\rho'(s, (\sigma, t)) = \begin{cases} \rho(s, \sigma) & s \neq s'_0 \\ \bigvee_{v \in \Upsilon}(v, s'_0) & s = s'_0 \text{ and } t = \bot \\ \bigvee_{v \in \Upsilon}(v, s'_0) \vee (\varepsilon, s') & s = s'_0 \text{ and } t = s' \end{cases}$$

Clearly, $\mathcal{A}'$ accepts a $(\Sigma \times S_+)$-labeled tree T' iff there is a node x in T' labeled by (σ, s) for some $(\sigma, s) \in \Sigma \times S$ and $\mathcal{A}$ accepts the projection of T' on Σ when it starts its run from node x in state s. Let $\mathcal{P} = \langle \Sigma \times S_+, P, p_0, \rho_1, \alpha_1 \rangle$ be the NPT that accepts exactly those trees accepted by $\mathcal{A}'$ [Var98]. If $\mathcal{A}$ has n states and index h then $\mathcal{P}$ has $(nh)^{O(nh)}$ states and index $O(nh)$.

Let $\mathcal{D} = \langle \Upsilon, \Sigma, Q, q_0, \eta, L \rangle$ be the transducer inducing the labeling τ of T. We construct an NBT $\mathcal{D}'$ that accepts $(\Sigma \times S_+)$-labeled trees whose projection on Σ is τ and have exactly one node marked by a state in S. Consider the NBT $\mathcal{D}' = \langle \Sigma \times S_+, Q \times \{\bot, \top\}, (q_0, \bot), \eta', Q \times \{\top\} \rangle$ where η' is defined as follows. For $q \in Q$ let $pend_i(q) = \langle (\eta(q, v_1), \top), \ldots, (\eta(q, v_i), \bot), \ldots, (\eta(q, v_k), \top) \rangle$ be the tuple where the j-th element is the v_j-successor of q and all elements are marked by $\top$ except for the i-th element, which is marked by $\bot$. Intuitively, a state $(q, \top)$ accepts a subtree all of whose nodes are marked by $\bot$. A state $(q, \bot)$ means that $\mathcal{D}'$ is still searching for the unique node labeled by a state in S. The transition to $pend_i$ means that $\mathcal{D}'$ is looking for that node in direction $v_i \in \Upsilon$.

$$\eta'((q, \beta), (\sigma, \gamma)) = \begin{cases} \{\langle (\eta(q, v_1), \top), \ldots, (\eta(q, v_k), \top) \rangle\} & \beta = \top, \ \gamma = \bot \text{ and } \sigma = L(q) \\ \{\langle (\eta(q, v_1), \top), \ldots, (\eta(q, v_k), \top) \rangle\} & \beta = \bot, \ \gamma \in S \text{ and } \sigma = L(q) \\ \{pend_i(q) \mid i \in [1..k]\} & \beta = \gamma = \bot \text{ and } \sigma = L(q) \\ \emptyset & \text{Otherwise} \end{cases}$$

Clearly, $\mathcal{D}'$ accepts a $(\Sigma \times S_+)$-labeled tree T' iff the projection of T' on Σ is exactly τ and all nodes of T' are labeled by $\bot$ except one node labeled by some state $s \in S$.

Let $\mathcal{A}'' = \langle \Sigma \times S_+, R, r_0, \delta, \alpha_2 \rangle$ be the product of $\mathcal{D}'$ and $\mathcal{P}$ where $R = (Q \times \{\bot, \top\}) \times P$, $r_0 = ((q_0, \bot), p_0)$, δ is defined below and $\alpha_2 = \langle F'_1, \ldots, F'_m \rangle$ is obtained from $\alpha_1 = \langle F_1, \ldots, F_m \rangle$ by setting $F'_1 = ((Q \times \{\bot, \top\}) \times F_1) \cup (Q \times \{\bot\} \times P)$ and for $i > 1$ we have $F'_i = (Q \times \{\top\}) \times F_i$. Thus, $\bot$ states are visited finitely often, and only the state of $\mathcal{P}$ is important for acceptance. For every state $((q, \beta), p) \in (Q \times \{\bot, \top\}) \times P$ and letter $(\sigma, \gamma) \in \Sigma \times S_+$ the transition function δ is defined by:

$$\delta(((q, \beta), p), (\sigma, \gamma)) =$$
$$\left\{ \langle ((q_1, \beta_1), p_1), \ldots, ((q_k, \beta_k), p_k) \rangle \;\middle|\; \begin{array}{l} \langle p_1, \ldots, p_k \rangle \in \rho_1(p, (\sigma, \gamma)) \text{ and} \\ \langle (q_1, \beta_1), \ldots, (q_k, \beta_k) \rangle \in \eta'((q, \beta), (\sigma, \gamma)) \end{array} \right\}$$

A tree T' accepted by $\mathcal{A}''$ has a unique node x labeled by a state s of $\mathcal{A}$, all other nodes are labeled by $\bot$, and if T is the projection of T' on Σ then $\mathcal{A}$ accepts T from (s, x).

The number of states of $\mathcal{A}''$ is $\|\tau\| \cdot (nh)^{O(nh)}$ and its index is $O(nh)$. We can check whether $\mathcal{A}''$ accepts the empty language in time exponential in nh. The emptiness algorithm returns the set of states of $\mathcal{A}''$ whose language is not empty [EJS93]. From now on we remove from the state space of $\mathcal{A}''$ all states whose language is empty. Thus, transitions of $\mathcal{A}''$ contain only tuples in which all states have non empty language.

We are ready to construct the NFW N. The states of N are the states of $\mathcal{A}''$ in $(Q \times \{\bot\}) \times P$ in addition to S (the set of states of $\mathcal{A}$). Every state in S is an accepting sink of N. For the transition of N we follow transitions of $\bot$-states. Once we can transition into a tuple where the $\bot$ is removed, we transition into the appropriate accepting states.

Let $N = \langle \Upsilon, R' \cup S, r_0, \Delta, S \rangle$, where $R' = R \cap (Q \times \{\bot\} \times P)$, r_0 is the initial state of $\mathcal{A}''$, S is the set of states of $\mathcal{A}$ (accepting sinks in N), and Δ is defined as follows. Consider a state $((q, \bot), p) \in R'$. For every tuple $\langle ((q_1, \top), p_1), \ldots, ((q_i, \bot), p_i), \ldots, ((q_k, \top), p_k) \rangle$ in $\delta(((q, \bot), p), (L(q), \bot))$, we add $((q_i, \bot), p_i)$ to $\Delta(((q, \bot), p), v_i)$. For every tuple $\langle ((q_1, \top), p_1), \ldots, ((q_k, \top), p_k) \rangle$ in $\delta(((q, \bot), p), (L(q), s))$, we add s to $\Delta(((q, \bot), p), \epsilon)$. In the full version we show that N accepts $w \in \Upsilon^*$ in a state $s \in S$ iff $\mathcal{A}$ accepts T from (w, s).

4   Two-Way Path Automata on Trees

Path automata on trees are a hybrid of nondeterministic word automata and nondeterministic tree automata: they run on trees but have linear runs. Here we describe *two-way* nondeterministic Büchi path automata. We introduced path automata in [KPV02], where they are used to give an automata-theoretic solution to the local linear time model checking problem. A *two-way nondeterministic Büchi path automaton* (2NBP, for short) on Σ-labeled Υ-trees is a 2ABT where the transition is restricted to disjunctions. Formally, $\mathcal{S} = \langle \Sigma, P, p_0, \delta, F \rangle$, where Σ, P, p_0, and F are as in an NBW, and $\delta : P \times \Sigma \to 2^{(ext(\Upsilon) \times P)}$ is the transition function. A path automaton that visits the state p and reads the node $x \in T$ chooses a pair $(d, p') \in \delta(p, \tau(x))$, and then follows direction d and moves to state p'. It follows that a *run* of a 2NBP on a labeled tree $\langle \Upsilon^*, \tau \rangle$ is a sequence of pairs $r = (x_0, p_0), (x_1, p_1), \ldots$. The run is *accepting* if it visits F infinitely often. As usual, $\mathcal{L}(\mathcal{S})$ denotes the set of trees accepted by $\mathcal{S}$.

We studied in [KPV02] the emptiness and membership problems for 2NBP. Here, we consider the global membership problem of 2NBP. Consider a 2NBP $\mathcal{S} = \langle \Sigma, P, p_0, \delta, F \rangle$ and a regular tree $\langle \Upsilon^*, \tau \rangle$. Just like in the case of 2APT, we first modify $\mathcal{S}$ into a 2NBP $\mathcal{S}'$ that starts its run from the root of the tree in an idle state. In this idle state it goes to some node in the tree. From that node, the new automaton starts a fresh run of $\mathcal{S}$ from some state in P. We then construct an ABW $\mathcal{A}$ such that $\mathcal{A}$ accepts the word a^ω iff $\mathcal{S}'$ accepts the tree T. We check the emptiness of $\mathcal{A}$, and from the emptiness information derive an NFW N that accepts a word $w \in \Upsilon^*$ in state $p \in P$ (i.e. the run ends in state p of $\mathcal{S}$; state p is an accepting state of N) iff $\mathcal{S}$ accepts $\langle \Upsilon^*, \tau \rangle$ from (p, w).

Theorem 3. *Consider a 2NBP $\mathcal{S} = \langle \Sigma, P, p_0, \delta, F \rangle$ and a regular tree $\langle \Upsilon^*, \tau \rangle$. We can construct an NFW $N = \langle \Upsilon, Q' \cup P, q_0, \Delta, P \rangle$ that accepts the word w in a state*

$p \in P$ iff $\mathcal{S}$ accepts T from (p, w). We construct N in time $O(|P|^2 \cdot |\delta| \cdot \|\tau\|)$ and space $O(|P|^2 \cdot \|\tau\|)$.

Proof. Consider the 2NBP $\mathcal{S}' = \langle \Sigma, P', p_0, \delta', F \rangle$ where $P' = P \cup \{p_0\}$ and $p_0 \notin P$ is a new state, for every $p \in P$ and $\sigma \in \Sigma$ we have $\delta'(p, \sigma) = \delta(p, \sigma)$, and for every $\sigma \in \Sigma$ we have $\delta'(p_0, \sigma) = \bigvee_{v \in \Upsilon}(p_0, v) \vee \bigvee_{p \in P}(\varepsilon, p)$. Thus, $\mathcal{S}'$ starts reading $\langle \Upsilon^*, \tau \rangle$ from the root in state p_0, the transition of p_0 includes either transitions down the tree that remain in state p_0 or transitions into one of the other states of $\mathcal{S}$. Thus, every accepting run of $\mathcal{S}'$ starts with a sequence $(p_0, w_0), (p_0, w_1), \ldots, (p_0, w_n), (p, w_n), \ldots$. Such a run is a witness to the fact that $\mathcal{S}$ accepts $\langle \Upsilon^*, \tau \rangle$ from (p, w_n). We would like to recognize all words $w \in \Upsilon^*$ and states $p' \in P$ for which there exist runs as above with $p = p'$ and $w_n = w$.

Consider the regular tree $\langle \Upsilon^*, \tau \rangle$. Let $\mathcal{D}_\tau$ be the transducer that generates the labels of τ where $\mathcal{D}_\tau = \langle \Upsilon, \Sigma, D_\tau, d_\tau^0, \rho_\tau, L_\tau \rangle$. For a word $w \in \Upsilon^*$ we denote by $\rho_\tau(w)$ the unique state that $\mathcal{D}_\tau$ gets to after reading w. In [KPV02] we construct the ABW $\mathcal{A} = \langle \{a\}, Q, q_0, \eta, F' \rangle$ where $Q = (P' \cup (P' \times P')) \times D_\tau \times \{\bot, \top\}$, $q_0 = \langle p_0, d_\tau^0, \bot \rangle$, and $F' = (F \times D_\tau \times \{\bot\}) \cup (P' \times D_\tau \times \{\top\})$. We use the following definitions. Two functions $f_\alpha : P' \times P' \to \{\bot, \top\}$ where $\alpha \in \{\bot, \top\}$.

$$f_\bot(p, q) = \bot \qquad f_\top(p, q) = \begin{cases} \bot \text{ if } p \in F \text{ or } q \in F \\ \top \text{ otherwise} \end{cases}$$

For every state $p \in P'$ and letter $\sigma \in \Sigma$ the set C_p^σ is the set of states from which p is reachable by a sequence of ϵ-transitions reading letter σ and one final $\uparrow$-transition reading σ. Now η is defined for every state in Q as follows.

$$\eta(p, d, \alpha) = \bigvee \begin{array}{l} \bigvee_{p' \in P'} \bigvee_{\beta \in \{\bot, \top\}} (\epsilon, \langle p, p', d, \beta \rangle) \wedge (\epsilon, \langle p', d, \beta \rangle) \\ \bigvee_{v \in \Upsilon} \bigvee_{\langle v, p' \rangle \in \delta'(p, L_\tau(d))} (a, \langle p', \rho_\tau(d, v), \bot \rangle) \\ \bigvee_{\langle \epsilon, p' \rangle \in \delta'(p, L_\tau(d))} (\epsilon, \langle p', d, \bot \rangle) \end{array}$$

$$\eta(p_1, p_2, d, \alpha) =$$
$$\bigvee_{\langle \epsilon, p' \rangle \in \delta'(p_1, L_\tau(d))} (\epsilon, \langle p', p_2, d, f_\alpha(p', p_2) \rangle)$$
$$\vee \bigvee_{p' \in P'} \bigvee_{\beta_1 + \beta_2 = \alpha} \left(\begin{array}{l} (\epsilon, \langle p_1, p', d, f_{\beta_1}(p_1, p') \rangle) \wedge \\ (\epsilon, \langle p', p_2, d, f_{\beta_2}(p', p_2) \rangle) \end{array} \right)$$
$$\bigvee_{v \in \Upsilon, \langle v, p' \rangle \in \delta'(p_1, L_\tau(d))} \bigvee_{p'' \in C_{p_2}^{L_\tau(d)}} (a, \langle p', p'', \rho_\tau(d, v), f_\alpha(p', p'') \rangle)$$

Finally, we replace every state of the form $\{\langle p, p, d, \alpha \rangle \mid p \in F \text{ or } \alpha = \bot\}$ by **true**.

In [KPV02] we show that $\mathcal{L}(\mathcal{A}) \neq \emptyset$ iff $\langle \Upsilon^*, \tau \rangle \in \mathcal{L}(\mathcal{S}')$ by translating an accepting run of $\mathcal{S}'$ on $\langle \Upsilon^*, \tau \rangle$ into an accepting run tree of $\mathcal{A}$ on a^ω and vice versa. As shown in [KPV02] the number of states of $\mathcal{A}$ is $O(|P|^2 \cdot \|\tau\|)$ and the size of its transition is $O(|\delta| \cdot |P|^2 \cdot \|\tau\|)$. It is also shown there that because of the special structure of $\mathcal{A}$ its emptiness can be computed in space $O(|P|^2 \cdot \|\tau\|)$ and in time $O(|\delta| \cdot |P|^2 \cdot \|\tau\|)$. From the emptiness algorithm we can get a table $T : Q \to \{0, 1\}$ such that $T(q) = 1$ iff $L(\mathcal{A}^q) \neq \emptyset$. Furthermore, we can extract from the algorithm an accepting run of $\mathcal{A}^q$ on a^ω. It follows that in case $(p, d, \alpha) \in P \times D_\tau \times \{\bot, \top\}$ the run is infinite and the algorithm in [KPV02] can be used to extract from it an accepting run of P on the regular tree $\langle \Upsilon^*, \tau_d \rangle$. If $(p, p', d, \alpha) \in P \times P \times D_\tau \times \{\bot, \top\}$ the run is finite and the algorithm in [KPV02] can be used to extract from it a run of P on the regular tree $\langle \Upsilon^*, \tau_d \rangle$ that starts in state p and ends in state p' both reading the root of Υ^*.

We construct now the NFW N. Let $N = \langle \Upsilon, Q' \cup P, q_0, \Delta, P \rangle$ where $Q' = (\{p_0\} \cup (\{p_0\} \times P)) \times D_\tau \times \{\bot, \top\}$ and P is the set of states of S (that serves also as the set of accepting states), $q_0 = \langle p_0, d_\tau^0, \bot \rangle$ is the initial state of $\mathcal{A}$, and Δ is defined as follows.

Consider a state $\langle p_0, d, \alpha \rangle \in Q'$. For every $v \in \Upsilon$ such that the language of $\langle p_0, \rho_\tau(d, v), \bot \rangle$ is not empty, and $\{(a, \langle p_0, \rho_\tau(d, v), \bot \rangle)\} \models \eta(\langle p_0, d, \alpha \rangle)$, we add $\langle p_0, \rho_\tau(d, v), \bot \rangle$ to $\Delta(\langle p_0, d, \alpha \rangle, v)$. For every state $p \in P$ such that the language of $\langle p_0, p, d, \beta \rangle$ is not empty, the language of $\langle p, d, \beta \rangle$ is not empty, and $\{(\varepsilon, \langle p_0, p, d, \beta \rangle), (\varepsilon, p, d, \beta)\} \models \eta(\langle p_0, d, \alpha \rangle)$, we add $\langle p_0, p, d, \beta \rangle$ to $\Delta(\langle p_0, d, \alpha \rangle, \varepsilon)$. For every state $p \in P$ such that the language of $\langle p, d, \bot \rangle$ is not empty, and $\{(\varepsilon, \langle p, d, \bot \rangle)\} \models \eta(\langle p_0, d, \alpha \rangle)$, we add (the accepting state) p to $\Delta(\langle p_0, d, \alpha \rangle, \varepsilon)$.

Consider a state $\langle p_0, p, d, \alpha \rangle \in Q'$. For every $v \in \Upsilon$ and for every $p' \in C_p^{L_\tau(d)}$ such that the language of $\langle p_0, p', \rho_\tau(d, v), f_\alpha(p_0, p') \rangle$ is not empty, and $\{(a, \langle p_0, p', \rho_\tau(d, v), f_\alpha(p_0, p') \rangle)\} \models \eta(\langle p_0, p, d, \alpha \rangle)$, we add the state $\langle p_0, p', \rho_\tau(d, v), f_\alpha(p_0, p') \rangle$ to the transition $\Delta(\langle p_0, p', d, \alpha \rangle, v)$. For every p' such that the language of $\langle p', p, d, f_\alpha(p', p) \rangle$ is not empty, and $\{(\varepsilon, \langle p', p, d, f_\alpha(p', p) \rangle)\} \models \eta(\langle p_0, p, d, \alpha \rangle)$, we add the state p' to the transition $\Delta(\langle p_0, p, d, \alpha \rangle, \varepsilon)$. For every state $p' \in P$ such that the language of $\langle p_0, p', d, \beta_1 \rangle$ is not empty, the language of $\langle p', p, d, \beta_2 \rangle$ is not empty, and we have $\{(\varepsilon, \langle p_0, p', d, \beta_1 \rangle), (\varepsilon, \langle p', p, d, \beta \rangle)\} \models \eta(\langle p_0, p, d, \alpha \rangle)$, we add the state $\langle p_0, p', d, \beta_1 \rangle$ to the transition $\Delta(\langle p_0, p, d, \alpha \rangle, \varepsilon)$.

This completes the definition of the automaton. In the full version we prove that N accepts $w \in \Upsilon^*$ in a state $p \in P$ iff S accepts $\langle \Upsilon^*, \tau \rangle$ from (p, w).

5 Global Model Checking

In this section we solve the global model-checking problem by a reduction to the global membership problem. The constructions are somewhat different from the constructions in [KV00,KPV02] as we use the global-membership of 2APT and 2NBP instead of the emptiness of 2APT and membership of 2NBP. We start with branching time model checking and then proceed to linear time.

Consider a rewrite system $R = \langle \Sigma, V, Q, L, T \rangle$. Recall that a configuration of R is a pair $(q, x) \in Q \times V^*$. Thus, the store x corresponds to a node in the full infinite V-tree. An automaton that reads the tree V^* can memorize in its state space the state component of the configuration and refer to the location of its reading head in V^* as the store. We would like the automaton to "know" the location of its reading head in V^*. A straightforward way to do so is to label a node $x \in V^*$ by x. This, however, involves an infinite alphabet. We show that labeling every node in V^* by its direction is sufficiently informative to provide the 2APT with the information it needs in order to simulate transitions of the rewrite system. Let $\langle V^*, \tau_v \rangle$ be the tree where $\tau_v(x) = dir(x)$.

Theorem 4. *Given a pushdown or a prefix-recognizable system $R = \langle \Sigma, V, Q, L, T \rangle$ and a graph automaton $\mathcal{W} = \langle \Sigma, W, w_0, \delta, F \rangle$, we can construct a 2APT $\mathcal{A}$ on V-trees and a function f that associates states of $\mathcal{A}$ with states of R such that $\mathcal{A}$ accepts $\langle V^*, \tau_v \rangle$ from (p, x) iff $G_R^{(f(p), x)} \models \mathcal{W}$. The automaton $\mathcal{A}$ has $O(|Q| \cdot \|T\| \cdot |V|)$ states, and has the same index as $\mathcal{W}$.*

The construction in Theorem 4 reduces the global model-checking problem to the global membership problem of a 2APT. By Theorem 2, we then have the following.

Theorem 5. *Global model-checking for a pushdown or a prefix-recognizable system $R = \langle \Sigma, V, Q, L, T \rangle$ and a graph automaton $W = \langle \Sigma, W, w_0, \delta, F \rangle$, can be solved in time exponential in nk, where $n = |Q| \cdot \|T\| \cdot |V|$ and k is the index of W.*

According to [Wil99], we can conclude with an EXPTIME bound also for the global model-checking problem of μ-calculus formulas, matching the lower bound in [Wal96]. Note that the fact the same complexity bound holds for pushdown and prefix-recognizable rewrite systems stems from the different definition of $\|T\|$ in the two cases.

We now turn to linear time specifications. As branching time model-checking is exponential in the system and linear time model-checking is polynomial in the system, we do not want to reduce linear time model-checking to branching time model-checking.

As before, the 2NBP reads the full infinite V-tree. It uses its location as the store and memorizes as part of its state the state of the rewrite system. For pushdown systems it is sufficient to label a node in the tree by its direction. For prefix-recognizable systems we label a node x, in addition to its direction, by the regular expressions β for which $x \in \beta$. We denote this tree by $\langle V^*, \tau_\beta \rangle$ and its size is exponential in $|Q_\beta|$.

Theorem 6. *Given a pushdown or a prefix-recognizable system $R = \langle \Sigma, V, Q, L, T \rangle$ and an NBW $N = \langle \Sigma, W, w_0, \eta, F \rangle$, we can construct a 2NBP S on V-trees and a function f that associates states of S with states of R such that S accepts $\langle V^*, \tau_V \rangle$ (or $\langle V^*, \tau_\beta \rangle$) from (s, x) iff $G_R^{(f(s),x)} \models N$. The size of the transition function of S is $O(\|T\| \cdot |N|)$ and it has $O(|Q| \cdot \|T\| \cdot |N|)$ states in the case of pushdown systems, and $O(|Q| \cdot (|Q_\alpha| + |Q_\gamma|) \cdot |T| \cdot |N|)$ states in the case of prefix-recognizable systems.*

Combining Theorem 3 and Theorem 6 we get the following.

Theorem 7. *Global model-checking for a rewrite system R and NBW N is solvable in time $O((\|T\| \cdot |N|)^3)$ and space $O((\|T\| \cdot |N|)^2)$ when R is a pushdown system and in time $(\|T\| \cdot |N|)^3 \cdot 2^{O(|Q_\beta|)}$ and space $(|T| \cdot |N|)^2 \cdot 2^{O(|Q_\beta|)}$ when R is a prefix-recognizable system.*

Our complexity coincides with the one in [EHRS00], for pushdown systems, and with the result of combining [EKS01] and [KPV02], for prefix-recognizable systems.

6   Conclusions

We have shown how to extend the automata-theoretic approach to model-checking infinite state sequential rewrite systems to global model-checking. In doing so we have shown that the restriction of automata-theoretic methods to local model-checking is not an inherent restriction of this approach. Our algorithms generalize previous automata-theoretic algorithms for local model-checking [KV00,KPV02]. The complexity of our algorithm matchs the complexity bounds of previous algorithms for global model-checking [EHRS00,EKS01,KPV02,Cac02] and show that a uniform solution exists in the automata-theoretic framework.

We believe that our algorithms generalize also to *micro-macro stack systems* [PV03] and to high order pushdown systems [KNU03,Cac03] as the algorithms for local model-checking over these types of systems are also automata-theoretic.

References

[ATM03]   R. Alur, S. La Torre, and P. Madhusudan. Modular strategies for infinite games on recursive game graphs. In *15th CAV*, *LNCS* 2725, 67–79, Springer-Verlag, 2003.

[BCM$^+$92]   J.R. Burch, E.M. Clarke, K.L. McMillan, D.L. Dill, and L.J. Hwang. Symbolic model checking: 10^{20} states and beyond. *IC*, 98(2):142–170, 1992.

[BQ96]   O. Burkart and Y.-M. Quemener. Model checking of infinite graphs defined by graph grammars. In *1st Infinity*, *ENTCS* 6, 1996.

[BR00]   T. Ball and S. Rajamani. Bebop: A symbolic model checker for boolean programs. In *7th SPIN Workshop*, *LNCS* 1885, 113–130, 2000. Springer.

[BS92]   O. Burkart and B. Steffen. Model checking for context-free processes. In *3rd Concur*, *LNCS* 630, 123–137. Springer, 1992.

[BS95]   O. Burkart and B. Steffen. Composition, decomposition and model checking of pushdown processes. *Nordic J. Comput.*, 2:89–125, 1995.

[Büc62]   J.R. Büchi. On a decision method in restricted second order arithmetic. In *Proc. Internat. Congr. Logic, Method. and Philos. Sci. 1960*, pages 1–12, 1962.

[Bur97]   O. Burkart. Model checking rationally restricted right closures of recognizable graphs. In *2nd Infinity*, 1997.

[Cac02]   T. Cachat. Uniform solution of parity games on prefix-recognizable graphs. In *4th Infinity*, *ENTCS* 68(6), 2002.

[Cac03]   T. Cachat. Higher order pushdown automata, the Caucal hierarchy of graphs and parity games. In *30th ICALP*, *LNCS* 2719, 556–569, 2003. Springer.

[Cau96]   D. Caucal. On infinite transition graphs having a decidable monadic theory. In *23rd ICALP*, volume 1099 of *LNCS*, 194–205. Springer, 1996.

[CES86]   E.M. Clarke, E.A. Emerson, and A.P. Sistla. Automatic verification of finite-state concurrent systems using temporal logic specifications. *TOPLAS*, 8(2), 1986.

[CKKV01]   H. Chockler, O. Kupferman, R.P. Kurshan, and M.Y. Vardi. A practical approach to coverage in model checking. In *13th CAV*, *LNCS* 2102, 66–78. Springer, 2001.

[CVWY92]   C. Courcoubetis, M.Y. Vardi, P. Wolper, and M. Yannakakis. Memory efficient algorithms for the verification of temporal properties. *FMSD*, 1:275–288, 1992.

[CW02]   H. Chen and D. Wagner. Mops: an infrastructure for examining security properties of software. In *9th CCS*, 235–244, 2002. ACM.

[EHRS00]   J. Esparza, D. Hansel, P. Rossmanith, and S. Schwoon. Efficient algorithms for model checking pushdown systems. In *12th CAV*, *LNCS* 1855, 232–247, 2000. Springer.

[EJ91]   E.A. Emerson and C. Jutla. Tree automata, μ-calculus and determinacy. In *32nd FOCS*, 368–377, 1991.

[EJS93]   E.A. Emerson, C. Jutla, and A.P. Sistla. On model-checking for fragments of μ-calculus. In *5th CAV*, *LNCS* 697, 385–396, 1993. Springer.

[EKS01]   J. Esparza, A. Kucera, and S. Schwoon. Model-checking LTL with regular valuations for pushdown systems. In *4th STACS*, *LNCS* 2215, 316–339, 2001. Springer.

[Eme97]   E.A. Emerson. Model checking and the μ-calculus. In *Descriptive Complexity and Finite Models*, 185–214. AMS, 1997.

[ES01]   J. Esparza and S. Schwoon. A BDD-based model checker for recursive programs. In *13th CAV*, *LNCS* 2102, 324–336, 2001. Springer.

[JW95]   D. Janin and I. Walukiewicz. Automata for the modal μ-calculus and related results. In *20th MFCS*, em LNCS, 552–562. Springer, 1995.

[KNU03]   T. Knapik, D. Niwinski, and P. Urzyczyn. Higher-order pushdown trees are easy. In *5th FOSSACS*, LNCS 2303, 205–222, 2003. Springer.

[Koz83]   D. Kozen. Results on the propositional μ-calculus. *TCS*, 27:333–354, 1983.

[KPV02]   O. Kupferman, N. Piterman, and M.Y. Vardi. Model checking linear properties of prefix-recognizable systems. In *14th CAV*, LNCS 2404, 371–385. Springer, 2002.

[Kur94]   R.P. Kurshan. *Computer Aided Verification of Coordinating Processes*. 1994.

[KV00]   O. Kupferman and M.Y. Vardi. An automata-theoretic approach to reasoning about infinite-state systems. In *12th CAV*, LNCS 1855, 36–52. Springer, 2000.

[LBBO01]   Y. Lakhnech, S. Bensalem, S. Berezin, and S. Owre. Incremental verification by abstraction. In *7th TACAS*, LNCS 2031, 98–112, 2001. Springer.

[MS85]   D.E. Muller and P.E. Schupp. The theory of ends, pushdown automata, and second-order logic. *TCS*, 37:51–75, 1985.

[MS87]   D.E. Muller and P.E. Schupp. Alternating automata on infinite trees. *TCS*, 54, 1987.

[Pnu77]   A. Pnueli. The temporal logic of programs. In *18th FOCS*, 46–57, 1977.

[PRZ01]   A. Pnueli, S. Ruah, and L. Zuck. Automatic deductive verification with invisible invariants. In *7th TACAS*, LNCS 2031, 82–97, 2001. Springer.

[PV03]   N. Piterman and M.Y. Vardi. Micro-macro stack systems: A new frontier of decidability for sequential systems. In *18th LICS*, 381–390, 2003. IEEE.

[Rab72]   M.O. Rabin. Automata on infinite objects and Church's problem. *AMS*, 1972.

[SW91]   C. Stirling and D. Walker. Local model checking in the modal μ-calculus. *TCS*, 89(1):161–177, 1991.

[Var98]   M.Y. Vardi. Reasoning about the past with two-way automata. In *25th ICALP*, 1998.

[VW94]   M.Y. Vardi and P. Wolper. Reasoning about infinite computations. *IC*, 115(1), 1994.

[Wal96]   I. Walukiewicz. Pushdown processes: games and model checking. In *8th CAV*, 1996.

[Wil99]   T. Wilke. CTL$^+$ is exponentially more succinct than CTL. In *19th FSTTCS*, 1999.

QB or Not QB: An Efficient Execution Verification Tool for Memory Orderings*

Ganesh Gopalakrishnan, Yue Yang, and Hemanthkumar Sivaraj

School of Computing, University of Utah
{ganesh,yyang,hemanth}@cs.utah.edu

Abstract. We study the problem of formally verifying shared memory multiprocessor executions against memory consistency models – an important step during post-silicon verification of multiprocessor machines. We employ our previously reported style of writing formal specifications for shared memory models in higher order logic (HOL), obtaining intuitive as well as modular specifications. Our specification consists of a conjunction of rules that constrain the *global visibility order*. Given an execution to be checked, our algorithm generates Boolean constraints that capture the conditions under which the execution is legal under the visibility order. We initially took the approach of specializing the memory model HOL axioms into equivalent (for the execution to be checked) quantified boolean formulae (QBF). As this technique proved inefficient, we took the alternative approach of converting the HOL axioms into a program that generates a SAT instance when run on an execution. In effect, the quantifications in our memory model specification were realized as iterations in the program. The generated Boolean constraints are satisfiable if and only if the given execution is legal under the memory model. We evaluate two different approaches to encode the Boolean constraints, and also incremental techniques to generate and solve Boolean constraints. Key results include a demonstration that we can handle executions of realistic lengths for the modern Intel Itanium memory model. Further research into proper selection of Boolean encodings, incremental SAT checking, efficient handling of transitivity, and the generation of unsatisfiable cores for locating errors are expected to make our technique practical.

1 Introduction

In many areas of computer design, formal verification has virtually eliminated logical bugs escaping into detailed designs (including silicon). However, in areas where the system complexity is high, and global interactions among large collections of subsystems govern the overall behavior, formal verification cannot yet cope with the complex models involved. The verification of multiprocessor machines for conformance to shared memory consistency models [1] is one such area. This paper focuses on verifying whether multiprocessor executions violate

* Supported by NSF Grant CCR-0081406 and SRC Contract 1031.001

R. Alur and D.A. Peled (Eds.): CAV 2004, LNCS 3114, pp. 401–413, 2004.

memory ordering rules. These executions may be obtained from multiprocessor simulators or from real machines. The current practice is to employ well-chosen test programs to obtain a collection of "interesting" executions from machines and simulators. These executions are then examined using *ad hoc* "checker" programs. Our contribution is to make the second step formal.

It is crucially important that multiprocessor machines and simulators conform to their memory models. Future high performance operating systems will exploit relaxed memory orderings to enhance performance; they will fail if the multiprocessor deviates from its memory model. However, as far as we know from the literature, none of the existing methods can *verify* executions against formal descriptions of industrial memory models. A tool such as what we propose can also help designers comprehend a given memory model by executing critical code fragments. Given that industrial memory models are extremely complex, an efficient execution verification facility is very important in practice.

In this paper, we show that Boolean satisfiability (SAT) based tools can be developed for verifying executions of realistic lengths. Our current work is aimed at the Intel Itanium memory model [2]; the technique is, however, general. Given a shared memory multiprocessor execution, e, and a formal specification of the memory model as logical axioms, r, we offer a formal technique to verify whether e is allowed under r. By the term *execution*, we mean multiprocessor assembly programs over *loads*, *stores*, *fences*, and other memory operations, with the *loads* annotated with returned values. The actual assembly program run on a machine may consist of instructions other than *loads* and *stores*; it may, for instance, include branches and arithmetic operations. In those cases, e retains a dynamic trace of just the *load* and *store* group of instructions, with the *loads* annotated with their returned values. In this paper, we will depict e in the form of assembly programs consisting of only *load* and *store* instructions, with the *loads* annotated with the returned values (such annotated programs are called "litmus tests"). We do not discuss here how such dynamic traces can be obtained.

Gibbons and Korach [3] have shown that the problem of checking executions against sequential consistency [4] is NP-complete. Generalizing this result, Cantin [5] has shown that the problem of checking executions against memory ordering rules that contain coherence as a sub-rule is NP-hard. Since the Itanium memory model contains coherence, and since executions serve as polynomial certificates that can be checked against the rules in polynomial time, we have an NP-complete problem at hand. Despite these results, we initially found it natural to employ a quantified boolean formula (QBF) [6] satisfiability checker. This is because of two facts: (i) the Itanium memory model is quite complex, and to write a formal specification in a declarative and intuitive style, we employed higher order logic (HOL) [7–9]; (ii) since we wanted to have a trustworthy checking algorithm, we took the approach of *specializing* the HOL description to a QBF description so as to check e. This specialization is natural, given that r captures the memory model in terms of quantifiers that range over program counters, addresses, and data values that have arbitrary ranges, whereas e has these quantities occurring in it over a finite range. However, the direct use of a

```
P0: st a,1;            ld r1,a <1>; st b,r1 <1>;
P1: ld.acq r2,b <1>; ld r3,a <0>;
```

[{id=0;proc=0; pc=0; op=St; var=0; data=1; wrID=0;
    wrType=Local; wrProc=0; reg=-1; useReg=false};
{id=1; proc=0; pc=0; op=St; var=0; data=1; wrID=0;
    wrType=Remote; wrProc=0; reg=-1; useReg=false};
{id=2; proc=0; pc=0; op=St; var=0; data=1; wrID=0;
    wrType=Remote; wrProc=1; reg=-1; useReg=false};
{id=3; proc=0; pc=1; op=Ld; var=0; data=1; wrID=-1;
    wrType=-1; wrProc=-1; reg=0; useReg=true};
{id=4; proc=0; pc=2; op=St; var=1; data=1; wrID=4;
    wrType=Local; wrProc=0; reg=0; useReg=true};
{id=5; proc=0; pc=2; op=St; var=1; data=1; wrID=4;
    wrType=Remote; wrProc=0; reg=0; useReg=true};
{id=6; proc=0; pc=2; op=St; var=1; data=1; wrID=4;
    wrType=Remote; wrProc=1; reg=0; useReg=true};
{id=7; proc=1; pc=0; op=LdAcq; var=1; data=1; wrID=-1;
    wrType=-1; wrProc=-1; reg=1; useReg=true};
{id=8; proc=1; pc=1; op=Ld; var=0; data=0; wrID=-1;
    wrType=-1; wrProc=-1; reg=2; useReg=true}]

Fig. 1. The execution of a multiprocessor assembly program, and the tuples it generates.

QBF solver[10] proved to be of impractical complexity. Therefore, we pursue the following alternative approach. We first derive a mostly[1] applicative functional program p from r . Program p captures the quantifications present in r via iterative loops (tail-recursive calls). It also stages the evaluation of the conditionals in an efficient manner. Such a program p, when run on execution e, evaluates all the *ground* constraints (constraints without free variables) efficiently by direct execution, and generates non-ground constraints in the form of a SAT instance b which is satisfiable if and only if e is allowed under r. Further we demonstrate that the derivation of p can be automated in a straightforward manner.

Related Work: Park et.al. [11] wrote an operational description of the Sparc V9 [12] memory models in Murphi [13] and used it to check assembly language executions. It is our experience is that this approach does not scale beyond a dozen or so instructions; it is also our experience that specifications for memory models as intricate as the Itanium are very difficult to develop using the operational approach [14]. Since our HOL specification follows the axiomatic style used in Intel's description [2], it can be more easily trusted. It also can be formally examined using theorem provers to enhance our confidence in it. In [15],

---

[1] The only imperative operations are file I/O.

we show that a whole range of memory models can be described in the same HOL style as we use here.

Yu [16] captured memory ordering rules for the Alpha microprocessor [12] as first-order axioms. Given an execution to be checked, they generated verification conditions for the decision procedure Simplify [17]. We believe that the use of SAT for this application will scale better.

In previous work [18], we presented the higher order logic specification of the Itanium memory model and its realization as a *constraint logic program*. We also sketched an approach to generate Boolean satisfiability constraints. Three major problems remained: (i) the constraint logic program version was unable to handle more than about 20 tuples (a dozen or so instructions); (ii) the SAT version was extremely difficult to debug owing to it being retrofitted into a logic program; (iii) since the logic program did not exploit the nature of the higher order logic axioms, it took far more time to generate SAT instances than to solve them – often with a ratio of 200:1. The present work is an improvement in all these regards and also offers several new directions. In particular, it offers a reliable formal derivation scheme to obtain the SAT instance generation program. This program can handle much longer executions – about 300 tuples. The SAT instances generated from such executions can be solved using SAT tools in reasonable time, thanks to the care exercised in selecting the Boolean encoding method. We have also identified many avenues to scale the capacity of our tool further.

2   Overview of Our Approach

As a simple example, consider the litmus test shown in Figure 1. Processor P0 issues a store (st) instruction to location a with data value 1. It then issues a load (ld) to location a, which fetches the value 1 into register r1 (shown via the annotation <1>). It then stores the contents of register r1 into location b (we show the value annotation <1> here also, as we can compute the value in r1 at this point). Processor P1 issues a *load acquire* (ld.acq) instruction to begin with. This fetches value 1 from location b into register r2. It then performs an ordinary ld instruction, obtaining 0 from location a that is stored into r3. The only strongly ordered operation in this whole program is ld.acq. Itanium rules require that the visibility of ld.acq must be before the visibility of all the instructions following it in program order (i.e., ld.acq acts as a "one-way barrier"). The question now is: "is this execution legal?"

Modeling Executions Using Tuples: Following earlier approaches [2, 19], we employ a set of tuples to model executions. One tuple is employed to capture the attributes of each ld instruction, and $p + 1$ tuples are employed to model the attributes of each st or st.rel instruction, where there are p processors in the multiprocessor (Figure 1). In our example, each store generates three tuples, giving us a total of nine tuples[2]. Of the $p + 1$ tuples modeling a store (st), one

---

[2] We have written an assembler to generate tuples from annotated assembly programs.

legal(ops) =

∃$order.$

StrictTotalOrder	ops $order$ ∧	**WriteOperationOrder**	ops $order$ ∧
ItProgramOrder	ops $order$ ∧	**MemoryDataDependence**	ops $order$ ∧
DataFlowDependence	ops $order$ ∧	**Coherence**	ops $order$ ∧
ReadValue	ops $order$ ∧	**AtomicWBRelease**	ops $order$ ∧
SequentialUC	ops $order$ ∧	**NoUCBypass**	ops $order$

StrictTotalOrder ops $order$ =   **IrreflexiveOrder** ops $order$
     ∧   **TransitiveOrder** ops $order$
     ∧   **TotallyOrdered** ops $order$

Irreflexive ops $order$ =   ∀($i ∈ ops$). ∀($j ∈ ops$). (i.**id** = j.**id**) ⇒ ¬$order$ i j

Transitive ops $order$ =   ∀($i ∈ ops$). ∀($j ∈ ops$). ∀($k ∈ ops$).
     ($order$ i j ∧ $order$ j k ⇒ $order$ i k)

TotallyOrdered ops $order$ =   ∀($i ∈ ops$). ∀($j ∈ ops$). ($i ∈ ops$) ∧ ($j ∈ ops$). ∧ ¬(i.**id** = j.**id**)
     ⇒ $order$ i j ∨ $order$ j i

ItProgramOrder ops $order$ =   ∀($i ∈ ops$). ∀($j ∈ ops$).
     ordByAcquire i j ∨ **ordByRelease** i j ∨ **ordByFence** i j
     ⇒ $order$ i j

ordByAcquire i j =   **ordByProgram** i j ∧ (i.**op** = **LdAcq**)

ordByProgram i j =   (i.**proc** = j.**proc**) ∧ i.**pc** < j.**pc**

ReadValue ops $order$ =   ∀($j ∈ ops$).
     (**isRd** j ⇒
       validLocalWr ops $order$ j
       ∨ **validRemoteWr** ops $order$ j
       ∨ **validDefaultWr** ops $order$ j)
     ∧ (**isWr** j ∧ j.**useReg** ⇒ **validRd** ops $order$ j)

validRd ops $order$ j =

     ∃($i ∈ ops$). **isRd** i ∧ (i.**reg** = j.**reg**) ∧ **ordByProgram** i j
     ∧(i.**data** = j.**data**)
     ∧ ¬(∃($k ∈ ops$). **isRd** k ∧ (k.**reg** = j.**reg**)
         ∧ **ordByProgram** i k ∧ **ordByProgram** k j)

atomicWBRelease ops $order$ =

     ∀($i ∈ ops$). ∀($j ∈ ops$). ∀($k ∈ ops$).
     (i.**op** = **StRel**) ∧ (i.**wrType** = **Remote**)
     ∧ (k.**op** = **StRel**) ∧ (k.**wrType** = **Remote**)
     ∧ (i.**wrID** = k.**wrID**) ∧ (**attr_of** i.**var** = **WB**)
     ∧ $order$ i j ∧ $order$ j k
     ⇒ (j.**op** = **StRel**) ∧ (j.**wrType** = **Remote**)
       ∧ (j.**wrID** = i.**wrID**)

Fig. 2. Excerpts from the Itanium Ordering Rules (For the full spec, see [18]).

t0 t1 t2 t3

t0	$[ord_{01}, ord_{00}]$		t0	0		1
t1	$[ord_{11}, ord_{10}]$		t1		0	
t2	$[ord_{21}, ord_{20}]$		t2		0	
t3	$[ord_{31}, ord_{30}]$		t3			0

Fig. 3. Illustration of the *nlogn* (left) and *nn* (right) methods.

is a *local store* and the remaining p are global stores, one for each processor. For example, consider the tuples with id=0, id=1, and id=2. These are tuples coming from the store instruction of P0 (proc=0), have program counter pc=0, employ variable `var=0`, and have `data=1`. The `wrID=0` says that these store tuples come from the store instruction with `id=0`. To distinguish where these stores are observed, we employ the `wrProc` attribute, the values of which are 0, 0, and 1 respectively. Notice that the tuple with `id=0` has `wrType=Local`, and the one with `id=1` has `wrType=Remote`. ("Remote" means "global" in the parlance of [2]). Notice that we employ two tuples, namely the ones with `id=0` and `id=1`, both for the local processor `proc=0` (P0). This is to facilitate modeling the the the semantics of *load bypassing* – the ability of a processor to read its own store early. For details, please see [2, 18].

The modeling details associated with *load* instructions are much simpler. We simply employ one tuple per `ld` or `ld.acq` instruction. The `useReg` field captures whether a register is involved, and the `reg` field indicates which register is involved. All fields with `-1` are don't-cares.

Overview of the Itanium Ordering Rules: Figure 2 provides roughly a fourth of the Itanium ordering rules from our full specification. The legality of an execution is checked by **legal** *ops*, where *ops* is the collection of tuples obtained from an execution, such as in Figure 1. Note how *order*, a binary relation, is passed around and constrained by all the ordering rules. Basically, the definition consists of four distinct parts: (i) **StrictTotalOrder**, which seeks one arrangement of the tuples into a strict total order, (ii) **ReadValue**, which checks that all reads in this strict total order either return the value associated with the most recent (in the strict total order) write to the same location, or the initial store values, if there is no write to that location, (iii) **ItProgramOrder**, which is weakened program order that orders instructions only if one of them is an *acquire*, a *release* or a *fence*, and (iv) all the remaining rules which try to recover some modicum of program order. For instance, an instruction *i* is ordered before an instruction *j* if *i* is of type *ld.acq*, as captured by the **ordByAcquire** rule.

This style of specification, adopted by [2], makes it easier to contrast it with sequential consistency. For instance, if we change **ItProgramOrder** into a regular program order relation, and retain **ReadValue** and **StrictTotalOrder**, we obtain sequential consistency. Since the combination of **ItProgramOrder** and the rules mentioned in (iv) above is weaker than the regular program order relation, the Itanium memory model allows *more* solutions under **StrictTotalOrder** than with regular sequential consistency. Hence the Itanium memory model is weaker than sequential consistency. However, the variety of instructions allowed under Itanium is more than just *load* and *store*. Hence, we can only hope to make qualitative comparisons between these models.

Overview of Boolean Encoding: As far as the relation **legal** goes, *ops* of Figure 1 is to be viewed as a set of tuples. Notice that **StrictTotalOrder** seeks to arrange the elements of *ops* into a strict total order such that the remaining constraints are met (the arrangement of the elements of *ops* is captured in the *order* relation). Total ordering among n tuples can be encoded using auxiliary Boolean variables in two obvious ways (Figure 3, also see [20] where these are called the *small domain* and the e_{ij} approaches): (i) the *nlogn* approach, in which a bit-vector of $\log(n)$ Boolean variables of the form $[ord_{i,j-1} \ldots ord_{i,0}]$ are augmented to the ith tuple (example tuples are shown as t0 through t3 in the figure). Here, n is the number of tuples, assumed to be a power of 2, and $j = \log_2(n)$; (ii) the *nn* approach, in which n^2 Boolean variables (denoted by $matrix_{ij}$, with $0 \leq i, j < n$) are introduced to represent how tuples are ordered. In the *nlogn* approach, **StrictTotalOrder** is implemented by the constraint $[ord_{i,\log_2(n)-1}, \ldots, ord_{i,0}] \neq [ord_{j,\log_2(n)-1}, \ldots, ord_{j,0}]$ for all $i \neq j$. In the *nn* approach, **StrictTotalOrder** is implemented via its constituents: **irreflexive, transitive,** and **totallyOrdered**. Constraint **irreflexive** is encoded by setting the diagonal elements of the matrix to 0. Constraint **transitive** is encoded by generating the formula $(matrix_{ij} \wedge matrix_{jk}) \Rightarrow matrix_{ik}$. Constraint **totallyOrdered** is encoded by generating the formula $matrix_{ij} \vee matrix_{ji}$.

The size of the formula which encodes **StrictTotalOrder** for the *nn* method is far greater than for the *nlogn* method. This is largely because of the transitivity axiom where we go through every triple of tuples and generate the transitivity clause. We plan to investigate other methods discussed in [20]. One key difference between our work and that of [20] is that in their setting, a collection of first-order equational formulae (or more generally speaking, formulae in *separation logic* involving $=$, $\geq$, and $<$) are to be checked for validity. In doing so, transitivity is applied over the given set of equations. In our case, we are *solving* for an *order* over the tuples. The number of these tuples is expected to be far higher. In a sense, our method searches for the few permutations of the given sequence of tuples that are consistent with the memory ordering rules. We hope to investigate lazy approaches to handling transitivity as discussed in Section 5.

A significant advantage of the *nn* method over the *nlogn* method in our context is that it generates much smaller formulae for the rest of the constraints other than transitivity. For example, suppose while processing a memory ordering rule we have to specify that some tuple, say t0, appears before another tuple, say t3, in any allowed total order. This encoding is achieved by $[ord_{01} ord_{00}] < [ord_{31} ord_{30}]$ in the *nlogn* method, while simply achieved by asserting $matrix_{03}$ in the *nn* method (see Figure 3 for a '1' in the matrix). These trade-offs are studied in Section 4. In effect, we found that despite the use of n^2 variables as opposed to $nlog(n)$, the *nn* method is more efficient during SAT checking. Similar results are obtained in [20] where SAT-checking is often faster under their e_{ij} method (similar to our *nn* method) than their small domain method (similar to our *nlogn* method).

In post-silicon verification, tests on multiprocessor machines are run multiple times in the hope of obtaining different load values due to non-deterministic interleavings. This naturally fits with the use of incremental SAT methods for execution verification.

3   Program Derivation from Memory Ordering Rules

We provide an example of how one rule of Itanium, namely **atomicWBRelease**, is transformed into a program; all other rules are handled similarly. The initial specification is in Figure 2. Recall from Section 1 that for every store instruction, we generate $p + 1$ stores, of which p are considered 'remote stores.' Rule **atomicWBRelease** says that all these remote stores form an 'atomic packet' in the sense that any other event e is strictly before or strictly after all the events in this packet. Notice how it is specified by the following axiom which says: if j is an event 'trapped' between i and k, then j also belongs to the atomic packet of all remote stores. (A note about our notation: we use the generic *order* relation to denote a total order over the set of tuple operations **ops**. When it comes to specifically generating the Boolean constraints, we choose *ord* or *matrix* depending on the encoding method used. This difference shows up in Table 1(e) in part b_2 of the results.)

We now pre-process this specification by applying the contrapositive rule. The general idea is to bring ground constraints to the antecedent so that we can evaluate them through direct execution. The SAT instances can then be generated from the consequent part. The result of this step is a formula with three outermost quantifiers (Figure 4, before *Quantifier Scope Reduction*). If we translate this directly into loops, we will obtain a very inefficient program. The *Quantifier Scope Reduction* step takes advantage of the limited scope of various sub-formulae and rewrites the quantified expression into a series of staged quantifications. This will allow many iterations of outer loops to be cut-off early, thus not suffering from the full brunt of the $O(n^3)$ complexity. This dramatically reduced our SAT-generation time. For example, $i.op = \textbf{StRel}$ depends only on i, and so the inner loops are not called for all those instructions that do not pass this test.

The last stage of our translation (*SAT-generation program sketch*) obtains a series of tail-recursive functions capturing the semantics of the quantified expression. Here, *foldr* reduces a given list of arguments (generated by *map*) using conjunction; this is because conjunction is the explicitly provided second operation '&' for *foldr*. The list that is reduced is obtained by mapping the function (**fn** $i \rightarrow e(i)$) (a Lambda abstraction) on the given list. Forms such as $f(i)(j)$ are employed as opposed to $f(i,j)$ to signify *currying* [21]. The main difference between the sketch we provide and the actual Ocaml [22] code we employ is that the latter emits constraints on-the-fly to a file instead of building an expression tree using **foldr** as shown in our sketch.

4   Results

Our program handles all the 17 litmus tests given in [2] except a few that involve partial word writes that are currently omitted. These tests ran considerably faster than those in [18].

Next, we considered executions with 32, 64, and 128 tuples in our experiments. The complexity of our algorithm depends primarily on the number of

atomicWBRelease($ops, order$) =
$\forall(i \in ops). \forall(j \in ops). \forall(k \in ops).$
$(i.\mathbf{op} = \mathbf{StRel}) \wedge (i.\mathbf{wrType} = \mathbf{Remote})$
$\wedge (k.\mathbf{op} = \mathbf{StRel}) \wedge (k.\mathbf{wrType} = \mathbf{Remote})$
$\wedge (i.\mathbf{wrID} = k.\mathbf{wrID}) \wedge (\mathbf{attr\_of}\ i.\mathbf{var} = \mathbf{WB})$
$\wedge \neg((j.\mathbf{op} = \mathbf{StRel}) \wedge (j.\mathbf{wrType} = \mathbf{Remote})\ \wedge (j.\mathbf{wrID} = i.\mathbf{wrID}))$
$\Rightarrow \neg(order(i, j) \wedge order(j, k))$

Quantifier Scope Reduction

atomicWBRelease($ops, order$) =
$\forall(i \in ops).$
$\quad (i.\mathbf{op} = \mathbf{StRel}) \wedge (i.\mathbf{wrType} = \mathbf{Remote})$
$\quad \wedge(\mathbf{attr\_of}\ i.\mathbf{var} = \mathbf{WB})$
$\quad \Rightarrow\ \forall(k \in ops).$
$\qquad (k.\mathbf{op} = \mathbf{StRel}) \wedge (k.\mathbf{wrType} = \mathbf{Remote})\ \wedge (i.\mathbf{wrID} = k.\mathbf{wrID})$
$\qquad \Rightarrow\ \forall(j \in ops).$
$\qquad\quad \neg((j.\mathbf{op} = \mathbf{StRel})$
$\qquad\qquad \wedge (j.\mathbf{wrType} = \mathbf{Remote})$
$\qquad\qquad \wedge(j.\mathbf{wrID} = i.\mathbf{wrID}))$
$\qquad\qquad \Rightarrow \neg(order(i, j) \wedge order(j, k))$

SAT-generation program sketch

atomicWBRelease(ops) = **forall**($i, ops, \mathbf{wb}(i)$);
$\mathbf{wb}(i)$ = **if**($\neg((\mathbf{attr\_of}\ i.\mathbf{var} = \mathbf{WB})$ & $(i.\mathbf{op} = \mathbf{StRel})$ & $(i.\mathbf{wrType} = \mathbf{Remote})))$
    then *true* **else** **forall**($k, ops, \mathbf{wb1}(i)(k)$);
$\mathbf{wb1}(i)(k)$ = **if**($\neg((k.\mathbf{op} = \mathbf{StRel})$ & $(k.\mathbf{wrType} = \mathbf{Remote})$ & $(i.\mathbf{wrID} = k.\mathbf{wrID})))$
    then *true* **else** **forall**($j, ops, \mathbf{wb2}(i)(k)(j)$);
$\mathbf{wb2}(i)(k)(j)$ = **if**($(j.\mathbf{op} = \mathbf{StRel})$ & $(j.\mathbf{wrType} = \mathbf{Remote})$ & $(j.\mathbf{wrID} = i.\mathbf{wrID}))$
    then *true* **else** $\neg(order(i, j)$ & $order(j, k))$;
forall($i, S, e(i)$) = **foldr**(**map**(**fn** $i \to e(i))(S)$, &, *true*)

Fig. 4. Sketch of SAT-generation Program Derivation.

tuples, and far less on the remaining attributes of the tuples. Thus, checking 8 tuples over 2 processors has nearly the same complexity as checking 2 tuples over 8 processors. We selected the instruction mix heavily skewed towards *stores* to reflect a worst-case behavior (more rules pertain to stores than loads). All runs were on an AMD Athlon XP2100+ CPU (1.733 GHz, 1GB memory, Red Hat Linux V.9). We used the Satzoo incremental solver [23].

We evaluated two approaches, one generating and solving the constraints monolithically, and the other using partial evaluation. To motivate the latter approach, note that the constraints generated from **TotallyOrdered** depends on the number of tuples – and not on the contents of the tuples. Capitalizing on this fact, we pre-generated the constraints pertaining to **TotallyOrdered** for various lengths; call these constraints b_{1n}, where n represents the number of tuples anticipated in a test program to be given in future. We then loaded these

Table 1. Result Tables.

(a). SAT generation times for *nlogn* encoding (parts b_1 and b_2).

#tuples	Part b_1			Part b_2		
	time (secs)	#vars	#clauses	time (secs)	#vars	#clauses
32	0.219	20,992	68,448	1.635	92,316	258,632
64	1.213	101,184	330,624	17.178	852,632	2,387,664
128	5.748	472,320	1,544,320	179.026	7,777,200	21,775,520

(b). SAT generation times for *nn* encoding

#tuples	Part b_1			Part b_2		
	time (secs)	#vars	#clauses	time (secs)	#vars	#clauses
32	0.509	67,552	233,376	0.100	8,044	22,760
64	4.311	532,416	1,851,200	0.967	63,832	179,792
128	34.255	4,226,944	14,745,216	9.095	509,104	1,431,200

(c). 'Monolithic' gives the SAT solver execution time for the full SAT instance. Column Part b_1 gives the SAT time for part b_1. Part b_2 gives the time for SAT after resuming from the checkpoint and adding the new constraints.

#tuples	*nlogn* encoding			*nn* encoding		
	monolithic	Part b_1	Part b_2	monolithic	Part b_1	Part b_2
32	9.61	0.6	4.3	0.33	0.69	0.05
64	247.17	29.53	37.6	2.73	6.17	0.5
128	aborted	1341.85	aborted	164.8	145.64	351.1

(d). *nlogn* encoding: 1-Cl, 2-Cl, and 3-Cl give the percentage of clauses with one, two and three literals.

#tuples	Part 1			Part b_2		
	1-Cl (%)	2-Cl (%)	3-Cl (%)	1-Cl (%)	2-Cl (%)	3-Cl (%)
32	1.449	46.376	52.173	0.064	71.387	28.547
64	1.219	46.341	52.439	0.024	71.419	28.555
128	1.052	46.315	52.631	0.010	71.430	28.559

(e). *nn* encoding: 1-Cl, 2-Cl, and 3-Cl give the percentage of clauses with one, two and three literals.

#tuples	Part b_1			Part b_2		
	1-Cl (%)	2-Cl (%)	3-Cl (%)	1-Cl (%)	2-Cl (%)	3-Cl (%)
32	14.479	57.013	28.506	0.738	70.685	28.576
64	14.382	57.078	28.539	0.329	71.006	28.664
128	14.333	57.110	28.555	0.154	71.143	28.702

constraints into the SAT solver, and created the checkpoint of a runnable image of the SAT solver using the `ckpt` tool [24][3]to obtain $ckpt_n$. Later, when presented with a litmus test of length n, we only generated the *remaining* constraints (other than $TotallyOrdered$) for it; call the resulting constraints b_{2n}. We then ran $ckpt_{1n}$ on b_{2n}. Table 1(a) provides the time to generate SAT instances for the *nlogn* encoding method for formula parts b_1 and b_2. Table 1(b) provides these for the *nn* encoding method. Table 1(c) gives the SAT solving time for the *nn* and *nlogn* methods for a monolithic run, and for running parts b_1 and b_2 separately.

The results show that under the *nn* encoding, it takes longer to generate SAT instances for part b_1, but considerably shorter for part b_2. The main reason is that in our implementation, the number of clauses nc grows as $7n^3 + \ldots$ and the number of variables as $2n^3 + \ldots$ (later code improvements have brought down nc to $n^3 + \ldots$). The SAT solving times are uniformly lower for the *nn* method. This is because of the preponderance of clauses with smaller numbers of literals, as shown in Tables 1(d) and 1(e). In particular, part b_2 of *nn* encoding has both lower number of clauses and a higher proportion of clauses with 1 or 2 literals than the *nlogn* encoding. To summarize: (i) The *nn* encoding is better in terms of SAT solving time. The SAT generation time is acceptably small till about 128 tuples. (ii) Verifying in two parts b_1 and b_2 can be advantageous for problems of reasonable sizes. The advantage is far more for the *nn* approach. (iii) Since the same test is re-run multiple times, partial evaluation and other incremental SAT techniques can play a crucial role in overall efficiency.

Recently we have run a more realistic test of 130 assembly language instructions[4]. These expanded into 239 tuples. Initially, since the constraint generation program could not handle the transitivity rule, we suppressed it, obtaining a SAT instance of 115,637 variables and 164,848 clauses. This SAT instance proved to be unsatisfiable. Upon deeper examination using the `Zcore` program (distributed with the latest Zchaff [25]), we discovered an unsatisfiable core of 9 clauses. By analyzing these clauses, it was discovered that the error we detected resulted from us forgetting to initialize the memory state prior to the test. Further experiments with these and other realistic tests are underway, and our latest results will be presented on our webpage [26].

To sum up, proper handling of transitivity is crucial to scale our tool further. Recent code optimizations have allowed us to handle this realistic example *without* suppressing transitivity. However, the complexity of transitivity still lurks – in the 400 tuples and above range as of now. Also, the use of unsatisfiability core generation tools can be of considerable help in finding the root cause of violations.

5   Concluding Remarks

We proposed a method for verifying shared memory multiprocessor executions where the reference semantics is that of shared memory consistency. We propose

---

[3] We resorted to binary checkpoints – as opposed to clause checkpoints – because the source code of Satzoo was not available.

[4] We are deeply indebted to Intel for providing us this test.

a method by which executions can be analyzed using programs that embody the shared memory consistency rules. The ground part of the constraints in these rules are evaluated by the program, and the non-ground parts are emitted as Boolean constraints to check.

Semaphores are currently omitted to retain focus on the overall scalability and usability of our tool. Partial-word writes are also not handled. These extensions are planned for the future. A rudimentary assembler has been written to generate tuples from value-annotated assembly programs. This assembler can model data and address dependencies. The Itanium memory model rules in HOL were hand-translated into a series of tail-recursive programs; this process is best automated to ensure correctness, using the transformation rules illustrated earlier.

If the generated SAT instance is satisfiable, the space of satisfying assignments will reveal the set of allowed executions. Future work will annotate the Boolean constraints (clauses) with the instructions as well as memory ordering rules that generate them. This way, if the SAT instance is unsatisfiable, the unsatisfiability core will reveal which instructions and which memory ordering rules are causing the execution to be invalid. Incremental SAT techniques will be of great importance to develop, as are hierarchical analysis methods that treat groups of instructions atomically.

Better methods for handling transitivity are needed. One approach would be to see if SAT returns a satisfying instance when transitivity is suppressed, and if so to selectively introduce transitivity on those elements corresponding to the SAT instance. The ability to analyze *symbolic* executions (where not all the execution results are ground) would also enhance the usability of our tool.

Acknowledgements

We thank our SRC mentor Kushagra Vaid and his colleagues at Intel for their discussions and comments on our work. Thanks also to Konrad Slind and Gary Lindstrom for their contributions to our research.

References

1. Sarita V. Adve and Kourosh Gharachorloo. Shared memory consistency models: A tutorial. *Computer*, 29(12):66–76, December 1996.
2. A Formal Specification of Intel(R) Itanium(R) Processor Family Memory Ordering, 2002. http://www.intel.com/design/itanium/downloads/251429.htm.
3. Phillip B. Gibbons and Ephraim Korach. Testing shared memories. *SIAM Journal on Computing*, 26(4):1208–1244, August 1997.
4. L. Lamport. How to make a multiprocessor computer that correctly executes multi-process programs. *IEEE Transactions on Computers*, C-28(9):690–691, September 1979.
5. Jason F. Cantin, Mikko H. Lipasti, and James E. Smith. The complexity of verifying memory coherence. In *Proceedings of the fifteenth annual ACM symposium on Parallel algorithms and architectures (SPAA)*, pages 254 – 255, San Diego, 2003.

6. Michael Sipser. *Introduction to the Theory of Computation.* PWS Publishing Company, 1997.
7. Alonzo Church. A formulation of the simple theory of types. *Journal of Symbolic Logic,* 5:56–68, 1940.
8. F.K. Hanna and N. Daeche. Specification and verification using higher-order logic. In *7th International Conference on Computer Hardware Description Languages and their Applications,* pages 418–419, 1985.
9. Michael Gordon. Why higher-order logic is a good formalism for specifying and verifying hardware. In *Formal aspects of VLSI design,* 1986.
10. Lintao Zhang and Sharad Malik. Conflict driven learning in a quantified boolean satisfiability solver. In *Proceedings of International Conference on Computer Aided Design,* November 2002.
11. David L. Dill, Seungjoon Park, and Andreas Nowatzyk. Formal specification of abstract memory models. In *Research on Integrated Systems,* pages 38–52. MIT Press, 1993.
12. David L. Weaver and Tom Germond. *The SPARC Architecture Manual – Version 9.* P T R Prentice-Hall, 1994.
13. D. L. Dill, A, J. Drexler, A. J. Hu, and C. H. Yang. Protocol verification as a hardware design aid. In *Computer Aided Verification,* pages 522–525, 1992.
14. Prosenjit Chatterjee and Ganesh Gopalakrishnan. Towards a formal model of shared memory consistency for Intel Itanium. In *ICCD,* pages 515–518, 2001.
15. Yue Yang, Ganesh Gopalakrishnan, Gary Lindstrom, and Konrad Slind. Nemos: A framework for axiomatic and executable specifications of memory consistency models. In *International Parallel and Distributed Processing Symposium,* 2004.
16. Personal Communication with Yuan B. Yu.
17. G. Nelson and D.C. Oppen. Simplification by cooperating decision procedures. *ACM Transactions on Programming Languages and Systems,* 1(2):245–257, 1979.
18. Yue Yang, Ganesh Gopalakrishnan, Gary Lindstrom, and Konrad Slind. Analyzing the intel itanium memory ordering rules using logic programming and SAT. In *CHARME,* pages 81–95, 2003. LNCS 2860.
19. Anne Condon, Mark Hill, Manoj Plakal, and David Sorin. Using Lamport Clocks to Reason About Relaxed Memory Models. In *Fifth International Symposium On High Performance Computer Architecture (HPCA-5),* January 1999.
20. Sanjit A. Seshia, Shuvendu K. Lahiri, and Randal E. Bryant. A hybrid SAT-based decision procedure for separation logic with uninterpreted functions. In *Design Automation Conference (DAC),* pages 425–430, 2003.
21. Michael Gordon. *Programming Language Theory and Implementation.* Prentice-Hall, 1993.
22. www.ocaml.org.
23. Satzoo Incremental SAT Solver. Author: Niklas Een. Also competed in SAT'03. http://www.math.chalmers.se/~een/Satzoo/An_Extensible_SATsolver.ps.gz.
24. http://www.cs.wisc.edu/~zandy/ckpt/.
25. Lintao Zhang and Sharad Malik. The quest for efficient boolean satisfiability solvers. In *Computer Aided Verification,* pages 17–36, 2002. LNCS 2402.
26. http://www.cs.utah.edu/formal_verification.

Verification of an Advanced MIPS-Type Out-of-Order Execution Algorithm*

Tamarah Arons

The John von Neumann Minerva Center for Verification of Reactive Systems
Weizmann Institute of Science, Rehovot, Israel
tamarah.arons@weizmann.ac.il

Abstract. In this paper we propose a method for the deductive verification of out-of-order scheduling algorithms. We use TLPVS, our PVS model of *linear temporal logic* (LTL), to deductively verify the correctness of a model based on the Mips R10000 design. Our proofs use the *predicted values* method to verify a system including arithmetic and memory operations and speculation. In addition to the abstraction refinement traditionally used to verify safety properties, we also use fairness constraints to prove *progress*, allowing us to detect errors which may otherwise be overlooked.

1 Introduction

Modern out-of-order microprocessors use dynamic scheduling to increase the number of instructions executed per cycle. These processors maintain a fixed-size window into the instruction stream, analyzing the instructions in the window and executing them *out of order* so as to improve performance. However, it is typically required that the results of this out of order execution be the same as that of a sequential execution of the program. Proving this correlation is non-trivial: The out of order scheduling algorithm is often complex, and may use a variety of data-structures not used in the sequential algorithm.

The two prevalent methods for the formal verification of hardware designs are *model checking* (e.g. [ABHS99,BCRZ99,JM01]) and *deductive verification* (e.g. [SH98,HGS00,CGZ96]).

There are obvious advantages to the model-checking techniques, the most important being that it is fully automatic and requires no strong familiarity with the internal details of the design. A very serious limitation of model-checking techniques is the limited size of designs which can be fully automatically verified.

The alternative approach based on deductive verification suffers from no such limitations and, in principle, can be used to verify very big designs provided their structure is based on regular patterns. The main drawback of the deductive approach to reactive system verification (as outlined, for example, in [MP95]) is that it is not fully automatic and requires much user ingenuity and supervision.

---

* Research supported in part by the John von Neumann Minerva Center for Verification of Reactive Systems, and the European Community IST project "Omega".

R. Alur and D.A. Peled (Eds.): CAV 2004, LNCS 3114, pp. 414–426, 2004.

In the past several years we have considered several out-of-order execution designs, developing the *predicted values* method for proving correctness using *refinement*. This method was applied to Tomasulo / Pentium II-like models [AP99,AP00] and to a much simplified Mips model [AP01]. None of these models included memory operations, and progress was not proved. The significant amount of human interaction required was a limiting factor in the complexity of the model, and the types of properties, we could verify.

For this reason, we developed TLPVS [PA03], a system for the formal verification of linear temporal logic (LTL) properties built on the PVS [OSRSC01] verification system. Using TLPVS we were able to apply the predicted values method to a significantly more complex model, based on the Mips R10000. In verifying what is arguably the most elaborate out-of-order execution mechanism verified within the academic community to date, we demonstrate the generality of our methods with respect to different execution models, and the feasibility of their use on more complex models.

Furthermore, TLPVS allows us to use fairness conditions to prove progress properties, checking for a class of errors likely to be missed otherwise. Most abstraction based verification methods for verifying out-of-order execution algorithms prove that there is an abstract state matching every concrete one, but do not ensure that the fairness requirements in the abstract system are met. They are therefore unlikely to detect a livelock or deadlock situation. We demonstrate progress in the concrete system by refinement to a weakly fair abstract system.

This paper makes a number of contributions: It is the first report of the successful verification of a detailed model based on the Mips architecture. In it we demonstrate that the predicted values method is general enough to be used on different architectures and extend its use to systems with memory. Furthermore, we extend the verification method to include progress, thus verifying that deadlock does not occur. We also demonstrate the use and advantages of TLPVS in microprocessor verification.

In the next section we discuss related works. Section 3 describes our model, MIPS, Section 4 explains the use of predicted values and Section 5 overviews TLPVS. In Section 6 we describe our proof of correctness. Space constraints limit the detail in this paper; annotated PVS files are available at [Tlpvs].

2   Related Works

Out-of-order execution mechanisms have been a very popular area of research in the last few years. Quite a number of techniques have been developed and applied to a variety of models. However, the models used and simplifications made are not standardized, making comparisons difficult.

The method of *completion functions* proposed by Hosabettu et al [HGS00] is, like ours, purely deductive, and uses PVS. Completion functions are used to complete every unfinished instruction in the implementation system which can then be compared with the specification system. Whereas the completion functions recursively compute the future value of the instruction, we use predicted values to obtain the same value without flushing, and without constructing completion functions. We believe that in the examples we have examined predicted values are easier to calculate and support than completion functions.

Whereas completion functions can be seen as implicit flushing mechanisms, explicit flushing mechanisms have also been used in out-of-order verification. In Burch and Dill's seminal paper [BD94] a pipelined systems is verified using refinement and flushing. After flushing the implementation state it is compared with the specification model. However, this approach does not work for out-of-order architectures as flushing the large buffers of partially completed instructions is too complex [SJD98a]. In order to verify out-of-order scheduling an *incremental flushing* mechanism [SJD98a] was proposed, as well as induction [SJD98b].

More recently, Lahiri and Bryant [LB03] used *shadow variables*, as well as refinement maps, to verify various processor models using UCLID, a deductive system based on the logic of CLU. Their shadow variables are taken directly from the abstract system – it is verified that the values computed in the concrete state match these auxiliary values. These auxiliary variables are similar to our predicted value fields, however conceptually our proof of the correctness of prediction is independent of the abstract system, while this proof is dependent on both. They also verify models including superscalar dispatch and retirement (though not, apparently, in conjunction with speculation / memory operations.)

Jhala and McMillan [JM01] use refinement maps to modelcheck out-of-order execution systems. Like [LB03] they use auxiliary variables calculated by the abstract system. This proof has a fundamentally deductive flavor although invariants are proved using model checking. This has the advantage of increased automation. However, the amount of user understanding needed to construct the correct refinement maps, and use the co-induction and abstraction mechanisms is, in our experience, far from negligible. Furthermore, this method relies heavily on symmetry, and it is unclear how it would work in asymmetric systems.

In [SH98] a model including speculation, memory operations, external interrupts and precise exceptions is deductively verified. An intermediate model comprising a table of history variables (MAETT) is used to verify the system in ACL2. The entire system state is stored in this table at dispatch time, and removed if a flush occurs. Like them, we also use auxiliary variable to allow for roll-backs in the case of a mispredicted branch, however we save only memory values, and only when branches are executed. Far more, and more complex, auxiliary variables are used than in our proofs, but none are used to 'predict' future values. The model is impressively detailed, but the proof has the disadvantage of being specific to one configuration and limited to bounded resources.

Our fully parameterized model, MIPS, is not restricted to bounded resources, and we do not explicitly use symmetry in our proofs. However, we exclude exceptions, a feature included in most of the models mentioned above. In the past we have used predicted values to verify systems with exceptions [AP00], and believe that there is no difficulty, in principle, in doing so in this case also.

While other researchers chose to extend their models and thus demonstrate how their methods scale up in the face of increasing complexity, we chose to test

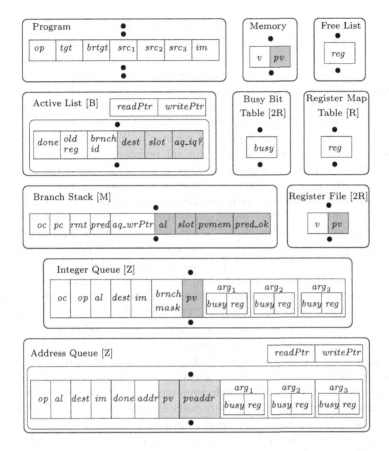

Fig. 1. Data structures for MIPS. Shading indicates auxiliary variables.

the flexibility of our methods by trying them on a totally different out-of-order execution mechanism – that of the MIPS model. To the best of our knowledge no other method has yet been used to verify this out-of-order execution mechanism. Its varied data structures and complex control algorithm make it more challenging than our Tomasulo-based models; we believe that it is the most complex model verified in the academic community to date. Furthermore, this is the first out-of-order processor verification effort which includes a proof of progress – a necessary feature which appears to have been universally overlooked.

3   A Model Based on the Mips R10000

In this section we detail our model, MIPS, based on [Yea96,Gwe94]. We have tried to make our model as accurate as possible, but made some simplifications, and took some assumptions in cases where the exact implementation was unclear to us. The more significant of these are explicitly noted. Our model includes arithmetic and memory operation, load forwarding, branch prediction and speculation, but not exceptions. The two most prominent differences between the Mips R10000 algorithm and the Tomasulo-like algorithms on which models are generally based are the register renaming and branch verification strategies.

Register renaming is effected by clearly distinguishing the logical register numbers, referenced within instruction fields, from the physical registers, which are locations in the hardware *register file* (*RF*). A *register map table* (*RMT*) maps each logical register to a physical register in *RF*. Other registers in *RF* may be used to hold prior values of logical registers. A *busy-bit table* (*BB*) indicates for each physical register whether it contains a valid value. The *free list* (*FL*) records the list of physical registers not currently in use.

The processor **verifies branch prediction** as soon as the branch condition is determined, even if earlier branches are still pending. If the prediction was incorrect the processor immediately aborts all instructions fetched along the mispredicted path, and restores its state to that before the misprediction. Every dispatched branch is stored in a *branch stack* (*BS*). In addition to the alternate branch address *pc* (program counter), the *BS* stores a copy of the current *RMT*, a *pred* bit indicating whether the branch was predicted taken, and the address queue write pointer position, aq_wrPtr[1]. This is significantly more complex than flushing the entire re-order buffer when retiring a mispredicted branch – the mechanism typically used in verification models.

The *active list (AL)* is a circular buffer which maintains program order between all dispatched but not yet retired instructions. (It is functionally comparable to the re-order buffer in Tomasulo-type models.) Arithmetic and branching instructions awaiting execution occupy entries in the *integer queue (IQ)*. Similarly, memory instructions occupy entries in the *address queue* (*AQ*)[2]. We model *memory* as a mapping from address to value, both of which are undefined.

The active list and address queue are both ordered circular buffers, with *write pointers* pointing to the next free entry, and *read pointers* noting the oldest queue entry. The integer queue and branch stack are unordered.

During **dispatch** an instruction is allocated the next entry in the active list. In addition, instructions are allocated entries in the *IQ* or *AQ* depending on their type. The current physical registers for operands are looked up in the *RMT*, their availability checked in the *BB*, and the information stored in the *IQ* (*AQ*). The *IQ* (*AQ*) entry also contains a *dest* field indicating the physical register in which the result will be stored, a tag *al* pointing to the active list entry associated with this instruction and any immediate value (*im*) encoded in the instruction. Address queue entries also have a *done* field recording whether the address has been calculated, and a field storing the address. A branch mask *brnch_mask* is calculated for new entries in the *IQ* by noting which entries of the *BS* are currently occupied. Intuitively, this mask will later be used to determine

---

[1] It appears that the write pointer and a prediction bit are stored, but this is not explicitly stated in the literature.

[2] The Mips R1000 also has a floating-point queue, very similar to the integer queue, which we have not modeled.

whether this instruction is along the path of a mispredicted branch and should be flushed.

If the instruction has a target register, t, it is also allocated a free physical register from the *FL*, and the *RMT* is updated accordingly. The identity of the previous physical register to which t was mapped is stored as *old_reg* in the *AL*.

Branch instructions are predicted, and the relevant information is stored in a new entry of the branch stack. The index of the *BS* entry is stored in the *AL* as the *bid* (branch id)[3].

Address calculation can be performed when all operand values are available. Using operand values obtained from the register file, the address is calculated and stored in the *AQ*. A *done* bit in the *AQ* is set after address calculation.

Load execution occurs after the load address has been calculated and the address of all preceding stores in the *AQ* have also been calculated. If any of these stores is to the same address as the load, then the value of the most recent preceding store is forwarded to the load. Otherwise, the value is obtained from the memory. The new value is written to the target register in the *RF*, the *BB* is updated, and the done bit in the *AL* entry is set.

Arithmetic instruction execution is enabled when all operands in the *IQ* are ready. The calculated value is written back to the *RF*, and the *BB*. The *AL* entry is updated, as are all matching operand fields in the *AQ* and *IQ*. The *IQ* entry is freed. If the instruction is a *correctly predicted* branch, then the *BS* entry is freed, and the corresponding branch mask bit is reset in all *IQ* entries. If the instruction is a *mispredicted* branch, then the program counter (pc) is set to the alternative value and all instructions succeeding are flushed: All *IQ* entries whose branch mask matches this branch are freed; the write pointer of the *AL* is set to the entry succeeding the branch (effectively freeing all entries after it); the *RMT* is restored to the values stored in the *BS*, i.e. all mappings due to instructions succeeding the branch are undone; physical registers allocated to instructions along the mispredicted path are returned to the free list; the write pointer of the *AQ* is restored to its position when the branch was dispatched.

The instruction at the head of the *AL* can be **retired** if its *done* bit is set. The physical register stored in its *old_reg* field is freed and added to the free list. Thus, a physical register is freed only when the next instruction targeting the same logical register is retired. The value in the *old_reg* register may be needed as an operand value for instructions dispatched after it but before the next instruction targeting the same logical register. The retirement policy ensures that register values are available as long as there is a possibility that they will be needed. If the instruction is a load or store, the entry at the head of the address queue (which must match this instruction) is also freed. In the case of a store memory is updated with the store value.

To this system we add a number of auxiliary variables (shaded in Fig. 1). Some auxiliary fields duplicate information in a more accessible form (the *aq_iq?* field of *AL* records whether it is an arithmetic or a memory instruction) or

---

[3] It is likely that the *AL* does not really have a *bid* field, and another mechanism, which we could not determine, relates *BS* entries to those in the *AL* and *IQ*.

provide pointers to related data structures (the *slot* fields in the active list points to the instruction's *IQ* or *AQ* entry). The auxiliary *BS.pvmem* field allows us to roll-back memory in the case of a mispredicted branch (Section 4.1). The system also contains many auxiliary *predicted value* fields, the use of which is explained in the next section.

4   Out-of-Order Execution and Predicted Values

Verification of out-of-order (OOO) systems often makes use of *refinement*. That is, the *concrete*, out-of-order *implementation* design is compared to an an *abstract* system *specifying* all the acceptable correct computations. Typically, the abstract system is taken to be a sequential system in which each instruction is completed (issued, executed, retired) in one step.

A difficulty with this comparison is that in the OOO execution systems the register file and memory are updated many cycles after the instructions are issued. Thus the program counter in the two systems may match if we synchronize at dispatch time, but the register file only if we synchronize at retirement time.

We developed the predicted values approach to deal with this disparity. *Predicted values* are auxiliary fields mapped to some or all of the value fields in the system, predicting the eventual value. This prediction is fully deterministic and depends only on other values in the system at the time of its calculation. Using the terminology of [AL91] these are *history*, not prophecy, variables. Predicted values form a "shadow" system mirroring the "real" computation except that all computations occur at dispatch time, using predicted values for operands.

Our method consists of two verification steps:

1. *Correctness of prediction*: We determine conditions under which values and predicted values in the OOO system agree. These are ordinary, single system invariants.
2. *Refinement*: We use refinement to prove a relationship between the predicted values in the OOO system, and values in the sequential system. The systems are synchronized at dispatch time.

This method has the advantage of allowing us to relatively easily synchronize the out-of-order and sequential systems at dispatch time, proving refinement without costly flushing or complicated roll-back mechanisms.

4.1   Using Predicted Values in MIPS

In the initial state all predicted value fields are equal to the real values. When the first instruction is dispatched its predicted value is calculated by applying the instruction operation to the predicted values of its operands. We consider, first, an arithmetic operation. When it is dispatched its predicted value is calculated from the predicted value of its operands in the *RF*, and stored in the *IQ* entry and as the predicted value of its target register in the *RF*.

Similarly, loads and stores calculate their predicted addresses (*pvaddr*) by using predicted values in the *RF*. The predicted value of a load is the predicted value at the *pvaddr* location in memory. Stores update the predicted value of the *pvaddr* location in the memory.

When branches are dispatched, the system speculates whether or not to take the branch using *value* fields in the system, a decision noted in the *BS.pred* field. (Note that this is not a predicted value – it is a system based branch prediction that may be incorrect. It records whether the branch is speculatively taken.) Using *predicted value* fields from the *RF* for the source operands, the branch condition is evaluated, determining whether it *should* be taken. This value is stored in the *pv* field if the *IQ*. The *pred_ok* field records whether the branch is mispredicted (by comparing *BS.pred* with *IQ.pv*). In addition, a complete copy of the memory predicted values is stored in the *BS.pvmem* field.

When a mispredicted branch is verified and flushed, it is necessary to restore the *RMT* and the *mem* to the state they were in before the misprediction. Instructions along the mispredicted path may have updated the *RMT* and these updates are undone by copying the *BS.rmt* field to the *RMT*. The real values in memory will not have been affected by these instructions as stores update memory only when they are retired. However, we do update the predicted values in memory when stores are dispatched. Analogously to the treatment of the *RMT*, we save the predicted memory values as *BS.pvmem* when a branch is dispatched, and restore them if it is verified as being mispredicted.

Predicted values are neither read nor written during address calculation, instruction execution (excluding misprediction verification) and retirement.

5   A Brief Overview of TLPVS

In order to reduce the enormous manual effort in conducting deductive proofs, we developed TLPVS which includes a formal PVS specification of LTL based on [MP95] and a framework for defining systems. A number of rules for proving safety and response properties are included in the system, each one accompanied by a strategy supporting its use. These rules and strategies greatly reduce the routine theorem proving interaction.

All proof rules used are defined and proved correct within TLPVS. In doing so we eliminate the pen-and-paper application of "known" rules typical in many proofs, and the validity of our final proof rests solely on the correctness of PVS.

5.1   Parameterized Fair Systems

The computational model of *parameterized fair systems* [PA03] is used for defining systems in TLPVS. This is a variation of the fair discrete systems of [KP00] which, in turn is derived from the model of *fair transition systems* [MP95].

A *parameterized fair system* (PFS) $S = \langle V, \Theta, \rho, \mathcal{F}, \mathcal{J}, \mathcal{C} \rangle$ consists of

- V : A finite set of typed *system variables*. We define a *state* s to be a type-consistent interpretation of V. A *(state) predicate* is a function which maps states into truth values. A *bi-predicate* defines a binary relation over states.
- Θ : The *initial condition*. A predicate characterizing the initial states.
- ρ: The *transition relation*. A bi-predicate relating a state to its successor.

- $\mathcal{F}$: A non-empty *fairness domain*. This is a domain which is used to parameterize the fairness requirements of justice and compassion.
- $\mathcal{J}$: The *justice (weak fairness) requirement*. This is a mapping from $\mathcal{F}$ to predicates ($\mathcal{J}$: $[\mathcal{F} \mapsto$ predicate]). For every $t \in \mathcal{F}$, a computation must contain infinitely many $\mathcal{J}[t]$-states.
- $\mathcal{C}$: The *compassion (strong fairness) requirement*. These were not needed in this proof. See [PA03] for details.

A *run* of a PFS is an infinite sequence of states satisfying the requirements of initiality and consecution. A *computation* is a run satisfying the justice and compassion requirements.

Our definitions of LTL are taken from [MP95], and for brevity are omitted.

6   A Proof of the Correctness of MIPS

In this section we use refinement to prove that every execution of MIPS has a matching sequential execution, thus proving the safety property that MIPS computes values correctly. Thereafter we prove progress by proving that a matching *computation* of the sequential system can be found, in which infinitely many non-idling steps are taken.

More precisely, we prove that our concrete system, MIPS: $S_C = \langle V_C, \Theta_C, \rho_C, \mathcal{F}_C, \mathcal{J}_C, \mathcal{C}_C \rangle$, *refines* an abstract system SEQ: $S_A = \langle V_A, \Theta_A, \rho_A, \mathcal{F}_A, \mathcal{J}_A, \mathcal{C}_A \rangle$ in which each instruction is completed in a single step. Since both MIPS and SEQ include a program counter (pc), memory (mem), and register file (RF), we subscript MIPS instances with "C", and SEQ instances with "A".

Let Σ_C and Σ_A denote the sets of concrete and abstract states respectively. Let Ω, referred to as the *domain of observations*, denote a set of elements. Let $\mathcal{O}_A : \Sigma_A \mapsto \Omega$ and $\mathcal{O}_C : \Sigma_C \mapsto \Omega$ be two functions termed the *abstract* and *concrete observation functions*, respectively. They indicate the parts of the systems compared in the refinement relations. We define an *interpolating system*

$$S_I = \langle V_I = V_C \cup V_A, \Theta_C \wedge \Theta_A^*, \rho_C \wedge \rho_A^*, \mathcal{F}_C, \mathcal{J}_C, \mathcal{C}_C \rangle$$

where $\rho_A^*(V_I, V_C', V_A')$ and $\Theta_A^*(V_C, V_A)$ may refer to all variables in $V_C \cup V_A$. Functions Θ_A^* and ρ_A^* allow us to "choose" from the possible transitions of SEQ, one that correctly matches the MIPS transition. We denote the V_C (V_A) component of V_I by $V_I\Downarrow_C$ ($V_I\Downarrow_A$, respectively).

Within TLPVS we define, and prove the validity of, rule REF (Fig. 2). Intuitively, R1 and R2 together ensure that the S_A component of a run of S_I is a run of S_A. Premise R1 requires that an initial S_A-state matching the initial S_C-state can be found. Premise R2 requires that an S_A-state satisfying ρ_A^* can always be found, ensuring that an S_I-successor state can be built. Premise R3 asserts that throughout the computation the observation functions of the two systems agree. The conclusion, that S_C *refines* S_A, denoted $S_C \sqsubseteq S_A$, is formalized as:

(1)   For every computation seq_C of S_C, there is a run seq_A of S_A, such that at every time t, $\mathcal{O}_C(seq_C(t)) = \mathcal{O}_A(seq_A(t))$.

Rule REF

R1. $\Theta_C(V_C) \longrightarrow \exists V_A : \Theta_A^*(V_C, V_A) \wedge \Theta_A(V_A)$
R2. $\rho_C(V_I \Downarrow_C, V_C') \longrightarrow \exists V_A' : \rho_A^*(V_I, V_C', V_A') \wedge \rho_A(V_I \Downarrow_A, V_A')$
R3. $S_I \models \Box(\mathcal{O}_C(V_I \Downarrow_C) = \mathcal{O}_A(V_I \Downarrow_A))$

$$S_C \sqsubseteq S_A$$

Fig. 2. Rule REF: Proving refinement.

Formula Θ_A^* initializes the pc, mem, and RF in S_A with the same values as in Θ_C. Transition relation ρ_A^* defines an instruction execution whenever ρ_C defines a dispatch which is not along a mispredicted path. All other ρ_C-transitions cause ρ_A^* to idle. Premises R1 and R2 are trivial to verify. We discuss the proof of R3:

We define $\mathcal{O}_A$ as the tuple (pc_A, mem_A, RF_A).

If the current state of MIPS does not include a mispredicted branch (detected by checking the auxiliary $pred\_ok$ variable in BS) then $\mathcal{O}_C$ is defined as

$$(pc_C, \lambda a : mem_C.pv(a), \lambda r : RF_C(RMT(r)).pv)$$

That is, we take the current program counter and the predicted values for memory. We use the predicted value of each logical register r, obtained from the RF by using the RMT to identify the physical register to which r is mapped.

Otherwise, $\mathcal{O}_C$ is derived from the branch stack. Letting $firstMis$ be the index of the first mispredicted branch, we define $\mathcal{O}_C$ as

$$(BS(firstMis).pc, BS(firstMis).pvmem, \lambda r : RF_C(BS(firstMis).rmt(r)).pv)$$

That is, we take the alternative branch address store in the BS, the copy of memory predicted values stored when the branch was taken, and the predicted values for logical registers obtained using the $BS.rmt$ mapping. Intuitively, $BS.pvmem$ and $BS.rmt$ record "snapshots" of the system before the misprediction occurred, and unlike RMT and mem, do not include changes made by instructions along the mispredicted path.

Result (1) refers to auxiliary variables in MIPS. From it we derive

(2) For every computation seq_C of S_C, there is a run seq_A of S_A, such that at every time t at which $seq_C(t).AL$ is empty:

$$pc_A = pc_C$$
$$\wedge\, RF_A = \lambda r : RF_C(RMT(r)).v$$
$$\wedge\, mem_A = \lambda a : mem_C(a).v$$

by proving that predicted values and real values match under certain conditions.

Verifying that R3 of REF holds required that a number of system properties be proved invariant. Similarly in deducing (2) from (1).

We proved the invariance of 19 general properties if MIPS, such as that if slot S of the IQ is occupied, then its al field points to an occupied entry in the

AL, in which the *done* bit is false. We also prove the invariance of 7 properties relating directly to predicted value. Properties in this group include prediction correctness (under which conditions value and predicted values are guaranteed to agree) and relationships between predicted values in different structures.

Most of the 26 properties whose invariance we proved, the bulk of the verification effort, fell into 1 of 4 groups of *mutually inductive* properties. We defined, and proved the correctness of, a simple compositional mutual induction rule which allowed us to verify each property in the group separately.

6.1   Proving Progress

The refinement proof described above is not very dissimilar from that of other researchers e.g. [LB03,JM01]. However, we claim that it is insufficient. There are errors that may not be found by the above method – errors which prevent the system from progressing. Consider, for example, a version of MIPS in which we do not return the *old_reg* register to the *FL* on retirement. Within a finite number of steps the system will flush itself out (*AL* empties) but be unable to dispatch the next instruction with a target as there are no "free" physical registers. The matching abstract run will be one with an infinite suffix of idling transitions.

To prove progress we define the justice condition for SEQ as $\lambda n : pc_A \neq n$. I.e., for every $n \in \mathbf{N}^+$, we require that infinitely often the program counter is not n. Intuitively, the sequential system can always progress, and doing so causes the program counter to change. However, it is possible for a program to violate this condition by containing a branch, at location m, with m as its branch target. We obviate this undesirable scenario by assuming that $\forall n : prog(n).brtgt \neq n$.

We now try to prove that

(3)   For any computation seq_C of S_C, there is a *computation* seq_A of S_A, in which infinitely many non-idling steps are taken, such that at every time t $\mathcal{O}_C(seq_C(t)) = \mathcal{O}_A(seq_A(t))$ and if $seq_C(t).AL$ is empty then: $pc_A = pc_C$
$$\wedge\ RF_A = \lambda r : RF_C(RMT(r)).v$$
$$\wedge\ mem_A = \lambda a : mem_C(a).v$$

That is, we try to show that every computation of MIPS matches a *fair* run of SEQ in which progress is made (infinitely many instructions are completed). It is easy to derive (3) from (1) and (2) once we prove the response property

(4)   MIPS $\models \forall n : \Box((getPC = n)\longrightarrow\Diamond(getPC \neq n))$

where *getPC* is defined as pc_C if the system contains no mispredicted branches, $BS(firstMis).pc$ otherwise.

We use a derivation of the WELL rule of [SPBA00] (Fig. 3) to verify (4).

The justice requirements we define for MIPS are that every sub-transition (dispatch, address calculation, execution, retirement) which is enabled infinitely often is eventually taken.

We define a ranking function which decreases every time a partially executed instruction which is not along a mispredicted path progresses (e.g. its address is

---

Rule WELL

For PFS $S = \langle V, \Theta, \rho, \mathcal{F}, \mathcal{J}, \mathcal{C} \rangle$,

Given initial and goal predicates p, q, helpful predicates $\{h_t : t \in \mathcal{F}\}$,

a well founded relation $\succ$ over $\mathcal{A}$, and ranking functions $\delta : \Sigma \mapsto \mathcal{A}$

W1. $$p \rightarrow q \vee \bigvee_{t \in \mathcal{F}} h_t$$

W2. $\forall t \in \mathcal{F}:$ $$h_t \wedge \rho \rightarrow q' \vee \bigvee_{u \in \mathcal{F}} (\delta \succ \delta' \wedge h_u') \vee (h_t' \wedge \delta = \delta' \wedge \neg \mathcal{J}'[t])$$

$$\Box(p \longrightarrow \Diamond q)$$

Fig. 3. Rule WELL. Primed variables refer to values in the next state.

calculated, or the instruction is retired). Instructions along mispredicted paths do not effect the rank. When an instruction which is not along a mispredicted path is dispatched (a *goal dispatch*), the *pc* changes and the goal state is reached.

The helpful predicate requires that if AL is empty then an instruction be dispatched, otherwise that the instruction at the head of AL progress. To prove that h_u' always holds for some u, we show that the instruction at the head of the AL (if any) can always progress, and that a dispatch is always enabled if the AL is empty. The latter required us to prove new safety properties regarding resource recovery, properties unnecessary for the proof of (2).

Justice conditions ensure that instruction at the head of the queue progresses, and thus the rank decreases. Well-foundedness ensures that as long as no goal dispatch occurs, the rank continuously decreases until the AL is empty. At this point justice conditions ensure that a goal dispatch occurs.

7 Conclusion

In this paper we present the predicted values method for the verification of out-of-order execution. Using predicted values we are able to prove refinement between a complex out-of-order execution system and a simple sequential system.

Our ability to verify a model of the size and complexity of MIPS is in no small part thanks to the use of TLPVS, which eliminates part of the drudge work. Despite this, our proofs are by no means automatic, and the effort required (two to three person months) is significant. However they are *fully* automated, with every rule being proved within the PVS theorem prover (as part of TLPVS). We have not sufficed at using a "known" refinement rule (or any other rule), but have verified the rule as well. In totally eliminating the pen-and-paper element, we believe that we provide a higher degree of certainty than most previous proofs.

Acknowledgments

I benefited much from the insight of Prof Amir Pnueli, my thesis adviser, particularly in the development of TLPVS. Many thanks to Orna Lichtenstein for valuable suggestions on an earlier draft of this paper.

References

[ABHS99]   A. Aziz, J. Baumgartner, T. Heyman, and V. Singhal. Model checking the IBM gigahertz processor. *CAV'99*:72–83, 1999.

[AL91]   M. Abadi and L. Lamport. The existence of refinement mappings. *Theoretical Computer Science*, 82(2):253–284, 1991.

[AP99]   T. Arons and A. Pnueli. Verifying Tomasulo's algorithm by refinement. In *VLSI'99*:306–309, 1999.

[AP00]   T. Arons and A. Pnueli. A comparison of two verification methods for speculative instruction execution. In *TACAS'00*:487–502, 2000.

[AP01]   T. Arons and A. Pnueli. A methodology for deductive verification of out-of-order execution systems based on predicted values. Technical Report MCS01-04, Weizmann Institute, 2001.

[BCRZ99]   A. Biere, E. Clarke, R. Riami, and Y. Zhu. Verifying safety properties of a PowerPC microprocessor using symbolic model checking without BDDs. In *CAV'99*:60–71, 1999.

[BD94]   J. R. Burch and D. L. Dill. Automatic verification of pipelined microprocessor control. In *CAV'94*:68–80, 1994.

[CGZ96]   E.M. Clarke, S.M. German, and X. Zhao. Verifying the SRT division algorithm using theorem proving techniques. In *CAV'96*:111–122, 1996.

[Gwe94]   L. Gwennap. MIPS R10000 uses decoupled architecture. *Microprocessor Report*, pages 18–24, October 1994.

[HGS00]   R. Hosabettu, G. Gopalakrishnan, and M. Srivas. Verifying microarchitectures that support speculation and exceptions. In *CAV'00*:521–537, 2000.

[JM01]   R. Jhala and K. McMillan. Microarchitecture verification by compositional model checking. In *CAV'01*:397–410, 2001.

[KP00]   Y. Kesten and A. Pnueli. Control and data abstractions: The cornerstones of practical formal verification. *STTT*, 2(1):328–342, 2000.

[LB03]   S.K. Lahiri and R.E. Bryant. Deductive verification of advanced out-of-order microprocessors. In *CAV'03*:341–354, 2003.

[MP95]   Z. Manna and A. Pnueli. *Temporal Verification of Reactive Systems: Safety*. Springer-Verlag, New York, 1995.

[OSRSC01]   S. Owre, N. Shankar, J.M. Rushby, and D.W.J. Stringer-Calvert. *PVS System Guide*. Menlo Park, CA, November 2001.

[PA03]   A. Pnueli and T. Arons. TLPVS: A PVS-based LTL verification system. In *Verification: Theory and Practice*:598–625, 2003.

[SH98]   J. Sawada and W.A. Hunt. Processor verification with precise excpetions and speculative execution flushing. In *CAV'98*:135–146, 1998.

[SJD98a]   J.U. Skakkebaek, R.B. Jones, and D.L. Dill. Formal verification of out-of-order execution using incremental flushing. In *CAV'98*:98–110, 1998.

[SJD98b]   J.U. Skakkebaek, R.B. Jones, and D.L. Dill. Reducing manual abstraction in formal verification of out-of-order execution. In *FMCAD'98*:2–17, 1998.

[SPBA00]   E. Sedletsky, A. Pnueli, and M. Ben-Ari. Formal verification of the Ricart-Agrawala algorithm. In *FSTTCS'00*: 325–335, 2000.

[Tlpvs]   TLPVS Homepage. http://www.wisdom.weizmann.ac.il/~verify/tlpvs.

[Yea96]   K.C. Yeager. The Mips R10000 superscalar microprocessor. *IEEE Micro*, pages 28–40, April 1996.

Automatic Verification of Sequential Consistency for Unbounded Addresses and Data Values[*]

Jesse Bingham[1], Anne Condon[1], Alan J. Hu[1], Shaz Qadeer[2], and Zhichuan Zhang[1]

[1] Department of Computer Science, University of British Columbia
[2] Microsoft Research

Abstract. Sequential consistency is the archetypal correctness condition for the memory protocols of shared-memory multiprocessors. Typically, such protocols are parameterized by the number of processors, the number of addresses, and the number of distinguishable data values, and typically, automatic protocol verification analyzes only concrete instances of the protocol with small values (generally < 3) for the protocol parameters. This paper presents a fully automatic method for proving the sequential consistency of an entire parameterized family of protocols, with the number of processors fixed, but the number of addresses and data values being unbounded parameters. Using some practical, reasonable assumptions (data independence, processor symmetry, location symmetry, simple store ordering, some syntactic restrictions), the method automatically generates a finite-state abstract protocol from the parameterized protocol description; proving sequential consistency of the abstract model, via known methods, guarantees sequential consistency of the entire protocol family. The method is sound, but incomplete, but we argue that it is likely to apply to most real protocols. We present experimental results showing the effectiveness of our method on parameterized versions of the Piranha shared memory protocol and an extended version of a directory protocol from the University of Wisconsin Multifacet Project.

1 Introduction

Shared-memory multiprocessors are the dominant form of multiprocessing. In such systems, the processors share a single address space and interact by reading/writing to a shared memory system. A *memory model* is the correctness condition for the memory system, defining the processor-visible behavior of the system.

Sequential Consistency (SC) [20] is the archetypal memory model. Informally, SC states that every execution of the system must behave as if it were some interleaving of the individual processors' executions on a single atomic memory. For example, Fig. 1 shows an execution that is not sequentially consistent, because there is no way to interleave the executions of the two processors on a single memory and obtain the observed results. SC continues to be important both from a verification perspective as a well-defined and extensively-researched challenge problem, as well as from an implementation perspective as a memory model balancing ease-of-programming with implementation flexibility [17].

---

[*] This work was supported in part by a research grant and a graduate fellowship from the Natural Science and Engineering Research Council of Canada.

R. Alur and D.A. Peled (Eds.): CAV 2004, LNCS 3114, pp. 427–439, 2004.

$proc_1$: (write $addr_2$ val_1), (write $addr_1$ val_2), (read $addr_2$ val_1), (read $addr_2$ val_2)
$proc_2$: (write $addr_1$ val_1), (write $addr_2$ val_2), (read $addr_1$ val_1), (read $addr_1$ val_2)

Fig. 1. Example execution that is not sequentially consistent. The values seen by the two reads on one processor imply that the other processor's second write appears to have occurred between the two reads; no interleaving can satisfy this property for both processors simultaneously. Note that the operations on each address, considered in isolation, **are** sequentially consistent, demonstrating that sequential consistency cannot be verified on a per-address basis. (In fact, the per-address operations satisfy the even stronger notion of *simple sequential consistency*, defined in Sec. 2.).

Memory systems use intricate finite-state protocols to implement the desired memory model. These protocols are notoriously complex and error-prone, because the primary objective is performance rather than simplicity. With the ascendance of finite-state model checking [9] as an automatic verification method, the verification of multiprocessor memory system protocols has been a major success story of the practical application of formal verification.

Finite-state model checking is limited, of course, to finite-state systems. In reality, memory system protocols are defined as parameterized systems — typically by the number of processors, the number of addresses, and the number of distinguishable data values. Most automatic protocol verification efforts have therefore considered only concrete instances of protocols. Furthermore, because of problems with state-space explosion, the instances verified are generally very small, e.g., for a detailed model of a typical industrial protocol, a successful model-checking run with 3 processors, 3 addresses, and 3 data values is a remarkable achievement. Far better would be a method to automatically verify an entire parameterized protocol family.

In theory, handling a parameterized number of processors is most interesting, because shared memory protocols are intended to facilitate complex interactions among processors. In practice, however, handling parameterized numbers of addresses and data values is a higher priority, because real shared-memory multiprocessors have few processors and many addresses and data values. For example, typical configurations have 2 to 8 processors, with even the largest installations having at most a few dozen processors. In contrast, even the smallest and most common configurations (e.g., a hyper-threading desktop PC) have at least 2^{32} data values and hundreds of millions of physical addresses (with much larger virtual address spaces) — far beyond the reach of the direct application of model checking for the foreseeable future.

This paper presents a fully automatic method for proving the sequential consistency of an infinite family of protocols parameterized in two dimensions: the number of addresses, and the number of data values. We consider the number of processors to be a fixed constant. Our approach relies on data independence to handle the parameterized data values; our main contribution is a means to handle parameterized addresses. Note that unlike easier-to-verify properties like seriality or linearizability [16], sequential consistency cannot be verified on a per-address basis. (See Fig. 1.) No previous fully automatable method for verifying sequential consistency can be parameterized by both the number of addresses and the number of data values. (See Sec. 7 for related work.)

Our method leverages a few common, practical assumptions about memory system protocols. Three of these — data independence, processor symmetry, and location symmetry — are standard and easily enforced syntactically. We impose some additional syntactic constraints to simplify the automatic generation of a finite-state abstract protocol from the parameterized protocol description; these are described in Sec. 4. Finally, our method verifies a slightly stronger form of SC in which writes to an address cannot be reordered. To our knowledge, all implemented SC protocols implement this stronger form. (The canonical example of a protocol that is SC, but violates this assumption is *Lazy Caching* [1].) With these restrictions, our method is, in principle, fully automatic.

2 Preliminaries

A *labelled transition system* (LTS) is a tuple $M = (S, \Sigma, I, \longrightarrow)$, where S is a set of states, Σ is a finite alphabet, $I \subseteq S$ is the set of initial states, and $\longrightarrow \subseteq S \times \Sigma \times S$ is the transition relation. The language $L(M)$ of the LTS M is the subset of Σ^* defined in the usual way. Given an alphabet Σ and some string x, define $x \uparrow \Sigma$ to be the string obtained by deleting all symbols of x that are not in Σ. We extend $\uparrow$ to act on sets of strings in the obvious way.

Denote by $\mathbb{N}$ the set of positive integers, and by $\mathbb{N}_n$ the set $\{1, \ldots, n\}$. For sets P, A, and V, let $MemEvents(P, A, V)$ be the set $\{R, W\} \times P \times A \times V$. Then $MemEvents(\mathbb{N}, \mathbb{N}, \mathbb{N})$ is called the set of *memory events*, also denoted simply *MemEvents*. An occurrence of memory event (R, p, j, d) is meant to represent processor p reading value d from address j, we call such an event a *read*. Similarly the *write* event (W, p, j, d) indicates processor p writing value d to address j. We call a finite string over *MemEvents* a *trace*. A shared memory protocol, hereafter simply *protocol*, is formalized as a LTS $\mathcal{P} = (S, MemEvents(\mathbb{N}_n, \mathbb{N}_m, \mathbb{N}_v) \cup E, I, \longrightarrow)$ for some $n, m, v \geq 1$, where S is finite and E (the *silent* action labels) is disjoint from *MemEvents*. The quantities n, m, and v are respectively denoted $Procs(\mathcal{P})$, $Addrs(\mathcal{P})$, and $Vals(\mathcal{P})$. Intuitively, these quantities are respectively the number of processors, number of memory addresses, and number of data values (per address) processed by the protocol. We define *PROTS* to be the set of all protocols. For a protocol $\mathcal{P}$, define $traces(\mathcal{P})$ to be $L(\mathcal{P}) \uparrow MemEvents$.

We aim to verify correctness of an infinite set of related protocols called a protocol *family*, defined as follows. For fixed $n \geq 1$, an *n-processor family* is a function $\mathcal{F} : \mathbb{N} \times \mathbb{N} \to PROTS$ where for all $m, v \geq 1$, $Procs(\mathcal{F}(m, v)) = n$, $Addrs(\mathcal{F}(m, v)) = m$, and $Vals(\mathcal{F}(m, v)) = v$.

A trace is said to be *serial* if every read event has the same value as the last write to the same address, and such a write always exists[1]. A trace σ is said to be *sequentially consistent* (SC) iff there exists a trace σ' (of the same length) such that (1) $\sigma' \uparrow MemEvents(\{p\}, \mathbb{N}, \mathbb{N}) = \sigma \uparrow MemEvents(\{p\}, \mathbb{N}, \mathbb{N})$ for each $p \geq 1$, and (2) σ' is serial. We call such a σ' a *serial reordering* of σ. Furthermore, σ is said to be *simple SC* (SSC) if there exists σ' with the above two properties plus the additional property (3) $\sigma' \uparrow (\{W\} \times \mathbb{N} \times \{j\} \times \mathbb{N}) = \sigma \uparrow (\{W\} \times \mathbb{N} \times \{j\} \times \mathbb{N})$ for each $j \geq 1$; here σ' is called a *simple serial reordering*. Intuitively, SC says that there must exist a reordering that is serial and preserves the per-processor order. SSC adds the requirement that the ordering of writes to each address is also preserved in the reordering. A protocol is said

---

[1] The *last write to the same address* is the rightmost write that is left of the read in question and has the same address, if the trace were written out from left to right as usual.

to be serial, SSC, or SC, if all of its traces are serial, SSC, or SC respectively. Similarly, an n-processor family is said to have any of these properties if all of its constituent protocols have the respective property.

3   The Big Picture

Our aspiration is to algorithmically verify that an n-processor family $\mathcal{F}$ is SSC. This section presents Theorem 1, which allows us to soundly reduce the proof that $\mathcal{F}$ is SSC to checking SSC of a protocol Q, where $Addrs(Q) = Procs(Q) = n$, and $Vals(Q) = 3$, provided that an infinite number of projected trace containments hold between certain members of $\mathcal{F}$ and Q (see condition 2 of Theorem 1). However, in Sec. 5 we show that if $\mathcal{F}$ is expressed in a certain formalism, then we can effectively produce a Q for which these containments hold "by construction". SSC of Q can be checked algorithmically using known methods based on model-checking [10, 29, 8, 7].

In Sec. 3.1 we define three assumptions that are required by Theorem 1; the theorem itself is presented in Sec. 3.2.

3.1   Assumptions

Here we define three common protocol assumptions: location symmetry (LS), processor symmetry (PS), and data independence (DI).

For a permutation λ on $\mathbb{N}$ define λ^{proc} to be the function on $MemEvents(n,m,v)$ specified by $\lambda^{proc}((op,p,j,d)) = (op,\lambda(p),j,d)$. Similarly, define $\lambda^{addr}((op,p,j,d)) = (op,p,\lambda(j),d)$. We extend λ^{proc} and λ^{addr} to have domain and range $MemEvents^*$ in the obvious way. A protocol $\mathcal{P}$ is *location symmetric (LS)* if for every permutation $\lambda : \mathbb{N}_{Addrs(\mathcal{P})} \rightarrow \mathbb{N}_{Addrs(\mathcal{P})}$ we have $\sigma \in traces(\mathcal{P})$ implies $\lambda^{addr}(\sigma) \in traces(\mathcal{P})$. Similarly, $\mathcal{P}$ is *processor symmetric (PS)* if for every permutation $\lambda : \mathbb{N}_{Procs(\mathcal{P})} \rightarrow \mathbb{N}_{Procs(\mathcal{P})}$ we have $\sigma \in traces(\mathcal{P})$ implies $\lambda^{proc}(\sigma) \in traces(\mathcal{P})$. A family is said to be location symmetric or processor symmetric if all protocols in its image have the respective property.

Intuitively, *data independence* (DI) in a system means that variables of a certain type can only be nondeterministically assigned, copied, and outputted [32]. When the system is a protocol, and the type is data values, one can define how DI manifests at the trace level. Qadeer [29] gives the following trace level definition of DI. A trace is called *unambiguous* if it has the feature that no two writes to the same address write the same value. Given $m, v, v' \geq 1$, we call a function $\lambda : \mathbb{N}_m \times \mathbb{N}_{v'} \rightarrow \mathbb{N}_v$ a *renaming function*, and define $\lambda^{val}((op,p,j,d)) = (op,p,j,\lambda(j,d))$. We extend λ^{val} to traces in the obvious way. Then an n-processor family $\mathcal{F}$ is said to be DI if for all $m, v \geq 1$ and traces σ, we have $\sigma \in traces(\mathcal{F}(m,v))$ if and only if there is $v' \geq 1$, an unambiguous trace $\sigma' \in traces(\mathcal{F}(m,v'))$, and a renaming function $\lambda : \mathbb{N}_m \times \mathbb{N}_{v'} \rightarrow \mathbb{N}_v$ such that $\sigma = \lambda^{val}(\sigma')$.

3.2   Reduction to Finite-State SSC

Theorem 1. *Let $\mathcal{F}$ be an n-processor family that is processor symmetric, location symmetric, and data independent. If there exists a protocol Q such that*

1. *Q is SSC, and*
2. *For all $m > n$ we have that $traces(\mathcal{F}(m,3)) \upharpoonright MemEvents(\mathbb{N}_n, \mathbb{N}_n, \mathbb{N}_3) \subseteq traces(Q)$*

then $\mathcal{F}(m,v)$ is SSC for all $v \geq 1$ and $m > n$.

Proof: The detailed proof is available from:

http://www.cs.ubc.ca/~jbingham/bchqz04-proofs.pdf

The proof relies on machinery developed in [29] to show that, under the LS, PS, and DI assumptions, if there exists $\sigma \in traces(\mathcal{F}(m,v))$ such that σ is not SSC, we can detect that σ is not SSC by considering only $\sigma \upharpoonright MemEvents(\mathbb{N}_n, A, \mathbb{N}_v)$, where $A \subset \mathbb{N}$ has cardinality n. By exploiting the symmetry assumptions, we can ensure that such a σ exists for which $A = \mathbb{N}_n$. Furthermore, we can ensure such a σ exists using only 3 data values. Hence, if Q is SSC, and the projected traces of all family members are contained in $traces(Q)$, then all family members must be SSC. □

We note that Theorem 1 does not allow concluding that $\mathcal{F}(m,v)$ is SSC for $1 \leq m \leq n$. This is not a deficiency, since we may verify correctness of these members via a finite number of model checks. Practically, these are the uninteresting cases, since multiprocessors always have many more addresses than processors.

Suppose we are given $\mathcal{F}$ and wish to determine if a candidate protocol Q exists for which the two conditions of Theorem 1 hold. Our approach involves automatically constructing a candidate Q such that condition 2 is guaranteed to hold; this construction involves abstracting $\mathcal{F}$ in some sense. The automatic construction of Q is possible because of the formalism we use to describe $\mathcal{F}$, presented in Sec. 4. Condition 1 is then checked algorithmically using known methods. If this check is successful, the conclusion of Theorem 1 follows. Otherwise, the approach has failed, and we can draw no conclusions; in other words the approach is *sound* but *incomplete*. Hence, to argue for the applicability of this approach, one must argue that real protocol families

1. adhere to the LS, PS, and DI assumptions, and
2. can be expressed in our formalism of Sec. 4, and
3. won't yield false negatives, i.e. if the family is SSC then the approach succeeds.

It is widely accepted that real protocols satisfy property 1 [29]. Our formalism of Sec. 4 is quite general, encompassing all real protocols that we have encountered. For instance, all of the protocols [1, 5, 22, 6, 19, 14] are expressible in our formalism. In support of item 3, we present successful experiments on two challenging protocols in Sec. 6.

4 A Protocol Description Formalism

To describe an automatic construction of a candidate finite-state protocol Q from a parameterized protocol description, we must choose some sort of protocol description formalism. Here, we will assume that the n-processor family $\mathcal{F}$ is expressible in a very general syntax based on first order logic that is inspired by the *bounded-data parameterized systems* of [27]. We have tuned our formalism to provide enough expressiveness for the real protocol descriptions we have encountered, while still allowing the efficient and automatic generation of a sufficiently finely abstracted protocol Q. For the sake of perspicuity, we will treat the number of data values as being fixed at 3, since condition 2 of Theorem 1 considers such family members. Standard restrictions can be imposed on our formalism to ensure that the family is PS, LS, and DI. For instance, DI can easily be enforced by syntactic constraints as observed by Wolper and others [32, 25, 29], and symmetric types such as Murφ scalarsets [18] can be used to ensure PS. LS is inherent to the syntax [27].

4.1 Syntax

We assume three sets of variables $X = \{x_1,\ldots,x_{|X|}\}$, $Y = \{y_1,\ldots,y_{|Y|}\}$, and $Z = \{z_1,\ldots,z_{|Z|}\}$. For a set D, let $Z[D]$ denote the variable set $\{z_i[d] \mid 1 \leq i \leq |Z| \wedge d \in D\}$ and let $\mathrm{Vars}(D) = X \cup Y \cup Z[D]$. Priming any of these sets has the effect of priming all constituent variables; semantically, primed variables will represent the next state. The variables of X are Booleans, while the variables in Z are arrays of Booleans indexed by addresses. The variables of Y will range over addresses, hence we call these variables *address ranged variables* (ARVs). Of course non-Boolean finite types and arrays of such can be encoded in this framework. In shared memory protocols, typical (though by no means exhaustive) examples of the variables in X, Y, and Z, are respectively fields corresponding to processor IDs or message types in messages, fields storing addresses in messages, and the permission bits and data value associated with each address in a local cache or main memory.

We will employ auxiliary ARVs a and a_1 to quantify over, and let ARVars denote the set $Y \cup Y' \cup \{a, a_1\}$. Define *quantifier-free actions* (QFA) as formulas with syntax:

$$\Phi ::= x \mid z[a] \mid z[a_1] \mid \langle \alpha = \beta \rangle \mid \neg\Phi \mid (\Phi \vee \Phi) \mid (\Phi \wedge \Phi)$$

where $x \in X \cup X'$, $z \in Z \cup Z'$ and $\alpha, \beta \in \mathrm{ARVars}$. For QFA ϕ, we write $\phi(a)$ (resp. $\phi(a, a_1)$) to emphasize that the set of auxiliary ARVs appearing in ϕ is a subset of $\{a\}$ (resp. subset of $\{a, a_1\}$). We call upon a set of action labels *Labels*, of which we require $(\{R, W\} \times \mathbb{N}_n \times \mathbb{N}_3) \subseteq Labels$. The transition relation of $\mathcal{F}$ must be expressible as a set:

$$\{r_\ell(a) \mid \ell \in Labels\}$$

where, for each $\ell \in Labels$, r_ℓ is a formula of the form

$$r_\ell(a) = \phi_\ell(a) \wedge \forall a_1 : \psi_\ell(a, a_1). \tag{1}$$

Here, $\phi_\ell(a)$ and $\psi_\ell(a, a_1)$ are arbitrary QFAs and we call formulas of the form (1) *restricted actions*. The initial state predicate *Init* must be of the form:

$$Init = \forall a : init(a)$$

for some QFA $init(a)$ that does not contain any primed variables.

Intuitively, a transition in a protocol expressed in our formalism must satisfy $r_\ell(a)$ for some ℓ and some "distinguished" address a. $\phi_\ell(a)$ dictates what happens to state related to address a, i.e. ath entries of arrays, while the conjunct $\forall a_1 : \psi_\ell(a, a_1)$ dictates the uniform effect on all other addresses. This restriction accords exactly with what we have observed in real protocol descriptions. We find that real protocol transitions have the property that ARVs are referenced and/or modified at no more than a single index a, with the exception that some more complex transitions will also modify entries at all other indices in some homogeneous way, hence the inclusion of $\forall a_1 : \psi_\ell(a, a_1)$ in restricted actions. Usually, $\psi_\ell(a, a_1)$ will simply state that if $\neg\langle a = a_1 \rangle$, then the a_1th entries of arrays are left fixed. However, several transitions in one of the protocols we experimented with have a more involved ψ_ℓ, e.g., a state change for one address forces all other addresses to abandon an optimization mode. A theoretical limitation of our formalism is that the auxiliary ARVs a and a_1 are the only ARVs that can be used to index into arrays. However, typical instances of indexing using another ARV $y \in Y$ can be performed by, for example, $\langle y = a \rangle \wedge some\_array'[a]$.

4.2 Semantics

In this section we formally define the set of LTSs represented by our family syntax.

Let s be a valuation of the variables $\mathrm{Vars}(D)$ such that variables of X and $Z[D]$ are assigned Boolean values, and variables of Y are assigned values of some type R, and let s' be a valuation to $\mathrm{Vars}(D)'$ with analogous typing. Then we call s a D,R-*valuation* and (s,s') a D,R-*valuation pair*, respectively. Intuitively, D is the index set for the arrays in Z, and R is the type of the variables in Y; for the protocols of $\mathcal{F}$ these will be the same, but in Sec. 5 we construct a protocol for which they differ. For D,R-valuation pair (s,s') and restricted action $\theta(a)$, we write $(s,s') \vDash_m \theta(j)$ if $\theta[j/a]$ is satisfied when variables are valuated by (s,s'), and quantified ARVs are taken to range over $\mathbb{N}_m$. If θ is a QFA, we may omit the subscript on $\vDash$.

For each $m \geq 1$, our syntax defines a LTS $\mathcal{F}(m,3) = (S,L,I,\longrightarrow)$ where

- S is the set of all $\mathbb{N}_m,\mathbb{N}_m$-valuations
- $L = Labels \times \mathbb{N}_m$. In a slight abuse, we will identify the memory event $(op,p,j,v) \in$ *MemEvents* with $((op,p,v),j) \in L$.
- $I = \{s \mid s \vDash_m Init\}$
- $\longrightarrow$ is the set of all tuples $(s,(\ell,j),s')$ such that $(s,s') \vDash_m r_\ell(j)$ and $j \in \mathbb{N}_m$.

5   A Candidate Q

Here we define a candidate Q for Theorem 1, which can be viewed as a modified version of $\mathcal{F}(n,3)$; hereafter Q will refer to such. These modifications involve syntactic transformations; the transition relation and initial state assertion can easily be realized automatically given $\{r_\ell \mid \ell \in Labels\}$ and *Init*. Intuitively, the modified protocol is a finite-state abstraction of the protocols in $\mathcal{F}(n,3)$, where everything related to addresses greater than n has been conservatively abstracted away. Note, however, that our abstraction is a finer abstraction than the typical abstract interpretation [11] in which addresses greater than n are replaced by an information-destroying $\top$ value that propagates throughout the interpretation. We need our more accurate abstraction to successfully verify real protocols.

In Q, address-ranged variables have type $\mathbb{N}_n \cup \{\xi\}$. The ξ symbol represents addresses in $\mathbb{N} \setminus \mathbb{N}_n$. Counter-intuitively, the arrays in Z will still be indexed by $\mathbb{N}_n$ because the variables of $Z[\{\xi\}]$ are existentially quantified out; for brevity we will let $\vec{z}[\xi]$ denote the variable list $z_1[\xi],\ldots,z_{|Z|}[\xi],z'_1[\xi],\ldots,z'_{|Z|}[\xi]$ throughout the paper. An important part of the transformation is the operator $sub(\cdot)$. For any action r, the action $sub(r)$ is obtained by performing the following substitution: each occurrence of $\langle \alpha = \beta \rangle$ falling under an odd number of negations (where $\alpha,\beta \in \mathrm{ARVars}$) is replaced with[2]

$$(\langle \alpha = \beta \rangle \wedge \neg (\langle \alpha = \xi \rangle \wedge \langle \beta = \xi \rangle))$$

---

[2] This syntactic substitution gives the same effect on the transition relation as the usual abstract interpretation with ξ conservatively abstracting the values greater than n. (The existential quantification of the Z variables is the key difference between our abstraction and the typical one.)

For restricted action $\theta(a)$ and integer $j \in \mathbb{N}_n \cup \{\xi\}$, we write $(s,s') \vDash_Q \theta(j)$ if $\theta[j/a]$ is satisfied when variables are assigned by (s,s'), and the universal quantifier in θ is taken to range over $\mathbb{N}_n \cup \{\xi\}$.

We now define $Q = (S_Q, L_Q, I_Q, \longrightarrow_Q)$:

- S_Q is the set of all $\mathbb{N}_n, (\mathbb{N}_n \cup \{\xi\})$-valuations.
- $L_Q = Labels \times (\mathbb{N}_n \cup \{\xi\})$. We note that labels of the form $((o,p,v),\xi)$ are not in *MemEvents*.
- $I_Q = \left\{ s \mid s \vDash_Q \exists \overrightarrow{z}[\xi] : sub(Init) \right\}$. The existential quantification notation $\exists z : f$ where z is a Boolean variable and f is a formula is simply syntactic sugar for $f[\text{tt}/z] \vee f[\text{ff}/z]$.
- $\longrightarrow_Q$ is the set of all triples $(s,(\ell,j),s')$ such that $j \in \mathbb{N}_n \cup \{\xi\}$ and

$$(s,s') \vDash_Q \exists \overrightarrow{z}[\xi] : sub(r_\ell(j)) \tag{2}$$

The existential Boolean quantification in (2) blows up the formula by a factor of $2^{2|Z|}$ in the worst case. However, in practice we find that only a small number of the variables $\overrightarrow{z}[\xi]$ are actually mentioned in r_ℓ, which mitigates this effect. For example, the only dependencies on $\overrightarrow{z}[\xi]$ might be the 2 or 3 bits representing the access permissions at the ξth entry of a single processor's cache.

We conclude this section by asserting that the trace set of Q overapproximates that of $\mathcal{F}(m,3)$ for all $m > n$, i.e. Q satisfies condition 2 of Theorem 1.

Theorem 2. $traces(\mathcal{F}(m,3)) \!\upharpoonright\! MemEvents(\mathbb{N}_n, \mathbb{N}_n, \mathbb{N}_3) \subseteq traces(Q)$ *for all* $m > n$.

Proof: The detailed proof is available from:

http://www.cs.ubc.ca/~jbingham/bchqz04-proofs.pdf

The construction of Q naturally corresponds to an abstraction function mapping concrete states from $\mathcal{F}(m,3)$ to abstract states in Q. This mapping turns out to be a weak simulation relation, and the projected trace containment follows. $\qquad\Box$

6   Experimental Results

To evaluate our technique, we experimented with two protocols, which we call PIR and DIR. Both of these protocols are SSC but not serial, hence trace reordering requirements are nontrivial. PIR is a simplified abstraction of the Piranha protocol [5]. Our implementation is consistent with the details of the simplification presented in [29]. DIR is a simplification of a directory based protocol with Scheurich's optimization [30]. Our implementation is based on, but is simpler than, the description of Braun et al. [8], which was obtained from the University of Wisconsin Multifacet group. We explain part of the design of both protocols here and describe the ways in which our implementation of DIR is simpler than the description of Braun et al. [8].

In both PIR and DIR, each processor p has a cache that contains, for certain memory locations j, a data value $d(p,j)$ and an access permission $access(p,j)$. The permission may be modifiable (M), shared (S), or invalid (I). Processor p may read the data value for location j if access(p, j) is S or M, and may write (change) the data value if access(p, j) is M.

In PIR, in addition to the caches, the system state has a queue per processor and an owner per memory location. The state maintains the invariant that the owner of location j is either some processor p for which access$(p, j) = S$ or M, or the owner is null. Requests of a processor to change its access level or to get a data value for a location are not modeled explicitly. Rather, if owner$(j) = p$, in one transition (step) of the protocol the triple $(\mathrm{d}(p, j), j, X)$ may be placed on the queue of any processor $p' \neq p$, in which case an invalidate message (INV, j) is placed on the queues of any processor p'' (other than p and p') with access$(p'', j) \neq I$. Also, owner(j) is set to null and access(p, j) is set to INV. In a later transition, when triple (d, j, X) is at the head of p''s queue, the triple may be removed from the queue, in which case $\mathrm{d}(p', j)$ is set to d, access(p', j) is set to M, and owner(j) is set to p'. Also, if (INV, j) is at the head of the queue of p'', in one transition the message may be removed from the head of the queue, in which case access(p'', j) is set to I. Other access permission changes are modeled similarly.

The state space of PIR is relatively small because requests of processors are not modeled explicitly, and moreover, no directory is used to store the set of processors with shared access to a memory location. However, the use of queues ensures that the traces generated by PIR are interesting and realistic, in the sense that if in some trace, the lth event σ_l is a read to location j which inherits its value from an earlier write event σ_k, then arbitrarily many operations (indeed, arbitrarily many write operations to location j) may separate σ_k from σ_l in the trace.

The DIR protocol contains many low level details that are not modeled by PIR. In DIR, a directory maintains information on which processors have exclusive or shared access to a memory location. Each processor and the directory has both a request *and* a response input queue, with different uses. For example, invalidate messages to processors are placed on the request input queue, whereas messages containing data values are placed on the response input queue.

In order to get exclusive access to a memory location, processor p sends a request to the directory, which arranges for the data value and the number of current sharers of the location to be sent to p. Before reading the data value, p must wait to receive acknowledgement messages from each current sharer. Because of the multiple queues, several race conditions can arise. For example, the directory might authorize processor p' to have exclusive access to location j after p, and p may receive a request to send j's data value to p' before p has even received the data value itself. As a result, a processor has 9 permission levels per location in its cache in addition to the I, S, and M levels. For example, access(p, j) may be IMS, indicating that p requested M access when access(p, j) was I, p has not yet transitioned to M access, but already another request for p to downgrade to S access has been received.

To keep the state space within manageable proportions, our implementation of the DIR protocol does not model a certain queue of Braun et al. [8]. This queue is used for transmission of data within a processor, rather than between processors, and its removal does not significantly change the protocol.

Both PIR and DIR were modeled at a fairly detailed level, resulting in substantial descriptions in the Murφ language (165 and 1397 lines of code, respectively, excluding comments). The Murφ language is more expressive than the formalism of Sec. 4, but the protocol family implementations used only constructs that conform to this formalism. Although the construction in Sec. 4 is obviously automatable, we do not yet have an implementation for the Murφ language, so we performed the construction by hand, exactly following the described syntactic transformations.

In addition, for the DIR protocol, the verification runs against the "automatically"-generated Q spaced out, so the protocol was manually abstracted further, yielding Q'; the numbers in Table 1 refer to the completed verification runs against Q'. The essential difference between Q and Q' is that in the latter, all fields (except for the *address* field) in messages pertaining to the abstracted address ξ were abstracted. The same approach was taken with a local record at each processor called the *transaction buffer*. Since Q' is an over-approximation of Q, the fact that the verification succeeded for Q' proves that verification would have succeeded for Q, *had we had sufficient memory resources*. In other words, our automatic construction of Q was accurate enough to prove SSC of the protocol family. In general, one could envision a tool that automatically attempts such additional abstractions if model checking the original Q is intractable.

Table 1 gives our experimental results. The 2-processor runs were successful, showing that our generated abstraction is accurate enough, even for these protocols with non-trivial reordering properties (which are therefore hard-to-prove sequentially consistent).

Table 1. Results for the PIR (Piranha) and DIR (Wisconsin Directory) Protocols. All runs are with the number of processors $n = 2$, except for PIR3 with $n = 3$. We experimented with two versions of PIR: with processors' queue depth $q = 1$ and $q = 2$. We use a method of Qadeer [29] to prove SSC of our generated finite-state abstract protocol. This method requires separate model-checking runs for each $k = 1, \ldots, n$, to check for cycles of length $2k$ in a graph of ordering constraints. Times are in seconds, on a 2Ghz Intel Xeon with 4GB memory running Linux. "prob" is an upper-bound on the probability of missing states due to hash compaction, as reported by Murφ [31] (40 bit hashes for PIR; 42 bits for DIR). The $n = 2$ runs concluded successfully, enabling us to conclude SSC for each example over all address counts m and data value counts v where $m > n = 2$. The PIR3 results are a preliminary attempt with $n = 3$ processors. For PIR3 with $k = 2$, we used 35-bit hashes. We have not yet completed a $k = 3$ run at press time.

Protocol	$k = 1$				$k = 2$			
	#states	time	depth	prob	#states	time	depth	prob
PIR $(q = 1)$	49365	7	18	≈ 0	138621	9	20	≈ 0
PIR $(q = 2)$	3782880	100	21	≈ 0	10558306	278	23	≈ 0
PIR3 $(q = 1)$	125865495	9244	36	≤ 0.000024	374557312	25640	38	≤ 0.021101
DIR $(q = 1)$	171088424	49660	53	≤ 0.000013	375967684	110211	59	≤ 0.000324

7 Related Work

There is a rich and successful literature pertaining to the verification of assorted safety and liveness properties on non-parameterized protocols, which we do not have space to summarize. We focus here on work pertaining to verification of SC for *parameterized families* of protocols. The problem of determining whether a finite state protocol is SC is undecidable [2], and so clearly also is the problem of determining whether a family of parameterized protocols is SC. Therefore, all methods are necessarily incomplete.

Some works verify weaker properties than sequential consistency, over parameterized memory protocols. For example, McMillan [23] uses compositional model checking to generate invariants that can be used to verify safety and liveness properties of the FLASH cache coherence protocol. Pong and Dubois [28], Delzanno [12], and Emerson and Kahlon [13] have produced automatic methods to verify safety properties over parameterized memory protocols, but these methods model the protocols at a very high level of abstraction, where implementation details are hidden. Pnueli et al. [27] and Arons et al. [4] present a general, sound-but-incomplete method for verifying parameterized systems. This work is similar in spirit to ours (and inspired our specification formalism) in that an incomplete procedure is used to guess a candidate, whose verification proves the property for the entire family. Their method, however, attempts to derive an inductive invariant for proving simple assertions, whereas ours derives an abstract protocol that preserves violations of SSC. All of these works can handle protocol families with parameterized number of processors, which we cannot. On the other hand, our method proves SSC rather than weaker safety properties, and applies to any protocol that can be expressed in the syntax of Sec. 4.

Several proofs of SC for parameterized protocols are manual in nature. Some [21, 26, 3] use theorem-provers, while others use formal frameworks to provide a rigorous proof [24]. In either case, a human must develop insights needed to build up the proof, and the process is quite time-consuming.

Qadeer's method [29] for verifying sequential consistency of finite-state cache coherence protocols actually provides a parameterized proof in one dimension, namely data values. Our work can be viewed as an extension of Qadeer's to two dimensions (data values and addresses). The only other approach known to us that uses model checking to verify sequential consistency of parameterized families of protocols is that of Henzinger et al. [15]. Their semi-automatic method, which builds on a method for structural induction on processes, can handle families of protocols that are parameterized in the number of processors, in addition to the number of addresses and data values. However, a limitation of their method is that its soundness relies on the assumption that the protocol to be verified is *location monotonic*, in the sense that any trace of the system projected onto a subset of locations is a trace of the system with just that subset of locations. Henzinger et al. do not provide a method (automated or otherwise) for testing location monotonicity of a parameterized family of protocols. (Nalumasu [25] does provide a framework for expressing protocols that guarantees location monotonicity, but the framework has very limited expressiveness.) Moreover, the Henzinger et al. method works only for protocols whose set of traces can be reordered by a finite state machine to form serial traces, a restriction that typically holds in practice only for protocols that are already fully serial. While protocols with traces that are not in simple SC can be handled, many protocols do not have finite-state observers; examples include both protocols described in this paper and the lazy caching protocol of Afek et al. [1]. (Although Henzinger et al. state in their paper that the lazy caching protocol has a finite state observer, this is only true of their simplified version.) In summary, while the Henzinger et al. method does allow the number of processors to be parameterized (unlike ours), their method is not automatic and applies to a limited protocol class that excludes important real protocols.

438   Jesse Bingham et al.

References

1. Y. Afek, G. Brown, and M. Merritt. Lazy caching. *ACM Trans. on Prog. Lang. and Sys.*, 15(1):182–205, 1993.
2. R. Alur, K. L. McMillan, and D. Peled. Model-checking of correctness conditions for concurrent objects. In *11th IEEE Symp. on Logic in Comp. Sci.*, pages 219–229, 1996.
3. T. Arons. Using timestamping and history variables to verify sequential consistency. In *Computer-Aided Verification: 13th Int'l. Conf.*, pages 423–435. Springer, 2001. LNCS Vol. 2102.
4. T. Arons, A. Pnueli, S. Ruah, Y. Xu, and L. Zuck. Parameterized verification with automatically computed inductive assertions. In *Computer-Aided Verification: 13th Int'l. Conf.*, pages 221–234. Springer, 2001. LNCS Vol. 2102.
5. L. A. Barroso, K. Gharachorloo, R. McNamara, A. Nowatzyk, S. Qadeer, B. Sano, S. Smith, R. Stets, and B. Verghese. Piranha: a scalable architecture based on single-chip multiprocessing. In *27th Int'l. Symp. on Comp. Arch.*, pages 282–293, 2000.
6. E. E. Bilir, R. M. Dickson, Y. Hu, M. Plakal, D. J. Sorin, M. D. Hill, and D. A. Wood. Multicast snooping: a new coherence method using a multicast address network. In *26th Int'l. Symp. on Comp. Arch.*, pages 294–304, 1999.
7. J. D. Bingham, A. Condon, and A. J. Hu. Toward a decidable notion of sequential consistency. In *15th ACM Symp. on Parallel Algorithms and Architectures (SPAA03)*, pages 304–313, 2003.
8. T. Braun, A. Condon, A. J. Hu, K. S. Juse, M. Laza, M. Leslie, and R. Sharma. Proving sequential consistency by model checking. In *IEEE Int'l. High Level Design Validation and Test Workshop (HLDVT)*, pages 103–108, 2001. An expanded version appeared as University of British Columbia Dept. of Computer Science Tech Report TR-2001-03, http://www.cs.ubc.ca/cgi-bin/tr/2001/TR-2001-03.
9. E. M. Clarke and E. A. Emerson. Design and synthesis of synchronization skeletons using branching time temporal logic. In D. Kozen, editor, *Workshop on Logics of Programs*, pages 52–71, Springer, 1981. LNCS Vol. 131.
10. A. Condon and A. J. Hu. Automatable verification of sequential consistency. In *13th ACM Symp. on Parallel Algorithms and Architectures (SPAA01)*, pages 113–121, 2001.
11. P. Cousot and R. Cousot. Abstract interpretation: a unified lattice model for static analysis of programs by construction or approximation of fixpoints. In *4th Symp. on Princ. of Prog. Lang.*, pages 238–252, 1977.
12. G. Delzanno. Automatic verification of parameterized cache coherence protocols. In *Computer-Aided Verification: 12th Int'l. Conf.*, pages 53–68. Springer, 2000. LNCS Vol. 1855.
13. E. A. Emerson and V. Kahlon. Exact and efficient verification of parameterized cache coherence protocols. In *12th Conf on Correct Hardware Design and Verification Methods (CHARME)*, pages 247–262, 2003.
14. G. Gopalakrishnan, R. Ghughal, R. Hosabettu, A. Mokkedem, and R. Nalumasu. Formal modeling and validation applied to a commercial coherent bus: a case study. In *Conf on Correct Hardware Design and Verification Methods (CHARME)*, pages 48–62, 1997.
15. T. A. Henzinger, S. Qadeer, and S. K. Rajamani. Verifying sequential consistency on shared-memory multiprocessor systems. In *Computer-Aided Verification: 11th Int'l. Conf.*, pages 301–315. Springer, 1999. LNCS Vol. 1633.
16. M. Herlihy and J. Wing. Linearizability: a correctness condition for concurrent objects. *ACM Trans. on Prog. Lang. and Sys.*, 12(3):463–492, 1990.
17. M. D. Hill. Multiprocessors should support simple memory-consistency models. *IEEE Computer*, pages 28–34, August 1998.

18. C. N. Ip and D. L. Dill. Better verification through symmetry. In *Int'l. Conf. on Computer Hardware Description Languages*, pages 87–100, 1993.
19. J. Kuskin, D. Ofelt, M. Heinrich, J. Heinlein, R. Simoni, K. Gharachorloo, J. Chapin, D. Nakahira, J. Baxter, M. Horowitz, A. Gupta, M. Rosenblum, and J. Hennessy. The Stanford FLASH multiprocessor. In *21st Int'l. Symp. on Comp. Arch.*, pages 302–313, 1994.
20. L. Lamport. How to make a multiprocessor computer that correctly executes multiprocess programs. *IEEE Trans. on Computers*, C-28(9):690–691, September 1979.
21. P. Loewenstein and D. L. Dill. Verification of a multiprocessor cache protocol using simulation relations and higher-order logic. *Formal Methods in System Design*, 1(4):355–383, 1992.
22. M. M. K. Martin, M. D. Hill, and D. A. Wood. Token coherence: low-latency coherence on unordered interconnects. In *Int'l Symp. on Comp. Arch.*, pages 182–193, 2003.
23. K. L. McMillan. Parameterized verification of the FLASH cache coherence protocol by compositional model checking. In *Conf. on Correct Hardware Design and Verification Methods (CHARME)*, pages 179–195. Springer, 2001. LNCS Vol. 2144.
24. M. Merritt, ed. *Distributed Computing*, 12(2-3), 1999. Special issue devoted to proving sequential consistency of lazy caching.
25. R. Nalumasu. *Formal Design and Verification Methods for Shared Memory Systems*. PhD thesis, University of Utah, 1999.
26. S. Park and D. Dill. Verification of the FLASH cache coherence protocol by aggregation of distributed transactions. In *8th Symp. on Parallel Algorithms and Architectures*, pages 288–296, 1996.
27. A. Pnueli, S. Ruah, and L. Zuck. Automatic deductive verification with invisible invariants. In *Tools and Algorithms for the Construction and Analysis of Systems, 7th Int'l. Conf., (TACAS)*, pages 82–97. Springer, 2001. LNCS Vol. 2031.
28. F. Pong and M. Dubois. Verification techniques for cache coherence protocols. *ACM Computing Surveys*, 29(1):82–126, March 1997.
29. S. Qadeer. Verifying sequential consistency on shared-memory multiprocessors by model checking. *IEEE Trans. on Parallel and Distributed Systems*, 14(8):730–741, August 2003. Also appeared as Compaq Systems Research Center Report 176, December 2001.
30. C. Scheurich. *Access Ordering and Coherence in Shared Memory Multiprocessors*. PhD thesis, University of Southern California, May 1989. USC Tech Report CENG 89-19.
31. U. Stern and D. L. Dill. Improved probabilistic verification by hash compaction. In *Conf. on Correct Hardware Design and Verification Methods (CHARME)*, pages 206–224, 1995.
32. P. Wolper. Expressing interesting properties of programs in propositional temporal logic. In *13th Symp. on Princ. of Prog. Lang.*, pages 184–192, 1986.

Efficient Modeling of Embedded Memories
in Bounded Model Checking

Malay K. Ganai, Aarti Gupta, and Pranav Ashar

NEC Laboratories America, Princeton, NJ USA 08540
Fax: +1-609-951-2499
{malay,agupta,ashar}@nec-labs.com

Abstract. We describe a viable approach for memory abstraction that preserves memory semantics, thereby augmenting the capability of SAT-based BMC to handle designs with large embedded memory without explicitly modeling each memory bit. Our method does not require examining the design or changing the SAT-solver and is guaranteed not to generate false negatives. The proposed method is similar, but with key enhancements, to the previous abstract interpretation of memory that captures its forwarding semantics, *i.e.*, a data read from a memory location is same as the most recent data written at the same location. In our method, we construct an abstract model for BMC by eliminating memory arrays, but retaining the memory interface signals and adding constraints on those signals at every analysis depth to preserve the memory semantics. The size of these *memory-modeling constraints* depends quadratically on the number of memory accesses and linearly on the bus widths of memory interface signals. Since the analysis depth of BMC bounds the number of memory accesses, these constraints are significantly smaller than the explicit memory model. The novelty of our memory-modeling constraints is that they capture the exclusivity of a read and write pair explicitly, *i.e.*, when a SAT-solver decides on a valid read and write pair, other pairs are *implied invalid immediately*, thereby reducing the solve time. We have implemented these techniques in our SAT-based BMC framework where we demonstrate the effectiveness of such an abstraction on a number of hardware and software designs with large embedded memories. We show at least an order of magnitude improvement (both in time and space) using our method over explicit modeling of each memory bit. We also show that our method of adding constraints boosts the performance of the SAT solver (in BMC) significantly as opposed to the conventional way of modeling these constraints as nested *if-then-else* expressions.

1 Introduction

Formal verification techniques like SAT-based Bounded Model Checking (BMC) [1-4] enjoy several nice properties over BDD-based symbolic model checking [5, 6]; their performance is less sensitive to the problem sizes and they do not suffer from space explosion. Due to the many recent advances in DPLL-style SAT solvers [7-11], SAT-based BMC can handle much larger designs and analyze them faster than before.

R. Alur and D.A. Peled (Eds.): CAV 2004, LNCS 3114, pp. 440–452, 2004.

Designs with large embedded memories are quite common and have wide application. However, these embedded memories add further complexity to formal verification tasks due to an exponential increase in state space with each additional memory bit. In typical BMC approaches [1-4], the search space increases with each time-frame unrolling of a design. With explicit modeling of large embedded memories, the search space frequently becomes prohibitively large to analyze even beyond a reasonable depth. In order to make BMC more useful, it is important to have some abstraction of these memories. However, for finding real bugs, it is sufficient that the abstraction techniques capture the memory semantics [12] without explicitly modeling each memory bit. In the following, we discuss some of the existing abstraction techniques.

In bottom-up abstraction and refinement techniques [13-18], starting from a small abstract model of the concrete design, counter-examples discovered are used to refine the model iteratively. In practice, several iterations are needed before a property can be proved correct or a real counter-example can be found. Note that after every iterative refinement step the model size increases, making it increasingly difficult to verify. In contrast to the bottom-up approaches, top-down approaches [19, 20] use resolution-based proof techniques in SAT to generate the abstract model, starting from a concrete design. As shown in [20], one can use iterative abstraction to progressively reduce the model size. Since these approaches use the concrete model to start with, it may not be feasible to apply them on designs with large memories. Moreover, both approaches, in general, are not geared towards extracting the memory semantics.

To capture the memory semantics, Burch and Dill introduced the interpreted *read* and *write* operations in their logic of equality with un-interpreted functions (EUF) [12] instead of naïve un-interpreted abstraction of memories. These interpreted functions were used to represent the memory symbolically by creating nested *if-then-else* (ITE) expressions to record the history of writes to the memory. Such partial interpretation of memory has also been exploited in later derivative verification efforts [21-24]. Specifically in [21], Velev *et al.* used this partial interpretation in a symbolic simulation engine to replace memory by a behavioral model that interacts with the rest of the circuit through a software interface that monitors the memory control signals. Bryant *et al.* proposed the logic of Counter arithmetic with Lambda expressions and Un-interpreted functions (CLU) to model infinite-state systems and unbounded memory in the UCLID system [25]. Memory is modeled as a functional expression whose body changes with each time step. Similar to [12], the memory is represented symbolically by creating nested ITE expressions. One can use BMC to verify safety properties with this restricted CLU logic.

In this paper, we describe a viable approach for memory abstraction that preserves memory semantics, thereby augmenting the capability of SAT-based BMC to handle designs with large embedded memory without explicitly modeling each memory bit. Our method does not require examining the design or changing the SAT-solver and is guaranteed not to generate false negatives. The proposed method is similar, but with key enhancements, to the abstract interpretation of memory [12, 21] that captures its forwarding semantics, *i.e.*, a data read from a memory location is the same as the most recent data written at the same location. In our method, we construct an abstract model for BMC by eliminating memory arrays, but retaining the memory interface signals and adding constraints on those signals at every analysis depth to preserve the semantics of the memory. The size of these *memory-modeling constraints* depends quadratically on the number of memory accesses and linearly on the bus widths of memory interface signals. Since the analysis depth of BMC bounds the number of memory accesses, these constraints are significantly smaller than the explicit memory model. The novelty of our memory-modeling constraints is that they capture the exclusivity of a read and write pair explicitly, *i.e.*, when a SAT-solver decides on a valid read and write pair, other pairs are *implied invalid immediately*, thereby reducing the solve time. We have implemented these techniques in our SAT-based BMC framework where we demonstrate the effectiveness of such an abstraction on a number of hardware and software designs with large embedded memories. We show at least an order of magnitude improvement (both in time and space) using our method over explicit modeling of each memory bit. We also show that our method of adding constraints boosts the performance of the SAT solver (in BMC) significantly as opposed to the conventional way of modeling these constraints as nested *if-then-else* expressions [12].

Outline. In Section 2 we give basic idea used in our approach, in Section 3 we give relevant background on BMC and memory semantics, in Section 4 we discuss our approach in detail, in Section 5 we discuss our experiments, and in Section 6 we conclude with summarizing remarks and future work.

2   Basic Idea

For typical designs with embedded memory, a *Main* module interacts with the memory module *MEM* using the interface signals as shown in Figure 1. For a single-port memory at any given clock cycle, the following observations can be made: a) *at most one address is valid*, b) *at most one write occurs*, and c) *at most one read occurs*.

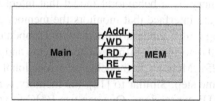

Fig. 1. Design with embedded memory

As BMC-search-bound k becomes larger, the unrolled design size increases linearly with the size of memory bits. For designs with large embedded memories, this increases the search space prohibitively for any search engine to analyze.

It can be observed in this memory model that memory read at any depth depends only on the most recent data written previously at the same address. Therefore, to enable the SAT-based BMC to analyze deeper on such designs, we replace an explicit memory model with an efficient memory model as follows:

a) We *remove* the *MEM* module but *retain* the memory interface signals and the input-output directionality with respect to the *Main* module.

b) We *add constraints* at every analysis depth k on the memory interface signals that preserve the forwarding semantics of the memory.

To improve the SAT solver (in BMC), we also do the following:

c) We *add constraints* such that when the SAT-solver decides on a valid read and write pair, other pairs are *implied invalid immediately*.

Note that although a) and b) are sufficient to generate an efficient model that preserves the validity of a correctness property, c) makes the performance of the SAT-based BMC superior as observed in our experiments. Moreover, we do not have to examine the *Main* module while adding these memory-modeling constraints. Though we consider a single-port memory for the ensuing discussion, our method is also extendable to multi-port memories. In the next two sections, we will give some relevant background and then formalize our contribution.

3 Background

Bounded Model Checking

In BMC, the specification is expressed in LTL (Linear Temporal Logic). Given a Kripke structure M, an LTL formula f, and a bound k, the translation task in BMC is to construct a propositional formula $[M, f]_k$, such that the formula is satisfiable if and only if there exists a witness of length k [26, 27]. The satisfiability check is performed by a backend SAT solver. Verification typically proceeds by looking for witnesses or counter-examples (CE) of increasing length until the *completeness threshold* is reached [26, 27]. The overall algorithm of a SAT-based BMC method for checking (or falsifying) a simple safety property is shown in the Figure 2. Note that P^i denotes the property node at i^{th} unrolling. The SAT problems generated by the BMC translation procedure grow bigger as k increases. Therefore, the practical efficiency of the backend SAT solver becomes critical in enabling deeper searches to be performed.

```
BMC(k,P){//Falsify safety property P within bound k
  for (int i=0; i<=k ; i++) {
    Pⁱ= Unroll(P,i);//Property node at iᵗʰ unrolling
    if (SAT_Solve(Pⁱ=0)=SAT) return CE;//Try to falsify
  }
  return NO_CE; } //No counter-example found
```

Fig. 2. SAT-based BMC for Safety Property P

Memory Semantics

Embedded memories are used in several forms such as RAM, stack, and FIFO with at least one port for data access. For our discussion, we will assume a single-port memory, as shown in Figure 1, with the following interface signals: Address Bus (Addr), Write Data Bus (WD), Read Data Bus (RD), Write Enable (WE), and Read Enable (RE). The *write* phase of the memory is a two-cycles event, *i.e.*, in the current clock cycle *when* the data value is assigned to *WD* bus, the write address location is assigned to the *Addr* bus and the *WE* signal is made active, the new data is *then* available in the next clock cycle. The *read* phase of memory is a one-cycle event, *i.e.*, when the read address location is assigned to the *Addr* bus and *RE* is made active, the read data is assigned to the *RD* bus in the same clock cycle.

Assume that we unroll the design up to depth k (starts from 0). Let S^j denote a memory interface signal variable S at time frame j. Let the Boolean variable $E^{i,j}$ denote the address comparison between time frames i and j and be defined as $E^{i,j}=(Addr^i=Addr^j)$. Then the forwarding semantics of the memory can be expressed as:

$$RD^k = \{WD^j \mid E^{j,k}=1 \wedge WE^j=1 \wedge RE^k=1 \wedge \forall_{j<i<k}(E^{i,k}=0 \vee WE^i=0)\}, \text{ where } j<k \qquad (1)$$

In other words, data read at depth k equals the data written at depth j if addresses are equal at k and j, write enable is active at j, read enable is active at k, and for all depths between j and k, either addresses are different from that of k or no write happened.

4   Our Approach

In our approach, we augment SAT-based BMC (a part of our formal verification platform) with a mechanism to add memory-modeling constraints at every unroll depth of BMC analysis. We use a hybrid SAT solver [10] that uses hybrid representations of Boolean constraints, *i.e.*, 2-input OR/INVERTER gates to represent the original circuit problem and CNF to represent the learned constraints. In this work, we extend the use of hybrid representation to model memory constraints efficiently. We specifically compare it with only a 2-input uniform gate (instead of a multi-input gate) representation, as it was already shown in [11] that efficient Boolean constraint propagation can be achieved using a fast table lookup scheme on such a representation.

In order to add the constraints for the forwarding semantics of memory as in (1), one can use a conventional approach based on the selection operator ITE[1] in the following way. Let the Boolean variable $s^{j,k}$ denote the *valid read signal* and be defined as $s^{j,k} = E^{j,k} \wedge WE^j$. Then the data read at depth k (given $RE^k=1$) is expressed as:

$$RD^k = ITE(s^{k-1,k}, WD^{k-1}, ITE(s^{k-2,k}, WD^{k-2}, ...ITE(s^{0,k}, WD^0, WD^{-1}))...) \qquad (2)$$

where WD^{-1} denotes the initial data value, same in all memory locations. We can extend (2) to handle non-uniform memory initialization as well.

Note that when constraints are added as above, the decision $s^{j,k}=1$ does not necessarily imply $RD^k=WD^j$; other pairs need to be established invalid through decision procedures as well, *i.e.*, $s^{j+1,k}=0, s^{j+2,k}=0,...,s^{k-1,k}=0$. Instead we add explicit constraints to capture the read and write pairs exclusively. Once a read and write pair is chosen by the SAT-solver, the other pairs are implied invalid immediately. Let the Boolean

---

[1] ITE when applied on three Boolean variables is defined as $ITE(s,t,e) = (s \& t) \mid (!s \& e)$.

variable $S^{i,k}$ denote the *exclusive valid read signal* and the Boolean variable $PS^{i,k}$ denote the intermediate exclusive signal. They are defined as follows:

$$\forall_{0 \leq i < k} \quad PS^{i,k} \quad = !s^{i,k} \wedge PS^{i+1,k} \qquad (= RE^k \text{ for } i=k)$$

$$\forall_{0 \leq i < k} \quad S^{i,k} \quad = s^{i,k} \wedge PS^{i+1,k} \qquad (= PS^{0,k} \text{ for } i=-1) \qquad (3)$$

Now equation (1) can be expressed as

$$RD^k = (S^{k-1,k} \wedge WD^{k-1}) \vee (S^{k-2,k} \wedge WD^{k-2}) \vee \dots \vee (S^{0,k} \wedge WD^0) \vee (S^{-1,k} \wedge WD^{-1}) \qquad (4)$$

Note that $S^{i,k}=1$, immediately implies $S^{j,k}=0$ where $j \neq i$ and $i,j < k$.

4.1 Efficient Representation of Memory Modeling Constraints

As mentioned earlier, we use a hybrid representation for building constraints. We capture equations (3) and (4) efficiently

1) by not representing the constraints as a large tree-based structure since such a structure adversely affects the BCP performance as observed in the context of adding large conflict clauses [10], and
2) by not creating unnecessary 2-literal clauses since they too adversely affect a CNF-based SAT-solver that uses 2-literal watch scheme for BCP [28].

We implemented the addition of memory modeling constraints as part of the procedure *EMM_Constraints,* which is invoked after every unrolling as shown in the modified BMC algorithm (*m-BMC*) in Figure 3. The procedure *EMM_Constraints,* as shown in Figure 4, generates the constraints at every depth k using 3 sub-procedures: *Gen_Addr_Equal_Sig, Gen_Valid_Read_Sig,* and *Gen_Read_Data_Constraints.* It then returns the accumulated constraints C^i up to depth i. As we see in the following detailed discussion, these constraints C^k capture the forwarding semantics of the memory very efficiently up to depth k.

```
//BMC with efficient memory modeling
m-BMC(k,P) {
  C⁻¹=φ; //initialize memory modeling constraints
  for (int i=0; i<=k ; i++) {
  Pⁱ=Unroll(P,i);//Get property node at iᵗʰ unrolling
  Cⁱ=EMM_Constraints(i,Cⁱ⁻¹);//update the constraints
  if (SAT_Solve(Pⁱ=0∧Cⁱ=1)=SAT) return CE;}//Try to falsify
  return NO_CE; } //No counter-example found
```

Fig. 3. Improved SAT-based BMC with Efficient Memory Modeling

Gen_Addr_Equal_Sig: Generation of Address Comparison Signals

Let m denote the bit width of the memory address bus. We implement the address comparison as follows: for every address pair comparison ($Addr^j = Addr^k$) we introduce new variables $E^{j,k}$ and $e^{j,k}_i$ $\forall_{0 \leq i < m}$ (for every bit i). Then we add the following CNF clauses for each i:

$$(!E^{j,k} + Addr^j_i + !Addr^k_i) , (!E^{j,k} + !Addr^j_i + Addr^k_i),$$
$$(e^{j,k}_i + Addr^j_i + Addr^k_i), (e^{j,k}_i + !Addr^j_i + !Addr^k_i)$$

Finally, one clause to connect the relation between $E^{j,k}$ and $e^{j,k}_i$, i.e.,

$$(!e^{j,k}_0 + ...+!e^{j,k}_i + ... + !e^{j,k}_{m-1}+E^{j,k})$$

Note that these clauses capture the relation that $E^{j,k}=1$ if and only if ($Addr^j=Addr^k$). The naïve way to express the same equivalence relation structurally would be to use an AND-tree of X-NOR ($\otimes$) gates as follows:

$$E^{j,k} = (Addr^j_0 \otimes Addr^k_0) \wedge ... \wedge (Addr^j_{m-1} \otimes Addr^k_{m-1})$$

Clearly, this representation would require *4m-1* 2-input OR gates, amounting to *12m-3* equivalent CNF clauses (3 clauses per gate). Our representation on the other hand, requires only *4m+1* clauses and does not require any 2-literal clause. Thus, at every depth k, we add only *(4m+1)k* clauses for address comparison rather than the *(12m-3)k* gates clauses required by the naïve approach.

```
//Modeling of memory constraint at depth k
//where C is cumulative constraints up to depth k-1
EMM_Constraints(k, C){
 //Generate address equal signals
 Gen_Addr_Equal_Sig(k);
 //Generate exclusive valid read signals
 Gen_Valid_Read_Sig(k);
 //Generate constraints on read data
 C(k) = Gen_Read_Data_Constraints(k);
 return C ∪ C(k);}
```

Fig. 4. Efficient Modeling of Memory Constraint

Gen_Valid_Read_Sig: Generation of exclusive valid read signals

To represent the exclusive valid read signals as in equation (3), we use a 2-input gate representation rather than CNF clauses. Since each intermediate variable has fan-outs to other signals, we cannot eliminate them. If we were representing those using CNF clauses, it would introduce too many additional 2-literal clauses. This representation adds *3k* 2-input gates (or *9k* gate clauses) at every depth k.

Gen_Read_Data_Constraints: Generation of constraints on read data signals

By virtue of equation (3), we know that for a given k, at most one $S^{j,k}=1$, $\forall_{-1 \le j < k}$. We use this fact to represent the constraint in equation (4) as CNF clauses. Let n denote the bit width of the data bus. We add the following clauses $\forall_{0 \le i < n}, \forall_{-1 \le j < k}$

$$(!S^{j,k} + !RD^k_i + WD^j_i), (!S^{j,k} + RD^k_i + !WD^j_i)$$

To capture validity of read signal, we add the following clause

$$(!RE^k + S^{-1,k}+...+S^{j,k}+...+S^{k-1,k})$$

Thus we add $2n(k+1)+1$ clauses at every depth k. On the other hand, if we use gate representation, it would require $n(2k+1)$ gates and therefore, $3n(2k+1)$ gate clauses.

Overall, at every depth k, our *hybrid exclusive select signals* representation adds $(4m+2n+1)k+2n+1$ clauses and $3k$ gates as compared to $(4m+2n+2)k +n$ gates in a purely circuit representation. Note that though the size of these accumulated constraints grows quadratically with depth k, they are still significantly smaller than the explicit memory-model.

5 Experiments

For our experiments, we used three well-known recursive software programs *Fibonacci, 3n+1,* and *Towers-of Hanoi* with an embedded stack as shown in Figure 5 and one hardware design with embedded RAM. In each of these cases, we chose a safety property that makes the modeling of the entire memory imperative, *i.e.*, we simply cannot remove away the memory from the design. We translated each of the software programs into equivalent hardware models using Verilog HDL using a stack model. For each of the software designs, we use an inverse function to describe the negated safety property that requires a non-trivial state space search, e.g., given a certain value of *fibonacci* number does there exist a corresponding n? (Similar queries are made for a given number of recursive calls to terminate *3n+1*, and for a given number of legal moves required in *Towers-of-Hanoi*.)

```
 1.  //Fibonacci                16. 3nPlus1(n) {
 2.  //cache and recursion       17.   if (n==1) return;
 3.  fib(n) {                     18.   if ((odd(n))
 4.    if (n<2) return n;         19.     3nPlus1(3*n+1);
 5.    //cache lookup             20.   else
 6.    if(lookup(n,&f))           21.     3nPlus1(n/2);
 7.      return f;                22.   period++; }
 8.    f = fib(n-1)+fib(n-2);
 9.    //insert cache             23. //Towers of Hanoi
10.    store(n,f);                24. //count tracks # of moves
11.    return f; }                25. //req.; initialized to 0
                                  26. toh(n,s,d,a) {
12. //3n+1                        27.   if (n==0) return;
13. //period tracks # of         28.   toh(n-1,s,a,d);
14. //calls req. to converge;    29.   count++;
15. //initialized to 0           30.   toh(n-1,a,d,s); }
```

Fig. 5. Software programs with embedded stack used in experiments

We conducted our experiments on a workstation composed of dual Intel 2.8 GHz Xeon Processors with 4GB physical memory running Red Hat Linux 7.2 using a 3 hours time limit for each BMC run. We compare the performance of augmented SAT-based BMC (m-BMC) for handling embedded memory with basic SAT-based BMC using *explicit* memory modeling. We also compare the performance of m-BMC using our hybrid exclusive select signal representation (*hESS*), with that of a hybrid nested ITE representation (*hITE*). In addition, we show the effect on their performance with increasing memory sizes for a given property and design.

We performed our first set of experiments on the hardware models of the software programs with several properties selected as described above. Each of the properties has a non-trivial witness and is listed in Tables 1-4 in the order of increasing search complexity. We used a fixed memory size in each of the models. We also used one industrial hardware design with a safety property that is not known to have a counter example. For these properties, we show the performance and memory utilization comparison of the memory modeling styles, *i.e.*, explicit memory modeling, memory modeling using our *hESS* representation and that using *hITE* representation in the Tables 1-4. In Tables 1-3, we show comparison results for *Fibonacci*, *3n+1*, and *Towers-of-Hanoi*, respectively. We used address width (AW)=12, data width (DW)=32 for *Fibonacci*, AW=12, DW=2 for *3n+1*, and AW=12, DW=22 for *Towers-of-Hanoi* models. In Table 4, we show comparison results for the industrial hardware design with a given safety property S for various intermediate analysis depths as the property was not violated within the resource limit. Without the memory, the design has ~400 latches and ~5k gates. The memory module has AW=12 and DW=12.

In Tables 1-4, the 1st Column shows the properties with increasing complexity, the 2nd Column shows the witness depth (intermediate analysis depth in Table 4), 3-7 Columns show the performance figures and 8-12 Columns show the memory utilization figures. Specifically in the performance columns, Columns 3-5 show the BMC search time taken (in seconds) for explicit memory modeling (P1), using *hITE* (P2), and using *hESS* (P3) respectively; Columns 6 and 7 show the speed up (ratio) using *hESS* over the explicit memory modeling and *hITE* respectively. For the memory

Table 1. Comparison of memory modeling on *Fibonacci* model (AW=12, DW=32)

Prp	Wit Depth	Performance					Memory Utilization				
		Explicit P1(s)	hITE P2(s)	hESS P3(s)	Speed P1/P3	Speed P1/P3	Explicit M1(mb)	hITE M2(mb)	hESS M3(mb)	Red. M3/M1	Red. M3/M2
1-1	14	179	1	1	146	1.1	517	7	6	0.01	0.86
1-2	25	1050	5	4	248	1.3	1411	12	10	0.01	0.83
1-3	38	2835	20	15	184	1.3	2239	22	17	0.01	0.77
1-4	51	NA	79	47	NA	1.7	MO	41	34	NA	0.83
1-5	64	NA	125	100	NA	1.3	MO	63	52	NA	0.83
1-6	77	NA	252	311	NA	0.8	MO	100	75	NA	0.75
1-7	90	NA	587	362	NA	1.6	MO	175	92	NA	0.53
1-8	103	NA	625	557	NA	1.1	MO	163	161	NA	0.99
1-9	116	NA	1060	674	NA	1.6	MO	189	187	NA	0.99
1-10	129	NA	1674	1359	NA	1.2	MO	343	204	NA	0.59
1-11	142	NA	3782	2165	NA	1.7	MO	353	372	NA	1.05
1-12	155	NA	2980	2043	NA	1.5	MO	421	303	NA	0.72
1-13	168	NA	4349	4517	NA	1.0	MO	319	623	NA	1.95
1-14	181	NA	5573	4010	NA	1.4	MO	485	335	NA	0.69
1-15	194	NA	6973	4889	NA	1.4	MO	558	531	NA	0.95
1-16	207	NA	> 3hr	7330	NA	NA	MO	541	461	NA	0.85

Table 2. Comparison of memory modeling on *3n+1* model (AW=12, DW=2)

Prp	Wit Depth	Performance					Memory Utilization				
		Explicit P1(s)	hITE P2(s)	hESS P3(s)	Speed P1/P3	Speed P2/P3	Explicit M1(mb)	hITE M2(mb)	hESS M3(mb)	Red. M3/M1	Red. M3/M1
2-1	44	2736	85	51	54	1.7	293	25	20	0.07	0.8
2-2	47	3837	109	138	28	0.8	314	30	37	0.12	1.23
2-3	50	2811	167	160	18	1.0	412	44	37	0.09	0.84
2-4	53	3236	205	207	16	1.0	407	42	58	0.14	1.38
2-5	56	5643	258	264	21	1.0	569	48	44	0.08	0.92
2-6	59	4518	312	277	16	1.1	432	56	49	0.11	0.88
2-7	62	9078	324	368	25	0.9	479	58	59	0.12	1.02
2-8	65	9613	426	483	20	0.9	585	72	85	0.15	1.18
2-9	68	10446	487	522	20	0.9	648	73	64	0.10	0.88
2-10	71	9903	562	590	17	1.0	668	82	74	0.11	0.90
2-11	74	> 3hr	674	692	NA	1.0	981	83	92	NA	1.11
2-12	77	> 3hr	910	746	NA	1.2	719	110	83	NA	0.75
2-13	80	> 3hr	820	861	NA	1.0	875	106	89	NA	0.84
2-14	83	> 3hr	969	990	NA	1.0	586	113	80	NA	0.71
2-15	89	> 3hr	1292	1201	NA	1.1	659	127	113	NA	0.89

Table 3. Comparison of memory modeling on *Towers-of-Hanoi* (AW=12, DW=22)

Prp	Wit Depth	Performance					Memory Utilization				
		Explicit P1(sec)	hITE P2(s)	hESS P3(s)	Speed P1/P3	Speed P2/P3	Explicit M1(mb)	hITE M2(mb)	hESS M3(mb)	Red M3/M1	Red. M3/M2
3-1	10	4	0	0	149	1.3	71	3	3	0.04	1.00
3-2	24	182	1	1	264	1.2	664	6	5	0.01	0.83
3-3	52	2587	13	10	255	1.2	2059	16	12	0.01	0.75
3-4	108	NA	229	129	NA	1.8	MO	68	43	NA	0.63
3-5	220	NA	1266	838	NA	1.5	MO	214	143	NA	0.67
3-6	444	NA	8232	6925	NA	1.2	MO	845	569	NA	0.67

utilization columns, Columns 8-10 show the memory used (in MB) by explicit memory modeling (M1), using *hITE* (M2), and using *hESS* (M3) respectively; Column 11 and 12 show the memory usage reduction (ratio) using *hESS* over the explicit memory modeling and *hITE* respectively (Note, $MO \equiv$ Memory Out, $NA \equiv$ Not Applicable).

Observing the performance figures in Column 6 of the Tables 1-4, we see that our approach improves the performance of BMC by *1-2 orders of magnitude* when compared to explicit memory modeling. Similarly, as shown in Column 11 of these tables, there is a reduction in memory utilization by *1-2 orders of magnitude* by the use of our approach. Moreover, our modeling style of using the hybrid exclusive select signals representation is better than the hybrid nested ITE, as shown in Column 7 and 12. Noticeably, in the last row of Table 1 and 4, *hITE* times out while our approach

Table 4. Comparison of memory modeling on industrial hardware design (AW=12, DW=12)

Prp	Inter Depth	Performance					Memory Utilization				
		Explicit P1(s)	hITE P2(s)	hESS P3(s)	Speed P1/P3	Speed P2/P3	Explicit M1(mb)	hITE M2(mb)	hESS M3(mb)	Red. M3/M1	Red. M3/M2
	68	10680	1264	925	11	1.3	2049	91	64	0.03	0.7
S	150	NA	9218	7140	NA	1.3	MO	770	261	NA	0.3
	178	NA	>3hr	10272	NA	NA	MO	NA	908	NA	NA

Table 5. Comparison of memory modeling (for $3n+1$) with DW=12 and varying address width

Prp	AW	Performance					Memory Utilization				
		Explicit P1(s)	hITE P2(s)	hESS P3(s)	Speed P1/P3	Speed P2/P3	Explicit M1(mb)	hITE M2(mb)	hESS M3(mb)	Red M3/M1	Red M3/M2
	4	64	85	60	1.1	1.4	23	22	20	0.87	0.9
	5	81	72	47	1.7	1.5	21	22	17	0.81	0.8
	6	110	77	79	1.4	1.0	25	23	24	0.96	1.0
	7	117	99	53	2.2	1.9	28	25	19	0.68	0.8
	8	146	87	78	1.9	1.1	41	24	24	0.59	1.0
2-1	9	265	79	73	3.6	1.1	49	25	22	0.45	0.9
	10	767	86	59	12.9	1.4	95	27	22	0.23	0.8
	11	1490	89	56	26.4	1.6	153	27	20	0.13	0.7
	12	2736	85	51	54.1	1.7	293	25	20	0.07	0.8
	13	3759	83	54	69.6	1.5	569	24	21	0.04	0.9
	14	11583	81	46	249.2	1.7	1452	25	18	0.01	0.7

using *hESS* completes the analysis within the 3 hours time limit. Note that due to tail recursive nature of the $3n+1$ program, the search complexity is not severe and therefore, we don't see the consistent benefit of exclusive select signals for this example in Table 2. On average, we see a performance improvement of 30% and a reduction in memory utilization of 20%, noticeably more at higher analysis depths.

In the second set of experiments, we used different memory sizes for the model $3n+1$ and the property $2-1$. We varied the address bus width AW from 4 to 14 bits and compare the performance and memory utilization of the three approaches as shown in Column 2 of Table 5. The description of the remaining Columns in Table 5 is same as that in Tables 1-4. As shown in Columns 6 and 10, the performance improvement and memory usage reduction gets more pronounced, about 2 orders of magnitude, with increasing memory size. Clearly, the merits from adding memory-modeling constraints outweigh its quadratic growth. Moreover, our approach show on average 50% performance improvement and 20% memory usage reduction over nested ITE expressions.

6 Conclusions

Verifying designs with large embedded memories is typically handled by abstracting out (over-approximating) the memories. Such abstraction is generally not useful for finding real bugs. Current SAT-based BMC efforts are incapable of handling designs with explicit memory modeling due to enormously increased search space complexity. In this work, we are the first to use memory-modeling constraints to augment SAT-based BMC in order to handle embedded memory designs without explicitly modeling each memory bit. Our method does not require transforming the design and is also guaranteed not to generate false negatives. This method is similar to abstract interpretation of memory [12, 21], but with key enhancements. Our method can easily augment any SAT-based BMC effort. We demonstrate the effectiveness of our approach on a number of software and hardware designs with large embedded memories. We show about 1-2 orders of magnitude time and space improvement using our method over explicit modeling of each memory bit. We also show that our method of adding constraints boosts the performance of a SAT solver significantly as opposed to the conventional way of modeling these constraints as nested ITE expressions [12]. While the growth of memory modeling constraint clauses is quadratic with the analysis depth, we also observed that though the constraint clauses are sufficient they may not be necessary in every time frame. As an ongoing effort, we are further investigating the possibility of adding these clauses only as and when required.

References

1. A. Biere, A. Cimatti, E. M. Clarke, M. Fujita, and Y. Zhu, "Symbolic model checking using SAT procedures instead of BDDs," in *Proceedings of the Design Automation Conference*, 1999, pp. 317-320.
2. P. Bjesse and K. Claessen, "SAT-based verification without state space traversal," in *Proceedings of Conference on Formal Methods in Computer-Aided Design*, 2000.
3. M. Ganai and A. Aziz, "Improved SAT-based Bounded Reachability Analysis," in *Proceedings of VLSI Design Conference*, 2002.
4. P. A. Abdulla, P. Bjesse, and N. Een, "Symbolic Reachability Analysis based on {SAT}-Solvers," in *Proceedings of Workshop on Tools and Algorithms for the Analysis and Construction of Systems (TACAS)*, 2000.
5. E. M. Clarke, O. Grumberg, and D. Peled, *Model Checking*: MIT Press, 1999.
6. K. L. McMillan, *Symbolic Model Checking: An Approach to the State Explosion Problem*: Kluwer Academic Publishers, 1993.
7. J. P. Marques-Silva and K. A. Sakallah, "GRASP: A Search Algorithm for Propositional Satisfiability," *IEEE Transactions on Computers*, vol. 48, pp. 506-521, 1999.
8. H. Zhang, "SATO: An efficient propositional prover," in *Proceedings of International Conference on Automated Deduction*, vol. 1249, *LNAI*, 1997, pp. 272-275.
9. M. Moskewicz, C. Madigan, Y. Zhao, L. Zhang, and S. Malik, "Chaff: Engineering an Efficient SAT Solver," in *Proceedings of Design Automation Conference*, 2001.
10. M. Ganai, L. Zhang, P. Ashar, and A. Gupta, "Combining Strengths of Circuit-based and CNF-based Algorithms for a High Performance SAT Solver," in *Proceedings of the Design Automation Conference*, 2002.
11. A. Kuehlmann, M. Ganai, and V. Paruthi, "Circuit-based Boolean Reasoning," in *Proceedings of Design Automation Conference*, 2001.

12. J. R. Burch and D. L. Dill, "Automatic verification of pipelined microprocessor control," in *Proceedings of the sixth International Conference on Computer-Aided Verification*, vol. 818, D. L. Dill, Ed.: Springer-Verlag, 1994, pp. 68--80.

13. D. E. Long, "Model checking, abstraction and compositional verification," Carnegie Mellon University, 1993.

14. R. P. Kurshan, *Computer-Aided Verification of Co-ordinating Processes: The Automata-Theoretic Approach*: Princeton University Press, 1994.

15. E. M. Clarke, O. Grumberg, S. Jha, Y. Lu, and H. Veith, "Counterexample-guided abstraction refinement," in *Proceedings of CAV*, vol. 1855, *LNCS*, 2000, pp. 154-169.

16. E. M. Clarke, A. Gupta, J. Kukula, and O. Strichman, "SAT based abstraction-refinement using ILP and machine learning techniques," in *Proceedings of CAV*, 2002.

17. D. Wang, P.-H. Ho, J. Long, J. Kukula, Y. Zhu, T. Ma, and R. Damiano, "Formal Property Verification by Abstraction Refinement with Formal, Simulation and Hybrid Engines," in *38th Design Automation Conference*, 2001.

18. P. Chauhan, E. M. Clarke, J. Kukula, S. Sapra, H. Veith, and D. Wang, "Automated Abstraction Refinement for Model Checking Large State Spaces using SAT based Conflict Analysis," in *Proceedings of FMCAD*, 2002.

19. K. McMillan and N. Amla, "Automatic Abstraction without Counterexamples," in *Tools and Algorithms for the Construction and Analysis of Systems*, April 2003.

20. A. Gupta, M. Ganai, P. Ashar, and Z. Yang, "Iterative Abstraction using SAT-based BMC with Proof Analysis," in *Proceedings of International Conference on Computer-Aided Design*, 2003.

21. M. N. Velev, R. E. Bryant, and A. Jain, "Efficient Modeling of Memory Arrays in Symbolic Simulation," in *ComputerAided Verification*, O. Grumberg, Ed., 1997, pp. 388-399.

22. R. E. Bryant, S. German, and M. N. Velev, "Processor Verification Using Efficient Reductions of the Logic of Uninterpreted Functions to Propositional Logic," in *Computer-Aided Verification*, N. Halbwachs and D. Peled, Eds.: Springer-Verlag, 1999, pp. 470-482.

23. M. N. Velev, "Automatic Abstraction of Memories in the Formal Verification of Superscalar Microprocessors," in *Proceedings of Tools and Algorithms for the Construction and Analysis of Systems*, 2001, pp. 252-267.

24. S. K. Lahiri, S. A. Seshia, and R. E. Bryant, "Modeling and Verification of Out-of-Order Microprocessors in UCLID," in *Proceedings of Formal Methods in Computer-Aided Design*, 2002, pp. 142-159.

25. R. E. Bryant, S. K. Lahiri, and S. A. Seshia, "Modeling and Verifying Systems using a Logic of Counter Arithmetic with Lambda Expressions and Uninterpreted Functions," in *Computer-Aided Verification*, 2002.

26. A. Biere, A. Cimatti, E. M. Clarke, and Y. Zhu, "Symbolic Model Checking without BDDs," in *Proceedings of Workshop on Tools and Algorithms for Analysis and Construction of Systems (TACAS)*, vol. 1579, *LNCS*, 1999.

27. M. Sheeran, S. Singh, and G. Stalmarck, "Checking Safety Properties using Induction and a SAT Solver," in *Proceedings of Conference on Formal Methods in Computer-Aided Design*, 2000.

28. S. Pilarski and G. Hu, "Speeding up SAT for EDA," in *Proceedings of Design Automation and Test in Europe*, 2002, pp. 1081.

Understanding Counterexamples with explain

Alex Groce, Daniel Kroening, and Flavio Lerda

Computer Science Department, Carnegie Mellon University
Pittsburgh, PA 15213

Abstract. The counterexamples produced by model checkers are often lengthy and difficult to understand. In practical verification, showing the existence of a (potential) bug is not enough: the error must be understood, determined to not be a result of faulty specification or assumptions, and, finally, located and corrected. The explain tool uses distance metrics on program executions to provide automated assistance in understanding and localizing errors in ANSI-C programs. explain is integrated with CBMC, a bounded model checker for the C language, and features a GUI front-end that presents error explanations to the user.

1 Introduction

In an ideal world, given a detailed error trace, a programmer would always be able to quickly identify and correct the faulty portion of the code or specification. Practical experience, however, indicates that this is not the case. Understanding a counterexample often requires as much effort as preparing a program for model checking. As software model checking has become more concerned with practical applicability, the need for automated assistance in understanding counterexamples has been recognized [2, 6]. The explain tool provides users with assistance in focusing on the relevant portions of source code and in understanding the causal dependencies involved in an error.

CBMC [7] is a tool for verifying ANSI-C programs. CBMC is a bounded model checker (BMC) [3]: it produces from a C program a Boolean formula satisfiable by executions of the program that violate its specification (counterexamples). The model checker supports pointer constructs, dynamic memory allocation, recursion, and the float and double data types. CBMC also features a graphical user interface designed to resemble an IDE (Integrated Development Environment) that allows users to interactively step through counterexample traces.

explain uses the same bounded model checking engine to further analyze counterexample traces produced by CBMC. In particular, explain uses *distance metrics* on program executions [5], in a manner inspired by the counterfactual theory of causality [8], to provide a number of automatic analyses:

- Given a counterexample execution, explain can automatically produce an execution that is as similar as possible to the failing run but *does not* violate the specification.

R. Alur and D.A. Peled (Eds.): CAV 2004, LNCS 3114, pp. 453–456, 2004.
© Springer-Verlag Berlin Heidelberg 2004

- explain can also automatically produce a new counterexample that is as *different* as possible from the original counterexample.
- Finally, explain can determine causal dependencies between predicates in an execution.

explain is used through the same GUI as CBMC. The interface allows users to step through explanatory traces as they would in a debugger (with the ability to step forwards and backwards). Portions of the code that explain suggests may be faulty are highlighted for the user.

2   Using explain

Using explain is an interactive process. The tool assists the user in understanding counterexamples, but knowledge of the program (and the specification) is necessary to guide the tool. As an example, we will use explain to narrow in on an error in a small but non-trivial C program.

2.1   Debugging TCAS

TCAS (Traffic Alert and Collision Avoidance System) is an aircraft conflict detection and resolution system used by all US commercial aircraft. The Georgia Tech version of the Siemens suite [9] includes 41 buggy versions of ANSI-C code for the Resolution Advisory (RA) component of the TCAS system. A specification for this code (in the form of assertions) is available from another study [4].

The first step in using explain to understand an error is to produce a counterexample. We load tcas.c into the GUI and run the CBMC model checker. After a few seconds, the GUI reports that the assertion on line 257 has been violated.

The counterexample execution passes through 112 states. Single-stepping through the trace looking for a bug is not an appealing prospect, so we turn to explain for assistance in understanding what is wrong with our code. We run explain on the counterexample to find a successful execution that is as similar as possible to the failing run. explain uses the PBS [1] pseudo-Boolean solver to produce this trace, and lists the changes made to the original counterexample. The GUI highlights the lines that are involved in the changes[1].

Unfortunately, the explanation is less than useful. The failed assertion in the counterexample is an implication:

```
P3_BCond = ((Input_Up_Separation >= Layer_Positive_RA_Alt_Thresh)&&
            (Input_Down_Separation >= Layer_Positive_RA_Alt_Thresh)&&
            (Input_Own_Tracked_Alt < Input_Other_Tracked_Alt));
assert(!(P3_BCond && PrB)); // P3_BCond -> ! PrB
```

The successful execution most similar to the counterexample changes the value of Input_Down_Separation such that it is now < Layer_Positive_RA_Alt_Thresh, and *no other values*. We are really interested in finding out why, given that

---

[1] explain uses a causal slicing algorithm [5] to remove changes unrelated to the error.

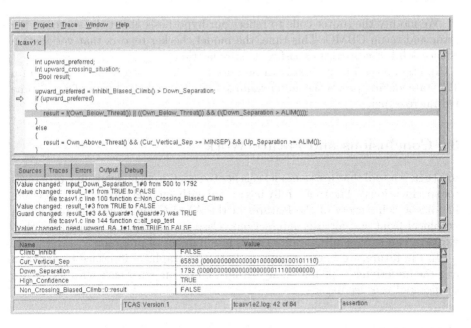

Fig. 1. Correctly locating the error in tcas.c.

P3_BCond holds, PrB also holds. In other words, we want to know the cause for the value of the consequent, not the antecedent, of the implication. Requesting the more precise explanation is a simple matter of adding the constraint assume(P1_BCond) and then rerunning explain.

The new explanation is more interesting (Figure 1). Input_Down_Separation is, again, altered. This time the value has increased, maintaining the original value of P3_BCond. Stepping through the source code we notice the first highlighted line in the run:

result = !(Own_Below_Threat()) || ((Own_Below_Threat()) &&
           (!(Down_Separation > ALIM())));

Most of the values in the expression are unchanged from the erroneous run. Only Down_Separation has changed, causing result to be FALSE instead of TRUE. In the original run, Down_Separation was 500, and now it is 1792. A quick examination of the other 4 highlighted lines shows that they simply propagate the value of result computed. If the comparison of Down_Separation and ALIM() had resulted in TRUE in the original run, the assertion would have held. Looking at the code, we notice that the ALIM function returns Positive_RA_Alt_Thresh[Alt_Layer_Value]. The variable watches window reveals that ALIM() has the value 500 in both runs.

Suspiciously, the value of Down_Separation in the counterexample was also 500, and the error did not appear when that value changed. It seems likely that the value of this expression is the source of the problem. In order to make the expression's value in the faulty run match the value in the successful run, we need to change the > into a >= comparison.

We modify the source code to reflect our hypothesis about the source of the error and rerun CBMC. This time, the model checker reports that verification is successful: the program satisfies its specification.

In other experiments, `explain` produced a 1 line (correct) localization of a 127 state locking-protocol counterexample for a 2991 line fragment of a real-time OS microkernel.

3   Conclusions and Future Work

`explain` is a tool that uses a model checker to assist users in debugging programs (or specifications). The tool is fully integrated with a model checker that precisely handles a rich variety of the features of the ANSI-C language, and provides a graphical front-end for user interactions. Case studies have demonstrated that `explain` can successfully localize errors in a number of programs.

In the future, we hope to improve both the graphical interface to `explain` and the underlying explanation algorithms, based on experience with more case studies and user feedback.

References

1. F. Aloul, A. Ramani, I. Markov, and K. Sakallah. PBS: A backtrack search pseudo Boolean solver. In *Symposium on the theory and applications of satisfiability testing (SAT)*, pages 346–353, 2002.
2. T. Ball, M. Naik, and S. Rajamani. From symptom to cause: Localizing errors in counterexample traces. In *Principles of Programming Languages*, pages 97–105, 2003.
3. A. Biere, A. Cimatti, E. Clarke, and Y. Zhu. Symbolic model checking without BDDs. In *Tools and Algorithms for the Construction and Analysis of Systems*, pages 193–207, 1999.
4. A Coen-Porisini, G. Denaro, C. Ghezzi, and M. Pezze. Using symbolic execution for verifying safety-critical systems. In *European Software Engineering Conference/Foundations of Software Engineering*, pages 142–151, 2001.
5. A. Groce. Error explanation with distance metrics. In *Tools and Algorithms for the Construction and Analysis of Systems*, pages 108–122, 2004.
6. A. Groce and W. Visser. What went wrong: Explaining counterexamples. In *SPIN Workshop on Model Checking of Software*, pages 121–135, 2003.
7. D. Kroening, E. Clarke, and F. Lerda. A tool for checking ANSI-C programs. In *Tools and Algorithms for the Construction and Analysis of Systems*, pages 168–176, 2004.
8. D. Lewis. Causation. *Journal of Philosophy*, 70:556–567, 1973.
9. G. Rothermel and M. J. Harrold. Empirical studies of a safe regression test selection technique. *Software Engineering*, 24(6):401–419, 1999.

ZAPATO: Automatic Theorem Proving
for Predicate Abstraction Refinement

Thomas Ball[1], Byron Cook[1], Shuvendu K. Lahiri[2], and Lintao Zhang[1]

[1] Microsoft Corporation
[2] Carnegie-Mellon University

Abstract. Counterexample-driven abstraction refinement is an automatic process that produces abstract models of finite and infinite-state systems. When this process is applied to software, an automatic theorem prover for quantifier-free first-order logic helps to determine the feasibility of program paths and to refine the abstraction. In this paper we report on a fast, lightweight, and automatic theorem prover called ZAPATO which we have built specifically to solve the queries produced during the abstraction refinement process.

1 Introduction

SLAM is a symbolic software model checker for the C language which combines predicate abstraction together with counter-example guided abstraction refinement. SLAM's overall performance critically depends on the automatic theorem prover that is used during the refinement process. Two of SLAM's modules, NEWTON [1] and CONSTRAIN [2], generate many theorem proving queries during their analysis[1]. As an example, when SLAM was used to check 30 properties of the Microsoft Windows Parallel Port device driver, NEWTON and CONSTRAIN called the prover 487,716 times. On average, these queries contained 19 unique atoms and 40 instances of Boolean operators per query. In the worst case, one query contained 658 unique atoms. Another query contained 96,691 instances of the Boolean operators. For the scalability of SLAM it is paramount that these queries are solved in less than a half a second in the average case.

In this paper we briefly describe SLAM's theorem prover – called ZAPATO. ZAPATO's overall architecture is similar to VERIFUN [5]. However, rather than using the Simplex or Fourier & Motzkin arithmetic decision procedures, ZAPATO uses an algorithm due to Harvey & Stuckey [6] for solving constraint problems over sets of *unit two-variable per inequality* integer terms.

---

[1] C2BP [3] can also be configured to use the theorem prover described in this paper. However, by default, C2BP actually uses a special purpose symbolic theorem prover called FASTF which is similar to the work of Lahiri, Bryant & Cook [4] but optimized for speed and not precision.

R. Alur and D.A. Peled (Eds.): CAV 2004, LNCS 3114, pp. 457–461, 2004.
© Springer-Verlag Berlin Heidelberg 2004

2   Lazy Theorem Proving Based on Propositional Logic SAT

ZAPATO takes a query in quantifier-free first-order logic (FOL) and returns valid if it can prove the query to be true. In the case that it cannot prove the query true, it returns invalid. Note that invalid does not actually mean that the query is not valid – only that ZAPATO could not prove it valid. ZAPATO operates by negating the FOL query passed to it and then trying to prove unsatisfiability. ZAPATO creates a propositional logic (PL) abstraction of the negated query in which each atomic formula is replaced by a fresh representative propositional variable. A mapping between formulae and propositional variables is maintained throughout the execution of the algorithm.

An incremental PL SAT-solver is used to determine if the propositional abstraction is satisfiable. In the case that it is unsatisfiable, the query is determined to be valid. In the case that the abstraction is satisfiable, the model found is converted to FOL (via a reverse application of the mapping) and passed to a FOL SAT-solver for conjuncts. This model is often *partial* – meaning that variables which can be of either Boolean value in the model are typically eliminated by the SAT-solver in a post-backtracking analysis. Since these values are not important in the model they can be ignored when determining the satisfiability of the model in FOL.

If the input FOL conjunct solver determines that the found model is satisfiable, then the original query is determined to be invalid. In the case that the set of conjuncts is unsatisfiable, the *core reason* that the model is unsatisfiable is determined. This core reason is a subset of the original conjuncts and is found by visiting the leaves of the proof tree constructed by the FOL conjunct solver. The core reason is then converted to PL using the mapping and inserted into the PL SAT-solver's database of learned clauses. A third possible output from the conjunct solver is a set of case-splits, which is translated into additional conflict causes. This case is due to the way some axioms are instantiated. The loop is repeated until the PL SAT-solver returns *unsatisfiable* or the FOL solver returns *satisfiable*.

ZAPATO's FOL conjunct solver uses Nelson & Oppen's method of combining decision procedures with equality sharing. Currently we are using this technique to combine congruence closure for uninterpreted functions with Harvey & Stuckey's decision procedure. Each of the procedures must produce the reasoning behind their decisions in order to allow for the construction of proofs. ZAPATO's FOL solver also implements several axioms that express facts about C expressions with pointers by searching the set of input conjuncts and adding additional conjuncts.

2.1   Harvey & Stuckey's Decision Procedure

Harvey & Stuckey's procedure is a complete algorithm with polynomial time complexity that can be used to solve conjuncted integer constraints. In this procedure each input constraint is expected to be of the form $ax + by \leq d$

where x and y are variables, d is an integer and a and b must be elements of the set $\{-1, 0, 1\}$. Harvey & Stuckey call this subset the *unit two-variable per inequality* (UTVPI) constraints. Note that ZAPATO uses homogenization and term rewriting to remove terms that contain both arithmetic and uninterpreted function symbols. ZAPATO also rewrites arithmetic terms into canonical form. For example, $x < y$ is converted into $1x + (-1)y \leq -1$.

The algorithm is based on iterative transitive closure: as each conjunct is added into the system, all possible consequences of the input are computed. Several strengthening transition rules on the state of the set of known facts are applied at each conjunct introduction to produce the complete closure. In the case that the conjuncts are unsatisfiable, a conjunct and its negation will eventually exist in the set of facts. In the case that no contradiction is found, the constraints must be satisfiable.

An interesting aspect to note about Harvey & Stuckey's algorithm is that it can be used to prove the unsatisfiability of sets of constraints which may include non-UTVPI terms. For example, it can prove the unsatisfiability of

$$n > k' + n' \wedge x < y' \wedge v + 5 < l \wedge y' < z \wedge \neg(x < z) \wedge k < v + z$$

In these cases we can simply prune away the conjuncts that are not UTVPI terms because the non-UTVPI constraints (such as $k < v + z$) may not factor into the reason for unsatisfiability. The above expression is unsatisfiable because the following is unsatisfiable: $x < y' \wedge y' < z \wedge \neg(x < z)$. This allows us to solve many queries that may appear at first to be non-UTVPI.

The logic supported by ZAPATO dictates that SLAM's predicates are always UTVPI constraints with the possibility of uninterpreted function symbols. This is due to the fact that SLAM's NEWTON module only adds new predicates in the case that validity is proved by the theorem prover. At first this may sound disastrously limiting. However, it is not. Both NEWTON and CONSTRAIN can refine the abstraction if they can find *any* spurious transitions in the path that they are examining. Paths are often spurious for multiple reasons. So long as at least one of those reasons can be proved valid using ZAPATO, the refinement algorithm will make progress. In the worst case, ZAPATO's limited arithmetic support could cause SLAM to report a false bug. In the 10 months that we have been using UTVPI in ZAPATO we have only seen this occur once while model checking real device drivers.

The completeness of Harvey & Stuckey's procedure allows us to prove the validity of queries other automatic provers struggle with. Consider, for example, the validity of $x < 3 \wedge x > 1 \Rightarrow x = 2$. Because VERIFUN uses a decision procedure for the real numbers the only way that this can be proved is through the use of special purpose heuristics or with additional axioms.

3   Experimental Results

To evaluate the effectiveness of ZAPATO we used SLAM to check 82 safety properties of 28 Windows OS device drivers and recorded statistics about the theorem prover queries. In total, SLAM passed 1,748,580 queries to ZAPATO. Note that SLAM caches the interface to the prover. These 1,748,580 queries are the cases in which a pre-computed result could not be found in the cache. Of these queries, 148,509 were proved valid by ZAPATO. ZAPATO resolved the remaining queries as invalid. 607,251 queries caused ZAPATO, at least on one occasion, to invoke Harvey & Stuckey's decision procedure on a set of conjuncts with a non-UTVPI term. Of those 607,251 queries, ZAPATO was still able to prove 62,163 valid.

To compare Harvey & Stuckey's algorithm versus a more traditional arithmetic decision procedure we also compared the functional result of ZAPATO to SIMPLIFY on the benchmark queries. SIMPLIFY was able to prove 248 queries valid that ZAPATO could not. ZAPATO proved 560 queries valid that SIMPLIFY could not. Because the provers support different logics, a performance comparison is difficult to analyze. But generally, as also reported by Flanagan et al. [5], the new lazy PL SAT-based approach scales better on larger benchmarks. In the case of the hardest invalid query from the benchmarks, ZAPATO's runtime was 8 seconds while SIMPLIFY's was 10 seconds. Both SIMPLIFY and ZAPATO were able to prove the hardest valid query in 3 seconds.

4   Conclusions

ZAPATO's architecture is based on the prover VERIFUN. What makes ZAPATO unique is that it does not use Fourier & Motzkin or Simplex as its decision procedure for arithmetic. Instead, it uses a decision procedure proposed by Harvey & Stuckey which has better worst-case asymptotic complexity and a completeness result for a useful subset of arithmetic terms over the integers. The expressiveness of this subset appears to be sufficient for the verification of Windows device drivers using SLAM. We are currently integrating the Simplex decision procedure into ZAPATO, which we envision could be optionally combined with Harvey & Stuckey's algorithm in applications where full linear arithmetic is required.

Acknowledgements

The authors would like to thank Cormac Flanagan, John Harrison, Rajeev Joshi, Sava Krstic, Rustan Leino, Ken McMillan, and Sriram Rajamani for their suggestions related to this work.

References

1. Ball, T., Rajamani, S.K.: Generating abstract explanations of spurious counterexamples in C programs. Technical Report MSR-TR-2002-09, Microsoft Research (2002)
2. Ball, T., Cook, B., Das, S., Rajamani, S.K.: Refining approximations in software predicate abstraction. In: TACAS 04: Tools and Algorithms for Construction and Analysis of Systems, Springer-Verlag (2004)

3. Ball, T., Majumdar, R., Millstein, T., Rajamani, S.K.: Automatic predicate abstraction of C programs. In: PLDI 01: Programming Language Design and Implementation, ACM (2001) 203–213
4. Lahiri, S.K., Bryant, R.E., Cook, B.: A symbolic approach to predicate abstraction. In: CAV 03: International Conference on Computer-Aided Verification. (2003) 141–153
5. Flanagan, C., Joshi, R., Ou, X., Saxe, J.B.: Theorem proving using lazy proof explication. In: CAV 03: International Conference on Computer-Aided Verification. (2003) 355–367
6. Harvey, W., Stuckey, P.: A unit two variable per inequality integer constraint solver for constraint logic programming. In: Australian Computer Science Conference (Australian Computer Science Communications). (1997) 102–111

JNuke: Efficient Dynamic Analysis for Java

Cyrille Artho[1], Viktor Schuppan[1], Armin Biere[1],
Pascal Eugster[2], Marcel Baur[3], and Boris Zweimüller[1]

[1] Computer Systems Institute, ETH Zürich, Switzerland
[2] Avaloq Evolution, Zürich, Switzerland
[3] Al Dente Brainworks, Zürich, Switzerland

Abstract. JNuke is a framework for verification and model checking of Java programs. It is a novel combination of run-time verification, explicit-state model checking, and counter-example exploration. Efficiency is crucial in dynamic verification. Therefore JNuke has been written from scratch in C, improving performance and memory usage by an order of magnitude compared to competing approaches and tools.

1 Introduction

Java is a popular object-oriented, multi-threaded programming language. Verification of Java programs has become increasingly important. *Dynamic analysis,* including run-time verification and model checking, has the key advantage of having precise information available, compared to classical approaches like *theorem proving* and *static analysis.* There are fully automated dynamic analysis algorithms that can deduce possible errors by analyzing a single execution trace [1, 7, 14].

Dynamic analysis requires an execution environment, such as a Java Virtual Machine (VM). However, typical Java VMs only target execution and do not offer all required features, in particular, backtracking and full state access. Code instrumentation, used by JPaX, only solves the latter problem [9]. JNuke, our run-time verification and model-checking framework, contains a specialized VM allowing both backtracking and full access to its state. Custom checking algorithms can be implemented.

Related work includes software model checkers that apply directly to programs, for example, the Java PathFinder system (JPF) developed by NASA [17], and similar systems for checking Java programs [4, 7, 12, 13] and other software [6, 8, 10, 11]. JPF, as a comparable system, is written in Java. Hence it effectively uses two layers of VMs, the system layer and its own. Our benchmarks show that JNuke is more efficient.

2 System Design

The static part of JNuke includes a class loader, transformer and type checker, including a byte code verifier. When loading a Java class file, JNuke transforms the byte code into a reduced instruction set derived from the abstract byte code in [16], after inlining intra-method subroutines. Additionally, registers are introduced to replace the operand stack. A peep-hole optimizer takes advantage of the register-based byte code. Another

R. Alur and D.A. Peled (Eds.): CAV 2004, LNCS 3114, pp. 462–465, 2004.
© Springer-Verlag Berlin Heidelberg 2004

component can capture a thread schedule and use code instrumentation to produce class files that execute a given schedule on an arbitrary VM or Java debugger [15].

At the core of JNuke is its VM, providing check-points [5] for explicit-state model checking and reachability analysis through backtracking. A check-point allows exploration of different successor states in the search, storing only the difference between states for efficiency. Both the ExitBlock and ExitBlockRW [2] heuristics are available for schedule generation. These algorithms reduce the number of explored schedules in two ways. First, thread switches are only performed when a lock is released, thus reducing interleavings. Second, the RW version adds a partial-order reduction if no data dependencies are present between two blocks in two threads. If no data races are present, behavioral equivalence is preserved. The supertrace algorithm [10] can be used to reduce memory consumption. For generic run-time verification, the engine can also run in *simulation mode* [17], where only one schedule defined by a given scheduling algorithm is executed. Event listeners can implement any run-time verification algorithm, including Eraser [14] and detection of high-level data races [1].

For portability and best possible efficiency, JNuke was implemented in C. A lightweight object-oriented layer has been added, allowing for a modern design without sacrificing speed. We believe that the choice of C as the programming language was not the only reason for JNuke's competitive performance. The ease of adding and testing optimizations through our rigorous unit testing framework ensured quality and efficiency. The roughly 1500 unit tests make up half of the 120,000 lines of code (LOC). Full statement coverage results in improved robustness and portability. JNuke runs on Mac OS X and the 32-bit and 64-bit variants of Linux (x86 and Alpha) and Solaris.

3   Experiments

The following experiments were used to compare JNuke to JPaX and JPF: two task-parallel applications, SOR (Successive Over-Relaxation over a 2D grid), and a Travelling Salesman Problem (TSP) application [18], a large cryptography benchmark [3] and two implementations of well-known distributed algorithms [5]: For Dining Philosophers, the first number is the number of philosophers, the second one the number of rounds. Producer/Consumer involves two processes communicating the given number of times through a one-element buffer. The experiments emphasize the aim of applying a tool to test suites of real-world programs without manual abstraction or annotations.

All experiments were run on a Pentium III with a clock frequency of 733 MHz and 256 KB of level II cache. Table 1 shows the results of run-time verification in simulation mode. Memory limit was 1 GB. Benchmarks exceeding it are marked with "m.o.".

The columns "Eraser" refer to an implementation of the Eraser [14] algorithm. Mode (1) distinguishes between accesses to individual array elements and is more precise. Mode (2) treats arrays as single objects and therefore requires much less memory for large arrays. Columns "VC" refer to the view consistency algorithm [1] used to detect high-level data races. Again, modes (1) and (2) concern array elements.

For comparison, the run times using the JPaX [9] and JPF [17] platforms are given. In the JPaX figures, only the time required to run the instrumented program is given, constituting the major part of the total run time. This refers to both the view consistency

Table 1. Execution times for run-time verification in simulation mode, given in seconds.

Application	Sun's VM		JNuke	JNuke Eraser		JNuke VC		JPaX	JPF
	JIT	no JIT	VM	1	2	1	2	2	2
SOR	0.7	0.7	3.6	934.1	21.5	34.0	19.2	45.9	error
TSP, size 4	0.6	0.4	0.7	1.7	1.5	1.2	1.1	2.7	m.o.
TSP, size 10	0.6	0.4	1.8	10.0	9.3	9.1	8.4	56.3	m.o.
TSP, size 15	0.8	1.2	24.5	228.7	203.0	207.0	192.7	1109.5	m.o.
JGFCrypt A	6.6	19.1	415.0	m.o.	1667.7	m.o.	1297.7	m.o.	m.o.
Dining Phil. (DP 3 5000)	1.2	1.9	11.0	15.7	15.6	987.0	987.0	83.2	m.o.
Prod./Cons. (PC 12000)	1.6	1.5	5.6	8.1	8.1	71.8	71.8	error	m.o.

Table 2. Results for model checking. Time is in seconds, no. of instructions in thousands.

	JNuke (EB/RW)			JNuke (EB)			JPF (lines)			JPF (byte codes)		
	time	#ins	#ins/s	time	#ins	#ins/s	time	#ins	#ins/s	time	#ins	#ins/s
DP 2 10	4.8	171	35.8	7.9	323	40.7	84.7	503	5.9	816.9	2,770	3.4
DP 3 1	0.2	3	16.7	1.7	60	35.3	29.7	151	5.1	845.7	2,457	2.9
DP 3 2	0.5	11	23.9	20.8	693	33.4	186.7	1,112	6.0	t.o.	t.o.	t.o.
DP 3 3	6.5	190	29.1	99.1	2,992	30.2	597.6	3,670	6.1	t.o.	t.o.	t.o.
PC 100	0.9	67	72.8	1.0	80	78.4	48.4	279	5.8	390.8	1,363	3.5
PC 1000	9.1	661	72.3	10.0	794	79.2	409.4	2,795	6.8	t.o.	t.o.	t.o.

and Eraser algorithms, which can use the same event log. JPaX currently only offers mode (2). View consistency is currently not implemented in JPF [17]. In its simulation mode, it ran out of memory after 10 – 20 minutes for each benchmark.

Generally, JNuke uses far less memory, the difference often exceeding an order of magnitude. Maximal memory usage was 66.7 MB in the SOR benchmark in mode (2). Analyzing a large number of individual array entries is currently far beyond the capacity of JPaX and JPF. Certain benchmarks show that the view consistency algorithm would benefit from a high-performance set intersection operation [14]. Because file I/O is not available in JPF, most benchmarks required manual abstraction for JPF.

The focus of our experiments for explicit-state model checking capability is on performance of the underlying engines, rather than on state space exploration heuristics. Therefore correct, relatively small instances of Dining Philosophers and Prod./Cons. from [5] were chosen where the state space can be explored exhaustively. JPF supports two modes of atomicity in scheduling, either per instruction or per source line. JNuke offers both ExitBlock and ExitBlockRW (EB and EB/RW, [2]) relying mainly on lock releases as boundaries of atomic blocks. Hence, a direct performance comparison is difficult. For this reason, Tab. 2 provides instructions per second in addition to absolute numbers. Timeout ("t.o.") was set to 1800 s.

JNuke often handles 5 – 20 times more instructions per second than JPF. Atomicity in scheduling has a large impact, as shown by the number of instructions executed for different heuristics. In absolute terms, JNuke is usually an order of magnitude faster.

4   Conclusions and Future Work

JNuke implements run-time verification and model checking, both requiring capabilities that off-the-shelf virtual machines do not offer. Custom virtual machines, however, should achieve a comparable performance, as JNuke does. Scheduler heuristics and verification rules can be changed easily. JNuke is more efficient than comparable tools.

Future work includes a garbage collector and a just-in-time compiler. The segmentation algorithm [7] would reduce false positives. Static analysis to identify thread-safe fields will speed up run-time analysis. Finally, certain native methods do not yet allow a rollback operation, which is quite a challenge for network operations.

References

1. C. Artho, K. Havelund, and A. Biere. High-level data races. *Journal on Software Testing, Verification & Reliability (STVR)*, 13(4), 2003.
2. D. Bruening. Systematic testing of multithreaded Java programs. Master's thesis, MIT, 1999.
3. J. Bull, L. Smith, M. Westhead, D. Henty, and R. Davey. A methodology for benchmarking Java Grande applications. In *Proc. ACM Java Grande Conference*, 1999.
4. J. Corbett, M. Dwyer, J. Hatcliff, C. Pasareanu, Robby, S. Laubach, and H. Zheng. Bandera: Extracting finite-state models from Java source code. In *Proc. Intl. Conf. on Software Engineering (ICSE'00)*. ACM Press, 2000.
5. P. Eugster. Java Virtual Machine with rollback procedure allowing systematic and exhaustive testing of multithreaded Java programs. Master's thesis, ETH Zürich, 2003.
6. P. Godefroid. Model checking for programming languages using VeriSoft. In *Proc. ACM Symposium on Principles of Programming Languages (POPL'97)*, 1997.
7. J. Harrow. Runtime checking of multithreaded applications with Visual Threads. In *Proc. SPIN Workshop (SPIN'00)*, volume 1885 of *LNCS*. Springer, 2000.
8. R. Hastings and B. Joyce. Purify: Fast detection of memory leaks and access errors. In *Proc. Winter USENIX Conf. (USENIX'92)*, 1992.
9. K. Havelund and G. Roşu. Monitoring Java programs with Java PathExplorer. In *Proc. Run-Time Verification Workshop (RV'01)*, volume 55 of *ENTCS*. Elsevier, 2001.
10. G. Holzmann. *Design and Validation of Computer Protocols*. Prentice-Hall, 1991.
11. G. Holzmann and M. Smith. A practical method for verifying event-driven software. In *Proc. Intl. Conf. on Software Engineering (ICSE'99)*. IEEE/ACM, 1999.
12. M. Kim, S. Kannan, I. Lee, O. Sokolsky, and M. Viswanathan. Java-MaC: a run-time assurance tool for Java programs. In *Proc. Run-Time Verification Workshop (RV'01)*, volume 55 of *ENTCS*. Elsevier, 2001.
13. Robby, M. Dwyer, and J. Hatcliff. Bogor: an extensible and highly-modular software model checking framework. In *Proc. European Software Engineering Conf. (ESEC'03)*, 2003.
14. S. Savage, M. Burrows, G. Nelson, P. Sobalvarro, and T. Anderson. Eraser: A dynamic data race detector for multithreaded programs. *ACM Trans. on Computer Systems*, 15(4), 1997.
15. V. Schuppan, M. Baur, and A. Biere. JVM-independent replay in Java. In *Proc. Run-Time Verification Workshop (RV'04)*, ENTCS. Elsevier, 2004.
16. R. Stärk, J. Schmid, and E. Börger. *Java and the Java Virtual Machine*. Springer, 2001.
17. W. Visser, K. Havelund, G. Brat, and S. Park. Model checking programs. In *Proc. IEEE Intl. Conf. Automated Software Engineeering (ASE'00)*, 2000.
18. C. von Praun and T. Gross. Object-race detection. In *OOPSLA 2001*. ACM Press, 2001.

The HiVy Tool Set

Paula J. Pingree[1] and Erich Mikk[2]

[1] Jet Propulsion Laboratory, Pasadena, CA 91109
Paula.J.Pingree@jpl.nasa.gov
[2] Erlangen, Germany
Erich.Mikk@epost.de

Abstract. Our aim is to validate mission-specific components of spacecraft flight software designs that are specified using state-charts and translated automatically to the final flight code for the mission. We established an automatic translation tool set from state-charts to the input language of SPIN for the validation of such mission-specific components. To guarantee compliance with auto-generated flight code, our translation tool set preserves the StateFlow® semantics. We are now able to specify and validate portions of mission-critical software design and implementation using the exhaustive exploration techniques of model checking.

Keywords: state-charts, model checking, translation, Stateflow, SPIN

1 Introduction

The HiVy Tool Set enables model checking for state-charts [1]. This is achieved by translating state-chart specifications into Promela, the input language of the SPIN model checker [2]. The HiVy Tool Set transforms output of the commercial tool Stateflow® provided by The Mathworks. HiVy can also be used independently from Stateflow. An abstract syntax of hierarchical sequential automata (HSA) is provided as an intermediate format for the tool set [3]. The HiVy Tool Set programs include *SfParse, sf2hsa, hsa2pr* and the HSA merge facility.

Rationale
The authors of Stateflow adopted the graphical notation of state-charts as proposed by D. Harel [4] but designed a different semantics to this notation. The Statemate by ILogix tool supports the original semantics developed by D. Harel and there are some advances that extend Statemate specified designs to model checking facilities [5], [6]. The following partial list illustrates differences in semantic design between Stateflow and Statemate state-charts, which make clear that Statemate-based tools cannot be used for Stateflow state-chart verification.

R. Alur and D.A. Peled (Eds.): CAV 2004, LNCS 3114, pp. 466–469, 2004.
© Springer-Verlag Berlin Heidelberg 2004

- In Stateflow semantics there is at most one event active at a time. In Statemate semantics any finite number of events are allowed.
- Emitting an event in Stateflow semantics means to pass control to the receiver chart of the event at the moment of emitting the event. In Statemate semantics events are collected until the end of the step and then broadcast to the chart.
- In Stateflow the execution order within an AND-state is determined by the graphical placement of the AND-composed charts. In Statemate all AND-states are executed simultaneously.
- In Stateflow semantics the effect of changing variables takes place immediately. In Statemate semantics a variable change takes effect only at the end of the step.

We propose a new format called hierarchical sequential automata (HSA) that accurately reflects the semantics of Stateflow for implementation within the HiVy Tool Set. Each state-chart is associated with an equivalent hierarchical sequential automaton that consists of a finite set of cooperating sequential automata that can be implemented as parallel processes in Promela. State-chart states, events and variables are encoded as Promela variables and Promela processes change the values of these variables in order to simulate state changes, event generation and variable changes according to the semantics of Stateflow. The observable behavior is defined with respect to the variables representing state-chart states, events and variables. These ideas are very close to those for translating Statemate state-charts to Promela as presented in [6].

2   Overview of the Tool Set

Constructing a State-Chart
A state-chart model of the system to be verified must first be constructed. Access to and general familiarity with the Stateflow application is needed.

Syntactic Restrictions. In order to use the HiVy Tool Set the state-chart must be designed in a sub-set of the Stateflow language. This sub-set does not include:
- Implicit event generation* (See Figures 1 & 2)
- Inner transitions with the same source and destination*
- Transition actions on transition segments that end on a junction
- History junctions
  * Alternate implementations are supported within HiVy

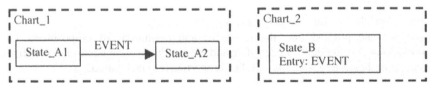

The diagram above represents the following state-chart activity. In Chart_1, State_A1 is active. In Chart_2, State_B is or becomes active. Upon entry into State_B an EVENT is internally generated. This EVENT is sensed by Chart_1 and causes the transition from State_A1 to State_A2 to be made.

Fig. 1. Implicit Event Notation Example

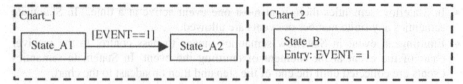

The diagram above represents an equivalent execution to that shown in Figure 1. We set a variable EVENT = 1 in State_B and create a conditional guard on the transition from State_A1 to State_A2 that evaluates to TRUE when EVENT==1. This notation is suitable for HiVy translation.

Fig. 2. Equivalent Implicit Event Notation

It is significant to note that HiVy supports state-chart events generated by an external environment (e.g., emitted non-deterministically from an included Promela if-loop).

There are additional, simple rules for state-chart model development to support successful translation with HiVy that pertain to scoping (dictation of where non-graphical object types can exist in the hierarchy), support for embedded state-charts or sub-charts, and closed-system verification with SPIN.

Performing Model Translation

This section describes how to parse Stateflow models to produce the HSA intermediate format, merge sub-charted state-charts with their parent charts (if desired), and generate Promela input for the SPIN model checker.

Parsing & HSA. Two programs of the HiVy Tool Set: *SfParse* and *sf2hsa* are used to prepare the model file for translation. If parsing is successful, a file is produced that contains an ASCII representation of the abstract syntax tree in HSA-format. HSA is given by a set of *events*, a set of *states*, a *root* state, a set of Boolean variables *bvars*, a set of integer variables *ivars*, a set of states denoting the initial configuration *iconf*, a hierarchy function *hi*, a typing function *ty*, a transition map *trmap* and OR-state mappings to their initial states *initmap* [3].

Merging State-Charts. Models consisting of several files may be merged into one HSA file before translating into Promela for SPIN using the HiVy program *hsacomplete*.

File Generation for SPIN Model Checking. The following files are generated by the HiVy translation program *hsa2pr*:

- stmodel.pr: the Promela model of the original state-chart.
- prop_list and propositions: the name list and definitions of propositions. One proposition is generated for each state and event. Proposition names are suitable in generating linear temporal logic (LTL) properties for verification.

3   HiVy Metrics and Optimization

A Plain Ol' Telephone System (POTS) model was developed to prototype HiVy's translation capability and performance. The Stateflow model contains 36 states and 7 events. The Promela file containing 1300 LOC (including comments) is immediately produced by executing the HiVy Tool Set programs. The translated model contains 13 Promela processes. The number of Promela processes directly affects SPIN verification performance. To minimize system compute time and memory utilization, it is desirable to limit the number of processes in a SPIN model. A HiVy optimization algorithm that produces a valid translation to a model with a single Promela process is currently in development. Preliminary model verification metrics as reported by SPIN for the original and optimized Promela POTS models are provided in Table 1 below.

Table 1. POTS Example Metrics

Parameter	Original HiVy	HiVy Optimization	Reduction
Real/user time	3.5 seconds	1.5 seconds	57%
Total actual memory use	8.87 Mb	4.67 Mb	47%

4   In Conclusion

The full capability of the SPIN model checker may be used to verify models generated by **HiVy** because they yield valid Promela code. The development of our approach for verification of NASA Spacecraft Fault Protection designs has been presented previously [7], [8]. The validity of HiVy generated models for SPIN model checking has been prototyped. State-space explosion effects are the significant challenge to the translation technique. Optimization approaches are under evaluation with initial results showing significant (> 40%) reduction in verification parameter values.

Acknowledgements

The authors acknowledge the work of Gordon C. Cucullu III in developing the POTS model. The research described in this paper was carried out at the Jet Propulsion Laboratory, California Institute of Technology, under a contract with the National Aeronautics and Space Administration.

References

1. The Mathworks Stateflow Users Guide, http://www.mathworks.com
2. G.J. Holzmann. The Model Checker Spin. *IEEE Trans. on Software Engineering*, 23(5):279-295, May 1997. Special issue on Formal Methods in Software Practice.
3. E. Mikk. HSA-Format, *private communication* 2002.
4. D. Harel, Statecharts: A Visual Formalism for Complex Systems. *Science of Computer Programming*, ASSP-34(2):362, 1986.
5. E. Mikk, Semantics and Verification of Statecharts. PhD Thesis. *Technical Report of Christian-Albrechts-University in Kiel,* October 2000
6. E. Mikk, Y. Lakhnech, M. Siegel and G. Holzmann, Implementing Statecharts in PROMELA/SPIN. In *Proceedings of the 2nd IEEE Workshop on Industrial-Strength Formal Specification Techniques.* pages 90-101, 1999.
7. K. Barltrop, P. Pingree, Model Checking Investigations for Fault Protection System Validation. *2003 International Conference on Space Mission Challenges for Information Technology,* June 2003
8. P. Pingree, E. Mikk, G. Holzmann, M. Smith, D. Dams, Validation of Mission Critical Software Design And Implementation Using Model Checking. *The 21st Digital Avionics Systems Conference,* October 2002.

ObsSlice: A Timed Automata Slicer
Based on Observers

Víctor Braberman[1,*], Diego Garbervetsky[1], and Alfredo Olivero[2,**]

[1] Departamento de Computación – FCEyN, Universidad de Buenos Aires, Argentina
{vbraber,diegog}@dc.uba.ar
[2] Centro de Estudios Avanzados, Universidad Argentina de la Empresa, Argentina
aolivero@uade.edu.ar

Abstract. ObsSlice is an optimization tool suited for the verification of timed automata using virtual observers. It discovers the set of modelling elements that can be safely ignored at each location of the observer by synthesizing behavioral dependence information among components. ObsSlice is fed with a network of timed automata and generates a transformed network which is equivalent to the one provided up to branching-time observation. Preliminary results have proven that eliminating irrelevant activity mitigates state space explosion and has a positive -and sometimes dramatic- impact on the performance of verification tools in terms of time, size and counterexample length.

1 Introduction

A common practice in the verification of concurrent systems is to express safety and liveness requirements as virtual components (observers) and composed in parallel with system under analysis (SUA). Our tool ObsSlice, based on [1], is fed with a SUA and an observer specified as a network of Timed Automata (TAs) and statically discovers, for each observer location, a set of modelling elements (automata and clocks) that can be safely ignored without compromising the validity of TCTL formulas stated over the observer (i.e., an exact reduction method wrt. branching time analysis). Eliminating irrelevant activity seems to mitigate state space explosion and have a positive impact on the performance of verification tools in terms of time, size and length of counterexamples.

ObsSlice seems to be well suited for treatment of models comprising several concurrent timed activities over observers that check for the presence of event scenarios (e.g, [2]).

2 ObsSlice Architecture

Figure 1 illustrates in a modular view the way ObsSlice solves this slicing problem by combining concepts presented in [1]. Currently, the tool takes a network

* Research partially supported by UBACyT 2004 X020, ANCyT grant BID 1201/OC-AR PICT 11738, Microsoft Research Embedded Innovation Excellence Award
** Research partially supported by UADE projects ISI03B and TSI04B

R. Alur and D.A. Peled (Eds.): CAV 2004, LNCS 3114, pp. 470–474, 2004.
© Springer-Verlag Berlin Heidelberg 2004

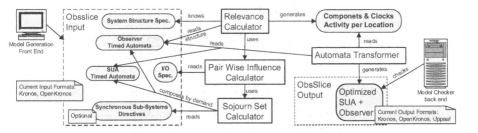

Fig. 1. ObsSlice architecture

of TAs compatible with Kronos [3] and OpenKronos [4] formats and an I/O classification of the labels in the TAs. The main goal of `Relevance Calculator` is to estimate, for each observer location, a set of components and clocks whose activity can be safely ignored during the observed evolution of the SUA. To achieve that goal, it relies on `Pair Wise Influence Calculator` which statically calculates if a given component C may influence the behavior of another component C' when sojourning a given observer location. Currently, I/O classification of events for each automata helps to check potential influence due to communication, assignments or predicates. I/O declarations are, in general, intuitively known by verification engineers or can be automatically provided by high-level front-end modelling languages. ObsSlice is robust in the sense that a wrongly specified I/O label classification would only compromise the exactness of the method but reachability results would still be conservative. On the other hand, `Sojourn Set Calculator` provides an over-approximation of the set of locations that may be traversed by a given component when sojourning an observer location. This information serves as a way to obtain a more precise pair-wise influence prediction. `Sojourn Set Calculator`, by default, performs an untimed composition of each of the SUA TAs with the observer. Optionally, the sojourn set calculus can be improved by specifying which sets of TAs should be composed together due to a suspected synchronous behavior among them (`synchronous subsystem directives`). In addition to SUA TAs, constraint automata can be used to compactly express ordering of events in the composed system (e.g., FIFO ordering in a communication chain of components). Such constraints can be derived through abstraction techniques or directly proposed by verification engineers, in order to keep `Sojourn Set Calculator` from performing large compositions.

Finally, the `Automata Transformer` receives the *activity tables* and generates the network of transformed TAs. The enabling and disabling of modelling elements is achieved differently depending on the target dialect. Currently, the transformed models can be checked by Kronos [3], OpenKronos [4] and Uppaal [5]. The reduction is performed through the addition of sleep locations and their corresponding transitions (when possible, deactivation of clocks is also informed together with the model).

Table 1. Examples sizes

SUA		SUA+O	Observer	
Name	#TAs	#Clocks	#Loc	#Tran
Fddi10	21	32	21	221
Pipe6	13	14	15	197
Pipe7	15	16	17	227
RemoteS.	12	13	29	395
MinePump	8	8	9	58

3   Experiments

Being a preprocessing tool based on an exact reduction technique, OBSSLICE is suited for integration with virtually any verification strategy built in current modelcheking tools. For a discussion on related work, please refer to [1]. OPENKRONOS tool was run using DFS search order and DBMs as state space representation when error is known to be reachable. UPPAAL was run using -Was option and BFS order generating the whole state space when error is not reachable, -Was -t1 to generate the shortest trace to the error, and -Was -A to apply a conservative abstraction (convex hull) for some of the unreachable error cases. Table 1 shows the examples sizes: number of TAs of the SUA, clocks of SUA+observer and the number of locations and transitions of the observers. Table 2 shows times and memory consumed by the modelchecking tools over the original and "obssliced" models. We also provide the length of the shortest trace (including committed synchronization with the observer) and the time consumed to generate it. Time consumed by OBSSLICE itself is not reported since it is negligible compared with verification times (less than a couple of seconds).

Fddi10 is an extension of the FDDI token ring protocol similar to the one presented in [1] where the observer monitors the time the token takes to return to a given station. Pipe6 and Pipe7 are pipe-lines of sporadic processes that forward a signal emitted by a quasi periodic source [1] (with 6 and 7 stages resp.). The observer captures a scenario violating an end-to-end constraint for signal propagation. The rest of examples are designs of distributed real-time system generated using the technique presented in [6]. Observers were obtained using VTS [2], a tool that automatically produces timed observer from scenario specifications. Remote Sensing [2], is a system consisting of a central component and two remote sensors. Sensors periodically sample a set of environmental variables and store their values in shared memory. When the central component needs them, it broadcasts a signal to the sensors. Each sensor runs a thread devoted to handle this message by reading the last stored value from shared memory and sending it back to the central component. The latter pairs the readings so that another process can use that piece of information to perform certain actions on some actuators. The observer captures scenarios where a request for collecting a pair of data items is not fully answered in less than a given amount of time. MinePump is a design of a fault-detection mechanism for a distributed mine-drainage controller [7]. A watchdog task periodically checks

Table 2. Verification benchmarks (Time expressed in seconds, Mem in MB)

SUA	OpenKronos Original Time	OpenKronos Obssliced Time	Uppaal (property satisfied) Original Time	Original Length	Obssliced Time	Obssliced Length	Uppaal (prop. not satisfied) Original Time	Original Mem	Obssliced Time	Obssliced Mem
Fddi10	630.08	1.21	835.95	32	0.65	32	O/M	O/M	0.44	5.09
c.h. (-A)							1141.24	230.28	0.15	5.02
Pipe6	994.20	0.05	306.76	103	31.59	56	21.11	16.06	6.77	9.59
Pipe7	O/M	0.03	O/M	O/M	324.44	65	407.36	162.79	84.02	49.87
RemoteS.	O/M	1.10	O/M	O/M	1.69	101	O/M	O/M	1.75	6.23
c.h. (-A)							29.72	19.68	0.93	8.60
MinePump	O/M	0.86	368.75	81	10.82	54	2856.47	139.43	65.66	20.02

the availability of a water level sensing device by sending a request and extracting acknowledgements that were received and queued during the previous cycle (by another sporadic task). When the watchdog finds the queue empty, it registers a fault condition in a shared memory which is periodically read, and forwarded to a remote console, by a proxy task. The proposed scenario verifies that the failure of the high-low water sensor is always informed to the remote operator before a given deadline. Experiments were run on a SunBlade 2000 with 2GB RAM and show important savings in verification times (even using convex hull abstraction[1]), memory consumed and length of counterexamples. A Java version of our tool together with a set of examples can be found at http://www.dc.uba.ar/people/proyinv/rtar/obsslice.

4   Past and Future

OBSSLICE evolves from a manually-integrated proof of concept tools [1]. Currently, it features improved transference algorithms, a weakened set of influence rules, clock deactivation rules, and a brand new set of transformation rules that work for broadcast model of communication (produces transformed networks ready to be checked with UPPAAL). Besides, it provides flexible mechanisms to guide sojourn set calculus. Future extensions comprise end-to-end support of more timed automata dialects. We also plan to extend the concept of influence at a finer grain of analysis (not only at the location basis) and to use time information to make a more precise analysis of sojourn sets. On the other hand, we believe that our abstraction based on activity, can be cheaply performed on-the-fly by adapting verification engines. We believe that slicing over observers is an idea that may also be applied to other fields such as the verification of concurrent and distributed applications where asynchronicity exacerbates state space explosion.

References

1. Braberman, V., Garbervetsky, D., Olivero, A.: Improving the verification of timed systems using influence information. In: Proc. TACAS '02, LNCS 2280. (2002)

---

[1] Moreover, for Minepump, -A option is useless since it yields a MAYBE result.

2. Alfonso, A., Braberman, V., Kicillof, N., Olivero, A.: Visual timed event scenarios. In: Proc. of the 26th ACM/IEEE ICSE '04 (to appear). (2004)
3. Daws, C., Olivero, A., Tripakis, S., Yovine, S.: *The Tool KRONOS*. In: Proc. of Hybrid Systems III, LNCS 1066, Springer-Verlag (1996) 208–219
4. Tripakis, S.: L'Analyse Formelle des Systemès Temporisés en Practique. PhD thesis, Univesité Joseph Fourier (1998)
5. Behrmann, G., David, A., Larsen, K., Möller, O., Pettersson, P., Yi, W.: UPPAAL - present and future. In: Proc. IEEE CDC '01, IEEE Computer Society Press (2001)
6. Braberman, V., Felder, M.: Verification of real-time designs: Combining scheduling theory with automatic formal verification. In: ESEC/FSE '99, LNCS 1687. (1999)
7. Braberman, V.: Modeling and Checking Real-Time Systems Designs. PhD thesis, FCEyN, Universidad de Buenos Aires (2000)

The UCLID Decision Procedure[*]

Shuvendu K. Lahiri and Sanjit A. Seshia

Carnegie Mellon University, Pittsburgh, PA
shuvendu@ece.cmu.edu, Sanjit.Seshia@cs.cmu.edu

Abstract. UCLID is a tool for term-level modeling and verification of infinite-state systems expressible in the logic of counter arithmetic with lambda expressions and uninterpreted functions (CLU). In this paper, we describe a key component of the tool, the decision procedure for CLU. Apart from validity checking, the decision procedure also provides other useful features such as concrete counterexample generation and proof-core generation.

1 Introduction

Decision procedures for fragments of first-order logic form the core of many automatic and semi-automatic verification tools. Applications include microprocessor verification (e.g., [3]) and predicate abstraction-based software verification (e.g. [1]). Decision procedures also find use as components of higher-order logic theorem provers, such as PVS [10].

UCLID [4, 15] is a tool for modeling and verifying infinite-state systems expressible in a logic called CLU. The logic is a decidable fragment of first-order logic with restricted lambda expressions, uninterpreted functions and equality, counter arithmetic (i.e. addition by constants) and ordering ($<$). Thus, the only arithmetic constraints permitted in this logic are of the form $T_1 \bowtie T_2 + c$ where T_1 and T_2 are integer expressions and $\bowtie \in \{<, =\}$.

One of the key components of the tool is an efficient decision procedure for CLU. Apart from the logic it handles, there are several distinguishing features of the decision procedure that set it apart from other decision procedures such as SVC [2], CVC [14] and ICS [6]:

- *Eager translation to SAT:* The decision procedure performs a satisfiability-preserving translation of the first-order formula to a Boolean formula, which in turn is checked with a Boolean Satisfiability (SAT) solver. This is in contrast to other SAT-based procedures (e.g., [5, 14]), which compute a Boolean abstraction of the first-order formula and *lazily* refine the abstraction based on inconsistent SAT assignments. In contrast, UCLID performs an *eager* translation.
- *Integer interpretation:* Most queries in hardware and software verification require using an integer interpretation of symbols. However, most available decision procedures are not complete for integers even if one restricts oneself to CLU logic. UCLID, on the other hand is complete for integers, which, e.g., makes it extremely useful in reasoning about systems with arrays.

[*] This research was supported by the Semiconductor Research Corporation, Contract RID 1029 and by ARO grant DAAD 19-01-1-0485.

R. Alur and D.A. Peled (Eds.): CAV 2004, LNCS 3114, pp. 475–478, 2004.

- *Reducing the domain of interpretation:* The decision procedure exploits optimizations that allow it to interpret symbols over smaller domains by analyzing formula structure. The small model property for CLU permits considering only a finite but often small set of values for the integer symbols in the formula. This set is further reduced by exploiting *positive equality* [3, 8].

The tool has been implemented in Moscow ML and contains around 30K lines of code. It can interface to both SAT solvers and BDD packages. The CLU formulas are internally represented using a directed acyclic graph (DAG) structure which facilitates effective sharing of common subexpressions. The DAG storage manager uses heuristics to detect and collapse certain semantically equivalent but syntactically distinct expressions.

2   CLU Logic via Examples

Consider an example of a valid CLU query which contains uninterpreted functions and lambda expressions for arrays where *ITE* stands for the *if-then-else* construct. Below, the first three lines define temporary names for sub-expressions, and the decide command is used to invoke the decision procedure.

```
t1   :=   f(a) != f(b) ;
m'   :=   Lambda x. ITE(x = a, 0, m(x)) ;   (* m' <- m[a:=0] *)
t2   :=   t1 => (m'(b) = m(b)) ;

decide (t2); (* is t2 valid? *)
```

Here is an example[1] that cannot be modeled using traditional select-update arrays, since an arbitrary number of entries in the array m gets updated in a single step.

```
t1   :=   f(m(b)) = f(m(a)) ;
m'   :=   Lambda x. ITE(m(x) < a+1, a, m(x)) ;
t2   :=   t1 => (m'(b) = m(b)) ;

decide (t2); (* is t2 valid? *)
```

This is an example of an invalid formula. The tool produces a counterexample which looks as follows:

```
+++ Counter-Examples Found : Formula Not Valid +++
a=23, b=32, m(23)=18, m(32)=22, f(22)=3, f(18)=3
```

This is a partial interpretation to all the function symbols which are relevant to the counterexample. The *concrete* counterexamples have been found extremely useful for debugging and verifying non-trivial systems [9].

The logic also supports very limited quantifiers (at the cost of incompleteness) at the top-level of a formula. One can assert a universally quantified formula in the antecedent while deciding a CLU formula as follows:

---

[1] The syntax is slightly different for the actual tool.

```
decide((FORALL x,y. f(x) = f(y) => x = y) => f(a) != f(a+1));
```

This limited capability has been found very useful in practice, e.g., in automating non-trivial proofs for out-of-order processor verification with unbounded resources [9].

3   Decision Procedure

Operation. The decision procedure performs a series of transformations to reduce a first-order formula to a Boolean formula. The quantifiers are first eliminated using quantifier instantiation techniques [9]. The resulting CLU formula is translated to an equi-satisfiable Boolean formula using the following sequence of steps: (i) First, lambda expressions are removed using Beta-reduction; (ii) Second, function applications are replaced with symbolic constants using optimizations like exploiting positive equality; (iii) Finally, integer-valued symbolic constants are either instantiated over a finite domain (which is sufficient to preserve satisfiability) or atomic predicates (e.g. $x < y + 3$) over these symbolic constants are encoded using fresh Boolean variables and transitivity constraints are imposed [13]. The generated formula is checked using a SAT solver. Since the nature of encoding greatly affects the SAT solver's performance, UCLID employs problem-specific hybrid encoding strategies [12] to improve the quality of the final encoding.

Counterexample Generation. The assignment produced by the SAT solver over the Boolean variables to an assignment over the first-order symbols including function constants. First, assignments for the integer variables are constructed, and then for each function application, the arguments and the result of the application are evaluated from the integer variables that represent them.

Proof-Core Generation. Many SAT solvers generate an unsatisfiable core of Boolean variables. This can be used to generate a proof core for the original CLU formula. These variables can be mapped back to atomic predicates in CLU logic, since the mappings generated by the translation to SAT are preserved. The atomic predicates find use in, for instance, predicate discovery for predicate abstraction-based verifiers.

Benchmarking. We have benchmarked the decision procedure on a diverse set of verification benchmarks arising in verifying high-level microprocessor designs, cache coherence protocols, model checking software device drivers, and compiler validation. UCLID outperforms other decision procedures including SVC and CVC on these benchmarks; results may be found in a recent paper [12].

Extensions. The decision procedure code has also been used for performing symbolic predicate abstraction [7]. Ongoing work includes extending UCLID's logic to include quantifier-free Presburger arithmetic [11].

Acknowledgments

We are grateful to Randal E. Bryant for his invaluable support and feedback.

References

1. T. Ball, R. Majumdar, T. Millstein, and S. K. Rajamani. Automatic predicate abstraction of C programs. In *Programming Language Design and Implementation (PLDI '01)*, pages 203–213, 2001.
2. C. Barrett, D. Dill, and J. Levitt. Validity checking for combinations of theories with equality. In *Formal Methods in Computer-Aided Design (FMCAD '96)*, LNCS 1166, pages 187–201, 1996.
3. R. E. Bryant, S. German, and M. N. Velev. Processor verification using efficient reductions of the logic of uninterpreted functions to propositional logic. *ACM Transactions on Computational Logic*, 2(1):1–41, January 2001.
4. R. E. Bryant, S. K. Lahiri, and S. A. Seshia. Modeling and verifying systems using a logic of counter arithmetic with lambda expressions and uninterpreted functions. In *Computer-Aided Verification (CAV '02)*, LNCS 2404, pages 78–92, 2002.
5. Leonardo de Moura, Harald Rueß, and Maria Sorea. Lazy theorem proving for bounded model checking over infinite domains. In *Conference on Automated Deduction (CADE '02)*, pages 438–455, 2002.
6. J.-C. Filliâtre, S. Owre, H. Rueß, and N. Shankar. ICS: Integrated Canonizer and Solver. In CAV '01, LNCS 2102, pages 246–249, 2001.
7. S. K. Lahiri, R. E. Bryant, and Byron Cook. A symbolic approach to predicate abstraction. In *Computer-Aided Verification (CAV '03)*, LNCS 2725, pages 141–153, 2003.
8. S. K. Lahiri, R. E. Bryant, A. Goel, and M. Talupur. Revisiting positive equality. In *Tools and Algorithms for the Construction and Analysis of Systems (TACAS'04)*, LNCS 2988, pages 1–15. Springer-Verlag, 2004.
9. S. K. Lahiri, S. A. Seshia, and R. E. Bryant. Modeling and verification of out-of-order microprocessors in UCLID. In *Formal Methods in Computer-Aided Design (FMCAD '02)*, LNCS 2517, pages 142–159, 2002.
10. S. Owre, J. M. Rushby, and N. Shankar. PVS: A prototype verification system. In *Conference on Automated Deduction (CADE '92)*, LNAI 607, pages 748–752, 1992.
11. S. A. Seshia and R. E. Bryant. Deciding quantifier-free Presburger formulas using parameterized solution bounds. In 19th *IEEE Symposium on Logic in Computer Science (LICS)*, July 2004. To appear.
12. S. A. Seshia, S. K. Lahiri, and R. E. Bryant. A hybrid SAT-based decision procedure for separation logic with uninterpreted functions. In *40th Design Automation Conference (DAC '03)*, pages 425–430, June 2003.
13. O. Strichman, S. A. Seshia, and R. E. Bryant. Deciding separation formulas with SAT. In *Computer-Aided Verification (CAV '02)*, LNCS 2404, pages 209–222, 2002.
14. Aaron Stump, Clark W. Barrett, and David L. Dill. CVC: A Cooperating Validity Checker. In *14th International Conference on Computer Aided Verification (CAV)*, volume 2404 of *LNCS*, pages 500–504. Springer-Verlag, 2002.
15. UCLID. Available at http://www.cs.cmu.edu/~uclid

MCK: Model Checking the Logic of Knowledge*

Peter Gammie[1] and Ron van der Meyden[2]

[1] Computing Science, Chalmers Institute of Technology, Sweden
peteg@cs.chalmers.se
[2] School of Computer Science and Engineering, University of New South Wales
and National ICT Australia, Sydney, Australia
meyden@cse.unsw.edu.au

Introduction

The specification formalism employed in model checking is usually some flavour of temporal or process algebraic language that expresses properties of the *behavioural* aspects of a system. *Knowledge* [5] is a modality that is orthogonal to the behavioural dimension, capturing properties of *information flow.* Logics of knowledge have been shown to be a useful framework for the analysis of distributed algorithms and security protocols, and model checking of these logics was first mooted by Halpern and Vardi [6]. Since that time theoretical aspects of model checking the logic of knowledge and its combinations with temporal logic have been studied [8–10]. The system MCK introduced in this paper implements parts of this theory.

The Model Checking Scenario

The typical scenario that can be analysed using the system consists of some number of *agents* (which might be players in a game, actors in an economic setting, or processes, programs or components in a computational setting) interacting in the context of an *environment.* The agents have the capacity to perform certain *actions* in this environment, which they choose according to their individual *protocols,* or sets of rules. The agents have *incomplete information* about the state of the system due to the fact that they are able to *observe* only part of the state at each instant of time.

The MCK system can be used to analyse this type of setting by the use of *model checking* techniques. The input to the MCK system describes: (1) the environment in which the agents operate, including a formal description of agent names, states, initial states, actions and how they affect states, and fairness conditions; (2) the protocol for each of the named agents, and a description of what parts of the state can be observed by which agents; (3) a number of

---

* Work of the first author conducted while employed at UNSW. Work funded by an Australian Research Council Discovery grant. National ICT Australia is funded through the Australian Government's *Backing Australia's Ability* initiative, in part through the Australian Research Council.

R. Alur and D.A. Peled (Eds.): CAV 2004, LNCS 3114, pp. 479–483, 2004.

specification formulas to be model checked, expressing how the agents' knowledge evolves over time. Both the possible state changes selected by the environment and the agents' choices of action may be non-deterministic.

The MCK system supports several different types of temporal and epistemic specifications. In the epistemic dimension, agents may use their observations in a variety of ways to determine what they know. In the *observational* interpretation of knowledge, agents make inferences about the actual state based just on their current observation. In the *clock* interpretation of knowledge, agents compute knowledge using both their current observation and the current global clock value. Even more information can be extracted by the agent if it uses a complete record of all its observations to date to determine what it knows – this is called the *synchronous perfect recall* interpretation of knowledge. In the temporal dimension, the specification formulas may use either linear time temporal logic, LTL, or the branching time logic CTL. The system supports different combinations of these parameters to different degrees, which in some cases is because the implementation remains to be undertaken and in others is due to inherent computational difficulties. In the case of the observational semantics, for example, the system supports arbitrarily nested combinations of either CTL or LTL operators with operators for knowledge and common knowledge, a type of fixpoint of the knowledge of many agents. In contrast, the perfect recall semantics only supports a linear or branching "next time" operator, although the theory for the full combination of knowledge with LTL has been developed [9].

The custom modelling language used in MCK is designed to cater for some specific issues arising from the semantics of knowledge and to allow maximum modelling flexibility; the intention is to support experimentation in this comparatively unexplored area rather than verification for a specific language.

Application Example

Figure 1 presents an example input file to the system which models a scenario where the single agent, a robot called `Robot` (running the protocol `"robot"`) operates in an environment of 8 possible positions. The environment provides noisy readings of the position to the robot via the `sensor` variable, which is declared to be an observable input to the agent. The robot's goal is to halt in the region {2..4}, which its protocol attempts to achieve by halting when the sensor value is ≥ 3. We would like to verify that this is the best the robot can do given its observations, which is to say that the condition `sensor` ≥ 3 characterises all situations in which the agent knows that it is in the goal region when it is running this particular protocol.

The `transitions` section represents the effects of the robot's actions (`Halt` and `skip`) on the state, by means of a program using non-deterministic `if` statements. This program is considered to run atomically in a single tick of the clock.

The example contains two specification formulas. The construct `spec_obs_ltl` indicates that the formula uses linear time temporal logic operators and that the knowledge operator `Knows` is to be interpreted using the

```
type Pos = {0..7}
position : Pos
sensor  : Pos
halted  : Bool

init_cond = position == 0 /\ sensor == 0 /\ neg halted

agent Robot "robot" ( sensor )

transitions
begin
  if Robot.Halt -> halted := True fi;
  if neg halted -> position := position + 1 fi;
  if True -> sensor := position - 1
  [] True -> sensor := position
  [] True -> sensor := position + 1
  fi
end

spec_obs_ltl = G (sensor >= 3 <=> Knows Robot position in {2..4})
spec_spr_xn = X 2 (sensor >= 3 <=> Knows Robot position in {2..4})

protocol "robot" (sensor : observable Pos)
begin
  do neg (sensor >= 3) -> skip
  [] break              -> <<Halt>>
  od
end
```

Fig. 1. A Sample MCK input file.

observational semantics. The operator G expresses truth at all future times. The model checker verifies that this formula is indeed true. The use of **spec_spr_xn** in the second specification indicates that the knowledge modality should be interpreted using synchronous perfect recall, and that the formula has the form $X^n\phi$, where ϕ is atemporal, expressing that ϕ holds in precisely n steps after an initial state ($n = 2$ in this example). The model checker verifies that this formula is false. Intuitively, the determinacy of the robot's motion allows it to derive its location from the number of observations made. This means that the test **sensor >= 3** is not complete — the right-to-left implication fails. If we alter the **transitions** part to allow **position** to either increment or remain static and add a fairness condition to ensure progress, this formula becomes true, but is still false for $n = 3$.

Implementation Sketch

The system constructs a BDD representation of a data structure that encodes the knowledge set of an agent, i.e. the set of states that are consistent with its local state. For the observational and clock semantics this structure is simply a set of states, but the synchronous perfect recall semantics requires a function that maps a fixed, finite sequence of observations to the set of final states of traces consistent with this sequence of observations, as detailed in [10]. The system is implemented in Haskell, and relies on David Long's BDD package, implemented in C, for efficient BDD operations.

Related Work

While other systems in recent years have implemented model checking for the logic of knowledge, MCK is unique in its support of a range of knowledge semantics and choices of temporal language. Additionally, fairness constraints and the common knowledge operator have not been treated in prior work, and the clock semantics has not previously been implemented.

The theoretical basis for MCK is largely described in [8–10], which employs LTL as the temporal language. Theory for model checking a combination of the perfect recall semantics and CTL is discussed in [2, 11].

Wooldridge and van der Hoek [7] use a connection between knowledge and the notion of *local proposition*, introduced in [3], to reduce model checking knowledge with respect to the observational semantics to temporal model checking in SPIN. This reduction works for positive occurrences of knowledge operators but leads to an explosion in the number of temporal formulas that need to be checked when there are negative occurrences. MCK handles negative occurrences directly without incurring such an explosion.

Our work is motivated more by issues of information flow in distributed systems than by distributed artificial intelligence concerns. Other work in the Distributed AI literature on model checking multi-agent systems, such as [1, 4], use epistemic modalities such as "belief" that are not given an information theoretic semantics as in Halpern and Moses [5]. The same remark applies to related work in the literature on cryptographic protocol verification.

Conclusion

MCK can be downloaded at http://www.cse.unsw.edu.au/~mck. The system is under active development and other instances of the known algorithms for model checking knowledge and time will be added in due course.

References

1. M. Benerecetti, F. Giunchiglia, and L. Serafini. Multiagent model checking. *Journal of Logic and Computation*, 8(3):401–423, Aug 1997.
2. P. Bertoli, A. Cimatti, M. Pistore, and P. Taverso. Plan validation for extended goals under partial observability (preliminary report). In *AIPS 2002 Workshop on Planning via Model Checking*, Toulouse, France, April 2002.

3. K. Engelhardt, R. van der Meyden, and Y. Moses. Knowledge and the logic of local propositions. In Itzhak Gilboa, editor, *Theoretical Aspects of Rationality and Knowledge*, pages 29–41. Morgan Kaufmann, July 1998.
4. R. H. Bordini, M. Fisher, C. Pardavila, W. Visser, and M. Wooldridge. Model checking multi-agent programs with CASP. In *CAV*, pages 110–113, 2003.
5. J. Halpern and Y. Moses. Knowledge and common knowledge in a distributed environment. *Journal of the ACM*, 37(3):549–587, 1990.
6. J. Halpern and M. Y. Vardi. Model checking vs. theorem proving: A manifesto. Technical Report RJ 7963, IBM Almaden Research Center, 1991.
7. W. van der Hoek and M. Wooldridge. Model checking knowledge and time. In *9th Workshop on SPIN (Model Checking Software)*, Grenoble, April 2002.
8. R. van der Meyden. Common knowledge and update in finite environments. *Information and Computation*, 140(2), 1998.
9. R. van der Meyden and N.S. Shilov. Model checking knowledge and time in systems with perfect recall. In *Proc. Conf. on Software Technology and Theoretical Computer Science*, Springer LNCS No 1738, pages 262–273, Chennai, 1999.
10. R. van der Meyden and K. Su. Symbolic model checking the knowledge of the dining cryptographers. In *IEEE Computer Security Foundations Workshop*, 2004.
11. N. Y. Shilov and N.O. Garanina. Model checking knowledge and fixpoints. In *FLOC workshop on Fixed Points in Computer Science*, 2002.

Zing: A Model Checker for Concurrent Software

Tony Andrews[1], Shaz Qadeer[1], Sriram K. Rajamani[1],
Jakob Rehof[1], and Yichen Xie[2]

[1] Microsoft Research
http://www.research.microsoft.com/zing/
[2] Stanford University

1 Introduction

The ZING project is an effort to build a flexible and scalable model checking infrastructure for concurrent software. The project is divided into four components: (1) a modeling language for expressing concurrent models of software systems, (2) a compiler for translating a ZING model into an executable representation of its transition relation, (3) a model checker for exploring the state space of the ZING model, and (4) model generators that automatically extract ZING models from programs written in common programming languages.

The goal is to preserve as much of the control-structure of the source program as possible. ZING's model checker exploits the structure of the source program, which is preserved in the model, to optimize systematic state space exploration. We believe that such an infrastructure is useful for finding bugs in software at various levels: high-level protocol descriptions, work-flow specifications, web services, device drivers, and protocols in the core of the operating system.

2 Architecture

We believe that the following features capture the essence of modern concurrent object oriented languages, from the point of building sound abstractions for model checking: (1) procedure calls with a call-stack, (2) objects with dynamic allocation, and (3) processes with dynamic creation, using both shared memory and message passing for communication. We designed ZING's modeling language to have exactly these features. ZING supports a basic asynchronous interleaving model of concurrency with both shared memory and message passing. In addition to sequential flow, branching and iteration, ZING supports function calls and exception handling. New threads are created via asynchronous function calls. An asynchronous call returns to the caller immediately, and the callee runs as a fresh process in parallel with the caller. Primitive and reference types, and an object model similar to C# or Java is supported, although inheritance is not supported. ZING also provides features to support abstraction and efficient state exploration. Any sequence of statements (with some restrictions) can be bracketed as atomic. This is essentially a directive to the model checker to not consider interleavings with other threads while any given thread executes an atomic sequence. Sets are supported, to represent collections where the ordering of objects is not important

R. Alur and D.A. Peled (Eds.): CAV 2004, LNCS 3114, pp. 484–487, 2004.

(thus reducing the number of potentially distinct states ZING needs to explore). A choose construct is provided that can be used to non-deterministically pick an element out of a finite set of integers, enumeration values, array members or set elements. An example ZING model that we extracted from a device driver, and details of an error trace that the tool found in the model can be found in our technical report [1].

Building a scalable model checker for the ZING modeling language is a huge challenge since the states of a ZING model have complicated features such as processes, heap and stack. We designed a lower-level model called ZING object model (or ZOM), and built a ZING compiler to convert a ZING model to ZOM. The compiler provides a clear separation between the expressive semantics of the modeling language, and a simple view of ZOM as labeled transition systems. This separation has allowed us to decouple the design of efficient model checking algorithms from the complexity of supporting rich constructs in the modeling language.

3   Model Checker

The ZING model checker executes the ZOM to explore the state space of the corresponding ZING model. Starting from the initial state, the model checker systematically explores reachable states in a depth-first manner. The biggest technical challenge, as with any model checker, is scalability. We have implemented several techniques that reduce the time and space required for state exploration.

Efficient State Representation. We observe that most state transitions modify only a small portion of the ZING state. By only recording the difference between transitions, we greatly cut down the space and time required to maintain the depth-first search stack. To further cut down on the space requirements, the model checker stores only a fingerprint of an explored state in its hash table. We use Rabin's finger-printing algorithm [3] to compute fingerprints efficiently.

Symmetry Reduction. A ZING state comprises the thread stacks, the global variables, and a heap of dynamically allocated objects. Two states are equivalent if the contents of the thread stacks and global variables are *identical* and the heaps are *isomorphic*. When the model checker discovers a new state, it first constructs a canonical representation of the state by traversing the heap in a deterministic order. It then stores a fingerprint of this canonical representation in the hash table.

Partial-Order Reduction. We have implemented a state-reduction algorithm that has the potential to reduce the number of explored states exponentially. This algorithm is based on Lipton's theory of reduction [12]. Our algorithm is based on the insight that in well-synchronized programs, any computation of a thread can be viewed as a sequence of transactions, each of which appears to execute atomically to other threads. During state exploration, it is sufficient to schedule threads only at transaction boundaries. If programmers follow the discipline of protecting each shared variable with a lock, then these transactions can be inferred automatically [6]. These inferred transactions reduce the number of interleavings to be explored, and thereby greatly alleviate the problem of state explosion.

Summarization. The ability to summarize procedures is fundamental to building scalable interprocedural analyses. For sequential programs, procedure summarization is well-understood and used routinely in a variety of compiler optimizations and software defect-detection tools. This is not the case for concurrent programs. ZING has an implementation of a novel model checking algorithm for concurrent programs that uses procedure summarization as an essential component [13]. Our method for procedure summarization is based on the insight about transactions mentioned earlier. We summarize within each transaction; the summary of a procedure comprises the summaries of all transactions within the procedure. The procedure summaries computed by our algorithm allow reuse of analysis results across different call sites in a concurrent program, a benefit that has hitherto been available only to sequential programs.

Compositional Reasoning. Stuck-freedom is an important property of distributed message-passing applications [14, 7]. This property formalizes the requirement that a process in a communicating system should not wait indefinitely for a message that is never sent, or send a message that is never received. To enable compositional verification of stuck-freedom, we have defined a conformance relation $\leq$ on processes with the following substitutability property: If $I \leq S$ and P is any environment such that the parallel composition $P \mid S$ is stuck-free, then $P \mid I$ is stuck-free as well. Substitutability enables a component's specification to be used instead of the component in invocation contexts, and hence enables model checking to scale. We have implemented a *conformance checker* on top of ZOM to verify the relation $I \leq S$, where I and S are ZING models.

4   Related Work

Model checking is an active research area [4]. The SPIN project [9] pioneered explicit-state model checking of concurrent processes. The SPIN checker analyzes protocol-descriptions written in the PROMELA language. Though PROMELA supports dynamic process creation, it is difficult to encode concurrent software in PROMELA due to absence of procedure calls and objects. Efforts have been made to "abstract" C code into PROMELA [10] to successfully find several bugs in real-life telephone switching systems, though no guarantees were given as to whether the generated PROMELA model is a sound abstraction of the C code. Over the past few years, there has been interest in using SPIN-like techniques to model check software written in common programming languages. DSPIN was an effort to extend SPIN with "dynamic" software-like constructs [11]. Model checkers have also been written to check Java programs either directly [18, 17, 15] or by constructing slices or other abstractions [5]. Unlike ZING, none of these approaches exploit program abstractions such as processes and procedure calls to do modular model checking. ZING supports a notion of conformance between two ZING models [7]. This feature of ZING is related to, but distinct from, the refinement checking feature of the FDR model checker [16, 8]. The SLAM project [2] has similar goals to ZING in that it works by extracting sound models from C programs, and checking the models. SLAM has been very successful in checking control-dominated properties of device drivers written in C. Unlike ZING, it does not handle concurrent programs, and it is unable to prove interesting properties on heap-intensive programs.

References

1. T. Andrews, S. Qadeer, S. K. Rajamani, J. Rehof, and Y. Xie. Zing: A model checker for concurrent software. Technical report, Microsoft Research, 2004.
2. T. Ball and S. K. Rajamani. The SLAM project: Debugging system software via static analysis. In *POPL 02: Principles of Programming Languages*, pages 1–3. ACM, January 2002.
3. A. Broder. Some applications of Rabin's fingerprinting method. In *Sequences II: Methods in Communications, Security, and Computer Science*, pages 143–152, 1993.
4. E.M. Clarke, O. Grumberg, and D. Peled. *Model Checking*. MIT Press, 1999.
5. M. Dwyer, J. Hatcliff, R. Joehanes, S. Laubach, C. Pasareanu, Robby, W. Visser, and H. Zheng. Tool-supported program abstraction for finite-state verification. In *ICSE 01: International Conference on Software Engineering*, pages 177–187. ACM, 2001.
6. C. Flanagan and S. Qadeer. Transactions for software model checking. In *SoftMC 03: Software Model Checking Workshop*, 2003.
7. C. Fournet, C.A.R. Hoare, S.K. Rajamani, and J. Rehof. Stuck-free conformance. In *CAV 04: Computer-Aided Verification*, LNCS. Springer-Verlag, 2000.
8. C. A. R. Hoare. *Communicating Sequential Processes*. Prentice Hall, 1985.
9. G. Holzmann. The model checker SPIN. *IEEE Transactions on Software Engineering*, 23(5):279–295, May 1997.
10. G.J. Holzmann. Logic verification of ANSI-C code with Spin. In *SPIN 00: SPIN Workshop*, LNCS 1885, pages 131–147. Springer-Verlag, 2000.
11. R. Iosif and R. Sisto. dSPIN: A dynamic extension of SPIN. In *SPIN 99: SPIN Workshop*, LNCS 1680, pages 261–276. Springer-Verlag, 1999.
12. R. J. Lipton. Reduction: A method of proving properties of parallel programs. In *Communications of the ACM*, volume 18:12, pages 717–721, 1975.
13. S. Qadeer, S. K. Rajamani, and J. Rehof. Summarizing procedures in concurrent programs. In *POPL 04: ACM Principles of Programming Languages*, pages 245–255. ACM, 2004.
14. S. K. Rajamani and J. Rehof. Conformance checking for models of asynchronous message passing software. In *CAV 02: Computer-Aided Verification*, LNCS 2404, pages 166–179. Springer-Verlag, 2002.
15. Robby, M. Dwyer, and J. Hatcliff. Bogor: An extensible and highly-modular model checking framework. In *FSE 03: Foundations of Software Engineering*, pages 267–276. ACM, 2003.
16. A. W. Roscoe. *The Theory and Practice of Concurrency*. Prentice Hall, 1998.
17. S. D. Stoller. Model-checking multi-threaded distributed Java programs. *International Journal on Software Tools for Technology Transfer*, 4(1):71–91, October 2002.
18. W. Visser, K. Havelund, G. Brat, and S. Park. Model checking programs. In *ICASE 00: Automated Software Engineering*, pages 3–12, 2000.

The Mec 5 Model-Checker

Alain Griffault and Aymeric Vincent[*]

LaBRI, Bordeaux University, 351 cours de la Libération, 33405 Talence, France
Firstname.Surname@labri.fr

Abstract. We present in this article the features of the model-checker we have developed: Mec 5. This tool makes it possible to handle models written in the AltaRica language and is characterized by the great expressiveness of its specification logic: μ-calculus on relations with first order quantifiers and equality.

Keywords: AltaRica, BDDs, model-checking, μ-calculus

1 Introduction

Mec 5 [10] is a model-checker for finite AltaRica [9, 2] models. The way to specify properties in Mec 5 consists in defining relations in a specification language we describe in section 2. In this setting, one can verify that a system satisfies a given property by testing that the set of states which violate the property is empty. This specification language is very expressive and allows the definition of complex relations between different models, e.g. bisimulation. Mec 5 is also open to more general problems like controller synthesis because it can compute winning strategies in parity games.

AltaRica is a rich formalism developed at the LaBRI jointly with industrial partners. Its goal is to provide a formalism with clear semantics, supported by a language offering powerful modeling facilities, itself supported by many tools in order to perform safety analysis of a given AltaRica model using several different techniques. Compilers exist to produce fault trees, Markov chains, Lustre programs, transitions systems.

The need for an AltaRica model-checker was real because the availability of commercial tools to model in AltaRica brings libraries of components whose correctness must be verified.

2 Specification Language

The specification language used by Mec 5 coincides exactly with Park's μ-calculus [8] which is first order logic extended with fixpoints over relations.

First-Order Logic

The propositions are built using the traditional boolean connectives (~ for negation, & for conjunction, | for disjunction). Variables range over finite domains like booleans (bool), finite intervals of integers ([0, 10]) or enumerations of constants ({on, off}).

---

[*] Currently a post-doc at the University of Warsaw in the European RTN "GAMES".

R. Alur and D.A. Peled (Eds.): CAV 2004, LNCS 3114, pp. 488–491, 2004.

A relation can be used in this context as a predicate, i.e. like the characteristic function of the relation it represents, returning a boolean value (R(x, 2)).

The introduction of first-order quantifiers in our language allows us to dispose of the existential and universal modalities *"for all successors..."* and *"there exists a successor such that..."* whose semantics are usually given explicitly and which are usually the only link between the specification language and the model under study. We use a concrete syntax which reminds those modalities: $\exists x.p$ is written `<x>p` and $\forall x.p$ is written `[x]p`.

Fixpoints over Relations

Given a monotonic function over relations, it is possible to compute the least (+=) or the greatest (-=) relation which is a fixpoint of this function. For example, computing the transitive closure T of a relation R can be written verbatim like this in Mec 5 using a least fixpoint:

`T(x, y) += R(x, y) | <z>(R(x, z) & T(z, y));`

Properties depending on several models are easy to express. Assuming an equivalence relation `eq(a,b)` on labels, bisimulation can be written like this:

```
bisim(s,s') -=
  ([e][t](R(s,e,t)=><e'><t'>(R'(s',e',t')&eq(e,e')&bisim(t,t'))))&
  ([e'][t'](R'(s',e',t')=><e><t>(R(s,e,t)&eq(e,e')&bisim(t,t'))));
```

It is also possible to use several interdependant fixpoint definitions by means of systems of equations [6], which gives Mec 5 the full power of μ-calculus.

Implementation

Mec 5 uses Binary Decision Diagrams [3] to represent relations. This choice fits exactly our specification language, because boolean as well as first order operations are efficient on BDDs. The test for equality can be done in constant time, which is valuable when computing fixpoints. Expressions which range over finite domains are handled with vectors of BDDs. As a side note, our implementation benefits currently from a few performance improvements: BDDs use negative edges so that negation can be computed in constant time, and the boolean variables used to encode a relation are interleaved and we are working on wiser heuristics to reduce the memory footprint.

3   Integration with AltaRica

The AltaRica formalism is based on constraint automata and provides facilities to allow the modeling of complex systems. An AltaRica *node* can be defined hierarchically, by first modeling small parts of the system (themselves nodes) and then gathering them as sub-nodes. The default semantics for sub-nodes is to run asynchronously, unless some events are explicitly synchronized. Indeed, two means of communication are provided:

Memory Sharing. The *assertion* of a node can relate local variables to variables of its sub-nodes and can be seen as an invariant of the node. By forcing two variables to be equal, it is easy to share information between nodes; more complex constraints can be used. (A.f1 = B.f) & (A.f2 < C.f)

Events Synchronization. Synchronization vectors <A.a, B.b> specify which events should be bundled together, preventing them from occurring independently, and allowing a transition to fire all the specified events in parallel.

Other mechanisms provided in AltaRica include the ability to specify priority constraints on events a<b as a partial order. *Broadcast vectors* <a,b?> extend synchronization vectors by allowing certain events (those with a ? mark) not to occur while maximizing the number of fired events: <a,b?> ≡ {<a>} < {<a,b>}.

The tight coupling between the AltaRica description language and Mec's specification language was one of our primary goals due to our need for an efficient model-checker in the AltaRica community. This was done by using the same basic types in the two languages (booleans, intervals and enumerations), and using the same concrete syntax wherever possible for the definition of new domains, for expressions and for type expressions. It makes Mec 5 a coherent tool.

Every AltaRica model A loaded in Mec 5 defines two types and two relations : the type of its configurations A!c, the type of its event vectors A!ev, its transition relation A!t⊆A!c×A!ev×A!c and its set of initial configurations A!init⊆A!c which is the set of all configurations by default. Given these new objects, any property on A can be expressed in Mec 5's specification language.

4   Example

We give a very simple AltaRica model which is a loop from which it is possible to escape non-deterministically; we define the product of two such loops and then compute the set of states from which it is unavoidable to go to a dead state:

```
NotEpsilon(e : main!ev) := ~(e.S1. = "" & e.S2. = "");
UnavDead(c) +=
    [e][c']((main!t(c, e, c') & NotEpsilon(e)) => UnavDead(c'));
```

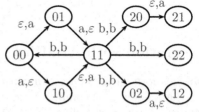

Semantics of main without ε loops

```
node LoopExit
    state s : [0, 2];
    event a, b;
    trans s = 0 |- a -> s := 1;
          s = 1 |- b -> s := 0;
          s = 1 |- b -> s := 2;
edon
```

```
node main
    sub S1, S2 : LoopExit;
    sync <S1.b, S2.b>;
edon
```

AltaRica description

({S1.s = 2, S2.s = 2})
({S1.s = 1, S2.s = 2})
({S1.s = 0, S2.s = 2})
({S1.s = 2, S2.s = 1})
({S1.s = 2, S2.s = 0})

Result

5   Conclusion

Mec 5 currently uses common techniques like Binary Decision Diagrams, and in that sense is very similar to tools like SMV [7] or NuSMV [4]. However, it departs from these model-checkers because it provides a more powerful logic that is not specifically designed for model-checking. In this respect, Mec 5 is closely related to Toupie [5] which implements Park's μ-calculus with decision diagrams but does not provide the means to load a model.

The experiments we made show that the specification language, although unusual at first glance, is extremely versatile and expressing properties with it is quite easy. Mec 5 and examples of AltaRica models are available from the following URL: http://altarica.labri.fr/

The ongoing evolution of Mec 5 follows two lines: performance improvement and implementation of satellite facilities to help in the verification process (either in the core of the tool, e.g. manipulating traces of executions, or in a graphical interface, e.g. a simulator). We expect to improve performance by using the knowledge we can extract from an AltaRica model to choose a good variable ordering for the BDDs, and we are investigating more symbolic methods which would delay the computation of BDDs, in the spirit of what was done with Boolean Expression Diagrams [1].

References

1. Henrik Andersen and Henrik Hulgaard. Boolean expression diagrams. *Information and Computation*, 179(2):194–212, December 2002.
2. André Arnold, Alain Griffault, Gérald Point, and Antoine Rauzy. The altarica formalism for describing concurrent systems. *Fundamenta Informaticae*, 40(2–3):109–124, 1999.
3. Randal E. Bryant. Graph-based algorithms for boolean function manipulation. *IEEE Transactions on Computers*, C-35(8):677–691, August 1986.
4. Alessandro Cimatti, Edmund M. Clarke, Enrico Giunchiglia, Fausto Giunchiglia, Marco Pistore, Marco Roveri, Roberto Sebastiani, and Armando Tacchella. NuSMV version 2: An opensource tool for symbolic model checking. In *CAV: International Conference on Computer Aided Verification*, volume 2404 of *Lecture Notes in Computer Science*, pages 359–364. Springer, July 2002.
5. Marc-Michel Corsini and Antoine Rauzy. Toupie user's manual. Research Report 586-93, LaBRI, 1993.
6. Angelika Mader. *Verification of modal properties using boolean equation systems*. PhD thesis, Fakultät Informatik, Technische Universität München, 1997.
7. Kenneth L. McMillan. *Symbolic Model Checking: an approach to the state explosion problem*. PhD thesis, Carnegie Mellon University, May 1992.
8. David Park. Finiteness is μ-ineffable. *Theoretical Computer Science*, 3:173–181, 1976.
9. Gérald Point. *Altarica : Contribution à l'unification des méthodes formelles et de la sûreté de fonctionnement*. PhD thesis, LaBRI, Université Bordeaux 1, January 2000.
10. Aymeric Vincent. *Conception et réalisation d'un vérificateur de modèles AltaRica*. PhD thesis, LaBRI, Université Bordeaux 1, December 2003.

PlayGame: A Platform for Diagnostic Games

Li Tan*

Department of Computer and Information Science, University of Pennsylvania
Philadelphia, PA 19104, USA
tanli@saul.cis.upenn.edu

Abstract. We introduce an integrated tool for implementing and playing various diagnostic games. The tool uses a *semantics hierarchy* introduced in [6] to improve code sharing among various diagnostic games
and reduce the cost of introducing a new game. PlayGame synthesizes
the winning strategy using the evidence that is an abstract and uniform
encoding of the proof computed by a checker, and hence instead of relying on any particular checker the tool works on a variety of checkers
that can be extended to produce such evidence. PlayGame implements
a μ-calculus game and a full range of equivalence/preorder games on the
Concurrency Workbench-New Century (CWB-NC).

1 Introduction

Games have been used in the verification community to model verification problems, to seek better solutions, and to understand verification results. The early
work by Stirling [5] on bisimulation games and μ-calculus games unveils the
potential of such games as diagnostic routines. In a diagnostic game the user
competes with the computer to show that the verification result is *incorrect*. By
losing each and every play to the computer the user shall be then convinced of
the correctness of the verification result. A diagnostic game can provide valuable
diagnostic information in an interactive way that a traditional diagnostic routine
such as counterexample mechanism cannot. Individual efforts have been made
to implement certain types of diagnostic games. The recent release of Edinburgh
Concurrency Workbench [1] includes the support for a μ-calculus game and a
strong bisimulation game. The verification tool Truth [3] also implements a μ-
calculus game. These tools are designed to use some specific checkers, mostly
game-based checkers, to build the winning strategy for the computer. It is left
to see how diagnostic games can be built on top of other existing checkers. Another problem in diagnostic games is that with so many verification semantics,
each of which requires different rules for game, defining and implementing them
separately is a daunting task. We introduce PlayGame, a tool that provides a
consistent interface for implementing diagnostic games and incorporating checkers. Figure 1 shows the architecture of the tool.

* Research supported by NSF grants CCR-9988489 and CCR-0098037, Army Research
Office grants DAAD190110003, DAAD190110019, and DAAD190110473.

R. Alur and D.A. Peled (Eds.): CAV 2004, LNCS 3114, pp. 492–495, 2004.
© Springer-Verlag Berlin Heidelberg 2004

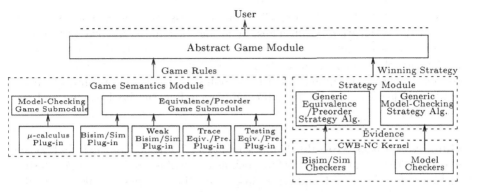

Fig. 1. The architecture of PlayGame

The tool is designed to use the evidence that is an abstract and uniform encoding of the proof constructed by a checker during verification. Its precise definition is given in our previous work [7,8]. Instead of relying on a particular checker, the tool works on a variety of existing checkers that can be extended to produce such evidence, as discussed in [7,8]. To support different verification semantics, we introduce a *semantics hierarchy* [6] that abstracts game rules to different layers. To introduce a new game, one only needs to provide the semantic layers unique to the game. PlayGame implements a μ-calculus model-checking game and eight different equivalence/preorder games including strong bisimulation/simulation games, weak bisimulation/simulation games, trace equivalence/preorder games, and testing equivalence/preorder games that cover all the equivalence/preorder semantics supported by Concurrency Workbench - New Century (CWB-NC)[2]. PlayGame also provides a consistent user interface for all the games that reduces the time required to learn a new game.

2 PlayGame

2.1 Designing PlayGame

The design of PlayGame reflects the game semantics hierarchy defined in [6]. The abstract game module implements an abstract version of games and the features common to all games. The game semantics module defines the rules for each individual game. The strategy module synthesizes winning strategies from the evidences submitted by checkers.

Abstract Game Module. A typical verification game has two players: player I, who insists a negative verification result, and player II, who believes otherwise. Each game has its own rules that must be *determined* in the following sense: if the correct answer to the verification problem is negative, then I has a *strategy* to win each and every play no matter how II moves; otherwise, II shall have a winning strategy. When a game is used as a diagnostic routine, it involves two *sides*: the computer vs. the user. The computer assumes the role of a player in favor of the verification result. Thus, by losing each and every play to the computer, the user is convinced of the verification result. The abstract game module implements the aforementioned abstract version of games. It also introduces the role of a *referee* that enforces the rules supplied by the game semantics module. It also implements the common functions including the bookkeeping and the user interface.

Game Semantics Module. Game semantics module defines the rules for each game. For the games studied before such as μ-calculus games and strong bisimulation games [5], our definition is close to previous results but also takes into account the human factor. Our revision intends to keep plays concise and informative. For example, the definition of a μ-calculus game by Stirling [5] requires two steps and the participant of a player to unroll a fixpoint expression ($\mu z.\Psi$ or $\nu z.\Psi$), while the choice of the player unrolling the expression is really irrelevant. In the revised rules, it takes only one step and becomes part of the *referee*'s job. For those games that to the best of our knowledge have not been defined in literature such as testing equivalence/preorder games, we define the games based on the target verification semantics. To further improve code sharing we exploit similarity among each category of games. For instance, in [6] we introduce a generalized equivalence game submodule and semantics *plug-ins*. To introduce an equivalence game, one only needs to supply a relatively small plug-in that specifies part of rules unique to this game. In our experience abstracting rules to different layers saves about 70-80% coding work when introducing a new game.

Strategy Module. Synthesizing a winning strategy for the computer is the key to diagnostic games. Traditionally winning strategies are constructed by a game-based checker [4]. In PlayGame the strategy is constructed from the evidence supplied by a checker. In [7, 8] we propose uniformly-encoded evidences for various verification semantics: for equivalence checking the evidence is a *partition refinement tree*; for preorder checking it is a *kernel-auxiliary partition refinement tree* [7], a variant of partition refinement tree in which each node contains a set of upper states (*auxiliary set*) in addition to a set of lower (and equivalent) states (*kernel set*); for model checking the evidence is a *support set* [8]. It turns out that winning strategies for the games of the same category are quite similar. For equivalence games, the strategy is to keep the states of two processes in different leaves of the partition refinement tree, and hence the algorithm for synthesizing the winning strategy from the evidence is implemented per category basis.

2.2   Using PlayGame

PlayGame is implemented on the CWB-NC. To activate a game, the user simply issues a verification command with a special flag. The CWB-NC with PlayGame calls a checker and enters the interactive game mode after the verification ends.

A play starts with the referee declaring the roles of the computer and the user based on the verification result, then it proceeds by rounds. Figure 2 shows a sample round in a weak bisimulation game. The look and feel of other games are quite similar. The referee judges the winner with an explanation. If no one wins yet, he decides how a round shall proceed. The user is prompted for his/her options of the next move. The user can also choose to take back a few steps.

```
################# Round 2###################
Starting configuration:
  Agent1: 'out_easy.Strongjobber | 'out_easy.Strongjobber
  Agent2: (Start_easy | Start_easy | Hammer | Mallet)
          \ {geth,puth,getm,putm}
Referee: User goes first to choose an agent and make a transition.
Which agent do you choose (1/2)?: 1
Available user options:
  Option 0: --<'out_easy>-->'out_easy.Strongjobber | Strongjobber
  Option 1: --<'out_easy>-->Strongjobber | 'out_easy.Strongjobber
Which transition do you choose?[Type (0-1), or (r)eview options]:1
Step 1: User chose agent 1 and made transition:
          --<'out_easy>-->Strongjobber | 'out_easy.Strongjobber
Step 2: Computer matchs user's choice by choosing
          the transition for agent 2:
          --<<'out_easy>>-->(Start_easy | Jobber
          | Hammer | Mallet)\ {geth,puth,getm,putm}
Continue game?[(c)ontinue, e(x)it or (b)ack]:c
```

Fig. 2. A sample round

3   Conclusions and Future Work

We introduce PlayGame, an integrated platform for diagnostic games. Two novel features in its design are the use of semantics hierarchy, which enables code sharing among different games, and the building of winning strategy using checker-independent evidences, which makes it easier to incorporate new checkers. It implements a μ-calculus game and the full range of equivalence/preorder games. In future we want to study and implement the diagnostic game for other logics.

Acknowledgments

The author would like to thank Rance Cleaveland for many interesting and fruitful discussions, and Madhusudan Parthasarathy for reviewing the draft of this paper.

References

1. The Edinburgh Concurrency Workbench. The University of Edinburgh, 1999.
2. R. Cleaveland and S. Sims. The NCSU concurrency workbench. In *Proceedings of CAV'96*, volume 1102 of *LNCS*, 1996.
3. M. Leucker and T. Noll. Truth/SLC — A parallel verification platform for concurrent systems. In *Proceedings of CAV'01*, volume 2102 of *LNCS*, 2001.
4. P. Stevens and C. Stirling. Practical model-checking using games. In *Proceedings of TACAS '98*, volume 1384 of *LNCS*, 1998.
5. C. Stirling. Games and modal mu-calculus. In *Proceedings of TACAS'96*, volume 1055 of *LNCS*, 1996.
6. L. Tan. An abstract schema for equivalence games. In *Proceedings of VMCAI'02*, volume 2294 of *LNCS*, 2002.
7. L. Tan. *Evidence-based Verification*. PhD thesis, State University of New York at Stony Brook, May 2002.
8. L. Tan and R. Cleaveland. Evidence-based model checking. In *Proceedings of CAV'02*, volume 2404 of *LNCS*, 2002.

SAL 2*

Leonardo de Moura, Sam Owre, Harald Rueß, John Rushby, N. Shankar,
Maria Sorea, and Ashish Tiwari

Computer Science Laboratory
SRI International
333 Ravenswood Avenue
Menlo Park, CA 94025, USA

1 Introduction

SAL (see http://sal.csl.sri.com) is an open suite of tools for analysis of state machines; it constitutes part of our vision for a **S**ymbolic **A**nalysis **L**aboratory that will eventually encompass SAL, the PVS verification system, the ICS decision procedures, and other tools developed in our group and elsewhere.

SAL provides a language similar to that of PVS, but specialized for the specification of state machines; it was first released with an explicit-state model checker as SAL 1 in July 2002; SAL 2, which was released in December 2003, adds high-performance symbolic and bounded model checkers, and novel *infinite bounded* and *witness* model checkers. Both the bounded model checkers can additionally perform verification by k-induction, and the capabilities of all the model checkers and their components are available through an API that is scriptable in Scheme.

2 The Language

The SAL language was originally conceived as an intermediate language and was developed in collaboration with the research groups of David Dill at Stanford and Tom Henzinger at UC Berkeley. Since then, our version of the language has evolved, principally through the addition of a richer type system, including structured types and subtypes so that, in addition to its role as an intermediate language, SAL is now a comprehensive specification language in its own right.

SAL's type system and expression language are similar to those of PVS, including higher types, predicate subtypes, datatypes, infinite types such as reals and integers (and their function types), recursive function definitions, and quantification. State machines are specified as parameterized modules with state variables explicitly identified as input, output, local, or global. The transition relation of a module may be specified using both guarded commands and SMV-style variable-wise invariants. Primes are used to indicate the values of variables

---

* This work was partially supported by the DARPA and USAF Rome Laboratory contract F33615-00-C-3043, NASA Langley Research Center contract NAS1-00079, National Science Foundation grant CCR-ITR-0326540, and by SRI International.

R. Alur and D.A. Peled (Eds.): CAV 2004, LNCS 3114, pp. 496–500, 2004.

in the new state and may appear in guards and in the right-hand sides of assignments and nondeterministic selections as well as on their left-hand sides. Modules may be composed both synchronously and asynchronously (and in combinations of these) to yield systems; a renaming construction allows inputs and outputs of different modules to be "wired up" appropriately.

The assertion language is not primitive in SAL but is defined in libraries associated with the analyzer concerned. Three of the model checkers that constitute the analyzers in SAL 2 provide LTL as their assertion language, while the witness model checker supports CTL. (Both notations can be used to specify formulas in their common subset and SAL translates automatically to the form required by the analyzer concerned).

To support its role as an intermediate language, SAL is defined in XML. Parsers and prettyprinters are provided for a human-readable ASCII representation, and for a Lisp-like LSAL syntax that is useful in scripting and is translated directly into internal representations by the Scheme scripting interface. Because the language is so rich, it is easy to translate most other state machine languages into SAL. We have a translator from the Stateflow notation of Matlab/Simulink, and we expect that ourselves and others will soon provide translators from other popular languages.

3 Preprocessing and Compilation

Because SAL is a rich language, compiling it into the representations used in the deductive cores of its analysis tools (e.g., as BDDs, or as propositional or ICS SAT problems) is a substantial task. All the SAL analysis tools share a common set of preprocessing and compilation routines that perform extensive optimizations. These include partial evaluation, common subexpression elimination, and slicing (i.e., cone of influence reduction). For the finite-state model checkers, arithmetic values and operators are compiled into bitvectors and binary "circuits" respectively, with comparable representations for other SAL types. Reverse translations allow counterexamples to be presented to the user as traces through the original SAL specification with variable assignments expressed in their original SAL types. LTL assertions are translated to optimized Büchi automata. Many transformations and optimizations can be controlled by the user.

SAL 2 provides a lightweight typechecker, called the SAL well-formedness checker, that operates like the typechecker of a programming language: it checks that functions and operators are applied to arguments of the correct types, but does not perform the deeper checks needed for some of SAL's richer constructs: these require proof obligations similar to TCCs in PVS (although SAL TCCs within modules need merely be invariants, not universally valid as in PVS) and will be supported by the full SAL typechecker, which is based on that of PVS.

4 Model Checkers

SAL 2 provides high performance symbolic and bounded model checkers (SMC and BMC, respectively) for systems defined over finite state types, and a novel "infinite bounded" model checker (inf BMC) that can handle infinite as well as finite state types; SAL 2.1 added the "witness" model checker (WMC) that performs finite-state CTL model checking using a new symbolic method.

The SMC and WMC symbolic model checkers use the CUDD BDD package and provide access to its options for controlling the ordering and dynamic reordering of variables. The representation of the transition relation as a BDD and the evaluation of the transformed assertion use many optimizations and deliver performance comparable to other state-of-the-art symbolic model checkers, most of which start from much more primitive notations. In a case study with Holger Pfeifer and Wilfried Steiner concerning fault-tolerant startup of the Time-Triggered Architecture (TTA), we routinely analyzed systems with many hundreds of state bits and hundreds of billions of reachable states in tens of minutes using commodity workstations.

The WMC model checker implements a novel approach that constructs both symbolic witnesses (positive) and counterexamples (negative) for assertions in full CTL. This symbolic evidence is useful in abstraction-refinement, vacuity checking and controller synthesis, and also allows explicit (trace or tree-like) witnesses and counterexamples to be extracted.

The BMC model checker uses a propositional SAT solver to search for counterexamples no longer than some specified "depth" (i.e., length); the model checker can be instructed to advance the depth incrementally, so that it will find the shortest counterexample, and it can also verify properties by k-induction (optionally using other formulas as lemmas). By default, SAL uses ICS as its SAT solver, but it can optionally be instructed to use zChaff or GRASP. In our TTA startup example, the SAL bounded model checker would often solve problems having hundreds of thousands of DAG nodes in their SAT representations (and more than 600 variables in a BDD representation) in a few minutes.

The inf BMC model checker uses the standard formulation of bounded model checking, but instead of translating into a purely propositional SAT problem, it translates to the theory supported by ICS. Although ICS is competitive as a pure SAT solver, it is actually a decision procedure and satisfiability solver for the combination of ground (i.e., unquantified) real and integer linear arithmetic, equality with uninterpreted function symbols, products (i.e., tuples) and coproducts (i.e., disjoint sums), propositional calculus and propositional sets, and restricted forms of lambda calculus, bitvectors, and arrays. Like its finite counterpart, the inf BMC model checker can advance its depth of search incrementally and can perform k-induction. Counterexamples are presented symbolically. Although inf BMC uses ICS as its default satisfiability procedure, it can also be instructed to use UCLID, SVC, CVC, or CVC-Lite, albeit with restrictions (e.g., UCLID decides less theories than ICS) and without counterexamples.

Using real or unbounded integer state types, SAL can represent infinite state systems such as hybrid or timed automata, and other formulations of continuous or real-time behavior. For example, with Bruno Dutertre, we have developed a timed formulation for TTA startup: instances with up to 10 nodes (whose representation uses 24 real and 99 discrete variables) can be verified in a few minutes using inf BMC to perform 1-induction on a series of lemmas. Instances of Fischer's real time mutual exclusion algorithm with as many as 39 nodes have been verified in the same way.

5 Scripting and the SAL Simulator

The preprocessing and model checking components of SAL can be accessed through an API defined in Scheme. The actual model checkers are simply Scheme scripts defined over this API. Users can write their own scripts to perform specialized analyses using the full resources of SAL. The SAL Simulator provides a convenient environment in which to develop such scripts: it is essentially a read-eval-print loop with the SAL libraries preloaded. Used as a simulator, it allows users interactively to explore a specification by executing selected transitions, filtering the current set of states, or finding a path to a state satisfying a given assertion. Used as an environment for scripting, all the capabilities described above can be employed within user-written Scheme functions. For example, with Grégoire Hamon we have used this capability to develop a prototype test case generator for Stateflow that first uses symbolic model checking to find a path to some previously unvisited state or transition, then alternates slicing and bounded model checking to extend the path to additional unvisited targets.

6 Plans for Further Development

SAL 1, which is still available, provides an explicit-state model checker for a subset of the language supported in SAL 2. We intend to redevelop this model checker and to integrate it with the others in forthcoming versions of SAL. We will also integrate the extensions for specifying and abstracting hybrid systems developed by Ashish Tiwari.

Over the longer term, we intend to integrate SAL with PVS (so that, for suitable specifications, it will be possible to translate SAL into PVS, and vice-versa), and to evolve both into an open scriptable environment for symbolic analysis in which numerous tools, developed by ourselves and others, will interact through a SAL *Tool Bus*. The tool bus will extend the SAL language with XML representations for the many artifacts and intermediate products of analysis: for example, invariants, abstractions, counterexamples, test cases and their outputs.

7 Current Status and Availability

SAL 2 with all the capabilities described is freely available for noncommercial research purposes (i.e., roughly, research that will be openly published) from http://sal.csl.sri.com. Binary versions of the system, which require an automatically-generated license key, may be downloaded for Linux, Solaris, MacOS X, and Cygwin (for Windows). The SAL binaries also install the ICS

500   Leonardo de Moura et al.

executable. The SAL and ICS source code is available with a signed license agreement. The top-level page for tools developed by our group is `http://fm.csl.sri.com`, from which you can find links to our Roadmap, papers, examples, and a tutorial illustrating all our tools.

For want of space, all references have been omitted here; they are present in an expanded version pf the paper available at `http://www.csl.sri.com/~rushby/abstracts/sal-cav04`.

Formal Analysis of Java Programs in JavaFAN

Azadeh Farzan, Feng Chen, José Meseguer, and Grigore Roşu

Department of Computer Science
University of Illinois at Urbana-Champaign
{afarzan,fengchen,meseguer,grosu}@cs.uiuc.edu

Abstract. JavaFAN is a Java program analysis framework, that can symbolically execute multithreaded programs, detect safety violations searching through an unbounded state space, and verify finite state programs by explicit state model checking. Both Java language and JVM bytecode analyses are possible. JavaFAN's implementation consists of only 3,000 lines of Maude code, specifying formally the semantics of Java and JVM in rewriting logic and then using the capabilities of Maude for efficient execution, search and LTL model checking of rewriting theories.

1 Introduction

JavaFAN (Java Formal ANalyzer) is a tool to simulate and formally analyze multithreaded Java programs at source code and/or bytecode levels. A novel feature of JavaFAN's design is that it is directly based on *formal definitions* of the Java and the JVM semantics in the form of *rewrite theories* that are efficiently executed and analyzed in the Maude language [2]. The following types of analysis are supported: (1) *symbolic simulation*, with Java and JVM specifications used as *interpreters* executing programs with actual or symbolic inputs; (2) *breadth-first search* (BFS) within a concurrent program's state space to find violations of safety properties; (3) *model checking* of linear temporal logic (LTL) properties for programs whose state space is finite. These forms of analysis are efficiently supported by Maude's underlying rewriting, breath-first search, and LTL model checking features [2]. To keep the framework user-friendly, JavaFAN wraps the Maude specifications and accepts Java or JVM code from the user as input.

JavaFAN's specification-based design has a number of important advantages: (1) formal specifications provide a rigorous semantic definition for a language that can be mathematically scrutinized; (2) such formal specifications can be developed with relatively little effort, even for large languages like Java and the JVM; (3) Maude's underlying formal analysis infrastructure is entirely *generic*, so that formal analysis tools become available *for free* for each language so specified; and (4) in spite of their generality, the formal analyses can be performed with *competitive performance*. Section 3 discusses several examples, providing analysis times and comparisons of JavaFAN with other related analysis tools.

The reason for JavaFAN's efficiency is twofold. On the one hand, Maude has a rewrite engine achieving millions of rewrites per second, an efficient BFS

R. Alur and D.A. Peled (Eds.): CAV 2004, LNCS 3114, pp. 501–505, 2004.
© Springer-Verlag Berlin Heidelberg 2004

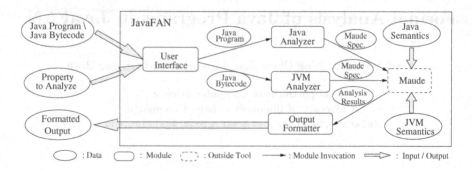

Fig. 1. Architecture of JavaFAN.

algorithm, and an explicit state LTL model checker with performance comparable to SPIN [3]. On the other hand, our approach in specifying the semantics of a concurrent language as a rewrite theory in Maude tries to maximize performance. A *rewrite theory* is a triple (Σ, E, R), with Σ a signature declaring types and function symbols, E a set of equations, and R a set of rewrite rules. Intuitively, the equations E specify the semantics of a language's *deterministic* computations, whereas the rules R specify its *concurrent transitions*. The point is that the *state space* is only defined by the rules R: the smaller R is, the more efficient the analysis. In JavaFAN, R is indeed small compared to E: for Java $|R| = 15$ and $|E| = 600$, and for JVM $|R| = 40$ and $|E| = 300$. A *continuation-based* semantics also increases performance, because most equations and rules then become *unconditional* and thus more efficient to execute. Finally, by distinguishing between the *static* and *dynamic* parts of a program, only the dynamic component is kept in the state representation, with huge resource savings for large programs.

2   Overview of JavaFAN

Figure 1 presents the architecture of JavaFAN. The *user interface* module hides the Maude back-end behind a user-friendly environment. It also plays the role of a dispatcher, sending the Java source code and/or the bytecode to Java and/or JVM analyzers, respectively. The analyzers wrap the input programs into properly defined Maude modules and invoke Maude, which analyzes the code based on formal specifications of the Java language and the JVM. The output formatter collects the output of Maude, transforms it into a user-readable format, and sends it to the user. We use Maude to specify the operational semantics of a sufficiently large subset of Java and the JVM, including multithreading, inheritance, polymorphism, object references, and dynamic object allocation. Native methods and many of the Java built-in libraries are not currently supported. Java and the JVM are modeled differently. For Java, a quite efficient continuation-based style is adopted, while for the JVM we use an object oriented style that makes the specification simpler and easier to understand.

Table 1. Thread Game Times.

N	JVM	Java
50	7.2	2.7
100	17.1	6.6
200	41.3	17
400	104	54.7
500	4.5m	2m
1000	10.1m	5.1m

Continuation-Based Semantics of Java. The semantics of Java is defined modularly – different features of the language are defined in separate modules – to ease extensions and maintenance. A state is a multiset of state attributes, such as threads, memory, synchronization information, etc. To support multi-threaded programs, we introduce the notion of *thread context*, which consists of three components: (1) a continuation, (2) the thread environment, and (3) the corresponding object. The continuation maintains the control context of the thread, which explicitly specifies the next steps to be performed by it.

Object-Based Semantics of the JVM. The state of the JVM is represented as a multiset of objects and messages in Maude. Objects in the multiset fall into four major categories: (1) objects which represent Java objects, (2) objects which represent Java threads, (3) objects which represent Java classes, and (4) auxiliary objects used mostly for definitional purposes. Rewrites (with rewrite rules and equations) in this multiset (modulo associativity, commutativity, and identity) model the changes in the state of the JVM. In each rewrite, there is usually one thread involved, together with classes and/or objects that may be needed to execute the next bytecode instruction.

3   Experiments

Using the underlying search and model checking features of Maude, JavaFAN can be used to formally analyze Java programs. *Breadth-first search analysis* (supported through Maude's `search` command) is a semi-decision procedure that can be used to explore all the concurrent computations of a program, looking for safety violations characterized by a pattern and a condition. This empowers JavaFAN to analyze programs with possibly infinite state spaces. For finite state programs, it is also possible to perform explicit-state model checking (using Maude's model checker) of properties specified in linear temporal logic (LTL).

JavaFAN has effectively been applied on a number of examples. Performance results are given in seconds on a 2.4 GHz Linux PC. Detailed discussions on the examples can be found in [4]. Results are given at both Java and JVM levels.

Remote Agent (RA) [5] has two running threads: a *planner* that generates plans from mission goals, and an *executive* that executes the plans. The code

Table 2. Dining Philosophers Times.

Tests	JVM	Java
DP(5)	4.5	9.9
DP(6)	33.3	81.7
DP(7)	4.4m	15.1m
DP(8)	13.7m	98m
DP(9)	803.2m	—
DF(5)	3.2m	19.2
DF(6)	23.9m	2.4m
DF(7)	686.4m	27m

contains a missing critical section, that leads to a data-race between two concurrent threads, which further caused a deadlock. JavaFAN finds the deadlock in 0.3 of a second in the bytecode level and 0.09 of a second in the source-code level, while the tool in [8] finds it in more than 2 seconds in its most optimized version.

Thread Game [7] is a simple multithreaded program which shows the possible data races between two threads accessing a common variable. Each thread reads the value of the static variable c twice and writes the sum of the two values back to c. The question is what values can c possibly hold during the infinite execution of the program. Theoretically, it can be proved that all natural numbers can be achieved [7]. JavaFAN (using the **search** command) addresses this question for any specific value of N. Table 1 presents the result for some numbers.

Dining Philosophers. We have model checked a deadlock-prone (DP) and a deadlock-free (DF) version of this problem. The property that we have model checked for this example is whether all the philosophers can eventually dine. The LTL formula is $\Diamond$Check(N), where N is the number of philosophers. The proposition Check(N) is specified in Maude by the user. For the deadlock-prone version, the model checker generates a counterexample – a sequence of states that leads to the deadlock – and states the property to be true in the deadlock-free version. Currently, JavaFAN can detect the deadlock for up to 8 philosophers at the bytecode level and up to 9 philosophers at the Java Language level in a reasonable amount of time (Table 2). It can also prove the program deadlock-free for up to 7 philosophers at both levels. This compares favorably with JPF [1,6] which for the same program cannot deal with 4 philosophers.

2-Stage Pipeline is a pipeline computation, where each pipeline stage executes as a separate thread. Stages interact through *connector* objects. The property we have model checked for this program states the "eventual shutdown of a pipeline stage in response to a call to **stop** on the pipeline's input connector". The LTL formula for the property is $\Box$(c1stop $\rightarrow$ $\Diamond$($\neg$stage1return)). JavaFAN model checks the property and returns **true** in 17 minutes (no partial order reduction was used). This compares favorably with the model checker in [8] which without using the partial order reduction performs the task in more than 100 minutes (both on a 2.4GHz PC).

4   Conclusions and Future Work

We have discussed JavaFAN's design, and experiments suggesting that it can analyze Java and JVM programs with competitive performance. Perhaps the most important experience gained is that a formal specification based methodology to develop formal analysis tools for concurrent programs is a rigorous, cost-effective, and practical approach when realized on a high-performance logical engine. The methodology itself is generally applicable to other languages. Future work will involve further experimentation, development of similar tools for other languages, partial order reduction optimization, and widening the range of formal analyses supported, including program abstraction and theorem proving.

References

1. G. Brat, K. Havelund, S. Park, and W. Visser. Model checking programs. In *ASE'00*, pages 3 – 12, 2000.
2. M. Clavel, F. Durán, S. Eker, P. Lincoln, N. Martí-Oliet, J. Meseguer, and C. Talcott. *Maude 2.0 Manual*, 2003. http://maude.cs.uiuc.edu/manual.
3. Steven Eker, José Meseguer, and Ambarish Sridharanarayanan. The Maude LTL model checker and its implementation. In *Model Checking Software: Proc. 10th Intl. SPIN Workshop*, volume 2648, pages 230–234. Springer LNCS, 2003.
4. A. Farzan, F. Chen, J. Meseguer, and G. Roşu. JavaFAN. fsl.cs.uiuc.edu/es/javafan.
5. K. Havelund, M. Lowry, and J. Penix. Formal Analysis of a Space Craft Controller using SPIN. *IEEE Transactions on Software Engineering*, 27(8):749 – 765, August 2001. Previous version appeared in Proceedings of the 4th SPIN workshop, 1998.
6. K. Havelund and T. Pressburger. Model checking Java programs using Java PathFinder. *Software Tools for Technology Transfer*, 2(4):366 – 381, April 2000.
7. J. S. Moore. http://www.cs.utexas.edu/users/xli/prob/p4/p4.html.
8. D. Y. W. Park, U. Stern, J. U. Sakkebaek, and D. L. Dill. Java model checking. In *ASE'01*, pages 253 – 256, 2000.

A Toolset for Modelling and Verification of GALS Systems

S. Ramesh, Sampada Sonalkar, Vijay D'silva,
Naveen Chandra R., and B. Vijayalakshmi

Center for Formal Design and Verification of Software
Department of Computer Science and Engineering, IIT Bombay
ramesh@cse.iitb.ac.in

1 Introduction

We present a toolset for design and verification of Globally Asynchronous Locally Synchronous(GALS) systems. Such systems consist of a network of reactive nodes which have independent clocks and I/O interfaces, and communicate using complex synchronisation mechanisms. GALS systems are gaining prevalence in avionics, embedded systems, and VLSI design. These systems are difficult to design and verify due to the concurrency and complex interaction involved.

The toolset is based on a visual formal language called Communicating Reactive State Machines(CRSM)[6], which builds upon Communicating Reactive Processes[2]. It seamlessly integrates a graphical editor, a simulator and a verification engine. It has several novel aspects in the areas of language design and verification. The semantics of CRSM consolidates ideas from the synchronous languages with classical concurrency constructs. The simulator implements a distributed protocol to incorporate pre-emption with asynchronous communication and supports distributed simulation with context switches. Properties are specified using *distributed observers* and verified using Spin[4]. The verification engine includes a non-trivial translation from CRSM, an open system with GALS semantics, to Promela, a closed system with asynchronous semantics. In addition, Spin has been modified to generate counter examples that can be viewed directly in the simulator.

We have used the tools to model and verify standard pedagogical examples, and for technology transfer in a company. We have found CRSM well suited for providing cycle accurate descriptions of control dominated architectures with multiple clock domains. Industrial case studies include a multi-processor System-on-Chip(SoC) application and a bus protocol. In this paper, we illustrate these tools using a case study. Section 2 introduces underlying theory, Section 3 discusses the tools, implementation issues, and our experience, and Section 4 concludes.

2 Communicating Reactive State Machines

A CRSM is a network of nodes built from communicating boolean Mealy-style automata using constructs for synchronous and asynchronous parallel composi-

R. Alur and D.A. Peled (Eds.): CAV 2004, LNCS 3114, pp. 506–509, 2004.
© Springer-Verlag Berlin Heidelberg 2004

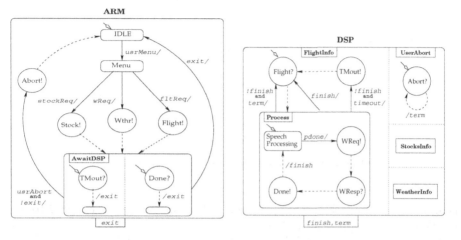

Fig. 1. *ARM* and *DSP* components of Infophone

tion, hierarchy, and signal hiding. The nodes are locally synchronous, execute concurrently, emit signals via synchronous broadcast, and communicate on point-to-point channels using CSP-style rendezvous. A formal description is provided in [9]. We illustrate CRSM using Infophone[1], a speech enabled Java application for information retrieval. It uses an ARM processor to control the user interface, a DSP to process speech commands, and a wireless web interface.

A CRSM description of Infophone is written as $ARM//DSP//WEB$, where $//$ is the operator for asynchronous parallel composition. Figure 1 shows simplified versions of *ARM* and *DSP*. The rectangles and circles represent passive and communication states respectively. The dashed arrows from communication states denote transitions taken when communication succeeds and solid arrows, transitions taken when their guards are true; guards describe the status of signals in the environment.

When activated by the signal usrMenu, *ARM* receives the user's request, say fltReq and forwards it to *DSP* on the relevant channel, in this case Flight. *DSP* receives speech commands, sends a request to *WEB* on WReq and notifies *ARM* when a response is received on WResp. A session ends in three ways: successfully, when *ARM* receives a message on the channel Done from *DSP*, times out, when a timeout is issued by *DSP* if *WEB* is not responding, and aborts, when the user issues usrAbort.

The state AwaitDSP in *ARM* has hierarchy and contains two automata. The transitions leaving AwaitDSP allow these automata to complete their ongoing reaction before passivating them, a policy of *weak pre-emption*. The automata FlightInfo, StockInfo, WeatherInfo and UserAbort in *DSP* execute in synchronous parallelism, written FlightInfo∥..∥UserAbort and interact

---

[1] Infophone was developed on the Open Multimedia Application Platform(OMAP), a trademark of Texas Instruments.

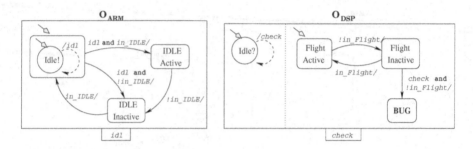

Fig. 2. Distributed Observers: O_{ARM} and O_{DSP}

using local signals such as exit, term and finish. Nodes are required to be deterministic and constructive[1, 9].

Safety properties of CRSMs are specified using distributed observers. An observer monitors the status of a node, communicates with other observers, and enters a special state Bug when a property is violated. Verification involves checking the system $(ARM\|O_{ARM})//(DSP\|O_{DSP})//(WEB\|O_{WEB})$ for the reachability of the state Bug. The observers in Figure 2 specify that a session terminated in ARM should be terminated in DSP within its next cycle. The conditional $in\_\langle state\rangle$ holds if the $state$ is active at the end of the reaction. A subtle error occurs when usrAbort is issued in ARM and timeout in DSP. ARM transits to the state $Abort!$, communicates with the automaton UserAbort in DSP and enters Idle. DSP consequently enters the state $TMout!$. The next time fltReq is issued in ARM, the system will deadlock.

3   Experience and Discussion

We have developed a graphical environment which integrates the design and verification flow described. CRSM models can be built using a graphical editor or a textual language tCRSM. The execution sequences can be viewed in the simulator, which performs a *must* and *can* analysis to determine the status of local signals[1] and implements a distributed protocol[7] to address issues due to pre-emption in the presence of communication[8].

Model checking is performed by translating the system to Promela[5, 10]. The Promela code for each node includes a reactive kernel and an environment process, and ensures that the status of signals and states in the system are evaluated correctly. Signal hiding requires *must* and *can* analysis to be incorporated in the Promela code. Spin is invoked automatically with the specification $\Box\neg$Bug(*always not* Bug) and counter examples generated are translated into traces and displayed in the simulator. Spin has been modified for this purpose.

The tools described have been implemented in approximately 30,000 lines of C and Java code. Our case studies include Infophone and a proprietary bus protocol used by Texas Instruments. The Infophone system with its observers was translated into 890 lines of Promela code with 107 boolean variables, while the bus protocol was translated to 270 lines of Promela code with 31 boolean variables. Boolean variables are required for state and signal encoding, performing analysis, providing observer related primitives and implementing rendezvous. The absence of local signals and asynchronous communication resulted in fewer booleans in the bus protocol code. We observed that CRSM models provided Register Transfer Level(RTL) style structure, yet complete and cycle accurate descriptions of the bus protocol. In addition, the designers find temporal logics intimidating and prefer state machine based specifications.

4 Conclusion

We have presented a tool set for modelling and verification of GALS applications. Tools such as SAL/PVS, Polis, Reactive Modules, and SMV capture both models of concurrency but significant semantic differences exist such as notions of acceptable programs and pre-emption mechanisms. Our work differs from most Statecharts based verification engines for similar reasons.

At present, we have developed static analysis[3] and refinement techniques[9] to ameliorate verification. These techniques are currently being incorporated in the tool. We are also exploring other techniques that might aid the designers and are conducting further case studies.

References

1. G. Berry. The constructive semantics of pure esterel. In *Book Draft, version 3*, July 1999.
2. G. Berry, S. Ramesh, and R. K. Shyamasundar. Communicating reactive processes. In *Twentieth Symposium on Principles of Programming Languages*, 1993.
3. Vinod Ganapathy and S. Ramesh. Slicing synchronous reactive programs. In *Synchronous Languages, Applications, and Programming*, Grenoble, France, April 2002.
4. Gerard J. Holzmann. The model checker SPIN. *Software Engineering*, 23(5):279–295, 1997.
5. Naveen Chandra R. Verification of communicating reactive state machines. M.Tech dissertation, Department of Computer Science and Engineering, IIT Bombay, 2002.
6. S. Ramesh. Communicating reactive state machines: Design, model and implementation. In *IFAC Workshop on Distributed Computer Control Systems*, September 1998.
7. S. Ramesh. Implementation of communicating reactive processes. *Parallel Computing*, 25(6):703–727, June 1999.
8. S. Ramesh and Chandrashekar M. Shetty. Impossibility of synchronization in the presence of preemption. *Parallel Processing Letters,*, 8(1):111–120, March 1998.
9. Sampada Sonalkar. Compositional verification of communicating reactive state machines. Master's thesis, Indian Institute of Technology Bombay, January 2004.
10. B. Vijayalakshmi. Verification of communicating reactive state machines. M.Tech dissertation, IIT Bombay, School of Information Technology, 2003.

WSAT: A Tool for Formal Analysis of Web Services

Xiang Fu, Tevfik Bultan, and Jianwen Su

Department of Computer Science
University of California
Santa Barbara, CA 93106, USA
{fuxiang,bultan,su}@cs.ucsb.edu

1 Introduction

This paper presents Web Service Analysis Tool (WSAT), a tool for analyzing and verifying composite web service designs, with the state of the art model checking techniques. Web services are *loosely* coupled distributed systems communicating via XML messages. Communication among web services is asynchronous, and it is supported by messaging platforms such as JMS which provide FIFO queues to store incoming messages. Data transmission among web services is standardized via XML, and the specification of web service itself (invocation interface and behavior signature) relies on a stack of XML based standards (e.g. WSDL, BPEL4WS, WSCI and etc.). The characteristics of web services, however, raise several challenges in the application of model checking: (**1**) Numerous competing web service standards, most of which lack formal semantics, complicate the formal specification of web service composition. (**2**) Asynchronous messaging makes most interesting verification problems undecidable, even when XML message contents are abstracted away [3]. (**3**) XML data and expressive XPath based manipulation are not supported by current model checkers.

WSAT, as shown in Fig. 1, tackles these challenges as follows: (**1**) **An Intermediate Representation:** We use automata with XPath guards (called GFSA) as an intermediate representation for web services. A translator from BPEL4WS to GFSA is developed, and support for other languages can be added without changing the analysis and the verification modules of the tool. (**2**) **Synchronizability and Realizability Analyses:** We define a set of sufficient *synchronizability* conditions to restrict control flows of a composite web service. When the analysis succeeds, LTL verification can be performed using the synchronous communication semantics instead of asynchronous communication semantics. We also define a set of sufficient *realizability* conditions that are used to synthesize a set of GFSA (called peers) which communicate with asynchronous messages from a single GFSA (called a conversation protocol) which specifies the set of desired global behaviors. The behaviors of the synthesized peers are the same as the behaviors of the conversation protocol if the conversation protocol is realizable [3]. (**3**) **Handling of XML Data Manipulation:** We developed and implemented algorithms for translating XPath expressions to Promela code [5], and we use model checker SPIN [7] as the back-end of WSAT to check LTL properties.

2 Guarded Finite State Automata

A composite web service can be specified in either bottom-up or top-down fashion. Formally, for a composite web service, its bottom-up specification (called a *web service*

R. Alur and D.A. Peled (Eds.): CAV 2004, LNCS 3114, pp. 510–514, 2004.

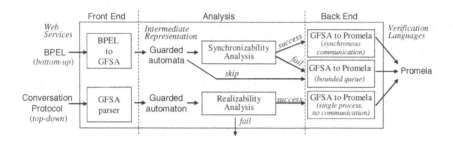

Fig. 1. WSAT architecture

composition) [4] is described as a tuple $\langle (P, M), \mathcal{A}_1, \ldots, \mathcal{A}_n \rangle$, and its top-down specification (called a *conversation protocol*) [2, 3, 6] is specified as a tuple $\langle (P, M), \mathcal{A} \rangle$. Here (P, M) is the composition schema where P is a set of peer prototypes, and M is a set of message classes. Guarded Finite State Automata (GFSA) $\mathcal{A}_1, \ldots, \mathcal{A}_n$ are the peer implementations (supposing $|P| = n$), and $\mathcal{A}$ specifies the desired set of global behaviors. Below, we present a fragment of the Stock Analysis Service (SAS) conversation protocol studied in [5]:

```
Conversation Protocol{              GFSA{
  Composition Schema{                 States{s1,s2,...,s12},
   PeerList{Inv,SB,RD},               InitialState {s1},
   MSL Type List{                     FinalStates{s3},
    Register[                         TransitionRelation{
     orderID[xsd:int],                  t14{s8 -> s12 : bill,
     reqList[stockID[xsd:int]{1,10}],   Guard{
     payment [                           $request//stockID =
      account[xsd:int] |                  $register//stockID[position()=last()]
      creditCard[xsd:int]                 =>
    ]], ...                              $bill//orderID := $register//orderID
  },                                    }
  Message List{                       } ...
   register{Inv->SB:Register},       }//end of TransitionRelation
   bill{SB->Inv:Bill},...           }//end of GFSA
  }}                               }//end of Conversation Protocol
```

As shown above, each message class has a type defined using MSL [1], a compact theoretical model of XML Schema. WSAT supports a fragment of MSL, where complex types can be constructed using sequence ',' (e.g. the Register) and choice '|' (e.g. the payment) operators. An MSL type can also have multiple occurrences (e.g. payment can have 1 to 10 stockID children), however, maximum occurrence must be bounded.

A GFSA is a tuple (M, T, s, F, Δ). M is the message class set in the composition schema. T, s, F are the set of states, initial state, and the set of final states, respectively. Δ is the transition relation. Each transition $\tau \in \Delta$ is of the form $\tau = (s, (c, g), t)$, where $s, t \in T$ are the source and the destination states of τ, $c \in M$ is a message class and g is the *guard* of the transition. Guards are written using XPath expressions. WSAT supports a subset of XPath which consists of the following operators: child axis (/), descendant axis (//), self-reference (.), parent-reference (..), basic type test (b()), node name test (t), wildcard (*), function calls position() and last(), and predicates ([]). Arithmetic and boolean constraints can be used as predicates in WSAT.

As shown in the SAS protocol, a guard consists of a guard condition and a set of assignments which specify the contents of the message that is being sent. For example the guard of transition t14 specifies that: if the stockID attribute in the request message is the last stockID in the register message, then send out a bill message whose orderID attribute matches the orderID of register. The powerful XPath language allows guards to express very rich semantics. In [4] we showed that static BPEL4WS web services can be translated into GFSA representation without loss of data semantics.

3   Synchronizability and Realizability Analyses

Consider the simple client-server web service composition given in the following figure. A requester and a server interact with each other via three request messages and one acknowledgment message. Recall that each peer is equipped with a queue to store incoming messages. It is not hard to infer that the composition has an infinite number

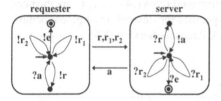

of configurations, because the requester can send arbitrary number of r_1 and r_2 messages (which are stored in the queue of the server) before any acknowledgment is sent back. However, another interesting observation is that the global behaviors, characterized by the sequence of messages, is a regular language $(r_1 \mid r_2 \mid ra)^* e$, which is the set of behaviors generated by the composition under synchronous semantics (i.e., the Cartesian product of the two automata). Since in our model [3], LTL properties are defined over the global behaviors, it is decidable to check LTL properties for such services.

We say a web service composition is *synchronizable* if it generates the same set of global behaviors for both synchronous and asynchronous semantics. In [4] we present three sufficient synchronizability conditions to identify synchronizable web service compositions. For each synchronizable web service composition WSAT will generate a Promela specification with synchronous (rendezvous) communication (by limiting the Promela channel size to 0), and then call SPIN to verify LTL properties on the synchronous specification. The verified LTL properties are guaranteed to be satisfied by the original asynchronous web service composition. For top-down specified conversation protocols, we developed a similar analysis called *realizability analysis* [3], which is further extended to consider message contents in [6].

4   Handling XML Data Manipulation

WSAT translates each GFSA into a Promela process. The central issue of the translation algorithm is how to handle XML data and XPath expressions. Each MSL type declaration is translated into a record type ("typedef") in Promela, and types with multiple occurrences are translated into Promela arrays. For example, the stockID in the SAS protocol is mapped into a Promela array of size 10. Based on the type mapping, XPath expressions can be translated into Promela code. When MSL types with multiple occurrences are involved, the translation is essentially a nested-loop. For example, consider the following boolean XPath expression: `$reg1//stockID = $reg2//stockID`, where `$reg1` and `$reg2` are two XML variables of type `Register` that is defined in the SAS protocol. Note each side of the equality is a location path which returns a set of `stockID` values. According to XPath standard, the expression evaluates to `true` if we can find one value from each side to satisfy the equality. Hence the expression captures the query: "Is there any `stockID` value which appears in both `$reg1` and `$reg2`?". The corresponding Promela translation is a two-layer nested loop which searches the two arrays (that correspond to the `stockID` array of `$reg1` and `$reg2` respectively), to find a pair of array elements that satisfy the equality. When function calls such as `position()` and `last()` are involved (e.g. the transition guard of `t14` in the SAS protocol), the translation is more complex. The main idea is to substitute the appearance of a function call with an integer variable, and properly update its value so that when the function is called the integer variable contains the right value. More details are available in [5].

We applied WSAT to a range of examples, including six conversation protocols converted from the IBM Conversation Support Project [8], five BPEL4WS services from BPEL4WS standard and Collaxa.com, and the SAS from [5]. Synchronizability and realizability analysis are applied to each example, and except two conversation protocols, all examples pass these checks. This implies that the sufficient conditions in our synchronizability and realizability analysis are not restrictive and they are able to capture most practical applications. For each example, we generated the corresponding Promela specification using WSAT, and we checked LTL properties of the form "$\mathbf{G}(p \rightarrow \mathbf{F}q)$" using SPIN. Our experience with these examples suggests that while exhaustive search of the state space may be very costly for verifying correct properties, SPIN's performance at discovering false LTL properties is satisfactory. For instance, we identified a very delicate design error (a misuse of XPath `position()` function in a transition guard) in the SAS example [5] using SPIN.

WSAT can be extended in the future, by supporting other web service specification languages at the front end, and targeting different verification tools at the back-end. We are especially interested in extending WSAT with symbolic verification techniques in order to handle large state spaces generated by XML data.

Acknowledgments

Authors are supported by NSF Career award CCR-9984822, NSF grant CCR-0341365, IIS-0101134, and IIS-9817432.

References

1. A. Brown, M. Fuchs, J. Robie, and P. Wadler. MSL a model for W3C XML Schema. In *Proc. of 10th Int. World Wide Web Conference (WWW)*, pages 191–200, 2001.
2. T. Bultan, X. Fu, R. Hull, and J. Su. Conversation specification: A new approach to design and analysis of e-service composition. In *Proc. of 12th Int. World Wide Web Conference (WWW)*, pages 403–410, May 2003.

3. X. Fu, T. Bultan, and J. Su. Conversation protocols: A formalism for specification and verification of reactive electronic services. In *Proc. of 8th Int. Conf. on Implementation and Application of Automata (CIAA 2003)*, volume 2759 of *LNCS*, pages 188–200, 2003.
4. X. Fu, T. Bultan, and J. Su. Analysis of interacting BPEL Web Services. To appear in the *Proc. of 13th Int. World Wide Web Conf. (WWW)*, 2004.
5. X. Fu, T. Bultan, and J. Su. Model checking XML manipulating software. To appear in the *Proc. of 2004 IEEE Int. Symp. on Software Testing and Analysis (ISSTA)*, 2004.
6. X. Fu, T. Bultan, and J. Su. Realizability of conversation protocols with message contents. To appear in the *Proc. of 2004 IEEE Int. Conf. on Web Services (ICWS)*, 2004.
7. G. J. Holzmann. *The SPIN Model Checker: Primer and Reference Manual*. Addison-Wesley, Boston, Massachusetts, 2003.
8. IBM. Conversation support project. http://www.research.ibm.com/convsupport/.

CVC Lite: A New Implementation of the Cooperating Validity Checker[*]

Category B

Clark Barrett[1] and Sergey Berezin[2]

[1] New York University
barrett@cs.nyu.edu
[2] Stanford University
berezin@stanford.edu

Abstract. We describe a tool called CVC Lite (CVCL), an automated theorem prover for formulas in a union of first-order theories. CVCL supports a set of theories which are useful in verification, including uninterpreted functions, arrays, records and tuples, and linear arithmetic. New features in CVCL (beyond those provided in similar previous systems) include a library API, more support for producing proofs, some heuristics for reasoning about quantifiers, and support for symbolic simulation primitives.

1 Introduction

Decision procedures for decidable fragments of first-order logic continue to attract users and interest in a wide variety of verification efforts.

CVC Lite (CVCL) is a tool for determining the validity (or satisfiability) of first-order formulas over a union of specific useful theories. It replaces the original Cooperating Validity Checker (CVC) [7], which, in turn, was a successor to the Stanford Validity Checker (SVC) [4]. The name does not imply that the new system is less powerful than CVC, but rather was chosen because after learning from our experience with CVC, we felt we could create a tool which, without sacrificing functionality, would be smaller, faster, and easier to use and maintain.

Although CVCL is a work in progress, in many respects it has already validated our vision and rewarded the effort involved in a reimplementation. In particular, the code base is one third the size of CVC, the performance is comparable, and it has been used and enhanced by a number of people outside the core group of developers. In addition, CVCL has many new features, not found in any of the previous systems.

In this paper, we will describe the theory and features of CVCL, with an emphasis on what is new as compared to the previous systems (especially CVC). We begin with a brief overview of the system and the theories which are currently

---

[*] This research was supported by a grant from Intel Corporation and by National Science Foundation CCR-0121403.

R. Alur and D.A. Peled (Eds.): CAV 2004, LNCS 3114, pp. 515–518, 2004.

supported in CVCL. Then we describe the features which are new in CVCL and conclude with some example applications.

2   Overview

CVCL accepts as input one or more assertion formulas and a query formula. It then checks whether the assertion formulas imply the query formula. Each formula must be a first-order formula whose parameters (non-logical symbols) must be from among the theories listed in the next section.

The algorithm used depends on the Nelson-Oppen method for combining decision procedures [6] and the implementation is based closely on an algorithm whose correctness is verified in the first author's Ph.D. thesis [3].

Although there is limited support for quantifiers in CVCL (see below), the algorithm is complete only for quantifier-free formulas. As with its predecessor, CVCL uses advanced SAT-based search heuristics and has the ability to produce a proof when a formula is successfully validated.

3   The Theories of CVCL

3.1   Equality with Uninterpreted Functions

The simplest supported theory is one which contains an arbitrary number of functions and predicates which are "uninterpreted", meaning that the theory does not provide any information about them other than that they are functions and predicates. Because the set of non-logical symbols in this theory varies according to the formulas being checked, the user must specify the set of such functions and predicates for a particular run of CVCL.

3.2   Arrays

CVCL includes a theory of abstract arrays with two operations, *read* and *write* which can be used to read from a location in an abstract array or to create a new array by *writing* a new value to a location in an existing array.

3.3   Records and Tuples

CVCL formulas can include simple aggregate datatypes like records and tuples. These are handled with a simple decision procedure for a set of operations used to create, read from, and write to these datatypes (much like the array operations).

3.4   Arithmetic

As with its predecessors, CVCL can decide the theory of linear arithmetic over the reals. However, CVCL also has some additional capabilities. The first is the ability to deal with linear arithmetic over integers. In fact, CVCL can reason about linear expressions over any combination of real and integer variables.

The other extension implemented in CVCL is the ability to handle some nonlinear arithmetic. Nonlinear expressions are transformed into a normal form, making it possible to verify simple identities like $(a+b)(a-b) = a^2 - b^2$. However, the nonlinear capabilities of CVCL are still very limited.

3.5   Additional Theories

Currently, new decision procedures are being developed for inductive datatypes, a subset of set theory, and a theory of bit-vectors.

4   New Features

4.1   Library API

One of the main features lacking in both SVC and CVC was a library interface. Interaction with the old systems was done using a small custom command language. Commands were either typed in manually or provided through a scripting mechanism.

CVCL has the same command language interface, but we also designed an abstract interface into CVCL from the start. The methods in this API mimic the command language, so that it is easy to move from one mode of interaction to the other. In fact, the command language interface is implemented using the API, minimizing the chance that the two modes of interaction will behave differently.

The API is available both as an abstract C++ class and as a set of C functions. It has been successfully used as a library from C++, and the C interface has been successfully used by the foreign function interface of other languages including Prolog and Ocaml.

4.2   Proof Support for Efficient Boolean Reasoning

A major feature of the original CVC system was the ability to produce a proof artifact as the result of successfully validating a formula. However, CVC could only produce proofs when using a slow search heuristic. When using advanced SAT-based heuristics, which are essential on large formulas, CVC was unable to produce a proof because it depended on an external SAT solver and had no way to extract a proof from this solver.

CVCL overcomes this difficulty by integrating a custom SAT solver and including proof rules for the kinds of reasoning done in modern efficient Boolean SAT solvers [2]. This enables CVCL to use advanced techniques like clause learning and conflict-directed backtracking while still producing proofs.

4.3   Quantifiers

One of the most significant new features of CVCL is native support for quantifiers. Adding quantifiers necessarily makes the logic undecidable, but in many practical examples, even very simple heuristics for quantifier instantiation can be sufficient.

The current heuristic used by CVCL is to collect the set of terms that have occurred in some previous formula, and then use these terms to instantiate the quantified variables of similar type. This is a very close reimplementation of the heuristic used by Das and Dill [5] for solving quantified formulas arising in predicate abstraction.

4.4   Symbolic Simulation

A primitive interface for symbolic simulation was built into CVC, and successfully applied to applications in hardware verification [1]. CVCL provides a more extensive and intuitive interface to symbolic simulation primitives.

5   Conclusion

Since becoming available in August 2003, CVCL has been downloaded by many research groups and used in a wide variety of verification efforts in both hardware and software.

One representative example is the work on compiler validation being done at NYU. CVCL is used to verify the verification conditions generated by a tool which checks the correctness of transformations done by an optimizing compiler [8].

CVCL has an active user and development community. More information, including instructions for downloading and installing the tool, is available at the CVCL web page: http://verify.stanford.edu/CVCL.

References

1. Husam Abu-Haimed, Sergey Berezin, and David L. Dill. Strengthening invariants by symbolic consistency testing. In Warren A. Hunt Jr. and Fabio Somenzi, editors, *CAV*, volume 2725 of *Lecture Notes in Computer Science*. Springer, 2003.
2. Clark Barrett and Sergey Berezin. A Proof-Producing Boolean Search Engine. In *CADE-19 Workshop: Pragmatics of Decision Procedures in Automated Reasoning (PDPAR)*, July 2003. Miami, Florida, USA.
3. Clark W. Barrett. *Checking Validity of Quantifier-Free Formulas in Combinations of First-Order Theories*. PhD thesis, Stanford University, 2003.
4. Clark W. Barrett, David L. Dill, and Jeremy R. Levitt. Validity Checking for Combinations of Theories with Equality. In Mandayam Srivas and Albert Camilleri, editors, *Formal Methods In Computer-Aided Design (FMCAD)*, volume 1166 of *Lecture Notes in Computer Science*, pages 187–201. Springer-Verlag, November 1996. Palo Alto, California.
5. Satyaki Das and David L. Dill. Counter-example based predicate discovery in predicate abstraction. In *Formal Methods in Computer-Aided Design*. Springer-Verlag, November 2002.
6. Greg Nelson and Derek Oppen. Simplification by cooperating decision procedures. *ACM Transactions on Programming Languages and Systems*, 1(2):245–57, 1979.
7. Aaron Stump, Clark W. Barrett, and David L. Dill. CVC: A Cooperating Validity Checker. In Ed Brinksma and Kim Guldstrand Larsen, editors, *14th International Conference on Computer Aided Verification (CAV)*, volume 2404 of *Lecture Notes in Computer Science*, pages 500–504. Springer-Verlag, 2002. Copenhagen, Denmark.
8. Lenore Zuck, Amir Pnueli, Benjaming Goldberg, Clark Barrett, Yi Fang, and Ying Hu. Translation and run-time validation of optimized code. *(to appear in) Formal Methods in Systems Design*, 2004. Preliminary version in *Third Workshop on Runtime Verification (RV), 2002*.

CirCUs: A Satisfiability Solver Geared towards Bounded Model Checking*

HoonSang Jin, Mohammad Awedh, and Fabio Somenzi

University of Colorado at Boulder
{Jinh,Awedh,Fabio}@Colorado.edu

Abstract. CirCUs is a satisfiability solver that works on a combination of And-Inverter-Graph, CNF clauses, and BDDs. It has been designed to work well with bounded model checking. It takes as inputs a Boolean circuit (e.g., the model unrolled k times) and an optional set of additional constraints (for instance, requesting that a solution correspond to a simple path) in the form of CNF clauses or BDDs. The algorithms in CirCUs take advantage of the mixed representation by applying powerful BDD-based implication algorithms, and decision heuristics that are *objective-driven*. CirCUs supports incremental SAT solving, early termination checks, and other analyses of the model that translate into SAT. Experimental results demonstrate CirCUs's efficiency.

1 Introduction

Efficient satisfiability (SAT) solvers [15, 18, 11, 6] have helped make Bounded Model Checking (BMC [2]) a widely used alternative to BDD-based model checking. The performance of BMC heavily depends on that of the SAT solver. At the same time, SAT-based model checking goes beyond the simple check for the existence of counterexamples, and involves a wide array of analyses such as early termination checks for invariants [13] and general LTL properties [1]. SAT solvers are also used in verification algorithms that combine BDDs and CNF [4], in the computation of concise proofs of satisfiability [12] and unsatisfiability [19], and in unbounded model checking [9, 10]. CirCUs is a SAT solver designed to be flexible enough to be used in all these tasks, while exploiting knowledge of the problem structure to provide better performance than generic SAT solvers in BMC.

CirCUs's input is a combination of And-Inverter-Graph (AIG [8]), CNF clauses, and BDDs. It combines the strengths of these different representations in a hybrid Boolean reasoning framework. The bounded model checker that uses CirCUs unrolls the model in the form of an AIG and applies optimizations like BDD sweeping and initial states propagation to it [8] to remove redundancy, which is a prime cause of inefficiency in SAT solvers. The constraints representing the property to be checked may be expressed as part of the AIG or as additional CNF clauses. Given these inputs, CirCUs transforms parts of the circuit into BDDs so as to apply powerful BDD-based implication algorithms [7]. It then looks for an assignment to the variables that satisfies all the outputs of the circuit and all additional constraints.

---

* This work was supported in part by SRC contract 2003-TJ-920.

R. Alur and D.A. Peled (Eds.): CAV 2004, LNCS 3114, pp. 519–522, 2004.

2   Objective-Driven Decisions

The speed of SAT solvers depends critically on their ability to choose good decision variables. In BMC, while the unrolled transition relation is always satisfiable, even after propagating the initial states, adding constraints on the target states makes most SAT instances unsatisfiable. CirCUs assumes that good decisions concentrate on proving that the *objective* cannot be satisfied, where the objective is an assertion on one of the outputs of the AIG. (If that assertion can be satisfied, then a counterexample is found.) Hence, decision variables are chosen from the cone of influence of the objective.

Even though the transition relation is satisfiable, a SAT solver will encounter conflicts in the attempt to derive consistent assignments for the inputs and outputs of subcircuits. These conflicts will produce *non-objective* clauses that express local satisfiability conditions for the transition relation and auxiliary objectives. Such clauses remain valid even when the objective changes as a result of further unrolling, and may prevent the search of fruitless parts of the solution space. When used as an incremental solver, CirCUs marks non-objective conflict clauses when they are created, and re-uses them for all successive runs and time frames. The clauses that depend on the objective, on the other hand, may be deleted by periodic clause deletion in CirCUs. Those that survive to the end of a run are "distilled" to bias the decision variable selection for the next run.

While this mechanism is not more powerful than the ones used in other generic incremental SAT solvers [17, 5] in identifying conflict clauses that remain valid from one run to the next, it either reduces the time required to detect what conflict clauses remain valid, or it removes the constraint that all conflict clauses must be kept. Compared to [14], CirCUs can identify more conflict clauses that remain valid.

3   Experimental Results

We have integrated CirCUs in VIS-2.1. To show the effectiveness of CirCUs, we compare the performance of four versions of BMC on the VIS benchmark suite [16]. All experiments have been performed on a 1.7 GHz Pentium IV with 1 GB of RAM running Linux. We have set the time out limit to 10000 s.

- Case A : VIS-2.0 [3, 16] BMC interfaced with Zchaff [11]
- Case B : VIS-2.1 BMC interfaced with Zchaff
- Case C : VIS-2.1 BMC interfaced with CirCUs
- Case D : VIS-2.1 BMC interfaced with Incremental CirCUs

We compare CPU times with scatter plots on logarithmic scale. The efficiency of optimizations like BDD sweeping and initial states propagation is shown in Fig. 1. In Case B, we run Zchaff on the CNF written from the optimized AIG. Since we use the same SAT solver for both case A and B, we can study the effects of removing redundancy. There are cases when redundancy gives an advantage in solving SAT. The score based decision heuristic may get a better initial decision order from redundant circuits. However, on average, redundancy elimination is very helpful.

In Fig. 2, we compare Zchaff's and (non-incremental) CirCUs's speed on the same BMC instances. CirCUs shows consistent improvement over Zchaff. CirCUs achieves the larger speed-ups on the harder examples (up to 10x). Incremental vs. non-incremental SAT in CirCUs are compared in Fig. 3. Incremental SAT shows improvement especially for the harder cases. Because an incremental SAT run starts with additional clauses transferred from the previous run, in small examples it may incur significant overhead. We summarize the overall improvement of CirCUs over VIS-2.0 BMC in Fig. 4. Each scatterplot shows two lines: The main diagonal, and $y = \kappa \cdot x^\eta$, where κ and η are obtained by least-square fitting. Student's t test confirms that the improvement visible in each plot is statistically significant.

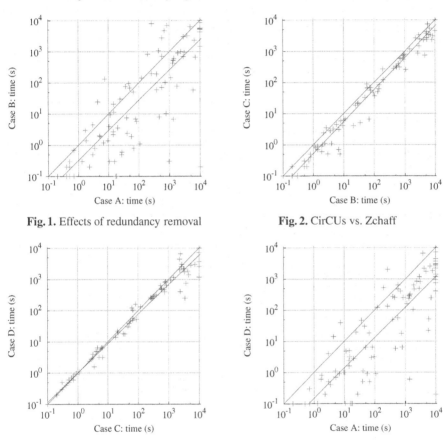

Fig. 1. Effects of redundancy removal   **Fig. 2.** CirCUs vs. Zchaff

Fig. 3. Incremental vs. non-incremental   **Fig. 4.** Overall gains

Thanks to its performance and flexibility, CirCUs is suited for the modular development of abstraction refinement algorithms and other complex SAT-based applications.

References

1. M. Awedh and F. Somenzi. Proving more properties with bounded model checking. These proceedings.

2. A. Biere, A. Cimatti, E. Clarke, and Y. Zhu. Symbolic model checking without BDDs. In *Fifth International Conference on Tools and Algorithms for Construction and Analysis of Systems (TACAS'99)*, pages 193–207, Amsterdam, The Netherlands, Mar. 1999. LNCS 1579.

3. R. K. Brayton et al. VIS: A system for verification and synthesis. In T. Henzinger and R. Alur, editors, *Eighth Conference on Computer Aided Verification (CAV'96)*, pages 428–432. Springer-Verlag, Rutgers University, 1996. LNCS 1102.

4. G. Cabodi, S. Nocco, and S. Quer. Improving SAT-based bounded model checking by means of BDD-based approximate traversal. In *Proceedings of the Conference on Design, Automation and Test in Europe*, pages 898–905, Munich, Germany, Mar. 2003.

5. N. Eén and N. Sörensson. Temporal induction by incremental SAT solving. *Electronic Notes in Theoretical Computer Science*, 89(4), 2003. First International Workshop on Bounded Model Checking. http://www.elsevier.nl/locate/entcs/.

6. E. Goldberg and Y. Novikov. BerkMin: A fast and robust SAT-solver. In *Proceedings of the Conference on Design, Automation and Test in Europe*, pages 142–149, Paris, France, Mar. 2002.

7. H. Jin and F. Somenzi. CirCUs: Speeding up circuit SAT with BDD-based implications. Submitted for publication, Apr. 2004.

8. A. Kuehlmann, M. K. Ganai, and V. Paruthi. Circuit-based Boolean reasoning. In *Proceedings of the Design Automation Conference*, pages 232–237, Las Vegas, NV, June 2001.

9. K. L. McMillan. Applying SAT methods in unbounded symbolic model checking. In E. Brinksma and K. G. Larsen, editors, *Fourteenth Conference on Computer Aided Verification (CAV'02)*, pages 250–264. Springer-Verlag, Berlin, July 2002. LNCS 2404.

10. K. L. McMillan. Interpolation and SAT-based model checking. In W. A. Hunt, Jr. and F. Somenzi, editors, *Fifteenth Conference on Computer Aided Verification (CAV'03)*, pages 1–13. Springer-Verlag, Berlin, July 2003. LNCS 2725.

11. M. Moskewicz, C. F. Madigan, Y. Zhao, L. Zhang, and S. Malik. Chaff: Engineering an efficient SAT solver. In *Proceedings of the Design Automation Conference*, pages 530–535, Las Vegas, NV, June 2001.

12. K. Ravi and F. Somenzi. Minimal assignments for bounded model checking. In *International Conference on Tools and Algorithms for Construction and Analysis of Systems (TACAS'04)*, pages 31–45, Barcelona, Spain, Apr. 2004. LNCS 2988.

13. M. Sheeran, S. Singh, and G. Stålmarck. Checking safety properties using induction and a SAT-solver. In W. A. Hunt, Jr. and S. D. Johnson, editors, *Formal Methods in Computer Aided Design*, pages 108–125. Springer-Verlag, Nov. 2000. LNCS 1954.

14. O. Shtrichman. Pruning techniques for the SAT-based bounded model checking problem. In *Correct Hardware Design and Verification Methods (CHARME 2001)*, pages 58–70, Livingston, Scotland, Sept. 2001. Springer. LNCS 2144.

15. J. P. M. Silva and K. A. Sakallah. Grasp—a new search algorithm for satisfiability. In *Proceedings of the International Conference on Computer-Aided Design*, pages 220–227, San Jose, CA, Nov. 1996.

16. URL: http://vlsi.colorado.edu/~vis.

17. J. Whittemore, J. Kim, and K. Sakallah. SATIRE: A new incremental satisfiability engine. In *Proceedings of the Design Automation Conference*, pages 542–545, Las Vegas, NV, June 2001.

18. H. Zhang. SATO: An efficient propositional prover. In *Proceedings of the International Conference on Automated Deduction*, pages 272–275, July 1997. LNAI 1249.

19. L. Zhang and S. Malik. Validating SAT solvers using an independent resolution-based checker: Practical implementations and other applications. In *Design, Automation and Test in Europe (DATE'03)*, pages 880–885, Munich, Germany, Mar. 2003.

Mechanical Mathematical Methods
for Microprocessor Verification

Warren A. Hunt, Jr.

Department of Computer Sciences
1 University Station, M/S C0500
The University of Texas
Austin, TX 78712-0233, USA
hunt@cs.utexas.edu

Abstract. The functional verification of microprocessor designs continues to represent one of the difficult challenges confronting the design of commercial microprocessors. In addition, test logic, transient errors, and power considerations complicate the problems by creating additional complexity and constraints on design solutions. Rigorous mechanized mathematics, often called formal methods, are being used to assist with functional verification and its use has spread to ensuring that test coverage and power limitations are met. While the successes have been notable, the wide-spread use of mathematical methods is still limited. Here we give a brief introduction to formal microprocessor verification, and then we present some scientific and engineering issues that need addressing to bring formal methods into the mainstream.

1 Introduction

The specification and formal verification of microprocessors represents an evolving science and a difficult to reach goal. There have been many efforts to verify abstractions of microprocessor designs, each with its own specific abstractions and detail. A number of related approaches have been reported, each with a slightly different twist, but in spirit similar. We discuss how we have partitioned the verification of a microprocessor, and make some remarks about why partitioning seems essential. This discussion will transform into a vision that an integrated capabilities a general-purpose verification system should possess. Finally, we present some research problems we believe need addressing if mechanical mathematical formal methods are to become mainstream design tools for industrial-sized designs.

We discuss several approaches that are typical for specifying the correctness of microprocessors. Even though many successful proofs have been done, there is no general agreement about what a suitable correctness statement is for microprocessors is, especially super-scalar, pipelined microprocessor designs that include memory delays, exceptions, memory management, and external interrupts. We discuss why the correctness specification of a processor possessing external interrupts can be particularly vexing. Instead of attempting to summarize all of the outstanding work that has been done, we refer the interested

R. Alur and D.A. Peled (Eds.): CAV 2004, LNCS 3114, pp. 523–533, 2004.

reader to Aagaard, et. al., paper *A Framework for Microprocessor Correctness Statements* [1], where an extensive reference list can be found.

To illustrate the kinds of integrated capabilities that a general-purpose verification system should have we describe a hypothetical verification tool **FMaAT** (Formal Modeling and Analysis Tool). Our description of **FMaAT** includes an integrated environment of language, database, checkers, provers, and autonomic regression and analysis routines. From our perspective, it is key that all of the design information and design meta data be represented in a unified database so that all manner of analysis can operate on the model of the design.

The excellent work performed by the formal verification community has shown the possibility of verifying microprocessor models, but we are far away from being able to apply our mechanical tools to complete industrial designs. Of course, we use mechanical tools all the time, and some, for instance, Boolean equivalence checkers, are regularly used on very large parts of modern designs. But we still seem far away from being able to process a complete high-level formal description of a microprocessor which includes all of its associated safety and liveness properties properties and (bi-)simulation relations that ultimately need to be checked on the actual RTL design description or an equivalent abstraction of the transistor-level design. If mechanical tools based on formal methods are to be used broadly, then it must be possible to compile and build a model of all specification levels.

We summarize a correctness statement that is sufficient to specify the correctness of a processor with exceptions, supervisor/user modes, memory delays, branch prediction and external interrupts. We present this specification in Section 2, and we discuss hierarchical verification in Section 3. We present a snapshot of what kinds of information that should be included with a design specification, and we argue in Section 5 that complete design data be available to all tools for manipulating and analyzing designs. We postulate what characteristics the **FMaAT** system should include to permit the wide-spread use of formal verification techniques in the design process. In Section 6 present some engineering obstacles that need addressing to ensure that formal analysis techniques are suitable for general use.

We note that this paper was written to provide some background for a microprocessor verification tutorial given by the author at this conference. Therefore, this paper is written in a conversational style, and it is provided as a partial record of what was presented and as a basis for further discussion. This paper was written not to explore a single topic in depth, but to present a vision for microprocessor verification techniques and tools. We conclude by describing areas of research we think need attention if formal mathematical verification techniques are to become mainstream.

2   Correctness Diagrams

The specification of correctness of a microprocessor can itself be subtle. This is obviously critical as it does no good to prove a vacuous or flawed theorem. In fact, there isn't general agreement about what suitable correctness is. Instead of attempting to justify a particular approach, we present several correspondence diagrams and conclude why we chose an approach we took.

Consider the correctness diagram in Figure 1. This diagram is meant to indicate that a micro-architecture (MA) design requires some number of steps to execute one ISA step; this is a slight generalization of Burch and Dill's approach [5] as it do not restrict the MA to only a single step. This was the correctness diagram was used to state the correctness of the FM8501 microprocessor [8]. This diagram, together with induction, can be used to show the correctness of any finite sequence of instructions. Such relationships between single and multi-step sequences has analyzed with the Microbox Framework [2].

The diagram in Figure 1 shows the ISA state being a proper subset of the MA state, and the correctness statement indicates that the MA state can be projected into a corresponding ISA state at certain points. The arrow moving from MA states to the ISA states are projection (abstraction) functions. In non-pipelined microprocessor implementations, these abstraction functions are simple projections but in the case of pipelines microprocessors, the MA implementation is often used to flush (or retire) in-flight instructions so a simple projection function can be used.

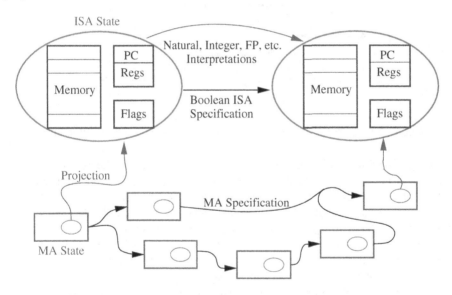

Fig. 1. Simple Microprocessor Correctness Diagram

Figure 1 is not general enough to verify processors that have non-deterministic external interrupts. What is the problem? In a modern microprocessor, (almost) all in-flight instructions are immediately flushed to keep the interrupt latency small, and to prevent a subsequent instruction from creating yet another exception. Consider an external interrupt event interrupting the first MA transition in the sequence of MA transitions. Normally, flushing from a particular state would permit the in-flight instructions to complete, but with an interrupt most, if not all, in-flight instructions are flushed without completion. The typical Birch-Dill flushing process lets all in-flight instructions complete before a projection is performed, but with an external interrupt in-flight instructions that will normally complete from an earlier MA state will be flushed. If we then project the corresponding ISA state from the MA state just after an interrupt, this may actually produce a state which, in some sense, is earlier in time than the state produced by letting the MA implementation only finish in-flight instructions.

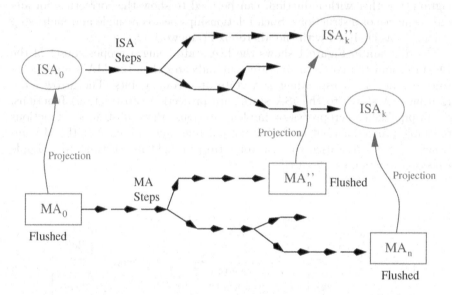

Fig. 2. Super-scalar Microprocessor Correctness Diagram with Interrupts

To provide for asynchronous external interrupts in the correctness statement, it is necessary for the ISA specification to accept external interrupts as well. That is, the different execution paths that can be taken by the MA-level machine must also be possible at the ISA level; otherwise, the ISA specification cannot be kept in correspondence with the MA-level implementation. Such a generalized correctness statement is pictured in Figure 2, where bifurcations represent possible execution path changes due to interrupts. Of course, the design of MA-level flushing mechanism must operate in such a manner that the diagram can be used. This diagram was the correctness diagram for the FM9801 microprocessor verification [11, 15–17]; the flushing mechanism in the FM9801 essentially "throws away" partially completed work, so it can quickly respond to external interrupts, and this mechanism prevents the problem mentioned above. Even though we believe we used correctness diagram in a sound manner, Manolios showed that it is possible to satisfy this type of diagram with trivial, wrong implementations [12]. Correctness statements can be very subtle.

In a companion paper [14], we describe another correctness diagram suitable for microprocessors with sophisticated features and external interrupts. All these correctness statements are designed to be hierarchical. We can construct another commuting diagram on top of these correctness statements, building a stack of verified layers [3]. In the next section, we discuss breaking down an individual commuting diagram proof into pieces.

3   Compositional Verification

The internal designs of modern microprocessors are very complex. In fact, the designs are so complex that attempting to just use symbolic simulation to satisfy one of the correctness specifications given in the previous section will not work. Instead a proof has to be broken down into smaller pieces so that can be later composed to produce a complete proof of the desired result.

There are many ways that a proof can be broken down, but whether the sublemmas are either single-step properties (or invariants) or multi-step properties certainly changes the ease with which the sublemmas can be composed. Single-step properties are easy to compose – so long as state-space restrictions are met. Multi-step properties are often much more difficult to compose because their environmental requirements and also their (possibly multi-step) conclusions may be very difficult to "stitch" together. Why? The assumptions (usage environments) can be very complex, and it may be difficult or impossible to satisfy both sets of assumptions simultaneously.

Composing two or more individual multi-step properties, or other multi-step invariants, into a single lemma may also produce a conclusion that itself is so specialized that is may difficult to state or prove. For instance, consider composing a four or more step property with a two-step property. Just how should the environments be aligned so the lemmas can be composed? Should the conclusion be about two steps or four steps? With single-step invariants, this is a much easier task as only environmental restrictions on the (reachable) states need to be considered when composing results. We used such single-step invariants to prove the correctness of the FM8501, FM8502, FM9001, Motorola's Complex Arithmetic Processor DSP, and the FM9801 microrprocessors [8, 9, 4, 10].

Industry has equiped itself with several kinds of FSM exploration tools, most notably model checkers and (G)STE engines. These tools have been used to great advantage, exploring various particular design questions in great depth. However, these tools can only be practically applied to subsets of modern microprocessor designs. Generally, the results from these tools provide multi-step property verifications, and as such, are very difficult to compose. This is a critical issue. When automatic FSM exploration tools are available, they can be put to profitable use on many parts of a design, but as the designs grow, and the number of different properties grows, the re-assembly process become extremely complicated.

We believe, if properties verified with FSM exploration tools are to be composed, then either a high-level theorem prover should be used to decompose the proof obligations into pieces that can be checked in a manner similar to McMillan's [13] approach or FSM property tools should be used to prove one-step invariant properties. In this way, the discoveries made with FSM exploration may be safely composed.

Even in light of the difficulties of composing results derives from various FSM exploration tools and checkers, we note that these tools have discoverd many design flaws and checked many complex properties. We have no doubt of the importance of FSM exploration tools as they are used today. These tools are productive and they will continue to be important, and the use of these tools has help defined what the state-of-the-art-of-the-practice is.

4   Current Practice

The state-of-the-art-of-the-practice of the use of formal mathematical methods with mechanically-implemented implementations varies from design to design. My impressions with the industrial use of formal methods comes from time I spent working for IBM Research in Austin, Texas, but through conversations with my colleagues at other companies, my experiences seem typical.

The application of formal methods to design projects varies widely, for many practical reasons: size and importance of project, available tools and people, confidence of architects and managers in the available technology, degree of integration of formal methods tools in the tool flow, size of the company, and duration of the project. The use of formal methods is primarily centered in a dozen or so of the largest companies, probably due to the cost of creating a critical mass of infrastructure (meaning tools, people, and design practice). Even in the larger companies, there are great differences in the degree to which such techniques are deployed. Many smaller projects did not use formal methods, while in larger design efforts, there may be a dozen or more people.

From the project management point of view, the use of formal methods represents a vexing challenge, due to the lack of available metrics to know when its use is efficient and sufficient. This is not so different from simulation, but over many years management has developed "coverage" metrics that help them gauge when there has been "enough" simulation. For complete designs, such intuition has not been developed for mechanical mathematical methods. We are optimistic that coverage metrics can be defined because with a proof, it is very clear what has been proved and what has been assumed.

5   Challenges

We see a number of challenges to improve mechanical mathematics tools so that they are regularly used on commercial-sized designs. First, we recognize that such tools are already being deployed, and are regularly being used to examine large parts of modern designs. For instance, equivalence checkers are now being regularly being used to ensure that low-level gate and transistor-level design specifications implement Boolean RTL micro-architectural descriptions. In addition, model checking [6] and (G)STE [18] are being successfully to validate various design elements. Theorem proving systems have been applied in niche areas, such as floating-point algorithms, and they may provide the "glue" to bind together different tools. Even so, we don't think of formal tools being part of the "model build" that is often done each evening during the design process.

After developing and using mathematical modeling and analysis tools in a commercial environment, we have identified several challenges that we believe need to be addressed before mathematical analysis will regularly occur at the higher levels of the design hierarchy. So, if we were to build a system called **FMaAT** (Formal Modeling and Analysis Tool), we would like it to have a number of properties.

- **FMaAT** needs to be able to read, compile, and "model build" the entire design specification. **FMaAT** should be able to read the entire design, and represent such a design as a formal object. Engineers do not trust tools that cannot manipulate the actual design specification. If one were to print the complete RTL description for a modern microprocessor, it may well require 30,000 or more pages.

- The **FMaAT** system must, in all respects, operate in a hierarchical manner. Every design is yet just another piece of an even larger design in the future.

- **FMaAT** needs to contain all embedded annotations. That is, if a module has a requirement that its inputs are one-hot and that its outputs are active-low, then this data must be included in the original design specification and it must also have a representation as a formal object that **FMaAT** can inspect, manipulate, and subject to analysis.

- **FMaAT** needs to be able to act as a database engine that allows every design module and interface to be identified. It must be possible to uniquely identify every primitive element, interface, and wire. A completely precise and unique naming convention is a requirement.

- Each time a change is made to the design, the effects of the change should be automatically propagated to the **FMaAT** database so when an analysis is requested, only the relevant parts are subjected to analysis.

- **FMaAT** needs to be able to compute cones-of-influence, bus conflicts, improper connections, and other user-definable queries.

- **FMaAT** must have a command-line interface. In a big design project, tools are always "taped" together with scripting languages to overcome deficiencies in the design flow. **FMaAT**'s command-line interface should itself be described formally.

- There has to be a way to re-run all checkers, simulators, etc., automatically whenever there is any change to the design. Automatic regression verification is a must.

- There must not be any way to get a false positive. There must be provisions for ensure vacuity checking for analysis requests.

- If possible, **FMaAT** should have some kind of analysis "coverage metrics". If included, then a formal definition of coverage should also be included, so that some kind of qualitative assessment can be made as to the thoroughness of an analysis.

- Along with having all of the design and associated property specifications directly available in a single database, it is critical that there be a semantics that allows the various tools (and the results derived from these tools) to be safely composed. This can only be done if **FMaAT** contains a general-purpose theorem prover.
- **FMaAT** must provide a means to write a truly rigorous high-level specification. System-C and System Verilog are not a long-term answer; in fact, these languages are creating yet more problems.
- A purely functional verification system is not sufficient. **FMaAT** must a way to specify non-functional properties such as power requirements, circuit sizes, wire types, physical location data, environmental requirements, and other critical design properties. And for each such property, suitable checkers and verifiers will need to be provided.
- **FMaAT** must deal with a distributed design process. No project of a significant size is all done in a single place.
- Finally, **FMaAT** must safely extensible; that is **FMaAT** should be no more difficult to extend than Emacs, but **FMaAT** should impose a discipline that ensures that extensions do not render existing checker and verifiers unsound.

A tool like **FMaAT** will require a much more general language than those commercially available, such as Verilog and VHDL and their derivatives. The limitations of the available languages are causing the specification problem to actually become worse because designers are forced to record their design properties as comments or in external files. The available existing design languages do not have associated specification languages. A community-wide effort has resulted in the Accellera [7] standardized property specification language, but even this language does not have a formal relationship to the systems (e.g., designs coded in Verilog or VHDL) it is meant to specify.

Future system design languages need to have fully integrated specification languages and fully integrated annotation languages. In this way, the analysis tools (checkers, simulators, theorem provers) can all get access to any or all of the design artifact, thus providing a unifying framework for designs and their specifications. And all such analysis tools must be defined using the same semantic foundation so results from one analysis tools can be immediately used by other analysis tools.

6 Research Problems

There are many technical and engineering challenges that remain before mechanical formal mathematical methods become fully integrated into the commercial design flow. We discuss these obstacles with the hope that our community will help solve these problems.

To make a system like **FMaAT** will require fundamental changes to the infrastructure of commercial design environment. With careful planning and execution, it should be possible to incrementally improve commercial design tools so that their foundation is suitable to allow the wide-spread use of mechanical formal methods.

- New formally specified design and annotation languages need to be defined that provide a semantically unified framework for designs and all associated specifications. These languages need to include mechanisms to represent all of the design "meta" data directly as a part of the design specification. For instance, that some inputs are "one-hot" and some outputs are "active-low" needs to be captured just as some safety or liveness property. All of this data needs to be expressible in this language. Such a design language also needs to be general enough to express non-functional properties such as area and power constraints. These languages must be hierarchical.
- To reduce power consumption, there is going to be a greater use of asynchronous circuit elements along with circuits that can trade execution speed with power requirements. Specification and analysis of mixed circuit types will be necessary, and we need to develop modeling and verification techniques capable of supporting designs with a mixture of digital, asynchronous, and analogue circuits.
- Typical two- and four-valued simulators need to be extended to symbolic simulator; that is, there should be a single simulation environment general enough to perform simulation with a mixed set of constants and symbolic variables. Moving from one simulation environment to another is error prone and confusing.
- All of the analysis tools (e.g., equivalence and model checkers, (G)STE engines, reachability analysis, theorem provers) should all read the same design data and all follow the same semantics. In other words, we must achieve integration between the various analysis tools so results from one tool can be used elsewhere. Implementations of these tools have chosen their own logics; we need some kind of unification so results can be shared and reused among the various tools.
- A new suite of non-functional checkers (e.g., for power, area, redundancy management) need to be developed. These checkers should receive the same level of rigor and development as existing formal analysis tools.
- Post-silicon design approaches need to be integrated into the design process. Post-silicon debugging tools (e.g., logic analyzers) have not improved much in the last decade and the amount of visibility continues to decrease as implementations become more and more integrated. Future formal design languages must be general enough to also permit the specification of the supporting chip sets and the systems themselves.
- Autonomic systems that automatically (re-)run all checkers and provers should be automatically started any time any part of a design is changed. This is necessary as no large design effort is now done in a single location. This system, if you will, is a *super-CVS*, ensuring that all design properties are pro-actively analyzed.
- Formal approaches to (microprocessor) security need to be developed. Future processors will be systems-on-a-chip, and the specification of security features and analysis of security properties is going to be critical.

These are some of the issues that need solving to broaden the impact of mathematics on the design of microprocessors, and computing systems in general. A sustained, long-term effort will be required to extend the state-of-the-art-of-the-practice.

7   Conclusion

The functional verification of microprocessor-sized designs will continue push the state-of-the-art and the state-of-the-practice of mathematical formal methods. As the complexity and sheer number of microprocessors continues to increase, we see no practical alternative to the use of formal mathematics supported by mechanical reasoning tools. Mathematics is the only technique that can scale with the ever increasing size and complexity, and mechanized mathematical specification and proof are the only practical infrastructure for correct, reliable, and secure microprocessor.

We would like computing systems to be specified by a *formula manual*, a complete precise set of formulas that exactly specifies computing systems (whether hardware, software, or both). We want mathematically specified, mechanically checked computing systems. Systems are increasing in complexity faster than our ability to manage them or control them. If we are aggressive, maybe we can achieve this vision on small commercial designs, e.g, cell telephones, pagers, routers, etc. Our ability to field secure, correct systems is based on our ability to specify and validate our computing, networking, and control systems.

The use of mathematical formal methods will continue to broaden. It is the most economical method to ensure correctness, reliability, power usage, and security, of future designs. No other analytical techniques known to us will be able to scale with future design requirements. We are impressed with the progress and we look forward the challenge of extending the use of mathematics for design.

References

1. M. Aagaard, B. Cook, N. Day, and R. Jones. A Framework for Microprocessor Correctness Statements. In *CHARME 2001*, LNCS 2144, pages 433-448, Springer Verlag, 2001.
2. M. Aagaard, N. Day, and M. Lou. Relating Multi-step and Single-Step Microprocessor Correctness Statements. In *Formal Methods in CAD, FMCAD 2002*, LNCS 2517, pages 123-141, Springer Verlag, 2002.
3. W. R. Bevier, W. A. Hunt, J S. Moore and W. D. Young. An Approach to Systems Verification. In *Journal of Automated Reasoning*, Volume 5, November, 1989.
4. B. C. Brock and W Hunt, Jr. Formal Analysis of the Motorola CAP DSP. In *Industrial-Strength Formal Methods*, edited by Mike Hinchey and Jonathan Bowen, Springer-Verlag, 1999.
5. J. R. Burch and D. L. Dill. Automatic Verification of Pipelined Microprocessor Control. In *Computer Aided Verification, CAV '94*, LNCS 818, pages 68-80, Springer Verlag, 1994.
6. E. Clarke, O. Grumberg, and D. Peled. Model Checking. MIT Press, 1999.

7. M. Gordon, J. Hurd, and K. Slind. Executing the Formal Semantics of the Accellera Property Specification Language by Mechanized Theorem Proving. In *CHARME 2003*, LNCS 2860, pages 200-215, Springer Verlag, 2003.

8. W. Hunt, Jr. FM8501: A Verified Microprocessor, LNAI Number 795, Springer-Verlag, 1994.

9. W. Hunt, Jr. and B. Brock. A Formal HDL and Its Use in the FM9001 Verification. In C.A.R. Hoare and M.J.C. Gordon, editors, Mechanized Reasoning and Hardware Design, pages 35-48, Prentice-Hall International Series in Computer Science, Engle wood Cliffs, N.J., 1992.

10. W. Hunt, Jr. and J. Sawada. Verifying the FM9801 Microarchitecture. In *IEEE Micro*, IEEE Press, pages 47–55, May-June, 1999.

11. M. Kaufmann and J S. Moore. ACL2: An Industrial Strength Version of Nqthm. Proceedings of the *Eleventh Annual Conference on Computer Assurance (COMPASS-96)*, pages 23-34, IEEE Computer Society Press, June 1996.

12. P. Manolios. Correctness of Pipelined Machines. In *Formal Methods in Computer-Aided Design, FMCAD 2000*, LNCS 1954, pages 161-178, Springer-Verlag, 2000.

13. K. L. McMillan. A Methodology for Hardware Verification Using Compositional Model Checking. In the *Science of Computer Programming*, Volume 37, Number 1-3, pages 279-309, 2000.

14. S. Ray and W. A. Hunt, Jr. Deductive Verification of Pipelined Machines Using First-Order Quantification. *Computer-Aided Verification, CAV 2004*, LNCS 3114, Springer Verlag, 2004.

15. J. Sawada and W. Hunt, Jr. Trace Table Based Approach for Pipelined Micro-processor Verification. *Computer-Aided Verification, CAV'97*, LNCS 1254, pages 364-375, Springer Verlag, 1997.

16. J. Sawada and W. Hunt, Jr. Processor Verification with Precise Exceptions and Speculative Execution. *Computer Aided Verification, CAV'98*, LNCS 1427, pages 135-146, Springer Verlag, 1998.

17. J. Sawada and W. Hunt, Jr. Verification of the FM9801 Microprocessor: An Out-of-order Microprocessor Model with Speculative Execution, Exceptions, and Self-Modifying Code. In *Formal Methods in Systems Design*, Kluwer Academic Publishers, Volume 20, Number 2, pages 187–222, March, 2002.

18. J. Yang and C. Seger. Generalized Symbolic Trajectory Evaluation — Abstraction in Action. In *Formal Methods in CAD, FMCAD 2002*, LNCS 2517, pages 70-87, Springer Verlag, 2002.

Author Index

Lecture Notes in Computer Science

For information about Vols. 1–3015

please contact your bookseller or Springer-Verlag

Vol. 3061: F.F. Ramas, H. Unger, V. Larios (Eds.), Advanced Distributed Systems. VIII, 285 pages. 2004.

Vol. 3060: A.Y. Tawfik, S.D. Goodwin (Eds.), Advances in Artificial Intelligence. XIII, 582 pages. 2004. (Subseries LNAI).

Vol. 3059: C.C. Ribeiro, S.L. Martins (Eds.), Experimental and Efficient Algorithms. X, 586 pages. 2004.

Vol. 3058: N. Sebe, M.S. Lew, T.S. Huang (Eds.), Computer Vision in Human-Computer Interaction. X, 233 pages. 2004.

Vol. 3057: B. Jayaraman (Ed.), Practical Aspects of Declarative Languages. VIII, 255 pages. 2004.

Vol. 3056: H. Dai, R. Srikant, C. Zhang (Eds.), Advances in Knowledge Discovery and Data Mining. XIX, 713 pages. 2004. (Subseries LNAI).

Vol. 3055: H. Christiansen, M.-S. Hacid, T. Andreasen, H.L. Larsen (Eds.), Flexible Query Answering Systems. X, 500 pages. 2004. (Subseries LNAI).

Vol. 3054: I. Crnkovic, J.A. Stafford, H.W. Schmidt, K. Wallnau (Eds.), Component-Based Software Engineering. XI, 311 pages. 2004.

Vol. 3053: C. Bussler, J. Davies, D. Fensel, R. Studer (Eds.), The Semantic Web: Research and Applications. XIII, 490 pages. 2004.

Vol. 3052: W. Zimmermann, B. Thalheim (Eds.), Abstract State Machines 2004. Advances in Theory and Practice. XII, 235 pages. 2004.

Vol. 3051: R. Berghammer, B. Möller, G. Struth (Eds.), Relational and Kleene-Algebraic Methods in Computer Science. X, 279 pages. 2004.

Vol. 3050: J. Domingo-Ferrer, V. Torra (Eds.), Privacy in Statistical Databases. IX, 367 pages. 2004.

Vol. 3049: M. Bruynooghe, K.-K. Lau (Eds.), Program Development in Computational Logic. VIII, 539 pages. 2004.

Vol. 3047: F. Oquendo, B. Warboys, R. Morrison (Eds.), Software Architecture. X, 279 pages. 2004.

Vol. 3046: A. Laganà, M.L. Gavrilova, V. Kumar, Y. Mun, C.K. Tan, O. Gervasi (Eds.), Computational Science and Its Applications – ICCSA 2004. LIII, 1016 pages. 2004.

Vol. 3045: A. Laganà, M.L. Gavrilova, V. Kumar, Y. Mun, C.K. Tan, O. Gervasi (Eds.), Computational Science and Its Applications – ICCSA 2004. LIII, 1040 pages. 2004.

Vol. 3044: A. Laganà, M.L. Gavrilova, V. Kumar, Y. Mun, C.K. Tan, O. Gervasi (Eds.), Computational Science and Its Applications – ICCSA 2004. LIII, 1140 pages. 2004.

Vol. 3043: A. Laganà, M.L. Gavrilova, V. Kumar, Y. Mun, C.K. Tan, O. Gervasi (Eds.), Computational Science and Its Applications – ICCSA 2004. LIII, 1180 pages. 2004.

Vol. 3042: N. Mitrou, K. Kontovasilis, G.N. Rouskas, I. Iliadis, L. Merakos (Eds.), NETWORKING 2004, Networking Technologies, Services, and Protocols; Performance of Computer and Communication Networks; Mobile and Wireless Communications. XXXIII, 1519 pages. 2004.

Vol. 3040: R. Conejo, M. Urretavizcaya, J.-L. Pérez-de-la-Cruz (Eds.), Current Topics in Artificial Intelligence. XIV, 689 pages. 2004. (Subseries LNAI).

Vol. 3039: M. Bubak, G.D.v. Albada, P.M. Sloot, J.J. Dongarra (Eds.), Computational Science - ICCS 2004. LXVI, 1271 pages. 2004.

Vol. 3038: M. Bubak, G.D.v. Albada, P.M. Sloot, J.J. Dongarra (Eds.), Computational Science - ICCS 2004. LXVI, 1311 pages. 2004.

Vol. 3037: M. Bubak, G.D.v. Albada, P.M. Sloot, J.J. Dongarra (Eds.), Computational Science - ICCS 2004. LXVI, 745 pages. 2004.

Vol. 3036: M. Bubak, G.D.v. Albada, P.M. Sloot, J.J. Dongarra (Eds.), Computational Science - ICCS 2004. LXVI, 713 pages. 2004.

Vol. 3035: M.A. Wimmer (Ed.), Knowledge Management in Electronic Government. XII, 326 pages. 2004. (Subseries LNAI).

Vol. 3034: J. Favela, E. Menasalvas, E. Chávez (Eds.), Advances in Web Intelligence. XIII, 227 pages. 2004. (Subseries LNAI).

Vol. 3033: M. Li, X.-H. Sun, Q. Deng, J. Ni (Eds.), Grid and Cooperative Computing. XXXVIII, 1076 pages. 2004.

Vol. 3032: M. Li, X.-H. Sun, Q. Deng, J. Ni (Eds.), Grid and Cooperative Computing. XXXVII, 1112 pages. 2004.

Vol. 3031: A. Butz, A. Krüger, P. Olivier (Eds.), Smart Graphics. X, 165 pages. 2004.

Vol. 3030: P. Giorgini, B. Henderson-Sellers, M. Winikoff (Eds.), Agent-Oriented Information Systems. XIV, 207 pages. 2004. (Subseries LNAI).

Vol. 3029: B. Orchard, C. Yang, M. Ali (Eds.), Innovations in Applied Artificial Intelligence. XXI, 1272 pages. 2004. (Subseries LNAI).

Vol. 3028: D. Neuenschwander, Probabilistic and Statistical Methods in Cryptology. X, 158 pages. 2004.

Vol. 3027: C. Cachin, J. Camenisch (Eds.), Advances in Cryptology - EUROCRYPT 2004. XI, 628 pages. 2004.

Vol. 3026: C. Ramamoorthy, R. Lee, K.W. Lee (Eds.), Software Engineering Research and Applications. XV, 377 pages. 2004.

Vol. 3025: G.A. Vouros, T. Panayiotopoulos (Eds.), Methods and Applications of Artificial Intelligence. XV, 546 pages. 2004. (Subseries LNAI).

Vol. 3024: T. Pajdla, J. Matas (Eds.), Computer Vision - ECCV 2004. XXVIII, 621 pages. 2004.

Vol. 3023: T. Pajdla, J. Matas (Eds.), Computer Vision - ECCV 2004. XXVIII, 611 pages. 2004.

Vol. 3022: T. Pajdla, J. Matas (Eds.), Computer Vision - ECCV 2004. XXVIII, 621 pages. 2004.

Vol. 3021: T. Pajdla, J. Matas (Eds.), Computer Vision - ECCV 2004. XXVIII, 633 pages. 2004.

Vol. 3019: R. Wyrzykowski, J.J. Dongarra, M. Paprzycki, J. Wasniewski (Eds.), Parallel Processing and Applied Mathematics. XIX, 1174 pages. 2004.

Vol. 3018: M. Bruynooghe (Ed.), Logic Based Program Synthesis and Transformation. X, 233 pages. 2004.

Vol. 3017: B. Roy, W. Meier (Eds.), Fast Software Encryption. XI, 485 pages. 2004.

Vol. 3016: C. Lengauer, D. Batory, C. Consel, M. Odersky (Eds.), Domain-Specific Program Generation. XII, 325 pages. 2004.